BLACK SPARTACUS

ALSO BY SUDHIR HAZAREESINGH

How the French Think: An Affectionate Portrait of an Intellectual People

In the Shadow of the General: Modern France and the Myth of De Gaulle

The Legend of Napoleon

The Saint-Napoleon: Celebrations of Sovereignty in Nineteenth-Century France

Intellectual Founders of the Republic: Five Studies in Nineteenth-Century French Republican Political Thought

From Subject to Citizen: The Second Empire and the Emergence of Modern French Democracy

Political Traditions in Modern France

Intellectuals and the French Communist Party: Disillusion and Decline

BLACK SPARTACUS

THE EPIC LIFE OF
TOUSSAINT LOUVERTURE

SUDHIR HAZAREESINGH

FARRAR, STRAUS AND GIROUX NEW YORK

Farrar, Straus and Giroux
120 Broadway, New York 10271

Printed in the United States of America
Published by Farrar, Straus and Giroux
Published simultaneously by Allen Lane, Great Britain
First American edition, 2020

Library of Congress Cataloging-in-Publication Data
Names: Hazareesingh, Sudhir, author.
Title: Black spartacus : the epic life of Toussaint Louverture / Sudhir Hazareesingh.
Other titles: Epic life of Toussaint Louverture
Description: First American edition. | New York : Farrar, Straus and Giroux, 2020. | Includes bibliographical references and index. | Summary: "A biography of the Haitian revolutionary leader Toussaint Louverture."—Provided by publisher.
Identifiers: LCCN 2020012455 | ISBN 9780374112660 (hardcover)
Subjects: LCSH: Toussaint Louverture, 1743–1803. | Haiti—History—Revolution, 1791–1804. | Revolutionaries—Haiti—Biography. | Generals—Haiti—Biography. | Haiti—History—Revolution, 1791–1804.
Classification: LCC F1923.T69 H39 2020 | DDC 972.94/03092 [B]—dc23
LC record available at https://lccn.loc.gov/2020012455

www.fsgbooks.com
www.twitter.com/fsgbooks • www.facebook.com/fsgbooks

1 3 5 7 9 10 8 6 4 2

For Karma

who knows all about revolutionary heroes

Contents

List of Illustrations

ILLUSTRATIONS IN THE INSERT

ILLUSTRATIONS IN THE TEXT

Acknowledgements

Although I have spent all my life studying various aspects of modern French history, politics and culture, before starting this book I had never ventured into the history of French colonialism in the Caribbean. One of the many pleasures of writing this biography has been discovering the extraordinary story of Haiti and the remarkable qualities of its people: their warmth, their creativity, their determination and their pride in the achievements of their revolutionary founders. It has been all the more gratifying to learn about this history in that it also took me back to my Mauritian roots. I already knew that the kreyol language in Mauritius shares numerous affinities with Haitian kreyol. Having written the book, I have also now come to appreciate how much my native island in the Indian Ocean had in common with late-colonial Saint-Domingue before it became the independent state of Haiti. In the 1790s, Mauritius (known at the time as Île de France) was a sugar-producing French colony, and its European colonial settlers brought thousands of African slaves there, as in Saint-Domingue. But although these men and women did not succeed in overthrowing slavery, as the Haitians did, they stood up to it by all the means at their disposal. Indeed, as a child in Mauritius I remember hearing stories about *marron* (runaway slave) rebellions against the plantation system, led by such charismatic figures as Diamamouve, Tatamaka and Madame Françoise, an enslaved Malagasy princess who spearheaded an effective resistance movement in the south-east of the island. Owing to the large number of runaway slaves who lived in its settlements and caves in the early nineteenth century, the area around Le Morne mountain came to be known as the 'Maroon Republic'.

Even more serendipitously, the bulk of the primary sources for the book, including most of Toussaint Louverture's manuscripts, have ended up in France. So the research for this biography was undertaken in many of my familiar haunts: the Bibliothèque Nationale, Archives Nationales, Archives de Paris, Archives Diplomatiques and the Service Historique de la Défense in Paris; the Archives Nationales d'Outre-Mer in Aix; and the departmental archives in Bordeaux and Nantes. This was supplemented by the extremely interesting material I found in British archives (the National Archives at Kew, the National Army archives, the British Library in London and the Bodleian Library in Oxford), as well as in the USA (notably at the Library of Congress in Washington DC and the New York Public Library's Schomburg Centre; I also drew on the University of Florida's extensive digital collections). I am grateful to all the librarians and archivists who assisted me in my work.

In researching and writing this book, I was most fortunate to benefit from the generous support of a number of institutions. I express my warmest thanks to the Department of Politics and International Relations at Oxford University, the British Academy's Small Research Grants Scheme and the Society of Authors' Travelling Scholarships fund for awarding me substantial grants to help me carry out my research in France, Britain, the USA and Haiti. I am likewise grateful to the Master and Fellows of Balliol College, Oxford (and in particular my PPE colleagues and the Senior Tutor Nicky Trott) for granting me sabbatical leave in Trinity and Michaelmas terms 2018, during which the bulk of this archival work was carried out.

Over the past couple of years I have discussed some of the book's central themes at a number of venues: at the History of Political Thought seminar at University College, Oxford; at a joint session of the European History and Modern French seminars at the Institute of Historical Research, London; at Bruce's Brunch at Balliol College, Oxford; and at the Oxford History Faculty's Early Modern World seminar. I am greatly indebted to all those who hosted me, as well as everyone who attended these talks: their encouragement, their observations and questions were enormously helpful in clarifying my thinking on many issues.

I would like to convey my warmest thanks to Jim Gill, who has been a true friend, a brilliant literary agent and a tower of strength throughout the writing of this book. A number of friends read through the text and provided immensely valuable comments and suggestions, as much on points of detail as on broader conceptual and historical arguments: my heartfelt gratitude to David Bell, Edward Berenson, Sophie Berlin, Richard Drayton, Nadia Hilliard, Karma Nabulsi, Julia Nicholls, Barnaby Raine, Calvin Runnels, Robbie Shilliam and Quentin Skinner. They all helped make this a much better book than it would otherwise have been. Julian Jackson and Robert Gildea supported my grant applications, and various forms of practical and moral support were provided by Jocelyn Alexander, Diana Berruezo-Sánchez, Chris Bongie, Henri Bovet, Tony Crowley, Edouard Duval-Carrié, David Ekserdjian, Ada Ferrer, James Fox, Oliver Franklin, Julia Gaffield, Adom Getachew, Jessica Hollows, Vinesh Hookoomsing, Yanick Lahens, Nathan Perl-Rosenthal, Neha Shah, Anne Simonin, Abdel Razzaq Takriti and Wolfgang Windel; I thank them all very warmly.

It has been a joy to be in Allen Lane's hands again and I am indebted to all the members of the team who produced the book: Isabel Blake, Richard Duguid, Anna Hervé, Linden Lawson, Imogen Scott, Ben Sinyor, Alice Skinner and the indexer, Christopher Phipps. Cecilia Mackay once more lived up to her reputation as an outstanding picture editor, discovering some superb illustrative material. I am especially thankful to my editor Stuart Proffitt, who worked closely with me at all stages, from the first intimations that Toussaint would be its subject to the meticulous discussions of my draft text; his comments were invariably insightful. It has been exceptionally stimulating – and huge fun – to work with such a true *artiste du livre*.

My ultimate inspiration, as ever, came from Karma Nabulsi. It was through her pioneering scholarship on eighteenth- and nineteenth-century democratic and revolutionary struggles against Empire that I first encountered Toussaint, and thus understood that he broadly belonged within this republican tradition of war, particularly as a powerful embodiment of its ideal of fraternity. Karma has been my muse on this exceptional journey, offering wise counsel on everything I wrote, shaping my thinking every step of the way, and listening patiently as I chatted excitedly about my discoveries in the archives or shared my treasure trove of Toussaint and Dessalines anecdotes with her. I am grateful to her for everything she has taught me, and for always being at my side. I dedicate this book to her.

S. H.
Oxford, December 2019.

Chronology

1697	September	Spain cedes western third of Hispaniola to France, which becomes the colony of Saint-Domingue
*c.*1740		birth of Toussaint on Bréda estate
1758	January	execution of François Makandal, leader of first major slave conspiracy
1763	November	expulsion of Jesuits from Saint-Domingue
1772		Bayon de Libertat becomes manager of Bréda estate (until 1789); appoints Toussaint as his coachman
1774	Jan, April	death of Hippolyte and Pauline, Toussaint's parents
*c.*1775		Toussaint emancipated from slavery
1782		Toussaint marries Suzanne Baptiste (with whom he has two children, Isaac, b. 1786, and Saint-Jean, b. 1791)
1784	December	royal ordinance calling for more 'humane' treatment of slaves rejected by Saint-Domingue settlers
1788	February	creation of liberal abolitionist Société des Amis des Noirs in France
1789	January	formation of colonial assemblies in Saint-Domingue
	July	French Revolution begins with fall of Bastille
	August	French National Assembly adopts Declaration of Rights of Man
	September	property-owning free people of colour petition French National Assembly demanding equal civil and political rights
	October	Saint-Domingue Colonial Assembly blocks reforms from France, and denies rights to free people of colour
1790	March	French National Assembly grants full legislative powers to Saint-Domingue, and avoids issue of rights of free people of colour
	May	Colonial Assembly declares Saint-Domingue's autonomy from France (Assembly closed down by loyalist local authorities in July)
	October	attempted rebellion by free mixed-race leader Vincent Ogé in north

1791	February	Ogé executed in Cap
	May	French National Assembly grants Saint-Domingue veto over colonial legislation
	July	new Saint-Domingue Assembly dominated by white supremacists
	August	slave insurrection begins in northern Saint-Domingue; involved in its planning, Toussaint becomes secretary of rebel leader Biassou
	Sept–Dec	Toussaint emerges as key figure in rebel leadership, protects white prisoners and advocates compromise with local Colonial Assembly
	November	death of Boukman, one of the slave rebellion's main leaders
1792	January	compromise efforts fail; Toussaint commands his own military force, composed largely of *marron* (runaway) slaves
	April	new French Legislative Assembly ends racial discrimination in colonies
	August	Toussaint attends celebration in honour of French king
	July	*Lettre originale des chefs nègres révoltés*
	September	arrival of French commissioners in Saint-Domingue; France becomes a republic
	December	Commissioner Sonthonax proclaims a republic in Saint-Domingue; Toussaint promoted to rank of general in rebel army
1793	January	after execution of French king, Spain declares war on France
	May	Spanish formal alliance with Jean-François and Biassou against French
	June	Toussaint becomes general in Spanish auxiliary forces; in ensuing months he takes Dondon, Marmelade, Verrettes, Petite-Rivière and Plaisance from French
	August	Sonthonax abolishes slavery in northern Saint-Domingue (abolition extended to west in September, and south in October); Toussaint adopts name 'Louverture'
	September	British forces begin five-year occupation of parts of southern and western Saint-Domingue

	November	Toussaint signs reconciliation agreement with Jean-François and Biassou, after Spanish mediation
	December	Toussaint captures Gonaïves, consolidating Spanish control of the whole of northern Saint-Domingue (except Cap)
1794	February	Convention decree abolishes slavery in all French colonies
	March	Toussaint denounces Biassou, begins rapprochement with French
	April	British capture Guadeloupe, after taking Martinique (in March)
	May	royalists massacred at Gonaïves; Toussaint rallies republican camp and brings territories under his control to French side
	June	Toussaint appointed commander of western territories under French control; British capture Port-au-Prince
	October	Toussaint captures Saint-Michel and Saint-Raphaël from Spanish
1795	June	Toussaint takes Mirebalais back from British, after five months' fighting
	July	Spain signs Bâle Treaty with France, abandons all positions in Saint-Domingue and cedes Santo Domingo; Toussaint promoted to brigadier-general
	August	Toussaint launches full-scale attack on British positions in Saint-Domingue
	October	new French constitution establishes Directory, with Conseil des Cinq Cents as its lower chamber
1796	March	Toussaint saves Governor Laveaux from attempted coup by people of colour in Cap, appointed as his deputy
	May	new commissioners arrive from France, including Sonthonax and Raimond
	July	Isaac Louverture and his half-brother Placide sent to France for their education
	August	British severely defeat Toussaint's forces and recapture Mirebalais
	October	Laveaux leaves Saint-Domingue to take seat in Conseil des Cinq Cents

1797	April	counter-revolutionary royalists win majority in French legislative elections
	May	Toussaint appointed commander-in-chief of Saint-Domingue army
	May	Viénot-Vaublanc speech at Conseil des Cinq Cents denounces black revolution in Saint-Domingue
	August	Toussaint forces Sonthonax to leave Saint-Domingue
	September	*coup d'état* of 18 Fructidor an V in Paris, royalists defeated
	October	Toussaint publishes *Réfutation de quelques assertions d'un discours prononcé au Corps Législatif le 10 Prairial an cinq par Viénot Vaublanc*
1798	January	law on colonies adopted in French legislature, fully incorporates Saint-Domingue
	April	new French agent Hédouville arrives in Saint-Domingue
	July	Hédouville's *Arrêté concernant la police des habitations* provokes widespread discontent among labourers
	August	British conclude negotiated withdrawal from Saint-Domingue with Toussaint; secret treaty on trade and non-aggression
	September	Toussaint challenges Hédouville by granting amnesties to émigrés
	October	Hédouville flees the colony after Toussaint orchestrates insurrection against him
	December	Philippe Roume appointed French agent in Saint-Domingue
1799	March	Edward Stevens appointed US consul to Saint-Domingue
	May	*Réponse du citoyen Toussaint Louverture aux calomnies et aux écrits mensongers du général de brigade Rigaud*
	June	attempted insurrection against Toussaint and beginning of *guerre des couteaux* (war of knives) against Rigaud in south; extension of 1798 treaty between Toussaint and Maitland
	August	Toussaint regains full control of north and west
	November	Bonaparte 18 Brumaire coup overthrows Directory; new constitution removes colonies' right to be represented in national legislature

	December	attempted republican plot in Jamaica foiled; Toussaint vessels seized by British
1800	March	Jacmel falls to Toussaint's forces, with American naval help (then Grand-Goâve in April)
	April	Toussaint coerces Roume approval of French takeover of Santo Domingo
	June	arrival of delegation appointed by consuls (Vincent, Raimond, Michel)
	August	Toussaint victorious in southern war, enters Les Cayes; Rigaud flees
	October	Toussaint labour decree establishes draconian regime in plantations
	November	Toussaint sends Roume into internal exile in Dondon
1801	January	Toussaint invades Santo Domingo, expels Spanish authorities and abolishes slavery; Hispaniola unified under French republican rule
	February	Toussaint announces creation of Central Assembly to draft new constitution for colony
	March	Central Assembly members appointed, and begin their deliberations
	May	Toussaint *Instructions aux fonctionnaires publics*
	July	Saint-Domingue constitution unveiled at Cap ceremony; Toussaint appointed governor of colony for life, and slavery abolished 'for ever'
	October	Bonaparte orders 20,000 troops to be sent to overthrow Toussaint; Moyse rebellion
	November	Toussaint 4 Frimaire an X decree: fight against 'sedition' expanded
	December	Toussaint proclamation announces impending French military invasion
1802	January	lead ships of Leclerc expedition sighted off Santo Domingo; French invasion begins
	February	Toussaint burns down Cap and refuses to submit; launches spring campaign against French forces
	March	Battle of Crête-à-Pierrot: French take fort, but suffer heavy losses
	May	Toussaint agrees ceasefire and retires to Ennery; Bonaparte restores slavery in Martinique, Tobago and Saint Lucia, soon followed by Guadeloupe and Guyana

	June	Toussaint and his family captured and deported to France
	July	government decree bans entry of black and mixed-race people into France
	August	Toussaint interned in Fort de Joux; news of restoration of slavery in Guadeloupe rekindles resistance in Saint-Domingue
	September	Toussaint dictates *Memoir*
	October	Dessalines and Pétion unite against French occupation, and issue general call to arms
	November	Leclerc dies of yellow fever, succeeded by Rochambeau
1803	April	death of Toussaint in Fort de Joux
	May	Arcahaie agreement: unification of Saint-Domingue's black and mixed-race insurgent forces under leadership of Dessalines
	November	final French defeat at Battle of Vertières, Rochambeau capitulates
	December	French forces evacuate Saint-Domingue
1804	January	Dessalines proclaims new state of Haiti

Glossary

Allada	Toussaint's ancestral ethnic group, named after African kingdom
agent	most senior French colonial envoy
ancien régime	French political system before 1789 Revolution
Artibonite	Saint-Domingue's largest river
blanc	white person (sometimes distinguished between *petit* and *grand*)
bossale	African-born person
cabildos	municipalities in Spanish territory of Santo Domingo
cercle	audiences at which Toussaint met members of the public
Code Noir	French rule book codifying treatment of slaves
colon	white settler
commandeur	slave-driver (after revolution, known as *conducteur*)
creole	native of Saint-Domingue
cultivateur	plantation worker
curé	priest
émigré	French person who fled the colony during the revolution
escalin	unit of currency created by Toussaint in Santo Domingo
Fatras-Bâton	(literally 'skinny stick') nickname given to Toussaint in his youth
Fon	language spoken by Alladas
gens de couleur	mixed-race people
gourde	unit of currency in Saint-Domingue
gourdin	a quarter of a *gourde*
habitation	plantation
Hispaniola	name given to island by Spaniards
houngan	*vodou* priest
kalinda	slave dance
Kongo	largest ethnic group among Saint-Domingue's black population
kreyol	vernacular of Saint-Domingue, combining French, African and local idioms
levée en masse	collective uprising of the people

liberté générale	emancipation from slavery
libre	person freed from slavery (*ancien libre*: freed before the revolution; *nouveau libre*: freed as from 1793)
lieue	unit of distance, equal to around three miles
livre	unit of currency
loa (*lwa*)	*vodou* spirit
Makandal	mid-eighteenth-century revolutionary slave leader
manumission	release from slavery
marron	runaway slave (hence *marronage*)
métropole	mainland France
morne	circular-shaped elevated terrain, hill or mountain
mulâtre, *mulâtresse*	mixed-race man, woman
National Guard	citizens' militia
Port-Républicain	Port-au-Prince's name from 1793 onwards
propriétaire	property owner
Ogoun Fer	*vodou* spirit of war
tafia	sugar cane molasses-based rum
Taino	original native American inhabitants of Saint-Domingue
vodou	spiritual system and way of life centring on the worship of spirits
war of knives	conflict between Toussaint and Rigaud (1799–1800)

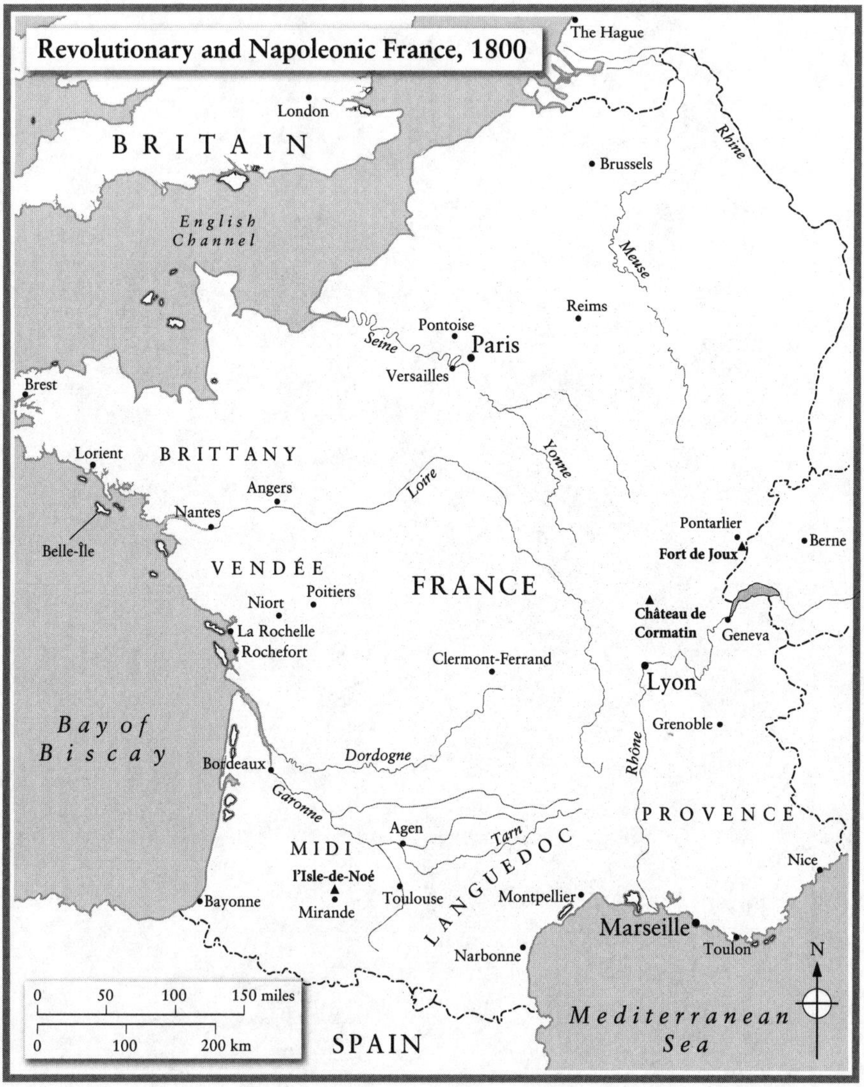
Revolutionary and Napoleonic France, 1800
The Hague
London
BRITAIN
Brussels
Rhine
English Channel
Meuse
Reims
Pontoise
Seine
Paris
Versailles
Brest
Lorient
BRITTANY
Yonne
Loire
Angers
Nantes
Belle-Île
Pontarlier
Fort de Joux
Berne
VENDÉE
Poitiers
FRANCE
Niort
Château de Cormatin
La Rochelle
Geneva
Rochefort
Clermont-Ferrand
Lyon
Bay of Biscay
Grenoble
Dordogne
Rhône
Bordeaux
Garonne
PROVENCE
Agen
Tarn
MIDI
LANGUEDOC
Nice
l'Isle-de-Noé
Bayonne
Mirande
Toulouse
Montpellier
Marseille
Narbonne
Toulon
N
0
50
100
150 miles
0
100
200 km
SPAIN
Mediterranean Sea

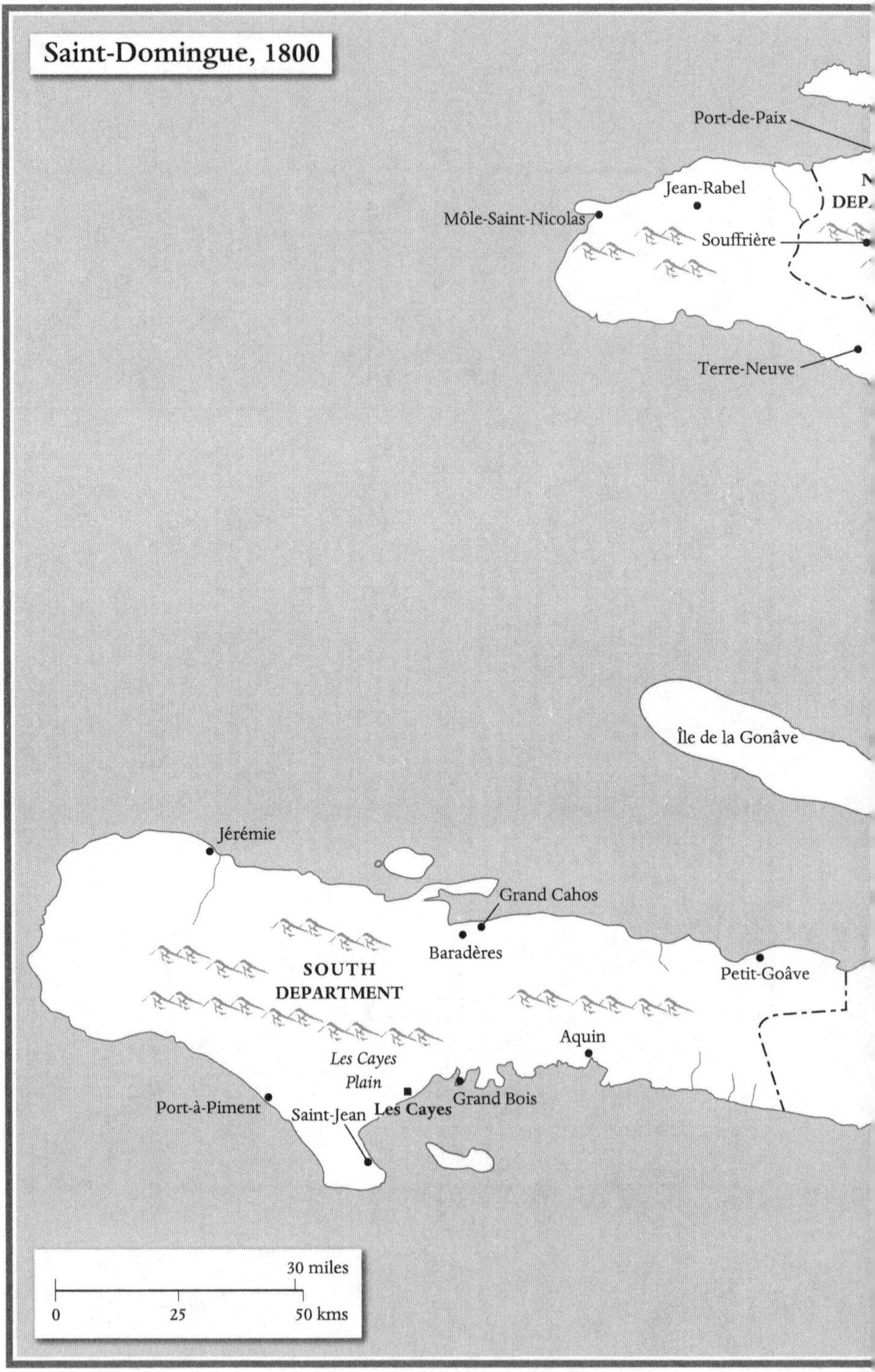
Saint-Domingue, 1800
Port-de-Paix
Jean-Rabel
Môle-Saint-Nicolas
Souffrière
Terre-Neuve
Île de la Gonâve
Jérémie
Grand Cahos
Baradères
SOUTH
DEPARTMENT
Petit-Goâve
Aquin
Les Cayes
Plain
Grand Bois
Port-à-Piment
Saint-Jean
Les Cayes
30 miles
0
25
50 kms

Île de la Tortue
Saint-Louis du Nord
Atlantic Ocean
N
Moustique
ORTH
ARTMENT
Port-Margot
Haut-du-Cap
Cap-Français
(Le Cap)
Volant-le-Thor
Massif du Nord
Gros-Morne
Limbé
Acul
Northern Plain
Sainte-Suzanne
Grande-Rivière
Fort-Dauphin
(Fort-Liberté)
Plaisance
Dondon
Mapou
Marmelade
Carrefour Vincent
Gonaïves
Ennery
Saint-Raphaël
Ouanaminthe
Vallière
Saint-Michel
Ravine-à-Couleuvres
Cahos peaks
Petit Cahos
Saint-Marc
Hinche
Petite-Rivière
Petite Montagne
Crête-à-Pierrot
SANTO
DOMINGO (SPAIN)
Bánica
Verrettes
Montagne Noire
Artibonite Plain
Artibonite river
Lascahobas
WEST
DEPARTMENT
Mirebalais
Grand Bois
Arcahaie
Charbonnière
La Croix des
Bouquets
Port-au-Prince
(Port-Républicain)
Léogâne
Neyba
Grand-Goâve
La Selle
Jacmel
Caribbean Sea
Main towns
DEPARTMENTS
Towns
Bréda plantation

St Paul
MICHIGAN
New Lisbon
Chicago
CANADA
Mon
NEW Y
Detroit
PENNSYLVANIA
INDIANA TERRITORY
NORTHWEST TERRITORY
COLONY OF LOUISIANA (FRANCE)
Alexandria
VIRGINIA
KENTUCKY
TENNESSEE
NORTH CAROLINA
SOUTH CAROLINA
DISPUTED TERRITORY
GEORGIA
Charleston
MISSISSIPPI TERRITORY
FLORIDA
Gulf of Mexico
NEW SPAIN
Havana
Santa Cruz
CUBA
Güines
Puerto
YUCATAN
Bayamo
Santia
SAINT
JAMAICA
Kingst
HONDURAS
Caribbean Sea
North Pacific Ocean
NICARAGUA
COSTA RICA
0
200 miles
0
200 kms
Cartagena

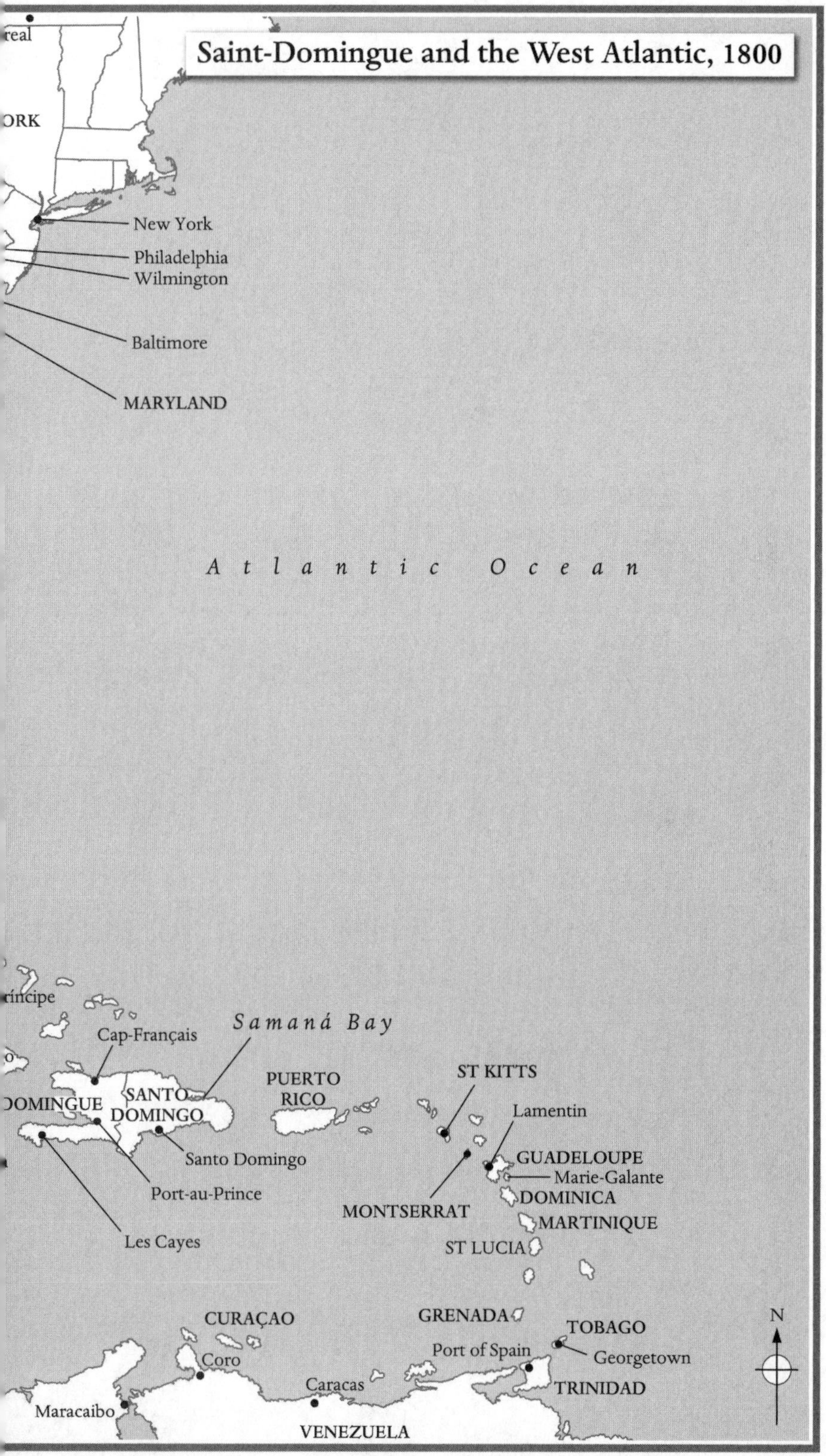

Saint-Domingue and the West Atlantic, 1800
real
ORK
New York
Philadelphia
Wilmington
Baltimore
MARYLAND
Atlantic Ocean
ríncipe
Samaná Bay
Cap-Français
SANTO DOMINGO
DOMINGUE
Santo Domingo
Port-au-Prince
Les Cayes
PUERTO RICO
ST KITTS
Lamentin
GUADELOUPE
Marie-Galante
DOMINICA
MONTSERRAT
MARTINIQUE
ST LUCIA
GRENADA
TOBAGO
Georgetown
Port of Spain
TRINIDAD
CURAÇAO
Coro
Caracas
Maracaibo
VENEZUELA
N

BLACK SPARTACUS

Introduction

The Originality of Toussaint Louverture

Toussaint Louverture was an emancipated black slave who became the emblematic figure of the Haitian Revolution. Lasting a decade and a half, this momentous process of social and political change began in 1789, in the aftermath of the fall of the Bastille in France, with demands for self-government and equal rights for free people of colour in the French Caribbean colony of Saint-Domingue. The revolution then took a radical turn with the launching of a massive slave revolt in August 1791, which led to the abolition of slavery by the colony's republican authorities in 1793, and their recognition that the black population shared the same social and political rights as white and mixed-race citizens. As Toussaint put it in one of his early proclamations: 'freedom is a right given by Nature'.[1]

These events, and the subsequent course of the Haitian Revolution, are narrated in this book.[2] The revolution in Saint-Domingue was part of a wider series of transformations in the late-eighteenth-century Atlantic world, which were reflected in growing challenges to monarchical and imperial rule, the emergence of the principle of popular sovereignty and the advent of the American and French republics.[3] Toussaint's rise perfectly symbolized the broader characteristics of this age of revolution: its global nature (his parents were African-born slaves who were forcibly transported to Saint-Domingue); its defiant martialism (he rose through the ranks to become a French general); its unsettling of existing social hierarchies (he went from being a slave herdsman to assuming the governorship of Saint-Domingue); its shaping by European ideals (he was brought up in the Catholic faith, and in sincere admiration of the French *grande nation*); its immersion in Enlightenment culture (he championed administrative and economic reforms, and profoundly believed in the power of scientific ideas); and its dedication to building a better society, and even a better species of humankind. In Toussaint's words: 'reason and education will spread across our regenerated soil; once crushed under a yoke of enslavement which was as odious as it was degrading, man will elevate himself on the wings of liberty'.[4]

At the same time, Toussaint epitomized the uniqueness of Saint-Domingue's revolution. It was the age's most comprehensive example of radical change, combining democratic and republican goals with an emphasis on racial equality, and became a just war of national liberation which foreshadowed the anti-colonial struggles of the modern era. Saint-Domingue was also exceptional in that the driving forces of its revolution were not white bourgeois liberals but black slaves, who were partly revolting against slave-owning supporters of the French Revolution, such as the merchants of Bordeaux and Nantes. It was a revolution, too, which forced French leaders locally and in Paris to face up to the issue of slavery and proclaim its general abolition in 1794. This revolution wiped out the colony's old ruling class, pioneered guerilla warfare and successfully confronted the military might of European imperialism. It shook the Enlightenment's belief in the inherent superiority of all things European – its primary agents drew on native American forms of spirituality and African political cultures, and embodied the mutinous spirit of the African American rebels who disrupted colonial authority across the black Atlantic in the late eighteenth century.[5]

In short, Toussaint embodied the many facets of Saint-Domingue's revolution by confronting the dominant forces of his age – slavery, settler colonialism, imperial domination, racial hierarchy and European cultural supremacy – and bending them to his will. Through his dynamism he acquired some striking epithets. His republican friends hailed him as the 'Black Spartacus', the modern incarnation of the legendary gladiator who led his fellow slaves against the Roman Republic; his miraculous appearance in Saint-Domingue had, in the words of one of his admirers, 'transformed the chaos of destruction into the seeds of new life'.[6] He was also described as the father of the blacks, the black son of the French Revolution, the black George Washington, the Bonaparte of the Caribbean, the African hero, the Hannibal of Saint-Domingue and the centaur of the savannah (a tribute to his horsemanship; his white steed Bel Argent was integral to his myth). By the early nineteenth century, Philadelphia's newspapers were referring to him as 'the celebrated African chief'.[7] Even liberal opinion in England was moved by the sight of such an uncommon hero: an article in the *London Gazette* in 1798 hailed Toussaint as a 'Negro King', a proud representative of the 'Black race whom the Christian world to their infamy have been accustomed to degrade'.[8] In 1802 the London *Annual Register* described him as 'the major public figure of the year, and a great man'.[9]

Toussaint also thrived in the collective imagination of the nineteenth century. It has been suggested that the revolutionary events in Saint-Domingue directly inspired Hegel's master-slave dialectic, in which the slave eventually transcends his alienation and achieves self-consciousness.[10] Precisely because of his subversive potential, his leadership caused panic among slave-owners across the Atlantic. In 1799 Thomas Jefferson denounced Toussaint and his revolutionary comrades as 'cannibals of the terrible Republic', warning that their 'missionaries' could provoke a 'combustion' in America,[11] while in 1801 the British War Secretary, Lord Hobart, shuddered at the thought of the 'power of a Black Empire under Toussaint'.[12] From London and Paris through Virginia and Louisiana to Jamaica, Cuba, Brazil and Venezuela, planters and merchants echoed these alarms and lambasted the man they saw as the 'Robespierre of Saint-Domingue'. Simon Taylor, the wealthiest sugar baron in Jamaica, 'tossed and turned in his luxurious bed linen, suffering repeated bouts of fever' as he imagined Toussaint and his revolutionaries arriving on his plantation and slitting his throat.[13] Their slaves, conversely, cherished him as an energizing figure, and celebrated his military successes against French, Spanish and British forces. From the late eighteenth century onwards, Toussaint and the Haitian revolutionaries became potent symbols in the United States: tales of their civil and military accomplishments were recounted in American newspapers, notably in Philadelphia and Washington;[14] their achievements helped inspire specific revolts such as those of Nat Turner and Denmark Vesey, frame social attitudes towards slave emancipation, and embody the very ideal of black heroism.[15] The anti-slavery campaigner Frederick Douglass, the most eminent nineteenth-century African American, was a Toussaint devotee who helped spread his legend across the United States, notably by using images of him in the publicity for his *New National Era* newspaper.[16] Toussaint's extraordinary after-lives in print, music, painting and legend are the subject of the last chapters of this book.

In the late eighteenth century, Saint-Domingue was a territory of around 10,600 square miles occupying the western third of Hispaniola, first claimed by Spain when Christopher Columbus landed in the north-west of the island in December 1492. Ceded to France by the Spaniards in 1697, the colony was divided into three provinces: the most populated, the northern, hosted the principal city, Cap Français, which was situated in a large and sheltered bay and was the first port of call for ships arriving from Europe and the Americas; it took around forty-five days to travel from France, and twenty from the eastern coast of the United States. Cap was surrounded by a wide plain, the most fertile land in the colony thanks to its regular rainfall and irrigation by rivers and streams; by the late eighteenth century it contained the colony's richest plantations.[17] The two other provinces were the western and southern, with Port-au-Prince and Les Cayes as their main towns. Port-au-Prince became the administrative capital in 1750 and was surrounded by two plains, the Cul-de-Sac and the Artibonite, named after the colony's most important river; also in the western province were the major ports of Gonaïves and Saint-Marc.[18] Urbanization was limited in the colony, with only 8 per cent of the population living in towns of over 1,000 inhabitants,[19] and its rugged inland regions were dominated by mountain ranges, steep ravines and elevated *mornes*; the indigenous native American inhabitants of Hispaniola, the Taino people, called the island 'Ayti', the land of high mountains. Covered in lush tropical forests, sparsely populated and little explored by Europeans (less than a third of the colony was properly mapped), this elevated hinterland separated the three provinces from each other and created contrasting landscapes and distinct regional climates.[20] Movement from one province to another was not easy: in the mid eighteenth century a passage was cut to build a road linking Cap and Port-au-Prince, but carriages were only able to travel on it from 1787. In the plains, roads joining smaller towns and plantations were often rudimentary, and the high terrains were a further hindrance to communications; rising water levels in rivers and lengthy rainy seasons made it impossible to use certain roads for long periods.[21] The south – the smallest of the three provinces – was especially isolated from the rest of the colony, and in many respects had closer connections with neighbouring Jamaica, with which it maintained regular exchanges in contraband merchandise. Indeed, the most common way people and goods moved from one region of Saint-Domingue to another was by sea.[22]

Late-colonial Saint-Domingue was widely known as the 'Pearl of the Antilles'. It was the world's largest producer of sugar and coffee, along with significant amounts of cotton, indigo and cacao. These valuable staples made the colony the strongest export economy of the Americas, a place where opulence and luxury were flaunted and 'colossal fortunes' made.[23] Cap was a bustling, cosmopolitan centre with a population of nearly 20,000 in 1789, offering a quality and diversity of urban life which matched that of Havana, Philadelphia or New York. Along with its busy port, it had a booming business sector, twenty-five bakeries and a buoyant cultural scene, including a theatre with a capacity of 1,500; there were also theatres in Port-au-Prince, Saint-Marc, Léogâne, Jérémie and Les Cayes. Cap was noted, too, for its vibrant scientific and intellectual life, with an active press, subscription reading clubs and private libraries stacked with the latest philosophical works from Europe.[24] There were twenty Masonic lodges in the colony at the time of the French Revolution, and many of their members were closely involved in Saint-Domingue's best-known scientific organization, the Cercle des Philadelphes. Based in Cap between 1784 and 1792, the Cercle published five volumes of scientific memoirs, on medical, agricultural, botanical and ethnographical topics; it had an international membership, and cultivated close ties with leading *savants* in Europe and the United States.[25]

Yet this material and cultural effervescence was rooted in extreme inequalities. Saint-Domingue's whole system of production was based on slavery. By the late eighteenth century there were 500,000 slaves in the colony, a majority of whom were born in Africa and worked under gruelling conditions in the plantations. Slaves had no civil or political rights and were often treated with barbaric cruelty by their masters; from the mid 1750s they began to develop various kinds of individual and collective resistance. They formed brotherhoods in the plantations and practised *vodou* spiritual rituals involving dance, song, possession and divination, while *marrons* escaped in increasing numbers, retreating to the bush where they formed bands, or hiding in plain sight in towns and cities, and spread ideas about emancipation. Among the extraordinary figures in this underground was Jean-Louis from Cap, a *marron* who possessed 'special talents' and could speak Spanish, Dutch, English, French and Saint-Dominguan kreyol – and no doubt several African languages too.[26] Whites were divided as well along class lines, with an enduring pattern of contestation of the metropolitan hierarchy – and especially its large and domineering bureaucracy – by the so-called *petits blancs* (small farmers, employees, artisans, soldiers and sailors).[27] Uneasily resting between the 40,000 settlers of European origin and the black majority was a mixed-race population, almost as numerous as the whites. Yet although free, often highly literate and in some cases wealthy, these people of colour (together with the small number of free black people) suffered from humiliating legal discriminations: they were banned from employment in the civil service, and denied entry into certain professions such as medicine; they were forbidden from eating at the same table as whites, or dressing like them, and in the later eighteenth century were not even allowed to travel to France.[28] Attempts by the local colonial administration to introduce modest reforms in the 1780s created bitter indignation among whites, and resentment against metropolitan France among settlers; in 1784 a royal ordinance prohibiting the 'inhumane' treatment of slaves was fiercely criticized by the planters, and the colony's courts refused to apply it until it was watered down.[29]

[N° 52.]

AFFICHES AMÉRICAINES.

Du Samedi 25 Décembre 1784.

Poids du Pain d'un escalin....... 21 onces.

ARRIVÉE DE NAVIRES.

AU PORT-AU-PRINCE, le 11 de ce mois, *le Marchais*, de Rochefort, Capit. Boureau, venant de Miquelon : le 14, l'*Aimable-Victoire*, de Bordeaux, Capit. Paul Oré, venant de la Martinique; & *le Timide*, de Bordeaux, venant de S. Marc: le 16, *le Mirebalais*, de Nantes, Cap. Yves Griffé, parti le 25 Octobre : le 17, *le Chêne-Vert*, de Bordeaux, Capit. Seignoret, de relâche du Cap, par une voie d'eau : le 21, l'*Euriale*, de la Rochelle, Capit. Belleville, venant de la côte d'Or & du Cap, avec 400 Noirs.

DÉPART DE NAVIRES.

DU PORT-AU-PRINCE, le 13 de ce mois, l'*Aimable-Adide*, de Bordeaux, Capit. Pigeon, pour ledit lieu; & l'*Alliance*, du Havre, Capit. Heurtaut, pour ledit lieu : le 14, *les Deux-Frères*, de Bordeaux, Capit Jalineau, pour la Nouv. Angleterre; & *le Saint-Esprit*, de Marseille, Cap. Vidal, pour led. lieu : le 15, *la Ville-de-Nantes*, de Nantes, Capit. Barré, pour ledit lieu; & l'*Hercule*, Cap. Raguideau, de relâche des Cayes, pour Nantes : le 18, *le Blouin*, Cap. Morin : le 21, *le Prince-de-Poix*, Cap. Boyer : le 22, *la Comtesse-de-Tréville*, Cap. Chalumeau : tous trois de Bordeaux, allant audit lieu.

NÈGRES MARRONS.

A SAINT-MARC, le 13 de ce mois, est entré à la Geole, *Marianne*, Thiamba, étampée sur le sein droit DUBOURG, au-dessous ST MARC, âgée de 12 ans, taille de 4 pieds 6 pouces, se disant appartenir à Mlle Ducernet, à Saint-Marc : le 15, *Céleste*, Congo, étampée sur le sein droit, autant qu'on a pu le distinguer, ƎTƎ, ayant des marques de son pays sur l'estomac & sur le ventre, âgée de 13 ans, taille de 4 pieds 2 pouces, ne pouvant dire le nom de son maître : le 19, *Neptune*, Congo, étampé sur le sein droit G, & d'autres lettres illisibles, âgé de 30 ans, taille de 5 pieds 4 pouces, se disant appartenir à M. Capdeville, Habitant à l'Artibonite; & *Adonis*, Congo, sans étampe apparente, marqué de petite-vérole, ayant la jambe droite courte âgé de 29 ans, taille de 4 pieds 10 p. se disant appartenir à M. *Moreau*, dans les hauts de S. Marc.

AU PORT-AU-PRINCE, le 16 de ce mois, un Nègre nouveau, Congo, étampé AL-RAS, le milieu de l'étampe illisible : le 18, un Nègre nouveau, Congo, sans étampe apparente, ayant des marques de son pays sur le visage; une Négresse nouvelle, Congo, étampée RESSEN, au-dessous COU, & d'autres lettres illisibles; & deux Négresses nouvelles, Taquoas, étampées MAHOT, au-dessous ST M : le 20, un petit Nègre nouveau, Congo, étampé PLANCHER; tous six ne pouvant dire leurs noms ni ceux de leurs maîtres.

ANIMAUX ÉPAVES.

AU PORT-AU-PRINCE, le 16 de ce mois, une Mule, sous poil bai, etampée, autant qu'on a pu le distinguer, M : le 19, une Jument, sous poil rouge, étampée ACC, en travers; & une Bourrique, sous poil brun, étampée illisiblement, ayant le bout d'une oreille coupé : le 20, un Mulet, sous poil brun, étampé illisiblement, ayant des marques d'anciennes blessures & du poil blanc sur le dos : le 21, un Cheval, sous poil rouge, étampé MP entrelacés, au-dessous J JHB entrelacés; une Jument, sous poil rouge, étampée, autant qu'on a pu le distinguer, IBP, longue queue & une étoile au front; un Bourriquet, sous poil brun, étampé à la cuisse & au cou illisiblement, ayant le bout d'une oreille coupé; & un Cheval, sous poil rouge, sans étampe apparente, ayant une étoile au front.

Published every week in Cap and Port-au-Prince between 1764 and 1790, the *Affiches Américaines* included travel news, information about events in the Caribbean region and France, and prominent notices about runaway slaves (*marrons*), with physical descriptions supplied by their owners.

In short, Saint-Domingue under the *ancien régime* was a boisterous territory where social and political conflict was rife, and white power ultimately maintained by brute force: as one planter recognized, slave-owners like him 'walked on barrels of gunpowder'.[30] When the explosion came in 1791, Toussaint Louverture joined the ranks of the rebels, like thousands of his fellow black comrades. Yet his path towards revolutionary leadership was complex and remains shrouded in mystery. Part of the reason for this elusiveness lay in Toussaint's own personality. He was a very private man who confided in no one, and went out of his way to conceal important information about himself, his movements and his ultimate goals. He spread misinformation and rumours, often put false locations on his letters, and his most confidential messages were dictated in separate parts to different secretaries. He once told a British diplomat that his preferred way of operating was to 'say little but do as much as possible'.[31] The only authoritative painting of him made during his lifetime has been lost,[32] and he was renowned for his almost magical capacity to appear in the most unexpected of settings and vanish without a trace. One of his adversaries described him as 'a man who managed to make himself, so to speak, invisible where he was, and visible where he was not; he seemed to have borrowed his spontaneity of movement from the tiger'.[33] The belief that he possessed supernatural qualities became, and remains to this day, an integral part of Haitian culture.[34]

Like all major revolutionaries, Toussaint was a controversial figure, and this is reflected in the crude and schematic ways he has often been represented after his death. French colonialist writers such as Louis Dubroca placed him among the 'most execrable monsters history has ever known' for daring to defy French imperial rule, while Thomas Prosper Gragnon-Lacoste's hagiography saluted him as 'the extraordinary individual whose fame has spread across the world'.[35] After the Haitian declaration of independence, Toussaint fared no better in the hands of the nation's leading mixed-race historians Thomas Madiou, Beaubrun Ardouin and Joseph Saint-Rémy, who attacked him as a racially divisive and tyrannical ruler who had betrayed the ideals of the revolution. They were particularly critical of his political authoritarianism, his alleged hostility towards their mixed-race brethren and his attempts to restore the plantation economy by forging an alliance with the old white ruling class, forcing the colony's black slaves to work for their old masters. These remain among the most controversial aspects of Toussaint's rule.[36]

More reflective biographies of Toussaint began to emerge from the later nineteenth century onwards. The French abolitionist Victor Schoelcher travelled to Haiti in 1841, and later used some of the archival sources available in France to produce a sympathetic and nuanced portrait.[37] The Haitian historian and diplomat Horace Pauléus Sannon's three-volume *Histoire de Toussaint Louverture* (1920–33) was the most significant work to emerge from Toussaint's native land. Drawing extensively on his speeches and proclamations, it recognized him as a founding father of Haitian independence.[38] The classic modern work in the English language was – and remains – C. L. R. James's *The Black Jacobins* (1938), an electrifying chronicle which educated generations of men and women in Europe, the Americas and the global South about the Haitian Revolution, and acted as a progressive handbook for revolution across the globe.[39] James stressed the role of mass mobilization against slavery in Saint-Domingue's radical politics, and saw Toussaint as the principal symbol of the interdependence of the Haitian and French Revolutions: in the later twentieth century, global historians hailed *The Black Jacobins* for its portrayal of the Haitian Revolution's prodigious combination of local, national, regional and universal elements.[40]

Yet, for all their merits, even these biographies in some senses further denatured our understanding of Toussaint. For example, Sannon's insistence on his black nationalism was an oversimplification of his views both on race and nationhood. Likewise, Schoelcher's portrayal of Toussaint as an orthodox disciple of French republicanism – a standard view among historians in France to this day – underestimated the Caribbean and African dimensions of his personality, as well as his deeply held religious values. James's representation of Toussaint as a French 'jacobin' ignored his monarchist leanings and the strong emphasis on local autonomy in his political thought, which eventually culminated in his 1801 constitution. More fundamentally, and despite its groundbreaking depiction of revolutionary activity outside Europe, *The Black Jacobins*' assessment of the events in Saint-Domingue as ultimately deriving from European ideals and political forms exaggerated the closeness of the links between radical movements in France and Saint-Domingue, and downplayed the breathtaking originality of Toussaint and his comrades.

Since the late twentieth century, as the Haitian Revolution has fully emerged from the shadows of its American and French counterparts, new waves of scholarship have sought to retrieve its remarkable intellectual richness and cultural diversity – whether in terms of the role of the local *vodou* religion, the impact of African political and military cultures, or the contributions of specific groups and communities (notably women, free people of colour, southerners and African-born citizens).[41] Jean Fouchard's *Les marrons de la liberté* (1972) and Carolyn Fick's *The*

Making of Haiti (1990) have recovered the historical and political significance of Saint-Domingue's tradition of *marronage*, placing the colony's *marrons* at the heart of the revolutionary process during the 1790s and the subsequent Haitian War of Independence.[42] Scholars have also mapped out the regional ramifications of the Haitian Revolution, highlighting the terror it provoked among the slave-owning classes and the encouragement it gave to slaves and free black people across the Caribbean and the Americas.[43] Yet this new research, too, has further displaced Toussaint from the centre of the revolutionary stage. For one thing, its emphasis on social and cultural history 'from below' has shifted the focus away from his heroic individual leadership. In Fick's account, Toussaint is represented as marginal to the colony's indigenous tradition of popular resistance, an adjunct to the main revolutionary protagonists, the *marron* slaves.

Toussaint's credentials as a revolutionary have been questioned, not least since the recent discovery of archival documents indicating that he was emancipated from slavery more than a decade before the revolution, and as a free black man for a time owned a number of slaves. Feminist scholars have highlighted the 'paradox' of Haitian republicanism, arguing that its democratic and egalitarian values were from the outset – in other words, from Toussaint's leadership onwards – undercut by the 'historical exclusion of women' from the realms of state politics and citizenship.[44] For other critics, Toussaint's rule began as emancipatory, but then degenerated into authoritarianism, further marred by his refusal to distribute land to the peasant masses: the 'liberator' became the 'liquidator'.[45] The revolutionary waters have been further muddied by the emergence of revisionist neo-imperial works, which have painted Toussaint as a conservative autocrat who aspired only to replace the white plantation class with a black oligarchy: this was the main thesis of the French historian Pierre Pluchon's biography.[46] This approach has been adopted most brazenly in the writings of the Guadeloupean-born historian Philippe Girard. In his recent biography of Louverture, Girard emphatically rejected any ideological basis for his actions, viewing him as a 'social climber' who was driven entirely by material greed and political self-interest, and a 'craving for social status'.[47] In an earlier study of the Haitian War of Independence, Girard expressed his 'positive' appreciation of the French colonial project, and his 'sympathy' for the members of the Napoleonic expeditionary force sent to exterminate Toussaint's black leadership in late 1801; he effectively justified the French attack on Saint-Domingue on the grounds of Toussaint's 'duplicitous' behaviour.[48]

Such claims show that in key respects the literature on Toussaint Louverture has tended to reflect the spirit of its times, as it so often does.

C. L. R. James's biography was influenced by a global anti-colonial revolutionary upsurge, and a quest among progressive intellectuals for an alternative to Stalinist communism. The recent resurgence of conservative and neo-imperialist views about colonial history is a reaction to the implosion of this *zeitgeist*. Indeed, since the late twentieth century, as that historic era gave way to a more melancholic and pessimistic one, Toussaint's ghost has even been sighted in the misty hinterland of postmodernism. David Scott used James's account of the Haitian Revolution to argue that, in today's age of disillusionment, Toussaint no longer stands for the emancipatory ideals of 'resistance and agency', but has become a tragic 'conscript' of Western modernity.[49] In her study of black heroism, Celeste-Marie Bernier took Toussaint as one her six iconic figures, but warned against any attempt to recover any 'essential or historically verifiable figure' through archival research: such an enterprise would be 'not only illusory but ultimately doomed to failure'.[50]

The ambition behind this biography is to cut through these thickets and find our way back to Toussaint: to return as far as possible to the primary sources, to try to see the world through his eyes, and to recapture the boldness of his thinking and the individuality of his voice. As a leader he was blessed – and sometimes burdened – with an extraordinary sense of determination, and his own official accounts of his military and political successes tended to dwell on his individual role.[51] Like all great revolutionaries, however, his power rested on strong collective foundations. It was grounded in his republican army as well as in the free black population, which after the abolition of slavery in 1793 embraced the principles of freedom, equality and justice. But Toussaint also built a wider coalition of support in the colony's administrative and municipal structures, among white planter and business leaders, as well as the Catholic Church; and he helped to establish a black clergy which became one of the pillars of his rule locally. For much of the 1790s he reported to the Minister of Navy in Paris, who had overall responsibility for the administration of the colonies. He also secured the backing of senior figures in the colonial bureaucracy, elected members of French assemblies and leading abolitionist figures such as Abbé Henri Jean-Baptiste Grégoire; in addition, he successfully cultivated American and even British diplomats. How Toussaint interacted with these networks, how they viewed him, and how his relationship with them evolved over the course of his leadership is key to assessing the basis of his authority.

Getting back to Toussaint is also a matter of putting him in his primary context – that of slave and colonial politics in eighteenth-century

Saint-Domingue – where he was exposed to the major influences which shaped his character and intellectual personality. This was not merely a matter of absorbing Enlightenment thinking. Saint-Domingue (and Caribbean colonies more generally) also witnessed a 'subtle creolizing movement', in which these European ways of thought were reformulated to fit local conditions.[52] Toussaint and the insurgents of Saint-Domingue thus evolved in, and shaped, a lively and fertile milieu in which ideas and practices were exchanged between Europe and the Caribbean, as well as between Africa and the Caribbean, where universal concepts such as freedom, justice and brotherhood were appropriated and given specific meanings. Conversely, they also took local ideals – such as the abolition of slavery, the rejection of racial hierarchy and the definition of blackness – and gave them a universal significance.[53]

The Haitian Revolution generated its own set of emancipatory principles, making it 'the most masterful political improvisation of the Radical Enlightenment'.[54] A striking example from the archives serves as illustration. Shortly after the outbreak of the slave revolt in August 1791, a planter named Leclerc returned to his lands in the parish of Limbé, in the north of Saint-Domingue. Even though Leclerc saw himself as a 'humane' slave-owner, his property had been taken over and burned to the ground by the insurgents. When he came back to the area after rebel forces had retreated, he found only one building standing, and was told that it had been occupied by the local commander of the insurgency. Upon entering, he saw that it contained all his best furniture, and was surprised to see that his property had been 'carefully maintained'. The planter was even more startled to find his quarto edition of Guillaume-Thomas Raynal and Denis Diderot's *Histoire philosophique des Deux Indes*, the revolutionary pamphlet of the late Enlightenment which denounced slavery. The rebel commander had taken the book from his library and placed it on a mahogany table; it was the only work from his collection which had not been burned. The commander had left the book open on a page which spoke of the 'terrible reprisals' which would be meted out on the colonists if they did not emancipate their slaves;[55] he had not only reappropriated the *Histoire philosophique*, but brought the text to life in a glorious display of erudition, swagger and wit.

This kind of synergy was central to Toussaint's thinking. Those who observed him closely highlighted his 'closeness to nature' and his 'intuitive genius', which were rooted in his local upbringing and experiences; he often compared his way of seeing the world to that of a bird of prey, both elevated and yet capable of discerning the slightest movement on the ground.[56] At the same time, he defined himself as a man fashioned by 'reason and sound philosophy', and sincerely believed that the struggle of the people of Saint-Domingue could serve as an example to 'the entire universe'[57] – which offers a better appreciation of the originality of his republicanism. His speeches and letters showed that he was familiar with Raynal's work, as well as the main ideas of Machiavelli, Montesquieu and Rousseau. His political thought had powerful echoes of what Quentin Skinner has termed the 'neo-Roman' conception of liberty – especially in his explicit identification with the Spartacus legend, his attachment to the common good, his constant definition of republican freedom as the opposite of 'enslavement to tyranny',[58] and his steadfast refusal to become dependent on the arbitrary will of other states (including the French).[59] His revolutionary republicanism was focused on the equal dignity of the citizenry and a commitment to the ideals of popular sovereignty and service to the general interest which arose from his own experience. This was a republicanism in which he fought to retain his self-esteem in the face of white-settler attempts to dehumanize him; a republicanism of war which was rooted in military practice, and in particular the battle to liberate Saint-Domingue from slavery and foreign occupation; a republicanism of *métissage* which integrated local traditions of natural mysticism, including those of the native Taino Indians, with elements of royalism and Catholic moral teachings; and a republicanism of brotherhood which held up the enticing prospect of a multiracial community of equals, while giving the colony's black citizens responsibility for defending the revolutionary order.[60]

Getting back to Toussaint is perhaps primarily an exercise in recovery, lifting the barriers which have made him increasingly distant from us. The 'erasure' of the Haitian Revolution which Michel-Rolph Trouillot denounced in his classic essay is no longer as pronounced as before, but its trivialization remains.[61] Especially in modern French writing, Toussaint and the Haitian revolutionaries are still not credited with much meaningful intellectual potency.[62] One of my primary resources in correcting this distortion has been the rich holdings on late-eighteenth-century Saint-Domingue in French, Spanish, American and British archives, which have unearthed a wealth of captivating material about Toussaint's life and career. Most are in France, in the Archives Nationales, the Bibliothèque Nationale, the archives d'Outre Mer in Aix-en-Provence, the military archives at Vincennes, the Archives Diplomatiques in Nantes and Paris, as well as in a number of regional archives. Many of these precious documents have been ignored, or only cited selectively, in studies of Toussaint. They have revealed a wealth of original material which sheds new light on key aspects of Toussaint's leadership: hence the chapters devoted to his distinct qualities as a republican military commander, his constitutional thinking, and the local foundations of his rule.

American and Spanish archives, for their part, have enabled a better understanding of the decisive turning points in his career, such as his decision to embrace the French cause, his defeat of his mixed-race rival André Rigaud and his invasion of neighbouring Santo Domingo; these sources have further confirmed his skilful diplomatic manoeuvring, which he used to carve out new political opportunities for himself and his people. The most gratifying haul has come from the British archives in Kew, which have uncovered some key Toussaint papers not available elsewhere, as well as detailed and often uniquely informative reports about the final years of his leadership, thanks to the observations of British consular officials based in Saint-Domingue between 1799 and 1801.

One of Toussaint's most distinctive qualities was his 'epic faith in the written word'.[63] For this reason, an essential source in the quest to recapture his voice is the large collection of his own speeches, proclamations and letters. The Haitian historian Joseph Boromé, who devoted his life to gathering and cataloguing these papers, listed more than 1,600 of them, held in more than ninety archives, libraries and private collections across the Atlantic.[64] Use of this mass of material, as Boromé rightly surmised, helps put to rest some of the absurd claims still repeated to this day about Toussaint (for example, that he could not read or write),[65] and resolve some of the mysteries surrounding his personality.[66] Toussaint's letters, in particular, are a crucial resource. They range from brief jottings, despatched in the heat of the moment, to elaborate and carefully constructed texts. He was a meticulous correspondent: his important letters often took several drafts, which he scrutinized to ensure that every word conveyed his precise intent. In their sheer number they bear witness to his intellectual energy: at the height of his career in the late 1790s he would send out dozens of letters every day, and 'wear down his five secretaries'.[67] The delivery of his messages preoccupied him constantly, and he often wrote supplementary letters to establish whether and when the initial ones had reached their destinations (and in at least one instance, he penned a third letter enquiring about the first two). His writings show his willingness to champion the causes of those in need – a widow looking to have her family property returned, a planter whose animals were being stolen, or even a gendarme slapped by his captain, 'in breach of his human rights'.[68]

This material is revealing, too, about the complex ways in which Toussaint reflected on his blackness, which was all at once a matter of heritage, pride, duty, and (a frequently cited term) 'honour'.[69] Acting with honour was a matter of standing up for black interests, as well as occupying the moral high ground. When a white French official who had once declared that he could not 'live under the orders of the blacks' later wrote asking for his help, Toussaint first reminded him of his earlier statement, before agreeing to assist him, on the principle that the best way to 'respond to evil' was by 'doing good'.[70] Blackness was integral to his sense of self, especially in a world which was rife with prejudice against men and women of African descent. It was also a concept forged in deliberate contrast to the behaviour of other groups – notably the colony's administrative overlords, its former white ruling class, as well as its mixed-race leaders, with whom he clashed on a number of occasions. At the same time, Toussaint's blackness had a powerfully modern resonance. It was a resolute affirmation of what Stuart Hall has termed cultural and spiritual 'hybridity', which brought together elements from multiple African, European and Caribbean heritages, while at the same time celebrating the fundamental equality of black people with other ethnic and racial groups.[71]

The letters reveal much about Toussaint's stoicism, his subtlety and his playfulness (as in one of his early missives, addressed to 'Monsieur Chanlatte, scélérat, perfide et trompeur').[72] These documents are not, unfortunately, as illuminating about his intimate life as a biographer might hope: when the French invaded Saint-Domingue in 1802, they destroyed a large collection of his papers, including a thick bundle of *lettres galantes* between Toussaint and his numerous white mistresses, such as the legendary Madame Fisson, a white woman 'of rare beauty' whose husband became one of his agents;[73] only the odd billet-doux to one of these ladies has survived.[74] Yet his remaining correspondence affords some tantalizing glimpses of his private self – his concern for the education of his children, his passion for horses and roses, his attachment to personal hygiene, and his famously spartan eating habits: responding to a request from him, a letter from his wife Suzanne in 1794 mentioned the despatch of fresh clothes and towels, and four loaves of bread.[75] Toussaint's love of music was noteworthy, too: one of his early letters showed him overseeing the formation of a trumpeter and a clarinetist, and one of his last notes was a signed payroll sheet for a group of thirteen musicians who were attached to the governor's office.[76]

All great leaders struggle with contradictions, and Toussaint's letters are at their most revealing in exposing the competing impulses with which he wrestled throughout his career: between his yearning for a quiet family life and his devotion to the *res publica*; between his congenital impatience (one of his favourite sayings was 'ne perdons pas notre temps') and his belief in allowing things to take their natural, divinely ordained course (or, as he would put it: 'man proposes and God disposes'); between his sincere French patriotism and his duty to defend Saint-Domingue's interests; between his commitment to bring people together and his appreciation that violence was a necessary evil in moments of political change; between his instinctive penchant for secrecy and his need to draw from the energy of his 'immense people'; and between his unabashed pragmatism and his wish to lead the men and women of Saint-Domingue towards a new world of revolutionary possibility, in which they could realize 'their crazy dream, arising from their absolute love of liberty'.[77]

PART ONE

A Revolutionary is Born

I
The Soul of a Free Man

'I was born a slave, but nature gave me the soul of a free man.'[1] This fleeting mention, in an administrative report written in 1797, was one of the few recorded instances in which Toussaint Louverture alluded to his personal predicament as a slave before the revolution. It was typical of his utterances: it was direct, elevated in tone, and gave little away about his emotions. The statement also did not, as we shall see, tell the entire story: he was a master in the art of calculated ambiguity. But he had a gift, too, for concision; and his closeness to nature, his single-mindedness and his unrelenting quest to emancipate his spirit were among the defining features of his personality from an early age. Contrasting his enslavement with his longing for freedom, Toussaint hinted at the two main qualities which set him apart from most of his contemporaries: his yearning to free himself from external constraints, and his visionary power – the capacity to 'see and foresee'.[2]

Toussaint's early years present the most daunting challenges for his biographer. When he became Saint-Domingue's revolutionary leader, he left a sizeable paper trail. In addition, the records of many contemporaries who dealt with him have been preserved, from his own collaborators and military subordinates to French officials and foreign dignitaries, as well as ordinary citizens in the colony. But, even though there is considerable documentation about Saint-Domingue's plantations in French public archives, Toussaint's pre-revolutionary existence barely features in them.[3] Unlike figures such as Olaudah Equiano and Frederick Douglass, Toussaint produced no autobiographical narrative, and none of the men and women who knew him intimately on the plantation he grew up in – his parents, his godfather, his fellow house slaves, the priests from nearby Haut-du-Cap, or the manager whose principal assistant he eventually became – left any written records about him. Apart from a handful of tantalizing documents, most of which have come to light only recently, archival sources about his slave years are sparse. What little we know comes largely from oral traditions in nineteenth-century Haiti – a valuable resource in many respects, but not one which can provide conclusive information, even about the most basic features of Toussaint's life.

His date of birth is a case in point. In the same 1797 administrative report, Toussaint mentioned that he was 'fifty years of age' at the time of the revolution. This tallies with the later memoir of his son Isaac, who drew on family memory to affirm that his father was born on 1 May 1740.[4] (Slaves were not issued with birth certificates.) Yet other sources – including statements by Toussaint himself – have hinted at different possibilities, so his year of birth remains uncertain. Some have suggested later dates, up to 1746, while one of the French administrators who was among his closest collaborators, and who spoke extensively with his relatives, claimed that he ruled until the age of sixty-six – which would put the year of his birth at 1736.[5] Oral tradition has also been the principal source of our knowledge about his ancestry. Family sources intimated that Toussaint's father was the second son of Gaou Guinou, a king of the warrior nation of the Alladas, a west African people living in the southern regions of the Gold Coast, in present-day Benin.[6] Recent research, however, has been unable to find any trace of an Allada monarch by this name: Toussaint's grandfather was perhaps a provincial governor, or a royal functionary with extensive regional authority.

At the same time, this invented tradition shows Toussaint's attachment, from a very early age, to the power of imagination, and imposing his own control over his life narrative. The story also hints at the richness of African social and political cultures in Saint-Domingue during the eighteenth century, with their music, dances, games, religious beliefs, concepts of nature and supernatural tales.[7] Elements of royalist ideology also flourished in the colony, surviving through rituals, preserved historical memories of wars fought in Africa, and specific cultural practices such as skin markings.[8] Toussaint shared in these collective beliefs and practices by absorbing vivid fables about his noble ancestry from his parents, and passing them on to his children; it is likely that these stories helped instil in him his lifelong allergy to fatalism, together with his sense of his own exceptional destiny.

Toussaint was born – this much, at least, is not disputed – on the Bréda sugar estate, where his parents worked as slaves, near the village of Haut-du-Cap. The property was acquired by Count Pantaléon de Bréda, a marine officer from south-west France who married a local heiress and amassed a large fortune in the colony during the early decades of the eighteenth century. He occasionally visited the Caribbean but was mainly based in France,

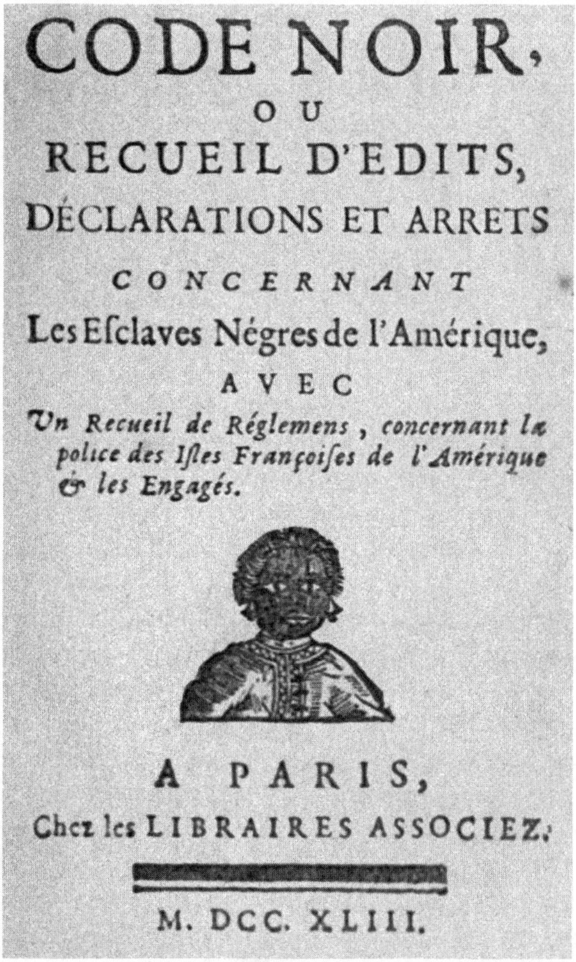
CODE NOIR,
OU
RECUEIL D'EDITS,
DÉCLARATIONS ET ARRETS
CONCERNANT
Les Eſclaves Négres de l'Amérique,
AVEC
Un Recueil de Réglemens, concernant la police des Iſles Françoiſes de l'Amérique & les Engagés.
A PARIS,
Chez les LIBRAIRES ASSOCIEZ.
M. DCC. XLIII.

First published as a royal decree in 1685, the *Code Noir* was the rule book which sought to regulate the treatment of slaves in French colonies. Regarded as property, slaves had no legal rights, and their masters could beat them with rods and straps.

like many wealthy landowners in Saint-Domingue.[9] His estate was part of a cluster of large sugar plantations on the northern plain around Cap, and had a workforce of around 150 slaves. According to the 1685 *Code Noir*, the rule book which governed the treatment of slaves in French colonies, a child automatically inherited the enslaved condition of his parents.[10] Nor did Toussaint have any choice about his surname: bonded labour was viewed as mere property, and so the young boy was formally known as 'Toussaint à Bréda' (or simply 'Toussaint Bréda'); the name 'Louverture' would emerge only at the time of the revolution. His health was poor during his early years, and at times he was so seriously ill that his family feared for his life; infant mortality rates in eighteenth-century Saint-Domingue were high, and especially so on the Bréda plantation, where one child in every three did not reach adulthood.[11] His scrawny physiognomy was mocked, too, and it was around this time that he earned the nickname 'Fatras-Bâton' (literally 'skinny stick') – a wordplay in the local kreyol dialect which lampooned his fragility.[12]

Fatras could also mean lazy, but there was nothing indolent about this young boy. Indeed, he more than made up for his physical deficiencies by his sheer determination. According to a nineteenth-century Haitian historian who talked to surviving members of Toussaint's family, by the age of twelve he had become the fastest runner, the most agile climber and the best swimmer of all the young slave children of the surrounding estates.[13] When he was in his teens, he began to master the horse-riding techniques which would later earn him the accolade of 'Centaur of the Savannah'; his favourite method was to attempt to tame the horses by mounting them when they were still wild. He often fell off, and on at least one occasion suffered a serious injury, breaking his thigh bone. But by the time he had reached young adulthood he had become one of the colony's most accomplished horsemen; people came from across the northern plain to learn from his equestrian expertise.[14] Even the best riders from France could not match him for speed or endurance, not to mention bravado – he once negotiated his way across a heavily swollen river by standing, fully upright, on his horse and guiding the steed to the opposite bank.[15] Such adventurous journeys across Saint-Domingue became one of Toussaint's hallmarks: they helped forge his sense of spiritual freedom, giving him, in the words of the historian Antoine Métral, 'an intimate knowledge of the tides, the torrents, the rivers, the lakes, the height and shape of mountains, gorges, passes, and the least practicable paths, the depths of forests, the return of the winds, the rain seasons, the approaching earthquakes, and the violent storms'.[16]

This communion with nature was enhanced by the fact that Toussaint spent most of his teenage and early adult years as a *gardien de bêtes*, tending to the Bréda farm animals. This occupation nurtured in him a somewhat melancholic disposition, and an enduring fondness for solitude. But the young shepherd also developed a feisty character from an early age. Any slave who laid hands on a white person could face severe punishment: according to article 33 of the *Code Noir*, a slave who struck a master or any member of his family could face the death penalty,[17] and in at least one instance a black freedman was hanged for a premeditated assault on a *colon*.[18] Yet Toussaint once confronted a young man named Ferret on the nearby Linasse plantation in 1754. Why he did so is unclear: perhaps Ferret taunted him with the familiar derogatory epithet 'Allada mangeur de chien' ('dog-eater'). They ended up trading blows under an orange tree, with the white boy coming off second best, even though he was two years older than Toussaint. On another occasion, the young Fatras-Bâton learned that Béagé, the manager of the Bréda plantation at the time, had tried to take possession of one of his horses. Toussaint responded by rushing to the stables and cutting the steed's saddle, infuriating the manager, who threatened to beat him. The young slave, however, stood up to him, telling him: 'Hit me if you dare!' The manager backed off and the story became a family legend.[19]

This self-confidence was no doubt in part a family heritage, but it was also shaped by Toussaint's Catholic beliefs. A daily public prayer was held for all the Bréda plantation slaves, and the young boy was exposed to the Christian religion from a very early age. The Catholic Church in northern Saint-Domingue was controlled by the Jesuit order; its headquarters were located in Cap, and some priests resided in the village of Haut-du-Cap and were well known to Toussaint. Oral tradition has it that they taught him to read and write; by the mid nineteenth century, as reported by a French schoolteacher who travelled across Haiti, the young Toussaint was widely believed to have been formally trained as a priest.[20] Jesuits certainly had a robust conception of their role as missionaries: they sponsored a special 'black Mass' at Cap, at which African elders led the congregation in song and prayer. They also appointed a 'priest of black people' to help disseminate the faith among the slaves. Unlike the rest of clergy in Saint-Domingue, these missionaries were respected by the slaves, who saw them as their protectors.[21]

Toussaint enthusiastically involved himself in the Jesuits' proselytizing activities, becoming one of their active surrogates in his neighbourhood. He may well have been one of the black slaves denounced in an official report for 'often and frequently spreading the gospel in the homes of the black population of the north'.[22] The order's efforts to provide spiritual comfort to the slave population were frowned upon by the colonial authorities. Planters complained that the Jesuits were undermining their material power and moral authority, notably by encouraging their slaves to marry; wedded couples were harder to sell than individuals. Some accused the missionaries of pushing their slaves to revolt against their masters, and to embrace reprehensible ideas of 'independence' and even 'equality'.[23] The Jesuits were duly expelled from Saint-Domingue in 1763, and the imposing building they occupied in Cap was taken over by the colonial administration. Toussaint, however, retained a close relationship with their successors, the Capuchins; and there is evidence that he was employed in the two Jesuit-founded hospitals which continued to operate in the Cap region.[24] By this point, his faith was fully entrenched and grounded in the values celebrated by the Catholic elders around him: harmony, compassion, sobriety and, above all, brotherhood. This Catholicism treated black slaves as integral members of the community, and Toussaint's religiosity was tinged with a specifically creole egalitarianism which challenged the colony's existing racial hierarchy.

Alongside his energetic physical activities, his spiritual bond with nature and his Catholic faith, the young Toussaint's personality was shaped by his African heritage. The extent of this influence remains a matter of dispute, and in fact Toussaint's relationship to his African roots has often been dismissed. Many historians have attempted to distinguish the minority of native 'creoles' such as Toussaint, born in Saint-Domingue, from African-born *bossales*, who constituted around 60 per cent of the adult population in the colony by 1790;[25] these slaves mostly came from the Kongolese-Angolan region.[26] It is typically suggested that creoles spurned their African past, which they associated with backwardness and humiliation, turning instead to their Caribbean roots, as well as to Roman Catholicism and Enlightenment thinking. In Toussaint's specific case, it has been claimed that his African past had 'remarkably little impact' on his public and private persona, that he tried to 'distance himself' from his father, and that his relationship to his African heritage was one of 'wilful denial'.[27]

Such assertions fail to convince, not least because they overstate the dissimilarities between creoles and *bossales* in eighteenth-century Saint-Domingue. There were undeniably material differences between the two groups: creoles tended to lead less precarious lives, often occupying established positions in the plantations, such as domestic servants, artisan craftsmen, coachmen and slave-drivers. There were also cultural contrasts: *bossales* were often more active in preserving their social rituals, languages and religious practices. Yet there were also numerous bridges between the two communities. As has rightly been pointed out, *bossales* 'became creolized in many ways', notably through baptism, the cultivation of their individual plots of land and the assimilation of the kreyol language, while creoles like Toussaint were only 'a generation away from Africa'.[28] This connection appears very clearly in Toussaint's upbringing: he learned and spoke kreyol, the vernacular of Saint-Domingue, but was also immersed in Allada culture from a very young age by his parents. Forcibly separated from his wife Affiba at the time of their capture and enslavement in the late 1730s, his father Hippolyte remarried once he reached Saint-Domingue, and he chose as his wife a young woman named Pauline, like him of Allada origin; Toussaint was the first of five children she bore him.

As a boy and young man, Toussaint would have heard himself described as an 'African': the term was loosely employed in colonial Saint-Domingue, typically as a racially pejorative description of the black population. Slaves were widely equated with domestic animals: one planter kept a notebook in which he listed the 'different remedies to be used for treating the ailments of negroes, horses, and mules'.[29] Local settlers complained about the difficulties of controlling their workforce ('malheureux qui a des nègres, plus malheureux qui n'en a pas'),[30] and there was a widespread view of black people as 'dangerous, superstitious and fanatical'.[31] As Frantz Fanon later observed, such portrayals were a key technique of colonial domination, reinforcing settler supremacy by depicting local populations as not only inferior but also menacing, 'the quintessence of evil'.[32] Encouraging ethnic division on a 'scientific' basis was another essential tool of white power, and French writers devoted much effort to attributing particular characteristics to groups of slaves on the basis of their African geographical origins. In the view of the colonial lawyer Moreau de Saint-Méry, one of the most widely cited apologists of the planter cause, members of the Allada nation were generally seen as 'well built and intelligent'; however, they were also thought to be 'deceiving, artificial, dissembling, lazy, and roguish'.[33] Many of these traits would continue to be pinned on Toussaint by his enemies in his later years.

Yet, despite the best efforts of the colonial order to dehumanize the 'African' population of Saint-Domingue, positive tropes also survived and in fact flourished. Alladas were the second largest group of African slaves in Saint-Domingue, for whom successive plantation managers at Bréda had a particular fondness, believing them to possess extensive agricultural skills.[34] Alladas were also highly rated as among the most effective African 'warrior races'.[35] Toussaint would have experienced this prestige as he was growing up: his father was recognized as a figure of authority by African-born slaves on his plantation and in the vicinity, and treated with deference by them – and even, it would appear, by plantation manager Béagé; this would cast further light on the latter's reluctance to confront young Toussaint in the incident mentioned earlier.[36] And although he could neither read nor write, Hippolyte passed on to his eldest son the practical knowledge of herbal medicine he had acquired from his African elders: this savoir-faire was also widely associated with Allada culture in eighteenth-century Saint-Domingue.[37]

It has been suggested that Toussaint fully embraced the emerging *vodou* religion, widely practised among black communities of Allada origin in Saint-Domingue's plantations at this time. Originating in West Africa, and drawing also on indigenous Taino Indian religious practices,[38] *vodou* was a cult which centred around the worship of spirits (known as *loa*), who were believed to preside over different aspects of earthly existence and communicate with humans during religious rituals.[39] Toussaint's embrace of *vodouism* has become an article of faith among many contemporary Haitians: one modern historian observes that he was 'thought to be a *bòkò*' (*vodou* priest).[40] Interestingly, there was a powerful link between herbal science and *vodou* in the *loa* known as Loko, who was the patron of healers; this spirit was passed on to the first *marron* communities of Saint-Domingue by the Taino Indians.[41] Toussaint undoubtedly made this connection, and drew upon the magical recipes of sorcerers in his practice of natural medicine;[42] this was one of the sources of his reputation as a healer who possessed supernatural powers, with many *bossales* hailing him as a priest who could communicate with the 'good spirits'.[43]

Toussaint not only treasured this traditional herbalist science, which earned him the officious title of *docteur feuilles*, but built upon it through his extensive journeys across the colony. Like his highly prized fellow-slave healers across Saint-Domingue, he eventually combined African, Caribbean and European forms of medical knowledge. His plant-based remedies helped nurse injuries sustained in the plantations and the sugar mills, combat illnesses such as malaria and yellow fever, and contain outbreaks of scurvy, one of the most common ailments to afflict newly arrived slaves.[44] Hippolyte also taught his eldest son the Fon language spoken by the Alladas, and we are told that the young boy frequently conversed in this African dialect with community elders on the plantation and in nearby Haut-du-Cap; the manager of the Bréda plantation confirmed that the slaves spoke 'in their own languages'.[45] Far from turning his back on this cultural heritage during the revolutionary era, Toussaint embraced it. His son Isaac later recalled an instance in which a group of African-born combatants came to visit Toussaint at his military headquarters: realizing that many of them were his Allada countrymen, he started haranguing them in the Fon language, to their immense delight.[46]

Perhaps the most eloquent testimony to the enduring importance of Toussaint's African roots was his reaction to the loss of his parents. Hippolyte and Pauline both died of chest infections within a few months of each other in early 1774, suddenly thrusting Toussaint – now in his early thirties – into the position of family elder. He became responsible for his two brothers and two sisters, together with a number of children of his own, as we shall see.

He handled the crisis by seeking out the assistance of an African-born woman called Pélagie, who effectively became the adoptive mother of the clan. Significantly, Pélagie was from the Aguia (Aja) nation, which originated from the same region as the Alladas. She was in all likelihood a close acquaintance of his mother, and her presence in the family setting was a crucial source of cultural continuity with Toussaint's African heritage, all the way up to the revolutionary era. Far from looking down on her, or trying to conceal her from public view, Toussaint protected and honoured his adoptive mother. He bought her out of human bondage in 1789, at a time when his own resources were still modest and the immediate members of his own family were still enslaved; he also found new lodgings for her in Haut-du-Cap. Later, when he became one of the leaders of the revolution, he invited Pélagie to come and live near him in Ennery, and sent a carriage to take her to Mass every Sunday.[47]

In one of his later pamphlets, Toussaint summed up the inhumanity of slavery in its systematic tendency 'to tear away the son from his mother, the brother from his sister, the father from his son'.[48] The impersonal turn of phrase served to disguise the extent to which he was speaking from personal experience. As a slave his entire existence was governed by the provisions of the *Code Noir*: he had no legal personality, could not marry without the permission of his master, was banned from carrying weapons, and could be physically punished by being chained and beaten with whips or rods.[49] Although Toussaint was not personally treated with this kind of savagery, he would have known of countless examples of inhuman violence inflicted on his fellow slaves across the colony. These atrocities were widely documented in late-colonial Saint-Domingue and horrified even those who defended the institution of slavery: they included throwing slaves into furnaces, burying them alive, blowing up their bodies with gunpowder and cutting off their limbs; various forms of torture, including castration and genital mutilation, were also widely practised, although they were technically banned by the *Code Noir*.[50]

Even though such gruesome horrors were not inflicted, as far as is known, on the Bréda plantation workers, Toussaint saw the ordinary violence of slavery on a daily basis, with its grim complement of disease, misery and death. It has been calculated that life expectancy on his estate was a mere thirty-seven years, and that the mortality rate of African-born plantation workers was among the highest in the region: by the time he reached his early forties, Toussaint would have seen around half his contemporaries at Bréda die.[51] He observed the crushing effects of slavery on his own family from a very young age. As noted earlier, his father Hippolyte had been separated from his wife Affiba at the time of their enslavement, and he believed that he had left her and their two children behind in their Allada homeland. However, unbeknown to him, Affiba and her offspring were also captured and transported to Saint-Domingue, and sold to a slave-owner in the colony. The young African woman was baptized and given the name Catherine, and her two children were called Augustin and Geneviève. By the time Affiba realized that she and her husband had ended up on the same island and was able to locate his whereabouts, Hippolyte was already remarried to Pauline and had started his second family; the news completely broke her and she died of sorrow shortly afterwards.[52] Toussaint spent time with his half-brother and sister, consoling them for the loss of their mother, and forging a particularly strong bond with Geneviève. She was, however, soon sold off to a *colon* named Fontaine, and he lost sight of her for several decades. But she continued to haunt his mind, and it is not unlikely that he was thinking of her in 1797 when he wrote of sisters being 'torn off' from their brothers. In the final years of his life, his perseverance would be rewarded when he was reunited with her in the southern town of Les Cayes.[53]

Another pivotal figure in Toussaint's extended family circle was Pierre-Baptiste, an Allada freedman who worked as gatekeeper at the Haut-du-Cap plantation. Educated by the Jesuits, Pierre-Baptiste was a tall, imposing man who spoke in parables and was recognized as one of the wise men of the locality; he was among the worthies who led the black congregation in prayer at Cap.[54] He adopted Toussaint as his surrogate son after the death of Hippolyte, and gave him lessons in history, geography and algebra (he also manifestly influenced Toussaint's own love of allegories). As with his adoptive mother Pélagie, Toussaint kept in close touch with his godparent throughout the later years of his life, and invariably stopped by Haut-du-Cap to pay his respects when he was passing through his area; even when he became famous, he described Pierre-Baptiste as the only man he obeyed unconditionally.[55]

Pierre-Baptiste was still alive – aged over 100 – when Toussaint was deported to France in 1802. He had particular cause to be grateful to his godfather: Pierre-Baptiste was an effective matchmaker and introduced Toussaint to his niece Suzanne, a fellow slave on the Bréda plantation, where her brother was one of the *commandeurs* (slave-drivers). She was also of Allada origin. They eventually settled down – according to oral tradition, sometime around 1782 – and lived together as a couple, Suzanne becoming the mother of his two sons Isaac and Saint-Jean, born in 1786 and 1791 respectively. Toussaint welcomed Suzanne's son Placide (an offspring from an earlier marriage) into his family, and later sent him to study in France along with Isaac. It is worth mentioning here, in light of later accusations of anti-mixed-race bias against Toussaint, that Placide's father was a person of colour.[56]

Suzanne was long believed to have been Toussaint's only wife. Recent research into the parish archives of Cap has, however, established that he was first married in the early 1760s, when he was in his early twenties, to a free black woman (*négresse libre*) named Cécile. This was remarkable given that he himself was still a slave at that time, and it was extremely unusual for a male black slave to marry a free black woman – indeed it was rare for men in such circumstances to marry at all. The couple had three children, the eldest being a boy named after his father;[57] a burial certificate from November 1785 records the death of a young man named Toussaint, born in 1761, who was interred in the presence of his father and his brother Gabriel. The document bore the hesitant signature of 'Toussaint Bréda' – his first recorded autograph, under the most tragic of personal circumstances. Toussaint's sorrow was compounded by the breakdown of his marriage with Cécile, who by the time of the death of their son appears to have left him for a building contractor named Pourvoyeur.[58]

Toussaint's family network was large, complex and multi-layered; towards the end of his life he claimed to have fathered no fewer than sixteen children. Taken together with his devotion to his godparents, his generosity towards his stepson Placide and his efforts to maintain close relations with his siblings, these wider ties highlight the value he attached to family bonds. He was in this respect entirely representative of prevailing social customs in late-colonial Saint-Domingue, and large, patriarchal, extended families have remained a prominent feature of social life in rural Haiti to this day.[59] These blood and clan affiliations also underpinned Toussaint's ideal of brotherhood. In republican terms, fraternity was a principle which served as a link between the private and public realms, and so it was for Toussaint: as a political leader and military commander he systematically recruited members of his family to serve in his immediate entourage. Moreover, as we shall see later, the family featured prominently in Toussaint's revolutionary political thought, both as a force for social cohesion and an idealized metaphor for the citizenry as a whole.

It was already clear before the revolution that Toussaint was no ordinary slave: his father's reputation as an Allada patriarch shielded him as a young boy, and in all likelihood enabled his marriage to a woman of higher status such as Cécile. His penetrating intelligence, immediately observed by those who came into contact with him, rapidly attracted the attention of the plantation hierarchy, and he was eventually recruited into the service of Antoine-François Bayon de Libertat, a white French *colon* who played a decisive role in Toussaint's pre-revolutionary life. Bayon had lived in Saint-Domingue since 1749, and he served as manager and attorney for the Bréda estate between 1772 and 1789, forging a close relationship with Toussaint. As Bayon's coachman, Toussaint effectively became his right-hand man, with the power to act in his name and travel across the colony on business for him. According to a French military officer who conducted extensive local research on Toussaint's early years, Bayon 'completely trusted [Toussaint] and consulted him on plantation work and even on his own affairs'.[60]

Toussaint never gave a full account of his activities as Bayon's coachman, but it is likely that he had considerable supervisory power over the Bréda estate, as well as assisting his boss in his numerous other business ventures. Bayon spent a great deal of time away from Bréda tending to these wider interests, which included his own sugar estate with 280 slaves, which he acquired in 1778 in the nearby parish of Limbé; he also bought a plot of land in 1782 and a house in 1789, as well as shares in two other plantations on the colony.[61] Toussaint's position of responsibility perhaps explains the interview he gave in 1799 to a local correspondent of the French *Moniteur Universel*, in which he was able to paint this idyllic portrait of his pre-revolutionary marital life with Suzanne: 'not only did we live in such abundance that we were able to make savings, but we also had the pleasure of giving food to the black plantation workers whenever they fell short. On Sundays and holidays, my wife, myself and my relatives would go to Mass; and once back home, after enjoying a pleasant meal, the family would spend the rest of the day together, ending with a prayer which we would all say together.'[62]

This edifying narrative asks the obvious question, already raised by some of Toussaint's early biographers: why he did not use his 'abundant' resources to buy his own freedom?[63] He provided part of the answer in another letter to the French Directory in 1797, where he acknowledged that the 'burden of slavery' had been lifted from his shoulders 'twenty years earlier' by his manager on the Bréda estate, 'the virtuous Bayon de Libertat'.[64] Toussaint did not state whether Bayon had formally emancipated him or merely given him de facto freedom, known as *liberté de savanne*.[65] For a long time, the latter was assumed to be the case. Recent research in the French archives has, however, conclusively established that Toussaint had been formally emancipated by 1776, and possibly earlier.[66] Even more dramatically, notarial documents show that after his liberation from servitude he owned at least one slave, and rented a coffee plantation with thirteen slaves from his son-in-law, Philippe-Jasmin Désir, between

1779 and 1781.[67] These revelations have opened the way for a new raft of questions about Toussaint's pre-revolutionary status and the sincerity of his later opposition to slavery.

The archives of the Bréda plantation provide some answers, and shed fresh light on Toussaint's position on the estate in the decades prior to the revolution.[68] Although the official document certifying his manumission has yet to be found, it does seem very likely that Toussaint obtained his freedom thanks to the intervention of Bayon de Libertat. According to the most plausible theory, Bayon approached the nephew of the owner of the Bréda plantation, count Louis-Pantaléon de Noé, who was based in Saint-Domingue between 1769 and 1775 and would later inherit the property. Bayon convinced Noé to free his coachman as a reward for his key role in bringing the *habitation* back to order after a period of major unrest in the early 1770s.[69] A significant number of slaves fled in 1773 in protest against their violent treatment by one of the Bréda managers, a man named Delribal, who had temporarily displaced Bayon. As one of the plantation's coachmen, Toussaint would have been an essential intermediary between the estate hierarchy and the workforce; it is likely that he would have helped broker the solution which ended this episode of *marronage* and brought the slaves back to the plantation. The arrangement included the dismissal of Delribal, the abandonment of his harsh treatment of the workforce, and the reinstatement of Bayon as manager – an outcome which would explain the latter's gratitude to his coachman.[70]

Toussaint, too, remained indebted to Bayon: he showed his appreciation by helping the manager's family escape from the plantation at the time of the outbreak of the revolution in 1791. He even sent funds regularly to his old boss when he went into exile in the United States in the 1790s, and later facilitated his return to Saint-Domingue, singing his praises to the French authorities and obtaining the release of his sequestrated property in Limbé;[71] he also recruited one of Bayon's nephews, Gilbert, as his personal aide-de-camp.[72] Later descendants of Bayon went so far as to claim that the Bréda manager brought up Toussaint 'like his own son'[73] – almost certainly an exaggeration, even though the bond between the two men was genuine and lasting. Yet once he became a freedman, Toussaint did not take his emancipation as a sign that his interests were now aligned with those of the slave-owners of Saint-Domingue. Rather it reflected the position of influence he had managed to carve out for himself at Bréda, through his talents as a conciliator. There is evidence that Toussaint's close relationship with Bayon allowed him to encourage a more humane treatment of the slaves on the plantation: the records of the Bréda estate in the decade prior to the revolution show a comparatively high level of expenditure on medical services for plantation workers. In the year 1788, for example, Bayon spent 3,703 *livres* on curing diseases that afflicted his slaves;[74] a year later, only around twenty of the 150 Bréda plantation workers were typically listed on the infirmary register, a much lower percentage than the colony average, which ranged from a quarter to a third of all slaves.[75]

And so, though terse, Toussaint's self-description in his 1799 *Moniteur* interview turned out to have been quite accurate. Even though he now belonged to a tiny aristocracy of black freedmen (fewer than 750 in the Cap and Port-au-Prince areas in the entire 1776–89 period),[76] his emancipated status did not fundamentally change his lifestyle. As was typically the case with black freedmen, he lived in more comfortable accommodation than the plantation slaves, with windows, beds and curtains, and enjoyed the use of a comparatively larger allotment. But, contrary to later rumours, he did not at this time accumulate a huge fortune or own large properties.[77] Indeed, in late-colonial Saint-Domingue, free blacks continued to be seen as inferior beings in the eyes of white society, which took every opportunity to prevent their assimilation: like people of colour, they were banned from engaging in games of chance, or (from the 1770s) travelling to France; their dress was strictly regulated and they were forbidden from taking the name of their former masters.[78] Recently uncovered documents from the Bréda estate show that Toussaint was still living on the plantation in the 1780s: a register entry from 1785 listed him as a slave, describing him as 'an intelligent subject, handy for treating animals, gentle in his manners but bigoted, and tending towards religious indoctrination and proselytism'.[79]

It may seem odd that a freedman would choose to continue to reside on the site of his former enslavement. But there is a simple answer. If Toussaint was now emancipated, the rest of his family were not: the names of Suzanne, Placide and Isaac appear on the same 1785 register. He had clearly made a choice to remain close to his wife and children, even if it meant being formally listed as a slave, and to use his influence to promote and protect them; Suzanne was noted in the same document as being 'the most valiant *négresse* of the plantation'.[80] Toussaint also watched over his extended family, notably the entire clan of his nephew Moyse: Moyse's mother Marguerite, the sister of Suzanne; his father Gilles, a mason; and his siblings Louison, Henri, Jeanne, Charles and Marie-Noëlle.[81] The Bréda coachman was thus able to see to it that many of his relatives were deployed in the estate house belonging to manager Bayon, as cooks, valets, housekeepers, seamstresses and washerwomen; these were comparatively privileged positions, which came with a lighter load and greater supplies of provisions. It is also a measure of his authority on the plantation – as well as his filial devotion – that he managed to secure especially favourable working conditions for his beloved Pélagie even before he bought her out of slavery. The 1785 register specifically indicated that Toussaint's surrogate mother was 'exempt of all labour' because of past services rendered to Bayon's family; she was clearly a popular figure on the plantation, as it added that she was 'robust and dances well in the style of her country'.[82]

The greatest challenge facing the historian of Toussaint's pre-revolutionary life is painting a coherent picture of his political values. No record has been found reliably connecting him to any particular event, group or sensibility before 1791, and much of what he himself later declared was clearly intended to be consistent with his position as an eminent French revolutionary leader. The only glimpses we catch from the 1785 Bréda registry are references to his 'gentleness' and his 'Catholic zeal', but we should not read too much into such observations – not least as the author of this annotation did not even know that Toussaint had been emancipated for the past decade. Bayon's coachman was no doubt able to give off an impression of meekness when it suited him, and was already adept at disguising his appearance and keeping a low profile – qualities which would serve him very well during his political life.

Oral tradition has it that the single most influential work to shape Toussaint's world view was Guillaume-Thomas Raynal and Denis Diderot's *Histoire philosophique des Deux Indes*, a sweeping indictment of European colonialism which denounced the barbarity of slavery. Its authors warned that if Europeans continued to 'massacre, imprison and plunder' the indigenous inhabitants, an 'avenger' would arise to destroy the practice of human bondage.[83] Toussaint was later likened to this liberator by his French admirers in Saint-Domingue, and he readily accepted the accolade – so much so that he became known as the 'Black Spartacus'. Yet even though the text was familiar in the colony, as we saw in the Introduction, it is unlikely that it shaped Toussaint's thinking about his condition as a slave before the revolution: rather, he later adopted it as a way of reassuring his French comrades about the robustness of his republican beliefs. A more fundamental reason to be sceptical is that the *Histoire philosophique* was not a call to arms to the black slaves, but primarily a warning to colonial authorities and slave-owning classes. For even the most radical fringes of the European philosophical establishment, the idea of a revolution carried out by black slaves in the name of universal republican principles, leading to the collective empowerment of the black population in the colonies, was simply

Guillaume-Thomas Raynal and Denis Diderot's *Histoire philosophique des Deux Indes* denounced the barbarity of human bondage, and announced the advent of an 'avenger' who would liberate the slaves. This nineteenth-century illustration shows Toussaint reading the text, with his wife Suzanne behind him.

'unthinkable'.[84] As the philosopher Louis Sala-Molins mused ironically: 'how did [Toussaint] manage to snatch from the Enlightenment what the Enlightenment never dreamt of?'[85] In addition, Toussaint's views on religion were diametrically opposed to the anticlericalism of Diderot. Raynal himself published a pamphlet specifically about Saint-Domingue in 1785, which did not call for the abolition of human bondage, merely the introduction of more humane treatment of slaves, and punishments which were 'less severe'.[86]

The sources of Toussaint's early political thought can be found much closer to home. Indeed, his Bréda plantation was located near the centre of the first slave revolts in mid-eighteenth-century Saint-Domingue. Under the charismatic leadership of François Makandal, *marron* slaves are thought to have formed secret societies across the north of the colony between the mid 1740s and the late 1750s, with the aim of destroying settler dominance and ultimately achieving black emancipation. Makandal was captured and publicly executed in 1758, and historians disagree about the scale and even the existence of this conspiracy. In the Haitian tradition, Makandal is hailed as one of the nation's early freedom fighters: one historian likened his movement to a 'black Carbonarism' whose members exchanged information and co-ordinated their actions, with the use of poison as one of their preferred methods.[87] It is suggested that they developed *vodou* religious rituals to cement their ties, and established a complex network of communication across northern towns and plantations;[88] Makandal is also believed to have been a *vodou* priest of Kongolese origin, and his agents included small merchants as well as slaves in senior positions, such as *commandeurs* and coachmen.[89] Whatever view one takes of Makandal himself and his organization,[90] there is widely documented evidence that he became a legend in late-colonial Saint-Domingue, inspiring terror among whites and capturing the imagination of black dissidents and rebels. Many of his supporters believed that their leader's supernatural powers had enabled him to survive; so widespread were the activities of the secret societies that they had their own spirit, Ezili Kawoulo, whose anniversary was celebrated every year.[91]

How actively Toussaint's Bréda plantation was penetrated by these revolutionary undercurrents is difficult to establish, especially as any rebels had to operate covertly, and 'resistance' took a variety of forms, ranging from mockery and foot-dragging to *marronage*, strikes and outright acts of rebellion. The correspondence between the estate management and the owners during the 1773 revolt mentioned slaves forming 'cabals' in order to resist punishment, suggesting the existence of some form of slave organization on the site, as well as a significant occurrence of *marronage* (which was much higher in northern Saint-Domingue than in the rest of the colony).[92] In the same year, Bayon de Libertat referred to the consultation of 'soothsayers' by plantation slaves, indicating that *vodou* practices were beginning to spread alongside traditional Catholic rituals.[93] A few years later Bayon pardoned two slave-drivers named Hippolyte and Jean-Jacques who organized a mass walkout from one of the Noé plantations. By the mid 1780s strikes had become widespread in the northern plain of Saint-Domingue. Other sources tell us that Bayon offered a reward for the return of two of his slaves who had gone into *marronage*, an Allada woman named La Garonne and a Martinique-born person of colour named Joseph.[94] A report to the Bréda owners by a disgruntled white official denounced the anarchic state of the plantation, likening it to a 'carnival' because of the absenteeism of the slaves, who often disappeared to nearby Cap for days on end; it also noted the 'penchant for idleness, promiscuity, and independence' among the domestic servants.[95]

At first sight, this Makandalist world of African stick fights, nocturnal *chica* and *kalinda* dances, *vodou* rituals and plantation brotherhoods seems far removed from Toussaint's practical preoccupations, to say nothing of his strongly held Catholic values. Yet the frontier between *vodou* and Catholicism (and between both of these and African herbal science) was highly porous.[96] There were substantial overlaps between Toussaint and the beliefs and personal traits attributed to Makandal, which were embraced by his followers – notably their deism, their visceral opposition to slavery, their intimate knowledge of natural medicine, their charisma, and above all their commitment to the ideal of fraternity. Furthermore, Toussaint's duties as Bayon's coachman required him to remain in very close touch with the plantation workers; it is also clear that he managed to retain their support and trust throughout this period, and, as noted, to renegotiate their working conditions during their conflict with Delribal. He could surely not have sustained such a position without engaging with, and fully understanding, the politico-religious culture of the dissident slaves.

In fact, everything we know about Toussaint's later methods suggests that his relationship with Makandalism was not one of complete identification, but of creative adaptation. He believed, through his personal experience, that the European settler population could be worked with, and indeed was vital for the colony's economic future. He would have been opposed, too, to the killings of black slaves by Makandal's agents: the shedding of blood, especially black blood, was always abhorrent to him. Above all, Makandal was eventually captured, and the teenage Toussaint probably witnessed his public execution at Cap in 1758: he would have taken his defeat as evidence that an all-out quest to confront the dominant order was unlikely to succeed. At the same time, his subsequent political thinking shows that he was inspired by the Makandalist ambition to create a common consciousness among black slaves, by the movement's appeal to their aspirations for liberty, and by its goal to forge an efficient revolutionary organization which could project its influence across the different parts of the colony.

It was in this ability to take existing social and political forms, absorb them fully and then redeploy them to his own ends that Toussaint's genius lay. In the later 1790s, he followed the same approach with Catholicism, adapting for his political purposes the religious networks instituted by the Jesuits in the mid eighteenth century. He also borrowed creatively from *vodou* culture, as was illustrated in the emergence of his own form of Makandalist mysticism, with his use of particular rhetorical expressions and contrasts (light-dark, bitter-sweet, good-evil, earth-heavens) and his fondness for vivid natural symbols. Makandalist rituals typically ended with the chant, 'après Bon Dieu, c'est Makandal', and Toussaint frequently used this turn of phrase in his own speeches in the 1790s (but replacing 'Makandal' with other names). He also borrowed Makandal's techniques of displaying different-coloured substances to convey his political messages, and used a variety of subterfuges to appear and disappear rapidly; these added to the supernatural aura already associated with him, with some of his people hailing him as a sorcerer who was a reincarnation of Makandal.[97]

Toussaint's depiction of himself as a man who had acquired the soul of freedom before the revolution was amply justified. It was a gruelling journey, as Frederick Douglass later observed: 'other liberators and saviors of men come from heaven, this man came from the hell of slavery'.[98] But he laboured tirelessly to liberate himself from the material and spiritual constraints of his condition. This independence of spirit was one of the most compelling features of his personality, and it would go on to become a defining characteristic of his politics: in the words of the Haitian poet Roger Dorsinville, his 'vocation for freedom' was expressed in his endeavours 'constantly to transcend the limits others sought to impose upon him'.[99]

This quest to liberate himself from external domination was the main element of continuity between his pre- and post-revolutionary life. Before the 1790s Toussaint had joined the ranks of the handful of black men in Saint-Domingue who managed, against all odds, to escape from human bondage. He did not gloat about this achievement during his later years, for obvious political reasons: indeed, in his speeches to his black brethren he emphasized that he had been 'a slave like all of you'.[100] Toussaint always took pride in his appearance in his later years, and we can guess that he dressed smartly – not least because the records show that Bayon de Libertat made generous allocations of funds for elite members of the Bréda workforce, including jackets (normally blue), hats and buttons.[101] More importantly, many of Toussaint's later character traits were already fully formed before the revolution: from his physical habits (pushing himself to his limits, being constantly on the move, getting by with little sleep and even less food) to his pride, his prudence, his religiosity, his talent for compromise and his secretiveness. Also in plain sight during the Bréda years was one of his most captivating human qualities: his abhorrence of violence, which probably stemmed both from his medical activities as a natural healer and his humanistic religious values.

It has been suggested that Toussaint shared the common ideology of black freedmen in late-colonial Saint-Domingue: one which both opposed slavery and white domination and, at the same time, stressed the virtues of individual effort, hard work and advancement by merit.[102] There is perhaps something in this, although it underestimates the significance of fraternity in Toussaint's scheme of values. Ideals of brotherhood had deep roots in Saint-Domingue's various cultural and religious traditions, and Toussaint identified with them all in different degrees before 1791 – well before the advent of the French Revolution. For him, fraternity was less a philosophical concept than a lived experience, expressed through active engagement in a variety of networks. From his base at the Bréda estate he seamlessly moved across a range of overlapping circles, drawing strength from his extended family, from his Allada culture, from his creole and *bossale* brethren, and from the men and women who shared his Catholic faith; by the 1780s he had secured his own bench in the Cap church, where he brought his entire family on Sundays and festive occasions.[103] As a patriarch he combined idealism and generosity with pragmatism and self-interest, watching over his personal interests while involving himself in the complex affairs of his boss, Bayon de Libertat, and on occasion entering the shadowy worlds of natural healers, *vodou* followers and Makandalist itinerant traders, who linked the plantations to the cities.[104] In all these activities he made precious contacts which would serve him during his later career.

At some point in the later 1780s, as we shall see in the next chapter, he also forged strong bonds with fellow slave elites (coachmen, drivers, valets) in Saint-Domingue's northern plain, taking part in regular Sunday meetings which would eventually prepare the ground for the August 1791 insurrection. Recent archival research has uncovered further layers of this brotherly sociability. A number of Saint-Domingue's future black insurgents interacted closely with Toussaint at Bréda in the decade prior to the 1790s: they included Jean-François Papillon and Jeannot Bullet, two of the early revolutionary leaders, and the *bossale* rebel Sans-Souci, who would later become a senior commander in his army.[105] Perhaps the most startling of these revolutionary affiliations *avant la lettre* is the connection recently discovered between Toussaint and Jean-Jacques Dessalines, one of his most successful generals, who later became the first leader of the independent state of Haiti. It turns out that Dessalines was quite probably one of the thirteen slaves Toussaint supervised when he watched over the affairs of his son-in-law Philippe-Jasmin Désir, and that he was eventually inherited by his own daughter Marie-Marthe.[106] This astonishing fact highlights the complex web of relationships that could develop among the black slaves of Saint-Domingue in the years preceding the revolution.

Contrary to the insinuations of some of his later critics, Toussaint did not suffer from an inferiority complex about his blackness, and his contempt for the white slave system of *ancien-régime* Saint-Domingue was profound. He had first-hand experience of its brutality, inhumanity and racism, as well as its immorality, in particular the depraved pursuit of luxury in places such as Cap, the lurid symbol of colonial greed and opulence. At the same time – and remarkably for a man who knew of scores of atrocities carried out against black people by the white settlers of Saint-Domingue that went unpunished[107] – his view of human nature was not racialized. His encounters with the Jesuit missionaries, and later with Bayon de Libertat, nourished his enduring belief that there was a capacity for goodness in all human beings. This is perhaps one of the areas where Toussaint formed spiritual links – mediated through *vodou* and Catholic traditions – with the culture of the indigenous Taino Indians, who were renowned for their gentleness and their love of nature.[108]

He was not – yet – a revolutionary. But the atmosphere of rebellion in which he was steeped during his Bréda years unquestionably shaped his character and values, and paved the way for his later emergence as the colony's Black Spartacus. It is no coincidence that the northern province of Saint-Domingue, with its large plantations and high concentration of *bossale* slaves, was the centre of all the major insurrections in the colony, starting with Makandal's underground conspiracy in the mid eighteenth century and continuing with the 1791 slave revolt, which launched the Saint-Domingue revolution, and ending with the 1802 popular rebellion against the French invading army. In other words, when Toussaint grew up a fully fledged revolutionary culture was already active in the colony; it rejected the slave system in the name of liberty and independence, and promoted a radical vision of black brotherhood which inspired large numbers of slaves.[109]

Even if he did not fully embrace its political agenda, this revolutionary culture shaped key traits of Toussaint's character. It helped nurture his capacity to operate silently, without revealing his true intentions, as well as his prodigious stamina and willpower, which allowed him to transcend his physical limitations. It also gave him an inner moral strength which could resist the pressures of the outside world, even at their most perverse. For despite the best efforts of the colonial system to crush his spirit and deny him a personality, like other men of African origin, Toussaint emerged into adulthood fully conscious of his humanity, and armed with a powerful yearning for freedom. His sentiments of brotherhood were reinforced by his Catholic faith, which cemented his belief in the potential for social regeneration: there was an underlying meaning and purpose to human existence, and all men and women were equally worthy of God's grace, irrespective of their race or colour. Finally, his strategic intelligence enabled him to exploit the weaknesses of the plantation order so as to protect those dearest to him. This capacity to build collective freedom within a structure of constraint would be replicated on a much grander scale in the relationship he later sought to develop between Saint-Domingue and France.

It is worth noting that the main language Toussaint spoke, and used on a daily basis during the first five decades of his life, was kreyol. One of Saint-Domingue's late-colonial memorialists who heard him speak noted how precise, but also how vivid and colourful his expression was.[110] In its combination of French, African and indigenous motifs and its capacity for ambiguity, irony and wit, the language was a perfect reflection of the cultural forces which shaped Toussaint's personality and intellect. The kreyol of northern Saint-Domingue was distinct from that of the west or the south: it was richer and more dynamic, as it absorbed a range of African influences. It was the language of unity, which brought together black populations from the towns and cities and the slaves in the plantations and conveyed their distinctness from white society. It also drew on their common experiences of oppression and their shared hopes for a better future; in this sense, it was the language of freedom.[111]

2

The Gates of Destiny

'I am Toussaint Louverture, you have perhaps heard my name. You are aware, brothers, that I have undertaken vengeance, and that I want freedom and equality to reign in Saint-Domingue. I have been working since the beginning to bring it into existence so as to establish the happiness of us all.'[1] With these words, Toussaint made a stylish entry into the public arena. The French Revolution of 1789, with its Declaration of the Rights of Man, its ideal of popular sovereignty and its principles of liberty, equality and fraternity, had unleashed powerful political rivalries in the colony. By the early 1790s, battle lines were drawn between advocates and opponents of granting rights to free people of colour, French loyalist *pompons blancs* and colonial autonomist *pompons rouges*, and among the principal racial groups in the colony: whites, mixed-race and black people. The touchstone issue was slavery, and Toussaint would eventually emerge as the champion of black emancipation and its revolutionary ideal of brotherhood.

The familiar world which the Bréda coachman had known for the first fifty years of his life completely disintegrated in the early 1790s. A massive slave insurrection, launched in August 1791, destroyed the moral and political authority of the white settlers, as well as their economic power: by the middle of the decade, thousands of whites had fled the colony, seeking refuge in neighbouring Caribbean islands, the United States and France, and production in the prosperous plantations of the northern plain essentially ceased. The anarchy was further inflamed by the collapse of French authority in Saint-Domingue, with the burning of Cap in 1793 and the fierce struggle for control of the territory among French, Spanish and British regular and auxiliary forces. Against this backdrop of civil war and foreign intervention, these early years of Toussaint's political activity between 1791 and 1794 have long been mired in controversy. His position in this changing sequence of events is generally seen as 'mysterious',[2] and his role in almost all the key episodes has been debated: the precise nature of his involvement in the 1791 uprising; the extent of his initial commitment to the principle of *liberté générale*, as emancipation was known; the significance of his allegiance to the Spanish monarchy, whose forces controlled significant portions of northern Saint-Domingue and under whose banner he fought for over a year; his motivations for refusing to join the republican side, even long after the French authorities had proclaimed the abolition of slavery in the colony in August 1793; and the precise date, and underlying rationale, of his *ralliement* to the republican camp in 1794. His critics have portrayed Toussaint throughout this period as a shadowy figure with few apparent principles of his own, a mere opportunist who sailed with the prevailing winds.

Yet closer scrutiny of the French and Spanish archival sources brings up a more coherent picture of Toussaint's early revolutionary years. Armed with his unshakeable belief in his natural liberty and a strategic commitment to the liberation of his people, his overriding goal was to preserve his freedom of manoeuvre and to avoid becoming compromised in the schemes of other individuals or groups. His political style was already beginning to crystallize: he preferred small steps to bold or ostentatious moves; to seek common ground where possible, and to bring people of all races together; and to limit the use of violence, if necessary by relying on ruse. He also went to some lengths to disguise his own objectives, and disarmed both his allies and his opponents by making them believe he posed no threat to them. Indeed, even though the years 1791–4 were in effect his period of apprenticeship in public life, many of his views as a revolutionary leader were already well in evidence.

One of these convictions, for example, was that black emancipation could not be pursued in isolation from the interests of whites and people of colour in the colony. This was plainly spelled out in the 29 August proclamation, where he pledged to respect the rights and properties of white landowners who agreed to work with him. He explicitly addressed the mixed-race population, urging their members not to form a 'separate party', ending with this striking formula: 'equality cannot exist without liberty, and for liberty to exist we need unity'. Also in plain sight was Toussaint's combination of creole, republican and Christian values. He defined himself as a 'true brother' who was working for the 'public good' and was committed to the precepts of 'goodness, integrity and humanity'. At the same time, he appealed to the principle of forgiveness: Toussaint distinguished between the 'darkness' which blinded his enemies and the 'light' which he sought to bring to them, and he further noted that God would 'punish the wicked and have pity on the innocent who have been led astray'.[3]

Most striking was Toussaint's self-confidence, captured in the new name he had chosen for himself, which would soon become legendary. In the early moments of the insurrection he fully assumed his slave name: an eyewitness in a rebel camp saw him referred to as 'Toussaint esclave nègre de l'habitation Bréda'.[4] As he established his authority as an insurgent military commander, he then became 'Monsieur Toussaint'. In the course of 1793 the name 'Louverture' emerged, soon accompanied by a flamboyant signature. What precisely lay behind the metaphor of 'opening' is still a matter of debate: there are suggestions that French officials first used the term to describe Toussaint's talent for conciliation, or, conversely, his astonishing capacity to snatch territories from their control; a French commissioner allegedly exclaimed in 1793, after the rebel commander had seized several of their strategic positions: 'comment cet homme fait donc ouverture partout!'[5]

Toussaint, so the tale goes, appropriated the title and turned it into a personal badge of honour. Yet there was much more to it. 'Louverture' symbolized not just an individual ambition, but Toussaint's aspiration to provide a brighter future, in particular for black people; the 'opening' was to be taken as a new departure. He would have known, in this context, that one of the most revered *vodou* deities was Papa Legba, the spirit of crossroads; a popular kreyol chant at the beginning of ritual ceremonies was 'Papa Legba, ouvri barriè pour moins!'[6] As he galloped across Saint-Domingue on his steed, Toussaint was poised to open the gates of destiny.

The insurrection of 1791 was conceived and executed by the black slaves of Saint-Domingue and their leaders. But events in metropolitan France, especially in the immediate aftermath of the 1789 revolution, also acted as a major catalyst. The repeated incapacity of the French revolutionaries in Paris to engage in any meaningful process of colonial reform – and in particular to apply the universal principles of liberty and equality to the free mixed-race and black populations – left a deep mark on Toussaint, and fortified his belief that the rights of Saint-Domingue's black citizens would be secured only if they themselves seized the political initiative.

The symbol of the revolution's colonial impotence was the Société des Amis des Noirs, established in France a year before the 1789 revolution. Inspired by the ideals of the radical Enlightenment which brought about the abolition of feudalism and the Declaration of the Rights of Man in France, the Société denounced slavery and called for greater equality in the colonies, notably by recognizing the civil rights of the colony's free people of colour, who were as numerous as the whites. It was committed to abolitionism in principle but only in the long term, and without any empowerment of the slaves themselves – especially not by means of a 'revolution'.[7] And so, despite the eloquence of its luminaries such as Brissot, Mirabeau,

Lafayette and Condorcet, the Société failed to shape public opinion and the early political acts of the revolution. The abolition of slavery was advocated in only around sixty *cahiers de doléances* (revolutionary registers of grievances) in France – out of a total of 60,000 – in early 1789.[8] Furthermore, the national revolutionary legislature, the Constituent Assembly, was dominated by the interests of the slave-owning and mercantile bourgeoisie, and the colonies accounted for two-thirds of France's overseas trade in 1789. It was their representatives, grouped in the Club Massiac, who exercised the greatest influence on the French Assembly.[9]

Stridently opposed to the principle of racial equality, and terrified at the prospect of any extension of the Declaration of the Rights of Man to people of colour, this colonial lobby oversaw the promulgation of the 8 March 1790 decree which criminalized any criticism of slavery and put the 'properties' of the settlers – including their slaves – under the protection of the nation. A year later, in its decree of 15 May 1791, the Constituent Assembly recognized the constitutional basis of slavery, and gave the white settlers an effective veto over any reforms by resolving that the status of 'non-free' inhabitants could be deliberated only on the basis of 'proposals made by colonial assemblies'. The rationale for this decision was that slaves were 'individuals of a foreign nation'; changing their circumstances would be contrary to their own interests, as well as that of the 'common good'.[10] Despite the prophetic warnings of Abbé Grégoire that all peoples deprived of their liberty would eventually reclaim it, the French Revolution had manifestly sided with the slave-owners.[11]

Triumphant in Paris, this counter-revolutionary spirit became rampant in Saint-Domingue. In August 1789 one of the leading mixed-race spokesmen warned that the French had become 'drunk with liberty', and asked the colonial authorities to arrest any 'suspicious' person coming from France and to seize writings in which the word 'freedom' appeared.[12] Colonial assemblies were rapidly formed in the north (Cap), west (Port-au-Prince) and south (Les Cayes) to protect the interests of Saint-Domingue's planters and merchants. While the provincial assembly of the north, being dominated by lawyers and big merchants, remained broadly loyal to France, the General Assembly of Saint-Marc adopted an increasingly mutinous position; its members were for the most part middling planters, largely drawn from the assemblies of the west and south.[13] Operating between April and July 1790, the Saint-Marc Assembly produced a constitutional charter which declared that the right to self-government belonged 'essentially and necessarily' to the colony;[14] its members embraced the principles of independence and free trade, and rejected the granting of any political rights to free black and mixed-race people.[15] There was a general consensus, across the different assemblies, that the 1789 Declaration of Rights could not be applied to Saint-Domingue, as it would destroy the 'imperious necessity' of retaining the division among the colony's three races.[16]

So fiercely were the white *colons* opposed to change that those suspected of sympathy for slaves were denounced, subjected to public humiliation, and in many cases murdered. As one of the leading *colon* figures asserted: 'in Saint-Domingue there can only be masters and slaves'.[17] Despite their protestations of loyalty to the plantation system, people of colour were denied the 'rights and privileges of all worthy citizens'[18] by the new colonial assemblies – even though mixed-race spokesmen had at this stage shown no inclination to challenge slavery. This was hardly surprising: on the eve of the revolution, people of colour owned around a quarter of the colony's slaves, notably in the south, and a swathe of valuable properties in main cities such as Port-au-Prince.[19] Indeed, the wealthy mixed-race merchant Vincent Ogé specifically excluded 'the fate of the black people living in slavery'[20] from his demands, and appealed to the whites to forge an alliance with them in order to prevent a slave revolution.

The main argument used by mixed-race reformers was that the colonial hierarchy should be based on property rather than skin colour, and that a white and mixed-race alliance would strengthen slavery.[21] When this union of reactionary forces was rejected by the whites, Ogé launched a rebellion in October 1790, with the assistance of another free person of colour named Jean-Baptiste Chavanne, who had fought in the American War of Independence. The revolt was rapidly contained, as its leaders refused to appeal to slaves to join the struggle, and fierce repression ensued; black and mixed-race people believed to support the insurgency were lynched, mutilated and murdered by white militias. Ogé and Chavanne were eventually captured and gruesomely executed by being broken on the wheel in Cap in early February 1791, in the presence of the members of the northern assembly; after their deaths their heads were cut off and exposed on stakes, Ogé's on the road leading to Dondon and Chavanne's on that to Grande-Rivière. Saint-Domingue's new Colonial Assembly, elected in July 1791, was dominated by white supremacists who rejected any dilution of their exclusive rights; these diehard elements were especially strong in Port-au-Prince and Cap, where Grégoire's effigy was burned by demonstrators. To compound the perversion, the *colons* justified their counter-revolutionary claims in the republican language of patriotism, natural liberty and resistance to oppression.[22]

Though the colony's 500,000 black people formed the majority of the population, they were excluded from the formal political processes. They remained completely absent from the discussions of the local white assemblies between 1789 and 1791, irrespective of whether they were loyal to France or pro-independence – confirming that, in the minds of the settlers, slaves were literally invisible. Yet these black men and women gained considerable exposure to the revolution, not least by the sight of colonial assemblies vigorously practising democracy through local elections and collective deliberations. They were emboldened, too, by the radical ideas which came from France. In the colony's ports, newly arrived soldiers and sailors enthusiastically repeated the latest maxims on liberty and equality from French revolutionary clubs and shared them with slaves in the docks.[23] In his memoirs, a disgruntled *colon* described Saint-Domingue's coastal towns at this time as a 'smouldering school of insurrection'; he also personally witnessed slaves buying revolutionary images and carrying copies of subversive works such as Raynal and Diderot's *Histoire philosophique*.[24] Despite the best efforts of the colonial authorities, scores of revolutionary publications – books, pamphlets and newspapers – found their way to Saint-Domingue, where they were publicized by white jacobins and literate blacks and people of colour. Domestic slaves also learned of these writings by overhearing the conversations of their masters, and passed on their contents in markets, on the roads and in the fields of the colony. A plantation manager reported in October 1790 that the sight of the revolutionary symbol, the blue, white and red cockade, was giving 'ideas' to his slaves, and 'even more the news from France, which is flaunted indiscreetly'.[25] A European visitor to the colony was appalled to hear his white hosts openly discuss ideas of liberty and equality in the presence of their slaves: 'talking about human rights in front of such men can only teach them that power resides in force, and force in numbers'.[26]

As in France, the revolution especially appealed to the collective imagination, providing a fertile ground for rumours to take root in the colony. Stories began to circulate that, despite the opposition of the Constituent Assembly in Paris, the king had granted the slaves of Saint-Domingue their freedom, but that their cruel white masters were refusing to comply; a number of slaves arrested in 1790 and early 1791 testified to this effect during their trials.[27] Even more remarkably, slaves adapted the French Revolution to fit in with their own aspirations for liberty: one widespread account circulating in Saint-Domingue was that 'white slaves in France had killed their masters, and they are now free, govern themselves, and have recovered possession of the land'.[28] This blending of French and creole revolutionary ideas was reflected in the possessions found on a black insurgent captured in late 1791: around his neck was a *vodou* fetish consisting of 'a little sack full of hair, herbs, and bits of bone', while his pockets were filled with 'pamphlets printed in France, filled with commonplaces about the Rights of Man and the Sacred Insurrection'.[29]

The August 1791 slave insurrection began when a few thousand rebels attacked a number of plantations in northern Saint-Domingue. Among the first to be burned to the ground was one of the Gallifet plantations, where, according to white plantation mythology, slaves led lives of blissful contentment.[30] Within a matter of days the entire northern plain was ablaze, as the plantations which produced the colony's finest sugar were devastated; the flames from the fires were visible from Cap, where one inhabitant wrote that he had never seen such a 'terrible spectacle'.[31] Although some individuals were spared or protected by their slaves, hundreds of white men, women and children were put to death, and others taken prisoner.[32] The insurgents told one of their captives that their aim was 'nothing less than the destruction of all the whites except some who did not own property, some priests, some surgeons, and some women,

Incendie de la Plaine du Cap. Massacre des Blancs par les Noirs.

The launching of the slave insurrection in August 1791 led to the massacre of white settlers across northern Saint-Domingue and the destruction of many plantations. Toussaint protected the Bréda estate and escorted the wife of Bayon de Libertat to safety.

and making themselves masters of the country'.[33] By the end of August, the ranks of the black insurgent army had risen to 10,000, and reached 80,000 by November – nearly half the slave population in the northern area. Although they failed to take Cap, despite three attempts, the rebels successfully pushed east during a second wave of attacks in October, and by the end of 1791 they had secured control over most of the northern and eastern parts of Saint-Domingue, right up to the border with the Spanish-controlled territory of Santo Domingo.

Saint-Domingue's 1791 black insurgency was launched in the wake of two meetings: the first, on 14 August, was a gathering of elite slave representatives from about 100 northern plantations; it almost certainly included the Raynal-reading rebel commander from Limbé we encountered in the Introduction. The second, around a week later, was the famous 'Bois-Caïman' ceremony, in which the conspiracy was sealed in a religious ritual which brought together a variety of spiritual practices.[34] The ceremony, which has become one of the founding myths of modern Haitian culture, marked the culmination of the actions of a 'vast network' which had been operating across the northern plain for some time.[35] Toussaint's role in these early moments of the revolution has been a matter of much debate. He prevented the Bréda plantation from being overrun during the first weeks of the insurrection, and protected Bayon de Libertat's wife, who had remained on the premises. It was long believed, including by some of his most ardent admirers, that he played no active part in the August uprising. Schoelcher noted that he was at this time a 'defender of order, and a conservative by instinct',[36] while C. L. R. James, in a rare lapse, observed that he 'lacked the boldness of the rank and file' rebels, and 'waited to see how things would go'.[37]

In this view, he only formally joined the insurgency later that year, after having Madame Bayon escorted to Cap by his brother Paul Louverture, and sending his own wife and children to safety in Spanish-controlled territory. Toussaint himself, however, stated in his 29 August 1793 proclamation that he had been part of the revolutionary movement from its inception – a cue for other historians to insist that he had 'played a large part in the secret preparation of the insurrection', even as he continued to reside on the Bréda plantation.[38] To add to the confusion, it was widely believed among French republicans that the slave insurrection had been stirred up by 'agents of the king';[39] in a colourful twist to this version, the nineteenth-century Haitian historian Céligny Ardouin alleged, on the basis of the oral testimony of a Saint-Domingue war veteran, that Toussaint was at the heart of the 1791 insurrection, but as a French royalist *agent provocateur.* The claim was that, thanks to the contacts he established through Bayon de Libertat, serving in the loyalist Cap militia at the time, he helped mastermind the rebellion so as to decapitate the colony's landowners, who had effectively taken control of Saint-Domingue's regional assemblies and were agitating for greater autonomy and even independence. And so, far from enabling black people to seize power, his purpose was to restore authority to Governor Rouxel de Blanchelande and put a brake on the colony's drift away from metropolitan France.[40]

The archives of the colony offer no evidence of this conspiracy. Indeed, it seems well beyond the intellectual and material capacities of the hapless governor, whose administration was in meltdown (a letter sent to Blanchelande in April 1790 from Port-au-Prince took two months to reach Cap).[41] The Spanish archives, however, contain a 'Certificate' signed by Toussaint in July 1793 in which he recognized that at the time of the slave revolt he had been part of a plot to restore the French king to his throne.[42] However, one of Toussaint's characteristic qualities was his ability to mislead his adversaries; in the volatile context of mid 1791 he may well have been in touch with agents from the royalist camp and led them to believe that the slave revolt could serve their interests. Defenders of the conspiracy theory also point to the use of royalist slogans and insignia by black insurgents, many of whom called themselves 'amis du roi'. However, as Toussaint later clarified with robust common sense, in 1791 France was still a monarchy and not a republic: 'it was therefore natural for us to address our grievances to the king, the nation's chief'.[43] Black citizens would have seen no contradiction between royalist ideas and belief in their emancipation: as noted earlier, royalist administrators had attempted to introduce labour reforms in the colony in the 1780s, such as lessening the harshness of the slave regime, but had been blocked by the *colons* – hence the widespread perception of the king as a counterweight to the planters.[44] Slaves would have needed no reminding that revolutionary authorities in Paris had failed utterly to further the cause of emancipation between 1789 and 1791, and that the most ardent defenders of slavery in Saint-Domingue had appropriated revolutionary language for their own ends.

The royalist conspiracy theory ultimately falters because the events surrounding the planning and execution of the 1791 insurrection bear all the hallmarks of what would later become Toussaint's style. In many respects, the uprising was the first formal coming-together of the Louverture coalition: slaves and free blacks (one of the early ringleaders, Jean-Baptiste Cap, was a freedman with substantial means), African-born and creole blacks, house slaves and *marrons*, slave-drivers and plantation workers, warriors and clergymen (a large majority of Catholic priests in the northern parishes of Saint-Domingue supported the slave rebellion;

they included Abbé Guillaume Sylvestre de Lahaye, the *curé* of Dondon).[45] Nor was it fortuitous that the gathering on 14 August 1791 was held at the Lenormand de Mézy plantation, where Makandal had been a slave before he escaped into *marronage*, going on to become a mythical figure in Saint-Domingue's black imagination. This was exactly the sort of symbolism at which Toussaint excelled, and it is very likely that this Makandalist connection would have prompted the idea of sealing the plans for the insurrection in a *vodou* pact.

Equally typical was the fact that Toussaint went out of his way in the early moments of the insurgency to appear as a lowly figure. As we shall see, even after he formally joined the rebellion, he continued to use a number of different pseudonyms, obscuring the true extent of his implication in events. As a French officer later concluded, not without admiration: 'hidden behind a curtain, it was Toussaint who directed all the strands of the plot, and he was the one who organized the revolt and prepared the explosion'.[46]

Toussaint's real influence on the 1791 insurrection can most plainly be inferred from the names and backgrounds of the main leaders who emerged from the 14 August meeting. These were drawn from the elite slave circles with whom he had been in regular contact since the late 1780s; an eyewitness from Limbé observed that it was 'the valets and the coachmen, and those who were the closest to their masters, who generally struck the first blows'.[47] Indeed, three of the four men entrusted with directing the rebellion, Dutty Boukman, Jean-François and Georges Biassou, were also coachmen, like Toussaint: 'Zamba' Boukman, as he was known, had worked at the Clément plantation, one of the first to be torched; before becoming a *marron* slave, Jean-François had been employed by a landowner from the northern province called Papillon; and Biassou, a person of colour with whom Toussaint was close, was a former slave of the Capuchin order which ran the military hospitals of Cap. As noted in the previous chapter, the fourth rebel leader, Jeannot, was also very well known to Toussaint before 1791, as he had worked on the plantation of Guillaume Bullet – who was none other than the brother-in-law of Bayon de Libertat. Toussaint was the only significant common link between these four men.[48]

Yet the leaders of the rebellion were not mere figureheads: Boukman, in particular, was a brave and determined fighter who was feared by his adversaries for his charismatic appeal;[49] his death in combat in early November 1791 (his head was cut off and paraded on a pike in Cap) was lamented by the rebels, who held religious services in his honour.[50] But neither Biassou nor Jean-François, who thereafter emerged as the public face of the rebellion, were particularly menacing figures. As one of the few men in their entourage who could read, Toussaint was in a favourable position to shape the rebellion's strategy and tactics from the very outset. Possible evidence that he sought to do so is revealed in a letter addressed to Biassou in October 1791. This message, written from a rebel camp in Grande-Rivière, was signed 'Médecin Général', which could have been one of Toussaint's pseudonyms at the time because of his knowledge of herbal medicine. If he was indeed its author,[51] this would be the first of his political writings from the early rebellion era to have survived. In any case, the letter sheds a fascinating light on rebel activities at the time. It shows that they were in contact with a Spanish emissary, who may have helped supply them with arms and munitions.[52] The rebels were planning the defence of the camp, and had also devised a cunning scheme to seize the powder magazine of Haut du Cap, thanks to information given by a spy (this was the kind of subterfuge which would later become another of Toussaint's hallmarks, and adds credence to the claim that he wrote the letter). There was a touch of Louverturean humour, too: the note concluded with a disparaging comment about Jean-François, known for his frivolous inclinations, who had not 'deigned to write' for several days, probably being too busy 'riding his carriage with his *demoiselles*'.[53]

As a revolutionary leader, Toussaint was later known for his ability to assess his position pragmatically and carry out tactical retreats when necessary; this too was in evidence in his early activities in the rebellion. In November and December 1791, when fears of the imminent arrival of military reinforcements from France were growing, Toussaint encouraged Jean-François and Biassou to begin negotiations with the governor, and with the French commissioners who had just landed in the colony. His hand is especially visible in the letter of 12 December 1791, in which the rebels undertook to help bring the slaves back to work in exchange for an amnesty for the senior officers of the insurgency; in an effort to secure agreement, Toussaint weighed in specifically to bring this number down to fifty. Despite its appeal to 'moderation and wisdom'[54] and suggestion of a date for the ending of hostilities (1 January 1792), the offer was torpedoed by the diehard elements in the Colonial Assembly and provoked some consternation among the rank-and-file slave insurgents – especially the women rebels, who often advocated the most radical and uncompromising positions.

But, given Toussaint's ability to think in strategic terms, it was unlikely that he saw this ceasefire as an endgame. Rather, he would have viewed it as the start of a political sequence in which the rebellion gained legitimacy; moreover, the offer was plainly an attempt to divide the more pragmatic white colonists in Cap from the hardliners. He knew, deep down, that the freedom which the slaves had conquered through their insurrection was irreversible. According to an eyewitness account by two white prisoners, Toussaint gave a rousing speech in kreyol – the first recorded instance of his charismatic rhetorical power – in which he explained his reasoning fully and appealed to the rebels present to endorse his logic. He would no doubt have referred to his own past experiences as a slave, and promised that he would fight for the rights of his black brothers and sisters. His 'touching speech' had an 'electrifying effect', and the slaves declared that they were willing to 'return to their plantations if their commanders ordered them'.[55]

Toussaint was later noted for his magnanimity, particularly towards whites, and these humane sentiments were already in plain view at the beginning of the slave insurrection. We have clear testimony of this in an account written by another white prisoner captured by the rebels in October 1791. First published in Saint-Domingue in 1792, Gabriel Le Gros's narrative described, often in gruesome detail, the atrocities perpetrated by the insurgents against the white settlers. But, despite himself, Gros could not help giving positive accounts of some 'brigands' he encountered, such as the insurgent commander Michaud, who took pity on him and 'alleviated his misery whenever he could'.[56] There were also many favourable references to Jean-François, who recruited him as his secretary; at one point, Jean-François confirmed to Gros that he had not sought the leadership of the rebellion[57] – although the reluctant generalissimo failed to mention that he had had himself crowned king by a local priest.[58]

The real hero of Gros's tale was Toussaint. When in December 1791 news broke that the negotiations with the colonial authorities had collapsed, Biassou was so infuriated that he ordered all the prisoners (including Gros) to be killed. They were immediately brought out and lined up, and their fate seemed sealed. Toussaint intervened and, braving Biassou's wrath, persuaded his commander that a summary execution would reflect poorly on the rebellion, and justice would be served only by a proper trial. The general agreed, and the prisoners' lives were spared; no doubt after further interventions by Toussaint, Biassou pardoned them the next day. On their way back to Cap, the prisoners came under further threat from furious rebel combatants, and it was Toussaint, who was leading the escort, who again helped ensure their safe return to their families.[59] Other eyewitnesses confirmed this account, one noting that 'all the white prisoners owed their lives to Toussaint the slave from the Bréda plantation, who protected them from the fury of the different camp chiefs'.[60]

*

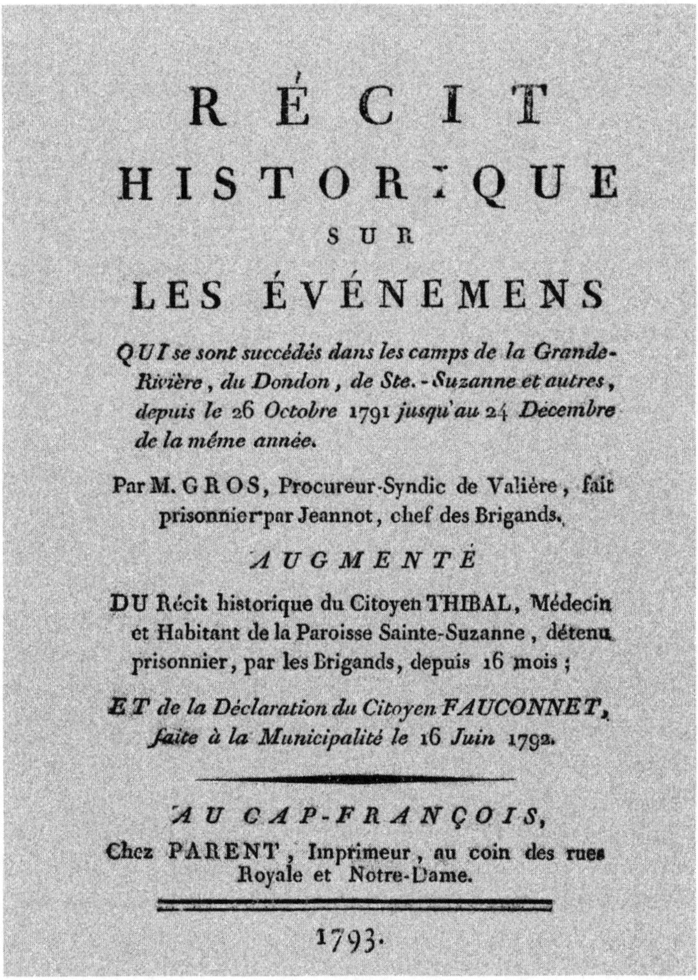

RÉCIT
HISTORIQUE
SUR
LES ÉVÉNEMENS

QUI se sont succédés dans les camps de la Grande-Rivière, du Dondon, de Ste.-Suzanne et autres, depuis le 26 Octobre 1791 jusqu'au 24 Décembre de la même année.

Par M. GROS, Procureur-Syndic de Valière, fait prisonnier par Jeannot, chef des Brigands.

AUGMENTÉ

DU Récit historique du Citoyen THIBAL, Médecin et Habitant de la Paroisse Sainte-Suzanne, détenu prisonnier, par les Brigands, depuis 16 mois;

ET de la Déclaration du Citoyen FAUCONNET, faite à la Municipalité le 16 Juin 1792.

AU CAP-FRANÇOIS,
Chez PARENT, Inprimeur, au coin des rues Royale et Notre-Dame.

1793.

First published in 1792, Gros's eyewitness account of the slave revolution included details of Toussaint's role in the early months of the insurrection, and praised his successful efforts to protect white prisoners.

As the conflict resumed in 1792, Jean-François (who called himself 'great admiral', even though he had no navy) and Biassou (self-styled 'governor general' and 'viceroy') divided up the territories still under rebel control. Although nominally under the authority of Biassou, Toussaint increasingly established himself as an autonomous agent, initially commanding a force of around 600 men. He had already made a considerable mark on the insurrection in the first six months, influencing the choice of its leadership, shaping its initial direction, pushing for compromise and restraining the tendencies towards indiscriminate violence of both the high command and the rank-and-file fighters.

The fundamental strategic question facing the insurgency was its stance over slave emancipation, and it was long believed that Toussaint's early views on the issue – and that of the rebel leadership more generally – were at best ambiguous and at worst hostile. Especially in standard French accounts of the Haitian Revolution, abolitionism in Saint-Domingue is typically portrayed as a product of the 'stimulating winds of the French Revolution', notably through the ending of slavery by Commissioner Sonthonax in August 1793, rather than an expression of radical thinking among the rebels.[61] Yet it has been convincingly shown that the Sonthonax decree was only made possible by the sustained actions of the black revolutionaries.[62]

Early proclamations of the slaves were adamant about the need for emancipation. When Governor Blanchelande issued a call for the rebels to surrender in September 1791, Jeannot issued a fiery response, retorting that they were seeking 'only that dear and precious object, freedom', and were prepared to defend it with their 'last drop of blood'.[63] The common expression of the slave fighters was 'bout à blancs',[64] which implied the elimination of slavery through the physical destruction of its most active agents. Yet we also know that some leaders of the insurgency did not support abolition, or believe it would be desirable in the short run: Jean-François admitted to his secretary, Gros, that the principle of *liberté générale* was a 'chimera', as it was both unacceptable to the French and unsuitable for the majority of 'uncivilized' slaves.[65] Also, as the demands of the insurgents took a more political turn, tactical considerations sometimes called for more modest objectives. So in November 1791, when the first overtures for peace were made by the rebels, their main petition was for 'a general amnesty for all the slaves'.[66] The implication was that, once pardoned, workers would return to the plantations – still as slaves, but hopefully to enjoy better conditions, such as the right to three free days per week, one of the widespread demands of the rank-and-file rebels. It is also worth noting that from the outbreak of the Saint-Domingue slave insurrection until the end of 1792, there was little support for the abolitionist cause from the so-called 'Amis des Noirs' in France. On the contrary: when news of the rebellion reached France in October 1791 a dismayed Brissot asserted that it had to be a counter-revolutionary conspiracy, as black slaves did not possess the moral, intellectual and material capacities to launch an insurrection on such a scale.[67]

It is against this background that one of the most remarkable documents of the early Haitian Revolution appeared: the *Lettre originale des chefs nègres révoltés*. Dated July 1792 and addressed to the colonial authorities, the French commissioners and the citizens of Saint-Domingue, it made the philosophical case for abolition by highlighting the absolute contradiction between the 1789 Declaration of the Rights of Man and the maintenance of slavery in French colonies. How was it possible, the *Lettre* exclaimed, that 'freedom, property, security and resistance to oppression' could be regarded as 'universal natural rights' and emblazoned in the 1789 Declaration, and yet these very same rights be denied to the half-million black inhabitants of the colony? The notion that black people could be treated as property was fanciful, as legitimate power could be founded only on the principles of 'virtue and humanity'. Calling on the authorities to recognize the principle of *liberté générale*, the *Lettre*'s signatories swore to reject any attempt to divide them from each other through the offer of partial amnesties: black unity had now become a cardinal principle. Equality of rights was the only basis upon which a prosperous future could be enjoyed by all the inhabitants of the colony. Specifically addressing the white population, the *Lettre* promised that the liberated slaves would treat them with affection, respect and gratitude, and would allow them 'full enjoyment' of their properties and revenues. Yet, in contrast with the rebel writings of late 1791, the tone here was not one of deference but of implacable strength: the text ended by warning the defenders of slavery that they faced 'total destruction' if they refused to meet the demands of the rebellion, and that the insurgents would prefer 'a thousand deaths' rather than capitulate.[68]

The *Lettre* was first published in 1793 in *Le Créole Patriote*, a Parisian newspaper edited by the jacobin abolitionist Claude Milscent, a former Saint-Domingue planter who became radicalized by the revolution.[69] But its authorship has remained something of a mystery. The names of three signatories appeared at the bottom of the text: Jean-François, Biassou and Gabriel Belair. Some historians believe they actually produced the document, but this is highly improbable.[70] Neither of the two leading generals of the rebellion could have contributed much, if anything, to this text: there is no evidence that they were familiar with radical Enlightenment thinking. Moreover, as we have seen, Jean-François did not believe in general emancipation, and Biassou, as one of his letters demonstrates, was at the time only interested in designing a monarchist constitution.[71] Indeed, the notions of equality, justice and natural law do not appear in any of the contemporaneous writings of Jean-François and Biassou.[72] As for Belair,[73] he was one of Biassou's young aides-de-camp. There were some intimations that Abbé Delahaye, the radical Dondon cleric, may have been the author of the text, but the *Lettre*'s language and tone are not consistent with his recorded beliefs at the time.[74] And so, given Toussaint's fondness for 'directing all the strands of the plot', it is very plausible that this text was written by him or under his auspices. He would have aimed both to radicalize the position of the insurgency on this crucial question, and also to move the black revolutionaries away from the Makandalist position of 'bout à blancs': the *Lettre*'s explicit appeal to the ideal of a community of equals was the first glimpse of the later Louverturian vision of a multiracial Saint-Domingue.

There are marked similarities between the *Lettre* and Toussaint's later style and imagery: from his celebration of modesty (the letter claimed to speak for men 'who do not choose big words') to his specific turns of phrase ('our lives depended on your whims') and appeals to nature (which 'takes pleasure in diversifying the colours of the human species'), together with his trademark combination of republican and Christian egalitarianism ('we are all created in the same image as our Father, and are therefore your equals in natural law'). The *Lettre* also contained a passage about Vincent Ogé which used almost identical terms as in Toussaint's 29 August 1793 proclamation, where the mixed-race martyr was described as having been 'put to death for having taken the side of liberty'. Last but not least, the *Lettre* foreshadowed one of Toussaint's favourite rhetorical moves in his later dealings with the French: holding them to their best image of themselves. Appealing to French soldiers who had just been shipped to Saint-Domingue to fight the rebellion, many of whom were known to be ardently committed to revolutionary ideals,[75] he urged them to remember their own struggles for liberty and equality, and to recognize that their black brothers were merely following their lead in preferring the exaltation of freedom to a life of servitude.[76]

On 24 August 1792, a year after the launching of the slave insurrection, Toussaint was one of the chief guests at a ceremony organized by Biassou in Grande-Rivière to honour the feast day of Louis XVI. The invitation from the general (who also awarded himself the sonorous title of 'chevalier de l'ordre royal militaire de Saint-Louis') insisted that all rebel officers and their men should be punctual, and attend fully armed and in their best attire. Toussaint was more than happy to oblige.[77] Such an overt manifestation of monarchism on his part may seem perplexing at a time when the *Lettre* was signalling his underlying adhesion to the ideals of liberty and equality. Along with the extent of his commitment to abolitionism, Toussaint's royalism during this period has been subject to speculation, with some claiming that it represented his true beliefs, and others that it was merely a tactical stance.

The evidence suggests – as usual with Toussaint – a more complex and original scheme of thinking. The royalist banner was flown with enthusiasm by Biassou and Jean-François, and it would have been impolitic of Toussaint to distance himself too overtly from the two rebel commanders at this stage. The monarchy also offered a welcome symbolic berth for the insurgents at a time of considerable political uncertainty in revolutionary Europe; in fact, within a matter of months, France would become a republic. Royalism was a useful rallying point, too, because its focus on the figure of the strong, charismatic ruler had an ongoing appeal to many African-born slaves, and because it provided the 'brigands' with a badge of respectability which their white adversaries in Saint-Domingue constantly sought to deny them. Indeed, Toussaint was genuinely drawn to certain aspects of royalism – notably its belief in providential leadership and the values of duty, sacrifice and honour; its commitment to politeness and gentility of manners; and of course its profound religiosity. A Spanish royalist official who was in contact with the rebels at this time reported attending a Catholic Mass which was officiated, in the absence of a priest, by a senior black officer; he did not formally identify him, but it is very likely that this was Toussaint, who was always known for his willingness to leap to the pulpit, metaphorically and sometimes literally.[78]

Toussaint also used this period to consolidate his military position, and train his own forces at the fortified camp of La Tannerie; his growing authority is alluded to in one of Biassou's letters, which refers to him as 'Monsieur le Maréchal' and depicts him doing the rounds in rebel-controlled areas, 'establishing order, peace and tranquillity'.[79] This is our first glimpse of his belief in the critical virtue of discipline – and no doubt he was ably assisted in this task by his brothers Paul and Jean-Pierre and his nephew Moyse, who became key members of his entourage, and by Jean-Jacques Dessalines, one of his future generals, whom he recruited around this time. Such reinforcements proved timely, as 6,000 French troops landed in Saint-Domingue in October 1792, launching a major counter-offensive which led to significant losses of rebel-held positions – notably Ouanaminthe, on the border with Santo Domingo, and Dondon. Toussaint himself came under severe pressure as he sought to defend the Morne Pélé (the advanced outpost protecting La Tannerie), and although he fought gallantly he was eventually forced to retreat after sustaining significant losses. Impressed by his military valour, Biassou, who barely knew one end of a rifle from another, promoted Toussaint to the rank of general in December 1792; from this moment on, Toussaint appeared in Biassou's proclamations as 'notre général d'armée'.[80]

As French military pressure on the insurgents mounted in the early months of 1793, they began to make formal overtures to Spain, which controlled the neighbouring territory of Santo Domingo. As noted earlier, there is evidence that the August 1791 uprising had enjoyed some undercover assistance from local Spanish agents, always happy to make mischief for the dastardly French. Although the official position of the Santo Domingo authorities was one of neutrality, there were a number of contacts between local military and religious officials and rebel leaders, especially in border areas; according to the testimony of a prisoner in 1792, the insurgent camps were regularly supplied with Spanish munitions, alcohol, tobacco, dried fish, salt and fresh meat;[81] it has also been revealed that Biassou was in correspondence with the Santo Domingo governor, Joaquín García y Moreno, in the early months of 1792.[82] But conditions were now favourable for a proper alliance, as Spain had joined the coalition which had declared war on France, in the wake of the execution of Louis XVI in January 1793.

In the early months of 1793, Toussaint was despatched to make contact with the Spanish, and they duly came up with extremely satisfactory terms: the immediate emancipation of all slave combatants and their incorporation as auxiliaries in the Spanish forces, and the enjoyment of all the 'freedoms, exemptions, properties and prerogatives' available to Spanish subjects.[83] By June 1793 Toussaint had become a general in the Spanish auxiliary army, and commanded a force of 4,000 men.[84] A month later he took back the town of Ouanaminthe with such distinction that the Spanish government gave him an award of 400 pesos.[85] He contemptuously turned down attempts by the French to get him to recognize their authority, responding that his men were 'under the protection of the Spanish king';[86] by September 1793 Toussaint's letters were headed 'Général des Armées de Sa Majesté Très Catholique et Chevalier de l'Ordre Royal et Militaire de Saint-Louis'.[87] In the course of these months he took on the French with relish. Dondon, Marmelade, Verrettes, Petite-Rivière and Plaisance fell into his hands, more often by ruse rather than by dint of military force; most of the ordinary soldiers in the French camp were black, and he sought at all costs to avoid spilling their blood. For example, he gained Marmelade by recruiting one of its main mixed-race republican defenders, André Vernet, who immediately joined his secretariat (and later married one of his nieces).[88] He crowned this astute campaign by taking the coastal town of Gonaïves in December, after having again been invited in by the republican forces defending it. He was received in triumph, and from that moment this town became a Louverturian bastion.[89] Governor García was so delighted with Toussaint's 'efficiency and skill', which were so 'unlike those of his colour', that he hailed him as a 'brave warrior' and awarded him a gold medal on behalf of the King of Spain.[90]

Meanwhile, the political situation in France was evolving. The procolonial Constituent Assembly was replaced by a more progressive legislature, which in April 1792 promulgated a decree abolishing all racial discrimination in the colonies: it had taken the French Revolution nearly three years to arrive at this basic point. In September 1792 France became a republic, and the new regime's commissioners arrived in Saint-Domingue; among them was Léger-Félicité Sonthonax, one of the key figures in the colony's revolutionary history, who formally proclaimed the Republic in December 1792.[91] He was seen as an advocate of colonial reform, and in 1790 had written an article denouncing the slave trade and slavery, and welcoming their demise.[92] Contacts were established between the French envoys and the rebels, and Toussaint and Biassou were exchanging correspondence with Sonthonax in the months following his arrival in the colony.[93] However, Toussaint was not tempted to join forces with the French at this point, as he had little reason to trust the republicans. One of the commissioners' first announcements upon reaching Saint-Domingue was to reaffirm that 'slavery was necessary for the culture and prosperity of the colonies', and that they would not challenge the 'prerogatives' of the planters in this respect; Sonthonax even went to the trouble of having the *Code Noir* (euphemistically renamed 'code républicain du servage') translated into kreyol.[94] Such gestures were intended to reassure the white *colons*, and offered little comfort to the black slaves. Moreover, the French camp was unappealing during these times, with rampant administrative chaos; four successive governors were sent to the colony in the space of a year. This spectacle of anarchy culminated in the burning of Cap in June 1793, after a bout of lethal infighting among rival French forces which left thousands dead.[95]

Even in these exceptionally difficult circumstances, Toussaint did not abandon the abolitionist cause. He devised a daring military plan for the unification of the island of Hispaniola under Spanish control, on condition that the latter agreed to emancipate all black slaves, not just those who were fighting in their army. He took the proposal to his immediate superior, the Marquis Matias de Armona – who rejected it after consulting with Governor García.[96] Toussaint sounded out the French during the first half of 1793, hoping to secure an alliance with them on similar terms to those offered by the Spanish: full amnesty to all rebels, and a general emancipation of all slaves. Even though the French were moving in the direction of abolition, they only offered limited emancipation, and Toussaint vented his bitterness in a proclamation published in early August 1793. He accused the republicans of 'perfidiousness', of 'destroying thousands of desperately poor people' and 'putting to death an innocent king on a wretched scaffold'. He did not particularly care about poor Louis XVI's fate, but this was a good opportunity to throw back the traditional charge of barbaric behaviour at the French, whose country had now become 'a land of crime and carnage', where the 'innocent blood' of religious believers was shed 'in the name of the republic'. He rounded on the new French commissioners in Saint-Domingue, whom he described as 'scoundrels sent to put [the black people] in chains' and to wage a war of extermination against the insurgents, inflicting 'torture and hardship' on them and pursuing them 'like wild beasts'.[97] This strident rhetoric should not be taken entirely at face value, as we know from other sources that Toussaint was in contact with several French military officers at the time, and even allowed food supplies from areas under his control to be sent to Cap; he also had meetings scheduled with republican commanders in early August 1793.[98]

Toussaint's declarations during this period sought to convince his people that it was he who was the most ardent defender of their emancipation from slavery, rather than any other rebel leaders, or the French republicans. He also stressed repeatedly that freedom needed to be recognized as a universal principle. A few weeks later, in an appeal to the men of colour who were still supporting the French, he returned to this theme, urging that there could be no liberty in Saint-Domingue until 'all were free'. Those who launched the August 1791 rebellion had been the 'originators' of the struggle for abolition, and had laid its 'foundations'. He then added: 'I was the first to favour a cause that I have always upheld', before concluding: 'what we have begun, I will finish'.[99]

Yet assuming the leadership of the black revolution was impossible for Toussaint as long as he remained, at least technically, a subordinate of Jean-François and Biassou, and an auxiliary general in the Spanish royal forces. However much praise Don García and his men lavished on their new ally, their internal correspondence shows that they still viewed him with suspicion, the black rebels with contempt, and the idea of universal emancipation as an utter abomination. The French position also shifted decisively from mid 1793 onwards, with the unilateral abolition of slavery in northern Saint-Domingue by Sonthonax in August. The move was dismissed as a stunt by Toussaint, not without reason: the commissioner only broke his earlier pledge to maintain slavery in the French territories because he realized that emancipation was the price to be paid for preserving the support of the colony's northern black citizens – especially the men who were fighting on the French side. Toussaint also observed that Sonthonax initially struggled to convince his fellow commissioners of the need for the decree, and was unable to enforce it even in the pockets of territory nominally under his control. Meanwhile the desperate slave-owning *colons*, perfidious to the last, invited the British to take control of Saint-Domingue in order to safeguard their interests: the towns of Jérémie, Môle Saint-Nicolas and Saint-Marc were handed over to British forces, soon to be followed by Arcahaie and Port-Républicain, in all of which human bondage was restored by the new occupying forces, which eventually numbered over 20,000.[100]

As 1793 came to an end, the question of slavery had become the critical divide in Saint-Domingue and Toussaint now needed to reassess his position. The first rupture came with Jean-François. There had never been much of a romance between the two men, and as Toussaint's stature and authority grew the generalissimo tried repeatedly to trim his sails, provoking skirmishes with his forces and on one occasion in late 1792 even capturing and imprisoning him in Vallière, from where he had to be delivered by Biassou.[101] Toussaint was grateful for this intervention and later claimed it had saved his life – but by early 1794 his relationship with Biassou, too, had begun to deteriorate sharply. Believing that Toussaint was trying to upstage him, the 'viceroy' set an insidious trap for his subordinate: he arranged for his own men to rough up the commander of one of the rebel outposts at Barade, an officer named Thomas, and to pretend that they were acting on Toussaint's orders. When Toussaint arrived at the camp soon afterwards Thomas's forces opened fire, wounding him and killing seven of his lieutenants; one of them was Jean-Pierre, who was riding by his brother's side.[102]

In a long, breathless letter dated 20 March 1794, an enraged Toussaint denounced Biassou to the Spanish authorities. The general was a 'simple, vulnerable man without much knowledge', and he was 'easily led astray by the scoundrels surrounding him', in particular his personal secretary, a 'dangerous man who seeks only to spread confusion among us'. Among Biassou's greatest failings were his weakness of mind ('his impressions are always formed by the last people who speak to him') and his 'impetuous, confused and scatty character'. He blamed Biassou for instigating the murderous attack which had claimed his brother's life, and accused him of systematically stirring up dissension among the auxiliary troops. Toussaint at this point formally declared his military autonomy, claiming that from his Marmelade headquarters he was now the 'general commander' of the black forces, and that Biassou was 'not his superior and had never been'; there was more than a touch of poetic licence in the latter claim, but by this point Toussaint's flow was irrepressible.[103]

Under pressure from the colony's black revolutionaries, French commissioner Sonthonax issued a decree abolishing slavery in August 1793. This kreyol version of the proclamation was widely circulated at the time.

A week later Toussaint penned a second, equally vitriolic, letter, this time lambasting Biassou for refusing his offers of reconciliation and plotting another attempt on his life 'at the Carrefour-à-Vincent'; Toussaint heard about the scheme, no doubt from one of his spies in the Biassou camp, and took another route. The general had also sent his men to steal his livestock and tafia liquor and plunder areas under Toussaint's control, while again trying to lay the blame on him; in addition, he claimed that Toussaint 'was planning to take up arms against the King of Spain' and would begin with an attack on Saint-Raphaël, where his wife and children remained the guests of the Spanish authorities. The aim was manifestly to discredit him in the eyes of the Spaniards.[104] Behind these clashes with Jean-François and Biassou lurked a fundamental difference over emancipation. Not only was this issue not even remotely on their agenda, but to Toussaint's indignation both leaders of the black insurgency were themselves actively involved in buying and selling slaves. He provided specific details of Biassou's participation in the 'odious trade of women and children': he would despatch his agents to capture the families of insurgents while they were away on front-line military duty and 'sell them into slavery'.[105]

Appalled by such despicable behaviour, Toussaint was championing the cause of emancipation in the parishes of Gonaïves, Ennery, Plaisance, Marmelade and Dondon, encouraging slaves from plantations to defect to his army and promising them their freedom and his protection. Radically different from the positions of Jean-François and Biassou, this stance also put Toussaint on a collision course with the counter-revolutionary *colons* residing in the areas under Spanish control. Many of these were by now inhabited by embittered white refugees from French areas who openly supported slavery (which was still legal in Spanish-held Santo Domingo); they set up armed militias which advocated the use of terror to 'bring the negroes back to order', and some even dreamed of reconquering French territories.[106] In April 1794 Jean-Baptiste Laplace, one of the spokesmen for the local *colons*, denounced Toussaint in a letter to Don García for 'preaching disobedience' and 'promising to grant freedom to the slaves who had returned to work in the plantations'. For such crimes of 'treason and sedition', Laplace thundered, Toussaint's 'head should roll'.[107]

Pressure was mounting from all sides. Then Toussaint's relationship with his Spanish protectors, too, began to unravel from the end of 1793. On the surface, the picture seemed idyllic: Toussaint was feted as an intrepid warrior by the authorities and he continued to pledge his unconditional allegiance to the Spanish monarchy. In November 1793 he attended a 'reconciliation' ceremony organized by the Spaniards in Saint-Raphaël with Jean-François and Biassou, where he agreed to bury the hatchet with the two generals; the detailed memorandum signed by the three men included a pledge never to speak ill of each other and to 'forget past dissensions', and ended with a solemn undertaking that they would remain 'faithful vassals of the greatest and best of all monarchs, the King of Spain'.[108] Even the March 1794 letters in which he attacked Biassou, after the reconciliation had failed, reiterated Toussaint's support for the cause of the monarchy, 'until the last drop of his blood'. He described his fidelity to the Bourbon king as 'unshakeable' and 'as firm as a rock'; for good measure he also invoked his Catholic faith, comparing his monarchist beliefs to a 'religion', and his own persecutions to the sufferings of Jesus Christ.[109]

But the martyr's cross was getting heavier to bear. García's forces could scarcely conceal their racial prejudice against the former slaves who made up the auxiliary army, and in early 1794 Spanish troops sent to garrison the town of Gonaïves clashed repeatedly with Toussaint's combatants, brutalizing a number of his former republican senior officers; in this instance, ideological and racial divides coincided perfectly. Worse still, Toussaint's main contact, the Marquis de Armona, with whom he had developed a cordial relationship (it was in his house that the reconciliation ceremony with Biassou and Jean-François had been held), was replaced by Don Juan Bautista Gemir y Lleonart, who was much more receptive to the *colons*' gripes against Toussaint and treated his black auxiliary forces with open disdain. Significantly, Lleonart and his superiors took Biassou's side as the conflict between the two men escalated in early 1794. For a while local Spanish forces kept Toussaint's wife and children under house arrest, and also detained his nephew Moyse; this provoked a bitter outburst by Toussaint, who declared himself 'distressed' by the way the Spanish commanders had treated his family.[110]

Even though uncertainty remains about the exact date of Toussaint's transfer of allegiance from Spain to France, it is manifest that by early May 1794 he was in close contact with the colony's authorities, and by the middle of the month he had clearly signalled his embrace of the French cause.[111] He prudently arranged for his wife and children to be removed from Saint-Raphaël and brought to him, cheekily making the Spaniards pay for the travel costs. One of the turning points in this transition was a conflict which broke out in Gonaïves in late April, in which the black auxiliary forces demanded the surrender of the Spanish garrison; the latter fled, and around 150 white *colons* were massacred in early May. Toussaint wrote to the Gonaïves vicar and the white community expressing regret for the killings,[112] but it may well have been a premeditated strike against the most hardline counter-revolutionary elements among the settlers. Legend has it that before giving the orders for the culling, Toussaint went to Mass.

Yet it is a measure of Toussaint's mercurial qualities that even now he did not sever relations with his erstwhile Spanish allies, and led them to believe that he might still co-operate fruitfully with them. He wrote to Biassou, urging him to forget their past differences, and invited him to join the French camp too (he tried to sweeten the offer by congratulating him on his recent marriage). The black commander rebuffed his advances. It seems, however, that Don García and Lleonart fell for the ploy, even as Toussaint was boldly flying the French flag in their former possessions, from Gonaïves, Ennery and Petite-Rivière to Dondon and Marmelade. Toussaint claimed that his going over was a mere 'rumour' peddled by his enemies, and also pretended that Gonaïves had been threatened not by the French but by the British. Whether Lleonart fell for these tales is unclear – but he was gullible enough to send livestock and even munitions to Toussaint long after he had rallied to the French side, and continued to exchange letters with him;[113] as late as early October 1794 Toussaint was still swearing his 'fidelity' to Spain. At this point, the man whom Lleonart had dismissed as a 'vindictive and arrogant negro' presented the Spaniard with an ultimatum, and unceremoniously booted him out of Saint-Michel and Saint-Raphaël.[114] Don García was left to lick his wounds, and fulminate against the 'deceptive and perfidious impulses' of his former officer.[115]

By mid 1794, as Toussaint's tumultuous apprenticeship as a revolutionary was coming to an end, another, more exalted, journey was beginning. From the time he joined the 1791 insurrection to his *ralliement* to the French he had kept his mental compass resolutely focused on one fixed point: the emancipation of his 'brothers', the black slaves of Saint-Domingue. He was inspired by the extraordinary qualities of these men and women: their intellectual creativity, their courage, their humanity and, above all, their spirit of freedom, which echoed his own sense of natural liberty. At the same time, he sought to move them away from the Makandalist project of confronting the white-settler presence in the colony towards a vision of a political community of equals, in which black, white and mixed-race people could coexist peacefully. This fraternal ideal was still a long way from being universally accepted, let alone implemented – but for the moment its contours were clearly etched in Toussaint's mind, and already embodied in the values and practices of his now 6,000-strong revolutionary army.

Seen in this light, it would be misleading to view Toussaint's decision to join the French camp in 1794 in terms of a 'conversion' to jacobin republicanism – or, for that matter, an 'abandonment' of Spain. From the time he joined the 1791 insurrection, his ideas were shaped through his own reasoning, and combined Saint-Domingue's revolutionary tradition with his own, home-grown elements of royalism and republicanism. There was a significant gap between his position and the French colonial republicanism of the 1790s, as we shall later see. For example, even after they abolished slavery, the French revolutionaries never recognized the legitimacy of the 1791 slave insurrection in Saint-Domingue. More generally they had given Toussaint no reason to trust them, collectively or individually: he saw them betray the revolution by rejecting any application of the 1789 Declaration of the Rights of Man to the colonies, and then allow their policy towards Saint-Domingue to be shaped exclusively by the mercantile slave-owning bourgeoisie and the most racist settlers. Even though it was an important symbolic act, Commissioner Sonthonax's abolition of slavery in 1793 was driven more by necessity than by principle, reflecting his belated recognition of the fact that it was the slaves themselves, by their insurrection, who had made slavery impossible, as Toussaint had understood from the very outset. Hence Toussaint's contemptuous reply to an offer from a local French commander to join the republican camp: 'I will present arms to you', he replied, 'when you recognize my king.' This is generally seen as evidence of his royalist sympathies, but the most telling part of his response was that he called himself 'Toussaint Abréda' – his slave name.[116] Likewise, the French Convention's abolition decree of February 1794 was marginal to Toussaint's decision: news of it reached Saint-Domingue only in July 1794 – several months after he had joined the French camp.

Yet there was one senior French figure whose interactions with Toussaint did matter, and would play a pivotal role in his subsequent political career: Étienne Maynaud de Laveaux, an aristocratic radical who embraced the French Revolution with fervour and came to Saint-Domingue as an officer in the French army. The relationship between the two men did not begin under auspicious settings: in early January 1793 Laveaux stormed the fortified camp at La Tannerie and forced the rebels to retreat; among the thousands of 'brigands' he faced was Toussaint, and the two men almost certainly fired at each other from across the trenches.[117] Within a matter of months, however, Toussaint was reaching out to the French commander, who had been appointed as the colony's governor.[118] Toussaint sensed that 'Papa' Laveaux was that rarest of French envoys, a man who was sincere both in his republicanism and in his commitment to the cause of black emancipation. Replying to one of the first letters he received from Laveaux, Toussaint acknowledged that he had been 'led into error' by the Spaniards, 'the enemies of the republic and of the human race' – but he also pointedly reminded Laveaux that the French had spurned his offer of alliance in 1793. He had been forced to turn to the Spaniards because they had offered him and his combatants freedom and protection; he now realized, however, that the 'contemptible monarchists' had only wanted to divide and weaken the black citizens, so as eventually to bring them 'back into servitude'. Urging Laveaux to 'forget the past', Toussaint pledged that he would henceforth be 'wholly devoted to crushing the enemies of the republic'.[119] When he finally heard that the Convention in Paris had decreed the abolition of slavery, Toussaint acknowledged to Laveaux that it was 'a great consolation for all the friends of humankind'. But he did not dwell on the matter: most of his letter focused on his successes on the military front against his old rival Jean-François.[120]

Laveaux could barely contain his enthusiasm for the new recruit to the French cause. He vouched for Toussaint's devotion to the principle of *liberté générale*, noting that he had confirmed that one of his main reasons for defecting from the Spanish camp was his realization that Jean-François and Biassou were 'selling into slavery children, women and men who were deemed to be "bad subjects"'.[121] After meeting him the governor praised this 'brave and meritorious citizen' to his superiors, commenting that if Saint-Domingue's gendarmerie were to be reorganized, he would be its 'ideal commander'.[122] Had he found out about this rather patronizing commendation, Toussaint would have smiled: his ambitions were on a much grander scale.

3
Brave Republican Warriors

'As I have already made clear to you,' Toussaint told his officers sharply in early 1795, after they had failed to abide by his exact instructions, 'a good soldier should appear cold from the outside, and be methodical, loyal and fiery in the inside.'[1] This exhortation summed up his own character, but it also highlighted the challenges he faced now that he had embraced the republican cause, which focused on the campaign to expel the Spanish and British, and their treasonous French settler allies, from the colony. The British invasion of Saint-Domingue was a key element in the wider strategy adopted in 1793 by William Pitt and his Home Secretary, Henry Dundas: to conquer France's rich West Indian colonies, eradicate the French naval menace in the region and preserve the system of plantation slavery.[2] By mid 1794 the British had seized Martinique, St Lucia and Guadeloupe, and had taken Port-au-Prince; as noted in the previous chapter, they would eventually hold a large tranche of the western province, notably Saint-Marc and Léogâne, as well as a strip around the coastal town of Jérémie. Spanish forces, allied to the British, controlled significant parts of the northern province, as well as most of the colony's eastern territory bordering Santo Domingo, from Fort-Dauphin all the way down to Mirebalais.

Toussaint joined the French side at a particularly critical moment: with the exception of the still-loyal southern province, only small enclaves around Cap and Port-de-Paix remained in republican hands. For him, dislodging his enemies from his native soil was an absolute priority, especially as the British immediately brought back slavery in the areas under their control, as they did elsewhere, for example in Martinique, with the enthusiastic support of royalist French settlers. As one of the *colons* who enlisted with the British put it: 'to carry arms against the revolting slaves of Saint-Domingue is not to be traitorous to one's country; it is to serve it'.[3] The British were in a strong tactical position, enjoying command of the seas as well as superiority in equipment and in financial resources

('Pitt's gold', as it came to be known, was liberally deployed to bribe locals).[4] And so the greatest challenge for Toussaint – hence the impatience in his tone – was to transform his own bedraggled combatants, most of whom came from local *marron* bands, into an effective fighting force. Within three years he had achieved his goals, first defeating the Spaniards and then driving the British and their French royalist allies off the colony, creating in the process a disciplined black army of 'brave republican warriors'[5] under his leadership.

Toussaint began his campaign briskly, with a series of victories against his erstwhile Spanish allies. His troops inflicted heavy losses on his former comrade Jean-François, who had retained his allegiance to the Spanish king and was rapidly forced to leave the colony when the Spaniards signed the Bâle Treaty with France in July 1795, in which they abandoned all their positions in Saint-Domingue and formally ceded control of neighbouring Santo Domingo to the French.[6] From his base in the western Artibonite sector, a ninety-mile area in which he installed some thirty military camps, Toussaint then subjected the British and their French royalist auxiliaries to a fierce onslaught, with more than 200 encounters in the opening months; this effort succeeded in pushing them out of much of the western province. A stalemate then ensued, and the British regained some ground in 1796 – although by the end of that year they were privately acknowledging that their position had become unsustainable. Indeed, by mid 1797, after a further campaign by Toussaint's republican forces, the royalists had been driven out of key strategic positions, notably in Mirebalais, the mountains of Grand Bois and the areas of Lascahobas, Bánica and Saint-Jean. Toussaint's army – now 15,000 strong – pinned them down to a narrow coastal strip on the west, which included Port-au-Prince and St Marc, as well as Môle Saint-Nicolas in the north-west and Jérémie in the south.

After a final campaign in early 1798, Toussaint concluded an armistice with the now exhausted British, who agreed to evacuate all their positions on the colony, having lost 15,000 men and spending over 10 million pounds to retain their position. By October 1798, Toussaint had achieved his goal of ridding republican Saint-Domingue of British and French royalist troops. How he and his men achieved these exploits will be the central theme of this chapter. The scale of their accomplishment was prodigious, for by their victories these hardy black combatants overturned prevailing racial stereotypes about European military superiority and the perceived incapacity of black soldiers to wage war. Such views were commonly held in the late eighteenth century, not only by Toussaint's military and political adversaries but also by most of his French allies. They were avidly embraced by Adolphe Thiers, who viewed Toussaint's military skills as 'mediocre', consisting mainly in the 'art of ambushes', and by a number of modern historians.[7] In this perspective, Toussaint's 'modernizing' approach to warfare, with its emphasis on regular troops and European training techniques, was a temporary hiatus from the grass-roots, guerilla-style rebellions which defined the slave revolts of the early 1790s, and were later revived during the successful popular Haitian War of Independence against the French invading army.[8]

As a commander, Toussaint was notable for his precise planning of every military operation. He led by example, galvanizing his men by his presence and his willingness to expose himself to mortal danger. He also developed a distinct and highly original set of military techniques, combining the methods of guerilla warfare with conventional forms of combat, while also deploying the skills of his African-born warriors. This represented the military dimension of his conception of fraternity. At the same time, Toussaint's objectives were not limited to the conventional ones of territorial acquisition and power projection, but were anchored in a wider set of principles about equality, political autonomy, humanity and freedom from foreign occupation. They constituted an early manifestation of what Karma Nabulsi has called the modern 'republican tradition of war'.[9]

Toussaint never tired of reminding his soldiers, and the citizens of Saint-Domingue, that the battle against the Spanish, the British and their local slave-owning stooges was one of political emancipation. The point of the struggle, as he put it to his commanders, was to 'bring liberty to those parts of our territory which are soiled by the presence of the enemy, and where our people are still lamenting their oppression'. The elimination of human bondage was at the heart of Toussaint's ideal of brotherhood, and it also offered the black people of Saint-Domingue an opportunity to demonstrate their sense of 'honour' by proving that 'the men who have gone from servitude to dignity are worthy of enjoying the benefits of freedom'.[10]

One of the principal sources for understanding Toussaint's art of war is his correspondence with Étienne Laveaux, the French governor general who oversaw his *ralliement* to the French camp in mid 1794. Laveaux remained in post until October 1796, and Toussaint sent him regular and often extensive reports about his military engagements. In the same way as Bayon de Libertat had been a pivotal figure in his pre-revolutionary life, Laveaux played a decisive role in Toussaint's early revolutionary career. From the outset, the governor recognized that he was dealing with an exceptionally gifted fighter. Soon after he had entrusted him with the command of the military front in the western province in 1794, he sent this ringing endorsement of Toussaint to the French authorities: 'this is a citizen about whom I cannot speak highly enough. He is bursting with virtues, with talent, and with martial qualities; he is full of humanity, truly conquering, and indefatigable in his activities as warrior.'[11]

Toussaint reciprocated, referring repeatedly to Laveaux as his 'father' – even though the governor was at least five years younger than him; he described himself as his 'respectful son', who would follow his superior's injunctions with 'gratitude' and 'unconditional submission'.[12] In 1796 he expressed his devotion in lyrical terms:

> there are, no doubt, pure friendships, but I am not convinced that any surpass the one I have with you or are more sincere. Yes, General, Toussaint is your son! You are dear to him. Your tomb will be his. He will risk his life to defend you. His arms and his head are always at your disposition. If ever he were to succumb, he would take with him the sweet satisfaction of having defended a father, a virtuous friend, and the embodiment of freedom.[13]

Laveaux was very widely read in eighteenth-century European literature on military strategy, and Toussaint also drew readily on his intellectual expertise;[14] what he appreciated above all was the firm grounding of the governor's political and military practices in the principles of republican fraternity. In his base at Port-de-Paix Laveaux treated his soldiers well, assisting them in their material tasks and sharing the scarce rations equally among European and black soldiers.[15] Toussaint also warmed to Laveaux's commitment to defending the economic interests of the *nouveaux libres*, the former black slaves of Saint-Domingue who formed the majority of the population in the colony. Since their emancipation in 1793 they were now wage labourers: if they worked on a plantation they were entitled to a quarter of its income (after government tax),[16] and Laveaux travelled far and wide across areas under French control, successfully confronting white landowners and managers who were refusing to pay their workforce.[17]

Toussaint admired Laveaux, in short, for his 'exceptional love of black people'.[18] He wore a plume the French general sent him on his hat, as a gesture of friendship and respect but also for personal protection: a wonderful example of how Toussaint could readily combine European symbolism and local magical traditions (the plume was widely used in *vodou* rituals). And he felt, too, that Laveaux's disposition was based not on paternalistic condescension but on a real commitment to republican equality. This principle was tested when the wealthy American merchant Stephen Girard petitioned Laveaux in 1795 to return his slave Crispin, who had absconded from Philadelphia and found his way to Port-de-Paix.

Marcus Rainsford was a British soldier who visited Saint-Domingue in 1799, where he met Toussaint. First published in 1805, his *Historical Account of the Black Empire of Hayti* paid tribute to Toussaint's skills as a political and military leader.

The governor replied indignantly: 'you must know very little of me to dare to hope that in defiance of our Glorious Constitution, I would consent to force a man against his own will to leave the land of liberty where he has taken refuge. In Philadelphia [Crispin] was a slave. Have I the right to order him to take up his chains again? Assuredly not.'[19] In one of his later letters, Toussaint congratulated Laveaux for 'not treating black people as children' but rather 'directing and encouraging them towards the public good': this was exactly his own philosophy.[20]

This shared value system came across in Toussaint's military proclamations during this period, where he often claimed to speak 'in the name of the governor general'. For example, when he called on a group of French rebels to surrender in early 1795, he observed that both he and Laveaux believed in the principles of 'humanity' and 'peace', and in 'leading our brothers away from error and extending them a helping hand'. Toussaint added: 'like all republicans, I am driven by the ardent desire to find only brothers and friends wherever I will lead the troops under my command'.[21] In honour of the French Revolution Toussaint named one of his regiments after the *sans-culottes*, and his soldiers' musical repertoire included a number of French revolutionary chants, including the 'Marseillaise' and the 'Carmagnole'.[22]

The absolute dedication Toussaint expected of his soldiers on the battlefield was more than exemplified by their commander. He was the epitome of the charismatic military leader: a model of sobriety, he slept only a few hours every night, drank no alcohol, and his capacity for physical endurance was greater than even the hardiest of his men.[23] His daily diet consisted of a modest plate of vegetables, served with a few pieces of chicken or salted beef – or, when meat was not available, eggs or cheese. He was kept constantly informed of military operations by means of an efficient courier system, which saw messages delivered to him at all times of the day or night wherever he happened to be; his staff were instructed to wake him up for especially urgent missives.[24]

Locating Toussaint was not easy as he was constantly on the move, and rode so fast that he frequently left his own guards trailing a long way behind him – even though they were chosen for their exceptional equestrian abilities. His ubiquitousness was such that he was able to give his military forces the comforting impression that he was always nearby – a sense which was reinforced by his remarkable memory for places and names: he often had better topographic knowledge of specific sites than the scouts who had been sent there, and he could almost always call out his soldiers and officers by name, even if he had only met them fleetingly years earlier. These qualities gave him a quasi-mystical aura among his men, many of whom regarded their commander as a divinity. Toussaint's authority rested, too, on his capacity to appeal to the supernatural beliefs of his men; for example the red handkerchief he often wore around his head, the corners tied in delicate knots, was seen as a symbol of Ogoun Fer, the *vodou* spirit of war and anger who led his followers into combat and kept them safe (in West African cosmology this spirit was also represented as a blacksmith, and was associated with healing and reconciliation).[25] There was a widespread belief that his military decisions were dictated to him by his spirit protector.[26]

Daring was among Toussaint's primary attributes as a commander, and he was often in the very front ranks as he directed the charge against enemy lines. There are numerous examples of his heroic actions, many of which became the stuff of legend in his lifetime. In October 1794, when he recaptured Saint-Raphaël from his former Spanish allies, he found that their position was defended by an elevated fortification armed with heavy artillery and surrounded by a wide moat. His republican cavalry charged twice, but on both occasions was forced to retreat under intense fire, with the loss of more than 200 men. Toussaint finally broke through by driving the remnants of his mounted forces into the camp through a hail of bullets and cannon fire; this third cavalry charge routed the enemy.[27] Similarly, in August 1795, as he fought to reclaim the Mirebalais region from Spanish and British control, Toussaint personally directed the attack on a fort at Lascahobas which was held by 400 heavily armed men, and led the victorious cavalry assault which left a quarter of the enemy dead.[28]

Toussaint's bravery as a front-line combatant was versatile, drawing on the full range of military instruments available to him. In July 1794 he captured the positions held by Jean-François in Dondon and Fort-Dauphin 'sabre in hand', and chased his retreating foe into the bush, forcing him to abandon all his equipment, supplies and papers; as he gleefully reported to Laveaux, 'he saved only his shirt and trousers'.[29] His skills as a marksman were also excellent and he put them to good use: during the attack on another Spanish outpost he pursued their troops, which had taken refuge in the woods, and manoeuvred them into an exposed position, where he led his dragoons and picked them off with his rifle.[30] In early 1795, when he captured the fort of Saint-Malo, the decisive action was a bayonet charge which he piloted.[31] And when all else failed, there was just his sheer, almost foolhardy, audacity: at the height of one battle against British forces, Toussaint's troops tried repeatedly to take a redoubt tenaciously defended by the enemy. When several assaults by his soldiers failed to dislodge the entrenched British dragoons, Toussaint and his chief of staff, General Pierre Agé, led a small platoon and overwhelmed them in hand-to-hand combat. Toussaint embraced Agé and told him that he was 'as brave an infantryman as he was an outstanding general';[32] the same was true of his commander.

These campaigns demanded extraordinary feats of bravery, but also vast reserves of physical stamina. On one occasion Toussaint mentioned that he had been engaged in combat for fifteen successive days; it certainly helped that he did not need more than a few hours' sleep each night.[33] But these long stretches of fighting, coupled with consistent exposure to fire, did at times affect Toussaint's health. In one encounter he rushed to the rescue of a local commander in Petite-Rivière who had pleaded for his help after coming under royalist attack: he rode through the night even though his body was burning with fever, and helped his republican troops repel a series of royalist raids.[34] Returning from an inspection round in the Artibonite in December 1795, he informed Laveaux that the trip had 'heated him so much' that he was suffering from a 'high temperature'.[35] Travel across the choppy seas of northern and western Saint-Domingue could also unsettle him: on another inspection trip his boat journey left him 'seriously indisposed'.[36]

In July 1796, as he struggled to recapture British positions around Arcahaie, Toussaint confessed that he had been 'very ill for the past seven days'.[37] He had had dozens of horses killed under him, and was seriously wounded in battle seventeen times; the most visible (and permanent) trace of these injuries was the loss of most of his front teeth, which he suffered when a cannonball exploded near him – hence the widely held but mistaken belief that the name 'Louverture' referred to the opening in the front of his mouth. Toussaint laid siege to British-controlled Saint-Marc on two occasions and was injured both times: first by a cannon barrel which he was helping his soldiers to mount, and which fell and crushed all the fingers of one of his hands; and second when he sustained a serious arm injury and was forced to wear a sling. This wound, however, did not stop him from leading the charge at a column of British troops and driving them back.[38] Invited by Laveaux to spare himself, Toussaint responded with stoicism: 'it is best I suffer but keep doing good things'.[39] In 1799 the commander-in-chief admitted that he was 'suffering cruelly from a pain which had fixed itself' on his left leg, following an injury in the final stages of the campaign against the British in the previous year.[40]

Such hyperactivity, together with Toussaint's apparent physical invulnerability on the battlefield, confirmed his soldiers' belief that he was in close touch with the *vodou* spirits and that they gave him supernatural powers. This mystical quality was reinforced by remarkably timed natural events, which seemed miraculously to turn the tide in his favour. One such moment occurred in 1797 during an engagement with the royalist troops of Dessources, a *colon* commander who was retreating back to his Saint-Marc base from Verrettes to avoid an encounter with Toussaint's advancing forces. As the royalists reached an open road a torrential downpour fell upon them and drenched all their weapons, rendering them unusable; the rain, however, spared Toussaint's forces, which were less than two miles away. Left to defend themselves only with their bayonets, the exposed royalists were decimated.[41] Dessources must have felt especially cursed: three years earlier, after a seven-hour battle, Toussaint had crushed his forces and sent him back to Saint-Marc 'without cannon, without baggages, without hats, without shoes, without horses, in sum, without any kind of fanfare'.[42]

One of the abiding mysteries about Toussaint was how a man with no military background before the revolution, and whose physique was hardly an exemplar of martial virility, could have come to acquire such formidable fighting skills. Like most great revolutionary leaders, he was largely self-taught and learned from his own experiences. But he also knew where to turn to for help. According to the memoirs of his son Isaac, Toussaint started to undergo regular military training immediately after the 1791 slave insurrection: he asked a former officer from Cap to give him lessons in fencing and in military strategy, and every morning, under the guidance of this instructor, he dutifully trained in the 'handling of weapons'. The novice was a quick learner: he was soon able to direct the manoeuvres of the battalions of Biassou's guard. Another figure who helped with Toussaint's practical military training at this time was a black officer named Gille Lavette, who had served in Saint-Domingue's colonial militia. After Toussaint joined the republican camp in 1794, several French officers also provided him with the rudiments of theoretical instruction, notably General Edme Desfourneaux, who guided Toussaint through standard French manuals such as the Chevalier de Clérac's *Treatise* on military fortifications.[43] Toussaint's library was well stocked with the historical classics of the republican tradition of war, which included Herodotus' *History of the Wars of the Persians against the Greeks*, Vegetius' *Scriptores de re militari*, Caesar's *Commentaries*, d'Orléans' *History of Revolutions in England and Spain* and the inescapable *Lives* of Plutarch.[44]

Toussaint's ultimate strength in the domain of military strategy – as in many other areas – lay in his capacity for creative adaptation. He was able to draw on the full range of materials and techniques available, whether from the annals of the distant past or the experiences of the immediate present, from seasoned European military experts or Saint-Domingue *marron* rebels, from the closest of allies or the bitterest of foes. When it came to the formation of his own troops, for example, he wrote to Laveaux in mid 1794 asking for a copy of the governor's military training manual, so that he could 'educate the troops, both the infantry and the cavalry, and so that the officers can learn the commandments'.[45] This republican bible was not sufficient, though, and a year later he revealed that he had captured an instruction manual from a royalist officer employed in the training of Dessources' legion: he thought it would be very handy for his own purposes and planned on using it, even though it would be 'at the expense of the British sire's Majesty'.[46] Within a few years the best of his soldiers had developed prodigious skills in the manipulation of weaponry. A former British military officer who visited Saint-Domingue in the late 1790s was particularly struck by the dexterity with which Toussaint's infantry handled their bayonets: 'With that dreadful weapon, fixed on musquets of extraordinary length in their hands, neither cavalry nor artillery could subdue infantry, although of unequal proportion; but when they were attacked in their defiles, no power could overcome them'.[47] This training was all the more effective in that it required no munitions, which were always in short supply.

At the same time, and contrary to the conventional view of his philosophy of war, Toussaint did not believe that European techniques were the only recourse available to him; his strategic and tactical thinking was imaginative, and frequently departed from the European military tradition. He insisted that his troops carry very little with them, and trained them to guide themselves by the night stars and move with lightning speed. This mobility was also emphasized in Toussaint's adaptation of military training to the Saint-Domingue terrain, and in particular to the prevalence of woods, bushes, hills, ravines and mountains. The technique led to the development of combat skills which were aimed at building flexibility of movement, without losing the overall sense of group cohesion among his fighters. The originality of these combinations, too, caught the eye, as when Toussaint's republican army was observed conducting a military drill:

> Each general officer had a demi-brigade . . . [They] performed equally well several manoeuvres applicable to their method of fighting. At a whistle a whole brigade ran three or four hundred yards, then separating, threw themselves flat on the ground, changing to their backs or sides, keeping up a strong fire the whole of the time, till they were recalled; they then formed again, in an instant, into their wonted regularity.[48]

Toussaint's originality as a military strategist lay not only in his unconventional training of his regular troops, but also in the novel ways he prepared his forces for irregular combat. This is where he drew extensively upon the techniques developed by the *marron* slave rebels in Saint-Domingue: the systematic exploitation of the advantages of terrain; the entrapment of the enemy and capture of his equipment; camouflage; the psychological intimidation of the adversary by a variety of means; and the use of deceptions such as false ceasefires and surrenders.[49] Toussaint's tactical plans often relied on misleading the enemy, and here too he led the way. The most elaborate of these ruses, which became part of his legend, involved a plan in August 1794 to capture one of the most capable British officers, Major Thomas Brisbane. A few months after switching to the republican side, Toussaint pretended that he was having second thoughts about the French and was open to joining the British camp; he instructed his lieutenants to hand over the republican-controlled territories of Verrettes and Petite-Rivière, which they duly did. Hostilities ceased, soldiers fraternized, and Toussaint held a series of meetings with Brisbane and his staff over an eight-day period during which he exchanged seventeen letters with him and swore allegiance to King George III. But all the while he was secretly plotting to entrap the British officer with the help of the latter's secretary Morin, whom he won to the republican cause. Toussaint promised to hand over Gonaïves to Brisbane and invited him to come and take possession of the town with his retinue; the British commander sent one of his royalist deputies. Two days later Toussaint arrived with a large force and retook the town, arresting a number of senior enemy officers; he only narrowly missed capturing Brisbane.[50]

Successful entrapments also involved the ambushing of enemy convoys, as for example in early 1795, when Toussaint's troops lay in wait for a royalist detachment sent from Saint-Marc to supply its neighbouring camps: they captured 'seven carriages laden with comestibles', and the unfortunate Dessources, who rushed to the rescue, was yet again thrashed, losing more than sixty of his combatants and receiving a complimentary republican bullet in the thigh.[51] A year later, 500 British troops were ambushed by Toussaint's men near Petite Montagne, with considerable enemy losses and the taking of 'seven carts laden with comestibles': the surprise effect, and the careful positioning of his men, allowed Toussaint to achieve this success with a force which was less than half the size of the enemy's.[52] Such tactics were used throughout the war against the British. In the final campaign in early 1798 he ordered a small contingent of his forces to present themselves to British outposts in the area of Charbonnière, on the outskirts of Port-au-Prince, and to 'pretend that an attack on these posts was imminent'; the majority of his troops, meanwhile, were deployed on the roads leading out of town so that they could attack the British when they made a sortie to rescue their besieged comrades. 'Make yourselves as small as possible,' Toussaint instructed his commanders, 'because he who lies in wait is much stronger than he who is surprised.'[53]

These deceptions were combined with another of Toussaint's favourite tactics, which also came straight out of the popular slave-rebellion repertoire: the constant intimidation of the enemy. In a letter to Laveaux, he even ascribed the majority of his victories to this form of psychological warfare.[54] Further credence can be given to his claim if we examine the testimonies of Toussaint's enemies, most notably the *Journal* of Lieutenant Howard of the York Hussars, who fought in the final years of the British campaign in Saint-Domingue. His diaries tell of the torments suffered by the British at the hands of Toussaint's 'brigands', the most notable of which was the permanent fear of being 'murdered from behind the bushes' or 'from wherever they could find an opportunity of cutting [us] off'.[55] Just as undermining was Toussaint's practice of sending small, highly mobile units to unsettle British-held outposts late at night, to cause chaos and prevent the soldiers from getting a proper night's sleep. On one occasion Howard recounted how 'a party of several men' had come up to the gate of his camp at 11 p.m. and fired several times before retreating into the darkness; the officer rallied a group of his men and gave chase for five miles, but was unable to find the assailants. Howard returned, went to sleep, only to be awakened at 4 a.m. by yet more shooting; this time he roused every man under his command and searched the entire plain around his camp, but 'could not fall in with a single soul'. He later learned that other British-held positions had been attacked that night in exactly the same way by Toussaint's invisible fighters.[56]

These techniques of harassment, perfected to a fine art by Louverture and his men, created a state of permanent unease among British forces, which steadily undermined their confidence – especially as they knew they were under constant surveillance by an adversary they could neither see nor hear. Toussaint was highly resourceful in gathering information about enemy activity: whether through spies, informers, the interception of communications, or drawing upon refugees, deserters and local citizens with first-hand accounts such as peasants and fishermen.[57] These 'grandes intelligences', as he called them, provided invaluable knowledge about enemy schemes which he used to prepare his own actions.[58] Natural elements were also used as camouflage for military operations. For example, Toussaint developed the habit of attacking the British during thunderstorms, especially severe ones, which could be spectacular in Saint-Domingue. Howard described one such event, which lasted six hours, as 'one of the grandest effects of Horror I have ever experienced'; this association of thunderstorms with potential attacks clearly provoked dread among enemy troops.[59] Toussaint's men also resorted to the kind of intimidating sounds produced by *marron* rebels in early 1790s, such as 'screams, hissing noises, and the loud beating of drums' during certain combat operations; faced with this 'deafening noise' in one encounter, British troops fled in 'tumultuous terror'.[60]

Thanks to all of these skills, Toussaint's forces were able to carry out bold raids into the very heart of British-held territory: on the night of 16 April 1797, Howard noted that a 'party of brigands' came at night 'into the middle of the regiment in Saint-Marc without being perceived' and made off with six saddle horses. This theft from the army barracks astounded the British, and was characterized by Howard as 'one of the most audacious attempts ever committed in the Annals of Military History'.[61]

Toussaint's writings offer fascinating glimpses of his military operations, but he left few comprehensive accounts of his campaigns. In one of his later letters, he listed more than fifty of his major victories against Spanish and British forces between 1794 and 1798.[62] But although we can broadly piece together his movements on the ground during these episodes, notably through his correspondence with successive French governors, we often lack specific dates and locations, information about his strategic plans and troop movements, and precise battle descriptions. One significant exception is his successful fifteen-day campaign to recapture the Mirebalais basin from the British in April 1797, in the aftermath of which he produced a detailed report.

The region was of considerable military significance as it was a natural fortress, serving as a gateway to the interior from the provinces of the north, the west and the south, as well as offering a potential escape route into Spanish territory. Its ranches, farmed by whites and free people of colour, were a vital source of beef, and its plantations of cotton, indigo and coffee had been largely spared the devastation of the early revolutionary years.[63] The area was invaded and held by the British until early 1795, allowing royalist forces to extend their control east towards the border with Santo Domingo. Toussaint counter-attacked and reclaimed much of the region by June 1795. But the British and their allies regrouped and eventually fought back, and in August 1796 inflicted a severe defeat on his forces: gathering all their troops from Grand-Bois, Arcahaie, Croix-des-Bouquets and Port-au-Prince, the royalists overran republican positions around Lascahobas and almost completely wiped out the 4th regiment of the republican army; barely fifty men survived.[64] By the time Toussaint prepared to take the fight back to the British in early months of 1797 they had consolidated their positions in the area, with a network of camps protected by blockhouses generally perched on elevated sites.

Toussaint left Gonaïves on 15 March and travelled across the western cordon, inspecting his troops and assembling a force of over 12,000 men from his 4th, 6th, 7th and 8th regiments around Verrettes on 24 March. On his way to Petite-Rivière, he sustained a serious injury when his horse attempted a difficult passage too brusquely and flung him off; he had to make his way to Verrettes by carriage. He established his headquarters there, and organized his forces into three columns, entrusting one of them, under the command of Christophe Mornet, with the task of occupying the principal road joining Mirebalais to Port-au-Prince, so as to prevent the arrival of any possible British reinforcements. Mornet's troops fought their way to the location and held the position, defeating a force of royalist auxiliaries; during this engagement the son of Desbruges, the enemy commander of the region, was killed. Toussaint then ordered his other columns under Clervaux and Dessalines to advance immediately on two major British positions, the Bourré and La Selle fortifications, both situated on high ground, whose defenders taunted their assailants with chants of 'Vive Le Roi'; the republican soldiers responded with revolutionary chants as they hauled their artillery pieces up narrow mountainous paths. The forts did not resist Dessalines' cannons, and as the fleeing royalists tried to reach the River Artibonite they were cut to pieces by the republican cavalry. The town of Mirebalais soon fell into republican hands, with the royalists pulling back into the Grand Bois mountains. Toussaint noted that the British made little effort to defend Mirebalais, even though it was protected by an imposing fortress; the enemy 'retreated in panic at the sight of republican bayonets'.[65]

At this point, although still struggling with his injury, Toussaint himself joined the battle: as he put in his report, 'I was still in agony, but the success of republican arms made me insensitive to the pain, and I was eager to complete the victory, and rout the enemy from the region.'[66] One of the key tactical advantages he had was his personal knowledge of the terrain, which he now exploited to the full. He took command of Clervaux's column, to which he joined his own cavalry regiment, and pursued the retreating royalists into the Grand Bois area; over a thirty-six hour period he surrounded and burned down the enemy blockhouses of camp Cotineau, camp Coupé, camp Guerrier, camp Bobin and camp Sainte-Victoire, while Dessalines cleared the fortified positions of camp des Cayettes, camp Dattis and camp Basile. By the end of the campaign, Toussaint and his men had recaptured Mirebalais and cleared the Grand Bois mountains;

slave-owning *colons* in the area had surrendered, several hundred royalists had been killed and a considerable supply of enemy equipment captured, including cannons of various sizes, rifles, pistols and ammunition. When Toussaint learned that the inhabitants of the towns of Bánica, Lascahobas and Neyba had looted British army stores after their retreat from the area, he demanded that the munitions be immediately handed over to his troops; if they failed to do, he threatened to have their homes searched.[67] Around sixty prisoners were taken and sent back to Gonaïves; the majority were local French royalists and black mercenaries and a small number were British and German.

Consolidating such victories was often a frustrating affair; within a month of his troops' successes in Mirebalais the British crept back in, and Toussaint was forced to return and drive them out again.[68] One additional factor which made it hard for his men to hold on to captured territory, as Toussaint frequently noted, was the poor quality of their equipment: one of his constant preoccupations as a military commander, especially in the initial years of his struggle against the Spanish and the British, was the lack of weapons and supplies for his soldiers. Throughout the 1797 Mirebalais campaign, his troops were each given a daily ration of three biscuits.[69] His correspondence with Laveaux is full of complaints about the problems he faced: he once noted that his troops in the Artibonite had no salted meats, and were very short of clothing: three-quarters of his men were 'without shirt or trousers', and many were 'naked like earthworms'.[70]

Although his officers and soldiers endured these deprivations stoically, in true republican spirit, they occasionally grumbled: in January 1796 Toussaint received a petition signed by the officers of the 5th regiment, stationed in the remote Dondon region, informing him that they were facing 'the greatest of hardships'. They had not been paid and their rations had run out; they were surviving on a small supply of bananas and salted fish.[71] Such a predicament was by no means exceptional: another of his local commanders informed Toussaint that he was unable to keep hold of his men, as they had run out of provisions and clothing and had been 'forced to go marauding elsewhere in order to find subsistence'.[72] In July 1796, Toussaint himself informed his superiors that he would not be ready to launch an attack on British positions as his troops had been starved of supplies for three months. His flour reserves had dwindled, and torrential rains had destroyed the staple crops on which he traditionally relied, such as bananas and sweet potatoes, so that he had been forced to send soldiers to collect sugar cane from the fields. The men's daily ration had been reduced to a single piece of herring or salted cod.[73] A year later, despite the desperate shortage of supplies on the western front, he was able to send 250 barrels of flour to Cap, while noting that his troops in Jean-Rabel were 'acutely in need'; when he received news that a supply ship destined for his sector had been lost, he wept.[74] Even after the defeat of the British in 1798 the situation did not improve significantly: Toussaint reported that his troops on the western front were facing 'extreme food shortages' and were having to rely on local provisions, which were 'not in abundance';[75] he complained to his superiors that his soldiers were still overwhelmingly 'without coats, shirts, or trousers'.[76]

As if this was not enough, there was also a dire shortage of equipment. His horses lacked saddles, and Toussaint frequently complained to his superiors about this problem.[77] There was also an ongoing issue with munitions, which became an obsessive theme in Toussaint's correspondence with Laveaux. 'I am entirely short of ammunition, having spent it all on the various attacks against the enemy,' he wrote urgently in 1794; soon afterwards, as he prepared an offensive against Saint-Marc, he declared that he needed 'twice as many munitions' as were available in his military stocks. Later, as he reviewed the defence lines of Gonaïves, he asked for 'cannon, mortar, and bombs', and awaited their arrival 'trepidatiously'.[78] He compared the promise of 400 pounds of gunpowder to a wondrous deliverance: 'it is as though I had been ill,' he told Laveaux, 'and you are sending me the right cure for my disease'. But there could sometimes be problems: in 1796 he asked for and received 2,000 rifles; however, they turned out to be 'in very poor condition, with the loss of around 150 bayonets'. Toussaint pledged to try and 'patch them together' as best he could; improvisation was another indispensable skill in his art of war.[79]

Toussaint not only coped with these limitations, but in some senses turned them to his advantage. No shot was fired by his soldiers 'without good reason', he informed Laveaux, adding that he was 'very severe' in his exhortations to use munitions sparingly; he told one local group of commanders that he would hold them 'responsible for the gunpowder until the very last grain'.[80] He also insisted that all the rifles and ammunition captured from the British and their allies be handed over to the military depot, so that they could be recycled for the war effort. He demanded that his officers 'keep their eyes wide open' to ensure this order was faithfully executed.[81] There was for Toussaint, it seems, something especially poetic about a military success which was achieved on the back of enemy munitions.

It is a measure of the fortitude Toussaint instilled in his men that some of their greatest exploits were achieved from positions of numerical and tactical inferiority. Natural or man-made obstacles did not easily stand in their way, be they traditional defensive barriers erected outside fortifications, such as fascines or chevaux de frise, or elevated terrains. In early 1795, the troops of Toussaint's nephew Moyse launched an assault against Fort Bamby, an enemy position built on the top of a steep and almost inaccessible mountain. They slung their weapons on their shoulders and ascended the peak even though they were unable to return the sustained fire they were receiving from above; having reached the summit, and despite losing some of their comrades, they overran the enemy with bayonets.[82] In 1798, when Toussaint stormed the British position of Fort Churchill with his elite troops, his men realized that their ladders were too short, and so they stood on one another's shoulders for half an hour, taking heavy casualties but eventually succeeding in creating a breach in the enemy position.[83] The use of human ladders was clearly a valuable technique, as it was also deployed in a successful attack on another British-held position, the Camp Martineau, situated by Arcahaie: as Toussaint put it, 'our men were forced to join themselves together to reach the heights of the wall' – this was brotherhood taken to its ultimate limits.[84]

Toussaint's troops often found themselves facing a larger contingent of enemy forces. In late 1794, for example, thirty of his men were sent to repulse a royalist attack at Verrettes. When they arrived they were confronted by an enemy ten times their number which charged at them three times; on each occasion they were repelled, with the royalist commander Bisquet losing his life in the third attempt.[85] A year later, Toussaint received word that Moyse's troops were in difficulty during an engagement in the Dondon area with Jean-François's militia, whose forces were again overwhelmingly superior in number. By the time Toussaint arrived, with merely fifty troops from his *sans-culottes* regiment, Moyse's men were in difficulty, having run out of munitions and being left with 'one barrel of gunpowder'. Yet Toussaint was delighted to find that his men were still on the offensive and were attacking the enemy – with stones. He rallied his soldiers, who charged with such fierceness that Jean-François's troops fled in disarray.[86]

These examples of military valour, and many more, show that Toussaint often turned his troops' inferiority into a weapon, both by highlighting the importance of courage and by instilling in his men an unshakeable belief in the justice of their cause: an army fighting to liberate its black brothers could never be defeated by its adversaries, however well they might be equipped, financed and armed. A wonderful example of how well Toussaint schooled his soldiers in this republican philosophy came to light when they received an invitation from Jean-François to abandon the French cause and rally to the King of Spain. They greeted this summons to treachery with a magnificently contemptuous proclamation: 'Our liberty is very different from yours,' they responded, 'you are just the slaves of a king, and we are free republican men who despise your monarch.' As for the profusion of weapons and munitions Jean-François had received from his king, Toussaint's men laughed them off cockily: 'Be sure to use them to tighten your chains, as we need only sticks and stones to make you dance the Carmagnole.'[87]

Military fraternity was also about discipline, a central feature of Toussaint's military command, and it was recognized by his adversaries as one of the cornerstones of his army's successes in the field. A French general who later faced Toussaint in combat went so far as to assert that the unity he achieved among his fighters was 'Louverture's most remarkable accomplishment'.[88]

This cohesion began at the very top of his military hierarchy. Toussaint nurtured a talented group of senior officers, who rose through the ranks to assume commanding positions in his army; a number of them later became key figures in the Haitian Revolution. Some of these men, such as Henri Christophe, were gifted black commanders whom he put in charge of regiments he created when he first assumed responsibility for operations on the western front. Christophe eventually became the military commander of Cap, and was praised by Toussaint for his 'patriotism', his 'wisdom and prudence', as well as his robust adherence to 'order'.[89] The most flamboyant of Toussaint's senior military officers was Jean-Jacques Dessalines. From the very outset, when he was made commander of Saint-Michel, Dessalines emerged as one of Toussaint's most dependable lieutenants: tough, fearless and uncompromising, he was a formidable fighter, and was entrusted with important military operations against both the Spanish and the British. In his report following the recapture of Mirebalais in 1797, Toussaint singled out Dessalines for his 'firmness, valour and prudence'.[90] He was despatched, too, whenever local civil disorders needed to be quelled by the use of overwhelming force. It was best not to be loitering around the neighbourhood when Dessalines rode in with his fighters from the 4th regiment to execute one of his 'purges';[91] those involved in serious acts of violence were court-martialled on the spot and, if found guilty, executed.[92]

Toussaint's military entourage contained a number of his close relatives: notably his brothers Pierre (who served with him in the Spanish army) and Paul (who became a general), his brother-in-law Claude Martin (a colonel) and his nephews Moyse, Charles Bélair, Bernard Chancy and Jacques Chancy.[93] But it was also open to all available talents, representing, in a microcosm, the future fraternal society he hoped to construct in Saint-Domingue. Among his senior officers were gifted mixed-race fighters such as Augustin Clervaux, Colonels Morisset and Gabart, the heads of his elite cavalry regiments (Gabart later became the commander of the gendarmerie), and a colonel also called Dessalines (who bore no relation to his black namesake). There were, too, a number of white Europeans in Toussaint's inner military circle – notably General Agé, his chief of staff, whom we have seen in action, and several of his aides-de-camp, such as Dubuisson, Birète, and his most trusted subordinate, Augustin d'Hébécourt.[94] And, contrary to the widespread belief that his officer corps was dominated by black creole natives of Saint-Domingue, many of his military cadres were African-born *bossales*. Drawn from the dominant African ethnic group in Saint-Domingue, the 'Kongos', these fighters, many of whom were former *marron* slaves, were recruited as Toussaint unified the different black rebel forces under his command. They included his old acquaintance from the Bréda days, Sans-Souci, who rose to the rank of colonel and remained fiercely loyal to him until the very end; among other notable *bossale* commanders were Jasmin, Noël Prieur, Labelinaye, Mademoiselle, Sylla and Laplume.[95] 'The brave Laplume', as Toussaint called him, was a mild-mannered officer who entered the limelight when he arrested his boss, the militia leader Pierre Dieudonné, and brought his comrades into the republican camp; he was immediately promoted to colonel, and eventually became a general in Toussaint's army.[96] Mademoiselle was given the rank of colonel in the 12th regiment, which was composed entirely of former *marrons* from another African ethnic group, the 'Docos'; Toussaint had a particular fondness for these sturdy fighters, whom he called 'his indomitable montagnards'.[97]

In order to inspire a fraternal *esprit de corps* among these different elements, Toussaint constantly preached the virtues of republican unity. Whenever tensions flared up, as they invariably did in the early years, whether between whites and non-whites, black and mixed-race people or creoles and *bossales*, the commander gathered his troops and subjected them to a lengthy lecture in which he did not mince his words. After one such occasion, he informed Laveaux that he had given a 'vehement dressing-down' to his officers and soldiers during a troop review, and that 'a sense of unity' was 'now beginning to emerge among them'.[98] On another occasion, some of his black soldiers complained about his appointment of a white colonel as the military commander of Saint-Louis; Toussaint dismissed these grumblings, telling them that the man had saved his life during one of the battles around Saint-Marc and that he regarded him as 'his eldest son'.[99] The positive effects of these harangues can be seen in the petitions addressed to Toussaint by white members of his army, assuring their commander-in-chief that they had 'no problems whatsoever' with their black and mixed-race comrades, and that their relationship with them was based on 'friendship and fraternity' – assurances which demonstrated that the racial and ethnic integration of his army was one of Toussaint's consistent concerns.[100]

Toussaint also reminded his commanders of the absolute necessity of 'subordination and discipline'. 'These', he told them, 'are the two military virtues which once upon a time made the Romans the most warlike of peoples, and which today have enabled our republican armies in Europe to triumph over their enemies.'[101] He issued precise and detailed instructions to his senior officers before each military engagement, and expected them to report back to him regularly, and in detail, during their operations. For example, when he despatched his men to engage with the British in early 1798, his marching orders to Dessalines specified the manoeuvres to be carried out by individual columns, the locations where ambushes should be laid, the strategic positions to be held, the routes to be taken by the guides, the type of men to be employed for individual operations, the secret signals to be used to initiate co-ordinated actions, right down to the incentives which could be offered to soldiers carrying out especially dangerous missions.[102]

Toussaint kept his senior commanders on a very tight leash. When, in the final stages of the campaign against the British, he learned that Christophe had left his post without his permission and returned to Cap, he rebuked him sharply for allowing 'local intrigues' to get in the way of his military duty.[103] He reminded them all of the key virtues of co-ordination and communication: he told Dessalines that the timing of his specific manoeuvre was crucial, and that 'the slightest negligence' on his part 'could cause the whole operation to fail'.[104] He could at times needle and even taunt his commanders. Instructing Dessalines to capture a British-held fort, he not only gave him details as to how he should execute the operation, but also urged him to pick 'reliable, brave and experienced soldiers' who would 'lead the assault decisively' and not 'just go through the motions of firing at the enemy'.[105] (One can imagine that Dessalines, who rarely gave anything less than full-throttled commitment, would have bridled at receiving such an order.) Yet Toussaint was also humane, and mindful of the dangers to which he exposed his soldiers: if an enemy fortification could be taken only with considerable troop losses, he would normally instruct his commanders to surround the position and pin the enemy in rather than risk throwing away the precious lives of his fighters. He defended his officers, too, if he thought their actions were unfairly represented; he stood up for one of his captains when he was accused of treacherous conduct during an engagement in Dondon in 1797.[106]

Toussaint's expectations of his officers were always high, and he would rebuke any commander who failed to abide by his specific injunctions, especially if – as was frequently the case – he had made a personal trip to the field to demonstrate what exactly needed to be done. When in January 1795 the military chiefs of Petite-Rivière did not properly execute his plan to cross the River Artibonite to retake British-held positions on the opposite bank, Toussaint exploded with fury: 'I ordered you to carry out this manoeuvre three times, and you blatantly ignored my instructions . . . I told you to use 18 and 12 pounders, and even visited the site and showed you exactly where these artillery pieces should be placed . . . your attitude has been negligent and careless.'[107] The commander-in-chief did not always abide by his own injunction to be 'cold from the outside'.

Toussaint insisted just as much on discipline when it came to his soldiers; indeed, it was key to his conception of virtuous military behaviour. The first rule here, which he repeated before every single operation, was the duty to follow orders. Its absolute necessity featured prominently in all his harangues: in his stirring appeal before the final campaign against the British in 1798 he held up the discipline of French revolutionary armies, 'the most important weapon they used to defeat the tyrants of Europe'. He urged his men to follow their example: 'unconditionally obey the orders of your superiors, follow the strictest of disciplines, and observe the greatest subordination to your commanders: only then will we be certain of defeating the enemies of the republic'.[108]

Toussaint was constantly on the watch for British attempts to corrupt his soldiers. Early on in the campaign, the British sent two men of colour to Toussaint in an attempt to buy him off; he sent them on to Laveaux, who had them tried and executed for treason.[109] The royalists understood that Toussaint was beyond their reach, but this only encouraged them even further in their efforts to bribe his soldiers, forcing him to develop extremely strict rules to discourage any potential defections. During one attack on a British fort in early 1798, the enemy invited eight of Toussaint's soldiers into their compound and, after pulling them up with ropes, offered them food, drink and money if they agreed to try and win over their comrades when they returned to camp. This treacherous scheme was discovered by their commanding officer and the soldiers were executed near the fort, in sight of its British occupants.[110] His senior commanders would generally put British spies to death, but Toussaint himself tried whenever possible to spare their lives. On one occasion, upon hearing that General Laplume had found two spies and executed one of them, he rushed to the scene and not only prevented the killing of the other, but convinced the spy 'of the justice of republican ideals' and sent him back to Port-au-Prince to preach the cause to his black comrades who were fighting on the British side.[111]

The prohibition of pillage was Toussaint's cardinal principle of military virtue. His rules were equally draconian in this respect: his army's code of military practice stipulated that any officer or soldier who was caught pillaging would be court-martialled, and if found guilty would be sentenced to death; as with cases of treason, execution was to take place 'immediately and on site'.[112] Furthermore, every member of the army was asked to exercise supreme vigilance, and report any act of pillage he might have witnessed – whether by a fellow soldier or a commanding officer – directly to Toussaint. Pillage was defined broadly, to include 'the appropriation for personal purposes of guns, sabres, munitions and any military equipment from a camp, fort, or town'; the penalty here too was death.[113]

But Toussaint did not rely on the threat of punishment alone: the discipline he cultivated among his soldiers was also based on an education in the republican virtues. Steadfastness was among the key ones, and he incessantly reminded his men that they should remain confident, especially in the face of setbacks: 'a good republican', he wrote to an officer who had just been treacherously defeated, 'must not let himself be discouraged'.[114] He also insisted that liberated territories had to be safeguarded with the utmost care: 'now that we have planted the tree of liberty in these areas', he told his men, 'we have to become the first defenders of its properties'. He repeatedly admonished his officers and soldiers that no homes or plantations should be set on fire.[115] More fundamentally, he emphasized that they were fighting a just war in which 'the lure of material rewards' was irrelevant. Indeed, he turned the prohibition of pillage into a lesson in morality: 'we fight not for our fortunes: we will have ample time to think about such matters once we have chased our enemies from our lands, from our homes. We fight for our freedom, which is the greatest of riches we can aspire to, and we have to preserve it for ourselves and for our children, for our brothers and our citizens.'[116]

This appeal to an elevated morality was a striking success, as is shown by the generally scrupulous treatment of civilians by Toussaint's soldiers in combat zones – especially whites. When they overran a Spanish-controlled camp, they discovered a group of starving European women and took them under their protection. They fed and clothed them, even though they themselves had barely eaten for days.[117] In the aftermath of one of the many battles around Mirebalais, Toussaint's troops captured a convoy of twenty *colons* who were fleeing from the republican-controlled territory with all their worldly possessions: these included 200 horses laden with jewellery and precious objects of various kinds, as well as their slaves. Toussaint ordered that the *colons* be brought to him, and began by asking them if any of their belongings had been taken by his soldiers. When they confirmed that not a single piece of gold had been touched, he said they were free to continue with their journey and take all their possessions with them – except for their slaves, who were immediately released.[118]

This kind of behaviour, combining republican emancipatory practices with strict discipline and humanity towards civilians in combat areas, became the hallmark of Toussaint's soldiers. The rigorous sense of self-possession of his 'almost naked men' was noted when they entered Cap in late March 1796 to put an end to the mixed-race revolt against Laveaux.[119] The same virtuous conduct was demonstrated by Toussaint's troops – carefully chosen by the commander-in-chief from among his elite forces[120] – when they re-entered the British-held towns of Port-au-Prince and Saint-Marc in 1798. Toussaint credited his envoy Huin with preventing a mass exodus from Port-au-Prince thanks to his words of reassurance to local inhabitants, especially as those who had chosen to remain behind had been warned by the departing royalists that they would be massacred.[121] Local municipal officials went out of their way to commend Toussaint for 'the discipline and good order' observed by his men.[122] Noting that the liberating army which entered Port-au-Prince committed no acts of pillage, even though it went without rations for the first two days, a local inhabitant mused: 'what European troops would have maintained such tight discipline under the same conditions?'.[123] The contrast with the British takeover of Port-au-Prince in 1794, when dozens of republicans were massacred, was striking.[124]

More challenging was the issue of the treatment of enemy combatants. The fighting was often ferocious and it was wise to avoid finishing on the losing side: in October 1794 Toussaint informed Laveaux that, after he had stormed the Spanish fortified position outside Saint-Raphaël, he had 'put ninety or so Spaniards to the sword'; he added that these were 'mostly' those who refused to surrender, but it is not clear how closely their intentions were ascertained.[125] In September 1795, as his forces attacked the royalist position of Camp Dubuisson, the enemy put up such a fierce resistance that when the camp was eventually overrun, Toussaint confessed that 'it became impossible to hold back the fervour of the troops . . . everyone found inside the camp was massacred'.[126] Defeated enemies sometimes became macabre war trophies. When Jean Jeanton, a 'fanatical' royalist commander, was ambushed and killed in the mountains of

Saint-Marc on the anniversary day of the French Revolution, his head and epaulettes were paraded in the neighbourhood by the victors, and Toussaint gleefully reported the news to his superior.[127] Sometimes these enemy remains were sent to their chief by his lieutenants as evidence of their revolutionary zeal: one local commander informed Toussaint that his soldiers had 'cut off the heads of thirteen royalists' and were sending them to him.[128] During the occupation of the Spanish-controlled town of Bánica by Toussaint's troops in 1796, it was alleged that some of his black forces carried out acts of reprisal.[129]

But such incidents were more typical of the early years of the fight against the foreign occupiers and their auxiliaries; later periods were marked by consistent acts of humanity by Toussaint and his republican army. Black prisoners, in particular, were shown every possible courtesy and treated 'like brothers'; those who volunteered to do so were drafted into his army, and many subsequently distinguished themselves on the battlefield.[130] Desertions of black soldiers fighting on the British side were actively encouraged – for example, 250 fighters from Port-au-Prince came over to the republican camp in May 1797[131] – and the number increased steadily in the final months of the campaign.[132] Some of the gallantry displayed was quite extraordinary by any standards. After the 1797 encounter in which his troops were crushed the royalist officer Dessources fell into republican hands, but Toussaint's local commander had him escorted by ten of his men to the gates of Saint-Marc, where he was freed and allowed to return to his base.[133] The commander-in-chief himself regularly instructed his army that all prisoners of war should be treated humanely and according to the 'laws of war'; his own behaviour was typically meticulous in this regard. He often released them if they gave their word of honour to lay down their weapons: after capturing Mirebalais for the first time in 1795, he found 300 white Frenchmen who had come from the north of Saint-Domingue to enlist in the royalist militia; he permitted them to return to their homes after they swore an oath of allegiance to the republic; he had done this, he told Laveaux, out of 'humanity'.[134]

In one famous instance, Toussaint allowed the French royalist Marquis d'Espinville, whom he had just defeated on the battlefield, to leave Saint-Domingue for Cuba with his entire military staff. Toussaint incorporated the remnants of his troops into his own army, even though they could all technically have been prosecuted for high treason as they had taken up arms against France.[135] Always mindful of the example he was setting, Toussaint's merciful acts could verge on the theatrical. When four Frenchmen who had gone over to the British were recaptured by his troops in 1798, he ordered them to be brought to his church the following Sunday;

they were not told of their fate and must have expected to be executed, as they were guilty of aggravated treason. However, just as the priest's homily was extolling the virtues of Christian forgiveness, Toussaint walked up to the pew where the prisoners were seated and announced to the assembled congregation that they were to be pardoned.[136]

Toussaint also conducted prisoner exchanges with the British, and his correspondence with their officials shows that negotiations between the two sides took place regularly, and were generally implemented in good faith. In November 1795, for instance, he received fourteen republican prisoners from the British and undertook to send back a young man of colour named Davy, whose father had fought on the royalist side and was presently based in Jamaica.[137] These exchanges continued until 1798, even though Toussaint was irritated by the British habit of only exchanging white prisoners; he rightly suspected that they intended to keep the black captives as slaves.[138] The problem, however, was that such civilities were not observed by royalist fighters on the ground, especially when they were commanded by French *colons* or émigrés. In his report to his superiors, Toussaint highlighted separate incidents in which two of his brave local commanders, Brigadiers Biret and Michaud, were captured and summarily executed by royalists. Biret had laid down his weapons, and yet was hacked to death with bayonets; the manner of Michaud's killing was so gruesome that Toussaint could only report that he was executed with a 'refinement of cruelty'.[139]

Such incidents were manifestly encouraged by senior royalist officers. This was confirmed when, during the capture of a British fort, Toussaint discovered a letter by the sadistic commander Jean-Baptiste Lapointe to his officers, which concluded: 'no mercy should be shown to the brigands. No prisoners.'[140] Lapointe, a slave-owning mixed-race planter from southern Saint-Domingue, was given the command of a royalist regiment after handing over Arcahaie to the British; he detested Toussaint, whom he regarded as a 'miserable slave'.[141] After Lapointe massacred 200 men at Arcahaie and Saint-Marc, an outraged Toussaint penned a long letter of complaint to the commander-in-chief of the British forces in Saint-Domingue, Major-General John Whyte. He began, in the name of 'the principles of humanity and republican virtue', by denouncing the killings of his officers and Lapointe's 'barbaric' injunction to his forces, which were 'contrary to the laws of war'. He went on to list numerous instances of mercy shown to royalist prisoners by himself and by his own men, adding that the 'republicans of Saint-Domingue were incapable of murdering in cold blood an enemy whom they had just vanquished'. Indeed, despite the 'bitterness' he felt at the murder of his men, Toussaint had sent six captured soldiers from the Irish legion back to Saint-Marc, as well as a captain. He then sternly upbraided the British officer: 'even though I am just a black man, and even though I have not received as polished an education as you and your officers, I would feel that such dishonourable acts, were they committed by my forces, would tarnish my nation's glory'.[142]

The expulsion of the British occupying forces from Saint-Domingue in September 1798 raised the reputation of Toussaint and his hardy republican combatants to new heights. Shortly after the departure of British soldiers from the colony, the French Directory representative Philippe Roume wrote a report to his superiors in Paris in which he conceded that Toussaint's 'rebellious' tendencies sometimes made him difficult to handle. However, he added:

> this is a rebel whose will commands the assent of nine-tenths of the population of Saint-Domingue; a rebel whose courage, discipline and strategic intelligence in the conduct of colonial war have overcome the might and the ruses of the British; a rebel who hardly ever sleeps and seems able to multiply himself and be present in many different places at the same time; a rebel who knows the ideal locations for ambushes in every part of this territory which is littered with mountains, rivers, and passes; a rebel who commands a tireless army, that can feed itself on anything which can be digested and can even do without clothing.[143]

Toussaint's greatness as a military commander was not merely a matter of counting his victories on the battlefield. Indeed, even though he was often successful (his role in routing the Spanish was decisive), he suffered setbacks, too – especially against the British. Despite his determined efforts to force them out of their strongholds in the west (notably Port-au-Prince, Saint-Marc and Arcahaie), success consistently eluded him, and the final British withdrawal was achieved through negotiation rather than unconditional surrender. That said, Toussaint's massive troop build-up was one of the main reasons which forced the British to negotiate, and his strategy of pinning down and harassing his enemy undeniably achieved its primary psychological objective: by 1798 British forces were thoroughly demoralized.[144] Writing about the five-year campaign against the British, in which he participated from beginning to end, a European officer in Toussaint's army was categorical: the defeat of the occupying forces had been achieved by 'the force of our bayonets, and the courage, intelligence and wisdom of our commander-in-chief'.[145] Disease also played a role, of course, as yellow fever took a major toll on British troops; but Saint-Domingue's republican troops did not succumb to infection and disease to anything like the same degree. The reason for this lay partly in the natural immunity developed by his local-born soldiers, but also in their commander-in-chief's better preparation, notably his ability to maintain a network of military hospitals where his soldiers could receive effective treatment.[146]

It is also clear that Toussaint had ample reserves of what Napoleon defined as one of the great qualities of a general on the battlefield: *la chance*. He survived countless encounters with death, including a number of assassination attempts. Yet, unlike Napoleon, Toussaint was not a man of martial disposition: even though he readily confessed to having a great passion for military music, especially pieces for trumpets and percussion instruments, his Christian faith taught him the virtue of compassion (he described himself as someone with an 'open heart, always ready to forgive');[147] he was especially horrified, as he put it, by 'warriors with a fondness for spilling blood'.[148] If he could find a non-violent way of achieving his objectives, he preferred to take it. He always delivered ultimatums to his adversaries before attacking them, inviting them to surrender and promising to show clemency if they laid down their weapons: addressing the French royalists of Arcahaie in March 1798, he urged them 'in the name of the republic to rally to our army in order to avoid any inconveniences which might follow in the wake of the conflict; by this means, you will preserve yourselves and protect your properties'; he swore that there would be no acts of reprisal, 'on his honour as an honest man'.[149]

In this sense, the true measure of Toussaint's military success lay in his broader political objectives – notably the sense of fraternity he achieved among his republican troops, which had grown into an imposing force of nearly 20,000 men by 1798. He forged a group of commanders who were able and determined, and who faithfully executed his instructions – although, like every *grand capitaine*, he believed that his presence was the only effective guarantee of victory on the battlefield. As he once told Laveaux, after one of his subordinates suffered a military setback: 'when the principal chief is absent, things never go well'.[150] As for the junior officers and rank-and-file troops, they idolized their commander-in-chief and chanted his name after every victorious military operation; they followed him wherever he led them, across plains, mountains and rivers, through scorching heat and driving rain, typically surviving on the most meagre of rations. And despite being a strict disciplinarian, he joked with them too, often regaling them with anecdotes from his days on the Bréda plantation and reminding them that his nickname was 'Fatras-Bâton', which always provoked ripples of laughter.[151] Toussaint loved these men like a father: as he said, 'they are my children';[152] in return, they repeated his favourite expressions, playfully imitated his nasal voice, and called him 'Papa Toussaint' or 'vié [old man] Toussaint'.[153]

The paternal analogy was appropriate, because Toussaint did in a very real sense nurture these men, moulding them into a fighting force which exhibited all the military qualities he came to expect of them, such as discipline, bravery, resilience and collective pride. He did so against the odds, and against the expectations of his own friends and allies: even Toussaint's great admirer Laveaux reckoned that 'it would take a long time, and perhaps a generation, to turn Africans into good soldiers';[154] in the meantime, he thought republican rule in Saint-Domingue would need to be preserved by 'an imposing European force'.[155] One of the most remarkable testimonies of his black army's sense of self-esteem was a proclamation signed by its senior officers in late 1795, at a time when Toussaint was still only in charge of the western cordon; addressed to the French Convention, it expressed their implacable resolve to fight the enemies of the republic and show by their victories on the battlefield that 'the French soldiers of the Antilles, like their European brothers, know how to bear arms and use them effectively'. This text is one of the earliest documents to carry the signatures of the gallant men who would go on to become Toussaint's leading military commanders – Vernet, Maurepas, Noël Prieur, Moyse, Christophe and Dessalines.[156] By the late 1790s, this sense of black military superiority had become so entrenched that it was expressed in a popular kreyol saying in Saint-Domingue, directed at whites: 'zautres pas capable battre la guerre contre nègres'.[157]

Just as importantly, Toussaint's troops were educated in the military virtues, which they absorbed with gusto. He frequently affirmed that 'honour was [the] first',[158] and his soldiers and officers sought to emulate him in this respect. Their sense of solidarity was exemplary, too. They supported each other, fought for each other, and the loss of their comrades only fortified their resolve. As their commanding officer, Laplume, attested, one of the factors which motivated the soldiers who successfully stormed the Camp Martineau was their rage at the death of their fallen hero, Brigadier Biret: as they huddled together before launching their attack they swore to avenge his cowardly murder. What would have especially delighted Toussaint in Laplume's report was that all the different segments of his army were working in complete harmony, as ' true republicans': European soldiers, regular troops, as well militias made up of local *bossale* combatants – a fact all the more significant as Laplume himself, as we noted earlier, was a Kongo.[159]

Laplume added, and this too is worthy of note, that his men were fighting as 'good Frenchmen'. At one level, this illustrated the universality of the republican principles of fraternity and good citizenship, and demonstrated how they had been embraced by Saint-Domingue's revolutionaries. But Frenchness here came with a significant local twist, which was the key to Toussaint's success in mobilizing his men in the war against the Spanish and British forces. For they understood that this was not just a struggle against foreign occupiers: it was a fight to eradicate slavery from the colony. This republican spirit galvanized Toussaint's troops, as was symbolized by another telling moment during the Camp Martineau battle: at the height of the operation a sergeant named Gabriel, despite coming under intense fire, scaled the pole on which the British flag was flying and 'tore down this infamous banner of tyranny'.[160] For him and for his fellow fighters, Frenchness reflected the determination of Saint-Domingue's black people to retain their freedom and to resist any attempt to enslave them again. When he harangued his soldiers, Toussaint would often compare himself to a bird of prey who could not find a landing place as long as the 'freedom of his brothers' was still under threat.[161]

The cohesion of Toussaint's republican army can also be measured by its high ethical standards: his men's strict adherence to his injunctions against pillaging, and their humane treatment of prisoners of war. He boasted that the conduct of his forces had been exemplary: 'soldiers wanted to exceed the generosity shown by their officers, and officers that of their commanders'. There was perhaps an embellishment, but Toussaint clearly had good reason to commend his forces for their discipline. Indeed, the ultimate gratification for him was that this sense of compassion had not been limited to his troops: his calls for humanity had been heeded by black populations in republican-held territories. Noting several instances in which local peasants had come to the assistance of enemy soldiers in distress, he related the tale of one British soldier who told him that he owed his life to a *cultivateur* who had found him in a pitiful state at the end of a battle. This plantation worker – almost certainly a former slave – had taken him to his humble hut where he tended to his wounds, supplied him with food and drink, and then escorted him to the nearest republican military position, where he handed him over to Toussaint's forces.

The commander-in-chief beamed with pride: 'it is by this sort of behaviour that, despite the cruelty of her enemies, the people of Saint-Domingue will convince the entire universe that, even though they have only just begun their journey towards regeneration, they know how to appreciate liberty at its true value, and how to practise the republican virtues'.[162]

PART TWO

The Making of the Louverturian Order

4
A Single Family of Friends and Brothers

On 1 April 1796, the republican governor Étienne Laveaux organized a grand ceremony in Cap's main square in honour of Toussaint Louverture, whom he had just elevated as his deputy. By this point, the republicans had reclaimed the territories previously held by the Spanish, and were actively challenging the British in the enclaves they controlled. But tensions had been mounting between Laveaux and some of his mixed-race commanders, culminating in an attempted coup against him by a group of mixed-race rebels. During this 'conspiracy of 30 Ventôse' (20 March), he had been accused of advancing black interests at the expense of the people of colour; he had been manhandled and dragged to jail, and the plotters had issued a proclamation calling for his replacement by the mixed-race military commander of the northern region, General Jean Villatte. The coup had been foiled thanks to Villatte's equivocation, but also the providential intervention of black troops, commanded by Toussaint, who had arrived to confront the rebels and force Laveaux's release.[1] In presence of the senior officers of the French colonial army, and to the sound of cannons blasting from the nearby forts, Laveaux now saluted Toussaint as 'the saviour of legitimate authority', before hailing him as 'the black Spartacus, the leader announced by the philosopher Raynal to avenge the crimes perpetrated against his race'.[2]

This was the first time Toussaint was publicly likened to Spartacus. Nothing moves as swiftly as revolutionary time, but even he probably could not have imagined, when he embraced the slave revolt in 1791, that five years later the governor of Saint-Domingue would be comparing him to such an illustrious Thracian predecessor. Historians, too, viewed this moment as a turning point, and not just in terms of Toussaint's personal career. Pamphile de Lacroix saw it as a 'death blow for the authority of metropolitan France; it is from this declaration that the end of white rule and the birth of black power can be dated'.[3] Likewise, in the mid nineteenth century Thomas Madiou saw the 30 Ventôse episode as 'one of the most important moments in our history, definitely securing black preponderance in the North and the Artibonite'; henceforth, he added, mixed-race citizens only exercised 'subordinate' functions in these two provinces, while the authority of white French agents became 'null'.[4] For progressive historians such as C. L. R. James, there was an additional dimension: Toussaint's speech confirmed his credentials as Raynal's 'avenger of the new world', and as a true son of the French Revolution: his political thinking bore all the essential hallmarks of jacobin republicanism, with its cult of reason, its popular mobilization of the masses and its division of the world into good and evil.[5]

Defending the 'liberté générale' which the black slaves had won was at the heart of Toussaint's revolutionary politics, as we saw in the previous chapter. And even though Enlightenment thinking was not the decisive influence on him he readily, and proudly, accepted Laveaux's public presentation of him as a disciple of Raynal: according to a French visitor to Saint-Domingue, a bust of the radical philosopher occupied pride of place in his offices.[6] At the same time, his way of thinking was never merely imitative: in fact, by grappling with the specific circumstances of Saint-Domingue, notably the issue of race, Toussaint's views on citizenship represented a much bolder vision of brotherhood than that of the French jacobins. After he rallied to the French cause, his ideal of a future Saint-Domingue free of domination impelled him to fight an implacable war against Spanish and British forces and to resist any attempt to restore white supremacy. But it also led him to challenge the more subtle but no less demeaning paternalism of the French, whose administrative overlords at times tried to use him for their own ends.

Because Toussaint was all at once a soldier, a statesman and a man of ideas, his language could vary depending on the context; his ideas about fraternity drew upon republican as well as Christian, African and indigenous notions, and, especially when he was addressing peasant populations, were expressed in vivid creole parables and metaphors which spoke to his *bossale* brothers; one of his contemporary admirers wrote of Toussaint's 'African genius'.[7] Above all, his ideal of black power was never exclusive, but was balanced by his admiration for Laveaux and his sentiments of 'esteem and affection' for a number of white members of his entourage, such as the civil engineer Charles Vincent, with whom he conversed in kreyol and who was greatly loved by Toussaint's family (in particular by his wife Suzanne);[8] in a letter to him Toussaint said that the support of his 'sincere republican brothers' such as Vincent gave him much solace.[9] Indeed, Toussaint's ambition was to create, from the various white, black and mixed-race people of Saint-Domingue, a 'single family of friends and brothers'.[10]

*

A few days after the coup had been defeated, the released Laveaux prudently retreated from Cap to the nearby coastal town of Petite-Anse. A group of around 100 mixed-race women supporters of Villatte slipped into the neighbourhood at nightfall and began to spread rumours that the governor and his white allies had brought containers of slave chains on two ships. They alleged that the consignment had already been unloaded, and was part of a wider settler conspiracy to restore human bondage in Saint-Domingue. A general uproar ensued, in which armed black soldiers and residents arrived to confront Laveaux in front of the house where he was staying, with cries of 'kill the whites' – the Makandalist slogan of the 1791 slave insurrection. With an impeccable sense of melodrama, Laveaux appeared on his balcony and bared his breast to the crowd, warning them that if they shot him they would be killing 'the father who had always defended their liberty'. Parricide was fortunately averted when Toussaint again came charging in: he defused the situation in Petite-Anse by vouching for the besieged governor, the 'friend of the black people', and flinging open the doors of the local warehouse to reveal that it contained no slave chains, only bags of flour and salted meats.

The incident showed how fragile and vulnerable black populations felt about the possible return of slavery in Saint-Domingue, but also how easily their fears about their condition could be manipulated by unscrupulous local leaders, whether they were white, black or, in this case, mixed-race. Toussaint's conflicts with Villatte went back to 1794, when the latter offensively refused Toussaint's offer to abandon the Spanish cause and rally to the French camp because he could not bring himself to deal with a 'wretched slave'.[11] Villatte subsequently falsely accused him of threatening the peasants in the Gonaïves region with death for selling their produce in Cap, and, more seriously, encouraged Toussaint's soldiers to desert to his northern regiment with the promise of better pay and conditions. This kind of intrigue was not, Toussaint complained bitterly to Laveaux, the behaviour of a 'true brother'. Villatte was also a close ally of the southern mixed-race general André Rigaud (both men had fought in the Saint-Domingue American legion in 1779), and Toussaint suspected that Rigaud was involved in the attempt to undermine the French governor.[12] Laveaux had initially turned a deaf ear to Toussaint's warnings about intrigues from mixed-race leaders. But after the 30 Ventôse episode, Laveaux did not disguise his contempt: 'the people of colour', he wrote, 'are driven by an unsurmountable hatred against the whites . . . in their view, they alone should control the country and dictate its laws. But France has not made so many sacrifices for the cause of liberty and equality only to hand over power to a bunch of half-witted administrators.'[13]

Toussaint could not have agreed more: Villatte, the 'fin merle',[14] was just one in a long line of shady mixed-race figures he had encountered since the beginning of the revolution. In his view, Villatte's attempt to usurp power in 1796 was consistent with the misguided strategies pursued by the colony's mixed-race leaders since the early 1790s, when they refused to support slave emancipation and preferred to come to an arrangement with the white *colons*. In a letter to Laveaux, he pointedly referred to Vincent Ogé and Jean-Baptiste Chavanne, the leaders of the rebellion in 1790, as the 'so-called martyrs of freedom'; they were driven not by the love of general liberty but by the narrow self-interest of their caste, and he claimed to have 'proof' of their duplicitousness. Even though their gruesome execution had been deplorable, they did not deserve to be placed on the same pedestal as the black revolutionaries who had sacrificed their lives for their freedom.[15] Toussaint had glossed over this point when he had tried to win over the mixed-race leaders in 1793 – but now that Vilatte had challenged republican authority there could be little room for doubt. Toussaint also remembered that, in the aftermath of the 1791 slave uprising, people of colour had briefly made common cause with the black revolutionaries, before turning against them when they were granted political rights by the law of April 1792. Leading figures had publicly called for an alliance of whites and mixed-race people to 'destroy' the rebels, and force the slaves back to the plantations.[16] For Toussaint, this treacherous desertion stemmed from the mixed-race leaders' deep-seated racial prejudices against black people, and their fear that their interests would be adversely affected by the abolition of slavery.[17] The belief that people of colour were unreliable allies was also shared by French officials, especially after Villatte's attempted coup in 1796.[18]

Toussaint's distrust was increased by the military behaviour of local mixed-race groups in the war against the Spanish and the British. In October 1794 he blamed the loss of several positions in the region of Verrettes to the 'treachery' of mixed-race fighters, who went over to the Spanish side at a crucial moment in the battle and tried to have him captured by enemy forces. He railed against the 'perfidiousness of the people of colour of this region, who have never behaved with greater deceitfulness, and who have confirmed their ghastly character'.[19] In January 1795, a group of local republicans devised another scheme to capture the British officer Brisbane and hand over the town of Saint-Marc to the French; the plan was foiled because one of the conspirators, a person of colour, betrayed his comrades.[20] The following month, in the mountainous region of the Cahos, Blanc Cazenave, a mixed-race commander, was arrested by Toussaint for executing forty white prisoners, stealing supplies, encouraging his soldiers to desert, spreading malicious rumours against Laveaux and Toussaint, and aspiring to create an autonomous fiefdom under his personal control.[21] Cazenave died in his cell, after 'choking with bilious rage'.[22] To cap this catalogue of sedition, Toussaint arrested a number of regional commanders who were implicated in the 30 Ventôse conspiracy: Guy, in Petite-Rivière, Chevalier, in Terre-Neuve, and Danty, in Gros-Morne – again, all persons of colour. Danty's wife, accompanied by 'a hundred women of colour', pleaded in vain with Toussaint for her husband's release.[23] In June 1796 Toussaint uncovered a further plot to hand over the Verrettes region to the British; its leader was a mixed-race commander named Vallery.[24]

Toussaint was not always deaf to appeals for mercy – especially if they concerned rank-and-file combatants, who were easily misled by their leaders. So, for example, when he captured an enemy fort in the Grand Cahos area in March 1796, he found that most of the fighters were people of colour. Yet even though they had committed treason 'by firing on the tricolour flag', he pardoned them all after hearing the imploring pleas of their wives and children.[25] And crucially, Toussaint did not allow these many instances of betrayal to corrode his general view of the *gens de couleur*, or to undermine his vision of brotherhood among different communities. He was at pains to emphasize that he regarded the mixed-race community as his 'brothers', and that despite the events of 30 Ventôse he knew that there were a large number of 'virtuous' mixed-race citizens in Saint-Domingue.[26] When Laveaux visited Toussaint's stronghold in the Gonaïves region, he was delighted to find 'the greatest tranquillity and order among all: men, women, children, whites, blacks, people of colour, military servicemen, peasants, and *propriétaires*'.[27] He also praised Toussaint's key white allies in Gonaïves as 'patriotic and loyal men, who were devoted to the principle of *liberté générale*'.[28] And when, in the aftermath of the 30 Ventôse episode, Toussaint was allowed to create his own ninety-man cavalry regiment taken from 'the most dashing and bravest men in his army', he chose as its head a mixed-race officer, 'the intrepid Morisset', who would remain by Toussaint's side throughout his career.[29]

Forging a sense of unity among Saint-Domingue's black population – a majority of whom were African-born – was Toussaint's major preoccupation in the years after 1794. This was a military imperative, not least because the Spanish and British forces relied heavily on locally recruited mercenaries, most of whom were black. But it was also a political necessity, to ensure that the revolutionary gains achieved by the slaves during the early 1790s were consolidated. Fraternity was a multi-layered concept in his mind: all the black people of Saint-Domingue were potentially his 'brothers', but this brotherhood was not exclusive to one community, as it also included whites and people of colour, republicans from France and all the men and women across the Atlantic who were engaged in the just war against slavery. Learning that *marron* slaves had launched an insurrection in Jamaica in 1795, he expressed the hope that 'our brothers in this region will achieve their goal; I wish it with all my heart'.[30]

'My only objective', he told Laveaux, 'is the unity and happiness of all my republican brothers.'[31] The challenges, though, were formidable. His own *sans-culottes* troops were poorly equipped.[32] He could not match the salary of one *portugaise* a month offered by the Spaniards: 'at such a rate', he observed wistfully, 'they pay their recruits well'.[33] British forces were no less perfidious: writing about a military engagement on the Cahos highlands in early 1796, he noted that the British 'did not only harass us constantly, they send emissaries among the citizens of Petite Montagne and try to corrupt and seduce them by all means imaginable'.[34] Rumours stoked by the 'méchants' opposed to the republic could also damage Toussaint's ambition to rally the support of local communities, and by the middle of 1796 these were coming in thick and fast: 'I have become the white wolf: for some, I am out to destroy the yellow [mixed] race, for others, I am seeking to hand the colony over to the British and enslave the blacks.'[35]

How did Toussaint counter these damaging rumours and promote greater unity among the black citizens of Saint-Domingue? Within his military structure, as we saw in the previous chapter, he relied on his charismatic leadership and a strict disciplinary regime, but also the cultivation of a sense of republican comradeship among his soldiers. He had to use more diplomatic approaches to deal with situations of labour unrest in the plantations, which were sometimes inflamed by anti-French forces. This is where his skills as a peacemaker were most effective. Advising Laveaux in early 1796 about how to handle a group of 'unfortunate brothers' who had launched an insurrection in the Port-de-Paix region after suffering from abusive treatment by local whites and people of colour, Toussaint urged him to tread lightly: it was only by acting with the 'greatest prudence' that they would be able to bring them back to the path of 'righteousness'.[36] In a lengthy report, Toussaint explained how he regained the trust of local *cultivateurs* by holding a series of meetings with them, promising that any arrears owed to them would be paid, and asking them to come to him if they needed protection from unscrupulous plantation managers; he urged them to forget past conflicts and 'live like brothers and true French citizens'.[37] Julien Raimond, a mixed-race leader who became a very close ally of Toussaint and observed many of his interventions in such situations, marvelled at his remarkable rhetorical talents when addressing ordinary men and women, combining paternalism with just the right touch of sternness.[38] On these occasions his repertoire of homespun kreyol sayings came in very handy, too; among his favourites was this warning against charting a hazardous path: 'monde qui doit marcher pied nus, doit bien voir dans chemin à yo si pas gagné piquants'.[39]

An equally pressing concern was the neutralization of black militias, generally the remnants of *marron* fighting forces which had emerged during the 1791 slave uprising. These militias could be venal, such as those led by Toussaint's old companion-in-arms Jean-François, who issued a series of proclamations inviting his black 'brothers' to abandon the French cause in 1795. Toussaint described the situation in the Montagne Noire and Grande-Rivière region in these terms: 'the area comes under attack from time to time by Jean-François's *brigands*; but as soon as they presented themselves they were repelled by our brave French forces'.[40] Moreover, these combatants had a visceral distrust of whites and were ambivalent – often for valid personal reasons – about the French cause which Toussaint had embraced. He tried to broker agreements with them, notably by appealing to republican and racial unity. He wrote in February 1796 to the militia commander Pierre Dieudonné that he could not believe that a 'good republican' like him would consider supporting the British, who were the 'sworn enemies of his freedom and equality'. Toussaint also cited his own case: 'I have returned to the fold, and have been welcomed with open arms by the French, who have rewarded me for my services; I appeal to you, dear brother, to follow my example.' Noting that both of them were black men, and should trust each other on that basis ('my dear brother, you will not refuse your friendship to me, as I am a black man like you'), he said that disputes among their respective armed groups should be resolved through discussion, not force: 'the republic is the mother of all of us, and she does not wish to see brothers fighting each other'. He concluded with a characteristic motto: that 'when brothers fight among themselves, it is always the poor people who suffer as a consequence'.[41]

Toussaint went to extraordinary lengths to convince such people of the sincerity of the French republican cause. On one occasion in April 1796 he spent several hours with a militia leader named Noël Artaud, who was 'extremely suspicious and worked up' against Toussaint because he had arrived at their meeting accompanied by 'too many whites': 'I was forced to ride up to him by myself to reassure him, and prove to him that my intentions were sincere.' The two men then settled by a riverbank and had an extensive conversation, in which Toussaint used similar arguments to those he deployed with Dieudonné about republican and racial unity; he added that infighting among black people could only serve the interests of their common enemies. Toussaint also spoke at length to Artaud's officers; the deal was perhaps clinched when he sent 'four bottles of tafia' for Artaud's dragoons.[42] Toussaint would also cement his bond with black audiences with humorous asides about whites and people of colour; contrasting the steadfastness of the *nouveaux libres* with the mercurial disposition of many *gens de couleur*, he would remark: 'show a person of colour a piece of ham, and you can get him to run round the colony for you'.[43]

In another instance, in early 1796, Toussaint successfully reined in Étienne Datty, a black militia leader who had led a violent uprising against exploitative white plantation managers in the mountains of Port-de-Paix. He travelled to the area and sought out Étienne, who initially proved elusive; Toussaint considered using force at this point, but judged that it would make things 'worse not better'. He eventually tracked down the rebel leader and held several meetings with him, using his best rhetorical skills to win him back to the republican cause. He began by warning him to be wary of the sophistries of the enemies of freedom, such as the British and their slave-owning supporters, who slandered the republican cause by misrepresenting its aims and values, 'making good seem like evil, and evil like good; that which is bitter, sweet, and that which is sweet, bitter; and that which is light appear shrouded in darkness, and that which is in darkness seem light'. In any event, he added, the Holy Scriptures enjoined men 'to love their enemies, and to respond to evil by good deeds'. Toussaint also appealed to Étienne's sense of 'fraternity', describing himself as a 'brother who seeks the happiness of all the black people of Saint-Domingue'. Referring to himself in the third person, he added: 'Toussaint Louverture is the true friend of those of his colour, and his dedication to their cause is such that he would rather die a thousand deaths than see them fall back under the tyrannical yoke from which he has struggled to remove them.' After drawing upon this characteristic combination of creole, Catholic and republican values, Toussaint then injected a dose of charismatic power into the exchange: 'I am the person black people see when they look in the mirror, and it is to me that they must turn if they wish to enjoy the fruits of liberty.'[44]

Pacification also involved a series of face-to-face meetings with Étienne's *bossale* troops and local black peasants, to whom Toussaint preached what he called 'the morality of reason'. On one occasion, after they had violently rebelled against local French authorities, Toussaint admonished them sternly for the disorder they had provoked, again invoking religious ideals: 'God said, "ask and you shall receive", not "commit crimes to obtain what you need".' Even if their grievances were justified, he told them, their resort to violence had brought 'shame' upon them and upon him, and would only prove to the enemies of Saint-Domingue that 'black people are not fit for liberty'. The rebels asked for forgiveness and recognized Toussaint as their 'father'; they were particularly struck by the sense of harmony which reigned among the black, white and mixed-race members of his army: as one peasant put it, they all seemed to be 'brothers from the same mother'.[45]

In his speeches to the wider black population, Toussaint also dwelled on the abolition of slavery in Saint-Domingue, contrasted with its continuation in areas controlled by the Spaniards and its restoration by the British upon their arrival in the colony in 1793; in a letter to Laveaux he noted that 'a large population of citizens, both men and women, have left Saint-Marc, Mont-Rouy, Verrettes and other areas under enemy control, abandoning everything they possessed in order to come and live under the humane laws of the Republic'; a few months later he observed that these *ralliements* were occurring on a daily basis.[46] He made such speeches frequently. He apologized for the brevity of another of his letters to Laveaux, as he was 'busy rounding up the peasants and the *conducteurs* to instil in them the love of hard work which is inseparable from freedom'.[47] These homilies were sometimes delivered by trusted religious emissaries, 'educated persons' despatched to rural areas 'to instruct black citizens so that they might better appreciate who are their true friends and enemies'[48] (although he remarked that his own presence was much more helpful than that of any of these surrogates).[49] Such speeches were mostly successful – but not always: in one incident in June 1795, Toussaint travelled to a mountainous community after hearing that local peasants had revolted against French officials. No sooner had he started his 'sermon' than the *cultivateurs* picked up their weapons and took aim at him; 'the reward I received for all my efforts was a bullet in my leg, which still causes me a great deal of pain'.[50]

The greatest quandary Toussaint faced in rallying the support of the *nouveaux libres* was that the majority of them were not born in Saint-Domingue. In the turbulent and fragmented post-revolutionary landscape, the primary allegiance of many of these African *bossales* was ethnic and tribal: they saw themselves not as citizens of France (whose language very few of them even spoke) but as Kongos, Alladas, Ibos, Dahomets, Senegalese or Mozambiques. Militias were often formed along these 'national' lines, and their leaders were charismatic local figures whom Toussaint and the republican authorities sought to placate. One of the most majestic was Halaou, the dashing leader of the Cul-de-Sac rebels: a man of immense physical stature and 'herculean strength' who always carried a big white cock which, he claimed, directly transmitted the wishes of the heavens. In

February 1794 Commissioner Sonthonax invited him to a parley in Port-Républicain and he arrived with 12,000 warriors, who were able to see their sorcerer-king, almost naked and decked with talismans, treated to a lavish feast in the official palace, his trusted white cock seated next to him.[51]

This kind of mystical universe, with its *vodou* occultism, secret societies and pagan chants seems far removed from republican philosophical rationalism, and historians have often contrasted the instinctive, mystical Africanism of the *bossales* with Toussaint's 'European' military and political culture.[52] His language sometimes reflected this tension: one of his common expressions was the need to make black people 'entendre raison'.[53] He was undoubtedly appalled by the violence used by some of these African militias, and opposed their strategy of eliminating Saint-Domingue's white settlers. He also occasionally voiced his frustration at 'our unfortunate African brothers, who are too weak and too easily seduced'.[54] But Toussaint was nonetheless able to build bridges towards these African fighters. He was willing to treat them all with respect and dignity, and to open discussions with them in that spirit: even if they were misguided, or indeed had committed crimes, the *bossales* of Saint-Domingue were his 'brothers'. He sought to protect them from verbal insult, issuing an edict forbidding labourers to be called 'brigands' or 'rebels'.[55] One of the significant successes of this strategy was his alliance with his old Bréda acquaintance Sans-Souci, one of the chiefs in the Petite-Rivière area; in a letter to Laveaux he expressed his satisfaction at winning him over to the republican cause. Sans-Souci would remain a devoted Toussaint ally until the outbreak of the Haitian War of Independence in 1802.[56]

Toussaint also used the tribal and religious affiliations of his own soldiers and officers to his advantage, notably to open lines of communication with African militia leaders, or to encourage *bossale* recruits in the Spanish or British camp to defect; in July 1795 he explained to Laveaux that he had brought some African-born soldiers based in Saint-Marc over to his side 'by means of intelligences and relations'. The implication was that *vodou* connections (most probably the exchange of amulets and the performance of specific chants) were deployed – as no doubt in many other instances.[57] During a meeting in the Mirebalais region with the *marron* chief Mademoiselle and his band of hardy fighters, 'the Docos', Toussaint was pleased to find a number of Africans from his own Allada nation, to whom he delivered one of his vigorous harangues in the Ewe-Fon language; we can imagine that this linguistic versatility played a significant role in winning Mademoiselle over to the republican cause.[58]

The complexity of the connections between Toussaint and these African militia leaders can be seen in his volatile relationship with the

Kongolese-born Macaya. In the Acul region, his base of operations in the early 1790s, Macaya proudly celebrated his monarchism, describing himself as a subject of three kings – France, Spain and Kongo. Toussaint arrested and imprisoned him in Gonaïves a few years later, but he escaped and headed back to the Acul: there, as Toussaint grumbled to Laveaux, 'every day he holds dances and assemblies with the Africans of his nation and gives them bad advice'.[59] In early 1796 Macaya seems to have put himself under the protection of Villatte, no doubt because of their shared hatred of Europeans.[60] Yet the royalist ideology of Macaya and his followers contained much that Toussaint could identify with – notably its devout Christianity, its resolute anti-individualism and opposition to material greed, its belief in universal principles of justice and its commitment to cross-national harmony among black communities. With minimal adjustments, these ideals could just as readily be expressed in terms of republican fraternity. This was the common ground which Toussaint sought in his dealings with black militia leaders, rather than Macaya's recommendation to carry out a 'general massacre of whites'.[61]

Toussaint's rhetoric of republican brotherhood was thus an effective instrument in rallying black populations to his cause. Nowhere was this more powerfully displayed than in the proclamation he addressed to his 'African brothers' of Saint-Louis-du-Nord in April 1796, after they had violently rebelled against republican authorities by refusing to be enrolled in the National Guard. The blood they had spilled, Toussaint lamented, was that of a people who had sacrificed a great deal for 'general liberty, the rights of man and happiness and felicity of mankind'. By taking up arms against France they had behaved as 'misguided children', and allowed themselves to be led away from the righteous path 'by criminal monsters'. He ended by appealing not only to their sense of 'reason', but to the ideal of collective strength that they embodied: 'we, the black people, are the strongest and it is up to us to maintain order and tranquillity, and to set the right example'. But this could only happen if they responded to the proper guidance of their 'chief'; for there was no mistake, the black citizens of Saint-Domingue now had one, even if it would take a few more years for his leadership to be formalized.[62]

Laveaux left Saint-Domingue in October 1796. With Toussaint's encouragement, he was elected as one of the colony's deputies in the Conseil des Cinq Cents, the lower house of the French parliament under the Directory.[63] As the political situation in France shifted in a more conservative direction under the 1795 constitution, Toussaint believed that it was essential for Saint-Domingue's revolution to be powerfully represented in Paris.

Laveaux was the ideal person for this role, as he was 'the true friend of the black people'.[64] As a leading progressive member of the French legislature, he went on to play a crucial role in the passing of the law of 12 Nivôse an VI (1 January 1798), which sought to consolidate the achievements of the revolution in the colonies;[65] once back in Paris, Laveaux also championed Toussaint's leadership at meetings of the Société des Amis des Noirs, which he regularly attended.[66]

Laveaux's successor was Léger-Félicité Sonthonax, the former French envoy to the colony, who had proclaimed the end of slavery in August 1793. Because abolition was directly associated with his name, and with his powerful connections in French government circles, Sonthonax was a figure of real substance: he was genuinely popular in certain sections of the black community, and conversely was detested by Saint-Domingue's white *colons* and especially by those royalist émigrés whom he had sent into exile: their way of life had been destroyed by the revolution, and their plantation assets remained frozen. Over the next year, Toussaint's interactions with the self-styled 'founder of general liberty'[67] dominated the politics of the colony, and their clashes eventually culminated in Sonthonax's return to France. This victory was another political milestone for Toussaint, after the Villatte affair. But, more importantly, it provided the first significant indication of the difference between his vision for Saint-Domingue and that of his French colonial counterparts.

Even though the two men had not previously met – Sonthonax had left the colony a month after Toussaint rallied the French republican camp in mid 1794 – their initial contacts in 1796 were constructive. Sonthonax wrote a series of enthusiastic letters to Toussaint, and announced that he had arrived in the colony 'faithfully to second' his efforts to defend French territory and to 'organize the regime of general liberty'.[68] Toussaint reciprocated, writing to the government in France that Sonthonax's presence was 'essential for the well-being of Saint-Domingue, her full recovery and her prosperity', adding: 'this man has the entire confidence of the black people'.[69] The two men exchanged gifts: knowing Toussaint's love of music, the French commissioner offered him a trumpet, and in return he received a magnificent horse.[70] Within months of his arrival Sonthonax promoted Toussaint to the rank of division general, describing him to his superiors as 'a brave man worthy of the esteem of republicans through his courage, his humanity and his attachment to liberty';[71] he was 'exemplary in his public and private virtues' and saw 'all humans as his brothers'.[72]

Impressed with Toussaint's remarkable military achievements in the fight against the Spanish and the British, Sonthonax praised his 'indefatigability' and called him his 'best friend'.[73] He also went out of his way to endear himself to the Louverture family. Learning through Laveaux that Toussaint wished to send his two children to be educated in France, Sonthonax wrote to the Minister of Navy, Laurent Truguet, a progressive republican who was one of his key allies in Paris;[74] young Isaac and Placide set sail for France in early July 1796.[75] There was an even more personal connection between Toussaint and Sonthonax, whose wife was a woman of colour named Marie Eugénie Bléigat, whose first husband had been a manager at the Bréda plantation before the revolution; Toussaint was well acquainted with him.[76]

Yet it became apparent from the outset that there was a significant gulf between the two men. This was not just a matter of their different physical appearance (Sonthonax was plump, Toussaint wiry) or age (Sonthonax was twenty years younger). Toussaint presented himself, as he wrote to Laveaux in 1798, as a 'straight military man'[77] with an attachment to simplicity and order. Sonthonax was much more of a politician, a jacobin who revelled in intrigue and ambiguity. They also had sharply contrasting temperaments. Toussaint was reserved by nature and careful with his words; Sonthonax, a lawyer by profession, was irrepressibly, and at times imprudently, garrulous (or as the kreyol expression had it, 'there were no Sundays for his tongue').[78] Sonthonax was also effusive and tactile; Toussaint later pointedly noted that the French commissioner had taken his hand during their first encounter, and this overt show of intimacy did not go down well. His suspicion of Sonthonax was deepened by his recollection that during his first spell in Saint-Domingue in the early 1790s he had vigorously defended slavery and the exclusive rights of the white settlers – which was why Toussaint was initially so suspicious of France's conversion to abolitionism, which he believed was little more than a 'stratagem'.[79] In short, while it was easy for Toussaint to trust 'Papa' Laveaux, whose sincerity towards him and towards the cause of black emancipation was incontrovertible, he felt on much less certain ground with Sonthonax.

There was the additional difficulty that, from the outset, Sonthonax's conduct towards Toussaint was highly patronizing. Like most of his French metropolitan colleagues, his egalitarianism was no doubt sincere on an abstract level; but he could not actually bring himself to treat someone like Toussaint as an equal – especially since he regarded himself as the saviour of the black people by abolishing slavery in the colony in 1793. After their rupture Sonthonax revealed his real views in a report to the French government, in which he described Toussaint as 'a thick-headed man, as lowly as his first occupation as a slave herdsman; he normally speaks kreyol and barely understands the French language'. In the same report Sonthonax was also contemptuous of Toussaint's faith, which he took as evidence of moral weakness: 'his profound ignorance has left him completely beholden to the priests, who, in Saint-Domingue as in France, are seizing every possible means to destroy our liberties'.[80] Behind the façade of republican egalitarianism he was full of disdain for black people; he once told a fellow white French officer that 'blacks chase after military positions so that they can procure more liquor, money and women for themselves'.[81]

While Sonthonax did not reveal such thoughts openly, he certainly voiced his contemptuous feelings about Toussaint in his casual conversations with others. And as Saint-Domingue was small, and Toussaint had ears in all the right places, word eventually got back. In any case, this looseness was not limited to his tongue: Sonthonax's condescending attitude came across in his letters. For example, he altered the opening sentence of one of Toussaint's speeches before it was published, claiming that the change would make it more 'correct'.[82] When Toussaint wrote to Sonthonax asking him for better equipment for his exposed troops, the reply he received was a pompous history lesson in revolutionary virtue: the deprivation he and his soldiers were enduring was an inevitable feature of all wars of liberty against despotism, and 'every page in history is littered with such examples'. The commissioner-professor then went on to list various cases of numerically inferior and ill-equipped popular forces defeating their enemies, both during the French and American Revolutions, before instructing Toussaint to 'remind the republicans under your command of these heroic traits'. Even Sonthonax's mention of the British vilification of Toussaint's black soldiers as 'naked Kongos', which was intended as a compliment by analogy with the French revolutionary *sans-culottes*, came across as demeaning. For Toussaint, this was not the language of man who believed in real brotherhood.[83]

Substantial political differences also emerged between them, notably over the place of émigrés. Toussaint was keen to promote a generous amnesty to encourage those white planters and *propriétaires* who accepted the new order to come back to the colony and help rebuild it. Sonthonax was much more dogmatic, perceiving émigrés as incorrigible enemies of the revolution; he was therefore hostile to their return. These differing approaches to fraternity came to a head when Toussaint invited his former manager at the Bréda estate, Bayon de Libertat, to come back from the United States, where he had been living in exile. Toussaint had arranged for money to be sent to him, promising that he would be removed from the list of émigrés, and would have his property in Limbé returned to him.[84] He pressed Sonthonax to lift the sequestration on his assets and asked the French consul in Philadelphia to facilitate the return of this 'respectable old man' to Saint-Domingue;[85] he even wrote to the Directory offering a glowing testimonial for Bayon, describing him as a 'virtuous' manager who had treated his slaves with humanity and was regarded by his workforce as a 'father'.[86] Sonthonax, however, ordered that Bayon be arrested when he arrived in Saint-Domingue and sent to France to be charged with treason for his complicity with the British during the early years of the revolution.[87] Toussaint had to rush to Cap and plead with the commissioner, but met with a blanket refusal: he only agreed, out of 'consideration' for Toussaint, to expel Bayon back to the United States.[88] Sonthonax later tried to make amends by allowing him to provide financial support to his former boss, but continued to insist that Bayon's return had been 'criminal', not least because of his close connections with royalist traitors, and that the letter of the law on émigrés required that he receive the death penalty.[89]

The counter-revolution was not only a matter of the past: as from 1796, monarchist forces began to make a political comeback in Paris. These royalists were, as we shall see later, stridently hostile to the revolutionary regime in colonial Saint-Domingue. Toussaint and Sonthonax naturally agreed that their challenge had to be contained, but again they differed in their views on how this should be accomplished. Toussaint sought to concentrate his energies locally while relying on friendly voices in Paris (such as Laveaux), whereas Sonthonax flirted with grandiose schemes of turning Saint-Domingue into a 'secure outpost for French republican patriots'.[90] He also went on the ideological offensive, commissioning a play entitled *La Liberté générale ou les colons à Paris*, which was performed in Cap in 1796; it attacked the colonial faction in Paris and their allies in Saint-Domingue (many of whom were referred to by their real names).[91] More dramatically, he appears to have entertained the notion that the colony could follow a separate path from France by adopting its own constitution. Toussaint would later appropriate the idea, but for the moment he condemned it and used it to discredit Sonthonax.[92]

Military issues further aggravated the differences between the two men. Within a month of his arrival, Sonthonax was placed in charge of the overall war effort, and the bulk of his correspondence was concerned with military matters. In these, however, he proved to be highly incompetent, notably alienating the authorities from the southern province under Rigaud's control. Even worse, he meddled in Toussaint's responsibilities, to the latter's irritation.[93] He questioned his decision to grant an amnesty to the 'brigand' Noël Artaud, and claimed that one of the neighbourhoods controlled by Toussaint's men was 'in the greatest shambles'.[94] His revolutionary fetish for seeing conspiracies everywhere led him to take decisions which seemed erratic and arbitrary, such as the arrests of Generals

Desfourneaux and Pierre Michel, both popular officers whom he accused of conspiring against his authority without clear evidence.[95] The case of Michel was especially controversial: he was a black officer who led a group of insurgent slaves in 1792 and then fought gallantly against the British, earning a commendation from the national authorities;[96] he had just been promoted to the rank of brigadier-general because of his vigorous role in defeating the 30 Ventôse conspiracy. Even though Sonthonax appointed Toussaint commander-in-chief of the Saint-Domingue army in May 1797, his clumsy and chaotic interventions left a bitter aftertaste and did little to inspire Toussaint's confidence.

Toussaint's patience with Sonthonax eventually ran out, and after a meeting with him in May 1797 he got him to agree that he would leave Saint-Domingue and return to Paris to take up a seat in the Conseil des Cinq Cents, alongside Laveaux. But the unpredictable Sonthonax had a change of heart: he mobilized his supporters, both civilian and military, in Cap. Taking to the streets, they cheered his name; petitions and addresses signed by soldiers and officers from the northern division (including Toussaint's nephew Moyse, with whom Sonthonax had forged a close relationship) demanded that he remain in the colony.[97] To Toussaint's dismay, it was clear that the 'founder of liberty' still enjoyed considerable support among black citizens because of his abolitionist past; even the municipality of Toussaint's own fief in Gonaïves called for Sonthonax to stay in Saint-Domingue.[98] Charles-Cézar Télémaque, justice of peace (and future mayor) of Cap, wrote expressing his 'enormous regret' at the news of his departure, observing that no one could 'guarantee order' like him;[99] there were even stories that families prayed for his well-being.[100]

But bringing the contest into the open was a mistake, given Toussaint's superior resources. He sent a sharp letter to Sonthonax, asserting that 'the people and the troops have confidence in me' and warning that he, Sonthonax, would bear the responsibility for any ensuing conflict if he reneged on their agreement.[101] He also issued a stern proclamation to the municipality of Cap, which had also publicly called for Sonthonax to remain,[102] warning that 'cabals' were creating disorder and that it was their responsibility to prevent any further public demonstrations of support for the commissioner. Failure to do so, he hinted ominously, would have 'consequences'.[103] As Sonthonax still wavered, Toussaint despatched his chief of staff, General Agé, to the French commissioner's mixed-race colleague Julien Raimond, informing him that if he did not persuade Sonthonax to leave willingly he had orders from Toussaint to march on Cap with 20,000 troops and forcibly expel him from the colony.[104] The message was driven home by a proclamation signed by Toussaint and his leading military commanders.[105] Even after Sonthonax had embarked, Toussaint was concerned that he might try to land in nearby Port-de-Paix and attempt to rally troops against him; he ordered the local commander to oppose him by force.[106] He urged the citizens of Cap and the plantation workers of the northern plain to bury all their divisions and come together as 'a people of brothers'.[107]

At its core, the clash between Toussaint and Sonthonax was about the leadership of the black revolution in Saint-Domingue, and the scope of its ideal of fraternity which both men, in contrasting ways, aspired to embody. In a later letter to Laveaux, in which he listed Sonthonax's 'crimes' in exhaustive detail, Toussaint was at pains to reject the idea that Sonthonax was 'more of a friend of the black people than I am'.[108] This was not because of the difference in their skin colour, but rather because his own idea of brotherhood was much more comprehensive. Sonthonax was basically an enlightened white paternalist, who sincerely abhorred slavery but at the same time did not recognize black people as his true equals. Indeed, he believed that Saint-Domingue could not survive without the wise guidance of its European elites. He made this clear in his overbearing behaviour towards Toussaint and in his frequently expressed reservations about the fighting capacity of black soldiers, whom he believed were inferior to Europeans. He was even more emphatic about white supremacy in his private correspondence with his superiors in Paris: 'to organize general liberty with profit and to avoid making the inhabitants of this land a hoard of savages without laws or manners, the European must command in Saint-Domingue'.[109] A later letter asserted the incapacity of the 'savages' to exercise political sovereignty: if power was handed over fully to black people, he predicted, the colony would be 'for ever lost to the Arts, Civilization and Agriculture, and she will become another Guinea where the only commercial activity will be the slave trade'.[110]

Toussaint's view, naturally, was very different. He set it out in a lengthy report he addressed to the Directory in the aftermath of Sonthonax's departure, in which he provided salacious details of secret conversations he claimed to have had with the French agent over several months. The forty-four-page document was a magnificent piece of creative fiction, including dialogues between Toussaint and Sonthonax written almost for a dramatic performance; theatre was a thriving form of public entertainment in late-colonial Saint-Domingue. It was an eloquent response to Sonthonax's disparaging observations about Toussaint's limited intelligence (and linguistic deficiencies), a sharp and often witty exposé of Sonthonax's character flaws, and a devastating attack on the limits of his conception of fraternity. Toussaint alleged that Sonthonax had come to him with a scheme to declare Saint-Domingue independent from France, so that power could be exercised 'for the blacks'; he had also apparently suggested that all the whites of the colony were 'enemies of liberty' who should be 'massacred'.

Sonthonax vehemently denied ever expressing such ideas, and although he may have spoken in this way casually (notably in conversation with black soldiers and officers, with whom he liked to talk 'rough'), there is no evidence that he planned to eliminate all whites from the colony. But, as we have seen, there was also little doubt that he had entertained the idea of the territory's autonomy, and that he had a long history of contempt for the white *colons* in Saint-Domingue, among whom he had no friends and few allies. Toussaint's real purpose in the report, however, was to play the conspiracy card, which he knew would appeal to the French revolutionary imagination in Paris, while at the same time discrediting Sonthonax's claim to be a sincere friend of black people. He highlighted the numerous ways in which the French commissioner had tried to divide Toussaint's black soldiers and officers from their commander-in-chief, notably by calling them 'brigands', by starving them of supplies and equipment and by sending emissaries to sow dissent among his troops in the west; Toussaint claimed he had had to arrest sixty-seven of his own officers for insubordination as a result.

But most effective was Toussaint's portrayal of his own conversations with Sonthonax. Through the words he put in his mouth, Toussaint painted a scathing portrait of Sonthonax's contempt for black people, evidenced by his vanity ('I am the only friend of the blacks'), his arrogant selflessness ('I am doing this for you blacks, I don't need anything, my father in France is a rich man'), his narcissistic insecurity (he repeatedly asked Toussaint whether he 'loved' him), his transparently insincere flattery ('I regard you as the saviour of the colony') and his comical sense of hyperbole (he 'always spoke the truth', and loved black people so much that he was prepared to 'retreat to the mountains' with them 'and survive on a diet of roots'). Toussaint also had him repeat, in the style of one of Molière's buffoons, 'je suis philanthrope'. Sonthonax's only aim was to bring Toussaint under his control. Even his scheme to promote Saint-Domingue's independence came across as a self-serving subterfuge: 'we will be the masters of the colony', Sonthonax proclaimed to Toussaint, 'you will head the armed forces and I will be your advisor'. But this was no equal partnership, for the commissioner then added, 'I will direct you.'

In the end, however, it was Sonthonax who was shown the way out: reversing the formula he had used earlier, Toussaint now declared that it was the French official's departure which had been 'essential for the well-being of Saint-Domingue'. He also reclaimed Sonthonax's slur about his use of the kreyol language by citing a local proverb about how a pig which had tasted a chicken would always yearn for more, even if its eyes were covered: 'yon cochon qui déjà mangé poule, vous borgné yon yeux li, vous borgné l'autre yeux li, ça pas empeché li quand li passé côté poule, li va cherché mangé li toujours'.[111] The tale was both a none-too-subtle swipe at Sonthonax's porcine appearance and a summary of his moral failing: 'bad people are always incorrigible'. At the same time, Toussaint stressed that his notion of vice and virtue had nothing to do with race: 'there are good and bad among all colours'.[112]

Toussaint compounded Sonthonax's humiliation by publishing excerpts of his official report in Cap, including of course his most controversial assertions.[113] The aim here was to discredit Sonthonax among his local followers in Saint-Domingue. Toussaint went out of his way to denigrate Sonthonax's seditious 'faction' by inviting his own allies in municipalities to issue proclamations of support for his leadership. These messages were all written in florid republican prose, and mailed in a co-ordinated way to the Directory in Paris. This technique, which became one of Toussaint's most effective methods of political mobilization, saw the municipality of Jean-Rabel condemn the 'perverse schemes of the perfidious Sonthonax', notably his plan to 'murder all the French citizens born in the colony'.[114] Thankfully, noted the municipal officers of Petite-Rivière, Toussaint had been watching, and they praised his 'pure and virtuous heart, who was prepared to shed the last drop of his blood rather than consent to a crime' – although their description of him as 'incorruptible', three years after the elimination of Robespierre, was evidence that they were somewhat out of touch with the latest twists in Parisian politics.[115]

Perhaps the most revealing of the letters received by the Directory came from justice of the peace Lamontagne, based in the commune of Limbé. He praised Toussaint for his virtuous combination of 'prudence' and 'energy', noting that he had shown 'truly heroic courage' in confronting 'the external enemy Sonthonax', given that he had 'so little power, and such limited means at his disposal': in this imaginative reinvention of the battle between the French Goliath and the Saint-Domingue David, Toussaint's armed force of 20,000 men was quietly set aside.[116] But there was a deeper truth here: Toussaint's moral determination to 'preserve the liberty of his brothers' was in itself a powerful weapon, in some ways the most formidable of all.

Mixed-race rogues, dastardly Spanish and British imperialists, mercenary or misguided black people, arrogant republican administrators – Toussaint's battle to forge a new sense of fraternity among Saint-Domingue's different communities had to be waged on several local fronts. But he also needed to keep a close eye on events in France, especially with the re-emergence of a powerful colonial lobby representing the interests of the thousands of white settlers who had returned there and now sought to reverse the progressive advances of the early 1790s. Toussaint was able closely to monitor this counter-revolutionary trend by reading the French republican press, which he received regularly from mid 1796.[117] The most vocal advocates of the conservative cause were associated with the royalist movement, and Toussaint was particularly alarmed when they won a majority in the legislative elections of April 1797. Their representatives in the Conseil des Cinq Cents lined up to denounce the Directory's colonial policy, especially the granting of civil and political rights to the black citizens of Saint-Domingue; one of them asserted that the colony's slaves under the *ancien régime* were well treated and enjoyed 'abundant food, clean lodgings, access to medical treatment', adding that they were overall 'much happier than French peasants'; he concluded that the only way to restore order was through a military expedition to pacify the colony, as had been successfully done in the Vendée.[118] In the ongoing discussions about the future of French colonies a number of pamphlets defended the restoration of slavery; one writer, who had been a captive of the black rebels after the 1791 insurrection, summed it up simply: 'without slavery, there can be no colonies'.[119]

The speech which caused the greatest stir was delivered by Vincent-Marie Viénot, Count of Vaublanc, on 29 May 1797. Viénot, a fiery orator and polemicist, was one of the leading reactionary intellectuals of the royalist movement; he hailed from a slave-owning family which had lost its fortune in Saint-Domingue. He was a significant figure in expatriate *colon* circles, not just in France but also among the large community of French exiles in the United States, notably in Philadelphia, where the exiled colonial lawyer Moreau de Saint-Méry had a bookshop which served as a rallying point for counter-revolutionary resentments; it was from the Pennsylvanian capital that Toussaint received a copy of Viénot's speech.[120] What gave the speech even stronger resonance was that its denunciation of the alleged failings of the colonial administration in Saint-Domingue drew upon reports leaked to Viénot from official French sources, notably from General Donatien de Rochambeau. Viénot made a series of damaging allegations about the incompetent and tyrannical rule of successive French agents (notably Laveaux and Sonthonax), and lambasted the 'anarchy' which had developed in Saint-Domingue under the administration of these 'hotheads' ('têtes sulphureuses'). He lamented the 'extreme precariousness and pain' endured by the white population, claiming that Europeans had now become pariahs in Saint-Domingue: they were excluded from the colonial administration, hounded as counter-revolutionaries by French agents, marginalized in the army hierarchy, massacred by people of colour in the south and by black insurgents in the north, and abused and exploited in their fundamental property rights. They were even openly mocked and reviled in revolutionary plays in Cap's theatre, and accused of planning to murder the entire black population; the full measure of the horror, Viénot announced dramatically, was that these performances were 'attended by negroes'. The French nobleman's world had clearly turned upside down.

But there was even worse. In the name of that 'most monstrous doctrine of revolutionary equality', French officials such as Laveaux and then Sonthonax had gone out of their way to 'make the negroes happy', as a result of which Saint-Domingue effectively passed under the control of its black military commanders. 'And what a military government!' railed Viénot: 'it is made up of ignorant and uncouth negroes, who are incapable of distinguishing the most egregious licence from the austere sense of liberty which is governed by law'. Toussaint was not spared, and although Viénot paid tribute to his timely intervention in saving Bayon de Libertat from Sonthonax's vengeful hands, he cited a report which alleged that the black general 'was now giving instructions to the French representatives in the colony, rather than taking orders from them'. In another section of his speech Viénot went even further, suggesting that Toussaint's strategy was to incite local rebellions to intimidate French agents, progressively seize control of the main towns, lay his hands on food supplies and weapons and 'systematically massacre all the whites'.[121]

Toussaint was distressed by Viénot's speech: Julien Raimond, who discussed it with him on several occasions, noted that his face had lost its 'habitually serene expression'.[122] The commander knew that the intervention, with its scurrilous allegations and its disparaging portrayal of black people, was a full-blown counter-revolutionary manifesto, a threat to the 'liberté générale' which had been won by black citizens since the early 1790s. All the more so that the author was not some embittered *colon* but an influential member of the French legislature who sought to strike at the very heart of the Saint-Domingue revolution. There were some critical responses to Viénot's speech in France, notably a reply by Laveaux, who had by this point taken his seat in the legislature.[123] But although the former governor heaped praise on Toussaint ('an extraordinary man for the sheer range of virtues he possesses') and lauded the important role of black citizens in preserving Saint-Domingue for France, most of his reply focused on defending his own record during his years in office.[124] Toussaint therefore decided that it was imperative for him to produce his own rebuttal, engaging directly with Viénot's 'slanderous' arguments.[125] The pamphlet he wrote – a handwritten copy of which he immediately sent to the Directory in Paris[126] – was a polemic in the finest republican tradition: a spirited demonstration of some of Viénot's glaring inaccuracies; a defence of the Saint-Domingue revolution, and of the patriotic role black people played in it; and above all a powerful restatement of the ideal of fraternity in response to Viénot's racialist insinuations.

One of the leitmotifs of Viénot's speech, which played on stereotypes about black people in the European imagination, was their predilection for violence. Since they had been granted freedom from slavery, he claimed, the black people of Saint-Domingue had done nothing but pillage, steal, massacre and burn down buildings and plantations; he drew particular attention to the destruction of Cap in 1793, and the carnages perpetrated by the militias of Jean-François.[127] In response, Toussaint acknowledged that the civil war had seen terrible atrocities committed by Cap's black population. Yet, he noted, it was the European citizens who had placed the torches in the hands of his 'poor brothers' and were the prime instigators of the killings. Furthermore, the gruesome violence carried out by black militias was the work of a small minority of lawless 'brigands'. In any event, the behaviour of the black citizens of Saint-Domingue had to be judged in light of their subsequent eagerness to become law-abiding French citizens: 'by their acts of kindness and humanity, as well as their return to order and work, and by their attachment to France, they have partly atoned for the earlier mistakes which they were led to commit by their enemies, or by their own ignorance'. Toussaint recalled that the struggle between despotism and liberty in France during the early 1790s had also seen many appalling acts of violence, despite the nation's long traditions of civilization and sociability: if the 'ignorant and uncouth' black citizens of Saint-Domingue had done no worse during their own struggle for liberty, and had in many respects shown considerably more restraint against their oppressors, surely 'any impartial judge' should find in their favour?[128]

After rolling out this smooth piece of reasoning, Toussaint dealt firmly with Viénot's allegation that Saint-Domingue had fallen into utter chaos because black soldiers had taken over the military, which had accordingly become corrupt, ineffective and demoralized. This was another widely shared racialist trope which, as we saw earlier, Sonthonax also adopted: it affirmed that Africans were poor soldiers and only Europeans were truly capable of waging war. Toussaint lost no time in reminding Viénot that it was his French royalist friends who betrayed their nation and handed over large swathes of the colony to the Spanish and the British during the early

1790s, and that it was the Africans 'who used their weapons and their bare hands to keep the colony French'; black soldiers 'spilled their blood for the republic, and ensured her triumph'. It was they, too, who had rallied to the defence of Governor Laveaux during the 30 Ventôse conspiracy and restored power into rightful hands.[129] Toussaint also pointed out that the colony of Martinique, defended by white European troops, had easily fallen into British hands in 1794, whereas Saint-Domingue, protected by its black and mixed-race fighters, had remained true to the French cause. He seized this opportunity cheekily to double the size of his troops, claiming that he had '50,000' soldiers under his command in Saint-Domingue.[130]

In the confused demonology of slave-owners, black people were not only violent and chaotic but also indolent. Viénot seized on this image with relish, suggesting that since the revolution the *cultivateurs* of Saint-Domingue had abandoned the land, provoking anarchy on the plantations and a major crisis in agricultural production across the colony. Toussaint replied that peasants had left the plantations not out of laziness, but in order to take up arms to defend republican freedoms – and France's colonial interests – against her enemies. Despite this disruption, all the evidence showed that agricultural output was rising across the colony, in the north and west as well as in the south; in his own area of the Gonaïves, General Rochambeau had congratulated him on the 'good order and discipline' which he had seen on the plantations (Rochambeau went on to state the opposite in his report, which proved to Toussaint that he was not an honourable man). For Toussaint, the vast majority of black citizens understood that without work there could be no freedom, and they were fully committed to restoring Saint-Domingue to her former economic glory. But France also had to appreciate that this social contract would endure only if black people retained the freedom they had won through their revolutionary struggle; any attempt to enslave them again would be met with firm resistance. Toussaint reminded the Directory of the Blue Mountain *marron* people in Jamaica, who had forced the British to 'respect the rights they hold from nature'.[131]

What of the whites? Toussaint categorically rejected Viénot's accusation that black people in Saint-Domingue were seeking to eliminate them from the colony. He distinguished the minority of 'anti-republican whites', who had behaved treacherously and had therefore been rightly punished, from the majority of Europeans who had 'more or less sincerely' accepted the new order of things after the revolution, and who had been 'openly welcomed and protected' when they returned.[132] To confound Viénot's apocalyptic claim about the ethnic cleansing of the European population, he pointed out that the number of whites in Cap was on a par with that of mixed-race and black people; that more than half the sugar plantations in the fertile northern plain were still in white *colon* hands; and that this 'union and fraternity among men of all colours' was especially visible in the army: in the colony's northern province most of the military commanders were white, including General Agé, Toussaint's chief of staff, whom he had personally elevated to this position. Likewise in the administration and judiciary: almost all the executive roles were held by whites, and Toussaint noted that this hierarchy was fully accepted by the black citizens of Saint-Domingue as they realized they did not yet have the skills needed to occupy such functions. All they asked, in terms of equality, was to be allowed to serve in the military and expose their lives for the defence of their homeland.[133]

Underlying Viénot's entire approach was the old slavers' view that black people were not fully human and lacked the capacity to make moral judgements – a view which Toussaint believed was still widely shared in France and whose falsity he therefore had to expose. He first drew on Rousseau: while it was true that the black people of Saint-Domingue lacked formal education, they had nonetheless remained close to nature and were inspired by its teachings; this proximity to the elements gave them powerful intuitions about justice and goodness.[134] Such was the humanity of the black people of Saint-Domingue, Toussaint added, that they still showed a great deal of warmth and affection for their former white masters and were willing to regard them as their brothers, despite the terrible heritage of slavery.[135]

Viénot also claimed that black people lacked any notion of metaphysics and could not understand the concept of law: they only made sense of authority in individual terms, as embodied in the person of their master. This too, of course, came straight out of the slave-owner's manual, as did the perverse proposition that the victims only had themselves to blame for their bondage. In Viénot's mind, conclusive evidence of black people's depravity was their willingness to sell their own children into slavery, as had happened in the mountain peasant communities of Grande-Rivière. Yet if such abhorrent practices had survived in British-controlled territories in Saint-Domingue, Toussaint responded, they did not occur in any republican parts of the colony. Furthermore, responsibility for such actions surely lay not with those who had been forced into them through poverty and ignorance, but rather with those Europeans who had established, managed and profited from the system of slavery. The real 'monsters', Toussaint concluded, were not the dehumanized black community of Grande-Rivière, but men like Viénot, who claimed to be 'civilized' but who in their 'barbaric cupidity' had sent ships to the African coasts to enslave the local populations and now wanted to bring this odious system back to Saint-Domingue.[136]

The claim that black people were not fully human also served a political purpose in Viénot's racialist scheme, namely to deny their Frenchness. 'Not only do they claim that the territory belongs to them, and that they do not wish to see a single white man there: they also express an abiding hatred towards the whites, that is to say towards the real Frenchmen.'[137] This was an eerie echo of the language of the early French revolutionary era, which had denied black slaves equal citizenship on the grounds that they were 'foreigners'.[138] Toussaint offered Viénot a lesson in civic republicanism: patriotism was a matter neither of race nor of colour, but a quality which was expressed by the political will of men 'bound by their heart and their spirit to the French Constitution and its treasured laws'. This was how the black citizens of Saint-Domingue felt, and they would always cherish their Frenchness because it was synonymous with their freedom.[139]

By the time Toussaint's pamphlet reached France, the Directory had already taken decisive action against the most conservative royalists after discovering that a number of them had been plotting to overthrow the regime: in the *coup d'état* of 18 Fructidor an V (4 September 1797), many of their leading figures were arrested and deported to Guyana, and Viénot himself was forced to flee to Italy. Toussaint welcomed the news, and wrote to the Directory that the conspiracy was part of a wider counter-revolutionary movement to bring back slavery in Saint-Domingue, with the support of exiled *colons* in France and the United States.[140] Toussaint sent copies of his pamphlet to Charles Vincent and Sanon Desfontaines, whom he had despatched across the Atlantic to justify his actions against Sonthonax; he asked them to have further copies printed if necessary, so as fully to inform the French executive and legislature of the 'purity' of his intentions.[141] Toussaint also sent a copy of his response to Vaublanc to state councillor Daniel Lescallier, a member of the revived Société des Amis des Noirs and one of his staunch allies in the colonial administration in Paris, noting that he had taken up the pen to 'defend the honour' of his 'black brothers'.[142]

Toussaint was keen that his rebuttal of Vienot's arguments should be read as widely as possible in France. With its singular vision of brotherhood and its fierce commitment to upholding the rights of the newly freed black people, it was a powerful plea to the French authorities to stand by the new revolutionary order in Saint-Domingue. The most radical articulation of fraternity to emerge in the late Enlightenment, Toussaint's ideal was forged through resistance: against attempts by mixed-race leaders to reap the gains

RÉFUTATION

De quelques Assertions d'un Discours prononcé au Corps législatif, le 10 Prairial, an cinq, par VIENOT VAUBLANC.

TOUSSAINT LOUVERTURE,

Général en chef de l'Armée de St-Domingue,

AU DIRECTOIRE EXÉCUTIF.

CITOYENS DIRECTEURS,

AU moment où je pensais que je venais de rendre un service éminent à la République et à mes Concitoyens ; alors que je venais de prouver ma reconnaissance de la justice du Peuple français à notre égard ; alors que je croyais m'être rendu digne de la confiance que le Gouvernement a placée en moi, et que je ne cesserai jamais de mériter, un Discours prononcé dans le sein du Corps législatif, dans sa séance du 10 Prairial, an cinq, par Vienot Vaublanc, vient de m'être adressé des États-Unis, et j'ai la douleur, en le parcourant, d'y voir à chaque page mes intentions calomniées, et l'existence politique de mes frères menacée.

Un pareil Discours, dans la bouche d'un homme à qui la révolution, à Saint-Domingue,

A

After the publication of Viénot-Vaublanc's attack against the Saint-Domingue revolution, Toussaint produced this powerful rebuttal of his main arguments; his *Réfutation* also celebrated the role of the colony's black citizens.

of the revolution for their own interests; against mercenary royalist schemes to compromise black citizens' new freedoms; against patronizing republican colonialist efforts to take him for granted and treat black people in general with disdain; and against the resurgence of white racialist ideas which attempted – barely a few years after the abolition of slavery in Saint-Domingue and France – to exclude black citizens from their own political community, and indeed from the human race. His response was that citizens in a republic were all equal, and so the only real distinction that mattered was between those who lived up to their civic obligations and those who did not: 'blacks, people of colour and whites, when they submit themselves to the laws, should be protected by them, and they should equally be punished when they violate them'.[143]

Fraternity was about building a community in which citizens of all colours deliberately settled upon, and then chose to live by, a set of common values, such as equality and respect for the law; skin colour was for him, as his son Isaac put it, 'a matter of chance'.[144] In early revolutionary France, fraternity was at times associated with the exclusion of others and instances of violence; by contrast, Toussaint's ideal was about compassion: when in 1799 the exiled Count Noé, who had inherited the Bréda plantation on which Toussaint had lived as a slave, wrote to him pleading for financial assistance after he had been 'reduced to misery by the misfortunes of the revolution', Toussaint allowed his legal representative to come to Saint-Domingue to collect income from his assets;[145] he declared that 'fortune has changed my position but it has not changed my heart'.[146] He chose this path of generosity even though many of his associates opposed it, and he was aware that a large number of whites in the colony still viewed the *nouveaux libres* with contempt. At the same time, there was a strategic element to Toussaint's friendliness towards the *colons*: he understood that they alone possessed the material resources and technological skills needed to rebuild Saint-Domingue.

By characterizing Sonthonax's value system as 'false republicanism' and 'denatured patriotism',[147] Toussaint challenged French revolutionary thinking and combined universal values with the specific situation in Saint-Domingue. For within the shared republican framework, and careful not to stray too far from the watchful eye of the French motherland, Toussaint came up with an innovative concept of the civic order. It imagined citizenship as being based not only on abstract principles such as equality and brotherhood, but also on active participation in the defence of the community; in the process he also legitimized the slave revolt of 1791, and made it one of the pillars of his vision of republican Saint-Domingue. He pointedly observed that black citizens had fought for their emancipation by themselves, despite the active opposition they often faced from whites or people of colour; the black struggle for freedom deserved to be placed on the same footing as that of the revolutionaries who overthrew the *ancien régime* in France in 1789.[148] By celebrating their practical contribution to Saint-Domingue's revolution, Toussaint gave his fellow black citizens the power and legitimacy which was consistently denied to them by all French colonial regimes, from the revolutionary era to the Third Republic.[149]

But turning this fraternal dream into a living reality in the colony was to be no easy matter, because in Toussaint's scheme of things the privileged position of black people brought few entitlements and far more obligations. This was Toussaint's real challenge, to himself and to his people. It was up to his brethren to show, by their common endeavour under his leadership, that they were capable of rising above their internal divisions and acting as a united political force; by their collective example, that they were worthy of the freedoms they had conquered; by their willingness to forgive their former white oppressors, that they were equal to the noblest ideals of republican virtue and Christian compassion; and by their uncompromising readiness to fight to the death to safeguard their liberty, that they were the most effective guardians of Saint-Domingue's future. Hence the defiant note on which Toussaint concluded his response to Viénot: his people would prefer to 'bury themselves in the ruins of their country, rather than face the prospect of the restoration of slavery'.[150]

5
The Agent is Unwell

One of the defining moments in the history of colonial Saint-Domingue was Toussaint's expulsion of the Directory agent Gabriel de Hédouville in October 1798, barely six months after he had arrived to take up his post. This episode confirmed the steady consolidation of Toussaint's power in the wake of the departure of Laveaux in 1796 and the elimination of Sonthonax a year later. From then on, he seemed more able – and willing – openly to challenge the authority of France. The Black Spartacus was becoming more assertive, and his horizons were beginning to broaden.

Thanks to the preservation of the complete official correspondence between Hédouville and Toussaint in the French colonial archives, the conflict between the two men can be scrutinized. It allows us to observe Toussaint closely and to understand how he wielded his influence over his subordinates and allies, and how he actively defended his cherished principle of fraternity – through championing the interests of his republican army, promoting the ideal of national reconciliation, and saving his people from the prospect of British enslavement. The Hédouville episode also shines a light on certain traits of his character: his pride, his self-confidence, his mischievous sense of humour – and his prickliness, too. As the clash with the French agent reached its climax, we can gauge his skills as a revolutionary political operator: his shrewd judgement and sense of timing; his inventiveness in finding creative ways to achieve his ends; and his capacity to play to his strengths while exploiting his adversaries' weaknesses.

The clash with Hédouville is also significant because it coincided with Toussaint's first major foray into the diplomatic arena. By 1798, as the struggle to expel the British occupying forces from Saint-Domingue was coming to an end, Toussaint seized the opportunity to negotiate their withdrawal directly with local British commanders. Toussaint's status as an autonomous leader was reinforced by these exchanges, thus adding to the anxiety the black revolution in Saint-Domingue was provoking among colonial rulers and slave-owning planters across the Caribbean. The worry about potential revolutionary contagion was particularly intense in British-controlled Jamaica, which was only fourteen hours away from Saint-Domingue; its governor Alexander Lindsay, Earl of Balcarres, a Scottish aristocrat who had been in post since 1795, declared that the French colony had become a 'brigand island' which risked providing insurrectionary ideas to 'our negroes', and eventually compromising the island's 'safety'.[1] As we shall see, such views gave Toussaint leverage to increase his margin of manoeuvre regarding both the regional powers and the French and British authorities.

Toussaint also used his conflict with Hédouville to advance his domestic position, openly mobilizing his supporters for the first time. In this respect, the events of 1798 offer further insights into his political education of the colony's *nouveaux libres*, discussed in the previous chapter, again highlighting the eclectic nature of his value system with its blend of creole, European and African notions. This was especially important in Toussaint's dealings with his most loyal supporters, the *bossales* who made up the majority of the population. The conflict with Hédouville revealed graphically the political culture of revolutionary Saint-Domingue and the exuberant attachment of its black men and women to their new status as free citizens. Their bond with Toussaint took the form of a tacit social contract whereby he symbolized the promise of a better future for themselves and their children, the protection of their new rights, a guarantee of civil order and stability, the paternal authority to which they could appeal if necessary and a bulwark against any possible return to slavery. In local terms, Toussaint combined the boundless possibilities of Papa Legba with the warrior spirit of Ogoun Fer. Together these black citizens and their leader represented a formidable force capable of striking at the foundations of French power in Saint-Domingue.

Toussaint was under no illusions about Hédouville. Well informed about the latest political developments in Paris, he knew that the new agent was seen favourably by conservatives who believed the French Revolution had been too harsh towards white planters,[2] and that the Directory had explicitly instructed him to clip the commander-in-chief's wings, pitting black citizens against people of colour.[3] Hédouville's appointment was noisily welcomed, too, by the royalist and counter-revolutionary French émigré settlers in Philadelphia, who saluted him as a 'friend of the colons' who would 'put the blacks in their place'.[4] Hédouville was a forty-two-year-old impoverished nobleman from Lorraine who had rallied to the French revolutionary cause. He had acquired a military reputation as the chief of staff of the French army in western France, in which role he had actively fought the anti-republican *chouans* in the Vendée. He arrived in Saint-Domingue with a retinue of several hundred civil servants, signalling that one of his main tasks would be to reassert control over the colony's administrative affairs.[5]

At the same time, given the powerful position Toussaint had established and the esteem in which he was held in the colony by all communities – including the whites – Hédouville knew that he had to tread cautiously. Before he travelled to Saint-Domingue, Hédouville wrote to a *colon* of his acquaintance asking for confidential information about the principal administrative and military officials he would be working with. The summary he received about Toussaint noted that he was 'an excellent man' who was 'infinitely reserved' but 'capable of getting the full measure of those with whom he has dealings'.[6] Toussaint, too, began cordially enough, congratulating the French government on its appointment,[7] and promising his French ally Lescallier that General Hédouville would always find in him 'an obedient and faithful' servant of the law.[8] In this spirit he wrote to Hédouville stressing his willingness to assist him in whatever ways possible, even though his resources were 'weak and limited', not being 'on the same level as those who have received a brilliant education, but only on those provided by the Supreme Being'.[9] No doubt to lull the French envoy into a false sense of security, this show of modesty even extended as far as inviting Hédouville to act as his mentor: 'lacking the wisdom of a cultivated man, I can sometimes make mistakes, and that is why I would be delighted to find in you a man who could alert me to the errors I might commit'.[10]

But Toussaint could not resist a touch of insolence too, as when he told Hédouville, in one of his very first letters: 'I will treat you with the respect I always show to the representative of the French Republic'[11] – a sharp reminder of the fate of his predecessor, Sonthonax. In fact, even before their first face-to-face meeting in June 1798, the emboldened Toussaint had sent the French official a brisk warning: 'you should not listen to those who are driven by their personal interests, rather than those of the republic, which represents the general interest; nor should you be taken in by those who are motivated by personal ambition, rather than by a love for the common good: there are people who superficially claim to be committed to *liberté générale* but in their heart of hearts are its sworn enemies'.[12] This was an important letter, so much so that, when his relationship with Hédouville later soured, Toussaint referred to it again.

Whatever doubts Hédouville harboured about the difficulties he faced in gaining Toussaint's confidence would have been reinforced by the commander-in-chief's physical elusiveness upon his arrival in Saint-Domingue. Although he wrote saying that he was 'longing to meet' his new boss, and he was close by in his Ennery residence, Toussaint steered

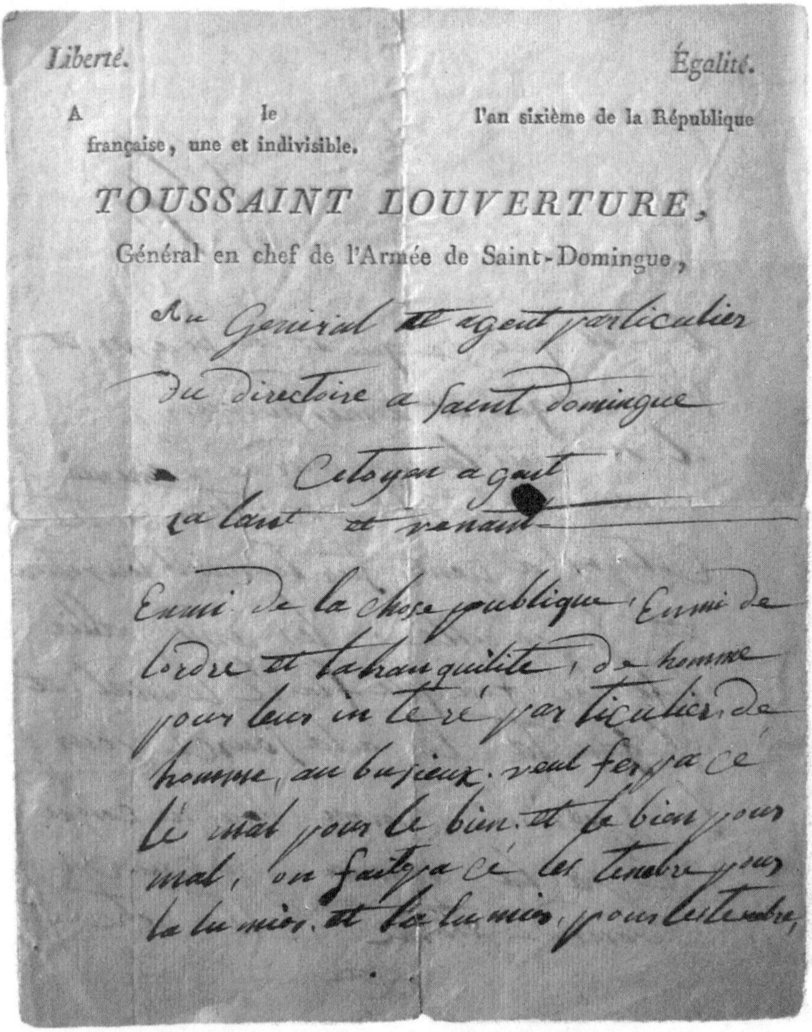

Liberté. Égalité.

A le l'an sixième de la République française, une et indivisible.

TOUSSAINT LOUVERTURE,

Général en chef de l'Armée de Saint-Domingue,

Au Genirial et agent particulier du directoire a saint domingue

Citoyen agent

ta lant et venant

Ennmi de la chose publique, Ennmi de lordre et tatranquilite, de homme pour leur in te ré par ticulier, de homme, au bu jeieux. veul fer ga ce le mal pour le bien. et le bien pour mal, on faitga ce les tenebre pour la lu mior. et la lu mior, pour les tenebre,

This handwritten letter captures Toussaint's phonetic French, and his fondness for contrasts (between good and evil, light and dark, sweet and bitter). It pointedly reminds Hédouville that he is new to the colony, and urges him not to doubt Toussaint's good faith and to work with him in the best interests of the republic.

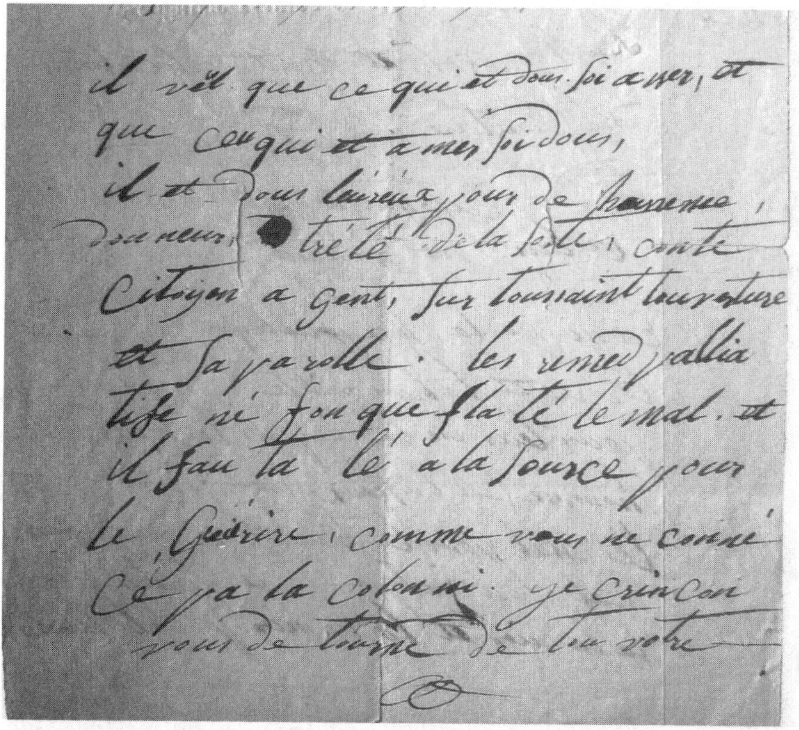

il vêt que ce qui et doux soi a mer, et
que ceu qui et a mer soi doux,
il et doux leureux jour de lhomme,
donneur, trèté de la sorte, conte
Citoyen a gent, sur toussaint louverture
et sa parolle. les remed pallia
tife ni fon que fla té le mal. et
il fau ta lé a la source pour
le guérire, comme vous ne conné
cé pa la colonni. je crin con
vous de tourne de tou votre

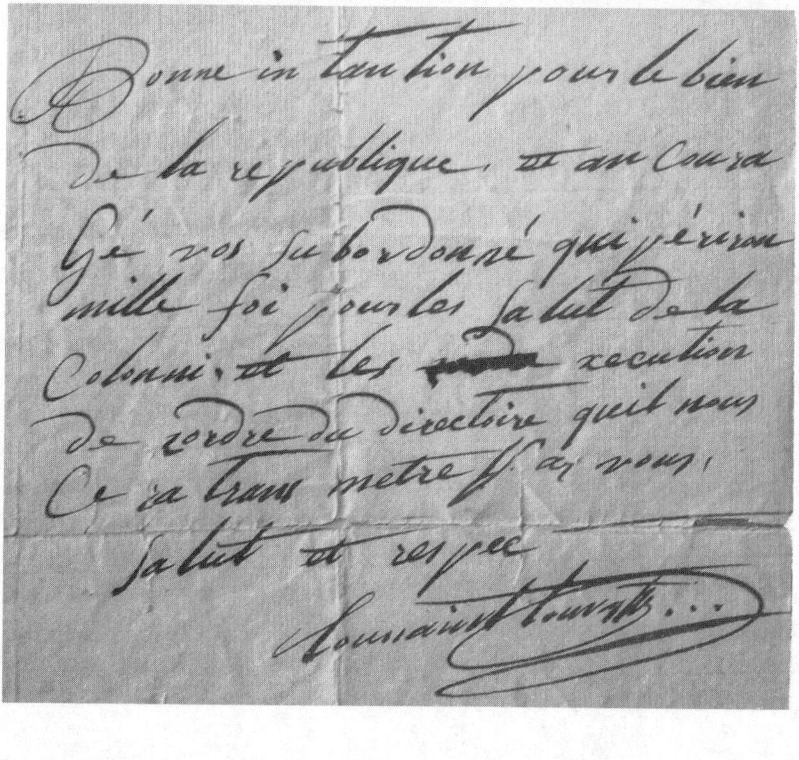

Bonne in tantion pour le bien
de la republique, et an coura
gé vos su bordonné qui périron
mille foi pour les salut de la
Colonni. et les ~~[illegible]~~ xecution
de zordre du directoire queil nous
cé za trans metre ſſ. ai vous,
salut et respec

Toussaint Louverture…

well clear. Days became weeks, and there was still no sign of him; Toussaint claimed that his urgent presence on the military front prevented him from making the journey, and that Hédouville would have to arm himself with 'patience'.[13] As yet more weeks passed Hédouville insisted, somewhat lamely: 'come to me as promptly as possible, the efficiency of our operations demands it and nothing can equal my impatience to make your acquaintance'.[14] Toussaint responded that he would arrive within a week. But still he did not appear, and his excuses began to sound almost insultingly frivolous: one day it was the need to attend a lavish banquet given in his honour at Port-Républicain; another, the messenger horse carrying an important message had died; and yet another, the River Artibonite was too swollen due to heavy rains to allow him – the colony's most accomplished horseman – to pass.[15]

When the two men finally met at the official *fête des victoires* celebration in Cap in June 1798 Toussaint was publicly effusive about Hédouville, saluting 'the high reputation he had justly acquired as the Pacifier of the Vendée', and pledging his absolute loyalty to him as the official agent of the republic. But an eyewitness noted that the speech was read out without any show of enthusiasm, and that the commander-in-chief's manner remained 'cold' during the entire occasion: 'not even the slightest smile lit up his face'.[16] His speech contained a pointed reminder about Saint-Domingue's historical singularity, which he expected the French agent to respect: 'here, more than anywhere else in the colonies, and indeed more than in Europe, man has suffered the most, and the different shades of skin colour have distinguished the oppressor from the oppressed'.[17] Hédouville was given to understand that he was still very much on probation.

To confuse him further, Toussaint initially gave the French agent alluring signs of his willingness to co-operate. This was in part a matter of self-interest: in order to maintain his growing system of political patronage, he needed Hédouville's imprimatur to proceed with nominations to various administrative positions, and the early correspondence between the two men demonstrates that he was successful. Toussaint also asked Hédouville to write to the French government supporting Bayon de Libertat's return to the colony, and, in marked contrast with Sonthonax's obstructiveness, he readily agreed to do so.[18] Clearly aware of the importance for Toussaint of his local Gonaïves municipality, Hédouville graciously asked him to provide him with the names of two men to serve as official commissioners on the town council.[19] After securing the appointment of his close ally Sanon Desfontaines ('a virtuous man and a good republican'), Toussaint fulsomely expressed his gratitude to the French agent: 'even before I met you, I had great faith in you, and since getting to know you this confidence has increased even more and I can see in all your deeds the signs of a real friendship, to which I attach the greatest value'.[20]

In the same spirit, Toussaint's first set of letters from the military front were long, detailed and even deferential, and repeatedly stressed his determination to abide by Hédouville's instructions.[21] This emphasis on discipline was one of the main themes in Toussaint's early missives. His intention was to reassure Hédouville not only about himself, but about his belief in the virtue of hierarchy and good order, in the civilian as much as the military sphere. So when Dessalines suspended a decree from Hédouville renaming the main streets of the recently liberated town of Saint-Marc, Hédouville ordered that he be punished for insubordination and placed him in detention for four days; Toussaint, however, proposed a much more severe tariff of fifteen days, and instructed Dessalines to write a grovelling apology to Hédouville, which he did, offering his 'great repentance' for failing to abide by his instructions and promising that henceforth his conduct would be exemplary.[22]

Even more remarkable was the speech Toussaint gave in July 1798 at the planting of the tree of liberty ceremony in Port-Républicain, shortly after it came back under republican control. Now that freedom from slavery had been won, he told the assembled plantation workers, there was no time to indulge in 'idleness'; indeed, he proclaimed, 'man can only realize his freedom through labour'. In a tropical echo of Mandeville's *Fable of the Bees*, he compared the perfect republic to the workings of a hive: 'the bees give us a great example of industriousness and happiness. Assembled in a hive they constitute a republic: they all work, and each individual creature through its endeavours participates in the happiness of the collectivity, and they even chase away those members who withhold their labour, refusing to tolerate any idleness in their midst'.[23] As we shall see, this praise of the regimentation of the workforce was partly a trap for the unsuspecting Hédouville, aimed at encouraging him to advance plans to regulate working conditions on Saint-Domingue's plantations. But its underlying philosophy, with its emphasis on unstinting collective effort, rigorous discipline and service to the common good, was also unquestionably Louverturian.

The cordiality between Toussaint and Hédouville was unlikely to last long, and it did not. Once he arrived in Saint-Domingue and took the full measure of Toussaint's power, the French agent realized that it was not limited to the military sphere but had spilled over into all sectors of the civil administration, including the entire system of local government. As he indicated in an early report:

> the assemblies in the countryside are made up of men from the plantations who are incapable of taking any decisions for themselves, and who allow themselves to be completely directed by Toussaint's regional military commanders. When I arrived I found all the judicial, civil and military powers in the hands of Toussaint as well, and he had also reduced the justices of the peace and the municipalities to positions of complete insignificance.[24]

Hédouville first attempted to rein in Toussaint by trying to set limits to his administrative interventions. Aware that the commander-in-chief's control over Saint-Domingue's institutions had grown partly through a combination of habit and military necessity (notably the need to fight the British in the pockets of territory still under their control), he reminded Toussaint that in the republican system of government military officials were subordinated to civilian rule; he could not presume to exercise the same powers in those parts of Saint-Domingue which were not in, or adjacent to, combat zones: 'there is a great difference between the powers of a commander-in-chief operating on enemy soil and one whose army is on the territory of the republic'.[25] The allocation of financial resources to different districts immediately became a contentious issue between the two men. Hédouville countermanded an instruction from Toussaint to move tax revenues from the areas of Charbonnière and Montagne Noire away from the southern coastal town of Léogâne to Port-Républicain: behind this innocuous-looking edict Toussaint was trying to pull off a double coup, taking resources away from his mixed-race rival General Rigaud, who controlled Léogâne, and transferring them to his own forces in Port-Républicain. Hédouville's response was blunt: 'no administrator can execute any instructions in this respect other than mine'.[26] Toussaint retreated immediately, and claimed that the whole thing had been a 'misunderstanding' (*malentendu*) – or as he put it, in a misspelling which was both amusing and portentous, a 'mal attendu'.[27]

But Toussaint did not always respond meekly to Hédouville's instructions to follow proper administrative procedures. On one occasion, after Toussaint had ordered the arrest of a planter named Bourges over an issue involving the theft of farm animals, Hédouville observed that this was a matter for the gendarmerie and the judiciary, not the commander of the army. He added, no doubt to soften the blow, that perhaps Toussaint had signed this particular order without careful scrutiny. The response was stiff: 'it is gravely insulting to suggest that I may sign either an order or a letter without reading or dictating it personally, it would amount to saying that I suffer from a great weakness in my character, and I cannot recognize myself in such a depiction. As I have the honour to repeat to you, I do not put my name to any document without reading or dictating it myself.'[28] This was true, but it was also typical of Toussaint's verbal chicanery, deploying attack as the best form of defence, and Hédouville immediately apologized for implying that his commander-in-chief could have acted carelessly. The unfortunate Bourges, for his part, remained in jail.

These sorts of skirmishes were manageable as long as Hédouville did not challenge Toussaint's protégés in the administration. Eventually, however, he began to do so: for example, he fired the chief army medical officer Lacoste, a close Toussaint ally, and replaced him with his own physician, Ferrié. At this point, his conflict with the commander-in-chief inevitably began to escalate. Toussaint was especially concerned about a senior financial administrator named Vollée, who was based in his stronghold in Gonaïves and was an invaluable subordinate (he was one of the very few men, along with his treasurer and diplomatic envoy Joseph Bunel, who knew everything about Toussaint's finances). Alerted that Hédouville was investigating Vollée for alleged financial irregularities, Toussaint wrote a long letter in person defending him against any 'slanderous allegations', and vouching for his competence and his integrity; indeed, according to Toussaint, Vollée was a man without any financial resources of his own, and had to depend on his son-in-law to make ends meet for his 'large family'; he was 'the poorest and the most dutiful administrator' on Saint-Domingue.[29] Despite Toussaint's continued protestations of his innocence, Vollée was removed from his position and threatened with prosecution, Hédouville stating darkly that 'the crime which has been committed here is of such great concern for public order that I am obliged to pursue its authors with the full severity of the laws'.[30] Now the gloves were definitely off.

One of the issues which did much to poison the relationship between Hédouville and Toussaint was the handling of negotiations for the British withdrawal from their final outposts in the colony, notably Port-Républicain and the coastal garrison town of Môle Saint-Nicolas. In the early months of 1798, the British government realized that its position in Saint-Domingue was no longer sustainable, and despatched Brigadier-General Thomas Maitland to end the conflict as rapidly as possible, in a way which was 'not dishonourable'.[31]

Maitland was an astute officer, and he knew that he arrived in Môle Saint-Nicolas with a weak hand – by this stage, as we saw in Chapter 3, the military situation was completely desperate. But exacerbating the tension between Hédouville and Toussaint was one of the few cards available to him and he proceeded to play it effectively, for example by giving both men the absolute assurance that he wanted to negotiate exclusively with them. Hédouville sent a warning to his commander-in-chief: 'General Maitland is manifestly trying to sow the seeds of division between us in order to benefit his cause; let us have absolutely no dealings with him other than those relating to our respective prisoners.'[32] Toussaint was in apparent agreement: 'the intention of the British is to divide us from each other, and I will have no correspondence with them, nor will I attempt any move without first consulting you and obtaining your approval'. This was more than a little disingenuous, as by this time Toussaint had already begun ceasefire discussions with Maitland and given his negotiator, Huin, 'full power' to reach a settlement with the British at Port-Républicain.[33]

Maitland quickly came round to the view that Toussaint was his more precious contact, both tactically and strategically. In late April the commander-in-chief discovered that his old boss and protector Bayon de Libertat had arrived in Port-Républicain, where he was being held by the British; he wrote to Maitland, asking for the former Bréda manager to be released and sent to him immediately. Maitland graciously agreed, and Bayon duly arrived in Gonaïves, where he was warmly welcomed by Toussaint.[34] The discussions between Huin and Maitland were rapidly concluded, leading to an orderly British retreat from Port-Républicain, Saint-Marc and Arcahaie; the main British condition – that the lives and properties of those *colons* who had supported the royalists would be fully protected – was readily accepted by Toussaint.[35] Agreements on Jérémie and Môle Saint-Nicolas soon followed, the latter evacuation taking place despite the vehement opposition of the governor of Jamaica, Balcarres, and the British naval commander Sir Hyde Parker, who in Toussaint's words were desperate to retain a foothold in Saint-Domingue.[36]

These agreements paved the way for a major breakthrough in late August 1798: the signing of a 'secret convention' between Toussaint and Maitland. This was much more than a cessation of hostilities, seeking to establish a framework for peaceful coexistence between the British government and the revolutionary authorities in Saint-Domingue. Maitland pledged that the British would not interfere either militarily or politically in the internal affairs of the French colony, while Toussaint undertook not to export his revolution to neighbouring Jamaica. Toussaint also secured a British commitment to allow some provisions to reach the ports of Saint-Domingue without interference from British cruisers.[37] Explaining the agreement to Balcarres, Maitland observed that it was 'strongly' in British interests, and urged him to begin 'friendly' negotiations with Toussaint about reopening commercial links with the French colony.[38]

Toussaint also made sure that word got out that the British regarded him as their privileged contact, and that Port-Républicain, Môle and Saint-Marc had been handed over to his forces, not to Hédouville.[39] Toussaint rubbed salt into the wound by telling Hédouville that the British had given him a house in Môle (the building formerly occupied by Maitland), and sending him a glowing report of the magnificent reception he had received from Maitland a few days later, just before the British commander sailed away from the colony: 'the British forces greeted me most majestically, and with full military honours. As a mark of his esteem, in consideration of my humane treatment of the prisoners of his nation, and of my generosity both during the war and in the course of the negotiations, General Maitland invited me to accept a bronze handgun and two exquisitely designed double-barrel shotguns.' Aware of his coup, Toussaint feigned surprise at the way he had been treated: 'I did not expect such deference.'[40] The date of this report was just as significant as its contents: Toussaint wrote to Hédouville a full four months after receiving the shotguns from Maitland – a measure of his growing self-confidence.[41]

The conclusion of the negotiations with the British was not just a personal diplomatic success for Toussaint. It showed that he was beginning to pursue a distinct strategy, based on a delicate balancing act. He remained true to his fundamental republican principles of eliminating the British presence from his native land and vigorously defending the interests of black citizens: in the name of his hallowed principle of fraternity he demanded from Maitland that all black soldiers and slaves who had been enlisted on the British side should be allowed to remain on Saint-Domingue, rather than follow their masters in their retreat to Jamaica; once released into Toussaint's hands, these 6,000 men were for the most part sent to work as paid labourers on the plantations.[42] The agreement with Maitland showed that Toussaint was looking not just to execute French policy, but to do so in a way which would secure the future political and economic interests of Saint-Domingue. And were the two objectives to come in conflict, it was plainly the good of the colony that took precedence for him.

A similar priority drove Toussaint's approach towards an even more contentious subject: the terms of the amnesty policy to be applied to the newly liberated territories. Right from the start, as Toussaint was negotiating the British exit from Port-Républicain, Hédouville informed him that, as commander-in-chief, he had a duty to uphold article 373 of the 1795 French constitution, which prohibited an amnesty to any person who had taken up arms against the republic or actively supported its enemies.[43] As we saw with his dealings with Sonthonax, Toussaint's approach towards these émigrés was much more flexible and arguably more far-sighted, as he was eager to extend forgiveness to them in the name of social peace and reconciliation. As the negotiations over the withdrawal from Môle Saint-Nicolas and Jérémie began, Hédouville again made his position clear: he issued a stern proclamation that not even the slightest exemption was to be made to the law, as pardoning any émigré would pose a 'serious threat' to public order.[44]

Toussaint not only ignored Hédouville's instructions, but publicly announced his intention to forgive all those who had sided with the British occupiers in the colony's coastal towns. At a Mass celebrated in Port-Républicain he granted a full amnesty to a group of French émigrés from Jérémie; according to an eyewitness, he first compared himself to Jesus Christ, who had absolved sinners in the name of his father, and then announced that he was pardoning them 'in the name of the republic'.[45] He wrote to Hédouville a few days later loftily quoting Luke: 'forgive us our sins, as we forgive those who sin against us'.[46] This was triply provocative, for he had not only disobeyed the French agent, but also taunted him by proclaiming the pardon publicly, and furthermore at a religious ceremony, which he must have known would annoy the anticlerical pacifier of the Vendée, who (like his predecessor Sonthonax) tended to see priests as potential 'disturbers of the peace'.[47] Sure enough, Hédouville wrote back crossly that Toussaint had no business granting pardons, especially in a church setting, which was in direct contravention of republican constitutional practice. Toussaint responded that his amnesty policy was aimed at the small group of men, 'more hapless than guilty', who had been misled into following the British; surely, he asked disingenuously, a 'generous pardon' was a more sensible policy towards such people?

Toussaint also claimed that most of his amnesties were granted to women, children, old men and plantation workers; in a very small number of cases, as with the black gunners from the disbanded Dessources royalist regiment, he cited military necessity: the need to bring these soldiers back into active military service because of the shortage of qualified artillerymen in his own ranks.[48] Then, typically, he went on the offensive: it was an outrage, he told Hédouville, even to imply that he could act against the constitution; in any case, an expression of faith in God could hardly violate French law. He then added, revealingly: 'I attribute to the Almighty, the sole author of all things, every good deed I have accomplished in my political life, and if only it were the case that our brothers shared my religious outlook: their timorous conscience would be guided towards good, and France would have no more ardent upholders of the constitution, and her constitution would have no more zealous and faithful defenders.'[49]

Hédouville attempted to regain control of the situation by issuing a decree reaffirming official French policy on émigrés. As he explained to

Toussaint, it would be particularly dangerous to pardon enemies of the republic, such as the military officers who had collaborated with British forces, as they might seize the opportunity to 'sow the seeds of discord' in Saint-Domingue. His decree cast the net very wide: he sought to exclude from any amnesty émigrés and those who had willingly served in the British forces, as well as 'all those who had never lived before in Saint-Domingue before the troubles, but had come to support the British occupation'.[50] It was actively sabotaged, as he later recognized, by elements of the Saint-Domingue colonial administration, with Toussaint's gleeful encouragement.[51] By the end of September 1798 Toussaint was not only granting pardons to local émigrés, but also inviting anti-republican exiles who were based outside Saint-Domingue to return,[52] and publishing his proclamations in local newspapers: *Le Citoyen véridique, ou gazette du Port-Républicain* carried the text of an edict granting amnesties to a group of French émigrés in the United States. In a resounding slap to Hédouville, he loftily declared that 'the best interests of the republic' would be served by reuniting hitherto divided families and reintegrating former enemies into the community, 'like the return of prodigal sons'. He added, in a characteristic expression of his Catholic and republican values, that his policy of amnesty was also consistent with 'the sublime sentiment of fraternity'.[53]

The confrontation over the granting of amnesties therefore ended as a major, and public, humiliation for Hédouville. It also laid bare the limits of the control he could exercise over his own administration, as Toussaint was able not only to pardon a large number of émigrés, in direct contravention of his decree, but to issue the very people Hédouville had labelled as renegades with official passports, allow them to return to a number of ports (including Cap), and parade them across Saint-Domingue as living proof of his commitment to reconciliation. Equally damagingly, the clash allowed Toussaint to start spreading negative rumours about Hédouville. Stories – which could only have come from Toussaint and his entourage – began to circulate that Hédouville was still full of aristocratic prejudices, that he and his commander-in-chief were not in agreement, and that these conflicts were damaging the integrity of the administration; naturally, the blame was pinned on Hédouville's 'rigidity' and 'arrogance'.[54]

Hédouville himself later admitted that his reputation was scarred by these rumours. In one of them it was claimed that, disguised as a woman, he was seen surreptitiously visiting the commander of Cap harbour in order to plan the surrender of the city to the British.[55] Another tale which began its life among the robustly republican plantation workers of Saint-Louis du Nord, before doing the rounds across the northern and western parts of the colony, claimed that Hédouville had tried to leave Saint-Domingue with 'two trunks full of money' (supplied by the perfidious British, of course), but had been stopped by the virtuous and vigilant citizens of Cap. Then, the tale continued, he had tried to have Toussaint arrested by the British: General Maitland had not only refused, but had shown the treacherous letter to the commander-in-chief.[56] In the popular imagination, Hédouville was beginning to be cast as a corrupt, devious and ultimately impotent figure, while Toussaint was cunning, steadfast and victorious.

These disagreements all contributed to the breakdown of the two men's relationship. But they could arguably have been overcome if Hédouville had not also chosen to wrangle with Toussaint in his primary sphere of responsibility: the military. Hédouville had arrived with instructions to reduce the size of Saint-Domingue's republican army, to put an end to the 'widespread abuses' which, he was told, were being committed by its black officers and soldiers, and ultimately to challenge Toussaint's authority as the head of the armed forces.[57] This confrontational agenda was bound to provoke a fierce reaction from Toussaint, all the more so because his long battle against foreign imperial occupying forces was reaching its climax during the first half of 1798. Toussaint rightly viewed the British exit from Saint-Domingue as a personal military triumph, and felt that his brave fighters were entitled to be treated with respect and honour by the official representative of France.

Instead, Hédouville issued a decree on 9 Messidor (27 June) removing food rations from various public officials – including Toussaint's soldiers. This measure was not based on necessity, but on Hédouville's belief that the rations were superfluous, and were not available to public servants in France.[58] The decree was, predictably, greeted with consternation in the army, especially as it was accompanied by strict instructions to the military administration to cease providing rations of flour and dried meats to Toussaint's senior officers. Toussaint, who had not been consulted, rapidly interceded with Hédouville, pointing out that those of his men who were posted in recently liberated territories were facing 'extreme hardship' because food supplies there were scarce and prohibitively expensive;[59] in Saint-Marc, when the republican army arrived after the departure of the British, soldiers and officers had been forced to pool their meagre resources to pay for their food.[60] In the end, Hédouville grudgingly allowed Toussaint to treat senior officers such as Laplume (who at the time had eight children) as special cases, but instructed that any such exemptions be made sparingly. He refused to rescind his decree, claiming that most soldiers sold on the bread they received – which was highly unlikely given that their daily ration was a mere eight ounces.[61] He showed remarkably poor judgement in forcing black republican war heroes like Laplume, who had known the harshest extremities of slavery and had risked their lives on countless occasions on the battlefield to preserve the French position in the colony, to plead for food rations for their families. With this petty episode Hédouville's relationship with Toussaint's black army got off to an unpromising start.

Far from regarding Toussaint's men with consideration, Hédouville seemed to go out of his way to treat them disparagingly. In his early letters to the commander-in-chief he complained of 'numerous, ongoing, and daily abuses' which were being committed by military officers and soldiers, including the theft of farm animals and the raiding of local plantations for food; Dessalines' regiment in Saint-Marc was explicitly accused of committing acts of 'brigandry'.[62] Toussaint responded indignantly, pointing out that the disciplinary regime to which members of his army were subjected was draconian, and that any soldier who transgressed these regulations was severely punished: he had issued strict orders that any soldier should be placed in detention if caught merely asking for food from a member of the public when stationed in a town or on a plantation.[63] Dessalines was so infuriated by the allegation against his regiment that he obtained sworn testimony from three neighbouring plantation supervisors, who confirmed that they had not been victims of any significant marauding.[64] It seems highly unlikely that there was any truth to these stories of mass indiscipline, given everything we know about Toussaint's insistence that his soldiers should set an example of virtue – especially as Hédouville also complained, with scant regard for consistency, that Dessalines had ordered the execution of one of his soldiers for thieving.[65]

Hédouville also refused to promote Christophe Mornet and Paul Louverture, Toussaint's brother, both of whom were strongly recommended by the commander-in-chief in light of their gallant services in the campaign against the British. Hédouville claimed that he was 'not allowed' to elevate officers to the position of brigadier-general, which sounded like the flimsiest of excuses; Toussaint responded with displeasure, saying that he was 'very cross'.[66] Likewise, in the run-up to the liberation of Saint-Marc and Port-Républicain, Toussaint had promised his victorious army that a quarter of revenues collected there (mostly through the sale of sugar) would be given to them as a 'war indemnity'; as he explained to Hédouville, his soldiers fully deserved these spoils given all the deprivations they had endured during the campaign.[67] Hédouville vetoed the request, arguing that any moneys found in liberated territories should be transferred into the public coffers and used to pay the salaries of all soldiers: a good republican response, perhaps, but hardly one which would have pleased

Toussaint's men – especially as their pay and material conditions remained an extremely sore issue.[68]

In Toussaint's correspondence with Hédouville, the soldiers' remuneration and equipment was a recurrent, almost obsessive theme. Not much seemed to have changed since his earlier pleas to Laveaux. Toussaint complained regularly that his brave warriors were not paid, and lacked even the most basic equipment such as clothing. He threw Hédouville's argument about equal treatment back at him: if all soldiers were meant to enjoy the same conditions, how come Rigaud's army in the south was paid on time, and smartly fitted out, while his own men were left in a state of destitution?[69] After receiving a series of vague reassurances, Toussaint wrote again, with mounting exasperation: the material situation of his troops was a source of 'extreme concern' to him; 'the sad position in which they find themselves can only touch a heart which is as sensitive as mine; it is very painful for a commander who has seen his forces endure thirst and hunger, and be exposed to the greatest dangers to expel the British from the territory of Saint-Domingue, it is painful, I repeat, to behold these very soldiers deprived even of such basic clothing as would cover their nudity'.[70] The situation, Toussaint told Hédouville in another letter, had become a personal embarrassment to him: he had promised his soldiers that they would be able to 'go into town fully dressed', and yet they were still naked and their arrears were unpaid. 'He who receives the blow', Toussaint concluded, 'feels the pain', before passing on this ominous warning from his soldiers: 'when the devil drinks too much of his own poison, he dies'.[71]

On 17 October 1798 Toussaint sent Hédouville a triumphant report announcing the liberation of the territory: 'I have finally succeeded, I have reached the goal I had set myself, namely to chase the English out of Saint-Domingue and to replace the banners of despotism with the flag of liberty and the standard of the French nation. I have nothing else to desire.'[72] This expression of patriotic pride was no doubt heartfelt, but Toussaint was not being entirely candid about his aspirations: by the time he sent this report, he had also clearly resolved to orchestrate Hédouville's removal from the colony.

When exactly Toussaint reached the conclusion that his relationship with Hédouville was fractured beyond repair can only be guessed at. His critics suggest that he intended to bring down Hédouville from the very outset, but there is no evidence to suggest this, and indeed their early exchanges imply the opposite. The ever-cautious Toussaint would not have wanted another major incident with the Directory so quickly after the departure of

Sonthonax the previous year – not least because he did not want to give any more ammunition to his royalist and conservative enemies in Paris. He therefore tried to establish a working relationship with Hédouville, but as time passed it became plain that their views diverged on too many issues. He also realized that the French envoy had been officially instructed to challenge him systematically, so as to reduce his political influence: as he put it in one frustrated letter, 'you have been countering everything I do, slandering my every move, and casting doubt on all my proposals'.[73]

Toussaint became convinced that these clashes were not just down to Hédouville: a number of his senior administrators, who had come with him from Paris, were out to undermine their relationship; Toussaint had ears everywhere, and Hédouville later realized that one of his mixed-race aides-de-camp was an informer.[74] One of the French agent's associates, for example, told Toussaint that he would be happy to have him transported to France, where he could take 'all the rest he needed'. Toussaint replied tartly: 'bâtiment à vous pas li gagné grandeur assez pour porter en France Général Toussaint'.[75] These 'enemies of the public realm, of order and tranquillity', he informed Hédouville, were trying to 'make evil pass for good, and good for evil, darkness for light, and light for darkness, what is sweet to be bitter, and what is bitter sweet'; he observed that it was 'painful for men of honour to be treated in this way'.[76] By September 1798 Toussaint was openly complaining about the evil role of this 'cabal', which contained men who were 'sworn enemies of the blacks'; the French agent, he claimed, was being consistently misled by 'insidious reports of men who aspire only to a general commotion'. Toussaint suspected that a plot was being hatched not only to contain his influence, but perhaps even to remove him altogether from his position of commander-in-chief. In an official speech celebrating the foundation of the republic, Hédouville pointedly stated that if the armed forces were not fully obedient, 'public order is threatened, and soon replaced by anarchy'.[77] This was a thinly veiled attack on Toussaint, who also complained – correctly, it turned out – that Hédouville was seeking to weaken his military power by encouraging the southern mixed-race General Rigaud to challenge his authority.[78]

Toussaint probably started his campaign to confront Hédouville publicly sometime in July 1798, for this is when he decided to ensnare him in a trap. He encouraged him to move forward with his plans to reform the system of agricultural labour, discussing them extensively with the French agent and privately describing them as 'very advantageous and useful to agriculture'[79] – so much so that Hédouville thanked him profusely for his help, and celebrated the fact that the principal provisions of the new regulations had been jointly agreed by the two of them.[80] Toussaint did not, however, associate his name publicly with the new decree. And for good reason: announced in late July 1798, Hédouville's *Arrêté concernant la police des habitations* provoked widespread discontent among plantation workers, as it forced them into binding contractual agreements with their employers. The new system was designed to favour the plantation-owners: the minimum length of these *engagements* was three years, and labourers were required to give a year's notice if they wished to take up employment elsewhere. The penalty for any *cultivateur* who left his plantation without prior agreement was drastic: a month's prison for the first offence, six months for the second and a year for the third.[81]

The new measures were widely perceived by the plantation workers as a threat to their freedom of labour, largely unrestricted since the abolition of slavery. Toussaint initially did little to alter this perception, while quietly stoking the *cultivateurs*' resentment against the decree in all areas under his influence. Exploiting the fact that Hédouville's officials made no effort to explain the new regulations to the workforce (the decree was sent to local municipalities in French, with no kreyol translation available), he played up fears that the measures were aimed at undermining both their freedom and their material interests. Spread through Toussaint's extensive political and military networks, darker rumours also began to circulate: the decree was portrayed as a menace to the 'liberté générale' which the black citizens of Saint-Domingue had gained since the revolution; there were even suggestions that the only way black freedom could be safeguarded was by 'a massacre of all whites'. Alarmed by the Makandalist undertones of such stories, Hédouville asked Toussaint to send a circular letter to his military commanders, asking them to quash these 'ridiculous' rumours.[82] He duly complied, and even reassured the French agent that whenever he saw his 'black brothers' straying from the righteous path, he would 'set them straight'.[83] But in fact he did exactly the opposite, actively – but still furtively – encouraging the growing unease against Hédouville's measures. In the Petit-Goâve district, for example, the revolt against the decree was led by a charismatic and influential local rebel named Singla,[84] whose links with Toussaint were carefully concealed – so much so that when the plantation workers in the area went on strike in late September 1798, the municipality frantically turned to Toussaint for assistance, little realizing that he was the source of the unrest.[85]

Given their role in encouraging these local rebellions against Hédouville, Toussaint would obviously have signalled to his regional military commanders that a public showdown with him was imminent. And since the French agent had done nothing to endear himself to the officers and soldiers of Saint-Domingue's republican army, they would have greeted this prospect with eager anticipation. Indeed, by September 1798 there was widespread evidence of anti-Hédouville sentiment being stoked within black ranks, both among ordinary soldiers and among the officer corps. One report from Saint-Marc claimed that Dessalines' 4th regiment was 'very unsettled' and that 'the existence of white officers is hanging by a thread'.[86] Hédouville had a series of sharp exchanges with Toussaint's nephew Moyse, whom he confronted over alleged 'abuses' (again, over food supplies); the confrontation ended with this brutal rebuke from Hédouville: 'he who wishes to be a commander of republican troops should also know how to obey'.[87]

Toussaint waited for Hédouville to make a serious tactical mistake before escalating the conflict. The French agent presented him with a golden opportunity in October 1798 by ordering the disarmament of the 700-strong northern military garrison of Fort-Liberté, where Moyse's 5th regiment was stationed. Hédouville sent a force of several hundred European soldiers to disarm the garrison, under the command of Manigat, a black justice of the peace from Fort-Dauphin. In the ensuing violence, Moyse's brother Charles Zamor was killed, together with more than 200 black soldiers. Hédouville's envoy further exacerbated the conflict by detaining a dozen black officers from the regiment and having them transported to Cap, and ordering that Moyse be suspended for insubordination. Troops loyal to Toussaint eventually took back control of the garrison, with the notable support of a peasant force of 3,000 men rallied by his ally Jean-Baptiste Sans-Souci from the mountains of Grande-Rivière, Vallière and Sainte-Suzanne.[88] The time to move against Hédouville had come.

In mid October 1798, just as events at Fort-Liberté were escalating, Toussaint seized the moment to launch a full-scale uprising against Hédouville. As he later explained to the French government, the agent's actions had provoked widespread anger: 'the spilling of the blood of the defenders of our territory in this unfortunate incident rekindled the flames of discord, and soon calls for vengeance were spreading everywhere, travelling to the furthest corners of the colony'.[89] From his headquarters in the d'Héricourt plantation, Toussaint co-ordinated these protests through his military commanders and organized several thousand *cultivateurs* to march on Cap, where Hédouville and his officials were based. As the large crowd – a significant number of whom were women – approached the town, the threat of pillage grew among the panicking inhabitants, especially the white population, as word spread that the protesters had come equipped with bags, baskets and ropes; many of them declared that they were 'grateful to God that their journey would not be in vain'.[90]

A French visitor described the 'horrifying' scene at la Fossette, just on the outskirts of Cap: 'imagine ten thousand blacks of all ages and sexes, almost naked, grouped around campfires, abandoning themselves without any inhibition to all their passions: obscene dances, contortions, screams'.[91] There was clearly more than a whiff of *vodou* in the air, and Hédouville later reported that Toussaint's mobilized *cultivateurs* had cast a spell on him in a ritual which involved 'dancing around a bull's head in which an illumination had been introduced'.[92] The Cap municipality sent a delegation to discuss the demonstrators' grievances. The self-styled 'popular army' responded ominously that they were coming to 'avenge' the treatment that had been meted out to the 5th regiment officers and soldiers at Fort-Liberté, and threatened to lay waste the town. They also declared that 'a bloodbath could be avoided' if Toussaint Louverture were to be called upon to intervene and restore order.[93] These exchanges were immediately communicated to the commander-in-chief, providing him with the cover he needed to step in.

Toussaint moved swiftly, first issuing a proclamation to the municipality of Cap, urging its officers to take all necessary measures to ensure that order was maintained, and promising to support their efforts to ensure that 'the laws and the constitution of the republic can be fully respected'. There was a delicious irony here, given that he was in the process of unseating the official representative of the French government in Saint-Domingue.[94] Toussaint followed this up with a public meeting with the Cap citizens, assembled somewhat uneasily outside the municipality, where he announced that he was 'only too happy' to have arrived in time to see that security was restored. He warned that there was a real threat of 'general upheaval', but promised to do his utmost to put everything back in 'good order'. The first step he took was to instruct his officers to take control of the military outposts around the town, and for good measure he also despatched the army into his old neighbourhood of Haut-du-Cap to 'guarantee the security of all inhabitants and properties'.[95] But even this gesture of reassurance was cloaked in menace, as the officer who rode at the head of his 4th regiment was none other than the formidable Dessalines. The real purpose of this move was to pin Hédouville down and prevent his escape from Cap, in particular to stop him from leaving the colony with official French Agency documents.[96]

In parallel with the tumultuous events in Cap, focused around the crisis at Fort-Liberté, Toussaint took steps to undermine Hédouville's authority in the plantations. In a series of co-ordinated actions across the north and west of the colony in October 1798, Toussaint mobilized thousands of labourers to down tools and begin a wave of protests in their localities. This strike movement was a direct snub to Hédouville's *arrêté* of 6 Thermidor, which stipulated penalties of up to two years' imprisonment for any *cultivateur* who 'fomented trouble and undermined order and discipline in the workshops'. But on this occasion the chief agent of sedition was none other than Toussaint himself, and so the plantation workers had little to fear. Indeed, he threw his full weight behind the movement: travelling to all the sites of protest, he harangued the striking workers and pressed them to convey their grievances to their municipalities, so that they could be noted and shared more widely.

With Toussaint's blessing, these encounters between the plantation workers and their municipal officials helped to inject a dose of popular revolutionary energy into Saint-Domingue's system of local government. For example, the protests prompted new forms of dialogue between municipal representatives and their local constituents. In some neighbourhoods the protesters came en masse to the municipality, whereas in others they nominated delegates who were sent to meet the municipal officers; at Gonaïves, as the municipal clerk scrupulously noted, there were twenty-two citizen protesters.[97] These meetings in turn radicalized the municipalities' representation of their own role: they now typically described themselves in revolutionary terms, as 'organs of the people'. Faced with a 'prodigious crowd of citizen plantation workers, both men and women', the municipal officers of Petite-Rivière announced that they were 'the sentinels of the people',[98] and that they had a sacred duty to hear and then transmit their voices.

As instructed by Toussaint, the plantation workers' petitions were transcribed by local municipalities and forwarded to Hédouville's office in Cap. The demands made depressing reading for the beleaguered French agent, as they all began with an emphatic expression of no confidence in him. After meeting with their constituents, the councillors and officers of Plaisance proclaimed that Hédouville had 'poisoned the atmosphere' in Saint-Domingue and provoked an outbreak of 'anarchy'; the only solution was for him to depart 'as soon as possible' from the colony.[99] In a gesture of magnanimity, the petitioners of Marmelade merely asked for the agent to be 'suspended'[100] – but this was the minority view. Hédouville's departure was insisted on by most of the mobilized citizens, and to avoid all ambiguity those of Gros-Morne spelled it out: 'Hédouville's presence here is the cause of the movement which has provoked the agitation of the plantation workers.'[101]

In contrast with the protests in Cap, it was Hédouville's agricultural reforms which were the primary issue for the provincial demonstrators, who denounced his *arrêté* in all their proclamations. The protestors from Gonaïves observed that the *engagement* system was nothing less than an attempt to 'infringe upon our freedoms', and they demanded that the contracts which they had been forced to sign be immediately torn up.[102] But this was no ordinary labour dispute, for its ultimate aim was to effect political change. The labourers of Port-à-Piment and Terre-Neuve solemnly declared: 'until Hédouville leaves the colony, we will not resume work'.[103] The plantation workers of Toussaint Louverture (by this point there was a town named after the hero of the revolution) stated in even more dramatic terms: 'we would rather live in the woods for the rest of our lives than work under these conditions'.[104]

At the same time, Toussaint saw to it that the dramatic scenes at Fort-Liberté were not ignored by the provincial protesters. Indeed, as the news of Moyse's arrest and the disarmament of the black troops spread across the plantations, events were further distorted by the rumour mill, and protestors' demands for the reinstatement of Moyse were mingled with more alarming stories, for instance that the entire 5th regiment had been massacred, or that all troops loyal to Toussaint might be disbanded. There may have been an element of deliberate misinformation here, as Toussaint sought to fire up local indignation against Hédouville. But such fears were not misplaced: as we noted earlier, there had been a considerable loss of black lives at Fort-Liberté, and the French agent had effectively arrived in Saint-Domingue with the explicit aim of reducing the size of Toussaint's army. This was the heart of the issue, and explained how Toussaint could be so successful in mobilizing thousands of plantation workers over the bloody skirmish at Fort-Liberté: in the minds of many *cultivateurs* the black army was the principal defender of their interests, and any attempt to undermine it was the prelude to an attack on their basic rights. This link was made explicit in one of the municipal proclamations: 'we demand that General Moyse be given back his command, so that he can defend us against those who would attempt to enslave us'.[105] Toussaint's nephew was beginning to emerge as one of the most powerful and popular figures in the northern department.

Toussaint's provincial supporters were remarkable for their energy, their determination and their discipline, which was noted admiringly by the military commander of Port-à-Piment and Terre-Neuve as he found a large number of them lined up outside his house.[106] But these men and women also bore witness to the range of Toussaint's appeal among the black citizens: he could mobilize the mountain peasants of Sans-Souci as well as ordinary agricultural workers, no doubt well reinforced by a sizeable cohort of *conducteurs*, who were Toussaint's key agents on the plantations. Their cohesion was visible both in their obedience of Toussaint's orders and the spirit of exuberant self-control they displayed: they combined the classic qualities of revolutionary crowds, namely festive celebration, derisive humour and thundering menace. Indeed, what was most striking about these men and women was their self-confidence and their powerful assimilation of republican ideas. In their declarations and petitions to their municipal officers, they framed their grievances about Hédouville not in terms of their own self-interest or in racial categories, but in the revolutionary language of freedom, justice and equality and in an appeal to the principle of the public good, in whose name they claimed to be acting, referring frequently to the constitution: at Petite-Rivière, for example, they affirmed that 'the rights of man are inalienable and unalterable, and they are guaranteed to all citizens by the constitution'.[107]

The most sacred right which the constitution had given the people of Saint-Domingue was that of citizenship. Toussaint's supporters showed that this was not just a philosophical abstraction for them, but a living reality. In their encounters with municipal officers they spoke not as humble petitioners but as *cultivateurs* and *cultivatrices* who were bearers of legitimate rights which they had earned through revolutionary struggle; the presence of large numbers of women both at Cap and in the provinces was particularly notable in this respect. They could be cheeky, too: taking advantage of their special patron, the petitioners of the town of Toussaint Louverture seized the opportunity to ask their beloved chief for a promotion for their local military commander.[108]

This confidence was further evident in the demand that their names be appended to the municipal proclamations. This was not a desire for individual recognition, rather a celebration of their collective strength, just as Toussaint had highlighted in his response to Viénot-Vaublanc. So, for example, alongside those of the municipal officers, the text produced at Marmelade listed the names of over 100 plantation workers: it was no doubt the first time that the likes of Cofie, Lespérance, Sansfaçon, Pompom, Fidelle and Gracia had been recognized in a public document of this kind. Some of their statements were even transcribed in kreyol. More than half of the text of the Petite-Rivière plantation workers was published in the Saint-Domingue vernacular, including this pithy dismissal of Hédouville: 'nous pas content avec li, d'abord li pas capable meté l'ordre dans pays-ci, li vlé meté désordre pitau'.[109]

*

Vilified by the revolutionary citizens of Saint-Domingue and outflanked by their leader Toussaint, whose forces blockaded him in Cap for several days,[110] Hédouville was literally driven out of the colony in late October 1798, along with his retinue of 1,800 civilian and military officials. He spent his final days contemplating his fate on board the *Bravoure*, a French ship anchored in the bay of Cap. It was a measure of his impotence that he did not feel secure enough even to spend his final moments on land, and rejected an invitation from Toussaint to come ashore for a discussion, fearing that he would be taken prisoner.[111] He ended his short career in Saint-Domingue in mortifying circumstances, 'treated', as his successor Roume put, 'as a defeated general forced to abandon a military position'.[112]

Before leaving the colony, Hédouville issued a dramatic proclamation blaming his departure on 'émigrés' whose return to Saint-Domingue had poisoned the political atmosphere. He accused them of spearheading a campaign of 'slanderous allegations' against him, notably by claiming that he was seeking to undermine the 'liberté générale' of the black population. These rumours had become potent because they were encouraged by those in the administration who had 'sold themselves to the British'. This was a predictable swipe at Toussaint, and it was not the only one: Hédouville claimed that those seeking 'independence' were now, finally, nailing their colours to the mast, and despite all appearances were showing themselves as the 'cruel enemies' of Saint-Domingue's liberty.[113] In a separate message, written on the same day, Hédouville also released Toussaint's mixed-race rival Rigaud from his obligations to obey the orders of his commander-in-chief, whom he accused of being 'in the pay of the British, the émigrés and the Americans'. He invited Rigaud to 'take control of the department of the south', in so doing directly encouraging the civil strife which would lead to the brutal *guerre des couteaux* (war of knives) a year later.[114]

But, for the moment, Toussaint's triumph was unquestionable. One of his great gifts was his sense of political theatre, and forcing the French agent onto a ship in the bay of Cap at the height of the sweltering Caribbean summer, right above the remains of the thousands of dead slaves thrown overboard before their vessels docked in the harbour, was a characteristic touch: this humiliation of a powerful *grand blanc* would have been greeted by his black soldiers – especially the *bossales* – as a fitting symbolic retribution, both for his contemptuous treatment of Toussaint's men during the previous months and for the suffering they and their families had endured on their way to Saint-Domingue from Africa. Toussaint emphasized this connection with his soldiers in a stirring speech he gave after taking back control of Fort-Liberté, in which he vowed to defend the achievements of the

Saint-Domingue revolution, most notably emancipation from servitude. He mocked his adversary with a vivid contrast: 'who is the greater defender of your freedom, General Hédouville, the former marquis and knight of Saint-Louis, or Toussaint Louverture, the slave from Bréda?'[115]

Toussaint's defeat of Hédouville enabled him to take his first strides into the diplomatic arena, with the conclusion of the 1798 convention with Maitland. The agreement elevated Toussaint's status in the region, and was the first step in the formal separation of the colony's interests from those of France. It also initiated a gradual rapprochement between Saint-Domingue and Britain, based not only on mutual interests but also a growing respect for Toussaint – even though he represented the negation of everything the British Empire stood for. Summing up his experiences in the French colony, Maitland savaged Hédouville ('a man of reputed talents, although as far as I had any concern with him he did not appear so to me'), while recognizing Toussaint's formidable military and political powers. But there was something more fundamental. Maitland paid tribute to Toussaint's 'moderation and forbearance' as a ruler, both in respect of his 'humanity' in warfare and in his honourable treatment of white émigrés, and urged his government to continue the policy of constructive engagement with him.[116] Maitland's emissary to Saint-Domingue, Edward Harcourt, likewise noted that his government's favourable policy towards Toussaint was a response to the 'good faith' he had shown towards British interests.[117]

These favourable impressions were also expressed in a glowing article about the agreement, published in the *London Gazette* in December 1798. It cast the British withdrawal from Saint-Domingue as a diplomatic triumph, as it brought the promise of 'exclusive commerce' with the colony, and of its 'independence' from French control. Most remarkable was the description of Toussaint, who was praised as 'a negro born to vindicate the claims of his species, and to show that the character of man is independent of exterior colour'. The fact that this 'chief' had raised 'the black standard' in Saint-Domingue was nothing less than a 'revolution', which was a matter of celebration for 'all liberal Britons': 'every virtuous man will rejoice to hear that the black race are now acknowledged as brothers'.[118] This was a somewhat rosy account of what had transpired between Toussaint and Maitland, and as we shall see there were many in the British political and military establishment who remained implacably opposed to the Saint-Domingue revolution. But the *Gazette* piece demonstrated the growing strength of the black general's appeal among enlightened British opinion.

The struggle between Toussaint and Hédouville illustrated the versatility of the revolutionary leader's power. Hédouville believed that he could achieve his mission to contain Toussaint and begin the disarmament of the black army by relying on the classic means available to a high-ranking representative of the French state with significant military experience to boot: he had, after all, helped bring the peasants of the Vendée to heel. Indeed, he was a white man. What chance could a former black slave, plagued by his 'extreme ignorance',[119] stand against such obvious superiorities? Yet Toussaint overpowered his adversary, and did so because he was much more imaginative and resourceful in his use of power. His summary of Hédouville's failure was that he was 'not doing well' ('li va pas bien') and would have done better to 'bend low in order to rise high, rather than rise high but fall flat'.[120] This was a typically shrewd observation: it reflected Toussaint's philosophy of moving forward in small steps, as well as his belief that power had to be exercised with finesse, coercive force only being deployed as a last resort.

This subtlety shines through the twenty-seven-page report Toussaint sent to the Directory shortly after Hédouville's flight from the colony. It was a powerful piece of Louverturian prose, combining fastidious attention to detail, forcefulness and more than a touch of bravado. He strenuously rejected any responsibility for the shambolic events of the previous weeks, and even began by asking for an 'honourable retirement' from his functions. He claimed to have played no part in the unrest in Cap and the plantations, and that 'no agent of the French government had received stronger support' from him than Hédouville. He feigned to be 'pained' by news that the large crowd of protesters was marching on the city, and 'surprised' that Hédouville and his entourage had been preparing to sail away from the colony. The French authorities would certainly not have been fooled by this protestation of innocence, but Toussaint's ensuing point was harder to dispute: the turmoil in Saint-Domingue had been provoked primarily by Hédouville's moral and political failings over the preceding months – notably his attempt to challenge Toussaint's military authority, his incapacity to understand local sensitivities and his 'despotic' behaviour towards loyal administrative officials, many of whom had been removed without consulting him. Hédouville's 'aristocratic' prejudices were also censured, notably his tendency to receive ordinary citizens who came to petition him with 'revolting rancour' ('aigreur repoussante').

After this rebuke to the Directory for sending a manifestly incompetent official to Saint-Domingue came the real sting: Toussaint cast the whole episode as a rearguard action to challenge black power in the name of white supremacy. He reminded the French authorities of the 'widespread alarm' provoked in the colony by Vaublanc's 'liberticidal speech' in 1797, and suggested that Hédouville had sought to follow in his tracks – notably by introducing an agricultural reform which was specifically shaped by Vaublanc's racist ideas. Toussaint quoted a passage in Hédouville's speech about the need to 'make the blacks remain on the plantations' (although he did not of course mention that he had quietly encouraged Hédouville in the matter); the labour reform was perceived by black plantation workers as 'the chains of a new form of slavery'. The report also made a number of references to the anti-royalist coup of 18 Fructidor, and portrayed Hédouville as a man who shared the plotters' ambitions.

In Saint-Domingue, Hédouville had attempted systematically to sow the seeds of division among black, white and mixed-race communities: by casting doubt on the patriotism of black officers in his army; by persecuting black officials in the administration; by challenging Toussaint's decision to grant an amnesty to the black gunners from the Dessources regiment who had been trained by the British, because he judged they could serve the republic honourably (at the same time allowing Rigaud to recruit such soldiers for his southern army); by seeking significantly to reduce the number of black soldiers, so that Saint-Domingue's defence would be provided by a 'purely European' army; and by slandering Toussaint as someone who had 'sold himself' to the British, and inventing false stories about his desire for independence, including the claim that in all the territories he controlled it was not the tricolour which flew on official buildings but his own personal standard, 'a white banner with a negro head' – an insult to Toussaint's 'honour'.[121] Any such action would of course be treasonous, Toussaint added, before pointedly observing that 'the black people are strong enough to defeat any conspiracy' – a coded but clear warning to the Directory that any further attempt to disarm his military force would be met with fierce resistance.

Yet the ultimate aim of the report was not to confront his French superiors, but to reassure them. Throughout the crisis he had done his utmost to prevent any serious threat to the security of persons and properties: no civilian blood had been spilled. In fact, Toussaint's report played up the 'constitutional' route taken by the plantation workers as they channelled their grievances through their municipal institutions – a canny way of suggesting that Hédouville was rejected not by Toussaint, but by the people and their elected representatives. The report claimed that both the municipal officers and the protesters had been acting according to republican principles, within the spirit of the French constitution. This emphasis on the legitimate functions of municipal government in times of crisis culminated in Toussaint's instruction that the Cap municipality should 'fully assume civil authority' now that Hédouville had departed.[122] This, too, was typical of Toussaint's more general approach, which was to further his revolutionary cause as much as possible from within official institutions; he emphasized this point to his supporters in Paris, notably in the French legislature, and specifically denied harbouring any ambitions for 'independence'.[123]

Toussaint was walking a tightrope, without doubt, but no one was more skilled at doing so than 'the virtuous commander-in-chief', as his supporters called him.[124] An anonymous report sent to the French government from Saint-Domingue shortly after Hédouville's departure noted that Toussaint's hold over the population was like 'a form of magic power': the colony was now clearly under his spell. This force could be used 'either to contain it, or to push it towards revolution'. Yet, it concluded, for all his flaws, Toussaint remained 'the only man who could guarantee that the colony remains in French hands'.[125]

6
Virtuous Citizens

The successful mobilization of Toussaint's supporters from the plantations in the final stages of his confrontation with Hédouville was anything but fortuitous. Saint-Domingue's slave revolution brought with it a thriving pattern of popular democratic activity which expressed itself in citizens' assemblies, plantation brotherhoods and networks of former *marron* slaves, often organized in small militia bands in the inland and more remote mountainous regions of Saint-Domingue. In the later 1790s this grass-roots tradition was still alive, and while it remained broadly supportive of Toussaint, especially in his conflicts with the French authorities and his battle against dissident factions, it was an independent social force which was never entirely under his control.

Partly for this reason, and also because of the low level of urbanization, Toussaint sought to develop his own networks across the colony. He understood – probably better than anyone else – the natural divisions between the north, the west and the south, and his compatriots' very particular territorial allegiances, which could at times spark fierce rivalries between neighbouring communities: he understood that, in post-revolutionary Saint-Domingue, politics was largely local in character. Seemingly parochial conflicts could very rapidly escalate into larger crises, as had occurred during the clashes at Fort-Liberté in 1798. In any event, building a secure base among local populations chimed naturally with his instincts as a leader: his painstaking attention to detail, his remarkable ability to remember individual names and situations, and his spiritual ties with the physical geography of Saint-Domingue. His closeness to the elements was one of the defining features of his character, making him, in the eyes of those who worked closely with him, 'the extraordinary man of the Caribbean, formed by Nature to govern the remarkable people whose leader he has become'.[1] His mobility, too, was legendary. He was constantly on the move – whether it was on scheduled *tournées* across regions, flying trips to localities to deal with disturbances, inspect specific sites or make impromptu visits to individuals; he once travelled from Gonaïves to Cap, a distance of thirty *lieues* (ninety miles) in twelve hours, riding continuously from three in the morning; news of his unexpected arrival produced large crowds at his house.[2] Announcements of his impending visit to a locality would provoke great excitement and trigger a wave of festive preparations in his honour, including the production of easily chewable foods such as sponge cakes, to help with the loss of his front teeth.[3]

Toussaint's critics believed that his authority was grounded exclusively on military force, his extensive powers of patronage and his ability to inspire an almost religious form of devotion among his followers. This messianic aura was particularly emphasized by his adversaries: in the words of the French general Pamphile de Lacroix: 'his soldiers viewed him as an extraordinary man, and the plantation workers worshipped him as a divinity'.[4] Yet there was much more to Toussaint's appeal than his power to inspire fear or fetishistic loyalty. From the outset his strategy was to co-opt various territorial groups and at the same time draw on existing social and political institutions, from Church officials and members of the National Guard to municipal administrators – a very republican enterprise, anchored in his belief in the natural goodness of man and the ideal of fraternity. But it was also a creole republicanism, a unique combination of European, African and indigenous elements.

This melange was most lavishly expressed in local festive celebrations in his honour, which were colourful displays of collective enthusiasm, tributes to Toussaint's power, and proof of the new social order, appealing to all the citizens of Saint-Domingue. The ceremonies often brought together civil and religious authorities, as when Toussaint entered the liberated Port-Républicain for the first time in 1798, shortly after the departure of the British. He was greeted on the outskirts of town by a huge crowd of finely attired men and women, led by the clergy, carrying crosses, thuribles and banners. He was invited to walk under a canopy carried by four of the town's most affluent white planters: he refused, stating that such an honour should be reserved only for a deity.[5] But there was no escaping the tribute these dignitaries had planned for him: after marching through a succession of triumphal arches which had been erected along his path into the town centre, Toussaint was met by the municipal authorities, who solemnly welcomed him as the liberator of Saint-Domingue and handed him a medal bearing the inscription 'After God, it is him'.[6]

It was an exquisite moment. This very slogan used to be chanted in Makandal's honour by his supporters at the height of their *vodou* ceremonies when they planned to eliminate the white planters of Saint-Domingue by poison: now it had been symbolically appropriated and transferred to their new hero.[7] This reincarnation of Makandal appealed equally to Catholic and Caribbean sensibilities, and at the same time to the more cerebral aspects of republican rationalism. Toussaint's approach to local politics fitted entirely with his style, which was progressively to adapt existing institutions to his own purposes and exploit opportunities to create new political arrangements over time. Hence one of his favourite kreyol sayings: 'doucement allé loin'.[8]

The methods Toussaint used to rally these local communities were varied and imaginative. One such group was the Freemasons. There is no evidence that Toussaint himself was a Mason, but his flamboyant signature included a standard Masonic symbol in the age of revolution: two slanted bars with three dots between them. His former boss Bayon de Libertat was a Masonic dignitary in Cap, whose lodges were particularly active in the decade before the revolution;[9] and the basic values of Freemasonry – solidarity, discretion, fraternity and charity – very much overlapped with his own. The membership list of the Port-Républicain lodge 'La Réunion Désirée à l'Orient' reveals that a number of his close associates were active Freemasons: among them were his brother Paul, who was the lodge's master of ceremonies, as well as Christophe Huin, the military commander of Port-Républicain and one of Toussaint's trusted subordinates; also affiliated to this lodge were many of his supporters among the white administrative, legal, commercial and plantation elites.[10] Toussaint's own entourage contained several officials from Gascony, notably his secretaries Pascal and Dupuis, his interpreter Nathan and Lacoste, the chief medical officer in the colony (whom Hédouville had tried to fire); many of these men were affiliated to Masonic networks. And one of his most ardent admirers among Saint-Domingue's administrative hierarchy was the engineer Charles Vincent, also a fervent Freemason.[11] So even though he may not himself have been a Freemason, Toussaint was surrounded by men who were, and he found ways of drawing upon their network to support his leadership and promote his goals and values.

Toussaint's local political style was most strikingly on display in his stronghold of Gonaïves, from which he had expelled the Spaniards. He rebuilt the town completely, paving its principal streets, widening its canal and embellishing its main buildings. After the departure of Laveaux in 1796, Toussaint turned the Gonaïves district into 'a more or less independent enclave' under his political and military command.[12] He ensured that the administration was staffed with loyal and competent men, and kept a very close eye on the deliberations of the municipal council. He also built strong and enduring ties with wealthy business figures such as Cazes, an opulent merchant (also known as 'Gros-Cazes'), who became one of his financial advisors and most dependable envoys (he was the man sent to Paris to deliver Toussaint's 22 Brumaire an VII report on the Hédouville episode).[13] Toussaint established his headquarters in an *habitation* in the nearby commune of Ennery, leased to him by Madame Descahaux, who hailed from one of the most powerful white families of the colony.[14] This legendary site, renowned for its long alleys, fragrant rose gardens and the splendour of its principal house, was Toussaint's favourite retreat: a secluded spot where he held secret meetings, both with his own agents and with foreign emissaries; a centre of military operations, where officers from across Saint-Domingue came to receive their instructions; and a base from which he managed the restoration of the colony's plantations.[15] It was also a court where he organized cultural evenings and social gatherings. He took 'ineffable pleasure' in the performance of music, especially military music, and often called on his trumpeters and drummers to play for him immediately after supper.[16]

Toussaint received visitors in his *grands cercles* (meetings by invitation) and *petits cercles* (public audiences) with 'politeness, grace and dignity', be they administrators, colonists, captains of American and Danish ships, planters or tradesmen. Here those who had fallen on hard times, in particular former white émigrés, could tearfully plead their case directly with the commander-in-chief.[17] One of his local visitors in the late 1790s described him as 'of a manly form, above the middle stature, with a countenance bold and striking, yet full of the most prepossessing suavity – terrible to an enemy, but inviting to the objects of his friendship or his love'. His outfit was always the same for these occasions: 'a kind of blue jacket, with a large red cape falling over the shoulders; red cuffs, with eight rows of lace on the arms, and a pair of large gold epaulettes thrown back; scarlet waistcoat and pantaloons, with half boots; round hat, with a red feather, and a national cockade'.[18]

From 1796 onwards Toussaint's position was strengthened when a string of his candidates obtained positions as surveyors, priests, medical officers, gendarmes and justices of the peace.[19] He constantly interceded with successive French agents and national authorities in Paris on behalf of his various protégés: for example, he wrote to the Minister of Navy asking that the son of one of the 'virtuous' citizens of Port-de-Paix, Granville, be admitted to the Institut National in Paris, where his own son Isaac and stepson Placide were studying. Granville was a mixed-race man of modest means who was the tutor of Toussaint's youngest son,

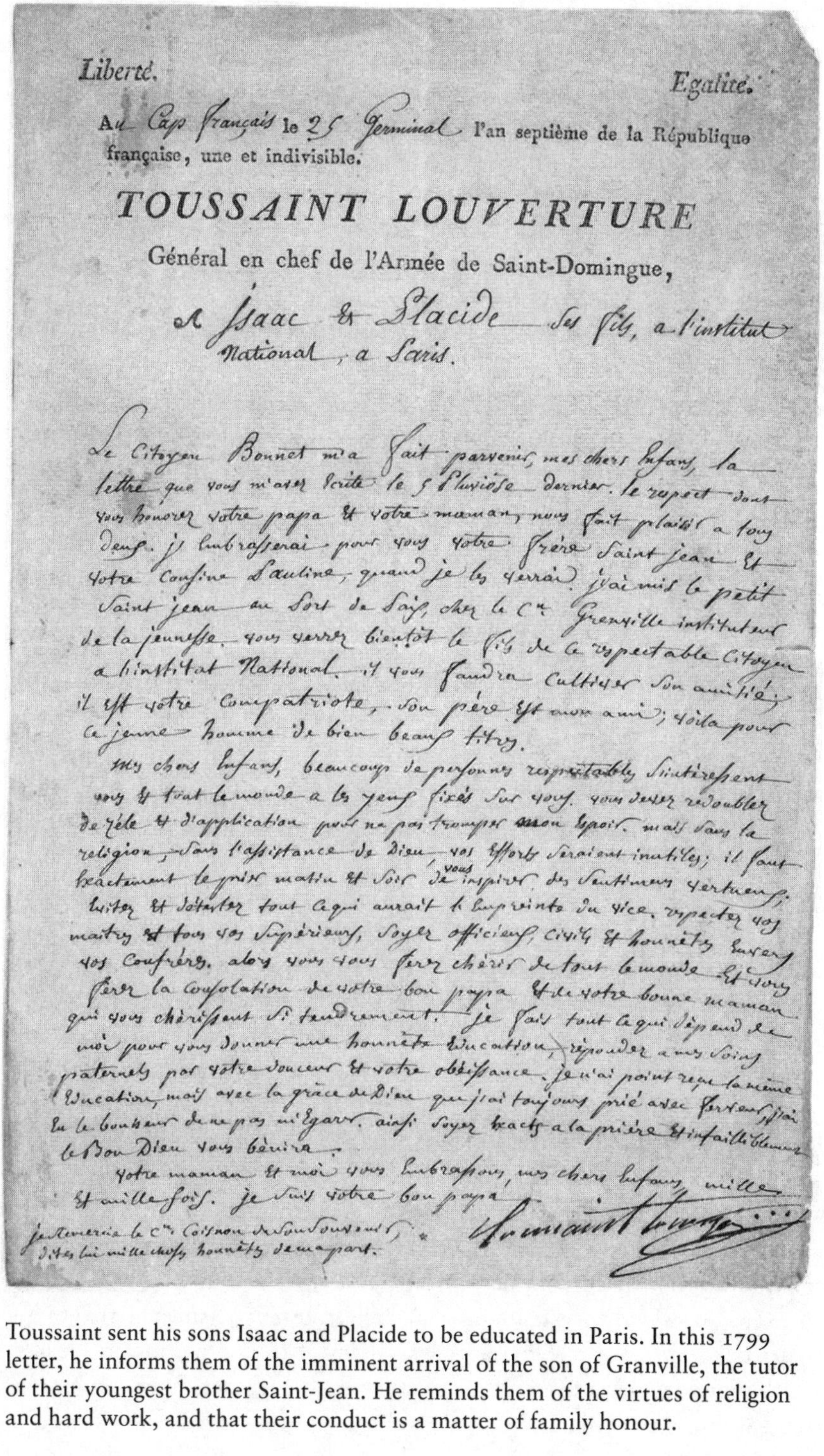

Liberté. Egalité.

Au Cap français le 25 Germinal l'an septième de la République française, une et indivisible.

TOUSSAINT LOUVERTURE

Général en chef de l'Armée de Saint-Domingue,

A Isaac & Placide ses fils, a l'institut National, a Paris.

Le Citoyen Bonnet m'a fait parvenir, mes chers Enfans, la lettre que vous m'avez écrite le 5 Pluviôse dernier. le respect dont vous honorez votre papa & votre maman, nous fait plaisir a tous deux. j'embrasserai pour vous votre frère Saint jean Et votre Cousine Pauline, quand je les verrai. j'ai mis le petit Saint jean au Port de Paix, chez le Cn Granville instituteur de la jeunesse. vous verrez bientôt le fils de ce respectable Citoyen a l'institut National. il vous faudra cultiver son amitié; il est votre compatriote, son père est mon ami; voila pour ce jeune homme de bien beaux titres.

Mes chers Enfans, beaucoup de personnes respectables s'intéressent a vous & tout le monde a les yeux fixés sur vous. vous devez redoubler de zèle & d'application pour ne pas tromper leur espoir. mais sans la religion, sans l'assistance de Dieu vos efforts seraient inutiles; il faut exactement le prier matin et soir de vous inspirer des sentimens vertueux, éviter et détester tout ce qui aurait l'empreinte du vice. respectez vos maitres et tous vos supérieurs, soyez officieux, civils et honnêtes envers vos confrères. alors vous vous ferez chérir de tout le monde et vous ferez la consolation de votre bon papa et de votre bonne maman qui vous chérissent si tendrement. je fais tout ce qui dépend de moi pour vous donner une honnête éducation, répondez a mes soins paternels par votre douceur et votre obéissance. je n'ai point reçu la même éducation, mais avec la grâce de Dieu que j'ai toujours prié avec ferveur, j'ai eu le bonheur de ne pas m'égarer. ainsi soyez exacts a la prière et infailliblement le Bon Dieu vous bénira.

Votre maman et moi vous embrassons, mes chers Enfans, mille et mille fois. je suis votre bon papa

Toussaint Louverture

Je remercie le Cn Coisnon de ses soins pour vous, dites lui mille choses honnêtes de ma part.

Toussaint sent his sons Isaac and Placide to be educated in Paris. In this 1799 letter, he informs them of the imminent arrival of the son of Granville, the tutor of their youngest brother Saint-Jean. He reminds them of the virtues of religion and hard work, and that their conduct is a matter of family honour.

Saint-Jean;[20] many of the leading black military commanders also sent their children to him.[21] Toussaint also paid close attention to the situations of distress in which the women of Saint-Domingue could find themselves, especially if they fell foul of civil and military administrations. In March 1798 he took steps to resolve the problems faced by Madame Flanet, a white resident of La Tortue island with four young children. She was the wife of a former officer who had served in his republican army and had returned to France; in his absence, their property had been occupied by Lesuire, one of the local military commanders. Ordering Lesuire to leave the premises, Toussaint noted that 'in the eyes of the law, the rich and the poor, the individual citizen and the public administrator, are equal, and are equally entitled to protection. So a leader who lends his support to those who find themselves oppressed is only practising this natural law.'[22] These individual gestures of support, repeated countless times, cemented Toussaint's reputation as a compassionate and generous leader, especially among the European *colon* population: as one French administrator noted, the black general was widely admired for his 'extreme humanity towards the white species'.[23]

As he intervened to solve these human problems at a local level, Toussaint's approach was creatively varied: with Madame Flanet, it drew upon republican ideals of equality and fairness. But Toussaint's philosophy was also driven by his highly original creole natural morality, typically rendered in the form of parables. So, for example, when a group of agricultural workers in Grande-Rivière revolted against their white and mixed-race overlords, whom they accused of domineering behaviour, Toussaint rushed from Gonaïves to the site accompanied by a retinue of his white, black and mixed-race officers. Facing the angry workers, many of whom were bearing clubs, rifles and lances, Toussaint defused the situation first by pointing to his officers and extolling the brotherly harmony they embodied. He then poured water into a glass of red wine and held up the mixture to the crowd: in all the towns and villages of the colony, he told them, the people of Saint-Domingue were like this compound, they were bound together organically, could not be separated and were destined to love each other; the use of coloured substances to convey political messages was a Makandalist art, now fully mastered by Toussaint.[24]

In these local homilies Toussaint often stressed the importance of the gentler virtues of compassion and forgiveness, which were integral to his republican value system and his Caribbean mysticism, but also to his Christian faith. Despite the anticlericalism of the revolution in France, Catholicism was a powerful inspiration for Toussaint, both personally (he saw to it that his children were brought up according to Catholic teachings) and in the civic regeneration of Saint-Domingue. Here, too, he carefully developed powerful networks which spread outwards from his Gonaïves fief. He exchanged letters with Abbé Grégoire in France, in which he occasionally complained about the anticlericalism of French envoys to Saint-Domingue.[25] He also cultivated strong links with the ecclesiastical hierarchy in his parish, and through them with the Catholic clergy across the colony. Every Sunday Toussaint would travel from Ennery to Gonaïves to attend the religious service, accompanied by his senior military officers and escorted by a detachment of his guides. He sometimes used a carriage but generally preferred to ride on horseback, which allowed him to race his guides to the destination. Needless to say, he always arrived before them.[26]

Toussaint had a number of chaplains who served on his staff, notably his confessors Antheaume and Molière, who were also his councillors. He entrusted them with important missions, including carrying his personal messages to military and civil authorities[27] – a practice which led some of his sworn enemies in Saint-Domingue and in France (notably, as we saw earlier, Sonthonax) to accuse him of being under undue clerical influence. But this was just a crude anticlerical and racialist stereotype which misunderstood Toussaint's view of the educative and social functions of religion. He maintained a sizeable network of female religious aides in strategic positions across the colony: the duties of these *aumonières* were to distribute charitable assistance to needy citizens (in particular to the indigent, women with large families, and wounded soldiers), and to teach catechism to young children. They were drawn from across the racial spectrum and were known throughout Saint-Domingue as much for their religious zeal as for their fervour for their beloved commander-in-chief: they included Madame Balthasar, a formidable black eminence from Cap; Madame Gariadete, a white lady of considerable means from Terre-Neuve; and Miss Nanete from Marmelade, a *mulâtresse* who tirelessly rode through her district on horseback ferrying food, drink and medical supplies to those in need.[28] Another key member of this female brigade was Madame Marie Fanchette, a black freedwoman married to Toussaint's treasurer, Joseph Bunel; rumoured to be one of Toussaint's former mistresses,[29] she was widely known as the 'protector of the poor' in Cap.[30]

Toussaint's religiosity was a combination of spiritual idealism and temporal self-interest. As we saw earlier, he was fully immersed in *vodou* culture and mythology and was widely believed to call upon the divination services of its priests, who acted as soothsayers, foretelling his future. His local speeches could deploy *vodou* notions whenever necessary, both to make serious points but also, on occasion, in jest; he often used to joke that he had picked up his nasal voice from a houngan's spell which had prevented him from speaking through his mouth.[31] He truly believed in the Christian virtues, and frequently composed his own prayers, which he declaimed at the altar during Mass.[32] He was sincere when he claimed that his political and military triumphs were guided by the Almighty. When he was appointed commander-in-chief of the army he declared that he was an 'instrument of God's power' and that his soldiers were executors of His 'vengeance'.[33] Likewise, in his victory proclamation after the British evacuation of Saint-Domingue he credited his success to the 'God of warriors', adding that 'man can achieve nothing without the assistance of his Creator'.[34]

He also understood the healing potential of religion in a colony which had been ravaged by slavery and war, pragmatically appreciating the importance of Catholicism as a source of discipline and social order. He intervened with municipal authorities to ensure that priests could practise their cult without undue constraints,[35] and regularly told his soldiers that their first duty (before even their service to their native soil) was to 'honour God'.[36] He gave instructions that all battalion commanders should lead their troops in prayer twice a day, in the morning and in the evening, and that the troops should be taken to Mass on Sundays fully kitted out and 'in the best possible order'.[37] Asked why he insisted on taking his officers with him to church, he replied that he hoped that the prayers and religious hymns would teach them 'to love and adore God, and also to fear Him'; he added, no doubt with a twinkle in his eye: 'and so that they might learn better to follow military discipline'.[38]

This was one of Toussaint's leitmotifs when he harangued his soldiers and officers: 'refer all your actions to the true principles of divinity and religion; and so, just as a commander demands the obedience of his subordinates, every mortal must bend before divine power'. Toussaint hoped that his virtuous military, through their example, could encourage the men and women of Saint-Domingue to abide by the teachings of the Gospels, and so serve the public interest. As he addressed his soldiers in May 1797: 'adore God and be irreproachable in your practice of religion: this will then inspire all the men and women of the colony, from the landowners to the agricultural workers, to be good citizens'.[39]

Alongside his Masonic, charitable and religious networks, Toussaint's support relied heavily on municipal institutions, which he described as representatives of the 'common good', guardians of the constitution and of the law, and guarantors of 'wisdom, prudence and tranquillity'.[40] He took advantage of municipal ceremonies directly to address local populations, and outline his hopes for Saint-Domingue's social and economic regeneration. One such gathering took place on the outskirts of the north-western coastal town of Môle Saint-Nicolas in October 1798. The inhabitants had just been liberated from British rule after the armistice negotiated between Toussaint and Maitland, and he used the occasion to plant a tree of liberty. He constructed his entire dedication speech around the tree – a rhetorical gambit which also enabled him to pepper his intervention with allusions to the *vodou loa* Gran Bwa (Great Wood), the guardian spirit of the sacred forest.

For Toussaint, the 'sacred sapling' of Môle Saint-Nicolas represented the accession of men and women of all ages, occupations and colours to 'the beautiful title of citizen'. Equating Frenchness with liberty, Toussaint further reminded his audience that liberation from British rule had brought them emancipation from 'the bonds of slavery'. He paid a glowing tribute to his soldiers, many of whom were in attendance from the nearby garrison, for their 'valiance and intrepidity' in this heroic struggle. But this was no time for empty triumphalism, and Toussaint pointedly reminded his fighters that he expected them to be, like him, bearers of the virtues of abnegation and selflessness. Nor were they to expect material rewards for their success on the battlefield, but rather the 'generous satisfaction' of seeing the former slaves of Môle Saint-Nicolas as free men and women, safely gathered around the tree of liberty.[41]

At the same time, the freedom symbolized by the tree of liberty was not just about the enjoyment of rights, but also the assumption of responsibilities. Those who had been part of the old order in town – the militia members who had fought for the occupying forces or the planters and merchants who had worked with the British, or even been involved in the buying and selling of slaves – had a duty to 'repent genuinely' for their past errors, and 'sincerely' pledge to follow the righteous path of republican virtue. This included all the French nationals who had been denounced as émigrés by the republican authorities, and who were generously granted an amnesty by Toussaint. The time for disunity was over: appealing to the ideals of 'concord' and 'fraternity', Toussaint invited these new French citizens to 'be of one heart, one soul, and to bury for ever at the foot of this sacred tree, the symbol of freedom, all our ancient divisions'. Again, the reference to Grand Bwa would have been obvious to most of the black citizens present: like the *loa*, the republican tree was a symbol of healing and protection. But to the former slaves, too, Toussaint had a special message, which he would almost certainly have uttered in kreyol to make sure it was clearly understood: 'may the sight of this tree remind you that freedom cannot exist without labour'. He followed this with one of his leitmotifs: 'without cultivation, there is no commerce; and without commerce, there is no colony'.[42]

With its effective blend of creole and republican elements, Toussaint's Môle Saint-Nicolas speech excitingly outlined his vision for Saint-Domingue's future, and the role he expected local communities to play in shaping it. It offered the promise of civil peace, the healing of past wounds in the name of national reconciliation, and the security and protection of equal rights for all citizens, whether they were men or women; white, mixed-race or black; landowner, merchant or labourer; from the north, the west or the south. But it was also a demanding prospect, as Toussaint made clear that rights came with political, moral and economic duties, and that he expected the citizens of his virtuous republic to live up to them.

From the outset, Toussaint paid special attention to the activities of municipal institutions. His correspondence with Laveaux from 1794 onwards contains regular updates about areas which had come under republican control: in 1795, for example, he informed the governor that he had summoned the citizens of Mirebalais to elect their municipal representatives.[43] The proper functioning of assemblies was one of his constant preoccupations, and as one of Saint-Domingue's best-informed memorialists wrote, it was in his 'private correspondence' with local administrative bodies that 'the secrets of Toussaint's power resided'.[44] Key members of municipal assemblies, such as Sanon Desfontaines in Gonaïves, were used to maintain Toussaint's links with local political dignitaries, and sometimes even travelled to France to deliver the commander-in-chief's messages to his metropolitan allies.[45]

Toussaint kept in close touch with the colony's local officials, who provided him with detailed information about social and political incidents, gossip and rumours. He scrupulously read the records of municipal councils, starting with those of Gonaïves, and regularly asked regional military commanders to keep him updated about the conduct of Assembly meetings.[46] Even though the regulation of municipalities was technically a matter for the French agent in Saint-Domingue and not the army, Toussaint's commanders effectively supervised the operations of local assemblies, as reflected in a proclamation addressed to municipal administrations in late 1798. Signed by Toussaint's senior military figures, it urged local officials to throw their full weight behind Toussaint's leadership, reminding them that he had constantly 'fought for their liberties'.[47] Toussaint also often intervened to offer his views on issues ranging from the performance of individual officers and the appointment of clergymen and interpreters to the reconstruction of towns, the clearing of canals and rivers, the mooring of boats, the exact specifications of the redesign of quay areas, the layout of streets and the issuing of passports to local inhabitants.

In moments of political turbulence, Toussaint also addressed municipal officers directly: during the 1796 attempted coup against Laveaux, for example, he asked the Cap Assembly members to warn the inhabitants not to support the 'cabal' which was attempting to undermine the republic.[48] When he heard that the municipality of Verrettes was spreading 'perfidious' information, he denounced them.[49] A few years later he summoned eighty local officials from Cap and the surrounding neighbourhoods to his home and upbraided them for not implementing his decrees with sufficient zeal;[50] he also dealt with requests from local assemblies to be exempted from specific administrative regulations.[51] His interventions provide glimpses of some of his major social and economic policies: his ordinance of December 1794, addressed to the commune of Gros-Morne, insisted that local agriculture should not be dominated by 'selfish interests', and invited the military commander of the region to 'take all necessary measures to hold the labourers on the plantations, so that they may endeavour to restore the colony to prosperity';[52] this was exactly the objective he sought to pursue on a general scale in the later 1790s.

Saint-Domingue's local government was a pyramidal system. Municipal officers were appointed for each commune by an assembly of local citizens. These councillors were drawn from among the propertied classes, and Toussaint was always active behind the scenes to ensure that the men chosen were favourable to the post-revolutionary order; mayors of important localities in the north and west of the colony, such as Bernard Borgella in Port-Républicain, were generally his close allies. Toussaint also understood that it was vital to recruit competent and public-spirited men from local communities. This was no easy matter given the turbulent history of Saint-Domingue since 1791, and especially the political and racial conflicts of the early revolutionary years. He summed up what he saw as the appropriate moral qualities for these officers:

> wise, honest, and progressive men, whose first passion is a devotion to the republic, to humanity and to freedom; citizens without prejudices, commendable as much for their reason as for their sense of virtue; enlightened, but open to receiving constructive ideas from their fellow citizens, and helping to translate them into measures which might be of profit to the common good; impervious to intrigue and corruption, and determined to eschew, at least for the duration of their honourable mandates, the petty passions which dull the collective spirit and debase the community.[53]

Les Généraux & Chefs de Brigade de divers Régimens Coloniaux des parties du *Nord*, *Est* & *Ouest* de Saint-Domingue, tant en leurs noms qu'en ceux des Officiers, Sous-Officiers & Soldats deſdits Régimens.

Aux Administrateurs Municipaux des divers Départements de Saint-Domingue.

CITOYENS MAGISTRATS,

SI les défenſeurs de la Patrie ont des inquiétudes ; ſi les atteintes réitérées que l'on porte à leur liberté & à celle de leurs frères les cultivateurs, leur font craindre pour elle, à qui doivent-ils s'adreſſer ? Dans le ſein de qui peuvent-ils épancher les chagrins qu'ils éprouvent ? Dans celui des Magiſtrats du Peuple, qui doivent, par la place qu'ils occupent, non ſeulement les raſſurer, mais encore déjouer les projets liberticides des oppreſſeurs, par des meſures ſages & fermes.

C'eſt aux Magiſtrats du Peuple à être leur organe & l'interprête de leurs ſentimens auprès du Directoire exécutif, lorſque le ſalut public l'exige. Oui, citoyens Magiſtrats, non-ſeulement le bonheur du Peuple de Saint-Domingue exige de vous que vous rendiez au Directoire, compte de la conduite de ſes Agens à Saint-Domingue, & de celle des Défenſeurs de la Patrie, mais votre devoir vous en fait la loi. Comme Magiſtrats du Peuple, vous êtes ſa ſentinelle, & comme chefs de la force armée, nous ſommes la vôtre ; & la loi nous ordonne de maintenir votre autorité. Que l'amour de la liberté vous anime ! embouchez ſans partialité la trompette de la vérité, & dévoilez ſans crainte, aux yeux du Directoire, la perfidie de ſes Agens. Si vous teniez, dans cette circonſtance, une conduite puſillanime, vous perdriez la confiance du Peuple, ſans laquelle vous ne pouvez parvenir à rendre, à Saint-Domingue, ſa tranquillité. Si, au contraire, toujours vrais, vous développez cette mâle énergie qui doit caractériſer toutes vos actions, en conſervant la confiance du Peuple, vous concourrerez ſans peine, au bonheur de cette infortunée Colonie ; rendus à eux-mêmes, les cultivateurs s'adonneront à leurs travaux agreſtes, & les militaires concourront, de leur côté, à faire reſpecter votre autorité & chérir les Lois bienfaiſantes de la République.

Prenez en main la balance de la juſtice, & vous verrez que notre conduite n'avoit pour but que le maintien de la liberté & le déſir de rendre à la France, ſes poſſeſſions. Que celle des Agens, au contraire, ne tendoit qu'à anéantir la liberté, & à priver la France de ſes Colonies.

Que l'homme impartial, ami de la liberté, analyſe la conduite que nous avons tenue, les ſervices que nous avons rendus depuis l'époque où la France, nous rendant nos droits politiques, que la cupidité & la ſoif de l'or nous avoient ravis, nous reçut au nombre de ſes enfans, & il verra que jamais nous n'avons trahis la Mère-Patrie.

Ayant à cette époque, à notre tête le Brave Général en Chef TOUSSAINT LOUVERTURE, n'avons nous pas combattu ſans relâche les ennemis de la liberté ? Sans ſecours, ſans moyens, ſans d'autres armes que celles que nous prîmes ſur l'ennemi, ne ſcûmes nous pas conſerver notre liberté & défendre nos droits ? n'eſt-ce pas à nos bras, à l'expérience de notre Général, à notre valeur & à celle des Soldats, que nous dûmes les conquêtes multipliées que nous fîmes ſur l'Eſpagnol & les Anglais ? qu'elles reſſources avions nous ? Qu'elles étoient alors nos moyens ? Aucun;

Signed by Toussaint's senior military figures, this proclamation was addressed to municipal administrations in late 1798. It urged local officials to throw their weight behind Toussaint's leadership, reminding them that he had constantly 'fought for their liberties'.

Cependant, supportant, à l'exemple du chef qui nous commande, toutes les fatigues & les privations, endurant la faim & la soif, nous sçûmes par notre persévérance & celle des soldats de la République, non seulement atterrer la puissance Anglaise, mais nous parvînmes à l'expulser pour jamais du sol de la Liberté.

La conduite du Général en Chef, la nôtre, & la valeur de nos soldats, méritoient, à n'en pas douter, la sollicitude de l'Agent du Gouvernement : Nous devions espérer la tranquillité à laquelle nous soupirons depuis si longtems; l'éloignement des Anglais devoit nous la faire espérer; en Officiers d'honneur, nous ne demandions pour toutes récompense que l'approbation de l'Agent du Directoire : Et certes nos prétentions étoient bien fondées; aulieu de nous l'accorder, l'Agent HEDOUVILLE, du fond de son cabinet, prépare le deshonneur des Officiers supérieures qui avoient si bien défendu la cause de la liberté, & trame l'assassinat des défenseurs de la patrie.

Un Général recommandable par son amour pour la liberté, qui a répandu son sang pour la défendre; qui perdit un oeil en combattant pour elle, est destitué, mis hors de la loi. La majeure partie d'un régiment est assassiné, & le vertueux Général en Chef est accusé de viser à l'indépendance; on projette son assassinat. Le deshonneur ou la mort sont la récompense des services qu'il a rendus. Nous nous arrêtons, parce qu'en écrivant, nous frémissons de toutes ces horreurs.

Que ces cruelles vérités vous fassent faire de sérieuses réflexions; qu'elles vous fassent déployer l'énergie nécessaire dans de pareilles circonstances; qu'elle vous oblige à dire la vérité : Car nous ne pouvons, ni ne devons nous le dissimuler; si nous espérons tout du Directoire, nous craignons tout de la perfidie de ses Agens qui nous ont si souvent & si cruellement trompés.

Nous vous supplions donc, au nom de la troupe que nous commandons, & au nom de l'humanité, de donner au Directoire les renseignemens basés sur la vérité, & dictés avec l'énergie qui doit les caractériser : en leur donnant la publicité que nous donnons à la présente, vous repandrés dans nos seins, dans ceux de tous les amis de la liberté, le baume consolateur de la tranquillité, & vous nous prouverés que comme Magistrats du peuple, vous savez défendre ses droits, lors qu'ils sont attaqués. Salut & respect, ont Signé.

Dessaline, général de brigade, Commandant l'arrondissement de Saint-Marc.-Clervaux, Commandant en chef les dépendances du Môle & du Port-de-Paix. — Laplume, général de brigade, Commandant en chef à Léogane — Henry Christophe, chef de brigade, Commandant en chef l'arrondissement du Cap. — Joseph Flaville, *Id.* Commandant en chef de la Cul. — Charles Mauvesin, chef de brigade, Commandant en chef au Port-Français. — Noël Prieur, *Idem*, Commandant à Caracol. — Romain, *Idem*, Commandant au Limbé. — Bodney. *Idem*, Commandant au Borgne. — Jean-Pierre Dumenil, *Idem*, Commandant à Plaisance. — Jean Baptiste Papare, *Idem*, Commandant à la Marmelade. — Vernet, *Idem*, Commandant aux Gonaïves. — Jean-Pierre Imbaud, Commandant au Gros-Morne. — Ignace, chef de bataillon, Commandant à Terre-Neuve. — Julien Audigé, *Idem*, Commandant au Quartier-Louverture. — Roussélot, chef de brigade, du 4e Régiment. — Dominique, Vaillant, Ferbos, chefs de bataillon dudit Régiment. — Adrien Zamor, chef de brigade, du 5e Régiment. — L'Africain & Charles Simon, chefs de bataillon dudit Régiment. — Laurent Bouché, chef de brigade du 6e. Régiment. — Raphaël, chef de bataillon du même Régiment. — Charles Belair, chef de brigade, du 7e Régiment, Commandant à l'Arcahaye. — Alexis & Montauban, chefs de bataillon dudit Régiment. — Christophe Mornet, chef de brigade du 8e Régiment & Commandant en chef l'arrondissement du Port-Républicain. — Pierre-Louis Valet & Pierre-Louis Masson, chefs de bataillon dudit Régiment. — Maurepas, chef de brigade du 9e Régiment Commandant au Port-de-Paix. — Gallard & Baudin, chefs de bataillon dudit Régiment. = Paul Louverture, chef de brigade du 10e Régiment, Commandant en chef l'arrondissement de la Croix-des-Bouquets. = Lacroix, chef de bataillon, du 11e Régiment, Commandant aux Verrettes. - Lafortune, chef d'escadron, Commandant en chef la Gendarmerie de l'Ouest. = Gingembre Trop Fort, Jean-Pierre Pavaut, chefs d'escadron du 1er Régiment de cavalerie.

Pour Copie Conforme,

Port-Républicain, le 19 Frimaire l'an 7e. de la République Française, une & indivisible.

Le Général en Chef.

TOUSSAINT LOUVERTURE.

Toussaint did not believe that 'petty passions' could be altogether excised from municipal life, and his expectations of what officials could achieve by their own devices were tempered by realism. One major concern, for example, was the maintenance of public order in Saint-Domingue's more remote towns and villages, especially in light of an alarming growth of low-level crime in the plantations in the later 1790s. Toussaint sought to contain this problem by relying on gendarme companies, which had been created by Sonthonax in 1796: they were attached to each commune and financed through local tax contributions.[54] Happily, one of the officers from the new corps he encountered was Ferret, the young white man with whom he fought under an orange tree on the Linasse plantation in 1754, and who had now become a senior commander in the gendarmerie. The two men embraced warmly and joked about their teenage adventures.[55] In 1797, as the commander of the Cap gendarmerie, Ferret went to Gonaïves to purchase horses for his unit, and Toussaint gave him advice.[56]

But even though Ferret and his colleagues undoubtedly helped to fight crime, the gendarmes were not numerous enough, and often lacked sufficient familiarity with the local areas where they were posted to maintain security effectively. One of Toussaint's proclamations illustrated both his intimate knowledge of local topography and the creative ways in which he sought to deal with ongoing criminality. Noting that a wave of thefts had been committed in the neighbourhoods of Petite-Rivière, Saint-Michel, Saint-Raphaël, Hinche and Bánica, he observed that the thieves were accustomed to taking their booty on a particular road by Petite-Rivière. He ordered that all citizens travelling on that particular causeway be required to carry valid passports, and that local farmers be given responsibility for ensuring that these travel documents were inspected by the nearest regional military authorities. Ever a stickler for detail, Toussaint entrusted the owners and managers of one particular plantation (the 'habitation Marion') with this duty of public safety; he also specified that the travellers' passports had to include 'the precise description of all the animals in their possession'.[57]

Toussaint sought to nurture a sense of public-spiritedness among the citizenry through the provision of primary schools, a major feature of his republican programme for the social regeneration of Saint-Domingue. He tried to ensure that each locality had a schoolmaster who could teach children to read and write.[58] He consolidated a network of educational institutions, including a central training school for teachers at Cap, thanks to which thousands of young black children between the ages of eight and fifteen were given a state education.[59] A 1799 report to the French government about the extension of education to black plantation workers was a further indication of how these values were taken up and acted upon locally. It turned out that since the revolution it had become common for these labourers to pay three-quarters of a *gourde* from their salaries so that their children could attend school, which they did readily, even though they sometimes had to walk several miles to attend the nearest one. This belief in the absolute value of learning showed how profoundly the former slaves' social attitudes had changed, and how broadly they now embraced Toussaint's ideal of virtuous citizenship.[60]

Local communities also received a series of exhortations from their leader about virtuous social behaviour, which included a sense of solidarity with the soldiers of his revolutionary army. Instances of the advancement of able senior officers were brought to the attention of local communities, as when Colonel Jacques Maurepas was promoted to the rank of brigadier-general: Toussaint despatched his assistant Augustin d'Hébécourt to Môle Saint-Nicolas, where the officer was based, to administer the oath. The ceremony took place in the presence of an enthusiastic local crowd, which heard Maurepas being commended by Toussaint for his 'zeal, patriotism and military talent', as well as his outstanding commitment to 'order, discipline and subordination'.[61] Ongoing military conflicts took a serious toll on Toussaint's republican army, and he periodically appealed to local communities to provide charitable assistance to injured soldiers – notably by requesting donations of old garments which could be used as bandages in hospitals.[62] Be they inveterate idlers, sluggish Assemblymen, insufficiently patriotic citizens, or indeed animals travelling on the road to Petite-Rivière without proper documentation, there was no place for them to hide in Toussaint's virtuous republic.

It is worth pausing here for a moment to consider how Toussaint's ideas for the regeneration of Saint-Domingue were received by the municipal officials. We are able to do so thanks to the survival of a comprehensive collection of *arrêtés* from the municipality of Môle Saint-Nicolas. Dating from 1798 to early 1802 – the final years of Toussaint's rule – these documents provide fascinating glimpses of the ways in which he was perceived and how his social and political philosophy was interpreted by these officials – and also how his injunctions were put into practice.

Situated on a beautiful bay, and blessed with an agreeable climate, Môle Saint-Nicolas was emblematic of the new type of society Toussaint hoped to build in Saint-Domingue. It also illustrates the severe challenges he faced. Môle was a town with few natural resources, whose local economy and urban infrastructure had been seriously damaged by the campaign against the British, with many inhabitants fleeing the town. So much so

Toussaint's fondness for urban design and reconstruction is submitted in accordance with the 'orders and instructions' of

that when Toussaint required all communes to use their local taxes to pay for the upkeep of their gendarmes, the Môle municipal officials met in an extraordinary session and pleaded for an exemption, arguing that such a charge would be too onerous for its finances, which were in a destitute state.[63] Toussaint also needed to keep the trust of local *propriétaires*, and prevent them from leaving the colony; addressing their concerns about their future, he issued a proclamation guaranteeing that they would all be covered by his amnesty, assuring them of 'the full protection of the republic' for themselves and their possessions.[64]

Môle's officials would have been personally vetted by Toussaint prior to their appointment: they were effectively the local relays of his power. Due to the meticulous record-keeping of Môle's municipal clerk, Rochefort – an ardent republican – we have details not only of the precise composition of the council throughout this period, but also of the wider parts of the community from which they were drawn. This broader group is described in a report entitled 'List of persons most capable of managing the affairs

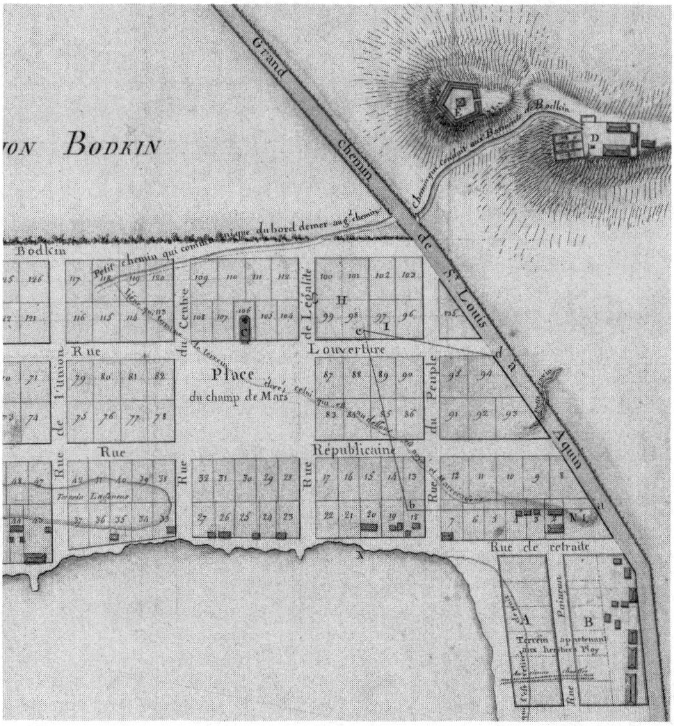

illustrated in this ambitious plan for the coastal town of Aquin, the commander-in-chief in October 1800.

of the commune of the Môle', produced by Rochefort in November 1800 in response to a formal request from the ever-vigilant Toussaint. The list of eighteen names contains details of the occupations of these Môle notables, as well as an evaluation of their moral and political values. Many were men of significant means, such as landowners, merchants and *propriétaires*. There were also two silversmiths, a builder and a health officer. The overwhelming majority (fifteen) were white. Many were typical of the *grands blancs* who had pledged their allegiance to Toussaint across Saint-Domingue: they included the government *commissaire* Pierre Ramadou, the chief justice of the peace, Pierre Prevost, and the president of the council, Joseph Jujardy, a wealthy planter who had earlier served under the British.[65]

Alongside these pillars of the community were a number of *petits blancs*, such as Bourgeau fils, Jacques Roumillat and Guillaume Kanapaux, described by the municipal clerk as 'men of simple lives, whose limited intelligence is compensated by their zeal' (young Bourgeau appears

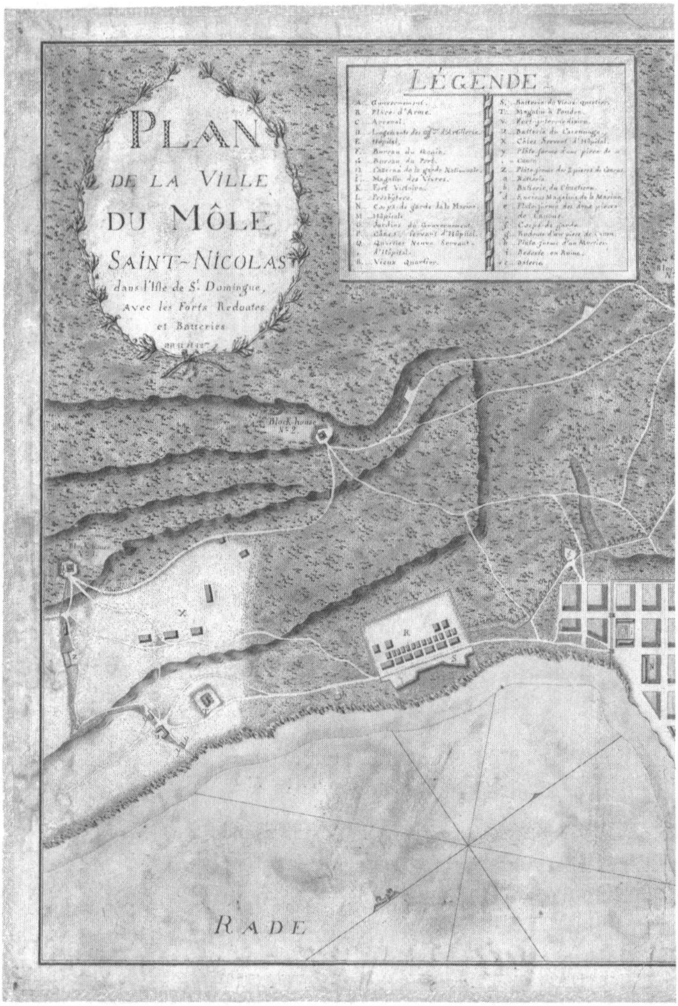

This early-nineteenth-century map of Môle Saint-
the final years of Toussaint's rule, as well as the

elsewhere in the Môle archives as a captain in the National Guard; he was obviously a man who enjoyed physical activity). In the same category were Pierre Noël, an administrative employee who was 'devoted to all good causes', and Barthélémi Boissieu, a *propriétaire* who 'conducted himself in a plausible manner' (not exactly a glowing endorsement: Boissieu had probably compromised himself in his dealings with the British). The two mixed-race councillors, Nicolas Dumai and Charles List, were listed as the only literate persons of colour in the town. The same was true of the sole black municipal councillor, 'citizen Toiny', described as 'the only

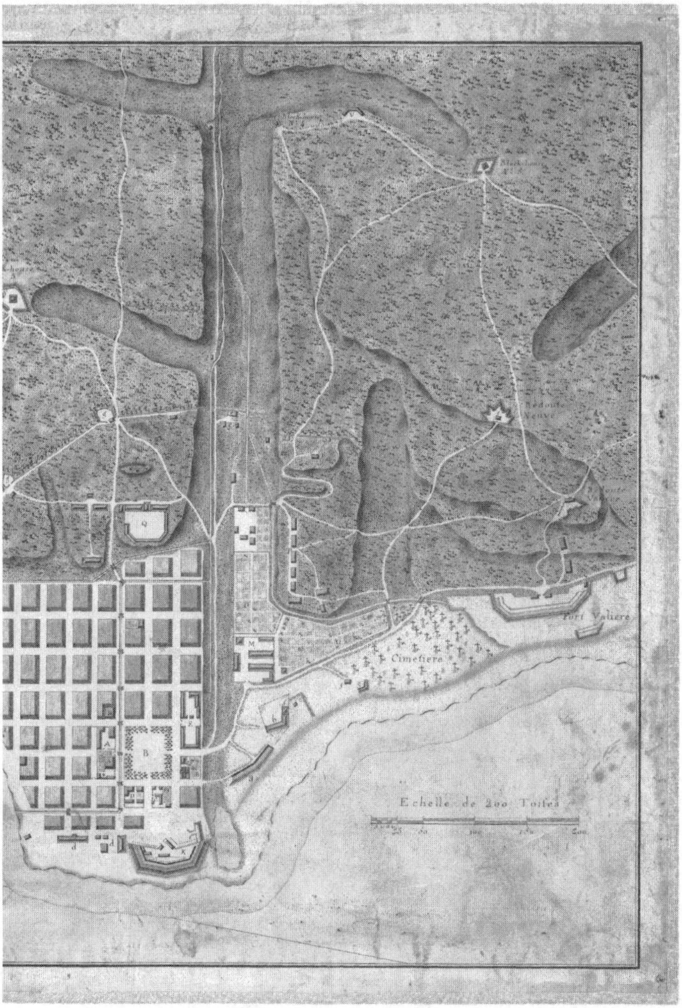

Nicolas shows the reconstruction of the town during recently erected military fortifications.

black man in the Môle who could sign his name' – and indeed his signature, prominently displayed at the end of every municipal *arrêté*, was very flamboyant.[66] The presence of these three men on a predominantly white council demonstrated that Toussaint was aiming to draw talented citizens from all racial groups into public life – but at a measured pace, in keeping with his 'doucement allé loin' motto.

Under the watchful eye of Toussaint's regional military commander Clervaux, the Môle councillors did their best to carry forward Toussaint's mission of civic regeneration. For example, they called a special meeting to endorse one of his general proclamations on the reconciliation of broken marriages, asserting that they saw it as their 'absolute duty' to give the edict the widest possible publicity.[67] But they also provided valuable political support to Toussaint, meeting in August 1800 in another extraordinary session to send a proclamation to the French Minister of Navy celebrating their leader's heroic qualities. The point of this missive, written by Rochefort, was to defend Toussaint against 'calumnies' which were being spread in Paris by his enemies. There can be little doubt that Toussaint encouraged them to send it, to demonstrate to the French government the breadth and resilience of his support in local communities. The piece began by describing him as a providential figure 'who seems to have been brought to this earth to lead his fellow humans'. It then provided an extensive list of Toussaint's exceptional virtues as a leader, before calling on the French government to entrust him with the 'reins of the colony'. Significantly, one of the qualifications singled out was the 'depth of his local knowledge', which was necessary to 'lead a new people, whose habits differ from the customs and traditions of Europe, as does its climate and its scorching sun';[68] this autonomist sentiment would later be used by Toussaint to justify his 1801 constitution.

Môle municipal officials also supported Toussaint's civic project by adopting his rhetoric of republican virtue, as can be appreciated in the annual public commemoration of the abolition of slavery in Saint-Domingue. This anniversary was known as the 'festival of general liberty', and was celebrated on 16 Pluviôse (4/5 February), to mark the French Convention's adoption of the decree abolishing slavery in Paris in 1794. The festival was announced by the Môle municipality in a proclamation which saluted this date as 'the first day of the emancipation of the French Caribbean'. Proceedings began early, at seven in the morning, with a rally of the National Guard in the town's main square; this was followed by a procession of local notables from the municipality to a specially designed 'patriotic altar', on which was inscribed article 18 of the 1793 version of the Declaration of the Rights of Man: 'no man can sell himself or be sold; his person is not an alienable property'. The citizens of Môle were warmly invited to attend the ceremony and to immerse themselves in its atmosphere of 'religious recollection'. To emphasize the solemnity of the occasion, the municipality decreed that all shops, businesses and factories should be closed.[69]

The climax of the ceremony was the speech given by the municipal clerk, Rochefort; the Môle register contains his deliveries on three successive years (1799, 1800 and 1801). These were remarkable pieces of republican oratory in themselves, but they also provide insights into the way Toussaint inspired local officials in their efforts to turn the page from the cruel divisions of the recent past, and harmonize revolutionary transformation with social order. Rochefort's challenge was to present the abolition of slavery as a living revolutionary principle, but not one which was intended to undermine French metropolitan interests, let alone damage the colonial social and political system. He therefore combined a progressive tribute with an idealistic reimagination of the event, opening the way for a vision of Saint-Domingue's future under the enlightened guidance of its commander-in-chief. Inspired by Toussaint's 1798 speech at the outskirts of the town, Rochefort began by equating the abolition of slavery with 'the symbolic tree of liberty', whose branches were 'now fruitfully being deployed across our colony'. The ending of slavery had marked the 'resurrection of a people' through the triumph of the principles of equality and fraternity, and the formation of a united citizenry in Saint-Domingue through the 'destruction of prejudice'.

Having celebrated its universality, Rochefort proceeded to dehistoricize the abolition of slavery and blunt any radical political connotation it might have possessed. He presented 16 Pluviôse not as a process but as a single event; not as the product of the actions of men and women but as a return to a 'natural' state of human perfection; and not as the result of a revolutionary struggle to which the slaves themselves had contributed – the 1791 revolt in Saint-Domingue, which played a decisive role in the abolition of slavery, was completely erased from his narrative. Instead, the act of abolition in 1794 had marked the victory of Enlightenment philosophy, 'the eloquent and courageous voice of Reason'. This, the defining feature of the French spirit, announced the real reason why 16 Pluviôse deserved to be commemorated: it bore witness to France's universal acclamation by the peoples of the world. Swept away by this tide of patriotism, Rochefort could find no geographical limits to the renown of the *grande nation*: 'even the wandering hordes of Arabia speak admiringly of our achievements in their deserts'.

The revolutionary principles of freedom and equality were the necessary basis for an orderly society. Addressing himself directly to the former slaves, his 'brothers and fellow citizens', Rochefort found an ingenious way to reconcile revolutionary change and political stability. He portrayed the end of human bondage as only the first stage in a wider process of social transformation: 'perfect regeneration is not only a function of the destruction of slavery,' he observed, 'it depends also on the necessary practice of all the virtues'. From the ancient splendour of the city states of Greece and Rome all the way down the ages, the republican spirit had flourished through the 'sacred empire of virtue'. The most important of these was a proper appreciation of freedom, which was not to be given 'dangerous extensions', as they could lead only to the 'mad frenzy of its abuse'. Freedom was a 'sacred duty', and it existed only in 'submission to the laws, and subordination to the legitimate authorities, who are charged with ensuring that these norms are religiously respected'.

The perfect symbol of the fusion of revolutionary principles with righteous order was Toussaint Louverture. Rochefort made no mention of the commander-in-chief in his 1799 speech,[70] but he more than made up for this omission in his next two. He hailed him as the 'successor to Spartacus', whose exemplary virtues were those of the archetypal republican hero: he was endowed with 'an indefatigable activity, geared towards the maintenance of social harmony'; 'an innate affection for all men, produced by a sensitive soul'; and 'a virile determination, never deterred by any obstacles'. But Toussaint was also the embodiment of the righteous legislator, giving the colonial system 'a new moral force' and providing a 'firm and zealous movement to our laws'– which was why every republican citizen had an absolute duty to abide by them. Rochefort completed the circle, turning the revolutionary slave into a guardian of the colony's stability and prosperity, and, with a daring rhetorical twist, 'the cherished benefactor of our colonial settlers'.[71]

Môle's officials backed this civic message up with practical recommendations aimed at promoting a sense of collective social responsibility. Toussaint's beliefs regarding the common good were an inspiration here too. For example, Rollin, the commander of the town's National Guard, observed that, in their capacity as 'representatives of the general in chief in the commune', local officials had a duty to promote a broad understanding of 'how to lead a good life'. This was not just a matter of 'passive' obedience of the law, but also an ardent embrace of private virtues: 'for no one can be a good citizen', he said, unless he was also, like Toussaint, 'a good husband, a good father and a good friend'.[72]

An equally robust message was conveyed about education. Soon after the town came under French republican rule, the Môle municipality established its first primary school, 'open to the children of all citizens, without distinction'; a quarter of the intake came from 'indigent' families. The municipal advertisement for the recruitment of the schoolteacher exactly echoed Toussaint's republican vision of the purpose of primary education: 'to preserve children from the dangers of ignorance, and to prepare them for individual happiness and contributing to the collective good'. One of the further tasks of the Môle teacher was to produce a biennial report on his students' progress, 'highlighting those who have distinguished themselves by their conduct and their application'. Toussaint used these municipal reports, which were passed on to him from across Saint-Domingue, to reward good students, the best of whom were sent to France for further studies.[73]

Môle officials also followed Toussaint's lead by inviting the inhabitants of the town to undertake socially responsible, practical civic tasks. The municipality was very keen on public hygiene, calling on citizens to clear the rubbish which piled up around their houses and dispose of it in the ravine outside town;[74] they also insisted on chimneys being regularly cleaned to avoid the risk of fires, which could have devastating consequences for entire neighbourhoods.[75] They regularly appealed for volunteers to clean the canal on the outskirts of the town, in order to remove the debris which obstructed and contaminated the water. A number of *corvées générales* (statute labour for public works) were decreed, with citizens being asked to arrive with their hoes and spades to carry out the work under the supervision of one of the town's civil engineers – not a task for the faint-hearted, especially as volunteers were expected to assemble at six in the morning.[76] The shift in the language used in these proclamations suggests that exhortation alone was not producing sufficient popular mobilization: one of the later edicts warned that 'any person who fails to participate in the *corvée* will be liable to a fine equal to the value of three days' labour'.[77]

Public-hygiene duties were not limited to the people of Môle: in 1800 Toussaint ordered the inhabitants of Cap – of all ages and colours – to participate in the clearing-up of a ravine on the outskirts of town; the penalty for any male who failed to attend was military conscription for a year, although citizens were allowed to buy themselves out.[78] Officials also took measures to curb profiteering by unscrupulous merchants. Prices of basic commodities such as bread, meat and fruit were fixed by the municipality, and a series of decrees warned tradesmen that their produce would be confiscated if they failed to abide by them; it was even specified that seized eggs would be donated to the military hospital, while bananas and figs would be handed to the gendarmes.[79] The latter were obviously the recipients of preferential treatment: another decree warned inhabitants to keep their pigs in their enclosures, adding that if their animals were found roaming around the neighbourhood only their bodies would be returned to their owners: the pigs' heads would be cut off and given to the gendarmerie.[80]

Above all, the municipality sought to back up Toussaint's efforts to promote an ethic of sobriety, taking specific measures to curb the inhabitants' penchant for revelry, which was liable to cause public nuisances. The 'inconsiderate amusement' of hunting at the edge of Môle's town walls was banned because residents were alarmed by the sound of gunshot – a reflection of the ongoing traumatic effects of war on civilian populations across Saint-Domingue.[81] Public houses were forbidden from allowing any gambling on their premises, notably roulette and craps.[82] A decree stipulated that balls were required to close 'two hours after sunset' at the very latest, and, in an obvious effort to contain *vodou* rituals, unauthorized assemblies were banned and citizens were explicitly forbidden from 'dancing before sunrise'. This proposal came more than a year before Toussaint's general ban on *vodou* – another example of how his policies were often tested locally before being decreed across the colony.[83]

Like Toussaint himself, Môle officials found that the appeal to noble sentiments could only go so far, and they increasingly resorted to regulatory measures. A strict regime of controls was imposed over the movement of people: citizens were required to notify their municipality of any foreign visitor, defined as a non-resident of the locality;[84] in an effort to contain the problem of vagrancy, all men and women employed as domestic servants were expected to be registered and issued with a card specifying the name and address of their employer;[85] and, to put an end to the widespread practice of military officers taking up lodgings in town rather than in their barracks (described as 'deeply damaging to order and discipline'), Môle's residents were banned from renting private accommodation to military personnel – a decree which suggested that, away from the battlefield, the iron discipline ascribed to Toussaint's valiant army was not always evident.[86]

Even though he occasionally vented his frustration with municipal officers and local populations, Toussaint knew full well that achieving his wider goals of social regeneration would require patience and forbearance. Asked by the French authorities whether he would recommend a public prosecutor named Fouqueau to serve as mayor of Saint-Marc, he replied: 'I have never thought he was a particularly strong republican, but I have always believed him to be a perfectly honest man.'[87] Fouqueau was brought in to serve on Saint-Marc's appeal tribunal, and was later appointed by Toussaint to a leading position in Saint-Domingue's judiciary. His policy was one of national reconciliation: integrity and competence were more important considerations than ideology or race. Putting it another way in a letter to Christophe about local assemblies, the key point was that their elected members should be 'true friends of liberty': men who recognized the scale of the revolutionary change which had taken place in Saint-Domingue since 1791, and had not only accepted it but reflected it to some extent in their public and private lives.[88]

His promotion of local black officials remained modest. Although councils elected some members of African descent, and a few leading black mayors came to prominence in late-revolutionary Saint-Domingue – notably

Charles-Cézar Télémaque at Cap – Toussaint made little attempt to institute any form of 'black power' among administrative and municipal elites: the example of Môle Saint-Nicolas, with its single black councillor, demonstrated this clearly. Toussaint's approach was to allow leaders of African descent to emerge naturally, while at the same time promoting civil equality and ensuring that surviving racialist mentalities did not go unchallenged. His preferred methods here, as in so many other respects, were persuasion and example. So when he was informed that some *colons* in Port-Républicain were still behaving contemptuously towards black and mixed-race citizens, he organized a musical soirée at which one of his mixed-race aides-de-camp, Captain Coupé, performed alongside Adjutant-General Médard, a black officer who was an accomplished harpist. Entirely funded by Toussaint, the evening was a great success and the guests, who included the town's municipal officers and their wives, returned home in a state of enchantment.[89]

There were, of course, drawbacks to such an approach, notably the disproportionate influence which it allowed traditional white planters and merchants to retain, and the limited scope it gave to the representation of black citizens' interests. This would become a more serious issue in the later years of Toussaint's rule. But, for the moment, and bearing in mind the modest material means available, his municipal policy was an unquestionable success. As with Môle Saint-Nicolas's commemoration of the abolition of slavery, it emphasized that the revolution had fundamentally transformed Saint-Domingue and that this change was irreversible. It brought into the public arena a number of competent men, genuinely dedicated to the common good and to improving the moral and material well-being of their communities; among their notable achievements were the promotion of hygiene, the more effective struggle against petty crime, and the protection of local people from extortionate commercial practices. Perhaps most importantly, Toussaint's municipal institutions gave war-torn and often deeply divided communities their first real glimpse of a peaceful social order. The population of Môle Saint-Nicolas was sharply reminded of this in mid 1799, when a rebellion in the garrison, fomented by dissident forces, briefly brought the town back under hostile control. Mayor Jujardy subsequently reminded his constituents of what they had achieved since the departure of the British, and urged them not to take their communal harmony for granted.[90]

From the perspective of Toussaint's own power, too, this local strategy brought handsome dividends. By 1798, as he expelled the British from the colony, he had built considerable support across all communities: as an observer noted, after following him on one of his galloping tours of the colony, 'the reception the general met in every town and village through which he passed, and at every port he visited, was such as to have gratified the vanity of the proudest potentate'.[91] The Haitian historian Placide David has argued that a key element of Toussaint's appeal to his many mistresses across the colony was the electrifying effect generated by these local appearances, enhanced by his imposing outfits and those of his cavalry guard.[92] Toussaint's trips around Saint-Domingue were such an important feature of his leadership that he even considered purchasing a frigate from the British and using it to speed up his travels still further.[93]

The relationship between Toussaint and the local communities of Saint-Domingue demonstrates the originality of the power system he built there in the late 1790s. As we have noted, Toussaint forged social bonds among the men and women of Saint-Domingue by appealing to a combination of republican and Catholic principles, mingled with his own creole form of natural morality, and colourfully illustrated with his homespun parables. This improvised blend was nonetheless ideologically coherent, for it was driven by his belief in natural goodness and the common good, and held together by the ideal of fraternity. He systematically drew upon notions of brotherhood to promote the values he deemed essential – friendship, solidarity and inter-racial unity; generosity, compassion and forgiveness; selflessness, discipline and industriousness.

It would be excessive to argue that Toussaint's words and deeds alone brought out these sentiments among Saint-Domingue's citizens. But his rhetoric of republican virtue reinforced them and gave them public legitimacy. It is a further measure of his success that the depth of his local support became a self-fulfilling prophecy. Bombarded with letters and proclamations from municipalities celebrating his appeal, French colonial officials adopted the message and began to convey it to their superiors in Paris: as one administrative report to the Directory put it, 'the commander-in-chief has the confidence, respect, and love of nine-tenths of the population'.[94] There was also a perceptible shift over time in Toussaint's local image, which followed his evolution in the 1790s from revolutionary hero to founding father. During official festivities organized in Saint-Domingue's towns and villages, he was still frequently cast as a modern Spartacus – the emblem of black emancipation, the liberator of the homeland and the embodiment of the warrior virtues of bravery and indefatigability.[95] In May 1797 the municipal officers of Ennery gave a literary twist to their 'veneration of the virtuous Toussaint', hailing him as the 'avenger of humankind', exactly as described by Louis-Sébastien Mercier in his novel *The Year 2440*.[96]

But the locals chose increasingly to dwell on his moral and political leadership, insisting for example on the way he symbolized Christian sainthood; they appreciated the fact that he ordered the celebration of Catholic festivals such as the Feast of Corpus Christi across the colony.[97] Others heaped praise on him as the incarnation of stability and constitutional legality; the local assembly of Arcahaie saluted him as a chief who enjoyed the 'full confidence of the *colons*',[98] while the municipal authorities of Terre-Neuve were in awe of his 'statesmanlike qualities' and waxed lyrical about his 'fine negotiation skills';[99] in a boldly empiricist twist, they went on to claim that 'Toussaint's sublime experience gives him the knowledge which even the most ingenious theories cannot provide'.[100] In Port-Républicain, where he was venerated as a 'father-figure and liberator', the municipality went one step further and offered him a plot of land as a tribute to his peerless leadership,[101] while a poem in his honour in the *Gazette du Port-Républicain* hailed him as the 'new Alcide';[102] after the departure of Hédouville, they asked the French government to entrust in his 'firm hands the reins of government'.[103]

For the municipal authorities in Gonaïves, Toussaint was the republican protector par excellence, steadfast in his support for 'brothers of all colours', as well as a 'law-giver, father, and friend';[104] two years later he had become 'the wise genius who has been sent from the heavens to protect the needy, avenge the crimes committed against humanity, defend the liberties of all, and consolidate the institutions of the republic'.[105] Their colleagues in Cap were no less lavish, lauding Toussaint for his unparalleled knowledge of local affairs and presenting him as motivated only by the promotion of the 'public interest'.[106] These accolades culminated in a Cap festive ceremony in 1801, where a crowd of women of all colours 'complimented, crowned and embraced' the local hero and prayed eagerly for him to throw his handkerchief in their direction, while the men 'pressed themselves around him, trying to get as close as possible, so that they could touch his hand'; as one observer noted, this was a ceremony worthy of 'a sovereign of the colony'.[107]

PART THREE

Toussaint in Power

7
Great Latitude

'How unfortunate it is for France and for us', wrote Toussaint to the Directory in late September 1798, 'that Saint-Domingue is so far away from the motherland, that relations between us are so infrequent, and communications sometimes interrupted for years on end.'[1] The statement bore witness to the general loosening of the ties between the colony and France since the mid 1790s, but also the commander-in-chief's increasingly frosty relationship with successive French governors: the warm loyalism of his rapport with Laveaux had given way to the *mésentente cordiale* with Sonthonax, and then the dramatic rupture with Hédouville. At the same time Toussaint was being rather disingenuous, for this separation was also an opportunity. He was convinced that Saint-Domingue needed to preserve a strong bond with France, but also develop its autonomy, in order to forge new relationships with neighbouring islands and regional powers around the Caribbean.

It is easy enough to understand why he had come to this conclusion. By the mid 1790s, after years of revolutionary turmoil, the colony was economically in ruins: the plantations were devastated, with the capital stock (especially the factories and sophisticated irrigation systems) in a state of complete abandon; tens of thousands of labourers had died during the conflict. The scale of the collapse in commodity production can be gauged by these simple figures: if the year 1789 is assigned the index of 100, by 1795 coffee exports had fallen to 2.8, sugar to 1.2, cotton to 0.7 and indigo to 0.5.[2] Toussaint was therefore desperate to reopen the colony's trading relations with nearby countries – especially the United States, which had become a vital source of Saint-Domingue's flour, salted fish and beef, lumber and horses since the 1770s. This goal, in turn, could not be achieved without some further understandings with the British, who were entrenched in Jamaica and commanded the seas.

In his agreement with Maitland in August 1798, Toussaint had obtained an assurance that provisions would be allowed into Saint-Domingue without British interference. But this was only meant to be the prelude to the restoration of full commercial links with regional powers, the necessity of which was widely recognized by Saint-Domingue's economic elites as well as informed observers in France. The point was made emphatically by the parliamentarian Louis Rallier, one of Toussaint's allies in Paris: 'the greatest disaster which could befall the colony [of Saint-Domingue] would be that plantations are turned away from production because of the impossibility of generating profits, and cultivation abandoned altogether. It is therefore indispensable that the colony maintains outside commercial relations not only with France, but also with her enemies, as well as with neutral powers.' He concluded that Saint-Domingue needed to be given 'great latitude' by France in determining her industrial, agricultural and taxation levels, as well as her trading relations.[3]

Such an outcome had long been desired by Saint-Domingue's white *colons*, both before the revolution and in its immediate aftermath. Toussaint embraced it, while characteristically refining it for his own ends. But he was careful not to articulate it publicly, as achieving it would be fiendishly complicated. The expulsion of Hédouville had caused a breach with France, and Toussaint knew that it was imperative that good relations be restored as quickly as possible. Furthermore, the interests of the regional powers he sought to court were in a state of flux. The Spaniards, who controlled neighbouring Cuba and the adjacent territory of Santo Domingo, were notionally France's allies since 1795. But they were extremely wary of revolutionary change and had no intention of following Saint-Domingue down the path of ending slavery, on which their plantation system depended; indeed, in 1799 the Cuban authorities blocked the sale of a sizeable schooner to Toussaint's envoys, and the slave regime in Cuba was brutally reinforced in the years following its abolition in Saint-Domingue.[4] Nonetheless, Toussaint established a line of communication with the Spanish governor of Santiago, taking advantage of his sense of isolation from his own capital, which was further away than the nearest port in Saint-Domingue; in 1800 Toussaint even offered to send provisions to the city, which was completely lacking in essential foodstuffs.[5]

Still smarting from their military defeat by Toussaint, the British were caught between their racial scorn for the black commander (the commander of the British navy objected to any 'coloured communication'[6] with the colony) and their desire to prise Saint-Domingue away from the French. It was in this spirit that Maitland had made 'seductive offers' to Toussaint, showering him with gifts and even offering to recognize him as an independent monarch.[7] The Americans, likewise, were divided. On the one hand they dreaded the prospect of Toussaint's slave revolution spreading to their cities and plantations, notably through the presence of 'black French' refugees from the colony. On the other, leading American newspapers carried favourable stories about Toussaint and his comrades from 1797 onwards, especially their military campaigns,[8] and their merchants yearned to build a lucrative commercial relationship with Saint-Domingue.[9] Even though France was a long way away she remained jealously watchful, and any overt move by Toussaint towards the United States and Britain could be viewed as potentially treasonous – especially after the imposition of a Congressional trade embargo on France and her colonies in June 1798, in retaliation against attacks on American ships by French privateers. To this 'Quasi-War' were added the ongoing hostilities between the French Directory and the British in Europe, the Levant and the Caribbean.

In Toussaint's mind, diplomacy was the continuation of domestic politics by other means. Rebuilding a healthy trading relationship with America was a way of consolidating his leadership, but also of strengthening his hand in dealing with his internal enemies. Before his departure, Hédouville had openly encouraged the southern mixed-race leader Rigaud to repudiate Toussaint's authority; as this rebellion developed into a full-scale insurrection from mid 1799, Toussaint sought to use his diplomatic leverage to gain political and military support against Rigaud among regional powers. But the commander-in-chief knew that he had to tread carefully here as well: too public a rapprochement with the British could weaken his position among the black *cultivateurs*, who had grim memories of their enslavement in the British-controlled parts of Saint-Domingue and sincerely embraced the republican depiction of England as a corrupt and bloodthirsty tyranny.

Undeterred by the scale of these challenges, Toussaint set about securing his objectives, fully conscious that he might need to be creative, and even crafty, to achieve his ends. He often railed against his adversaries, but he was well capable of the same Machiavellianism when he believed the greater interests of Saint-Domingue were at stake. Finesse and flexibility were the watchwords of his diplomatic approach, which he summed up, characteristically, as 'raffiner de politique'.[10]

Toussaint's most urgent diplomatic task was to secure a successor to Hédouville as French agent in Saint-Domingue. His ideal candidate was Philippe-Rose Roume de Saint-Laurent, the official French representative in Spanish-controlled Santo Domingo. Roume hailed from the Caribbean region (he was a white creole from Grenada); he was very well acquainted with Saint-Domingue, having briefly served as French envoy to the colony in the early years of the revolution;[11] he was an idealist who was fully committed to the new fraternal social order, and his companion Marie-Anne Elizabeth Rochard, whom he later married, was a mixed-race woman (Toussaint's name appears as a witness on the birth certificate of their daughter Rose-Marie).[12] Roume was a mild-mannered, gentle and humane figure, with neither the brashness of Sonthonax nor the arrogance of Hédouville; an ardent republican, he was an immense admirer of Toussaint. The intimacy between the two men was visible from their very early correspondence, notably when Roume hailed the commander-in-chief as 'the saviour of Saint-Domingue', but also urged him to look after his health, and especially to avoid too many of his 'breathless rides'; he signed off his letters with 'je vous aime tendrement'.[13] Toussaint gave Roume a portrait of himself which he took back to France, and was later thought to have been used by Nicolas Maurin for his classic lithograph of Louverture in 1832 (see Plate 1).[14]

Crucially, Roume was close by and could fill the vacuum quickly, before the French authorities had time to gather their wits and settle on a less accommodating alternative. Conscious that he did not have formal authority in the matter, Toussaint nevertheless skilfully managed to turn Roume's appointment into a fait accompli. He despatched letters to Santo Domingo with his emissary Charles Vincent, presenting the situation to Roume as a crisis of popular sovereignty. Hédouville had been forced to return to France after 'losing the confidence of the people', and Roume was the obvious person to succeed him because of his 'attachment to true principles, virtuous conduct, and love for France and for the republic'. Toussaint's invitation to Roume was issued in his own name, in his capacity as commander-in-chief of the army, but also in that of a 'people who does not and will never cease to cherish the republic and its constitution'.[15] To emphasize republican procedural legality further, Vincent also carried a letter from the Cap municipality, written at Toussaint's request. It emphatically endorsed his invitation to come to Saint-Domingue 'in the name of public safety and patriotism', adding that Toussaint 'has no wish to be entrusted with the reins of a government which frightens him all the more that he fears that he may not be able to support its burden'.[16] Toussaint observed, too, that he was 'too grateful to the motherland' to allow himself to deviate from the path of French patriotism – although there was ambiguity in his use of the term 'mon pays', as it could be taken as a reference to Saint-Domingue.[17]

These grand declarations of loyalty to the French representative, as we shall see, were not wholly consistent with Toussaint's true intentions. The real measure of his rapport with Roume was Toussaint's decision to relocate the Agency office to Cap from Port-Républicain, the traditional administrative seat of colonial power. True, he organized a large military parade in honour of the new agent upon his arrival – but even this was a double-edged homage, as it was also a reminder of Toussaint's coercive force.[18] Pretending not to notice this geographical demotion, Roume promised to work closely with the 'great man' and 'perfect republican' who had been the 'protector of Saint-Domingue', and pledged to assist all his efforts for the public good of its citizens. Roume also committed himself to be his true friend, making amends for the 'trouble' his predecessors had caused him, but also never hesitating to 'speak the truth' when he felt the commander-in-chief was straying off the path of righteousness.[19] Yet notwithstanding their disagreements, which eventually escalated beyond repair, Roume remained mesmerized by Toussaint. The French official was astonished by Toussaint's energy and intelligence, and impressed by his attentiveness to the plight of the needy; he frequently hailed him as a 'virtuous philosopher', and told him that he was already becoming a legend across France and Europe. He would, wrote Roume, come to be celebrated as 'a leader who transcended all genres: a remarkable French citizen, an outstanding political strategist, and one of the greatest generals of the world'.[20]

Toussaint was not the only *grand capitaine* who was attracting public attention as the eighteenth century was drawing to a close. Roume's assumption of his position in Saint-Domingue coincided with a turning point in France – the military and political ascension of Napoleon Bonaparte. It was Roume who brought Bonaparte to Toussaint's attention, frequently mentioning the rising star from Corsica in his exchanges with him, and finding many similarities between them; on one occasion he observed that Toussaint was 'greater even than Bonaparte'.[21] Knowing Toussaint's fondness for republican exemplars and his ability to learn from the military experiences of others, Roume highlighted Napoleon's exploits during the Egyptian campaign of 1799. He sent the commander-in-chief a copy of a popular Parisian brochure by Roux which detailed the successes of Bonaparte's army, noting in the process the parallels between Toussaint and Napoleon: 'the same courage, the same bravery, produced by genius, and the same capacity to be in all places at once, observing, judging, marching, acting and destroying the enemy even before it has realized what is happening, and above all the same vision, embracing the past, the present, and the future'.[22]

While Toussaint would have been flattered by these comparisons, there was one further, more political aspect of Bonaparte which would have struck him just as forcefully: his capacity for innovation and transgression. This quality came into the open in his challenge to the decaying system of the Directory, culminating in the *coup d'état* of 18 Brumaire (9 November 1799), through which he assumed power as part of a new triumvirate of Consuls. Toussaint was told of Bonaparte's coup by a letter from Vincent, written from Paris on the very day of the event, as well as by a long communication from Roume, detailing the measures taken by the new Consuls to restore order in France and seek to end the military hostilities with France's adversaries. For Toussaint the political strategist, the lessons of Napoleon's rise to supreme power were clear, and they would shape his fertile imagination in the months and years to come: it was legitimate to pursue peace with former enemies without impugning the integrity of the republic; it was appropriate, too, for a new social contract to be underwritten by the drafting of a new constitution, and for an individual to assume power in the name of the republic in order to end 'anarchy' and promote 'order and tranquillity'.[23] Like his French counterpart, the 'Bonaparte of Saint-Domingue' was ready to ignore convention in order to embrace his singular destiny.

After securing the appointment of Roume, Toussaint turned to the key economic crux of his strategy: restoring Saint-Domingue's commercial relations with her regional neighbours. The colony imported most of its foodstuffs, as well as military commodities such as gunpowder. Describing his arrival in Cap in May 1796 as he took up his post as administrator of the northern department, the French official Joseph Idlinger found a calamitous situation, with the harbour blockaded by British vessels to prevent the entry of any neutral ships, and warehouses 'completely devoid of foodstuffs'.[24] By the middle of 1798 the position was grave: exports were still crippled as a result of the destruction of the French merchant fleet during the naval war with Britain, and Saint-Domingue faced the prospect of food shortages. To compound the looming disaster, the American merchants who had become the territory's principal link with the external world were now officially barred from entering its ports by the Congressional trade embargo on French products.[25]

If Saint-Domingue's revolution was not to suffocate, Toussaint needed to act immediately. He decided to make direct contact with President John Adams, who had been in office since March 1797, despatching his treasurer, Joseph Bunel, to meet him. A wealthy white merchant from Cap, Bunel was a key member of Toussaint's inner circle. He was an ideal envoy to America: he was hard-headed, brash and more than slightly shady, and had developed a large network of commercial interests in the United States. Bunel met Secretary of State Timothy Pickering, who was well disposed towards Saint-Domingue's black revolution, and then dined with Adams in January 1799.

He sang Toussaint's praises as an effective and pragmatic leader to all he met, and handed Adams a friendly letter from the commander-in-chief.[26] In this missive Toussaint noted 'with the greatest surprise' that American ships had deserted Saint-Domingue's ports, and that the result had been mutually disadvantageous. The wider reasons for the embargo levied by Congress were irrelevant: the return of American vessels to Saint-Domingue, he told Adams, was 'in your interests, as well as ours'. Toussaint also undertook to protect American ships from attack by French privateers, and guaranteed that all vessels would receive 'exact payment' for their cargoes. In this manner, Toussaint concluded, they could work together to restore the harmonious relations which should exist between the American and French republics.[27]

Toussaint's nimble text appealed enticingly to America's mercantile aspirations, while treading the fine line between loyalty to France and the cultivation of Saint-Domingue's self-interests. Although Adams disappointed him by not replying directly, Toussaint rapidly obtained the result he hoped for: in February 1799 Congress adopted a bill lifting the trading restrictions on a number of French colonies, including Saint-Domingue: as a tribute to its architect, it was even referred to as the 'Toussaint Clause'. Within months of the passing of the bill, Edward Stevens, a West-Indian born physician from Philadelphia and boyhood friend of the founding father Alexander Hamilton, arrived in Saint-Domingue as America's diplomatic representative or 'consul'. This title was normally reserved for emissaries exchanged by sovereign states, and was not fortuitous: Stevens's instructions were to reach an agreement protecting American ships from 'the depredations of French privateers' and developing commercial links with Saint-Domingue – but also, in the longer term, to push Toussaint to declare independence from France;[28] there was a widespread view among merchants and Congressional representatives that Saint-Domingue was a 'mine of gold' awaiting American exploitation.[29]

Toussaint had no intention of breaking completely with France, but he did not reject this possibility out of hand in his conversations with Stevens. From the moment the American consul set foot in the colony Toussaint did his best to make him feel that he had privileged status, and that forging a special relationship with the United States was his highest priority. As soon as Toussaint was informed of Stevens's landing, he rushed to Cap to meet him – a courtesy which, as we saw, he had not extended to Hédouville, whom he kept waiting for several months. He also spoke to Stevens separately, and at length, before taking him to the Agency building in Cap for his initial meeting with Roume: this private conversation enabled him to be more candid about his commitment to the American presence in

Saint-Domingue than he could have been in the French agent's presence. During this first meeting with Roume, as they engaged in detailed discussion about the protection of American vessels from French privateers, Toussaint repeatedly sided with Stevens, and used his powers of persuasion to convince the sceptical French agent that American demands were not fundamentally prejudicial to French interests. Toussaint also came up with the ingenious solution eventually agreed by both parties: there was to be no outright ban on French privateering, but a commitment to recall all existing commissions and not to issue any new ones. A delighted Stevens wrote back to Secretary of State Pickering commending 'the powerful support, penetration and good sense'[30] of the commander-in-chief. Toussaint had clearly made a very strong first impression.

Toussaint did everything in his power to make this arrangement work. He worked on Roume, who was initially hostile to the American presence and kept trying to link the treatment of the Americans in Saint-Domingue with the fate of French ships in America; at one point he even suggested that Stevens and his associates should be detained and held in prison in retaliation for the capture of any French vessels off American shores.[31] Faithful to his strategy, Toussaint argued that such wider diplomatic considerations should not undermine the colony's own economic arrangements with the United States, and he eventually won Roume over – so much so that the French agent expressed his public appreciation of the helpful pragmatism of Consul Stevens, and heaped praise on Toussaint's 'patriotic measures for the renewal of American commerce'.[32]

Roume's contentment was understandable: within a few months of the agreement with Stevens, dozens of American ships (as well as vessels bearing flags from Spain and Hamburg) began to arrive in Saint-Domingue, replenishing local stores and markets with food. He thanked Toussaint, and looked forward to the prospect of 'the days of plenty';[33] he was also pleased to hear from Stevens that the Americans had sent three frigates to protect their trading vessels and would not 'tolerate any insolence' from the British.[34] A local observer welcomed the return of 'the greatest abundance of provisions', noting that increased competition led to a significant drop in the prices of key commodities such as flour – a boon for ordinary citizens.[35] American exports to Saint-Domingue, which had fallen to $2.7 million in 1799, bounced back to $5.1 million in 1800 and then $7.1 the following year.[36] A thriving commerce of colonial commodities from Saint-Domingue also resumed: a report from Cap in 1800 indicated that three-quarters of the sugar exports and two-thirds of its coffee went to the United States;[37] there was also a boom in exports of timber, with American merchants especially eager to lay their hands on local dyewood.[38]

Toussaint's correspondence showed that he spared no effort to encourage Americans to feel welcome in Saint-Domingue; for example, when the captain of a ship asked him for permission to celebrate an anniversary by firing a round of artillery in the bay of Cap, he readily obliged.[39]

Toussaint eased the integration of American traders into local communities, and issued clear instructions to his military commanders to protect their persons, interests and properties. He facilitated the appointments of Nathan Levy and Robert Ritchie as American consuls for Cap and the western department respectively, and even nominated some of the American merchants to administrative functions: Eugene Macmahon Sheridan was appointed as one of the assessors on the Léogâne tribunal.[40] An American expatriate community rapidly developed, notably in Cap, and its representatives regularly expressed their enthusiastic admiration for Toussaint, which was relayed back to the United States; articles favourable to the 'incorruptible General Toussaint' appeared regularly in the Philadelphia press.[41] When he was in Cap, the commander-in-chief regularly visited the Hôtel de la République, a tavern where leading American and Saint-Domingue figures mingled happily.[42]

The positive first impression that Toussaint made upon Stevens only grew. Stevens became close to him, often spending the night at his Ennery residence – a rare privilege.[43] Toussaint gave him messages for Roume; the protection afforded by American military vessels was so reliable that Stevens even helped transmit official letters destined for the French government through Philadelphia. His reports about Toussaint were glowing. He told Pickering that he had 'the most perfect confidence' in Toussaint's ongoing commitment to honouring his agreements with the United States and protecting American interests in Saint-Domingue.[44] Stevens was also struck by the support he enjoyed across the different communities through his 'humane and mild conduct'; he went out of his way to stress to his racially conscious superiors that Toussaint was endorsed not only by 'most of the black citizens' but also 'all the whites'.[45] There was little doubt, in his mind, that Saint-Domingue would thrive under Toussaint's leadership, commercially, agriculturally and in sound administration.[46]

In a blatant but cunning breach of etiquette, Toussaint also showed Stevens copies of his correspondence with the French agent, including a 'severe letter' in which the commander-in-chief accused his superior of 'weakness, indecision and criminal neglect of his duty'.[47] The point here, of course, was to undermine Roume's authority, while creating the impression that Toussaint was the Americans' only reliable ally in Saint-Domingue. Indeed, Toussaint, who had a gift for telling people what they wanted to hear, encouraged Stevens to believe that he was actively considering separation from France. The ploy worked: in one of his subsequent letters to his superiors, Stevens reported that 'all connections with France will soon be broken off', and that Toussaint would shortly declare the colony 'independent'.[48] With the obvious encouragement of Toussaint, Stevens also joined in the plotting against Roume: he associated himself with what the latter called a 'cabal of anglophiles' in Cap whose aim was to weaken the position of the French agent and eventually force his return to France; among these plotters was Christophe, the military commander of Cap.

Confronted by Roume, Stevens pulled back and promised to refrain from such undiplomatic activities in the future; as a goodwill gesture, he invited the French agent to come on board his ship for a reconciliatory tour of Cap bay. Roume accepted, but such was his paranoia that he suspected an Anglo-American plot to kidnap him, and ordered that the ship be sunk if it appeared to sail in the direction of Jamaica.[49]

Despite the importance of his diplomatic breakthrough with America, Toussaint realized that his strategy would prove futile unless Britain was also brought fully into the equation. In early 1799 a British proclamation allowed Jamaica to establish commercial links with Saint-Domingue, a move which suggested a continuing willingness to engage with Toussaint. While their material interests in the region were significant, the British were extremely concerned about the spread of revolutionary ideas from Saint-Domingue, especially as rumours of a Directory plan to invade Jamaica were beginning to circulate. While these stories strengthened Toussaint's hand, he also appreciated his own vulnerabilities. Even though the British had been expelled from Saint-Domingue, they still had the capacity to make local mischief – in particular by encouraging the dissent of Toussaint's southern rival Rigaud. British sea power was also such that it could effectively maintain a naval blockade on the colony and stifle the renewed commercial links between the United States and Saint-Domingue.

In January 1799 General Maitland wrote from London, announcing that he had been instructed by the British government to return to Saint-Domingue to negotiate an extension of the terms of their agreement; he concluded by reaffirming his 'personal esteem' for Toussaint.[50] After stopping in Philadelphia in April for discussions with Pickering, the British envoy then made his way back to Saint-Domingue and arrived at Cap in mid May.[51] Mindful that the sight of British officers in uniform in Saint-Domingue could be unsettling to many of his own supporters, and aware of the need to keep discussions with Maitland away from Roume, he swiftly decamped to Gonaïves.[52] He declined Roume's suggestion that he should arrest the British envoy and bring him to Cap as a 'prisoner': such a move, he replied, would be a betrayal of his country, and contrary both to his 'honour' and to the practice of 'civilized nations'. Highlighting the French agent's impotence and his own power, Toussaint showed Roume's letter, and his reply, to Maitland.[53] In his preliminary note setting out his position to the British envoy he described himself as acting in 'the interests of his country' ('mon pays'). This was no slip of the tongue: he was now getting used to thinking of Saint-Domingue as an entity distinct from France.[54]

After several weeks of hard bargaining, the two men signed what became known as the Maitland Convention on 13 June 1799, in the presence of Stevens.[55] Extending and formalizing the terms of the 1798 agreement, it stipulated that Cap and Port-Républicain would be opened to Anglo-American shipping, and that Britain and the United States would not molest any ships heading to these ports (provided they were not carrying weapons), and not engage in any hostile military actions against the parts of the territory controlled by Toussaint, or interfere in its political affairs. In return, the commander-in-chief repeated his pledge that Saint-Domingue would not be used as a base to mount any expedition against British colonial interests in the region or against the United States. Indeed, Toussaint promised Stevens and Maitland to do his utmost to oppose the Directory's plans to invade Jamaica, and again held up the prospect of a complete break from French control. The governor of Jamaica, Balcarres, understood how tricky it was to pin Toussaint down, reporting in late 1799: 'from what I have observed of [Toussaint's] general conduct, I must suspect that he is playing a game, not only with us, but also with the Directory, and that his aim is independence'.[56]

The Maitland Convention included an exhaustive list of restrictions on Toussaint's capacity to navigate and mount his own naval force – painful concessions, especially in light of his developing conflict with Rigaud, as we shall see shortly.[57] But the commander-in-chief also drove a hard bargain. Aware that the presence of British diplomatic and commercial representatives would be controversial, Toussaint also demanded that British merchants should sail into the colony under international or neutral flags, and that (unlike the American representative) the principal British envoy in Saint-Domingue envisaged by the agreement should not formally hold the title of consul; he initially refused to accredit the first British representative, Colonel Grant.[58] Maitland was even persuaded to recommend to Balcarres that Jamaica should provide military assistance to Toussaint, in the form of gunpowder, arms and flints.[59] The governor agreed, albeit reluctantly, and the supplies, consisting of 100 barrels of gunpowder, 200 stands of arms and 7,000 flints, were duly delivered.[60] As much as what it contained, the agreement itself was a major symbolic victory for Toussaint, as it represented an international confirmation of his diplomatic legitimacy.

The promotion of revolutionary change in the region provided the first major test of Toussaint's non-aggression pact with the British. There had been a number of French republican schemes to liberate British and Spanish colonies in the Caribbean during the revolutionary years, but none had been pursued systematically. In 1799, however, with the active encouragement of his superiors in the Directory, Roume hatched an audacious plan to throw the British out of Jamaica. It involved sponsoring a local insurrection through the mobilization of the Blue Mountain maroon rebels, while also recruiting support among the small contingent of French black and white exiles on the island; the *coup de grâce* was to be delivered by a French expeditionary force of 4,000 men, trained and equipped in Saint-Domingue and commanded by the mixed-race General Martial Besse. One of the key agents of the operation was an idealistic young Jewish textile merchant from Cap, Isaac Sasportas, who volunteered to 'be granted the honour of carrying death and desolation to the British enemy'.[61] In his formal letter of instructions to Sasportas, written in mid July 1799 (a month after the signature of the Maitland Convention), Roume rounded on the British, denouncing them as 'cannibalistic Machiavellians' for their global opposition to the French revolutionary cause, and for their enslavement of 'African peoples' in their colonies, where they captured free men and kept them 'like vile cattle'; he also condemned their despatch of agents and spies to foment chaos in Saint-Domingue.[62] Even though Roume did not yet know the precise terms of Toussaint's agreement, he had clearly been outraged by Maitland's recent presence in the colony; in late August 1799 he issued a decree banning British and American ships from Saint-Domingue's ports.[63] The Jamaica expedition was a direct challenge to Toussaint's accommodating policy towards the British.

Toussaint was now confronted with a serious dilemma. The expedition was approved at the highest levels of the Directory, and Toussaint could therefore not afford to express his misgivings openly. In fact, he pretended to go along with the plan, and actively involved himself in all its preparatory stages: he met Sasportas with Roume and agreed that he was the perfect candidate to lead the operation; he helped organize the young conspirator's first visit to Jamaica, during which he made contact with the Blue Mountain rebels, planned the outbreak of the insurrection (which was to include poisoning Governor Balcarres's morning coffee), and reported back that they were willing to launch an insurrection against the British, provided French military support was forthcoming; and he oversaw the training and equipment of the combat troops destined for Jamaica. Pressed by Roume as to whether the invasion had his support, Toussaint assented, even referring to it as 'our expedition'.[64] He made a point which struck Roume forcefully, noting that, while he was concerned at the prospect of the white-settler population in Jamaica being massacred by the insurgents, he believed that in the end they would not put up any significant resistance – not least because they would not want to suffer the same fate as Saint-Domingue's *colons* in the early years of the revolution.[65]

In principle, of course, Toussaint was sincerely committed to the liberation of black people in Jamaica from British rule. In a letter to Vincent in late 1798 he described the British as 'oppressors', adding that 'if it depended only on my will, Jamaica would soon be free'.[66] In his private discussions with his entourage, however, Toussaint was scathing about the Directory's plan – and not only because of his commitments to Maitland. The scheme cast a shadow over his strategy for autonomy, and was a waste of military manpower at a time when he needed to concentrate on containing the internal rebellions he was facing. He suspected, too, that some elements in the French government wanted to use the operation as a ploy to draw him and his black army into a risky foreign venture – rather in the same way as the Directory had sent Bonaparte to Egypt, in the hope that he might never return. Defeat would then enable the replacement of Toussaint with a more pliant leader, who would then have a free hand to restore slavery in the colony. This was not just his own view: it was widely shared among his senior officers, as well as by sympathetic observers such as the former French commissioner Raimond, who warned that the Jamaica expedition would imperil all the achievements of the revolution in Saint-Domingue, noting that one of its primary purposes was to 'get rid of Toussaint, his principal officers, and his army'.[67]

Faced with this dilemma, Toussaint resorted to an extraordinary series of moves: he first revealed the Jamaica plans to one of the British agents in Saint-Domingue, Charles Douglas, who passed them on immediately to Governor Balcarres; the documents included a twelve-page presentation by Martial Besse to Toussaint on 25 September 1799.[68] Toussaint then also leaked the plans to the American consul, who reported in a letter dated 30 September 1799 that the commander-in-chief was 'determined that the invasion shall not take place', adding that 'he appears to encourage it that he may the more certainly prevent it'. Toussaint urged Stevens to 'counteract the agent's operations by every possible means'.[69] His wishes were soon fulfilled: Sasportas was captured soon after his arrival in Jamaica in late November, tried, and executed on 23 December – three days before the insurrection was meant to begin.[70] There is little doubt that Toussaint's leaks were directly responsible for this outcome and that, in handing over confidential material about a forthcoming French military operation to representatives of foreign powers, he could easily have been accused of treachery.[71]

If Toussaint had anticipated that his acrobatic efforts to honour his non-aggression commitments towards Jamaica might earn him some British goodwill, he was to be disappointed. Writing to Stevens, Governor Balcarres expressed his belief in 'the good faith and honourable intention of general-in-chief Toussaint Louverture'.[72] The earl even credited Toussaint, in a report to his superiors, with making 'every effort to save Jamaica'. But he had done so, he added mulishly, only 'to favour the line of his own ambition'.[73] Balcarres flatly refused to consider Toussaint's request for the supply of further arms and ammunition, including 6,000 rifles, claiming that he did not have such material in Jamaica and would pass on his list to the British government in London – which was of course a diplomatic way of burying the request.[74] There was much worse to come. Very soon after the arrest of Sasportas, the British flexed their naval muscle and captured four of Toussaint's military vessels, which he had despatched to the south to assist in the war effort against Rigaud. The ships were seized and taken to Jamaica – even though they were carrying the proper authorizations signed by the British representative in Port-Républicain, Hugh Cathcart, as well as by Stevens. Despite Toussaint's speedy despatch of an emissary to Kingston, the British sold the vessels, confiscated the weapons and munitions they found on board and detained the crews.[75] Prior to this incident, Toussaint's naval capacity consisted of thirteen ships: the loss of four of them – and nearly half his mariners – was without doubt a significant setback.[76]

Toussaint fumed, telling Cathcart that the British behaviour was nothing less than 'dishonourable', and that he would never dream of acting in such a way, 'even though he was black'[77] – although he had, in fact, refused to release a British vessel captured by a French corsair just a few months earlier.[78] In a letter of protest to Balcarres, he described the news as 'afflicting to the highest degree'.[79] He acknowledged that the level of armament of the four ships had exceeded the limits imposed by the Maitland Convention; however, he stressed that the vessels were intended only for defensive purposes. He had not only obtained the requisite documentation for them, but had written to the commander of the British navy, Admiral Sir Hyde Parker, to inform him about his ships' movements; there had been no attempt to act deceptively.[80] By late January 1800 Toussaint was still complaining bitterly about the incident to the local British representatives, and declared that, even though he regarded Maitland as a 'friend' of

Saint-Domingue, he still felt personally 'injured' by the way he had been treated by the British admiral, whom he also described as a 'ferocious beast'.[81] He reminded the envoys that the British were 'indebted to him' for warning them about the Jamaica invasion – and that instead of treating him as a 'benefactor', they had dealt with him as an 'enemy'. 'After such behaviour,' he asked melodramatically, 'how can I ever trust you British again?'[82]

This was exactly the reaction of Roume, who expressed his satisfaction at the fact that the British, by taking Toussaint's ships, had revealed their true colours. He lectured Toussaint about his naïvety: 'you will now no longer be able to lend any credence to the lies and promises of these monsters whose only goal has ever been to destroy our colony, and you with it'.[83] Toussaint replied in two successive letters, stiffly upbraiding Roume for his lack of 'discretion' around the operation, and claiming that the French agent had failed to keep the information about the planned Jamaican invasion secret; by September 1799 its imminence was widely known, even by the women and children of Cap.[84] Toussaint brazenly claimed this leak had led to the capture of the French conspirators in Jamaica, and also provoked the seizure of his ships. Grasping the moment, he announced to Roume that the plans for the Jamaican invasion were now suspended indefinitely, given that the British were fully apprised of the French plans and that they were so terrified at the prospect of further revolutionary upheaval that they had expelled all French citizens from the island. Gratuitously twisting the knife in the wound, he blamed Roume for the entire debacle: 'your scheme, which you failed to keep secret, has done us much more harm than good, indeed it has ruined us comprehensively'.[85]

The conflict between Toussaint and Roume over the Jamaican expedition underlined the starkly different philosophies of the two men with respect to Saint-Domingue's future. The French agent's strategic goal was fully aligned with the interests of his national government: to 'extinguish the maritime despotism of England'; the duty of all French citizens in the colonies was to join in the collective effort to 'destroy the influence of the British government over its colonies, by all means possible'.[86] Toussaint, for his part, did not need reminding of the depravity of the British: he had fought them implacably, and would never forget 'as a former slave' that they were upholders of human bondage;[87] he repeated the point a few months later in a letter to Roume.[88] He certainly did not discard the objective of confronting the British position in Jamaica: in early 1800 he secretly offered to provide the Spaniards with 'armed volunteers' to recapture Jamaica (taken by the British in the mid seventeenth century), in exchange for supplying him with 20,000 rifles. The offer, conveyed through Toussaint's lieutenant Miguel de Arambarri, was turned down by the Cuban governor, Someruelos.[89] This showed, nonetheless, that Toussaint was willing to adopt an assertive external policy, provided it was not conducted in isolation. Roume's unilaterally aggressive policy towards British interests in the Caribbean seemed highly dangerous to him, as it did not take any account of Saint-Domingue's vulnerabilities, both to threats from outside and to internal subversion; as he put it revealingly, his priority was the 'safety of *my country*'[90] – the phrase he had also used to Maitland only a few months earlier.

In a later 'frank' letter to Roume, Toussaint expressed his position even more bluntly, asserting that he would never hesitate to 'use the English, even though they are our most cruel enemies, as long as I believe this might be in the best interests of Saint-Domingue'. The French agent's belief that a 'decisive blow' could be struck against British interests in the Caribbean was absurd, given that Saint-Domingue had no naval forces. For Toussaint, republicanism was not a matter of making grand rhetorical declarations, but of acting concretely, in the best interests of the colony's citizens. In light of the unequal balance of forces and their 'Machiavellianism', the only way to deal with the British was through a combination of conciliation and ruse, which Toussaint spelled out: 'I am prepared to use them in any way which might be of service to the safety, the preservation and the prosperity of the colony.' Perhaps seized by a pang of remorse at the extreme measures he had just taken to prevent the Jamaica expedition, he concluded that 'time will tell whether I have made the right or wrong decisions'.[91]

Roume remained unmoved by Toussaint's reasoning, and continued to argue against any further development of British commercial interests in Saint-Domingue; at one point he even demanded that all British-Jamaican commercial assets in Saint-Marc, Arcahaie and Port-Républicain be seized, along with any British vessels sailing under neutral or American flags.[92] The clash between the agent and the commander-in-chief came to a head in the early months of 1800, when Roume learned that the two British envoys, Hugh Cathcart and Charles Douglas, had been operating in Port-Républicain for some time under Toussaint's protection – despite the latter's repeated denials of their existence. He expressed his outrage to Toussaint, and issued a proclamation ordering that the two men be immediately arrested and expelled from Saint-Domingue, along with any other British nationals in the colony.[93] Toussaint rejected Roume's demands as 'impolitic' and 'ruinous to the commercial interests of the colony', adding that he could not allow his 'ill-judged policies' to prevail.[94]

*

Toussaint's diplomatic manoeuvres with the Americans and the British were further complicated by the eruption of a major domestic conflict with his southern rival André Rigaud. Before his departure from Saint-Domingue, as we saw earlier, Hédouville had released the mixed-race general from his military obligations to his commander-in-chief, and openly sponsored his dissidence. The relationship between the two men became increasingly tense, and in early February 1799 Roume had tried to broker a reconciliation during the 16 Pluviôse anniversary celebrations of the abolition of slavery in Saint-Domingue. At this meeting in Port-Républicain, Rigaud pledged his loyalty and, as a gesture of goodwill, agreed to hand over to Toussaint's forces the control of the towns of Petit- and Grand-Goâve, situated on the border between his southern department and that of the west.

However, Rigaud quietly continued to prepare his challenge to Toussaint and clashed with troops loyal to him; in one incident in Jérémie forty soldiers were killed, and in another gruesome atrocity thirty-one of Toussaint's supporters (thirty black and one white) suffocated in a cramped cell where they had been detained; their bodies were then dumped at sea.[95] As tensions rose, Rigaud issued a proclamation in early June 1799 denouncing Toussaint for preparing his troops to attack the south, handing over the colony to émigré and British interests and promoting 'civil war'.[96] A few days later Rigaud shattered the peace by violently seizing back control of Petit- and Grand-Goâve; again, dozens of men loyal to Toussaint were massacred. In early July Roume officially declared Rigaud a traitor, and gave Toussaint leave to use 'all the instruments and stratagems of war to destroy the rebellion'. The bitter war of knives had begun.[97]

The violence of the war of words was immediately apparent. Both leaders issued a barrage of pamphlets and proclamations denouncing each other: in a single missive, Toussaint described Rigaud as 'slanderous, deceptive, conniving, proud, pushy, jealous, unjust, vicious, callous, cruel, tyrannical, vindictive, divisive, murderous and treacherous'.[98] For Toussaint, the driving force behind the southerner's insubordination was 'his naked ambition', as well as his 'desire to rule over the entire territory'. This was not a recent phenomenon: as he observed in a letter to Roume, Rigaud's seditious disposition was already in evidence during the episode of 30 Ventôse 1796, when he had instigated Villate's rebellion to depose Governor Laveaux and undermine the colony's legitimate French authorities. According to Toussaint, Rigaud's commitment to the republican ideal of fraternity was a sham, as he was driven by a deep hatred of the white population. He claimed that Rigaud had once told him that only black and mixed-race people were the 'natural inhabitants' of Saint-Domingue, and that his secret aspiration was to 'eliminate' all European presence in

Liberté **RÉPUBLIQUE FRANÇAISE.** Egalité.

TOUSSAINT LOUVERTURE,

Général en chef de l'Armée de Saint-Domingue,

Aux Cultivateurs et aux Hommes de Couleur égarés par les Ennemis de la France et de la vraie Liberté.

CITOYENS, FRÈRES ET AMIS,

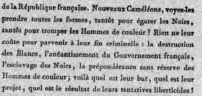

JE n'entrerai pas, mes Frères, dans le détail des manœuvres que la malveillance a employé jusqu'à ce jour pour égarer votre opinion, pour tromper votre bonne foi; vous avez appris par vous-même jusqu'où le désir de la domination, l'envie du commandement pouvaient porter ces Hommes méchans. La plupart d'entr'eux, tranquilles spectateurs de la lutte qui a existé entre les Anglais et les Républicains de Saint-Domingue, ils n'ont pas daigné seconder vos efforts courageux, qui ont forcé les Ennemis de la France à une fuite honteuse. Mais à peine avez-vous obtenu ce brillant succès, à peine les Anglais se sont-ils éloignés, qu'on les a vu s'armer et former une coalition impie pour abattre le Gouvernement de Saint-Domingue, pour anéantir vos Chefs légitimes, s'emparer du commandement, et forger pour vous les fers d'un nouvel Esclavage. Et voilà quel sera le fruit des manœuvres criminelles d'un seul Homme; la majeure partie des Hommes de couleur, qui devaient sentir que leur existence politique était attachée à la Liberté des Noirs, ont été assez aveuglés pour se laisser séduire par les mensonges de RIGAUD; ils ont épousé sa querelle et entrepris sa défense. Le désir de régner l'a emporté chez eux sur le bonheur résultant de la soumission aux Lois et aux Autorités légitimes. Ne voyez, mes Amis, dans cette conduite odieuse de ces Hommes perfides, qu'un désir bien prononcé d'anéantir à Saint-Domingue la Constitution qui vous assure imperturbablement la jouissance de vos Droits, une volonté ferme de saper jusques dans les fondemens l'Autorité nationale, et d'amener enfin une Indépendance qu'ils nourrissent depuis trop long-temps dans leur cœur, et dont ils ne craignent pas de rejeter l'odieux sur un Homme qui a affronté tous les dangers pour conserver à la France cette partie précieuse de la République française. Nouveaux Caméléons, voyez-les prendre toutes les formes, tantôt pour égarer les Noirs, tantôt pour tromper les Hommes de couleur? Rien ne leur coûte pour parvenir à leur fin criminelle: la destruction des Blancs, l'anéantissement du Gouvernement français, l'esclavage des Noirs, la prépondérance sans réserve des Hommes de couleur; voilà quel est leur but, quel est leur projet, quel est le résultat de leurs tentatives liberticides!

Mais, j'en jure par vous-mêmes, mes Amis, jamais ils ne parviendront à pervertir l'ordre établi; tant que le feu sacré d'un pur républicanisme animera nos ames, tant que la reconnaissance que nous devons à la France les échauffera, nous saurons venger ses droits, et faire repentir ses Ennemis de leur audace criminelle.

Pour moi, tous mes momens, que depuis long-temps je consacre à l'affermissement de votre bonheur, seront employés encore à vous débarrasser de vos nouveaux Ennemis, à maintenir l'Ordre constitutionnel dans toute l'étendue de cette Colonie, soumise à la France république.

J'invite les Administrations municipales de chaque Commune à éclairer la Religion de leurs Concitoyens, qui seraient assez faibles pour se laisser gagner par ces Hommes imbus de principes destructeurs; et ordonne à tous les Commandans desdites Communes de redoubler de surveillance pour arrêter leurs Émissaires et leurs Complices dans toute l'étendue de leur commandement.

Fait au Port-de-Paix, le 12 Thermidor, an sept de la République française, une et indivisible.

Le Général en chef de l'Armée de Saint-Domingue,

Signé TOUSSAINT LOUVERTURE.

Au Cap-Français, chez P. ROUX, imprimeur du Gouvernement, rues Nationale et du Panthéon.

Issued in late July 1799, this proclamation denounced the 'impious coalition of treacherous men' who rebelled against his authority under the leadership of the mixed-race General André Rigaud; the rebels' aim was to destroy the white population, break away from France and re-enslave the black people.

the colony; this was, of course, the antithesis of Toussaint's vision.[99] During the war, Toussaint received many reports about the mistreatment of whites by southern rebels: in Jérémie, for example, a large number of Europeans had been murdered, and many of the survivors had fled to Cuba; most of the men who had stayed behind had been forcibly conscripted into Rigaud's army.[100]

The intensity of the war with Rigaud was increased by its strong fratricidal undertones. In a private letter to Vincent, written at the beginning of the conflict, Toussaint asserted that he could only 'fully trust the white and the black people' of Saint-Domingue, and that the conspiracy against him was the work of the 'ungrateful and denatured' mixed-race supporters of Rigaud; as long as he was alive, he vowed, the colony would never become 'the property of people of colour'.[101] Shortly afterwards, after hearing of the murderous attacks carried out by the rebels against innocent civilians, Toussaint wrote to Vincent again, noting that 'three out of four men of colour were criminal';[102] in a public proclamation he declared that the 'major part' of the mixed-race population had allowed themselves to be 'seduced by the felonious manoeuvres of one man'.[103] Rigaud, for his part, presented himself as the leader of a beleaguered and victimized mixed-race population across the colony. He urged his compatriots everywhere to rally to his support in his battle against Toussaint, whom he accused of threatening to wipe out the mixed-race community – notably in a widely reported speech delivered in February 1799 at the main church in Port-Républicain, in which Toussaint allegedly declared that he would not hesitate to 'exterminate' the people of colour if they stepped out of line. They were, he observed, like greedy guests at a dinner table, trying to help themselves to all the dishes; but they should not touch the Toussaint Louverture plate as it would 'burn' them.[104]

Challenged by Roume, Toussaint claimed that he had only been referring to those who were engaging in acts of sedition in support of 'King Rigaud'. He added that there were undeniably some people of colour who could not bring themselves to take orders from 'Toussaint Louverture, a black man and a former slave'.[105] Nonetheless, he rejected viewing the conflict with Rigaud as a racial war, stressing that he still had absolute faith in the 'virtuous men of colour who were attached to their duties'. By way of example, he noted – accurately – that he entrusted his life every day to mixed-race officers who remained in his close entourage, and who served as his aides-de-camp and among his elite regiment of guides; there were also dozens of mixed-race officers in senior commanding positions in his army. This, he concluded, was simply not consistent with Rigaud's accusation that he had a 'visceral hatred of people of colour'.[106]

Confirmation that this was not primarily a racial war lay in the sheer scale of Rigaud's insurrection, which was not geographically confined to the southern province. In a series of carefully co-ordinated moves – which confirmed, as Toussaint noted, that the rebel general's sedition had been planned for at least six months[107] – uprisings were launched across the northern and western departments, notably in Arcahaie, Jean-Rabel, Gonaïves, Saint-Marc and Môle Saint-Nicolas; even Toussaint's control of Cap was briefly under threat. 'Almost all' the municipal and administrative officers who betrayed him in these localities were people of colour.[108] However, and to his immense chagrin, there were a number of *anciens libres* (black freedmen) who joined in the rebellion too, as well as some of his senior black officers – including Colonel Christophe Mornet, one of the heroes of the war against the British: recently nominated for promotion by Toussaint for his 'constancy and courage',[109] he conspired to open the gates of Port-Républicain and hand Toussaint over to the insurgents. Rigaud's rebels also carried out several assassination attempts against Toussaint, including one which failed on the outskirts of Saint-Marc and another near Gonaïves: in the former case his carriage was riddled with bullets, and he survived only because he was riding behind it on horseback; in the latter a couple of bullets went through his hat, and two of the officers travelling by his side were killed. He had reason to be grateful for the small plume which Laveaux had given him in 1796, and which he had worn ever since on his hat as a good-luck charm.[110]

Most disconcertingly for Toussaint, senior black commanders such as Pierre Michel and black citizens in a number of localities also joined the insurgency. For example, the 'entire mass' of the *cultivateurs* of Port-de-Paix went over to the rebels; Toussaint blamed a group of mixed-race troublemakers from Jean-Rabel and Moustique for deceiving these agricultural workers, adding that the agitators had always been 'agents of discord and destruction' in the locality.[111] While it was true that many joined the uprising for material reasons (personal advancement, financial reward or the promise of pillage), there was a more important reason why black communities across the colony were becoming uneasy about Toussaint's rule: Rigaud's propagandists effectively exploited his renewed diplomatic connections with Britain, notably by claiming that his agreement with Maitland included a secret clause to restore monarchical rule and slavery in Saint-Domingue.[112] According to one story, the price had even been agreed: three *gourdins* for a male slave and two for a female. Another rumour which circulated widely in 1799 among black peasants in the south was that, in the wake of his alliance with the British, Toussaint had already removed the tricolour flag from Port-Républicain; there were also various stories about Roume being placed under arrest by him.[113] The administrative capital was clearly the focus of the wildest imaginings: a European officer who joined Rigaud's side claimed that he had personally witnessed Toussaint fraternizing with British officers around a lavish banquet, and 'kicking black and mixed-race officers in the backside and tearing off their epaulettes'.[114]

The irony was that, far from giving Toussaint any support in his fight against the insurrection, the British were gleefully undermining him by strengthening Rigaud's hand, on the classic imperial principle that their interests would best be served by a Saint-Domingue which was divided by civil war. As Admiral Parker put it: 'for as long as Rigaud and Toussaint are carrying on the contest, no great danger can be apprehended from either'.[115] As he left Saint-Domingue after negotiating with Toussaint, Maitland noted that Rigaud was 'thoroughly supplied in arms and ammunition from Jamaica'.[116] So, just as he was censuring Toussaint for selling himself to Perfidious Albion, Rigaud was receiving weapons, money and supplies from the British – which ensured that his own soldiers, although fewer in number than Toussaint's forces, were better equipped (and paid) than their counterparts in the regular republican army.[117] The British also provided Rigaud with a fleet of naval vessels which intercepted Toussaint's communications and carried out numerous acts of piracy against French and American ships, murdering their crews and throwing their passengers overboard.[118] Toussaint denounced this British connivance with Rigaud to Roume, noting that the Spanish authorities in Cuba – including the dastardly governor of Santiago – had been sending assistance to the rebels too.[119]

The war of knives was a comprehensive challenge to Toussaint's social, political and military power, and his response was no less imperious. Conscious that rebel accusations of his collusion with the British were gaining traction, he issued a series of proclamations vigorously denying that he had reached any arrangement with them which might impinge on their freedoms. 'I took up arms so that you may be free,' he told the insurgents of the Môle Saint-Nicolas garrison, 'I alone have driven the English out of Saint-Domingue, and like you I was once a slave.'[120] He mobilized his supporters by promising an additional day of rest to plantation workers and organizing Catholic processions and *kalindas*, in which they playfully elected their kings and queens. He also sought to counter Rigaud's propaganda by sending emissaries to reassure concerned citizens across the colony: General Laplume, who was greatly admired among the black *bossales*, was despatched to quash the persistent rumour that the town of Léogâne had been handed over to the British forces.[121] Toussaint also used his network of municipal agents to drive home his fundamental advantage: he was the representative of legitimate authority, and it was Rigaud and his followers who had rebelled against the republic, thereby placing themselves, as the mayor of Saint-Louis-du-Nord put it, in the position of 'usurpers'.[122]

Toussaint took immediate charge of the military response to the insurrections in his own strongholds. He moved with speed across the different sites of unrest, here driving back rebels who had taken up arms, there surprising them before they had had a chance to organize themselves, and in several instances arriving just in time to save his own besieged officers and soldiers from death. In Port-de-Paix, for example, the local commander Jacques Maurepas had retrenched himself in the main fort and was nearly out of munitions when Toussaint arrived and, in one decisive cavalry charge, routed the insurgents.[123] Although the commander-in-chief grumbled that he was 'absolutely exhausted physically'[124] by these multiple operations, he prevailed rapidly, and by the end of August 1799 the entire western and north-western areas were back under his control; in Môle Saint-Nicolas the relieved inhabitants, who had in effect been taken hostage by the rebels, greeted him with festive illuminations.[125] Toussaint then focused his attention on the south, tasking the recapture of rebel territory to his faithful lieutenant Dessalines, whom he picked for his 'precision, bravery, prudence and impeccable republican principles'.[126] It would take Dessalines' forces a year fully to defeat Rigaud: their first major breakthrough was the port of Jacmel, which fell in March 1800, followed by Grand-Goâve in April, before Toussaint's entry into the southern capital of Les Cayes in early August. Rigaud had fled the colony a few days earlier; he returned to Saint-Domingue only in 1802, as a member of the French expedition sent by Bonaparte to overthrow Toussaint's regime.

This military victory was a logical outcome of Toussaint's numerical superiority, but it also reflected the resilient spirit of his republican army. The reports filed by Dessalines contain extraordinary accounts of gallantry, as when the 3rd battalion of *sans-culottes* (assisted by Laplume) were sent to clear out an enemy fortification built on top of a steep ridge in the Acul region. Despite coming under intense fire, they marched up fearlessly, charged their way through the rampart 'with bayonets forward' and took the position, along with a large supply of weapons and munitions; Dessalines noted that four enemy combatants were snatched from the soldiers by their officers and taken prisoner; the rest were 'put to the sword'.[127] The fury of the soldiers, in this instance, was caused by their desire to avenge the recent loss of more than 100 of their comrades from the 7th half-brigade who had been murdered in an ambush by Rigaud's men; the rebels had pretended to be farm labourers who had been forcibly enrolled in Rigaud's army, and were seeking to desert and return to their plantations. When the 7th half-brigade arrived to assist them, they were slaughtered. In his report of the incident to Roume, Toussaint noted that the ringleaders were all people of colour.[128]

It was this explosive combination of racial antagonism, fratricidal conflict and visceral sense of betrayal which accounted for the war of knives' horrific violence. Rigaud's atrocities, the long list of which were methodically reported by Toussaint's officers, were especially directed at the white population in the south: alongside Jérémie, there were mass killings in Les Cayes, and planters were systematically targeted and murdered, with no mercy shown even to women and children.[129] Although Toussaint never practised the same relentless ethnic cleansing, he too was drawn into the downward spiral of violence – not least as the rebels had tried to assassinate him. Even the genteel Roume had urged him to 'exterminate' the insurgents.[130] Little restraint was shown towards the officers who betrayed him: both Christophe Mornet and Pierre Michel were put to death, as were many of their subordinates who were accused of fomenting 'civil war'.[131] At least Michel faced a firing squad: Mornet was bayoneted, and the men who plotted against Toussaint in Gonaïves were executed by cannon; one of them survived the first discharge and the sentence had to be completed by firing squad.[132] There were stories of mass executions, both in territories controlled by Toussaint and by over-zealous officers in the south. According to expatriate French sources, reprisals took place against mixed-race soldiers and civilians in Port-Républicain, Arcahaie, Saint-Marc and Gonaïves after the failure of the insurrection: many were executed by firing squad, and some were chained to each other and thrown into the sea;[133] a letter sent to the French Minister of Navy estimated the number of people of colour killed at 6,000, and compared the atrocities to the massacres of Saint-Barthélémy.[134] Toussaint himself recognized that 'some poor innocents'[135] perished in the fighting, and blamed their deaths on Rigaud.

Even figures sympathetic to Toussaint, such as his emissary Vincent, noted that he sought to 'terrify those guilty of insubordination by dreadful and striking examples'.[136] Which is why, when he reprimanded one of his officers about the excessive spilling of blood, he hardly sounded as if he meant it: 'moué dit baliser, yo dessoucher même'.[137] Perhaps unsurprisingly, the officer responded laconically, quoting one of Toussaint's favourite sayings back to him: 'quand la pluie tombé, tout ca qui dehors mouillé'.[138] But not all were so bloodthirsty: despite his reputation for ferociousness, Dessalines, notably, did his best to protect mixed-race civilians. Toussaint subsequently attempted to rein in the violence of his troops, and his later proclamations offered amnesties to all those in the south who were prepared to lay down their weapons and return to their occupations; he promised to 'forgive and forget everything',[139] and sent Vincent to Les Cayes to negotiate an end to the conflict with Rigaud.[140] He also insisted on the virtues of humanity. A homily from the commander-in-chief was read out to his soldiers before one of their attempts to enter Jacmel, reminding them that the enemy they were about to fight were their brothers, many of whom had taken up arms because they had been misled by Rigaud; he urged them to 'respect the vanquished' and never to undermine their glory 'by spilling the blood of a man who has laid down his weapons'.[141]

This particular attack by Dessalines' forces was pushed back by the insurgents, who erected seven forts, each surrounded by a deep trench, to prevent the republican army from reaching their town; as Toussaint acknowledged after carrying out a reconnaissance of the terrain, 'great measures' were needed to overcome these defences.[142] This decisive contribution came in the end from American naval support: after holding out for six months, Rigaud's men surrendered when the USS *General Greene* bombarded Jacmel's fortifications; the *Experiment* and *Augusta* also participated in the blockade.[143] Indeed, from the moment the war in the south was declared, Consul Stevens extended his full assistance to Toussaint, promising food supplies, weapons and munitions to his under-equipped army.[144] Stevens also denounced Rigaud's 'capricious and tyrannical temper' to the US authorities, stressing 'the absolute necessity of supporting Toussaint by every legal measure'.[145] His calls were heeded, and the unstinting support of the United States not only enabled the crucial victory at Jacmel: American ships (including the USS *Constitution*) ferried Toussaint's troops and gunpowder to the southern front, and blockaded Rigaud's ports while Dessalines' forces attacked by land; they also patrolled the seas and engaged Rigaud's barges, inflicting severe losses on the rebels.[146] Toussaint expressed his delight to the American naval commanders, stressing his enormous debt of gratitude to them.[147] The operation was also hugely profitable to American merchants and even naval officers: Christopher Perry, the captain of the *General Green*, received a reward of 10,000 pounds of coffee from the commander-in-chief for his contribution to the liberation of Jacmel.[148]

As he entered the southern capital of Les Cayes in August 1800, Toussaint's mood was sober. He urged his compatriots across Saint-Domingue to remain vigilant, and declared that man was more inclined 'towards evil than good'[149] – a clear sign that the war of knives had taken its toll on him too. He appointed Laplume as the commander of the southern region: a sensible choice which reflected his desire to restore things to normal as quickly as possible.[150] He commended his soldiers for their bravery and discipline, and ordered them to mark their victory by attending Sunday Mass – perhaps to atone for some of the extreme violence they had resorted to.[151] He blamed the war entirely on Rigaud's 'criminality', stressing that he had 'declared war on the republic', while he himself was motivated by 'the principles of humanity, religion and love' for his compatriots; in this spirit, he extended the hand of forgiveness and reconciliation to the population of the south, whom he promised henceforth to consider as his 'friends and brothers'.[152] The rhetoric was wholly republican, right down to an ideal of fraternity couched in exclusively civic terms: there was no longer mention of white, black or mixed-race people. As Saint-Domingue now looked ahead to the prospect of peace and prosperity, Toussaint expressed his gratitude to the 'Supreme Being', concluding mystically: 'without His guidance, the work of men is perishable, and their designs are more ephemeral than the agitated tides of the sea'.[153]

Toussaint had good reason to be grateful to the Almighty at the end of the twenty-two-month sequence which began with the expulsion of Hédouville and ended with his victory over Rigaud. He had broken Saint-Domingue's economic and political isolation, survived a major challenge to his authority, and asserted the colony's autonomous diplomatic agency in the region. In the process he had consolidated his grip on Saint-Domingue's colonial bureaucracy, despite its notional subordination to Roume – so much so that all applications for passports, for example, now had to be personally sanctioned by Toussaint.[154] He was in absolute charge of the colony's finances, too, as evidenced by his control of all estate leases[155] and the terse instruction issued to one of his senior treasury officials: 'not a penny should leave the coffers without my permission'.[156] In his own mind, as well as in his actions, he had moved further away from France: in early 1800 he told the British representatives in Saint-Domingue that 'the power he possessed, he did not hold from France'.[157]

But these achievements had come at a considerable price, both human and political. He had become even more secretive in his ways, more reliant on his deepest intuitions, and less trusting of his comrades. Hundreds of his valiant republican soldiers had died in the war of knives. And to many of his own admirers, his dealings with the British, his betrayal of his own government's secret plans over Jamaica and his systematic conspiring behind the backs of successive French agents appeared to be inspired more by power politics than by the precepts of Christian or republican morality. Yet Toussaint's actions were driven by strong principles, whose underlying coherence seemed self-evident to him. As he explained to Roume, he would ruthlessly pursue the ideal of a Saint-Domingue which remained an integral part of the French Republic but which also had the freedom to pursue its specific interests – even if these flew in the face of France's diplomatic alignments and political goals.

It was not only to the French agent that Toussaint expressed the difference in his mind between France and Saint-Domingue. Responding to a request from Vincent to be allowed to leave the colony and return to the metropolis, he stated that he 'loved his country too much' to allow the engineer to return to France – a telling distinction.[158] This clash came to a head over his opposition to the Jamaica expedition. In his mind, his rejection of intervention in this case was fully justified by his own revolutionary calculus – whether it was sacrificing Sasportas's life to prevent the deaths of hundreds of his own republican soldiers, preserving his military forces in order to deal with Rigaud's treasonous insurrection, or sabotaging an ill-conceived and potentially unsuccessful French plan in order to safeguard years of patient republican consolidation in Saint-Domingue. Nor did he altogether jettison his dream of liberating his enslaved brethren: according to the memoirs of his son, in his later years he often talked about leading an expeditionary force to Africa to end the slave trade.[159]

Toussaint was no doubt disheartened at times by his dealings with the British. His four captured ships were never returned, nor their imprisoned crew members, although Balcarres tried to intercede in his favour with Hyde Parker. The Jamaican civil and military authorities remained wary of revolutionary Saint-Domingue, especially after Toussaint's victory over Rigaud.[160] Becoming frustrated with the lack of progress with its local agents, especially Parker, who regarded him as an 'enemy',[161] Toussaint decided to try and approach the British government directly. He despatched an envoy to London (a white *colon* named Pennetier) to reaffirm his claims to be a force for stability in the region.[162] With the support of Maitland in London,[163] Pennetier made a favourable impression, stressing that Toussaint was interested only in 'the happiness of his people'[164] – so much so that the Foreign Secretary, the Duke of Portland, eventually came round to the view that it would be in Britain's interests to 'cultivate a good understanding' with the ruler of Saint-Domingue.[165]

The message rapidly trickled down to British merchants, a number of whom established themselves profitably in Port-Républicain and Gonaïves after 1799. Another measure of Toussaint's diplomatic finesse was his ability to charm the British envoys in Saint-Domingue and persuade them to write favourable reports about him to his superiors. He was successful: one of the first of them, for example, commended Toussaint for the 'exactitude and faith' with which he had honoured his commitments so far; he also praised his 'mildness and humanity', and noted that he was 'beloved to a great degree by his people'.[166] But Toussaint was no pushover: especially after the seizure of his ships in late 1799, he was keen to keep the British in their place; their agent in Port-Républicain was not only denied the status of 'consul' but was asked to call himself an American, and got the distinct feeling that he was there 'on sufferance'.[167] Nor did the détente with the British undermine Toussaint's capacity for cheekiness: when another local British representative asked him why a recent batch of deliveries shipped from Jamaica had not been paid for, Toussaint 'coolly' replied that 'he was not the administration', and that 'as a soldier' he did not get involved in such trifling matters.[168]

Toussaint was delighted when his strategy of forging diplomatic links with the United States paid off handsomely under the presidency of John Adams. Thanks to the strong relationship he established with Consul Stevens, he was able to bypass the strict limitations imposed upon Saint-Domingue's naval activities by the Maitland Convention and eventually draw upon American assistance to crush Rigaud's rebellion. In September 1800, Toussaint received consignments of 20,000 rifles, 10,000 pairs of pistols and 60,000 pounds of gunpowder through trade with the United States.[169] Americans became so popular in revolutionary Saint-Domingue that they were known as the 'good whites'.[170] American trading ships brought hundreds of African American sailors to Saint-Domingue, who returned to the United States and spread stories about the revolution and its valiant leaders.[171] There were glowing articles about Toussaint in the American press: the *National Intelligencer and Washington Advertiser* hailed him as 'an extraordinary man'.[172]

Conclusive proof to Toussaint that Providence was by his side, as he brought the war of the knives to a conclusion in Les Cayes, came from a more intimate source. For many decades he had not seen or had news of his half-sister Geneviève, the daughter of his father Hippolyte's first wife Affiba. She had been torn away from the family when he was young and sold to a slave-owner who lived in the south. Hearing that she might be living in Les Cayes, he sought her out and found her happily married to Bernard Chancy, an affluent white planter who had freed her from slavery, and with whom she had had nine children. Toussaint spent some blissful moments with Geneviève, remembering their father and the days when they had been together on the Bréda plantation. He promptly recruited one of her sons as his aide-de-camp and invited two of her daughters to come and live with him. They did so, and one of them, the gracious Louise Chancy, ended up marrying his son Isaac.[173] Toussaint had managed to stand one of his own aphorisms on its head: out of bitterness there could, after all, come something sweet.

8
No Time to Lose

In June 1800 a three-man delegation arrived in Saint-Domingue from France. Its ostensible purpose was to inform the local authorities of the intentions of the consular regime which had replaced the Directory after the 18 Brumaire coup. In article 91 of their constitution of 22 Frimaire an VIII, the new French rulers had decreed that colonies were to be governed by 'special laws' which were adapted to their habits and interests.[1] But behind this lofty nod to the ideal of protecting local customs was a clear effort – led by First Consul Bonaparte – to restore central control over the affairs of Saint-Domingue; under the new arrangements, colonies were no longer to be entitled to their own representatives in the legislature. Aware that their proposals might provoke adverse reactions among the colony's *nouveaux libres*, the Consuls publicly pledged that the 'sacred principles of freedom and equality enjoyed by the blacks will never be encroached upon or modified'.[2]

In a further effort to placate Toussaint, one of the members of the delegation was none other than his own emissary, Charles Vincent. Even though the young engineer had not welcomed his expulsion of Hédouville, he was still highly regarded by Toussaint. Bonaparte was well aware of this, and after receiving a briefing from Vincent in Paris in late 1799 about the situation in the colony he sent him back across the Atlantic. After some initial difficulties – he was detained by an over-zealous military patrol on the road to Cap, beaten and then thrown in jail for three days, during which he survived on a meagre ration of bananas and water – Vincent finally reached Port-Républicain, where he gained access to Toussaint in late June 1800. Transcribed in minute detail, his ensuing conversations with Toussaint painted an absorbing portrait of Saint-Domingue's revolutionary leader at this pivotal juncture in the colony's history.[3]

What struck Vincent most forcefully was Toussaint's intellectual integrity: 'there is no man more attached to the ideal of French republicanism'. Striking, too, was his 'prodigious activity': a typical day at the office would normally last sixteen hours, and his 'indefatigable zeal' was such that every member of his entourage – be it his chief of staff General Agé, his aides-de-camp or his secretaries – was 'overwhelmed with work and exhaustion'. He sent out an average of 200 letters, and was capable of travelling up to forty *lieues*[4] a day, and at full speed no one could match his endurance. In one scene witnessed by the French envoy, Toussaint left Port-Républicain abruptly at two o'clock in the morning, ordering four of his secretaries to follow him on horseback; only one of them, however, was able to keep up with his frenetic pace. Having emasculated Roume's authority, Toussaint was now in charge of all matters, both civilian and military, managing this concentration of power by turning his carriage into a small office and relying on a system of prompt communication.[5] Whenever he arrived at a location, he would order the region's military commander to bring him any new messages or correspondence immediately – whether it came from his officers, from administrators, or from ordinary citizens. He always remained standing when reading these missives and would reply to some instantly. Teams of couriers travelled across the colony, urgently ferrying messages to and from the commander-in-chief. 'Nowhere', marvelled Vincent, 'is correspondence delivered as promptly as in Saint-Domingue.'

The emissaries from France arrived just as the war in the south was reaching its end; as we saw in the previous chapter, Toussaint took the opportunity of Vincent's presence to despatch him to Rigaud with a peace offering. This mission was inconclusive, but it enabled Vincent to observe Toussaint's soldiers and officers in action at close quarters. He was struck by their high morale and their fierce loyalty to their commander-in-chief, whom they regarded as 'a model of the essential virtues'. Their discipline and courage were no less impressive: he noted that all enemy positions taken in the final months of the conflict with Rigaud were captured after intense hand-to-hand combat. Vincent's eye was caught, too, by Toussaint's interactions with ordinary citizens. In addition to responding to their letters, every day at seven in the evening he received thirty men and the same number of women in his 'petits cercles', listening patiently to their petitions and issuing instructions that their complaints, when justified, be dealt with promptly. As he followed him across a number of towns, Vincent noted that, while citizens of all colours and backgrounds were present, from humble labourers to wealthy merchants, a significant proportion of his visitors were European, and that Toussaint was highly respected and even loved by them. They idolized him as their 'protector', and described him as 'the father of the *colons*'.

Watching Toussaint at work, Vincent glimpsed another facet of his efficiency: the papers in his office were meticulously filed, as he saw on one occasion when he went to fetch a letter he had received from the French Navy Minister, picking it out instantly from a mass of documents. Like all those who encountered the commander-in-chief close up, Vincent was in awe of his intellectual qualities: his memory and capacity for concentration, and his ability to reach quick decisions. Vincent's only reservation was about Toussaint's 'firm and absolute character', which stemmed from his total confidence in his own judgement, which 'had rarely led him astray'. Yet this self-assurance could be problematic: 'when he has set his mind on a scheme, he pursues it, without sufficiently worrying about the obstacles and costs incurred by its execution'. Indeed, Vincent could not help but notice that recent events – the rebellion in his own heartlands, the long and bitter war in the south, and the increasingly fraught relationship with national and local representatives of French authority – had all taken their toll on Toussaint. He grumbled that the *cultivateurs* were not working hard enough, and pledged that he would need to take 'measures' to deal with them once the war was over. Even though he had no doubt he was about to defeat Rigaud, there was an air of anxiety about him.

In particular, Toussaint sounded much less sanguine about his future relationship with France, whose politics he described as 'cruel', adding ominously: 'I do not know France and will never know it.' Even by his frugal standards, his consumption of food had diminished considerably: his main meal often consisted of a single piece of salted meat, and he was now extremely thin. In light of the numerous assassination attempts against him, most recently during the war of knives, he had become more secretive and suspicious, even of his inner circle. Vincent noticed that his guides and horses were ready for him to travel at any moment, day or night – but the exact destination of his journey was communicated only ten minutes before his departure. Toussaint still exuded a sense of revolutionary determination, but Vincent also detected a note of foreboding, summed up in an expression he frequently uttered: 'there is no time to lose'.[6]

Vincent was perceptive in detecting a strain of urgency. At the time of his meetings with the French envoy, Toussaint had already set in motion his latest military and diplomatic venture: the takeover by his republican forces of the Spanish-controlled territory of Santo Domingo.

By the Bâle Treaty of 1795, Spain had agreed to hand this province, which lay on the eastern part of the island of Hispaniola and was twice the size of Saint-Domingue, over to France. However, the French authorities at the time had decided to delay taking its possession, initially to avoid adding to the instability which was racking Saint-Domingue; indeed, for much of the 1790s Santo Domingo had remained largely insulated from the conflicts which had ravaged the French colony. It was understood by all parties, nonetheless, that the French would step in once order had been re-established in Saint-Domingue. Having eliminated Rigaud, Toussaint clearly believed that the time had come fully to implement the terms of the 1795 treaty – especially as he thought that the defeat of the Spaniards in Saint-Domingue had been made possible by the efforts of his hardy republican *sans-culottes*. More fundamentally – and this was the instinct of the Caribbean, creole Toussaint – he felt that the island of Hispaniola formed a logical whole, and that its political and administrative unification was consistent with 'the laws of nature'. It was on this basis that Toussaint declared to the American and British representatives in May 1799 that his ambition was to 'obtain supreme and sole authority over the *whole* of the island'.[7]

But by now the situation had become more complicated, locally, nationally and in terms of European diplomacy. The British, it is true, were resigned to Toussaint's takeover of the Spanish territory, even though they did not welcome the prospect; the ever-fearful Governor Balcarres was concerned that it might serve as the prelude for a concerted bid by France and Saint-Domingue to attack Jamaica.[8] However, the French Directory had become increasingly wary of Toussaint's power, and had even openly encouraged Rigaud's secession in order to weaken him; meanwhile the French agent in Santo Domingo, Antoine Chanlatte (a person of colour), had provided active support to 'his friend' Rigaud.[9] This policy of containment was shared after the 18 Brumaire coup by the new consular regime in Paris, which plainly did not relish the prospect of Toussaint's influence increasing across the neighbouring territory – especially as Bonaparte was, for the moment at least, seeking to move away from the Directory's revolutionary expansionism, and was therefore not keen to ruffle Spanish feathers.

Toussaint had his own compelling reasons for wishing to send his forces into Santo Domingo – and speedily. For one thing, he knew that the new French government was opposed to the operation, and he wanted to act pre-emptively: the Consulate's Minister of Navy, Pierre-Alexandre-Laurent Forfait, had written to urge him, in the name of 'sound politics as well as expediency', to 'refrain from making any move whatsoever on the Spanish territory'.[10] He was also only too aware that Santo Domingo was regularly used as a landing port by the French. Hédouville had arrived there in 1798, as had the three-man delegation sent by the consuls;

the territory could therefore serve as a potential base for any invading expedition.

This point was not purely theoretical: the conservative change of regime in Paris had shifted the balance of power towards forces opposed to Saint-Domingue's egalitarian order, and there was now talk of despatching a military contingent to overthrow Toussaint. In mid 1799, for example, a report by Godard, a senior official in the Ministry of Navy, warned that the black people of Saint-Domingue were out of control, and were being encouraged by their commander-in-chief to 'believe they were now above us whites'. He went on to describe Toussaint's rule as a form of 'despotic absolutism', in which the official representatives of the French government had become completely impotent; he further claimed that Europeans in the colony were living 'in a state of terror at least equal to that of slavery'. The time for persuasion, in his view, was over: the only way for things to revert to their rightful order was to 'use coercive force against these rebels so that they learn to respect and submit to the laws of the republic'.[11] As we have seen, Toussaint enjoyed significant support among the *colons* of Saint-Domingue, but there were some sullen locals who shared such views, for example the landowner Paul Alliot, who wrote to the Minister of Navy in 1800 affirming that the only way to bring Toussaint to his senses was by sending 'ten thousand European troops to the colony'.[12]

There was a deeper reason why Toussaint regarded the extension of republican rule to Santo Domingo as an absolute imperative: human bondage was still practised there, and gangs originating from Spanish-controlled areas routinely raided the settlements bordering the French colony to capture young black men and women and sell them into slavery. When General François-Marie de Kerverseau was the French agent in Santo Domingo, he not only turned a blind eye to the practice but allowed slaves captured in Saint-Domingue to be sold in other Caribbean colonies, notably in Cuba.[13] Toussaint demanded that the Cuban authorities return all the black victims of this trafficking.[14] Informed that this 'infamous trade' was being carried out 'every day',[15] Roume asked Commissioner Chanlatte to investigate. The latter eventually confirmed Toussaint's claims, reporting that he had found a young woman named Flore who had been sold to a Spaniard from Santo Domingo and bought back by the French for the sum of 200 *gourdes*;[16] a month later Chanlatte indicated that he had found several other such cases, along with evidence of organized criminal networks, and had officially complained to the Spanish authorities.[17] According to Toussaint's own enquiries, which included gathering direct testimony from French and Spanish citizens, the trade was not carried out in the main towns of Santo Domingo but in more remote regions such as the southern town of Azua, where the authorities did nothing about it.[18] Toussaint's critics have suggested that he fabricated the slavery claims as an excuse to invade the Spanish territory, but the issue was real.[19]

The assumption of French republican control over Santo Domingo was for Toussaint a matter of historical justice, strategic exigency and moral necessity. Already in 1795, shortly after the conclusion of the Bâle Treaty, he had warned 'Papa' Laveaux that the Spanish settlers were entirely untrustworthy and were so vehemently opposed to the abolition of slavery that they would prefer to give up the territory to the British than come under French republican rule.[20] In 1796, a gradual handover to French authorities had to be postponed when it emerged that the Spaniards were acting in bad faith and inviting local populations to rebel against French troops as they arrived.[21] Four years later, Toussaint believed that the moment to take action had come, but he faced a significant obstacle: he could not proceed without the formal agreement of Roume, who was implacably hostile to the takeover. As Vincent had rightly surmised, nothing could stop the commander-in-chief when his mind was settled on a particular scheme. Toussaint would get his way, but only at the cost of another spectacular rupture with the representative of the French government.

Toussaint did his utmost to persuade Roume that Santo Domingo's republican hour had arrived. He bombarded him with letters detailing the instances of enslavement which had been brought to his attention, repeatedly raised the matter in person, and encouraged his senior officers to lobby him. Faced with this barrage, Roume stonewalled: in response to a plea from Moyse, for example, he stated that the French occupation of Santo Domingo could not occur until the 'complete pacification of Saint-Domingue, and perhaps even the general pacification of Europe'. Drawing on his three years of service as a former French commissioner in the territory, Roume added that an invasion would undoubtedly provoke mass resistance from the white Domingans, at least 'ten thousand' of whom might be mobilized to bear arms against Toussaint's army.[22]

Toussaint then tried another approach, in a letter personally delivered by his aide-de-camp, d'Hébécourt: if the occupation of the whole of Santo Domingo could not be envisaged, Roume should sanction the takeover by French troops of neighbourhoods such as Azua and its surrounding areas, which had clearly become the operational centre for the slave traffickers; this was the least that could be done 'to preserve our black citizens from bondage'.[23] Realizing that he needed to address the matter constructively, the French agent replied a few days later. Toussaint was free to arrest anyone from Santo Domingo who might be involved in this slave trade and bring the suspects to Cap, where they would be imprisoned and put on trial; they would also be expected to hand over any slaves in their possession, or buy them back and release them to the French authorities. But on the wider issue of territorial control Roume remained inflexible. Given the continuing volatility in the French colony, the occupation of any part of Santo Domingo would be a 'betrayal of France, of Saint-Domingue, of yourself, and of the army under your command'. He presented three additional arguments: the populations of the Azua region had been 'energetically worked on by British agents', and would therefore be antagonized by any sustained French military presence; the former French commissioner Kerverseau, who had become a renegade, had spread rumours of an imminent French invasion before his departure and stirred up anti-republican sentiment in Santo Domingo; and any future French occupation could be carried out only by European forces, which were insufficient in number in Saint-Domingue at present.[24]

Toussaint would undoubtedly have been offended by the implication that his highly disciplined and gallant troops, who had liberated the colony from Spanish and British occupation, were now deemed unsuitable to carry out this operation. Beginning in late February 1800, he repeatedly summoned Roume to Port-Républicain: the well-being of the colony was at stake.[25] Roume refused, and so Toussaint decided to force his hand. Following the template he had successfully used against Hédouville, in the first week of April he organized a popular mobilization of his supporters from Dondon, Petite Anse, Grande-Rivière, Gros-Morne, Sainte-Suzanne and Limonade. Several thousand members of the National Guard from these communities – many in arms – rapidly converged towards Haut du Cap, where they assembled and demanded to see Toussaint, and threatened to march on Cap if their grievances against Roume were not immediately heard by representatives of the French government. On 11 April Roume, who kept a diary of the proceedings,[26] was escorted by Moyse to meet the demonstrators; he was accompanied by the entire municipality of Cap. This was classic *journée révolutionnaire* politics, in which public demonstrations were used to force specific concessions from the authorities. Except that now Toussaint introduced some Caribbean refinements: instead of lasting a day or two, as would a typical Parisian *journée*, the movement here went on for fourteen days and nights. During this ordeal, Roume and his associates were incarcerated in a chicken coop measuring barely 100 square feet, where they were exposed to the elements. The flimsy roof of the *poulailler* offered scant protection from the rain, and, as the diarist noted grimly, it poured heavily for four days.

In due course a string of popular petitions emerged, written in florid republican prose and signed by civic and military representatives from the different localities. Invoking the principle of the public good which Toussaint had cited in his earlier letter to the French agent, they presented a vote of no confidence in Roume, accusing him of heinous crimes against the republic such as supporting Rigaud, conniving with British agents in Jamaica (a touch of black humour by Toussaint here), squandering public funds, conspiring with émigrés and refusing to meet Toussaint, despite the latter's repeated requests. At the same time, the tone of the protesters was optimistic: the declaration from Gros-Morne expressed the citizens' pride in belonging to the French nation, which had 'laid down the law to all the powers of Europe and indeed even to the universe'.[27]

In the midst of all this revolutionary theatre, the hero himself – in keeping with his leadership style – was absent; the petitioners from Dondon noted anxiously that they had not seen Toussaint for several years.[28] Three successive letters were despatched, pleading with him to come to Haut du Cap, but he sent word back that he was unavoidably detained by more pressing military concerns (it was true that this episode coincided with the recapture of Jacmel in the south). Sensing that he had sufficiently softened up Roume, he announced that he was on his way, and even invited the mobilized citizens to return to their plantations. Finally, more than a week later, Toussaint arrived on horseback to huge cheers from the crowd, which Roume noted had now grown to 8,000 men and women. Toussaint brought the mobilization to an end by announcing grandly that he would take the necessary steps to 'bring tranquillity and respond to the concerns of the people';[29] on 24 April he ordered Moyse to escort Roume back to the Agency in Cap. At least the French agent was able to hitch a ride on horseback: the municipal representatives had to return on foot.

The final act in Roume's downfall opened three days later, on 7 Floréal (27 April), when he was summoned to Toussaint's residence at nine in the morning, again under Moyse's escort; the representatives of the Cap municipality were also present, along with Toussaint's treasurer Bunel. In a sombre tone, Toussaint again demanded Roume's endorsement of the proposed takeover of Santo Domingo. The French agent reiterated his well-rehearsed reasons for his opposition, adding a fresh argument: he had heard that the Spanish authorities were keen to retain Santo Domingo, but were prepared to offer up Louisiana instead – a highly advantageous proposition for the French. Toussaint responded tersely that 'a certain gain should not be sacrificed for a mere probability'. He also summarily dismissed Roume's other objections, notably the fear that a French occupation might provoke unrest and possibly armed resistance. At this point, Toussaint lost his temper. Accusing Roume of being an 'enemy of the colony', he turned melodramatically to the members of the Cap municipality and asked with a menacing air: 'What should I do with such a man?' Leaving the threat hanging, he dismissed the stunned representatives and sent Roume back to the Agency building, where Moyse locked him up in a small room on the first floor, threatening to 'cut off his head' and that of his wife and young daughter if he did not immediately concede. Roume replied that he was prepared to die as a republican martyr, at which point Moyse promised to launch a full-scale military invasion and to spread death and destruction across the Spanish territory. Roume capitulated, and drafted the decree promulgating the French takeover of Santo Domingo; it was signed a few hours later in the presence of a stern-looking Toussaint.[30]

The breach with Roume was now irreversible. Toussaint effectively confined him to the Agency offices in Cap, monitored his communications and stationed soldiers to guard the building and deny entry to visitors. Roume's wife Marie-Anne was also prevented from going into town, and on one occasion the guards stopped Roume's laundry from being taken out.[31] Yet, once he received the signature he wanted, Toussaint tried to mend fences with the French agent, at least on a personal level. He invited Madame Roume to his residence and confessed that he was ashamed of the indignities he had inflicted upon her husband, but the truth was that he could no longer trust him. Shortly afterwards, Roume collapsed from the strain and fell seriously ill. He was bedridden for over a month, during which Toussaint visited him on a number of occasions. At one point his condition took a turn for the worse, and was judged to be critical by his doctor. Toussaint rushed to his bedside and wept profusely – although he did let slip that his sorrow was mainly due to his fear that his enemies would blame him for Roume's death.[32]

The beginning of the Santo Domingo operation was disastrous. Confident that his envoy would meet no resistance from the Spaniards, Toussaint sent his chief of staff, General Agé, to the territory without even a military escort, armed only with 400 copies of Roume's decree of 7 Floréal and a mellifluous letter from himself, promising that France would 'respect all persons and properties, and the habits and customs of the Spaniards, while bringing them under the laws of the republic'.[33] Agé was duly introduced to Don Joaquín García, the wily and cruel old governor, whom Toussaint remembered very well from his days of service under the Spanish flag.[34] García welcomed Toussaint's envoy unctuously, and greedily accepted the beautiful jewels he brought as gifts. He entirely recognized France's entitlement to assume full control of Santo Domingo by virtue of the 1795 treaty, and even claimed such a move would be a relief, as he could then retire peacefully to Havana. However, he pleaded that he needed time to consult with his superiors and make the necessary arrangements for an 'orderly' withdrawal; he could not therefore accede to Toussaint's request 'with the desired speed'.[35]

Don García's response was merely a delaying tactic: when he first learned of Toussaint's plans, he had written to his superiors in Spain that 'this negro will find a stronger resistance among our inhabitants than he might expect'.[36] Indeed, within days of Agé's arrival, local opposition to the French takeover began to coalesce in the territory's *cabildos* (municipalities). Encouraged by García, a petition signed by leading Santo Domingo creole dignitaries called for the operation to be 'adjourned' while the matter was referred to the French and Spanish governments, and a delegation sent to Paris to seek an audience with Bonaparte; it was also to appeal to the First Consul's belief that colonies should be governed by laws which suited their local customs.[37] Another declaration noted that a handover to France given the present circumstances in Saint-Domingue would be 'inconvenient' – a coded expression of these notables' horror at the prospect of losing their slaves and coming under black republican rule.[38] Buoyed by this support from the territory's reactionary ruling classes, and quietly supported by the French representative, Chanlatte, García issued a decree effectively suspending the takeover, and calling on all French forces to withdraw from Santo Domingo until the dispute had been fully resolved.[39] As tensions rose, Toussaint's envoy had to be placed under military protection in the Santa Clara convent where he was residing, as crowds outside chanted 'death to Agé'. The French general was soon escorted out of town by the governor and a delegation from the *cabildos*. Toussaint's envoy had been humiliated – and Don García had kept the jewels.

At this point Roume, who had recovered from his illness, reminded Toussaint that he had predicted that things would go badly, and that his objections during their fraught discussion should have been heeded.[40] He endorsed a compromise position suggested by García (and which had originally been made by Toussaint himself) that the takeover be postponed, but that French commissioners be stationed in Azua and Santiago to prevent any recurrence of slave-trafficking. He also recommended – not without malice – that Agé be appointed as commissioner at Azua, an impertinent suggestion regarding Toussaint's chief of staff.[41] Roume rubbed more salt in the wound by blaming the entire debacle on Agé, whose 'indiscretions', he claimed, had unsettled the Spaniards, adding that his well-known 'fondness for drink' had probably not helped either.[42] He then issued a proclamation which declared his own 7 Floréal decree 'null and void' in light of the 'mass insurgency' it had provoked in Santo Domingo, and the ensuing possibility of 'war' between Saint-Domingue and her neighbour; he also welcomed the arrangements proposed by the Spanish authorities to prevent any further trafficking of French slaves.[43]

Toussaint was, predictably, exasperated by this turn of events. He told Roume that he was 'very distressed', especially at the prospect of the slave trade continuing across the border. He regarded the behaviour of the Santo Domingo authorities as 'deceitful', and the forcible expulsion of Agé as a 'grave insult' not only to the republic but also to himself. He particularly blamed the *cabildos* for creating an atmosphere of 'intrigue' and spreading wild rumours about the likely consequences of a French takeover. He pointedly observed that these generally placid local grandees were unlikely to have acted spontaneously, and suspected some underhand collusion between French and Spanish officials against him; it was hardly coincidental that one of Roume's employees, a natural scientist by the name of Gonzalez, had been seen in Santo Domingo during the upheavals.[44]

In a subsequent letter he was even more explicit, accusing Roume of personally inciting the Spanish revolt against Agé because of his visceral opposition to the takeover of Santo Domingo. He also defended the reputation of his chief of staff, who had carried out his mission with 'wisdom and prudence'; he had even given up drinking since his 'marriage to a good woman' (Toussaint had of course been the matchmaker; he made a habit of finding spouses for members of his military and administrative entourage).[45] Yet he ended the letter on a peaceful note, claiming that he had now reconciled himself to the indefinite postponement of the Santo Domingo operation: 'I have stopped thinking about it.'[46] This was absolutely not the case, as we shall see, but for the moment at least Toussaint decided to reassure Roume and the officials in Santo Domingo that he had moved on. Even in moments of revolutionary urgency, it was sometimes politic to bide one's time.

Roume understood that the disagreement over Santo Domingo had fractured his relationship with Toussaint. But he still cared passionately about the colony's future. He also shared the commander-in-chief's concern about the reactionary forces, both within and outside French government circles, which were now shaping the new regime's policy towards Saint-Domingue, and in particular their increasing contemplation of the use of military force against Toussaint. In June 1800 he produced a lengthy recommendation of an alternative course of action and sent it off to Paris. This report was remarkable for its elevated tone, for its probing analysis of the situation, for its capacity to project optimistically into the future and imagine a consensual relationship between Saint-Domingue and France. Above all it was perceptive in its sensitive portrait of Toussaint's leadership and the underlying sources of his power. At the same time, in its paternalistic tone it revealed the fault lines between even the best-intentioned French colonial officials and Saint-Domingue's revolutionary leaders.

Roume began by emphasizing the extent to which Toussaint's power was rooted in Saint-Domingue's revolutionary political culture. The slaves had conquered their freedom by revolting against their oppressors and forcing the French authorities to acknowledge their liberty. During this process the 'Africans', as he called them, had developed an extensive set of democratic practices centred around 'popular assemblies', where they conducted their affairs with 'sagacity and energy'. During the later years of the revolution, even as Toussaint's power became more entrenched, this vibrant local democracy survived and was given 'republican forms', notably in institutions such as Saint-Domingue's National Guard, which acted as a deliberative assembly, a 'grand council of the commune'. Its citizens participated in all the important decisions, and Roume insisted that while they generally followed their leaders' recommendations, their obedience was not 'blind'; indeed, on some occasions they refused to take the course of action prescribed to them. Roume had recently seen these principles in action during his fourteen-day escapade at Haut du Cap. There he had been at the receiving end of many vigorous harangues, but he paid a generous tribute to the robustness of the *cultivateurs*' republican sentiments. Order, tranquillity and secrecy were the characteristics of this African democratic spirit, he said, and it was no accident that they were also the hallmarks of Toussaint's power.[47]

For Roume, Toussaint enjoyed the 'unconditional' support of Saint-Domingue's black citizens precisely because of his consistent and zealous defence of their rights. He also had the 'absolute esteem and trust' of the colony's European population: Roume had personally witnessed this on countless occasions, and he noted with amusement that even when whites complained about one of Toussaint's decisions, they tended to lay the blame on his entourage, who exploited his 'goodness'. Having taken the lead in expelling first the Spaniards then the British from the colony, Toussaint had the republic's everlasting gratitude. And yet, precisely because he owed these accomplishments only to himself and the qualities he had harnessed from nature, he had not, in Roume's view, acquired any of the conventions of European military discipline; in fact, his political and military triumphs had 'exalted his *amour propre* beyond the limits of reason'.[48] Driven by his 'indomitable character' and his 'transcendental genius', as well as his fear that the French Revolution might be defeated by its European enemies, Toussaint was moving the colony towards a position where its fate no longer depended on that of France; he did not wish his people to be 'dismembered'. It was in this context that Roume issued his warning against any French military invasion of Saint-Domingue: such a war would be prolonged, costly in resources and in men, and would be resisted by black citizens 'to the final extremity'.[49]

To avert such a calamity Roume suggested a plan, to be implemented in two phases. The first would involve the French government formally withdrawing its agent – himself – from the colony, and entrusting Toussaint not only with military but also civilian executive functions. The idea here was to reassure him about France's intentions towards him, and also force him to take more efficient decisions. It was particularly important that his letter of appointment be signed by Bonaparte in person: its receipt would 'fill the commander-in-chief with gratitude', 'reconcile Toussaint with himself' and 'consume him with veneration for the First Consul'. The letter should be followed by more detailed instructions from the Minister of Navy, reminding Toussaint of his obligations towards France, of the need to run the affairs of the colony with financial rigour and impartiality, and warning him against getting too close to the dastardly British. This was the 'only practical solution'[50] for Saint-Domingue in the short run.

Upon the conclusion of a more general peace between France and her European rivals, the second phase of the plan could be set in motion: it would involve Bonaparte again writing to Toussaint, this time with a grand invitation to visit Paris to celebrate his achievements and also 'enlighten the French government with his suggestions about the future of the colony'. With characteristic faith in French universalism, Roume believed that spending time in the capital of the world would have a miraculous effect on Toussaint: 'within a month' of his stay, he would be 'fully cured of all his schemes for colonial autonomy'[51] and place himself 'at the level of our best French citizens'. Simultaneously – while Toussaint was away from Saint-Domingue – work could begin on a new 'organic code' overhauling the colony's political and administrative system, which would be promulgated after consultations among representatives of different racial and territorial groups in the colony. Toussaint would not be allowed to return until this task had been fully completed.

There was something naïvely enchanting about Roume's dream of Toussaint and Bonaparte riding into the Place de la Concorde alongside each other to the cheers of the Parisian crowds, having celebrated a *Te Deum* in Notre Dame Cathedral. It was greatly to his credit that he did not allow his stormy disagreements with Toussaint in the preceding months – not to mention his fortnight in the Haut-du-Cap chicken coop – to cloud his judgement. And though events took a very different turn, Roume's vision is a reminder that the breakdown between France and Saint-Domingue was not inevitable, and that alternative scenarios based on sustained co-operation were possible and indeed fully envisaged on both sides of the Atlantic. At the same time, in its infantilization of Toussaint and faith in the superiority of Gallic civilization, Roume's scheme reveals the limits of the French republican imagination when faced with the boldness of Saint-Domingue's revolution. Toussaint would not have been won over by being called to Paris and patted on the head by the Consuls like a fawning tropical bumpkin: he had his own ideas about what the good life for himself and his people should be – and they were very different from those of the French.

Toussaint, meanwhile, was also deploying his creative talents to carve out a line of communication with the new consular authorities. He decided to use General Claude-Étienne Michel, the head of the three-man delegation which had been sent to Saint-Domingue from Paris, as his principal conduit. He prepared the ground by psychologically destabilizing the French envoy, ordering Moyse to arrest him upon his arrival and detain him under severe conditions for five days in a remote village. When Michel eventually reached Cap, Moyse (manifestly on Toussaint's orders) prevented him from making contact with Roume, even though this was a key part of his mission, and also blocked him from meeting Toussaint. When, several weeks later, Michel finally gained access to Toussaint, he was grateful merely to be admitted into his presence: the revolutionary leader thus began the encounter with a strong advantage.[52]

This was merely the opening gambit. In the course of their two lengthy meetings, Toussaint put on a spectacular show for Michel. The French envoy had already formed a very negative opinion of Moyse, whom he described as 'vain, barbaric and despotic'; Toussaint claimed that he shared this view, and that he too felt intimidated by his nephew and did not 'dare contradict' him, or for that matter his other senior generals, such as Dessalines and Christophe, who were watching his every move. The only people in his entourage he claimed he could really trust were his chief of staff Agé and his spiritual councillor, the priest Antheaume; the others were all 'parasites'. He confided that his personal situation was precarious and that he could be 'removed from power at any moment' by his ambitious subordinates, who were pressing him to act decisively over Santo Domingo. His generals' power had spun out of control, he added melodramatically, and they were even carrying out 'exactions and atrocities' in his name (a reference to the military campaign against Rigaud); at this point, Michel noted, Toussaint became tearful and whispered that he 'feared for his own life'.[53]

The purpose of this theatrical performance was to impress upon the French government the urgent need to throw its weight unequivocally behind Toussaint: it was only under these circumstances, he told Michel, that 'the vacillating edifice' of his power could be stabilized. His ploy worked: the French envoy concluded his report by noting that Toussaint was the sole figure in the colony who could command the support of all sections of the population and at the same time serve the interests of the French government, to which he was 'sincerely attached'. He recommended that he be given 'full powers' so as to be able to deal with his opponents effectively, and that this measure be formalized through a 'handwritten letter by General Bonaparte', from whom Toussaint was eager to receive instructions.[54] Michel's advice was in this respect identical to Roume's, even though the two men did not exchange views prior to the despatch of his report.

Toussaint completed his approach by entrusting Michel with a letter for Bonaparte. He clearly regarded the First Consul as his appropriate interlocutor in Paris, rather than the Minister of Navy, Forfait, about whose name he used to joke.[55] Toussaint's letter began by regretting that Michel had not come to the colony bearing a note from the First Consul: such a 'precious letter' would have been 'a source of great consolation, and spread a comforting balm through his blood'. He trusted that the two of them would henceforth engage in a sustained correspondence. He had given Michel a 'full and frank' account of the situation in Saint-Domingue, and expressed his 'worries and concerns' about the challenges he was facing; he specifically mentioned the 'insulting treatment' received by Agé in Santo Domingo and condemned the 'intrigues' of the local Spanish authorities. Conscious that there were officials in the French government who were spreading hostile stories about him, Toussaint reaffirmed his loyalty to France and his personal integrity: he did not possess a large fortune, and indeed regarded money as a 'corrupting metal'.[56] To strengthen the personal bond he hoped to establish with France's new ruler he also talked about his pride in his two older children, Isaac and Placide, who were being educated at the Institut National in France, and asked Bonaparte to extend his 'paternal benevolence' towards them and to send one of them back to him in Saint-Domingue.[57]

But even though he sought to establish a direct dialogue with Bonaparte, Toussaint was under no illusions about him. At around the same time as he sent this letter, he despatched his lieutenants Huin and d'Hébécourt to France on a covert mission to try and bring back both his children.[58] Toussaint also flatly refused his request, conveyed through Vincent, to embroider on the banner of the Saint-Domingue National Guard the inscription: 'Brave blacks, remember that it is only France which recognizes your freedom and your equal rights'. As he told Vincent sharply: 'we are not looking for a circumstantial freedom, conceded just to us: we want the recognition of the principle that any man, be he red, black or white, cannot be the property of another man. We are free because of our struggle, and because we are stronger. The consul has maintained slavery on Bourbon island, and we too will become his slaves if he is strong.'[59]

And so, in his letter to Bonaparte, Toussaint asserted his version of the Santo Domingo crisis. He had 'strongly encouraged but not coerced' Roume into signing the decree of 7 Floréal – an inventive rendering of what had actually occurred. He lamented General Agé's demeaning reception when he tried to take possession of the territory 'in the name of the French Republic', noting also that this Spanish opposition had benefited from 'underhand connivances' on the French side. He went to considerable lengths to justify the takeover, speaking of the popular indignation felt across the colony at the capture and sale of French citizens. General Michel could independently attest to the reality of the phenomenon, and this was indeed the case: on his journey from Santo Domingo to Cap, the French envoy had personally encountered three black French citizens being led away to a jetty by a group of Spaniards in order to be sold into slavery; Michel had stopped and confronted the traffickers and freed their captives.[60] The implication was clear: the stand-off in the Spanish-controlled territory would not be allowed to endure for much longer.

In the months immediately following Agé's mortifying exit from Santo Domingo, everything went quiet. Toussaint seemed anxious to lower the tension. In addition to his letter reassuring Roume that the takeover was no longer in his mind, he wrote soothingly to Don García, expressing his relief that the matter was now in the hands of the French and Spanish authorities, and promising that he would await their decision.

He then made a series of well-publicized interventions to reinforce the impression that his thoughts were now turned squarely on domestic matters. In October 1800 he produced a proclamation on the reorganization of agricultural labour which was aimed at eliminating 'loitering and vagrancy' in the workforce, and ultimately placed managers, *conducteurs* and labourers under a draconian regime of military surveillance: the army's job, it clearly implied, was now to oversee the territory's economic productivity.[61] He ordered Vincent off to the western tip of the colony in Môle Saint-Nicolas, to survey the local fortifications, so that he would be out of the way. Toussaint was right to be wary of him: when he eventually returned to France in 1801 he supplied the government with detailed maps of the colony, as well as information about individual members of his entourage.[62] Toussaint also celebrated the pacification of Saint-Domingue. In late November 1800, after being feted as a hero in Gonaïves, he visited Cap, where he attended a lavish reception in his honour in the style of a Roman triumph: an arc de triomphe was erected to greet his arrival and a white woman 'of exceptional beauty' solemnly placed a crown of laurels on his head. The municipal representatives, who had not forgotten the terrifying scene with Roume a few months earlier, and clearly deciding that sycophancy was the wisest course, made a succession of speeches comparing him variously to Bacchus, Hercules and Alexander the Great; Bonaparte was also mentioned for good measure.[63]

But, just as his opponents' guard was lowered, Toussaint struck decisively. From Cap, amidst the ceremonial adulation, he sent Roume a letter accusing him of promoting 'discord and anarchy' in the colony by surrounding himself with 'wicked schemers' who were preying on the minds of the weak, spreading yet more rumours of his connivance with the British and making scurrilous accusations against him to his French superiors – a charge which confirmed that Toussaint was reading Roume's correspondence (as an American diplomat noted euphemistically, letters in Saint-Domingue were 'liable to casualties').[64] On the matter of Santo Domingo, he repeated his claim that Roume had colluded with García and the French commissioner, Chanlatte, to humiliate Agé and prevent the takeover of the Spanish territory.[65] Roume would have heard all of this before, but this time the sting came in the letter's tail: Toussaint ordered that the French agent be transported under military escort (inevitably, by Moyse) with his wife and daughter to the remote and humid region of Dondon, where he was to remain until he was recalled by the French government; the offices of the Agency in Cap were to be sealed off. Even though Toussaint promised that Roume would not come to any physical harm, this banishment of the official representative of the French government was an extreme punishment, especially as Toussaint immediately made the news public.[66]

The rationale for his action only became clear a few weeks later, when Toussaint sent a stiff letter to García. Demanding 'reparation' for the 'insulting' way in which the authorities of Santo Domingo had treated his envoy Agé, he announced his renewed intention to take control of the territory, promising again to respect the persons and properties of the

Spaniards as well as their religious customs. This time, the operation would be carried out by an 'armed force sufficiently powerful to ensure the execution of the [1795] treaty and the protection of the whole of this part of the colony from the machinations of the enemies of the republic'.[67] He warned the inhabitants against any resistance, offering them a simple choice: 'between happiness and misery, it is for you to choose'.[68] There would be no more diplomatic niceties: Toussaint was again on the warpath, and this time he had made absolutely sure Roume could not get in his way.

The military operation mobilized a force of over 10,000 men, assembled in three republican divisions which approached Santo Domingo's capital in a pincer movement. The northern column, under Moyse's command, had orders to make for Santo Domingo via the town of Santiago, while Toussaint himself headed a second force which took the southern route through San Juan and Azua, backed by a third contingent entrusted to his brother Paul.[69] Moyse reached Santiago in mid January 1801, after defeating a sizeable Spanish force at El Portezuelo; he placed Brigadier-General François Pageot in charge of the town and continued his advance at speed.[70] As they progressed, the black republican troops called on plantation slaves to revolt against their owners, and promised them full emancipation.[71] Toussaint entered San Juan in early January 1801, where he wrote again to Don García, who had ignored his previous communication: this letter arrived in the capital on the day of the Feast of the Epiphany, but was definitely not the kind of revelation the Spanish governor had been expecting. García responded evasively and sent out a force to confront Toussaint's troops, who by now had taken the towns of Azua and Bani, twelve *lieues* away from the capital. Among those who volunteered to fight on the Dominican side was the French commissioner, Chanlatte, who was appointed by García to lead the troops sent out to confront Toussaint. The main battle in the republican takeover of the Spanish territory was thus fought by French commanders on both sides. Chanlatte nominated as his chief of staff his predecessor Kerverseau, who happened to be in Santo Domingo at the time and eagerly seized the opportunity to take up arms against Toussaint.

Even with these treacherous reinforcements, the Spanish militia was no match for Toussaint's army. His infantry troops marched so quickly that they covered twenty-five *lieues* per day, even outpacing his cavalry, more than half of whose horses were unable to keep up with this frenzied pace.[72] Thanks to his effective network of informants, recruited from the local population, Toussaint's men knew precisely the enemy's whereabouts. Toussaint ordered his forces to set up camp on the right bank of the River

Nizao and hold their position so as to draw Chanlatte's men towards them. Once the Spanish troops had congregated on the opposite bank, Toussaint's forces crossed the Nizao by stealth, hid in the forest overnight and launched a surprise attack on the morning of 22 January. Charged at from three sides by Toussaint's columns, the bewildered Spanish militia fled and, in Chanlatte's own words, 'were absolutely routed'. Toussaint displayed his humanity – and his tactical good sense – by releasing all his Spanish prisoners immediately and issuing them with safe-conducts, stressing that his troops wished the citizens of Santo Domingo no harm and urging them to give up all resistance.[73]

The message was promptly received, and Don García capitulated shortly afterwards. The renegades Chanlatte and Kerverseau wisely took the first ship out of the territory to Venezuela.[74] The victor, whose troops had reunited with those of Moyse, entered Santo Domingo on 26 January 1801. He came through the gates slowly on his favourite horse, Bel-Argent, as if to exorcize the humiliation inflicted earlier on Agé, and stopped in front of the cathedral where the brother of Christopher Colombus was buried. A delegation of women of all colours came to greet him, accompanied by music and fanfares; they too were on horseback, and were carrying banners, branches of laurels and flowers. Toussaint was escorted to the government offices, where he was met by local notables who accompanied him to the office of Governor García.[75]

There had been many extraordinary episodes in Toussaint's life since 1791 but few could match this moment, when the black revolutionary leader found himself once again in the company of the Spanish governor, under whom he had served and whom he had already humiliated once before when he rallied to the French camp in 1794. The crushing defeat of García's militias was compounded when Toussaint refused his invitation to take a solemn oath to protect Santo Domingo; 'this would be the first time', the commander-in-chief retorted, 'that a victor yields to the vanquished'.[76] Toussaint loftily asked García to hand over the keys of the capital. The governor took him to the Assembly chamber and pointed to a set of ceremonial keys, laid out on a table, hoping that Toussaint would take them himself; but, ever conscious of the power of political symbolism, Toussaint asked García to hand them to him. He then reminded the governor of the early 1790s, when he had been an officer in the service of the Spanish Crown and had worked on an ingenious plan for the invasion and conquest of the French side of the island. García had contemptuously rejected the scheme; the tables had now turned and he was handing the keys of Santo Domingo to a French officer. Toussaint insolently added: 'if you had followed my original plan, I would still be at the service of his

Catholic Majesty, and Spain would be in possession of the whole of the island of Saint-Domingue'.[77]

'Ne perdons pas notre temps': never was Toussaint more faithful to his revolutionary motto than in the months which followed his successful campaign in Santo Domingo. He bundled Don García and his retinue off the island in February 1801, after relieving the governor of the 298,000 *gourdes* in his treasury;[78] 'not a single *gourde*' could be allowed to leave the colony, he wrote disingenuously to García, lest it fell into British hands.[79] With typical aplomb, Toussaint had fooled the Spanish government into thinking that his invasion of Santo Domingo had the full backing of Britain and the United States.[80]

The conqueror also sent Bonaparte a brisk message that the whole of Hispaniola was now under republican rule, and invited him to recall Roume to France, as the French agent's head had been poisoned 'by intrigue and malice'.[81] In a longer letter written to the First Consul on the same day he allowed himself to show off, praising his soldiers for their gallantry and fortitude during the Santo Domingo campaign. He also informed him that he had promoted Moyse and Dessalines to the rank of division general – the latter for his pivotal role in defeating Rigaud, the former for his prowess against the Spaniards.[82] Toussaint's praise for Moyse was a tragic irony, given that his nephew was soon to betray him. But there was little doubt that Moyse had earned the commendation: even his enemies conceded that he was a brave and formidable warrior.[83]

In Toussaint's mind the decommissioning of the Spanish and French envoys had edged Saint-Domingue further on its mercurial road towards autonomy. In April 1801, after nonchalantly giving him the news about Santo Domingo and enquiring about his health and that of his family, Toussaint ordered Roume to leave Saint-Domingue – but the real point of his letter was to underline that he had been right all along, against Roume's objections.[84] Roume had been kept in extreme confinement for five months, without any possibility of movement or communication; had it not been for the help discreetly provided by the American consul, Stevens, he and his family could have starved. He responded angrily, giving Toussaint an opportunity for a final touch of cruelty: he informed the Cap municipality that the agent had become mentally unbalanced, and that in light of his age and infirmities he needed to leave the colony forthwith.[85]

The protection of the territory's labourers was one of Toussaint's first priorities, especially when he learned that Spanish families were deserting Santo Domingo's plantations in droves and taking their house and field slaves with them. By late January 1801 it was estimated that more than

3,000 men and women had been forcibly removed by their owners and taken to nearby Spanish dominions, most notably Cuba. Toussaint took immediate action, reminding the Spaniards that many of these slaves were citizens of Saint-Domingue who had been captured illegally. When he learned that a vessel named *Trois Mâts* was about to set sail from Santo Domingo with a large contingent of slaves on board he ordered their release, adding that it was his duty to 'preserve this workforce for the cultivation of the land'.[86]

Did this mean, as some of Toussaint's critics have claimed, that he had no real desire to free the slaves of Santo Domingo and was only interested in their labouring capability? Beginning with Ardouin, who noted that there was no formal proclamation of emancipation, some scholars have questioned whether the slaves of Santo Domingo were actually freed;[87] others have even suggested that Toussaint only obtained the support of the Spanish planters by promising that they could keep their slaves, and that human bondage persisted 'in fact, if not in law'.[88] There is, however, clear evidence of Toussaint's emancipation of the slaves of Santo Domingo: on the day he took formal possession of the territory from García, 15,000 were freed.[89] He insisted that they received payment for work, and prevented any more local planters from leaving the territory with their slaves; Toussaint was also clear that the old system of institutionalized racism could no longer endure.[90] This is supported by the memoirs of local aristocrats, who complained bitterly about their new predicament, and indeed suddenly found themselves forced to tolerate new forms of social equality which they regarded as ignominious. At one ball given in honour of the French military, a Santo Domingo nobleman was invited to dance with his former black slave; as he put it sullenly, 'she owed her liberty to the entry of blacks in the country'.[91]

In fact, Toussaint challenged the racial hierarchies of Spanish colonial society as soon as he took control of the territory, notably by nominating black and mixed-race people to public offices in the army, the administration and the *cabildos*. The new municipality of Santiago, for example, was made up of three full members: a white person, a mixed-race official and a black military officer named Casimiro.[92] When Toussaint issued a proclamation in early February 1801 promising all slaves in Santo Domingo their liberty, he specified that they would receive a quarter of the crop as salary, exactly as in the French part of the island. At the same time, he was careful to warn the plantation workers that their new entitlements came with responsibilities:

> this is a good father speaking to his children, who is showing them the path to happiness, for themselves and for their families, and who wants to see

> them contented. I have never believed that freedom and licence are the same, and that men who have become free can abandon themselves to laziness or disorder; my clear intention is that all *cultivateurs* should remain attached to their respective plantations, where they should earn a quarter of the crop revenues, and any unjust treatment meted out to them should be sanctioned; however, I also want them to work even harder than before, be obedient, and fulfil their duties scrupulously.[93]

In another decree issued on the same day, Toussaint declared that all Santo Domingo's inhabitants were henceforth bound by the rule of French law, which explicitly prohibited slavery. He noted that 'enemies of the republic' were spreading vile rumours about the new order in Santo Domingo so as to encourage the flight of the Spanish population: in particular, it was being suggested that he had granted his soldiers 'four hours of pillage', and that his forces had drawn up a list of prominent Spaniards who were to be assassinated. After denying these stories, Toussaint declared that he personally guaranteed the safety of 'all persons and properties', and concluded that 'all citizens *without distinction*' were henceforth 'placed under the protection of the republic'.[94] The language could not have been clearer.

Over the coming weeks and months Toussaint threw all his energy into Santo Domingo, introducing a series of sweeping reforms which touched all sectors of public and private activity. He appointed a new keeper of the public archives, reorganized the tribunal of commerce in the capital, brought in new municipal officers, created a corps of gendarmes in every commune (with the important stipulation that each should have a trumpeter), set up public schools, appointed eight public defenders (four in Santo Domingo and four in Santiago), built new roads (notably one connecting Santo Domingo to Laxavon, separated by eighty *lieues*), and opened six ports to foreign trade, while at the same time lowering taxes and duties so as to attract outside investment; he also introduced horse-driven carriages to the territory, which were soon racing around Santo Domingo at Louverturian speed.[95] He even found time to act as marriage counsellor: he wrote to García requiring that one of his officers should honour his promise to marry the daughter of Doña Guerrero; 'morality', he observed, 'had to be protected'.[96]

In this torrent of proclamations, one of the most remarkable invited 'new settlers' from Saint-Domingue to seize the opportunities offered by the territory. This was Toussaint displaying his wonderfully eclectic qualities: visionary lyricism, closeness to nature and, in this instance, a touch of colonial entrepreneurship. He extolled the merits of the 'superb plain of Samanà', upon which 'Providence seems to have spread all her favours'.

This was an eldorado: 'fit for all types of agriculture, it enjoys an astonishing degree of fertility, and a milder temperature than all the other plains of Saint-Domingue; it is also blessed with easy access, and is irrigated by rivers from every direction, and in particular by the River Yuna which, after travelling a great distance from inland, flows into the magnificent bay of Samanà, which forms the vastest and safest natural harbour of the region'. Promising to grant plot concessions to 'any industrious French citizen' who wished to settle in the area, Toussaint guaranteed 'hundredfold returns' on their investment and labour – a pledge which also showed that he regarded the fates of France and Saint-Domingue as inextricably intertwined for the foreseeable future.[97] At the same time, in order not to encourage a sudden exodus of black plantation workers from the French side, he prohibited the sale of any plot of land of less than fifty *carreaux* (150 acres).[98]

Another of Toussaint's characteristics, which complemented his fondness for grand schemes, was his obsession with detail, and this too was was in plentiful evidence as he assumed the stewardship of Santo Domingo. Soon after the Spanish capitulation he toured the territory to carry out a meticulous evaluation of its agricultural capacities, and commissioned a detailed report from the forestry agent in Saint-Domingue.[99] He also authorized the French natural scientist Michel Descourtilz to catalogue the region's flora.[100] In his own journeys across Santo Domingo, Toussaint was struck by the conspicuous lack of development: there were only twenty-two sugar plantations, and no indigo or cotton in sight; coffee and tobacco were grown only for local consumption. He issued a proclamation inviting the population to concentrate on producing commodity crops, specifically sugar, coffee, cotton and cocoa. He suggested that farmers should move away from their traditional subsistence favourites, such as bananas, sweet potatoes and yams; it was only by making this transition that they would escape from poverty.[101]

Toussaint also took a particular interest in the fate of mahogany trees: he remembered from his earlier visits that Santo Domingo used to be covered in them, but this time he could barely find 'a thousand square feet'. He discovered, to his great irritation, that the trees had been over-exploited by the Spaniards, who had ruthlessly logged them for export; he noted with particular exasperation that the boles had been cut in such a way as to make it impossible to cultivate the trees further. He thereby issued a decree banning the export of mahogany wood and limiting its use only for local construction;[102] this was subsequently amended after complaints from local planters, but Toussaint pressed his customs officers to remain vigilant about mahogany exports, to ensure that the requisite export duties were

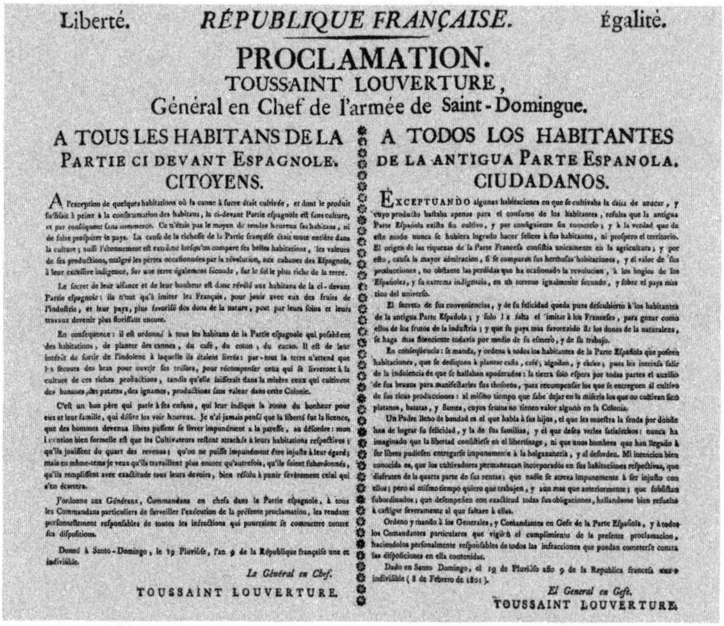

Liberté. *RÉPUBLIQUE FRANÇAISE.* Égalité.

PROCLAMATION.

TOUSSAINT LOUVERTURE,

Général en Chef de l'armée de Saint-Domingue.

A TOUS LES HABITANS DE LA PARTIE CI DEVANT ESPAGNOLE.

CITOYENS.

A l'exception de quelques habitations où la canne à sucre était cultivée, et dont le produit suffisait à peine à la consommation des habitans, la ci-devant Partie espagnole est sans culture, et par conséquent sans commerce. Ce n'était pas le moyen de rendre heureux ses habitans, ni de faire prospérer le pays. La cause de la richesse de la Partie française était toute entière dans la culture; aussi l'étonnement est extrême lorsqu'on compare ses belles habitations, les valeurs de ses productions, malgré les pertes occasionnées par la révolution, aux cabanes des Espagnols, à leur excessive indigence, sur une terre également féconde, sur le sol le plus riche de la terre.

Le secret de leur aisance et de leur bonheur est donc révélé aux habitans de la ci-devant Partie espagnole: ils n'ont qu'à imiter les Français, pour jouir avec eux des fruits de l'industrie, et leur pays, plus favorisé des dons de la nature, peut par leurs soins et leurs travaux devenir plus florissant encore.

En conséquence: il est ordonné à tous les habitans de la Partie espagnole qui possèdent des habitations, de planter des cannes, du café, du coton, du cacao. Il est de leur intérêt de sortir de l'indolence à laquelle ils étaient livrés: par-tout la terre n'attend que les secours des bras pour ouvrir ses trésors, pour récompenser ceux qui se livreront à la culture de ces riches productions, tandis qu'elle laisserait dans la misère ceux qui cultivent des bananes, des patates, des ignames, productions sans valeur dans cette Colonie.

C'est un bon père qui parle à ses enfans, qui leur indique la route du bonheur pour eux et leur famille, qui désire les voir heureux. Je n'ai jamais pensé que la liberté fut la licence, que des hommes devenus libres pussent se livrer impunément à la paresse, au désordre: mon intention bien formelle est que les Cultivateurs restent attachés à leurs habitations respectives; qu'ils jouissent du quart des revenus; qu'on ne puisse impunément être injuste à leur égard; mais en même-tems je veux qu'ils travaillent plus encore qu'autrefois, qu'ils soient subordonnés, qu'ils remplissent avec exactitude tous leurs devoirs, bien résolu à punir sévèrement celui qui s'en écartera.

J'ordonne aux Généraux, Commandans en chefs dans la Partie espagnole, à tous les Commandans particuliers de surveiller l'exécution de la présente proclamation, les rendant personnellement responsables de toutes les infractions qui pourraient se commettre contre ses dispositions.

Donné à Santo-Domingo, le 19 Pluviôse, l'an 9 de la République française une et indivisible.

Le Général en Chef.

TOUSSAINT LOUVERTURE.

A TODOS LOS HABITANTES DE LA ANTIGUA PARTE ESPANOLA.

CIUDADANOS.

EXCEPTUANDO algunas habitaciones en que se cultivaba la caña de azucar, y cuyo producto bastaba apenas para el consumo de los habitantes, resulta que la antigua Parte Española existe sin cultivo, y por consiguiente sin comercio; y à la verdad que de este modo nunca se hubiera logrado hacer felices à sus habitantes, ni prospero el territorio. El origen de las riquezas de la Parte Francesa consistia unicamente en la agricultura; y por esto, causa la mayor admiracion, si se comparan sus hermosas habitaciones, y el valor de sus producciones, no obstante las perdidas que ha ocasionado la revolucion, à los bogios de los Españoles, y su extrema indigencia, en un terreno igualmente fecundo, y sobre el pays mas rico del universo.

El secreto de sus conveniencias, y de su felicidad queda pues descubierto à los habitantes de la antigua Parte Española; y solo les falta el imitar à los Franceses, para gozar como ellos de los frutos de la industria; y que su pays mas favorezido de los dones de la naturaleza, se haga mas floreciente todavia por medio de su esmerò, y de su trabajo.

En consequencia: se manda, y ordena à todos los habitantes de la Parte Española que poseen habitaciones, que se dediquen à plantar caña, café, algodon, y cacao; pues les interesa salir de la indolencia de que se hallaban apoderados: la tierra solo espera por todas partes el auxilio de sus brazos para manifestarles sus thesoros, para recompensar los que se entreguen al cultivo de sus ricas producciones: al mismo tiempo que sabe dejar en la miseria los que no cultivan sino platanos, batatas, y ñames, cuyos frutos no tienen valor alguno en la Colonia.

Un Padre lleno de bondad es el que habla à sus hijos, el que les muestra la senda por donde han de lograr su felicidad, y la de sus familias, y el que desea verlos satisfechos: nunca ha imaginado que la libertad consistiese en el libertinage, ni que unos hombres que han llegado à ser libres pudiesen entregarse impunemente à la holgazaneria, y al desorden. Mi intencion bien conocida es, que los cultivadores permanezcan incorporados en sus habitaciones respectivas, que disfruten de la quarta parte de sus rentas; que nadie se atreva impunemente à ser injusto con ellos; pero al mismo tiempo quiero que trabajen, y aun mas que anteriormente; que subsistan subordinados; que desempeñen con exactitud todas sus obligaciones, hallandome bien resuelto à castigar severamente al que faltare à ellas.

Ordeno y mando à los Generales, y Comandantes en Gefe de la Parte Española, y à todos los Comandantes particulares que vigilen el cumplimiento de la presente proclamacion, haciendolos personalmente responsables de todos las infracciones que puedan cometerse contra las disposiciones en ella contenidas.

Dado en Santo Domingo, el 19 de Pluvioso año 9 de la Republica francesa una e indivisible (8 de Febrero de 1801).

El General en Gefe.

TOUSSAINT LOUVERTURE.

After the 1801 invasion of Santo Domingo, Toussaint called on the local population to concentrate on producing commodity crops, specifically listing sugar, coffee, cotton and cocoa. A Spanish translation is provided on the right-hand side.

paid and that any fraud was stopped. Toussaint warned the newly appointed senior customs officer of Azua that he had a 'terrible responsibility' and that he would answer for the slightest impropriety 'with his head'.[103]

The commander-in-chief's activism was unrelenting: he aligned the value of the *gourde* in Santo Domingo with that of Saint-Domingue;[104] he tracked down the widow of his old commander, General Biassou, to whom he had been sending a regular pension, and invited her to return to Saint-Domingue's capital, where she would receive further signs of public esteem;[105] after an explosion in livestock thefts he banned the sale of domestic animals, and ordered that anyone caught moving herds from one commune to another should be immediately arrested unless they had 'valid passports' for them, or had obtained a permission signed by himself or the military governors of the two departments.[106] Hearing about the unsatisfactory arrangements for religious worship in the region around Santiago, he promptly created four new parishes and laid down the precise number of priests who should officiate in each of them, the frequency of their presence and the services they should offer.[107]

Alongside his revolutionary ideals, Toussaint's religious faith was, of course, an important foundation of his political appeal; this proved to be the case in the deeply pious Santo Domingo too. Some racially prejudiced clerics were plainly unhappy with the new authorities, and there were some incidents between white and black people in Santo Domingo Cathedral; according to an eyewitness, Toussaint calmed things down with one of his quirky interventions, observing that he had the 'misfortune' of being a black man but that 'no one could surpass him in scientific knowledge'.[108] Most priests settled for at least the appearance of acquiescence. In ceremonies held in the new governor's honour in many towns and villages, the clergy rang church bells and came out to greet him carrying banners and incense; women placed crowns on his head.[109]

Toussaint's regime was supported across many sections of society, from black and mixed-race people to the commercial white bourgeoisie; only the racially prejudiced nobles were overwhelmingly hostile.[110] So when he returned for a visit in January 1802 he was greeted with rapture throughout the territory; an eyewitness noted that he 'was received with the greatest demonstrations of enthusiasm and joy by the former slaves'.[111] In a letter to her priest, a Spanish resident of Santiago called him 'Toussaint the Sublime' and observed: 'we would not have given a warmer welcome to our own monarch'.[112] He recruited a group of musicians from the Fijo battalion in Santo Domingo and sent them back to Port-Républicain to be included in his guard of honour.[113] Perhaps this popular ecstasy is what drove him shortly afterwards to order three coins to be minted in Santo Domingo, under the direction of a French goldsmith named Tessier. The new *double-escalins*, *escalins* and *demi-escalins* were to be legal tender throughout the island, and were adorned on one side with 'République Française' and on the other with 'Colonie de Saint-Domingue'.[114] Legend had it that some bore the inscription 'Toussaint Louverture', but this was perhaps merely a measure of how ubiquitous he had now become in the torrid imagination of the locals.

9
In the Region of Eagles

Toussaint's imagination was at its most fertile when he was on the move. In early February 1801, as his edicts were starting to transform Santo Domingo, he issued a proclamation to all the citizens of the island. After congratulating his army for executing his orders with 'courage and intelligence' and professing his wish for the happiness of Saint-Domingue (which he was now routinely calling 'mon pays'), he invited municipal authorities to select representatives to serve on a Central Assembly, which would meet in Port-Républicain in mid March. Its task would be to draft a set of laws which were 'suited to our habits, our customs, our climate, our industry, while at the same time strengthening even further our ties to the French Republic'. The document would be sent to the government in Paris for approval, after which it would become the law of the land. Having expelled foreign troops from the colony, established his military authority as commander-in-chief, subjugated the southern rebellion, neutered and then dismissed successive French envoys, outflanked the Spanish authorities in Santo Domingo and unified the entire island of Hispaniola under French republican rule, Toussaint was now embarking upon his boldest venture yet: a new constitution.[1]

It was a characteristically imaginative Louverturian ploy and caught everyone off guard. Article 91 of the 22 Frimaire an VIII constitution, which stipulated that colonies would be governed by 'special laws', was intended to enable tighter local control by the central government in Paris. Toussaint was taking it at its word, but in fact subverting it for his own revolutionary ends. He was also appropriating the reactionary Spanish creole arguments about historical and cultural specificity, which had been used just a few weeks earlier in objection to his invasion of Santo Domingo. The idea of a new constitution fitted perfectly with Toussaint's fondness for generalization and codification, and his consistent capacity for transgression. The move was also a natural culmination of his march towards supreme power – as he acknowledged when he confessed in conversation that he was 'unable to slow down his tremendous pace' and that he found himself 'pulled by an occult force which he could not resist'.[2]

Toussaint's biographers have generally viewed his constitutional project as the logical extension of his quest for independence. Starting with Louis Dubroca's anguished howl in 1802 against the 'fanatical African's solemn rupture of the ties which bind the colony and the motherland',[3] his conservative critics have portrayed it as the epitome of treacherousness, and unequivocal evidence of his ambition to sever his ties with France. His progressive admirers have seen it as the apotheosis of his struggle against slavery, though marred by his failure to communicate his real intentions to his people and his lapse into despotism.[4] For others still, Toussaint's constitutional plans were the hubristic extravagance of an impulsive man who had lost his way, 'dazzled by the favours of fortune, and driven by a kind of fatalism towards the abyss'.[5] More recently there has been a revival of scholarly interest in the 1801 constitution, particularly in terms of its broader philosophical implications.[6]

Yet in this flurry of argument and counter-argument, the dynamic nature of Toussaint's thinking has been lost. In his mind it had become imperative to create some distance between Saint-Domingue and France. This step was necessary both to promote better internal governance and also to protect the colony against French political instability, and against future legislation which could damage its social and economic fabric. As we noted, forces hostile to the revolutionary order in the colonies were systematically gaining ground in Paris: by April 1799 the Société des Amis des Noirs was effectively closed down,[7] and after Bonaparte's *coup d'état* the new French constitution of 22 Frimaire contained no declaration of rights and did not grant automatic citizenship to those born outside France. Worse still, it created a legal grey area in which slavery could be tolerated for some categories of people, such as household employees. It was widely believed that the vagueness of article 91 was intended to pave the way for the full-scale restoration of slavery in the colonies, and the recognition of full civic rights only to whites – as subsequently occurred in Martinique, Guadeloupe and Guyana in 1802.[8]

Saint-Domingue's constitution was also the result of Toussaint's increasingly strained relationship with French authorities throughout the war of knives. His clash with Rigaud had taught him a powerful lesson: even though he had only responded to the mixed-race leader's 'aggression' against his legitimate authority, the French government had done nothing to assist him and had in fact fuelled the flames of the conflict – and then blamed him for its continuation. Hence his sharply worded letter to the French Minister of Navy in February 1801: 'I took up arms to suppress the revolt of Rigaud;

had I not done so, the colony would still be consumed with the horrors of civil war. And in this important circumstance the government omitted to tell Rigaud that he should not turn the weapons which had been entrusted to him against the republic. I merely responded to force by force, and if blood was spilled it was only because it was a case of justified self-defence.'[9]

And so, if the French would do nothing to help him even against his internal enemies, Toussaint believed it was up to him to preserve the gains of the Saint-Domingue revolution and protect the colony from external attack. Both the spirit and the letter of his constitution were inspired by this republican goal: as its third article stated, 'slaves cannot exist in this territory and servitude is for ever abolished. Here, all men are born, live and die free and French.'[10] His lofty thinking was reflected in one of his typically vivid metaphors: 'I have taken my flight from the region of eagles; I must be prudent in returning to earth: I can alight only upon a rock, and this rock should be the edifice of the constitution, which will guarantee my power as long as I remain among mortals.'[11]

By the early 1800s, spirited exchanges were already taking place in different parts of the world about Saint-Domingue's constitutional future and Toussaint's place in it. As we saw in the previous chapter, Roume believed he should be involved in discussions to create a new organic code for the colony. Alexander Hamilton pictured him as the head of a feudal military regime,[12] while for the exiled slave-owning planters who had fought him in a desperate bid to reverse the tide of black emancipation, Toussaint remained 'a rebel slave' whose power needed to be 'paralysed' at all costs, otherwise it would spread to 'the negroes of all other colonies in the region'[13] – a point echoed in a report from the governor of Spanish-controlled Venezuela, who described Toussaint's new political order as 'pilfering the rights and tranquillity of states'.[14] Some of his more militant slave and free black supporters in the Atlantic area did indeed think that he was in the process of turning the colony into an exclusively black republic. The British were beginning to imagine him as king of an independent Saint-Domingue, while the local *colons* secretly prayed that he might preside over a sanitized restoration of the old plantation order. By mid 1801, thanks to some intentionally loose talk by one of his London envoys, the wily Toussaint had even led the British, whose 'foolish credulity'[15] he liked toying with, to believe that he might soon appoint a 'white government' in Saint-Domingue.[16]

While he was happy for Saint-Domingue's constitutional future to be the subject of speculation, none of the proposed schemes directly shaped

Toussaint's thinking. Indeed, there is compelling evidence that the constitutional process he followed was first conceived in discussions between Toussaint and his close ally the former commissioner Julien Raimond. The mixed-race notable was the third member of the delegation (along with General Michel and Charles Vincent) sent by the Consuls to Saint-Domingue in 1800 to reassure local elites about the 'special laws' promised by article 91 of the French constitution. In his own report to Bonaparte, Raimond welcomed the idea of different legal regimes between France and Saint-Domingue and proposed a short document consisting of three articles: about the particular status of the colony, its exclusive trade with France, and the banning of slavery; the latter as follows: 'in all the French colonies where human bondage has been abolished, it can never be restored'. Raimond added that these special administrative regulations, which he termed 'organic laws', must be drafted not by distant French legislators but by men with local knowledge and experience. Raimond proposed that the organic laws of Saint-Domingue be drawn up by an 'ad hoc commission' presided over by three men, one of whom should be Toussaint, and another a 'European who represented the Consul' who 'knew the colony and enjoyed the trust of its inhabitants'; they should be assisted by a number of representatives from each department.[17]

Toussaint drafted his constitution following the letter of these proposals, while subverting their spirit of prudent loyalism. After designating the members of the Central Assembly, he summoned them to Port-Républicain in March 1801 to begin working on the document. The presidency was entrusted to Bernard Borgella, the town's former mayor, an influential white planter who was a close political ally of Toussaint. Of a similar background and outlook were Gaston Nogérée and André Collet, who spoke for the interests of southern white planters, and three appointees from Santo Domingo: local notables Mugnoz and Roxas, and Mancebo, a Catholic priest, all three ardent supporters of the revolution (a fourth nominee died before the first meeting).[18] In addition to Raimond, there were two other persons of colour: a man named Lacour, whose first name is not recorded; and Étienne Viard, one of Toussaint's assistants, who acted as secretary. The only black member was General Moyse, picked to represent the department of the north, where he was immensely popular among the *cultivateurs*. He refused to serve on the Assembly, fearing it would concede too much ground to the *colons* – a first open gesture of resistance.

Toussaint's relationship with the Assembly's nine members has been a matter of much conjecture. For some historians the whole drafting process was merely a sideshow, and the real authors of the text were the commander-in-chief's secretary Henri Pascal (the son-in-law of Julien Raimond, presumably under his influence), assisted by his priests Marini and Molière.[19] For others, the Assembly members worked hard, but simply carried out their master's instructions: a contemporary local observer contemptuously referred to them as 'puppet legislators', while Sannon noted that 'these men were in truth the representatives of Toussaint Louverture rather than the people of Saint-Domingue'.[20] Yet for others still it was Toussaint who was manipulated by the Assembly: hence the over-representation of Saint-Domingue's plantation-owners, and the codification of laws about property and labour which served settler and émigré interests and paved the way for a kind of economic despotism. Laurent Dubois thus argues that the 1801 constitution was a 'charter for a new colonial order'.[21]

As always with Toussaint, the truth was more intricate. At the Assembly's opening ceremony he told the legislators not to divulge the contents of their discussions, and reminded them that their recommendations would only come into force once he had accepted them. He also offered them a precise road-map – as noted in the minutes of the first session, the only one whose records have survived.[22] The rationale for the constitution was to create a set of legal principles 'matured by the lessons of experience and the knowledge of localities', said Toussaint; its 'necessity' stemmed from the legal vacuum deliberately created by the French constitutions of 1795 and 1799 for the administration of colonies.[23] Having given the legislators their instructions, Toussaint then left them to their own devices. They met every day from nine in the morning until two in the afternoon; their deliberations were often animated, and shine a revealing light both on their vision of Saint-Domingue and on the centrality of Toussaint's leadership. It is clear that Raimond had some input into the wording of the article abolishing slavery, which used language very similar to his own earlier draft to Bonaparte. He had less luck, however, in defending the notion of exclusive colonial trade with France: Toussaint circumvented it with a clause which slyly gave the governor 'all necessary powers to secure provisions for the colony'.[24] At the same time, with his usual craftiness, Toussaint's briefing had omitted the most fundamental point. The primary function of the Assembly was outward-facing: to send a message of reassurance to the French government. He needed these respectable figures to vouch for his commitment to preserving French interests in Saint-Domingue; indeed, their very first formal discussion was about 'the island of Saint-Domingue in its moral relation with the metropolis'.[25]

The Assembly's draft text contained separate sections on Saint-Domingue's agriculture and commerce (title VI), the powers of its new chief executive, the governor (title VIII), the overhaul of the justice system (title IX), municipal reform (title X) and the rationalization of the colony's finances (title XII). The draft also reflected Toussaint's preoccupation with issues of public morality: it proposed that Catholicism be declared the official religion (title III), and divorce banned 'in the interests of encouraging and fortifying family unity' (title IV); among the governor's duties was the proscription of any subversive text which might 'corrupt collective morals' (article 39), and oversight of any activity which might threaten the 'public spirit, the security, the health or the fortune of the citizens' (article 69).[26]

Fascinating evidence of the legislators' thinking can be found in the notes of Gaston Nogérée, whose personal papers have survived; he took an active part in the body's deliberations, and also in drafting the series of 'organic laws' accompanying the constitution, which were adopted between mid July and mid August 1801. Nogérée was no revolutionary firebrand but a *grand blanc* who first met Toussaint in Port-Républicain in October 1798 after the evacuation of Jérémie by the British, with whom – like most southern white planters – he had collaborated actively; before 1791 he had also owned a large number of slaves. True to his philosophy of national reconciliation, Toussaint bore him no grudge and granted him permission to set up a mathematics school on the condition that he awarded four scholarships to outstanding black students. This too was typical of Toussaint's republican ethic: he made people atone for their past sins by performing charitable deeds.[27]

From that moment on Nogérée became a Louverture devotee, watching with wonder as this former slave presided over the return of order, prosperity and harmony in Saint-Domingue: 'I saw tranquillity develop wherever he was able to exert his influence.' He was particularly struck by the way in which his 'poor countrymen, the settlers' began to be 'treated with consideration again by the blacks, thanks to the orders and the example set by the commander-in-chief'. Nogérée noted the warmth with which Toussaint was greeted by the population whenever he returned to Port-Républicain after a prolonged absence: the inhabitants would put up 'spontaneous illuminations, which could last up to two or three days'. He summed up the attitude of the white *colons* towards their protector in this striking formula: 'if he happened to fall ill, we would all become greatly worried, we believed that our existence was attached to his'.[28]

Nogérée's notes – the only other record of the colony's constitutional discussions to have survived – provide tantalizing glimpses of the Assembly's discussions. He wrote down Toussaint's solemn injunction to the legislators when he first met them in March 1801: they were to see themselves as 'magistrates charged with securing the happiness of Saint-Domingue'. He took his duties very seriously, and at one moment of disagreement with

Toussaint even jotted down that while he was 'grateful for the leader Providence has sent us', his main ambition was to 'earn the esteem' of his fellow citizens. He was above all fiercely loyal to France: he completely accepted Toussaint's premise that the text they were agreeing was merely a draft, which would become law only when approved by the French government. Nogérée even volunteered to take the document to Bonaparte; Toussaint coaxed him into believing he was the 'ideal' person to carry out this patriotic task.[29] In his letter introducing Nogérée to the French authorities, Toussaint noted that he had 'witnessed all the events in Saint-Domingue since the revolution', and was therefore 'perfectly placed to inform the government about the present situation in the colony'.[30]

Nogérée's minutes show exactly why Toussaint believed he would be a suitable envoy to the French government and its allies in the French colonial lobby. He was an order-loving white planter whose social views were mostly conservative. He applauded the proposals for the restoration of the Catholic faith, and cited Toussaint as an 'exemplar of religious piety'. He loudly defended the ideal of a plantation economy enshrined in title VI, notably the priority given to agriculture, and the definition of the estate as 'the tranquil asylum of an industrious and well-regulated family, whose manager is necessarily the father'.[31] He railed against the practice of small plots of land being bought by black *cultivateurs*, which seemed to be continuing despite Toussaint's formal ban. Manifestly hostile to any form of small-scale black entrepreneurship, he also roundly condemned the proliferation of 'little huts along the main roads, where taffia and foodstuff are sold'. He thought the creole blacks and people of colour were disposed towards 'arrogance', and disapproved of the recreational habits of Saint-Domingue's domestic servants and plantation workers, noting that the traditional *kalindas* had a tendency to dissolve into 'bloody battles with shotguns and sabres'; no doubt his own head appeared in effigy on one or two spikes at these friendly gatherings.[32]

Most interesting of all are Nogérée's thoughts on the future arrangements of Saint-Domingue's executive. He strongly endorsed the proposition (in what eventually became article 28) that Toussaint should be appointed governor for life, which was no doubt unanimously agreed by the Assembly members: in his speech at the opening session, Lacour had hailed Toussaint as the 'saviour and restorer of the colony'.[33] Nogérée not only agreed, but expressed the hope that he would live on to rule for at least 'the next twenty years' – 'a recipe for twenty years of tranquillity and happiness for the colony and for my family'. But Nogérée was dismayed by the suggestion that Toussaint be given the power to appoint his successor: this prerogative, he announced, was a 'monarchical concept'.[34]

Nogérée's opposition was perhaps based on his evaluation of the likely line of succession: he believed that none of the military commanders in Toussaint's army were of the same political and intellectual stature as the commander-in-chief, and the most obvious contender to replace him would be Dessalines – a prospect which, given the latter's fearsome reputation, filled him with apprehension.

Yet it is likely that this fear, too, had played a part in Toussaint's thinking, and was one of the main reasons why Toussaint had wanted Nogérée to travel to Paris – to repeat the stories he had heard about Dessalines. One of these he had shared with Toussaint and other members of the Assembly. It was widely known that Dessalines had told his troops at the end of the war with Rigaud in mid 1800 that two more conflicts lay ahead for the republican army of Saint-Domingue: the first against the Spaniards in Santo Domingo, which would be simple, and the second against the French, if they sent an armed expedition to bring back slavery. If they did, Dessalines had warned, it would be a war of extermination, and 'il fallait tout le monde levé tous ensemble, les femmes commes les hommes'.[35] Even though he was sent to Paris with the constitution, Nogérée was never able to deliver this promise of a mass uprising to Bonaparte as Toussaint had intended. This was unfortunate: Dessalines' words exactly predicted what happened to the French invading army after its arrival in Saint-Domingue in 1802.

Toussaint received the draft text from the Assembly in early May 1801. Ever the perfectionist, he worked on the document and its related 'organic laws' for another two months before he felt they were ready to be made public. He was aware of the reservations of the legislators about a number of issues, especially the appointment of his successor and the scope of the governor's powers. But he knew that he had to assume full executive authority – all the more so since the idea of appointing a governor who combined all civilian and military functions was beginning to gain ground in Paris.[36] Such schemes almost invariably saw this governor as being a European, but Toussaint believed, of course, that he was the right person for the post, not least because he had effectively held it for the past few years. In this respect, as in many others, for him the constitution merely formalized Saint-Domingue's existing political reality.

All the evidence shows that there was wide-ranging enthusiasm across the colony for Toussaint's leadership. This was the case in Santo Domingo, as we saw previously, and there was no doubt about his overwhelming popularity among the colony's white population, who regarded him as their protector. As one of them put it, Toussaint had used his power 'only for the good of the *colons* and for the restoration of the colony';[37] another praised his 'humanity and respect for religion', and his understanding that the presence of Europeans was essential for the 'preservation of commerce and the arts'; he concluded that 'if he were to perish, it would be devastating for the colony'.[38] Such sentiments were widely echoed among the black citizens, and Toussaint witnessed them during his journeys across Saint-Domingue. Support for his assumption of full executive powers was also vigorously expressed whenever local communities conveyed their political views. For example, during its mobilization against Roume in 1799, when the municipality of Gros-Morne issued a proclamation demanding that the French agent be sent back to France, its views about governance were plain: 'we do not need [Roume], or any other agent. We have confidence only in the commander-in-chief, and he has earned our trust as much by his steadfastness and his attachment to France as by his zeal in defending our liberty, as well as by his humanity and his virtue'. It concluded by inviting the French government to 'grant all executive powers to the commander-in-chief'.[39] The assembly of La Croix des Bouquets declared that 'only the commander-in-chief can restore Saint-Domingue to its former glory; he alone knows the singularities of the different localities, which reflect their varying climates; he alone understands the spirit, the character, the habits and customs of the people who inhabit this colony'.[40] There were numerous similar instances.

Such was Toussaint's confidence in his popularity in the run-up to the publication of his constitution that he extended the hand of forgiveness to Rigaud's surviving supporters, a few of whom were still rotting in his jails. In late May 1801 he had a group of these men brought to the Cap church, where he addressed them from the pulpit in a typical homily: speaking to them 'as a father', he lamented all the pains they had suffered, and told them to return in peace to their families and be consoled, as they were pardoned 'with generosity' (Toussaint always took care of his own publicity). To make absolutely sure the message was received both by people of colour and by his own subordinates, he wrote to Dessalines a few days later, asking him to put the word out that these mixed-race *Rigaudins* were now his 'brothers and his children', and that his only wish was for them to 'take the righteous path, practise the Christian faith and bring up their children in the fear of God'.[41] We can be sure that the message got through: divine retribution was nothing compared to their fear of Dessalines.

In early July, Toussaint finally gave notice of the constitutional ceremony: it was to be held on the 7th in Cap.[42] Its citizens did not get much sleep the previous night, as the drummers and brass players of his cavalry began to sound the call to arms at three in the morning, and by five the army troops and National Guardsmen were assembled in their smartest attire at the Place d'Armes. Toussaint arrived at precisely half past five, preceded by a procession of civil and military authorities. By now a large crowd had gathered at the scene, including a number of schoolteachers and students, who formed a circle around the official platform; among the distinguished guests were the members of the Assembly, the new American ambassador, Tobias Lear, and his predecessor, Edward Stevens, who was still in the colony and had been personally invited by Toussaint. Moyse was there too: he was not going to be allowed to sulk indefinitely, and Toussaint clearly wanted him in plain sight, so that everyone could see who was in charge.

The whole ceremony was a meticulously crafted justification by Toussaint, both philosophical and practical, of the powers reclaimed by Saint-Domingue from France, and vested in him by the new constitutional proposals. The tone was now very different from that of his discussions with the Assembly members. After the secrecy surrounding the preparation of the text, this occasion was to be widely publicized across the island; an extensive account of the proceedings was immediately produced by the Cap authorities and sent to all municipalities. There were three speeches: the first by Borgella, followed by Toussaint himself, and finally by Fouqueau, the president of the civil tribunal; each presented complementary dimensions of the document's rationale. We can see from the language, imagery and sophistication of their arguments that Toussaint not only carefully vetted the other two speeches, but effectively channelled his views through Borgella and Fouqueau.[43]

This ventriloquism was perhaps most apparent in the bold move towards the end of Borgella's speech, just before he proceeded to read out the seventy-seven articles of the constitution. The president of the Assembly announced that, even though the original plan had been to 'submit' the constitutional draft to the French government for approval, the 'absence of laws' in Saint-Domingue had created a situation of 'imminent peril' for the colony. Given these circumstances, Toussaint had to be invited to 'put the constitution into immediate execution'. Toussaint could not but respond positively to such an urgent request – all the more so since he had obviously scripted it. So the draft text received its formal blessing at the Cap ceremony and Toussaint approved his own nomination as governor (the theatrical effect was slightly lost on the crowd, as his self-endorsement was drowned out by the enthusiastic roar, mingled no doubt with relief, which greeted the end of Borgella's lengthy speech). There was an even more audacious argument thrown in to justify this legislative fiat: such prompt and decisive action was needed, Borgella claimed, because the French government had failed to make its views

PROGRAMME

De la Cérémonie qui aura lieu le 18 Messidor, l'an neuvième de la République française, une et indivisible, pour la Proclamation de la Constitution.

TOUSSAINT LOUVERTURE,

Général en Chef de l'Armée de Saint-Domingue.

L'Assemblée centrale m'ayant prévenu qu'elle avait fixé le 18 Messidor pour proclamer la Constitution. Afin de donner à cet Acte important toute la pompe et la solennité qu'il exige, le Général de division, commandant le Département, donnera des ordres pour faire exécuter les dispositions suivantes.

Le 18 Messidor, à trois heures du matin, la Générale battra dans toutes les Sections. Les Corps de Musique seront également distribués avec les Tambours, pour jouer et battre tour à tour.

Toutes les Trompettes de la Cavalerie et le Corps de Musique attaché à la Garde du Général en chef, seront assemblés dans la cour du Gouvernement, d'où ils partiront, à trois heures du matin, pour sonner et jouer la Générale; ils recevront des ordres du Trompette major du 1er Escadron, qui leur tracera la marche qu'ils auront à suivre

La Generale cessera a quatre heures.

A quatre heures les mêmes Corps de Tambours, de Musique et de Trompettes, battront l'Assemblée.

A cinq heures précises toute la Troupe de ligne et la Garde nationale seront sous les armes, sur la place d'Armes, en bon ordre, bonne tenue, et le plus proprement possible. Chaque Officier, à son poste, aura l'attention de faire observer la plus exacte discipline.

Toutes les Autorités, civiles et militaires, en grand costume, se réuniront au Gouvernement à cinq heures et demie du matin, d'où elles se rendront, avec le Général en chef, au lieu de la Cérémonie.

La marche des Autorités, civiles et militaires, sera disposée ainsi qu'il suit:

La Commission du Commerce.
L'Administration de la Marine.
La Municipalité.
Le Tribunal de Commerce.
Le Juge de Paix.
Le Tribunal civil.
L'Assemblée centrale.

Le Général en chef, accompagné des deux Généraux commandant le Département et l'Arrondissement.

Tous les Officiers militaires qui ne tiennent à aucun Corps, ou qui ne sont pas en activité de service, seront à la suite du Général en chef.

La municipalité invitera tous les Instituteurs et Institutrices à se rendre sur la place d'Armes avec leurs Elèves; elle s'entendra avec le Commandant de la Place pour leur choisir une place convenable.

La Municipalité prendra également des mesures pour inviter tous les Citoyens à se trouver à cette Cérémonie.

Rendues sur la place d'Armes, les Autorités, civiles et militaires, seront placées en cercle, selon leur rang, pour entendre la proclamation de la Constitution, dont l'assemblée centrale doit donner connaissance au Peuple.

Au moment où la lecture de la Constitution sera terminée, une pièce de canon de 4, qui sera sur la place, tirera 5 coups de canon, pour servir de signal à tous les Forts de commencer une salve de 23 coups de canon pour chacun des Forts et pour chacun des bâtimens de l'Etat qui sont en rade.

La pièce de quatre restera sur la place pour saluer le Saint Sacrement, de vingt-trois coups de canon, au moment de son élévation

Les Ministres du Culte catholique sont et demeurent invités à faire leurs préparatifs, et à disposer tout ce qui sera nécessaire pour rendre cette Cérémonie auguste et imposante.

La lecture de la Constitution terminée, les Autorités, civiles et militaires, la Troupe, les Instituteurs, Institutrices et leurs Eleves, entreront dans la Cathédrale pour assister à une Grand'Messe solennelle qui sera chantée pour rendre des actions de grâces à Dieu, le prier de répandre ses faveurs sur la Colonie, ses bienfaits sur tous ses Habitans, éclairer le Peuple de Saint-Domingue sur ses devoirs, les Magistrats sur l'exécution des Lois, pénétrer tous les esprits d'affection et de respect pour la Constitution qui doit consolider la liberté publique, fixer la destinée, la paix et la prospérité de Saint-Domingue.

Le Général de division, commandant le Département, est chargé de donner les ordres les plus précis pour que le plus grand ordre soit observé pendant la Cérémonie, et le plus profond silence pendant la lecture de la Constitution. Le même ordre et le même silence sera observé à l'Eglise pendant toute la Cérémonie.

Le présent Programme sera imprimé, adressé, par le Secrétaire général, à toutes les Autorités civiles et militaires, afin de leur servir de règle dans les Villes de Départemens et les principales Villes de la Colonie, suivant leurs localités, lu, publié et affiché par tout où besoin sera, afin que personne n'en ignore.

Fait au Cap-Français, le 15 Messidor, l'an neuf de la République française, une et indivisible.

Le Général en chef,

Signé TOUSSAINT LOUVERTURE.

Au Cap-Français, chez P. Roux, imprimeur du Gouvernement.

In early July 1801 Toussaint invited the population of Saint-Domingue to celebrate their new constitution at a ceremony to be held on the main square in Cap. The constitution would 'consolidate public freedom and fix the destiny, peace and prosperity of the colony'.

about Saint-Domingue known, and been 'silent for too long'. This too was a splendidly Louverturian sleight of hand: the French government was being castigated, in effect, for not responding promptly enough to a document it had yet to receive.

The symbolic politics of the Central Assembly were entirely geared towards reassuring France about its national interests and those of its white *colons*; the justifications of the 1801 constitution at the Cap ceremony, in contrast, were all directed at Saint-Domingue's citizens and were steeped in classical republican arguments about liberty. Borgella argued that those in power in France for much of the 1790s had ignored the needs of the colony's citizens and at times violated their basic freedoms; worse, from a republican perspective, they had also forced them to accept laws which they had 'neither made nor consented to'. In any event, the rights of the citizens to govern themselves by laws of their own making were recognized not just by the French constitution but also by 'the laws of nature'. Hence Toussaint's wording of the abolition of slavery in article 3, which was cast not as a formal right tied to citizenship which could be taken away, but as an inherent quality of every man and woman born in the colony. Borgella celebrated the spirit of natural harmony which had guided Toussaint's battle against 'age-old prejudices', allowing him to reinforce 'those sweetest bonds of fraternity' among the citizens of Saint-Domingue.[44]

Alongside the principle of consent, further justification of the constitution was based on the need for the colony to be governed by good laws. Because of its distance from France, Fouqueau observed, and the absence of any direct contribution from Saint-Domingue's representatives, the legislation passed in Paris was often unsuitable for the colony and at times harmful to its interests; in fact, such had been the 'incoherence' of the French approach to colonial questions in the past few years, under the notoriously inefficient Conseil des Cinq Cents, that Saint-Domingue had been effectively deprived of proper laws and reduced to a state of 'complete anarchy'. The situation would be remedied by the forthcoming organic laws prepared by the Assembly. Fouqueau noted, as further evidence of this institutional chaos, that successive French governments had attempted to keep the powers of the military commander apart from those of the civilian administrator. Thankfully, he added, Toussaint had spotted this incoherence, recognizing that 'there could be no government worthy of the name if authority is allocated without clear rules, and different branches are in constant conflict with each other' (an entirely fair argument against Montesquieu's doctrine of separation of powers, although it omitted the crucial fact that here it was Toussaint who had been the chief source of these conflicts). And so Fouqueau now anointed Toussaint, the 'liberator and protector' of the colony, as its lawgiver ('législateur') too, rescuing its citizens from turmoil thanks to his extraordinary virtues and capacity to act in the general interest; this was straight out of Rousseau's *Social Contract*.[45]

Toussaint's speech – his first as governor of the colony – fortified this republican message by expanding on the theme of liberty. He praised France and vowed to cultivate a relationship of 'fraternity and friendship' with its people. However – and this was the real measure of the radicalism of the 1801 document – the colony's freedom was no longer dependent on French political thinking or practice. Alluding again to the article which abolished slavery on the colony, he observed that it was now Saint-Domingue's own constitution which guaranteed the freedom of its citizens, irrespective of their 'age, condition or colour'; the document's primary purpose was to 'immortalize liberty' in the colony. Toussaint was careful not to sound triumphant: this was not so much a victory speech as a call to all citizens to remain vigilant and mobilized to defend Saint-Domingue's collective sovereignty. Speaking 'the language of truth' to his fellow citizens, Toussaint stated that the constitution would defend their rights but also impose on them 'the duty to practise the virtues'. These included private qualities, notably the possession of 'sound morals and the religion of Jesus Christ', but above all public ones such as the pursuit of the common good.[46]

This went to the heart of Toussaint's ideal of freedom: an active citizenship in which all sections of society were mindful of the general interest. He appealed to public officials to ensure that they always served the people and behaved with honesty and integrity. Likewise, he told the *cultivateurs* that article 16 of the constitution guaranteed them their fair share of plantation revenues and would defend them vigorously against any violation of their rights. But the constitution would also impose upon them the obligation to 'avoid idleness, the mother of all vices'. This robust conception of freedom was expressed most forcefully in Toussaint's message to his soldiers and officers: their duty was not only to practise the virtues of discipline and subordination, but also to 'protect the constitution against its internal and external enemies, who might seek to attack it'.[47] The message could not be clearer: Saint-Domingue's integrity as a political community was inseparable from the defence of the revolution. This was underlined by the constitution's penultimate article: 'every citizen has a duty to serve the country which has given him life and nourishment, for the maintenance of liberty and the equal share of properties, whenever the law demands their defence'.[48]

The ceremony was followed by a *Te Deum* in Cap's church, and the day ended with a glittering banquet in Government House, attended by

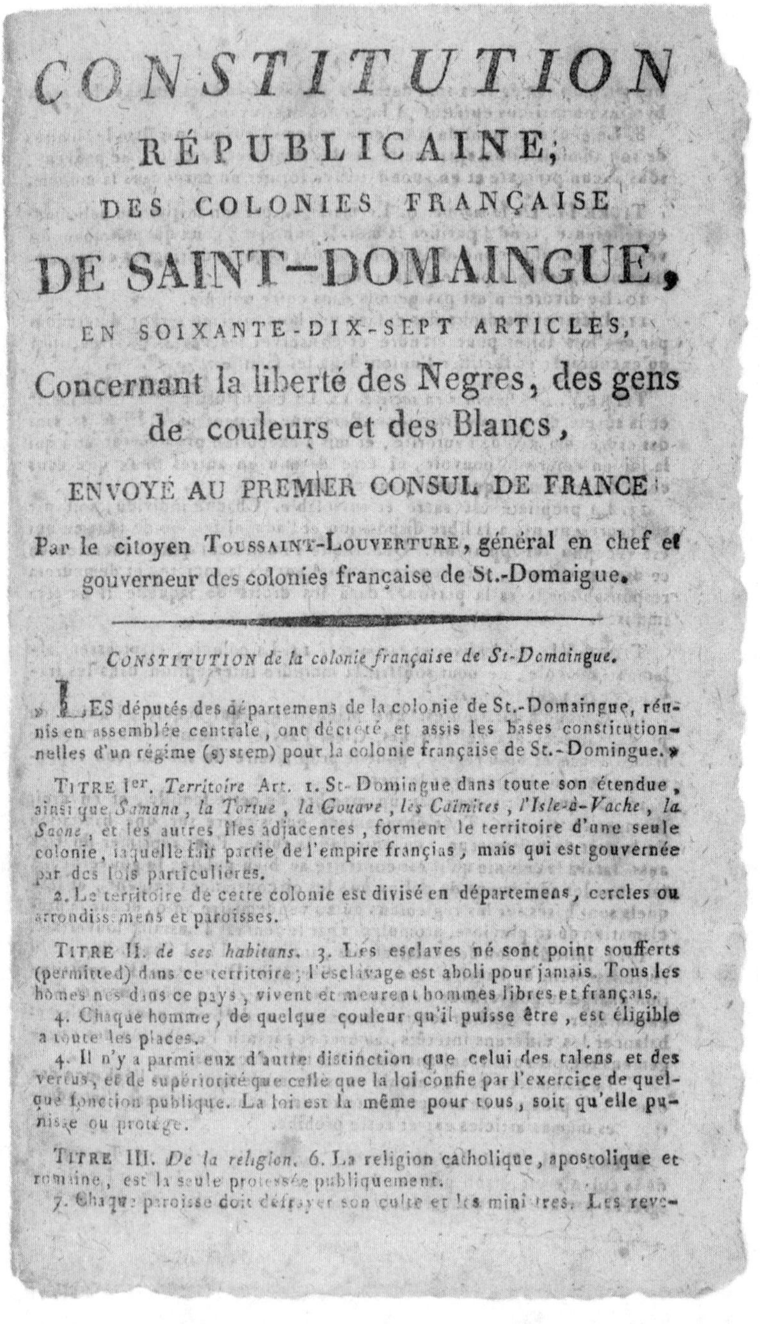

CONSTITUTION

RÉPUBLICAINE,

DES COLONIES FRANÇAISE

DE SAINT-DOMAINGUE,

EN SOIXANTE-DIX-SEPT ARTICLES,

Concernant la liberté des Negres, des gens de couleurs et des Blancs,

ENVOYÉ AU PREMIER CONSUL DE FRANCE

Par le citoyen TOUSSAINT-LOUVERTURE, général en chef et gouverneur des colonies française de St.-Domaigue.

CONSTITUTION *de la colonie française de St-Domaingue.*

» LES députés des départemens de la colonie de St.-Domaingue, réunis en assemblée centrale, ont décrété et assis les bases constitutionnelles d'un régime (system) pour la colonie française de St.-Domingue. »

TITRE Ier. *Territoire* Art. 1. St-Domingue dans toute son étendue, ainsi que *Samana*, *la Tortue*, *la Gouave*, *les Caïmites*, *l'Isle-à-Vache*, *la Saone*, et les autres îles adjacentes, forment le territoire d'une seule colonie, laquelle fait partie de l'empire françias, mais qui est gouvernée par des lois particulières.

2. Le territoire de cette colonie est divisé en départemens, cercles ou arrondissemens et paroisses.

TITRE II. *de ses habitans.* 3. Les esclaves né sont point soufferts (permitted) dans ce territoire; l'esclavage est aboli pour jamais. Tous les homes nés dans ce pays, vivent et meurent hommes libres et français.

4. Chaque homme, de quelque couleur qu'il puisse être, est éligible a toute les places.

4. Il n'y a parmi eux d'autre distinction que celui des talens et des vertus, et de supériorité que celle que la loi confie par l'exercice de quelque fonction publique. La loi est la même pour tous, soit qu'elle punisse ou protége.

TITRE III. *De la religion.* 6. La religion catholique, apostolique et romaine, est la seule professée publiquement.

7. Chaque paroisse doit défrayer son culte et les ministres. Les reve-

Toussaint's 1801 constitution affirmed the colony's continuing membership of the French Empire, while noting that it was governed by 'special laws'. Article 3 stipulated that slavery was abolished 'for ever', and that all citizens were born, lived and died 'free and French'.

600 invitees. There were toasts to the governor, to the Assembly members, to the French and American governments and to Generals Christophe and Moyse (but not, curiously, to Dessalines, who seems not to have attended the ceremony). According to an eyewitness, Moyse managed to make one impertinent intervention, asking the guests to raise their glasses to the 'French Republic' – a coded gesture of defiance to the new governor.[49] Needless to say, the official record made no mention of this brief chord of dissonance. But it noted that Toussaint's 'eyes were shining with contentment' as he savoured the remarkable accomplishments he had achieved by 'the sheer force of his character'. That was no doubt true. But perhaps his happiness also had another source: as he looked around the tables, he would have seen that the colony's mostly white civil and military dignitaries were breaking bread with guests whose names were Hector, Jean-Louis, Granjean and Lafricain.[50] These black men were born into slavery or came from slave families, and yet they could now, thanks to the constitution he had so artfully conjured, enjoy the rights of equal citizenship in Saint-Domingue, and the promise that they would never again suffer a life of servitude.

Soon after the Cap ceremony Toussaint summoned Charles Vincent, entrusting him with the task of taking his constitution to the French government. Although he disagreed vehemently with some of its contents – and with the very premise that Saint-Domingue should adopt a separate constitutional charter – Vincent agreed to carry out the mission. He later claimed that it was his only way out of the colony, but this was probably a retrospective justification, to avoid deeper trouble with the French authorities. In any event, his exchanges with Toussaint about the constitution, recorded with his usual scrupulousness, provide compelling insights into the governor's intentions and state of mind at this point.

The choice of Vincent is itself worthy of comment. In one sense, he was the obvious candidate. A man of great integrity and impeccable republican credentials, he was a fervent defender of the revolution; Henri Christophe, the military commander of Cap, described him as 'the only European who really loves the people of Saint-Domingue'.[51] Vincent had already represented Toussaint thrice in Paris and, as we saw at the beginning of the previous chapter, had recently been sent by Bonaparte (along with Julien Raimond) to reassure the colony about France's constitutional intentions; he was therefore the ideal conduit between the two parties. Raimond had told Vincent that Toussaint had singled him out for this mission a long while ago – which confirms that Raimond's ideas shaped Toussaint's thinking, and shows that he had been planning his constitution methodically.

At the same time Toussaint was becoming wary of Vincent, and felt that his presence in the colony could become burdensome. He had objected to the Santo Domingo operation, which he believed was motivated by Toussaint's desire 'to dominate the colony'.[52] And importantly, Vincent was also the colony's principal civil engineer, and Toussaint had given instructions for all coastal fortifications to be reinforced in 1801, just as he was moving forward with his constitutional project. Toussaint did not want Vincent involved in it, even though he was one of the most qualified persons to oversee it: he was obviously worried that Vincent might divulge sensitive information about the island's defences to his military superiors in Paris. Sending him to France with the constitution was therefore in several respects a shrewd manoeuvre.

Although he had long intended him for this important assignment, Toussaint did not initially divulge any of its contents to Vincent. He even sent him off on a diversion to Gonaïves to pay his respects to Madame Louverture a few days before the Cap ceremony, which he accordingly missed. Toussaint clearly did not want Vincent to know too much about his justifications for charting an autonomous path from France – however much they were cast in republican terms. The result was that when he first cast his eyes on the document, Vincent was greatly taken aback. Particularly unsettling to him was the mode of government proposed in title VIII, which granted absolute powers to the governor, and his sense that the text was casting aside 'all the colony's obligations to the *métropole*'. He immediately raised his objections with Toussaint, and asked him what he expected the French government to do once it received a document which effectively removed its right to appoint colonial officials. Toussaint replied grandly: 'they will send commissioners to negotiate with me'. This was a significant response, confirming that Toussaint envisaged further interactions with France over the text. Vincent then tried another angle: surely this constitution would encourage other nations, such as the United States, Spain and 'even' Britain, to establish formal diplomatic ties with Saint-Domingue in order to weaken her links with France? Toussaint sought to reassure him, giving this justification of his dealings with Maitland: 'I know that the British are the most dangerous for me and the most perfidious for France, they did everything in their power to gain exclusive commercial rights in the colony, but I granted them only what was impossible to refuse, for I needed them at the time.'[53]

Toussaint's responses sought to convey a sense not only of purpose, but also of mastery: he still believed that he was in control of events and could shape them to his advantage. But as Vincent pressed him further and their exchanges became more heated, his composure began to fray. Toussaint acknowledged that it was probably a mistake to send printed copies of the constitution to the French government rather than handwritten drafts, which might give less of an impression of finality (but the point was moot, as Toussaint had already publicly approved the constitution at the Cap ceremony). When Vincent told him that he owed his power to 'the protection of the French government and the force of European bayonets' he became very agitated and flatly rejected the claim, which clearly wounded his pride; it was also inaccurate, because it downplayed the popular legitimacy of Saint-Domingue's revolution. Faced with Vincent's persistent criticism of his apparent insubordination and ingratitude, Toussaint added disdainfully that he did not believe that he had erred in any way with respect to the French authorities. Emboldened by his imminent departure from the colony, Vincent held his ground, and retorted that Saint-Domingue's constitution was nothing less than a 'manifesto against the French government'.[54]

This conversation – the last that Vincent ever had with Toussaint – was never going to end well. Vincent did not improve matters by asking the governor whether he would like to receive any honour or gratification from the French authorities. This sounded too much like an attempt to buy him off or placate him with the prospect of a grand retirement, as Roume had imagined earlier. Toussaint replied stiffly: 'I want nothing for myself. I know that the French want to bring me down, and that my children will not enjoy the fruits of what I have managed to set aside. But I am not ready to become the consenting prey of my enemies.' He then added some further reflections which Vincent did not transcribe, noting only that they caused him 'the cruellest of pains'. The final meeting between the two men ended with a characteristic act of Toussaint flamboyance: he suddenly bolted out of a side door, jumped on his awaiting horse and rode away at breakneck speed, leaving the bemused Vincent with Toussaint's astonished retinue of guides, who had to break the news of his departure to the large throng of people who were waiting patiently to see him.[55]

Vincent set sail from Saint-Domingue on 21 July. Toussaint issued him with a letter of recommendation to the French consul-general in the United States, Louis-André Pichon, asking him to facilitate his speedy journey to France as he was carrying out an 'important mission'.[56] In the days preceding his departure, Vincent continued to voice his constitutional concerns to Toussaint's entourage. He shared his views with Pascal, the governor's secretary, who claimed that he agreed entirely with Vincent's criticisms – but suggested, with a bureaucrat's well-honed instinct for self-preservation, that it would be better if he passed on his objections directly to Toussaint.[57]

When interrogated by Vincent about the constitution created by his adoptive son, Toussaint's godfather Pierre-Baptiste was elliptical: 'ci là qui conné planté patate, cé ci là qui doit mangé patate'.[58] Vincent also had a frank exchange with two Assembly members, Lacour and the president, Borgella, telling them that the document he was about to take to Paris would have been more appealing to the French government if they had stood up to Toussaint on the issue of the governor's powers. The members did not agree, and vigorously defended their handiwork. A discussion with Henri Christophe showed how divisive the issue had become, even among those most loyal to Toussaint: speaking with 'great feeling', the Cap military commander declared that the constitution had been produced by the 'most dangerous enemies of Saint-Domingue', as it was appropriating 'powers which do not rightfully belong to us'. The volcanic Moyse was equally critical: upon hearing that Toussaint had complained to Vincent about Bonaparte's failure to respond to his letters even as the First Consul was writing to France's supreme enemy, the King of England, he exploded with anger, calling his uncle 'a mad and delusional old man' who now believed that he was the 'King of Saint-Domingue'.[59]

Despite the abrupt way in which their conversation had ended, Vincent did not give up hope of persuading Toussaint to change his course. Before embarking from Cap, he wrote to Toussaint acknowledging safe receipt of the copies of the constitution from Borgella and Toussaint's secretary. But he rebuked him for not handing him letters of greeting to his devoted allies in Paris, such as the elected representative Rallier and the state councillor Lescallier – men who greatly admired him, believed in the idea of greater colonial autonomy, and might prove helpful in the challenging task of getting the constitution endorsed by the French government. Vincent also expressed his 'deep concern' about Toussaint's condition, which he likened to an 'illness': he seemed no longer capable of placing his trust in anyone, and appeared to have cut himself off from the very people who cared most for him. He warned Toussaint of the dangers of this sort of isolation: 'there is nothing more cruel for a man than to think himself friendless, and alone on the earth'.[60]

A month later, Vincent reached New England. He first made his way to Georgetown to meet the French consul-general, Pichon, who issued him with travel documents. The two men were already well acquainted and shared the same progressive republican views. When briefed by Vincent about developments in Saint-Domingue, Pichon echoed his misgivings and decided to express them. He wrote to Toussaint, pointing out that the full text of the constitution had already been published in the American press and that it was unanimously seen to augur a 'separation' of

1. Lithograph of Toussaint by Nicolas-Eustache Maurin first published in France in 1832. According to the Haitian historian Joseph Saint-Rémy, it was based on an original painting offered by Louverture to the French agent Philippe Roume, who took it with him to France after he left Saint-Domingue.

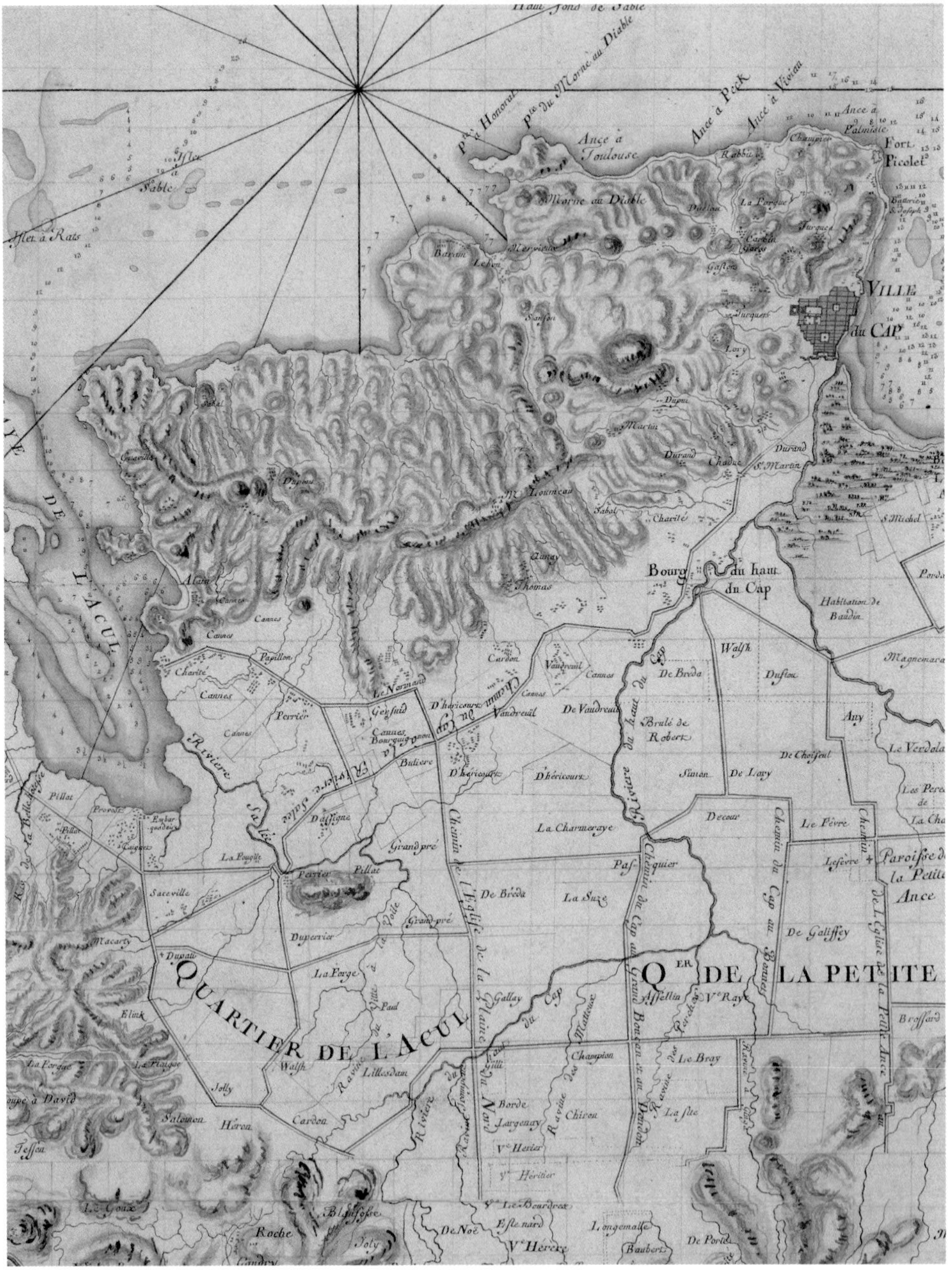

2. 'Carte topographique du Nord de Saint-Domingue, 1760', showing the fertile northern plain of Saint-Domingue, with the colony's largest and wealthiest plantations. Just south of the village of Haut-du-Cap is the Bréda *habitation* (estate), where Toussaint was born and spent the first five decades of his life before the revolution.

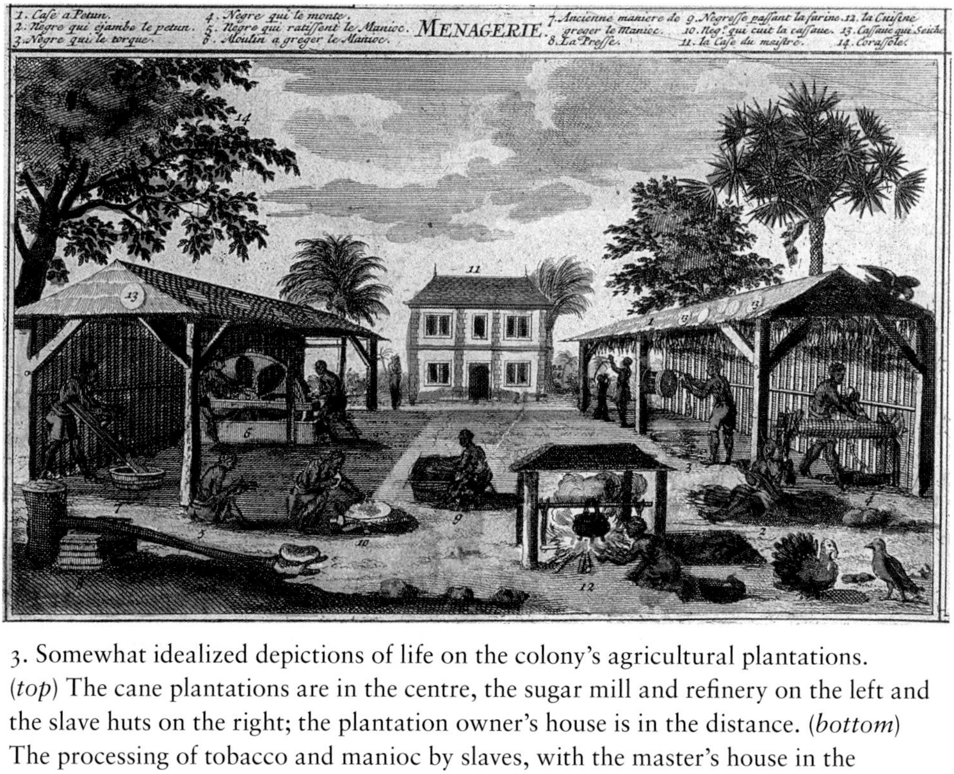

3. Somewhat idealized depictions of life on the colony's agricultural plantations. (*top*) The cane plantations are in the centre, the sugar mill and refinery on the left and the slave huts on the right; the plantation owner's house is in the distance. (*bottom*) The processing of tobacco and manioc by slaves, with the master's house in the background.

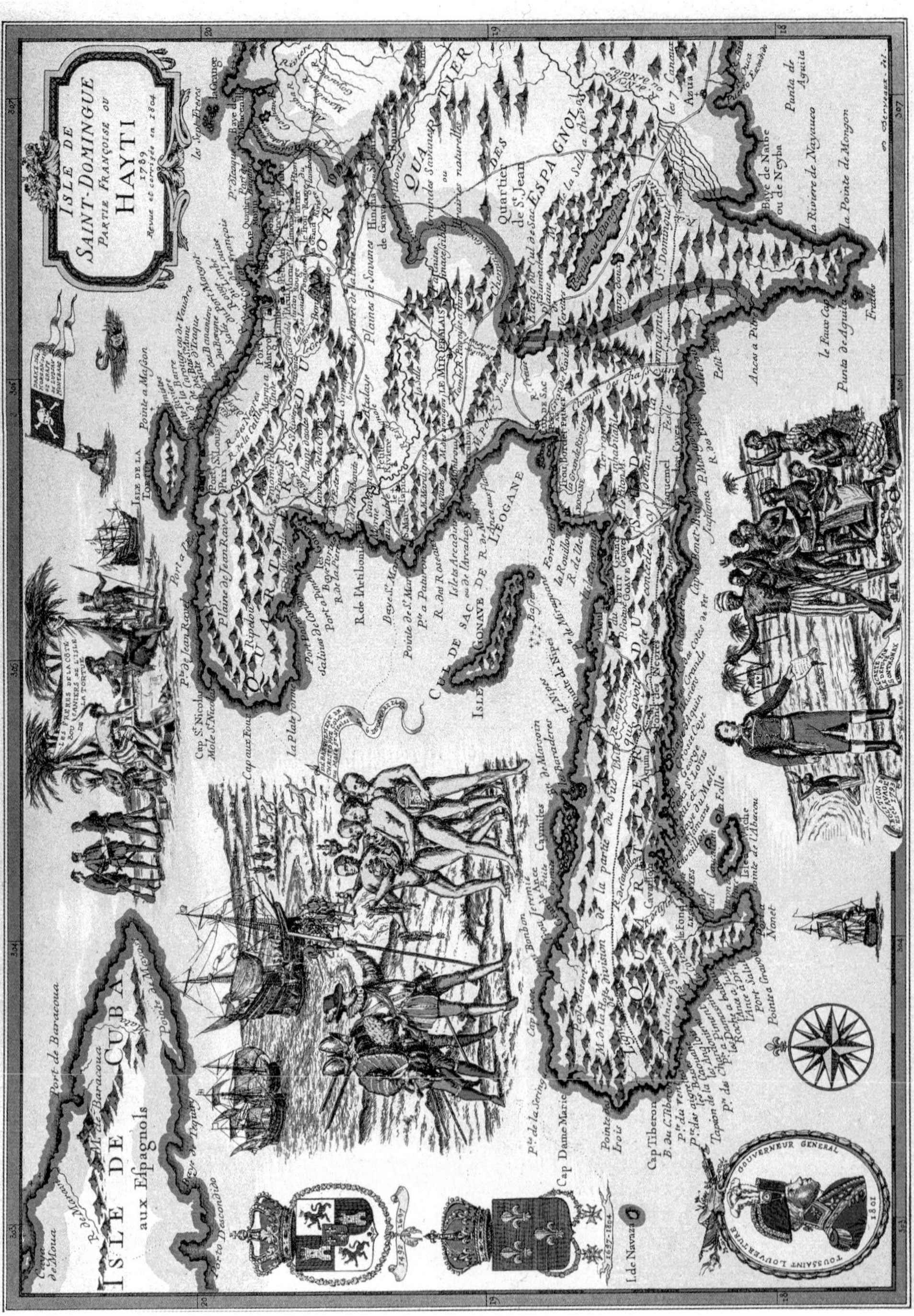

4. Based on an eighteenth-century original, this early twentieth-century French map of Saint-Domingue by Daniel Dervaux reflects the republicans' vision of events from the colonial past: the landing of Christopher Columbus, the arrival of Spanish and French settlers and the emancipation of slaves by the French Revolution (bottom middle). At bottom left is Toussaint Louverture as the last colonial governor of Saint-Domingue.

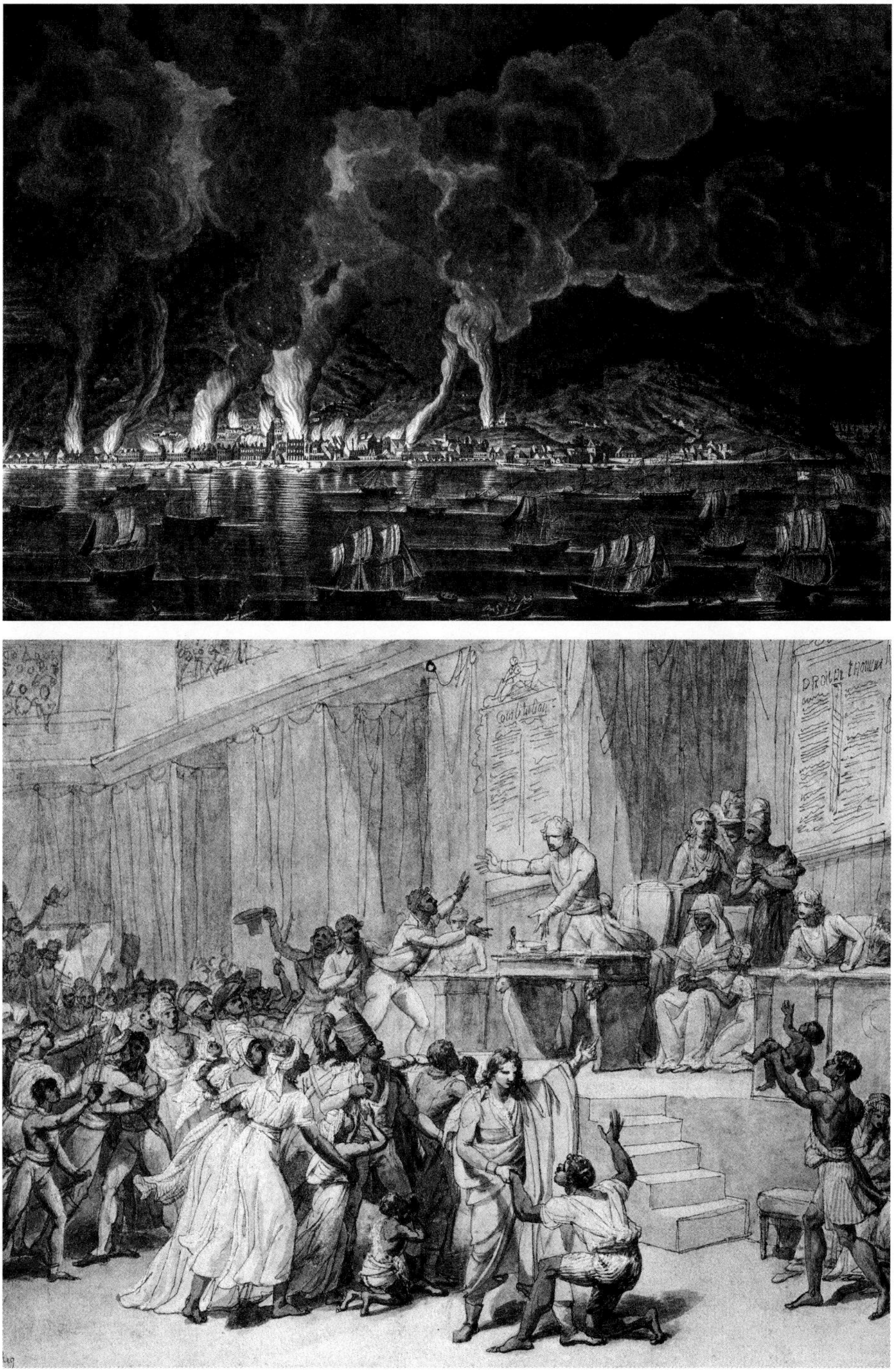

5. Two contrasting scenes from the early revolutionary years in Saint-Domingue and France: (*top*) *The Burning of Cap on 21 June 1793* and (*bottom*) a depiction of the French legislature in February 1794 following the 16 Pluviôse decree abolishing slavery; emancipated black citizens rejoice in the foreground, watched from the podium by a black woman believed to be over 100 years old.

6. Toussaint's principal interlocutors and adversaries: (*top left*) the French commissioners Léger-Félicité Sonthonax and (*top right*) Gabriel Hédouville, both of whom he outmanoeuvred; (*bottom left*) the British envoy Thomas Maitland, who supported him with the British authorities; and (*bottom right*) the commander of the French expeditionary force, Charles Emmanuel Leclerc, who captured him and sent him into exile in France in 1802.

7. Three portraits, once held by Toussaint's descendants, depict the key members of the Louverture family: (*above left*) his stepson Placide, (*above right*) his son Isaac, and (*far left*) Isaac's wife Louise Chancy, the daughter of Toussaint's half-sister Geneviève. On the left is an 1877 painting of Toussaint by the Haitian artist Louis Rigaud.

8. Théodore Géricault, *Épisode de la guerre coloniale: Noir sur un cheval cabré* (1818–19). Géricault was a fervent opponent of slavery and produced a number of striking portraits of black figures. This painting, believed to depict a battle scene during the Haitian War of Independence, conveys the heroic qualities of Toussaint's troops.

9. Portrait by Denis Volozan, dating from the early 1800s, showing Toussaint on his horse Bel-Argent in a classic martial posture. His features bear clear resemblance to the Maurin portrait; there is a marked similarity to David's famous 1801 painting of Bonaparte crossing the Alps.

10. Guillaume Guillon-Lethière's *Oath of the Ancestors* (1822) conveys the Haitian ideal of national reconciliation after independence through the alliance of black and mixed-race citizens, here symbolized by the revolutionary leaders Jean-Jacques Dessalines (left) and Alexandre Pétion (right).

11. These images by (*above*) Jacob Lawrence (from his 1938 series *The Life of Toussaint L'Ouverture*) and (*left*) William H. Johnson (*Toussaint l'Ouverture*, 1945) highlight Toussaint's continuing appeal to the African-American imagination in the mid twentieth century as a symbol of charismatic leadership, racial equality and resistance to imperial occupation.

12. *Toussaint Emanating Yellow* (2008). An enchanting evocation by the Haitian-born artist Edouard Duval-Carrié of the Caribbean creole Toussaint, and a homage to modern Haiti's vibrant political and religious traditions (in particular *vodou*) and their deep roots in African spiritual cultures.

13. Toussaint and the Haitian revolutionaries have been widely commemorated in stamps. (*left*) The 150th anniversary of the revolution in 1954, showing Lamartinière and his wife Marie-Jeanne at the Battle of Crête-à-Pierrot; (*below, from left*) the bicentenary of Toussaint's death in 2003, and a stamp from Dahomey (1963) and a cancellation from France (1991, alongside Charles de Gaulle), describing Toussaint as the 'liberator of Haiti'; (*bottom*) the bicentenary of the Saint-Domingue slave revolt commemorated in Cuba in 1991.

14. Toussaint's image has featured regularly on currency, as on (*above*) this Haitian ten-*gourde* silver coin (1968) based on a painting of Toussaint by Gustave Alaux and (*below*) this twenty-*gourde* note (2001). (*left*) In 2007, a Senegalese coin was minted for the bicentenary of the 1807 Act for the Abolition of the Slave Trade.

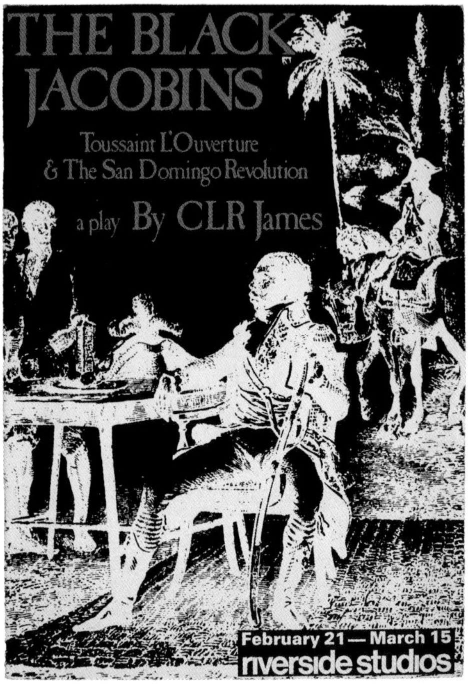

15. Toussaint and the Haitian Revolution have been the subject of plays, novels and films across the Caribbean, Europe and the Americas, as shown here by the cover of the first English edition of Alejo Carpentier's *The Kingdom of This World* (1957), the cover of the programme for a 1986 performance of C. L. R. James's play *The Black Jacobins* and a poster for Philippe Niang's 2012 television film *Toussaint Louverture*.

16. Toussaint's legend continues to thrive in our time. These sculptures show him (*top left*) in a martial pose in Allada, Benin (1989); (*top right*) defiant in his Fort de Joux prison cell (2002); (*left*) engrossed in his 1801 constitution at La Rochelle (2014), sculpted by the award-winning Ousmane Sow; and (*above*) resolute in the city of Montreal in Canada (2017).

17. A depiction by the Haitian-born contemporary artist Nicole Jean-Louis of the Bois-Caïman *vodou* ceremony held in August 1791, one of the founding myths of the modern Haitian nation. Many of the slaves carry knives in preparation for their insurrection; the scars on their backs bear witness to their cruel treatment by their masters. On the left, dressed in a white outfit and holding a book (hence his name), the *marron* leader Dutty Boukman harangues the assembled slaves. In the words of the artist: 'Haitians freed themselves from enslavement because they believe God created all of us equal.'

Saint-Domingue from France.[61] Such a move would cause immense 'pain' to all those who believed that Toussaint's attachment to the French Republic was sincere. And this separation would only lead to the colony's isolation: Pichon warned that Saint-Domingue was already seen as 'an Algiers in the Caribbean' by her enemies and would now face the active opposition of every other European state; she would perish without the support of the French motherland.[62] A few days later Pichon sent a second, more personal letter, this time urging Toussaint to remember everything that France had done for him and for his children; he also noted that Toussaint had removed three successive agents from the colony, and that his erratic behaviour seemed to be inversely proportional to the faith and trust which had been consistently placed in him by France. He urged the governor to pull back from a path which was contrary to his 'glory, honour and interests'.[63]

Before leaving Pichon, and no doubt bolstered by his conversations with him, Vincent wrote a second letter to Toussaint. This message was important because Vincent returned even more candidly to many of the themes he had broached with the governor during their final conversations at Cap and was his opportunity to have the last word. He began, like Pichon, by noting with dismay that the text of the constitution had already been published in America, and that the French authorities would clearly get wind of it before he could reach Paris – a situation all the more calamitous when the general view among Americans was that it amounted to a 'formal declaration of independence' from France. Now that Vincent had fully digested the contents, his verdict was even more scathing: Saint-Domingue's constitution, he told Toussaint, was nothing but a 'pale imitation'[64] of the French version and contained nothing which truly expressed the local particularisms of the colony.

Vincent further reminded Toussaint that the governor's powers were more extensive than those of the First Consul: he was to hold office for life, and was even given the right to choose his own successor – the same objection made by Nogérée. Ironically, Vincent did not know that Bonaparte was about to imitate Toussaint in both these respects. He pressed on: although the Assembly's role was formalized in the constitution it was a weak body, entirely subordinated to the governor: it could only vote on legislation proposed by him and had no influence on his decisions. This was an entirely fair criticism; and even though article 12 guaranteed the basic freedoms of all citizens and article 63 the security of their homes, Toussaint's sweeping powers created potential infringements of these protections, notably his right to ban any writings or popular assemblies he considered seditious and to arrest the 'authors and accomplices of any conspiracies against the tranquillity of the colony'.[65] Such a vaguely worded proposition could permit any arbitrary executive act.

Equally worrying, from Vincent's republican perspective, were the provisions for the colony's plantation system (as spelled out in title VI), which were coercive towards the colony's black *cultivateurs* and effectively tied them to their estates; this was not in his view a recipe for stability or fraternity. And those who stood to benefit most from Saint-Domingue's new arrangements were not the black men and women who had been the most vigorous defenders of the revolution, but British and American entrepreneurs, émigrés and European settlers – the very groups which despised the French Revolution's doctrine of human rights and regarded it as inconceivable that the white, yellow and black races could live together harmoniously and equally, as they had been doing in Saint-Domingue. The American businessmen whom Vincent had met had expressed crude, racially prejudiced views of black people, prompting this damning judgement: 'you have been abducted, my dear general, by the enemies of France and freedom, by vile men who are interested only in the riches of the colony and are full of contempt for its inhabitants'.[66]

Returning to the international implications of Toussaint's quasi-declaration of independence – one of the major aspects of their disagreement in Cap – Vincent suggested that the governor had effectively painted a huge target on the colony. Echoing Pichon's view, he stated that a black republic would be regarded as a threat by the imperial powers: not just the British, but also the Spaniards, the Portuguese and the Dutch, who were all known for being 'cruel masters' in their dealings with black populations. They would view Toussaint's constitution as a 'torch' which could be used to 'ignite their own settlements' and would do everything in their power to 'extinguish' the revolutionary flames as a matter of urgency.[67] This was not an inaccurate speculation. News of the constitution was indeed received with alarm in Jamaica, according to the French commissioner in Philadelphia, particularly among the planters, who believed that it was the first stage in Toussaint's ambition to attack the British colony and 'subjugate the whole of the Caribbean'.[68]

Vincent's fundamental point, which he now repeated to Toussaint, was that he had chosen the wrong strategy: even though he was in a 'delicate' position in his dealings with the French government, it would have been preferable for him to have sent his constitutional draft to them 'secretly', with sincere expressions of his attachment and gratitude to the French nation. 'France', he announced naïvely, 'can only have favourable dispositions towards you.' Vincent was particularly dismayed by what he saw as Toussaint's wrong-headed approach to Bonaparte, the 'extraordinary man who today commands the respect and admiration of the entire world', who, he claimed, was very well disposed towards Saint-Domingue. Bonaparte had sent him in 1800 with 'entirely satisfactory reassurances' about the preservation of the colony's revolutionary gains, notably the liberty and equality of black citizens – but Toussaint had foolishly spurned his overtures. This was, he concluded, a grievous error: he should not only have grasped this offered hand of friendship, but also trusted the First Consul to produce laws which would best serve the interests of the people of Saint-Domingue.[69]

Toussaint had not, as Vincent seemed to be saying, openly broken with France and did not intend the colony's new constitution to rupture the relationship between France and Saint-Domingue; as he had made clear privately, he fully expected the French to negotiate with him. This was not an unreasonable assumption: Bonaparte was, after all, preparing to negotiate with the British, his sworn enemies, so why not with the black people of Saint-Domingue, who were his allies? But Toussaint had none of Vincent's illusions about the First Consul's alleged benevolence towards him, or for that matter towards the revolution in Saint-Domingue. This wariness was amply justified in his mind by Bonaparte's ambivalent position on the issue of slavery, and by the silence which had so far greeted his letters to him. Faced with this quandary – he could not ignore Bonaparte, but nor could he pledge allegiance to him in the demeaning way Vincent and Roume expected – the governor came up with his own approach, a characteristic combination of singularity, boldness and impudence.

These qualities were all manifest in the letter he gave Vincent for the First Consul. It began by informing Bonaparte that he had embarked upon his constitutional project after the unification of the French and Spanish territories, making Saint-Domingue 'one and the same country, ruled by the same government'; this was not exactly a conciliatory start, given that the French authorities had opposed his annexation of Santo Domingo. Toussaint, however, gave his actions a positive gloss by stressing that the colony's new laws were entirely in keeping with article 91 of the 22 Frimaire an VIII constitution: his aim had been to come up with proposals which faithfully reflected 'local interests and customs'. Now that the document was ready, Toussaint went on, he was sending it for the 'approval and sanction of' his government. This loyalism was immediately qualified when he added that the Assembly had asked him 'provisionally' to put the constitution into effect, that he had acceded to this request, and that the decision had been 'received by all classes of society with delight'. Presented in this way, the document seemed to require little more than Bonaparte's rubber-stamp:

there was no mention of possible amendments or alterations. To emphasize the point, Toussaint assertively sent his letter on his new 'Governor of Saint-Domingue' letterhead, and briskly reminded the First Consul that he had written him several times but was still awaiting 'the pleasure of a reply'. This was not a subordinate addressing his superior: it was a letter purportedly between equals.[70]

In late August 1801 Toussaint followed up with another letter to Bonaparte; this time it was sent with Assembly member Nogérée, who, as we saw earlier, was eager to accept the mission. Contrary to the view that Nogérée was despatched because Toussaint lost confidence in Vincent, this double act had always been his plan. Sending two different intermediaries separately on the same assignment was typical of Toussaint: while Vincent's republicanism would hopefully placate his progressive allies, Nogérée would appeal to the more conservative and reactionary elements in Bonaparte's entourage – notably the colonial lobby. And so, unlike the mildly impertinent tone of his previous message, Toussaint's letter of introduction for Nogérée was immaculate, presenting him as an important landowner in the colony, a man 'respectable both for his personal qualities and his social virtues', 'just as attached to the colony as he is devoted to France'. By contrast, Toussaint had made no reference to French patriotism in the letter he had sent with Vincent.

Together with the constitution, Nogérée took with him a copy of the 'organic laws' which had been produced by the Assembly between mid July and mid August 1801. Toussaint was keen for Bonaparte to scrutinize these copious legislative details so that he could find out 'everything he might want to know' about Saint-Domingue's arrangements. (Someone had no doubt told him about the First Consul's consuming obsession with detail, one of the many qualities both men shared.) In short, the object of Nogérée's mission was to reassure Bonaparte about Toussaint's loyalty to France, and to confirm that the territory was now on the road to peace and prosperity 'under the administration of a black man'. Even on his best epistolary behaviour, Toussaint could not resist this little dig – but the point here was also to refute the 'slanders' about Saint-Domingue which were being spread by his enemies in Paris, who were pushing for 'measures which would bring about the disorganization of the order which has been established in the colony'.[71]

The day after writing the Nogérée letter, Toussaint took up his pen again, this time to inform Bonaparte that he was allowing Roume to leave Saint-Domingue. Toussaint did nothing by accident, and that he chose this particular moment to make this announcement – several months after he had decided to release the French agent from house arrest – was plainly significant. As so often with Toussaint, there were several motives at work. The most obvious was that he did not want Roume, who was sickly, to die while detained, especially as news of his position had reached the United States and rumours were beginning to spread that he had been executed; French Consul-General Pichon lobbied him repeatedly for his release, giving details about the undignified conditions of his detention which Toussaint probably found embarrassing.[72] But, just as plainly, he wished to signal that, with the departure of its agent from the colony, France's relationship with Saint-Domingue was now moving in a new direction – so Bonaparte had better take his constitution seriously. More obliquely, Roume's liberation was no doubt connected in Toussaint's mind to the fate of his own children. He had asked for them to be returned to him in his earlier letters to Bonaparte, and this had yet to occur: in effect, they had become hostages in France. By releasing Roume Toussaint was making a gesture of goodwill, and hoping that the French government would reciprocate.

Indeed, Toussaint was eager to show that he was still operating within a French chain of command. He informed Minister of Navy Forfait that his constitution had been 'temporarily' put into effect at the request of the Central Assembly (an economical version of the truth),[73] and also asked him for a list of émigrés who were to be denied access to their properties in Saint-Domingue, in accordance with article 73 of its new constitution.[74] Toussaint even recognized, in a further letter to Bonaparte, that he was in a hierarchical relationship with him, twice mentioning that he had been expecting to receive 'orders'[75] concerning Roume. Not having been sent any such directions, he had taken the initiative of releasing him: this was his way of emphasizing his humanity, of course, given Roume's 'considerable age and the natural weakness of his character'. But by declaring that he was allowing Roume 'the freedom to embark' to the United States, there was also a hint of menace, reminding Bonaparte, lest it might have slipped his mind, that the ruler of Saint-Domingue had power of life and death over the colony's French nationals.

The founding father was rather pleased with his constitution. He rewarded the members of the Assembly handsomely for their efforts, nominating them to high positions in the judiciary and in the financial administration; Borgella became the seneschal of Port-Républicain, and Raimond *intendant des finances*, although, dying in October 1801, he was unable to enjoy his new office for very long.[76]

Toussaint ensured that pocket-size copies of the constitution were widely circulated across the island, and public festivities were organized in its honour in which citizens pledged their allegiance to the new laws. He invariably brought the constitution to his audiences' attention during his regular journeys to different places. Actually, he became a bit of a bore about it: during a visit to Santiago, in the former Spanish territory, he took advantage of one of his *grands cercles* triumphantly to pull out a copy of the text from his jacket pocket. He then invited citizen Hatrel, one of his commissioners for war, to read the contents in full. Hatrel had to pause frequently to allow the governor to interject learned comments about the significance of particular titles or articles. The lecture was received with rapturous applause by the local guests; the only person who looked somewhat overwhelmed by the end was the unfortunate Hatrel, who was in 'much need of refreshment'.[77]

The 1801 constitution has been much commented on, both by Toussaint's contemporaries and by later generations of historians, political scientists and, more recently, political philosophers. Its significance has been debated in many contexts, such as the French and Haitian Revolutions, the spread of Enlightenment thought outside Europe, the global resistance to slavery, as well as the emergence of post-colonialism. From a biographical perspective, what does it reveal about the freshly minted governor's preoccupations at the time? Toussaint's thinking was driven neither by hubris nor by whimsy, but – as always – by rational political calculations.

When Bonaparte eventually responded to Toussaint, in a letter sent with his invading army, he observed that the text's greatest shortcoming was its failure to recognize the 'sovereignty of the French people'.[78] This was brazen coming from the man who had trampled over republican institutions in his 18 Brumaire *coup d'état*, who would restore slavery, and whose empire would turn its back on much of the revolution's heritage. But Bonaparte's claim has stuck and is one of the main criticisms of the constitution. Yet it is far too categorical to capture the subtlety of the document or of Toussaint's intentions. True, Saint-Domingue was referred to as 'ce pays' in the text: a semantic slide which reflected Toussaint's increasing confidence about the colony's emancipated status. But he set up the Assembly with the primary goal of reassuring the French government, and tried repeatedly to engage its attention on the matter; his two emissaries Vincent and Nogérée were staunch French patriots. There is little doubt, too, that placing the titles about plantation order and the Catholic religion in the early parts of the text was a tactical move, destined to show that he was intent on remaining within the French *grande nation*. His keenness to retain Saint-Domingue's status as a French colony was reaffirmed in the very title of the constitution, in its opening sentence, in the recognition that

French succession rights applied to properties in the colony, and in probably the most important article in the whole document: the clause abolishing slavery, which equated freedom with Frenchness; to be a citizen of Saint-Domingue was to be 'libre *et français*'.[79]

Toussaint's secretary, Pascal, testified to the governor's intentions in his twelve-page reply to a letter from the French consul-general, Pichon.[80] Writing shortly after Nogérée had been despatched to France, Pascal summarized Toussaint's thinking in the governor's own words. Responding to accusations swirling around Philadelphia and Paris that he was leading the colony towards independence, Toussaint asserted that a break from France was 'impossible, impractical and absurd' – not least because Saint-Domingue had no navy, but also because he had no intention of 'betraying' France and allowing himself to 'become a stooge of the British'. The colony was tied to France by history, by a shared struggle for freedom, by a common language and above all by a revolutionary leader who had 'never taken a step backwards' in his relationship with France and had devoted the past ten years to fighting 'the enemies of the republic and forcing them off our lands'.[81]

But Toussaint did not dwell too long on the past, or on the issue of sovereignty. The 1801 constitution and its associated organic laws were mostly concerned with matters of good governance, such as the rationalization of the colony's finance and justice systems, the organization of its municipal and religious institutions and the setting-up of educational establishments. All the legislative edicts produced by the Assembly, carefully combed through by the governor, bear witness to his meticulous preoccupation with the proper administration of Saint-Domingue and the well-being of its citizens.[82] The reorganized civil and commercial tribunals, for example, were staffed by ten highly respected figures, three of whom were black.[83] No detail was too minute for him, whether it concerned the exact number of parishes in each department; the operation of the appeals courts; the attribution of family pews in churches; the rights of children born out of wedlock (with one decree for fathers who were still alive, and another for those deceased); the activities of notaries, land surveyors, health officers, pharmacists, public vendors, prison guards and concierges; the regulation of debts; the administration of confiscated properties; and the (severe) sentencing guidelines for crimes such as theft, robbery, arson and physical attacks, including rape.[84] Toussaint's quirkiness was evident too, as when he devoted a special organic law to the attire required for all major public functionaries: mayors were expected to wear 'a round hat, upturned on one side, with a tricolour panache'.[85] He also recorded in the constitution that he would conceal the name of his successor in 'a sealed packet', but would leave 'clear instructions as to its location'[86] for the Assembly members. The appointment of the next governor would begin with a Louverturian treasure hunt.

Toussaint's 1801 constitution clearly met Rousseau's standard of serving the collective good. Yet from a republican perspective there remained two very contentious areas: the considerable, almost completely unconstrained powers assigned to the governor, and the way in which the colony's production system now favoured landowner interests, with measures which seemed to force Saint-Domingue's *cultivateurs* into the plantation system. Both have been highly criticized, and have often been blamed for the long tradition of institutional absolutism in post-independence Haïti.[87] Toussaint's republican rule was anchored in a highly paternalistic vision of society. He was celebrated as a providential figure and saw himself as the 'father' of Saint-Domingue: there were frequent references to the 'family' in his speeches and writings – this was one of the ways in which his republican, Caribbean and Christian values coalesced. This paternalistic principle was embedded in the constitution's description of the plantation system, built around the familial ideal, with the estate-owner or manager as a 'father' figure. But this hardly demonstrates, as Toussaint's critics have often asserted, that he ditched the principle of fraternity and abandoned black people to their fate: the constitution explicitly stated that the enforcement of planters' obligations towards their workforce was one of the governor's duties.[88]

It is in terms of revolutionary fraternity, too, that Toussaint's broader rationale for the consolidation of the colony's estates should be viewed. His agrarian policy was not an end in itself: his priority was to defend Saint-Domingue's gains against external intervention, and in his mind this could be achieved only through a revival of the plantation economy, which would generate tariff and export revenues on commodity crops such as sugar and coffee that could then be used for 'the common good'; this was also the logic of article 73, which sought to attract absent landowners back to the colony. The only alternative to Toussaint's system was the break-up of the large estates into small landholdings. But while that would have been welcomed by many of the colony's black citizens, it would have alienated the French government and the local white planters and destroyed Saint-Domingue's productive capacities in the short run. As we shall see in the next chapter, there were some in Toussaint's entourage who believed that this might be a price worth paying – but he did not agree, and it is hard to fault his logic from a strictly revolutionary perspective. It is also worth bearing in mind that, although there was no formal separation of powers in the constitution, it did in effect allow a form of social pluralism between the predominantly white elites, who wielded economic power in the colony, and the black army, from which his successor was expected to be drawn and which remained the ultimate guarantor of Saint-Domingue's political arrangements.[89]

The 1801 constitution also brought into focus one of the most fascinating aspects of Toussaint's personality: his complex conception of time. As with all the great revolutionaries of the modern age, time was an obsession: it was all at once an irreversible threshold, which allowed for progressive transformation; an infinite expanse, which bore witness to the boundless potential for human perfectibility; a precious commodity, not to be wasted; a physical constraint, which could be overcome by almost superhuman effort; and a horizon of possibility, which needed to be managed carefully. All these collided, in magnificent polyphony, in the constitution. Characteristically, the spirit of the text was one of restlessness: hence its immediate promulgation at the Cap ceremony, without waiting for Bonaparte's permission, and the urgent wording of article 14, which rejected 'even the slightest interruption' to the colony's agricultural works. Hence also the injunction in article 3 that all inhabitants should live *and die* free, echoing the French revolutionary slogan 'liberté-égalité-fraternité ou la mort', which placed an ongoing duty of active republican patriotism at the heart of Saint-Domingue's ideal of citizenship.

But Toussaint's constitution was also a work in progress: provision was made for its periodic revision by the Assembly, a rarely mentioned feature which shows that Toussaint genuinely thought it could be improved on. Hence, also, the five-year limit to the term of his successor, which reflected his prudence – and his insistence on having a say in everything, even from beyond the grave. In his sunnier moments, and despite his growing misgivings about Bonaparte, Toussaint continued to view Saint-Domingue's relationship with France as one for the long term – even though it had become less of an alliance of like-minded revolutionaries, as in the halcyon days of Governor Laveaux, and more a marriage of convenience. Likewise, governorship 'for life' suggested an optimistic sense of continuity, echoed in Nogérée's sanguine vision of 'twenty years of tranquillity' under Toussaint's rule. At the most expansive end of this spectrum there was the abolition of slavery 'for ever', reflecting Toussaint's belief that Saint-Domingue's revolution had created a novel set of political arrangements which uniquely combined African dynamism, European modernity and Caribbean voluntarism.

PART FOUR

The Leader and his Myth

10

Rapid and Uncertain Movements

Toussaint's constitution came with a personal homage: the creation of a new department named Louverture, which was inscribed in the very first organic law of 13 July 1801.[1] The idea was first mooted by the members of the Central Assembly, and the governor took little convincing: he was by now getting used to this kind of flattery from his supporters. But there was real historical significance to the honour, as the territory included many of the sites of his famous early military successes, such as Gros-Morne, Plaisance, Marmelade and Dondon.

The department's designated capital was Toussaint's beloved Gonaïves, which he hoped to transform into the colony's foremost city. Delighted by this opportunity to add to its lustre, he commissioned an ambitious plan for redesigning its commercial area. In an effort to attract investment, he decreed that all wood brought into the town for construction purposes would be exempt of tax, and levies on other merchandise would be significantly reduced. This preferential treatment was not entirely fair on other towns, but Toussaint did not mind, especially as his ambitions were not modest: 'the inhabitants of this new department in general, and the town of Gonaïves in particular, must make every effort to show themselves worthy of the honour which has been bestowed upon them. They must redouble their zeal and sense of emulation to make the capital of this new department as flourishing as the principal towns of the colony.'[2]

Toussaint's expansiveness was contagious: there was a real sense of confidence in the air immediately after the adoption of the 1801 constitution. It could be seen in the thriving public entertainments: in the main towns' theatres, where most of the leading actors were black, comedy and pantomime shows were hugely in demand. Commercial activities, too, experienced a boom: in the early July issue of the *Bulletin Officiel de Saint-Domingue*, alongside the usual news of arrivals and departures from the colony, it was announced that Graille's hardware store had just received a new consignment of door locks and copper cabinet liners, and that Pourcin and company were fully stocked in quicklime and slaked lime. Laforgue proclaimed that his shop was 'very vast and very spacious' and was laden with exquisite provisions from Bordeaux, while Hulin, not to be outdone, advised his clientele that he had an excellent collection of French garden seeds, as well as vermicelli and macaroni, and 'other quality comestibles'; Marthe Guenon announced that she was the sole depository of the magic potion which could cure those afflicted with scurvy. These were cheering times for thieves, too: the retiring American consul, Edward Stevens, posted a notice that burglars had entered his bedroom and made off with his English gold watch, seven silver teaspoons ('marked EHS'), one silver tablespoon, a pair of gold earrings and a woman's cap.[3]

In the old days, access to such luxuries was reserved exclusively to the white *colon* community. However, in the late Toussaint era a black bourgeoisie began to emerge, in the commercial sector, in the administration and in the senior levels of the military; its members sometimes flaunted their wealth ostentatiously, but there was also a graciousness and an elegance about their manner which was striking.[4] In the second half of 1801, Toussaint raced around the island, issuing scores of decrees, creating a postal service for the departments of the north and Samanà, attending the inauguration of new churches, inspecting plantations and fortifications, ordering the widening of roads, the digging of ditches and the building of new bridges. His staff strained even more than usual to keep up with his manic pace, which was also reflected in the high volume of letters he despatched.[5]

He maintained his diplomatic activism, too: in late 1800 he wrote to the British government suggesting that it would be mutually advantageous to build upon their existing relationship. In this constructive spirit, he sent Joseph Bunel to Jamaica, where he remained for several months and began negotiations with Balcarres and his successor as governor, George Nugent; among his principal objectives was the extension of the Maitland Convention to the colony's southern ports.[6] In parallel, and responding to a letter from Pichon, the French consul-general in the United States, Toussaint tried to use official channels to consolidate his commercial connections with American merchants. At the same time he was wary of the growing number of former Saint-Domingue *colons* residing in America who were applying for passports to return to reclaim their properties; he certainly wanted these whites back, but not at any price. Noting that most of them had not shed their 'old prejudices', he asked Pichon to send him their names so that he could first establish whether their arrival would pose any threat to 'established order'.[7]

Domestically he faced fresh hurdles, with growing challenges to his authority among the black *cultivateurs*, a minority of the white community and even senior cadres of his revolutionary army; later in the year he would have to resort to harsh measures to put down a rebellion in the northern region. For his critics, this show of force merely revealed the bankruptcy of Toussaint's regime and his betrayal of the revolutionary principles which had guided him during his career. However, even when he strayed from the republican path, Toussaint's actions were driven by what he believed were the best interests of Saint-Domingue and the moral and material well-being of its citizens; the common good remained the guiding principle behind all his key decisions during this period. He never lost sight of the oath he had sworn at the Cap ceremony: to defend Saint-Domingue against its internal and external enemies.

Keeping up with Toussaint during these months was almost an impossible task, as much for his exhausted entourage as for the spies who were trying to tail him: as a frustrated French diplomatic report put it, 'he is always on horseback, and in fact has no fixed residence; he is constantly charging from one place to the other'.[8] The new American consul, Tobias Lear, was bowled over when they met in early July, calling him 'an extraordinary man', he too observing that his movements were 'very rapid and uncertain'.[9] Toussaint graciously interceded on Lear's behalf to help settle unpaid debts owed to American merchants,[10] and involved him in securing the purchase of one of his horses: the governor made it clear that its colour did not matter as long the steed was 'swift'.[11] Summing up Toussaint's qualities at this time, his secretary Pascal listed his 'assiduousness for every kind of task, wisdom, strength of character, impenetrability, extreme sobriety, energy and almost foolhardy bravery when it becomes necessary to take action', and of course his 'all-consuming activity'.[12]

This relentlessness was most visible in the series of decrees promulgated by Toussaint in 1801 dealing with the colony's public administration. With typical impatience, he did not even wait for his own constitution to be formally adopted before launching these reforms: his *Instructions aux fonctionnaires publics* (May 1801) preached the virtues of 'subordination and military discipline' to all officials, in the name of 'the colony's public interest'. The most interesting aspect of this proclamation was Toussaint's clear attempt to prevent his senior military officers from encroaching upon the terrain of the civil service, notably on matters concerning justice, finance and the administration of public lands. For these purposes, he even found virtue in Montesquieu's ideal of separation of powers: 'military chiefs and senior civil servants must remain strictly within the limits of their respective attributions, and act independently of each other. There can be no good government unless the powers of its different branches are distinct.'[13] Needless to say, the governor granted himself a silent exemption from this general principle.

As no Louverturian regulation could be complete without an element of quirkiness, he inserted a gloriously complex system of controls for Saint-Domingue's senior paymasters, some of whom had obviously been less than straightforward in their accounting of public funds. Under the new guidelines, the colony's chief paymaster was to establish a reserve cash chest, separate from ordinary expenses, which was to be fitted with two independent locks, one of whose keys was to be held by Toussaint. The departmental paymasters were to proceed in the same manner, except that their chests were to be equipped with three locks, with one key deposited with the chief paymaster and the other with Toussaint. Whenever funds needed to be released from these general or departmental reserves, the governor's key would be sent 'with one of his trusted lieutenants'.[14] It was not specified what these officials were meant to do if they could not locate the elusive keyholder-in-chief, who was capable of disappearing from public sight for days and sometimes weeks at a time.

This aloofness was no doubt intentional, as Toussaint was always extremely careful before allowing any debits from the public purse: one of his favourite sayings, which his senior administrative officials would have heard countless times, was: 'money is a clever spirit, as soon you touch it, it all disappears; we must therefore be very prudent before opening our coffers'.[15] Yet this fiscal conservatism did not deter him from helping those in need. His correspondence for this period shows that he was just as receptive as before to the pleas of those facing financial distress, notably women. These included an 'unfortunate soul' who was trying to recover her property, and whose case he recommended to the administrator of national estates;[16] there was also Madame Flanet, the wife of a former officer in his army, whom he had already helped before.[17] When she was unable to raise the funds to travel back to France to be reunited with her relatives she turned to the governor, who paid for her trip to the United States and recommended her to the care of French Consul-General Pichon, asking him to provide her fare back to France. As he put it, extending this support to a French military family was for him a matter of 'humanity and honour'.[18]

As Toussaint consolidated his grip over power, the colony's revenues became one of his priorities. He demanded a full audit of the debts owed to the authorities either in taxes or property leases, and appointed two special commissioners to recoup them; no mention was made of special keys here.[19] Having heard 'the observations of learned men, champions of the common good', he also issued a decree comprehensively reforming customs and tariffs. According to the well-informed British representative in Port-Républicain, Saint-Domingue's monthly revenues from import and export duties in 1801 were in the region of $100,000.[20] In an attempt to reduce the widespread fraud committed by foreign trading vessels, who very often did not declare the full contents of their cargoes, he made it mandatory for every consignment to be underwritten by a French commercial institution; he reserved the right to grant concessions to foreign companies, but only in light of the 'services they may have rendered to the colony, their good faith, their credit-worthiness and their morality'. Mindful of the needs of the poor, Toussaint also reduced from 10 to 6 per cent the import tax on 'essential items' such as flour, biscuits, salted meat, construction wood, rope and agricultural implements. Contrary to the myth peddled by both his conservative and his progressive critics that he only cared about the propertied classes in these final years of his rule, the well-being of ordinary men and women remained one of his key concerns.[21]

The other important area on which Toussaint focused his attention in 1801 was the reform of Saint-Domingue's justice system, which had become chaotic. In late May he reorganized the civil tribunal of the department of the north, appointing competent officials to replace the well-meaning but inefficient men in post. Sixteen county courts were established across the colony to deal with civil, commercial and criminal cases.[22] There was a serious backlog in the criminal justice system, and immediately after the adoption of the constitution Toussaint asked for a full audit of Saint-Domingue's prisons, so that he could establish a complete list of the inmates and the reasons for their imprisonment. His aim was to grant an amnesty to those guilty of petty crimes, and to ensure that those accused of major breaches of the peace, such as murder and theft (a critical offence in his eyes), were referred to the tribunals 'within three months'. The proper administration of justice was for Toussaint 'one of the great benefits of Saint-Domingue's constitution'.[23]

To ensure that the justice system rested on proper foundations, he set up appeal tribunals at Cap, Saint-Marc and Santo Domingo, and a court of cassation in Port-Républicain, which he inaugurated with great pomp: 'after God', he announced, 'comes justice'.[24] But, for him, the real measure of the effectiveness of judicial institutions was their capacity to serve the public with probity. In a decree of late July 1801, he noted with dismay that it had become standard practice in Saint-Domingue for the public to be asked to pay for legal documents such as civil certificates and even tribunal judgments: this corrupt system was sustained both by 'speculators', who charged for providing the service, and by unscrupulous public servants, who only

Liberté. RÉPUBLIQUE FRANÇAISE. Égalité.

AVIS.

TOUSSAINT LOUVERTURE,

Gouverneur de Saint-Domingue.

INSTRUIT qu'on dit en Public que pour obtenir Justice du Gouvernement de Saint-Domingue, aux Réclamations qui sont journellement faites par les Particuliers, l'on est obligé de payer les moindres faveurs. Instruit qu'il y a des Agioteurs qui, colportant de Bureaux en Bureaux les Réclamations des Particuliers, et qui faisant valoir des prétendus sacrifices exigés, ont particulièrement donné naissance à ces bruits injurieux. Je préviens le Public que toute Pétition, de quelle nature quelle soit, tendante à réclamer Justice du Gouvernement, toutes Pièces ayant pour objet l'obtention de quelques faveurs, seront répondues et remises *Gratis*. En conséquence, tout Particulier de qui, à dater de ce jour, on exigerait une rétribution quelconque pour la remise de ses Papiers, soit par mes Secrétaires, Aides de Camp, ou autres Personnes de ma suite, soit par les Hommes qu'ils auraient fait agir, sont invités à m'en instruire de suite; et le Délinquant, n'eût-il exigé que *sept sous six deniers*, sera puni. Le Public est invité à me dénoncer sur-tout les Hommes qui se feront un métier d'accaparer les Créances des Particuliers pour les acheter à vil prix ou les remettre au poids de l'or à leurs légitimes Propriétaires; et immédiatement après la dénonciation qui m'en sera faite, avec preuve, ces Hommes seront jugés et punis conformément aux Lois les plus rigoureuses, les regardant comme de *Maîtres Voleurs*.

Comme Homme public, je dois rendre la Justice *Gratis*, ainsi tous les Actes qui émaneront de moi, seront remis gratuitement aux Particuliers; les Passe-Ports seuls, pour sortir de la Colonie, continueront à être payés, ainsi qu'il l'a été prescrit, pour leur produit, versé dans une Caisse particulière, être partagé, d'après mes ordres, aux Secrétaires du Gouvernement, en formes d'indemnités. Nulles Pièces, autres que ces Passe-Ports, ne pourront être payées.

Cette mesure sera générale pour toute la Colonie et pour toutes les Autorités. Nul Fonctionnaire public ne pourra exiger de rétributions, en raison des Opérations de son Ministère, que celles auxquelles il a pu être autorisé par la Loi ou par des Règlemens antérieurs à la présente.

Les Généraux et tous autres Commandans tiendront la main à l'exécution des présentes Dispositions, qu'ils feront publier si tôt leur réception, par les Commandans de Place, afin que Personne n'en prétende cause d'ignorance.

Donné au Cap-Français, le 9 Thermidor, l'an neuvième de la République française, une et indivisible.

Le Gouverneur de Saint-Domingue,

Signé TOUSSAINT LOUVERTURE.

Au Cap, chez P. Roux, imprimeur du Gouvernement.

Issued in late July 1801, this Toussaint notice declared that henceforth, with the exception of passports, official papers should be issued free of charge; any public servants who went against this rule would be prosecuted as 'master thieves'.

delivered the documents when they were paid for. Toussaint declared that henceforth, with the exception of passports, for which there would be a modest fee, 'justice will be rendered free of charge', and no public employee would be allowed to demand payment for issuing official papers. The public was invited to denounce functionaries who tried to contravene this edict: even if they merely asked for 'seven cents or six pennies', as he put it colourfully, they would be prosecuted as 'master thieves'.[25]

As we saw in the specific provisions of his constitution, a major priority for Toussaint in 1800–1801 was to defend Saint-Domingue against a possible foreign attack, and he continued to take appropriate measures even as he despatched his emissaries to France to appease Bonaparte. He hired a number of civil engineers who had evacuated to Jamaica with the British forces in 1798, and who agreed to return to work for him. In May 1801 he ordered a full review (he was clearly in the mood for audits) of the colony's defence structures, and ordered his senior military officers to ensure that all those under their command would be in a ready state, with any necessary repairs carried out 'at the lowest possible cost'; as an incentive, he promised to inspect the sites personally and commend the officers who had carried out the best work.[26] And so, during the months following the proclamation of his constitution, Toussaint travelled across the northern and eastern coastal areas, inspecting the fortifications of the main towns, visiting the elevated sites in their vicinity, and ordering that additional cannon be brought to particular locations. He personally supervised the construction of retrenchments around several towns by workforces composed of thousands of men.[27]

This consolidation of Saint-Domingue's defences was not based on hypothetical threats. Bellicose language about the need to restore order in Saint-Domingue was increasingly being heard in Paris, notably in Bonaparte's entourage, among senior officials and in the colonial lobby.[28] From mid 1800, there were a number of incidents in which British ships regularly intercepted local vessels sailing along Saint-Domingue's coasts for trading purposes, seizing their cargoes and in some cases landing ashore to carry out attacks against fishing communities. Toussaint vainly urged Balcarres to intervene with the British naval authorities and rein in his bête noire, Hyde Parker, who condoned these acts of piracy and remained bitterly hostile to his regime.[29] By early 1801, in a report to his brother, Paul Louverture noted that these attacks were occurring on a daily basis, in flagrant breach of the Maitland Convention. Toussaint complained to the British representative about such 'insulting' behaviour, pointing out that the reason his ships did not fight back was that he had 'religiously' observed the stipulations of the agreement with Maitland, which forbade the arming of Saint-Domingue vessels.[30] Toussaint demanded that these callous British attacks be halted, and stated that his 'faith' in Britain was 'almost completely destroyed';[31] in April 1801 he issued a proclamation putting the colony's coastal areas, 'desolated by the reiterated aggressions and insults of foreign vessels', on alert.[32]

Toussaint completed these preparations by ordering that his army be kitted out in brand-new uniforms,[33] and issuing a stirring proclamation to his soldiers and officers in late April 1801. He noted that the entire island was now united under a 'single republican government under French laws', and celebrated its military achievements in defeating the colony's foreign enemies, linking its emancipatory campaigns to his personal crusade for republican liberty: 'from the dawn of the revolution I fought for freedom, and I have sufficiently demonstrated by my conduct that I did not want this liberty only for myself. I have always treated you like my children, and in this capacity have constantly led you along the paths of glory.' He reassured his army that there would be no military adventures in distant lands: 'we will not fight in foreign countries', but only for 'the defence of our territories'. Mindful that some 'disturbers of the peace' might try to divide them and make them believe that 'darkness was light, and light darkness', he urged them to remain 'an army of brothers' and never to turn against each other: 'your weapons have been placed in your hands to protect your rights, the principles of liberty and equality, and your country'.[34]

The moral education of the citizenry continued to be just as important to Toussaint as its physical protection. At the zenith of his power, he assiduously promoted religion as the foundation of the social order. Even before his constitution was adopted, every ceremony he organized included a Mass, during which a *Te Deum* was performed. Church attendance by the colony's leading citizens was never higher than in this period – especially if there was a chance of taking Communion in Toussaint's presence. Across the island, army officers escorted their soldiers to church every Sunday after the traditional military review, and they heartily sang hymns in celebration of their commander-in-chief. In the main towns, Toussaint actively sponsored the formation of religious congregations, in which young women devoted themselves to spreading the gospel about the designs of God and the good deeds of the governor: the two were easily conflated in the popular imagination. Even Toussaint's mistresses were not exempted from their religious duties: one of the first questions he would ask them, as they entered his chambers, was whether they had been to Communion.[35]

Not surprisingly, one of the Assembly's early organic laws dealt with the organization of religious institutions, giving the governor close control over the appointment of local priests.[36] This merely codified existing practice: by mid 1801 Toussaint had quietly overseen the formation of a new class of black clergymen, under the supervision of the colony's ecclesiastical authorities; these 'priests of a new type', as a French report called them, were present in almost all parts of the island and were 'completely devoted' to the governor.[37] Here again, Toussaint took inspiration from French political convention and then adapted the process to his own ends. The principle of the subordination of spiritual institutions to temporal powers had been applied in France by the revolution in 1790, leading to a schism in the Church and the creation of a separate corps of *prêtres assermentés* (constitutional clergy); and indeed, back in 1797 Toussaint had written to his fervent ally Abbé Grégoire asking for twelves priests 'of exemplary conduct' to be sent to the colony 'to bring the lost sheep back to the fold'.[38]

However, when in early 1801, shortly before the signature of the Concordat with the State, French religious authorities eventually despatched Guillaume Mauviel to take up the position of Archbishop of Saint-Domingue, Toussaint refused to install him – not least because he was aware of his racial prejudice against black people. He confined him upon his arrival to Santiago, in the former Spanish territory, and cheekily encouraged a petition by the colony's local priests objecting to the presence of any religious minister who was not unconditionally devoted to the Pope.[39] The dim-witted Mauviel remained trapped in Santiago, and gained further experience of Toussaint's capacity for casuistry: exploiting the ultramontane and anti-revolutionary sentiments of local Catholics in Santo Domingo, Toussaint's religious emissaries depicted the French as a 'nation of monstrous atheists, without religion or morals'; Toussaint, in contrast, was portrayed as a profoundly religious and God-fearing leader.[40]

Of course, Toussaint did not leave the promotion of religious values to the priesthood: many of his decrees sought directly to shape the moral attitudes of his compatriots. In May 1801 he banned gambling houses 'in the name of ethics, the good running of commerce, the maintenance of public order, and the protection of family life'; he also promised severe punishment not only for anyone found hosting such activities, but also for any public servant or military officer caught gambling.[41] In addition to making Catholicism the official religion of the colony, the constitution and its organic laws confirmed Toussaint's prohibition of *vodou*, which had been proclaimed in his January 1800 decree banning 'nocturnal assemblies and dances'.[42] This was less an expression of moral opposition than a reflection of his unwillingness to allow any social institution which he did not fully control.[43]

A well-ordered state was not complete without an aesthetic dimension, and so, following his earlier ordinance on the dress of public officials, Toussaint designed the outfits of his own close assistants, including the secretary general, Pascal, and the interpreter of foreign languages, Nathan, as well as his private secretaries, right down to the uniform to be worn by the most hard-working members of his team: the copyists. The *couturier-en-chef* rewarded his top officials with a golden sabre, to be worn on a sling below their white waistcoat; Nathan, in addition, was to wear a medal 'on the left-hand side of his waistcoat', bearing an inscription which summed up the qualities Toussaint expected of all those who worked with him: 'trustworthiness and discretion'.[44]

Toussaint's doctrine of public interest was most forcefully – and controversially – put into practice in his agrarian policies. One of the rationales of the 1801 constitution was to revive the colony's agricultural exports, which had fallen to nothing by the mid 1790s: as noted earlier, coffee, sugar, cotton and indigo production, the backbone of Saint-Domingue's economy in its heyday, had completely collapsed in the years following the slave uprising. In his *Instructions*, Toussaint reminded civil servants and military officers that the island's prosperity depended entirely on its agricultural output, 'the condition of our freedom, the cause of our country's wealth, and of the happiness of all individuals, and the foundation of public order'.[45]

Toussaint believed that the only way to achieve a rapid increase in commodity exports was to restore the plantation economy. He never seriously considered dividing up the land into smallholdings, as such a system could operate only with a large and efficient bureaucracy and a highly developed transportation network – neither of which late-eighteenth-century Saint-Domingue had. The task of reviving the plantations was not entrusted only to white planters: abandoned properties were taken over by the state and leased to deserving public officials and senior military figures. This was a happy coincidence of public and private interests: the beneficiaries of the system included the likes of Christophe, Moyse and Dessalines, who amassed considerable fortunes (Dessalines alone controlled around thirty sugar plantations, each of which yielded an income of 100,000 francs a year).[46] For Toussaint, too, the times were good: he already owned a number of plantations, and in addition purchased a large estate in the Cap plain from a wealthy landowner named Lefevre, who lived in the United States; he entrusted the operation to the French consul-general, Pichon.[47] There were rumours that he deposited a large sum of money in a Philadelphia bank, but no evidence has emerged to support this claim – and it seems highly unlikely given the acute shortage of currency and gold in the colony during the 1790s.[48]

The challenge was herculean: in the late 1790s many plantations were still in disarray, with a workforce which was reluctant to return to the fields and lacked any stake in the system of production. Appealing again to the idea of 'the common good', Toussaint claimed that the revival of agriculture needed a 'salutary measure', which he was compelled to provide 'by the duties of his office'. His October 1800 decree was a draconian move, effectively imposing a martial order on agricultural production and demanding 'submission and obedience' of his labourers. But there was much more: vagrancy was denounced, workers were not allowed to leave their plantations without permission, and managers were expected to impose military-style discipline on the labourers; any fugitive was to be treated with the same harshness as a soldier who deserted his post, and severe penalties were imposed on any citizen caught harbouring a vagrant. Toussaint's army commanders were held 'personally responsible' for the operation of the labour system – a measure which was all the more effective because the senior officers had personal stakes in its success. The role of chief enforcer was devolved to Dessalines; his plantation inspections in the western and southern parts of the colony became infamous for their thoroughness and for his willingness to inflict severe beatings on underperforming managers and foremen – even, and especially, if they were white.[49] Dessalines also carried out regular sweeps of major towns such as Port-Républicain, and any person found without proper documentation was sent off forthwith to the plantations.[50]

This fierce regime inevitably brought back echoes of slavery for Saint-Domingue's black masses, even though they received the legal tariff – one quarter of the harvest – as payment for their labour. Whips, the hated symbol of the plantation system before the revolution, remained banned, but *cocomacacs* (clubs) were reintroduced and seem to have been used widely, causing enormous resentment. Some white planters believed that the October 1800 decree had given them licence to exercise absolute domination over their workers again, and that the latter no longer enjoyed any legal protections – forcing Toussaint to issue another proclamation punishing such 'incendiary' talk with a heavy fine for a planter, and demotion to the rank of ordinary soldier for an officer. But the very fact that some military officers were using this kind of demeaning language was revealing.[51] As they did in the times of slavery, labourers reacted to these harsh treatments by deserting their plantations in droves. Estimates of numbers vary, and there were different patterns across the island; but there is evidence that by 1800, in certain districts of the northern department, there were more *marrons* than before 1791.[52]

Faced with this worsening situation, Toussaint sought ways of increasing the supply of agricultural workers, and article 17 of the 1801 constitution specifically mentioned 'the introduction of labourers in Saint-Domingue' – a euphemism for the purchase of slaves. He asked Joseph Bunel, his negotiator in Jamaica, to enlist British help in securing labour from Africa.[53] Slaves were, of course, to be freed upon arrival in the colony and entitled to the standard wage: but given the already stringent agricultural code in operation, such a public pledge could not fail to alarm Saint-Domingue's labour force, fuelling rumours that the governor was intent on reintroducing human bondage and was now in cahoots with the enemies of the revolution. In the former Spanish part of the island, it was rumoured that Toussaint was looking to purchase as many as 40,000 slaves. These stories further damaged Toussaint's standing among Saint-Domingue's black *cultivateurs*.[54]

In the months after the proclamation of the constitution Toussaint was also preoccupied by the forcible abduction of black citizens from Saint-Domingue by slave-traffickers: in September 1801 he issued a decree mentioning a number of cases which had been brought to his attention in the United States, notably a resident of Cap called Bonhomme, who had been sold in Charleston, South Carolina. He called upon port authorities rigorously to scrutinize passenger lists to ensure that ships leaving the colony were not carrying men destined to a life of slavery in the United States.[55] He also wrote a number of letters to the French consul-general, asking Pichon to do everything in his power to locate citizens of Saint-Domingue who had been sold in the United States or were drifting in a state of vagrancy, and facilitate their return to the colony; he raised with him the plight of Joseph Petitoire, a black citizen who had been captured at sea and sold to a Frenchman named Fontaine in the port of Wilmington, North Carolina.[56]

Nonetheless, in his relentless drive to revive Saint-Domingue's plantation economy, Toussaint became increasingly trapped in an authoritarian spiral. His tone became more strident, and he relied less on exhortation, more on coercive measures. His interventions were now not restricted to citizens' performance of their public activities: he also sought to regulate their private behaviour. This paternalism was most spectacularly illustrated in his efforts to promote a sense of social responsibility among married couples. He banned divorce in his constitution, and in October 1801 issued two further edicts on marriage. In the first, Toussaint noted that this sacred institution was being denatured on the island by what he termed a spirit of 'corruption and vagrancy'. Dramatically – and no doubt painfully – he recognized that members of his own armed forces had contributed to the moral dissipation, notably by preying on young women. He decreed that no member of the military could henceforth get married without his express permission, which would be granted only if the military commander of the department vouched for the officer's 'morality' and confirmed that the parents of the bride had consented to the wedding. Likewise, Toussaint's personal consent was henceforth required for any union between men and women labourers based in different plantations; hopeful couples had to provide information about their employment and financial circumstances to their local municipality, which would then pass the information to Toussaint with an 'impartial' recommendation. Municipal and church officials were 'expressly forbidden' from celebrating any marriage unless these formalities had been completed.[57]

The second proclamation focused on the issue of broken marriages. Also addressed to all municipalities, which were still playing a critical role in promoting Toussaint's social policies, it began by pointing out that spousal disunity had disastrous social and economic consequences, leading to 'great unhappiness in families', especially for young boys and girls, who were increasingly condemned to lives of 'laziness, debauchery, promiscuity and irreligion'. In order to avoid this, the governor invited husbands and wives who were not legally divorced to make every effort at reconciliation. If this 'perfect harmony' still remained elusive, the separated couple were expected to provide a full account of their differences to their local town councillors, which then had to write up a report and send it to Toussaint for 'adjudication'. He also stressed that parents were responsible for providing for their children's education, and that those who failed to meet this standard would be publicly denounced as 'bad citizens' ('mauvais citoyens').[58]

So Toussaint drove the citizens of Saint-Domingue to the limits, seeking by the sheer force of his revolutionary will to hold them to his ideals of economic productivity, social concord and the common good. To what extent did this all-out mobilization succeed in reviving the colony's agricultural production? Toussaint's conservative critics claim that his economic strategy was a resounding failure: drawing on contemporary accounts from disgruntled white *colons*, one concludes that by the end of 1801 Saint-Domingue's economy offered a 'spectacle of African anarchy' in which the plantation system was 'in complete ruins'.[59] Toussaint reported that, thanks to his efforts, the colony's 'cultivation and commerce' had reached 'a degree of splendour' never seen before.[60] There was more than a touch of exaggeration here. Yet even if some sectors, such as indigo, failed to show any real signs of recovery and much more capital investment was still needed, there was significant evidence of improvement across many areas. An official table for the year 1800 showed that the total receipts from import and export duties reached 8.3 million francs.[61]

According to many contemporary observers, the effect of Toussaint's regulations on agricultural output was immediate, leading to tenfold increases in specific plantations; overall there was a surge in sugar and coffee production, which rose to a third of their 1789 levels by the end of 1801; a year later, cotton exports were up to nearly 60 per cent of their pre-revolutionary levels, and a report to the French government estimated that Toussaint's revenues from cargo taxes alone were in excess of 20 million francs for 1801.[62] In strictly economic terms, the governor's plantation system proved to be 'remarkably efficient'.[63] But, as we shall soon see, it came at a political cost.

The *cultivateurs* were not the only group who were unhappy: at the opposite end of the social spectrum, there were rumblings about Toussaint among Saint-Domingue's white inhabitants. There is little doubt that the governor continued to enjoy high levels of support among the *grands blancs* in the plantations and the mercantile bourgeoisie of the cities and larger towns, who were the principal beneficiaries of his economic measures; his generous policies of amnesty and national reconciliation, especially in areas formerly under British control, were also not forgotten.[64] The upper levels of Saint-Domingue's colonial administration were entirely white, and they too were still loyal to Toussaint; they included key figures such as his personal secretaries Allier and Guybre, his Port-Républicain legal stalwart Borgella, his financial chief Vollée, his treasurer and diplomatic emissary Joseph Bunel, the administrator of public estates Joseph Idlinger, the president of the tribunal Fouqueau, and government commissioner Lagarde.

This white backing, however, was broad rather than deep. It was contingent on Toussaint's continued support by the French government, and was due to his personal qualities, which were seen as exceptional, rather than the new social and political order which had emerged since the revolution. Above all, it was based on personal interests rather than any notion of the common good, as the *colons* (who tended to think in the short-term) banked on the governor as their most reliable protector. Describing the leading figures of the white commercial and plantation sectors, Charles Vincent noted that 'they only think about their fortune, and the only government they care about is the one which will enhance it to the greatest degree'.[65] Toussaint's endorsement by the whites coexisted with age-old beliefs about European supremacy and entrenched racial stereotypes about the black citizens of Saint-Domingue. A decade after the revolution, the world view of the old *colon* elite had changed but had certainly not been entirely transformed.

These views were reflected in the letters, reports, memoirs and reform proposals sent by individual *colons* to the French authorities in the early 1800s. The documents are a precious source for reconstructing the spectrum of white attitudes towards Toussaint. It is worth noting here that from the late 1790s he kept an increasingly close eye on correspondence sent to Paris, even resorting to searching and seizing the contents of mail bags at Cap (all of Roume's correspondence was read by Toussaint, for example).[66] While this was not done systematically, it occurred often enough to create a real sense of concern among Toussaint's potential critics on the island: one of them noted that he was taking a great personal risk in writing to the French authorities about the situation on the colony, as 'all communications here are observed, blocked and intercepted'.[67] The fact that this particular letter ended up safely in Paris was of course proof to the contrary. But even the exaggeration was evidence of the kind of power Toussaint was believed to wield.

We can see this too in the way settler endorsements of his policies were often phrased in more sober and practical terms than the buoyant public rhetoric officially deployed. Writing to a friend in Paris, a white inhabitant of Cap observed in December 1799: 'I have to be truthful: there is no doubt that General Toussaint is an honest man. He means to do good. It would be a major setback if we were to lose him: great misfortunes would befall us.'[68] This was exactly the view of the southern planter Nogérée, discussed in the previous chapter, and it was echoed in another letter despatched to France in October 1800, a few months after the end of the brutal war against Rigaud. Here, the predominant feeling about the triumph of Toussaint was summarized cautiously: the great majority of citizens of Saint-Domingue 'trusted' him, and saw him as 'less bloodthirsty than his rival, and a better friend of the whites'.[69]

White enthusiasm was based on Toussaint's capacity to maintain stability, especially in the plantations; this was a time when 'Europeans were happy and peaceful in their properties, and blacks worked hard'.[70] A letter by a planter from the Cul de Sac plain announced the revolutionary leader as a divine envoy: 'the grace of God is infinite, and it is not our fate to know the means by which Providence has elected to make use of Toussaint; but it is entirely possible that a black be destined to give the first example of a renewed submission to order'.[71] This power was often seen as one of his 'African' qualities: in the words of the memorialist Duboys, Toussaint's authority was rooted in a 'spirit of domination which was indigenous to slave countries'.[72] A month after the publication of Toussaint's labour code in October 1800, a Port-Républicain lawyer named Guilhou (a regular correspondent) wrote to the First Consul that this 'wise decree' was to be welcomed, as it would 'destroy vagrancy and anarchy, and restore order and diligence in the plantations'; and if anyone tried to undermine these new rules, he had every confidence that Generals Toussaint and Dessalines would 'deal with them'.[73] Guilhou also wrote to the governor, heaping praise on him for his 'constance, firmness, wisdom and humanity', and celebrating the fact that he had triumphed over all the 'disturbers of the peace who change their opinions like shirts'.[74] This appreciation was by no means all political. Praise was heaped on Toussaint for his religiosity, his generosity and his personal integrity; as might be expected in a colonial setting, his horsemanship also drew much favourable comment; the chief medical officer of the southern department, plainly an enthusiastic amateur botanist, wrote admiringly to the French authorities about the governor's knowledge of plant life, and his success in promoting the cultivation of certain seeds such as musk mallow and hemp in Saint-Domingue; he even sent them some samples, advising that they would thrive in the fertile soil of southern France.[75]

Toussaint's white critics, too, came in many varieties. They did not always hide their views, and some addressed themselves directly to him. One of the most fascinating such letters came from Jean-Michel Deseulle, a Cap-based doctor who was universally respected as a friend of the black community, whose medical needs he had tended to with dedication long before the revolution. Toussaint entrusted him with the delicate mission of explaining the expulsion of Sonthonax to the French authorities in 1797;[76] he also recommended him very warmly 'as a virtuous citizen' to Roume.[77] Deseulle loved Toussaint, but he was an ardent republican, a devout Christian and a passionate French patriot, and he wrote candidly in early September 1801, objecting to the colony's new political arrangements on all three grounds. He pulled no punches, accusing the governor of giving in to 'ambition, impetuous behaviour and malevolent passions'. Adapting the classic saying that there was no salvation outside the Church, Deseulle pronounced that 'there can be no freedom beyond the republic', warning Toussaint against drifting towards 'despotism' and treating his fellow citizens as 'slaves'.[78]

As a good patriot Deseulle was especially incensed by the constitution's apparent break with France, and he brought Rousseau into the argument to challenge Toussaint's justifications of his actions in terms of the common good: 'the law in a republic is the expression of the general will, and therefore it is not conceivable for a minority to dictate its wishes to the majority'. He went on: 'since Saint-Domingue is an integral part of the

French Empire, can it adopt a constitution which isolates it from the motherland and from the great French family?'. The question was rhetorical, but in case the governor was in any doubt the good doctor added an emphatic '*Non!*'. Toussaint's constitution was therefore an illegal and 'anti-political act' which represented an attempt to 'secede from France'. He urged the governor to return to 'the bosom of the motherland', whereupon 'all sins would be forgiven'.[79]

The theme of Toussaint's excessive concentration of powers was frequently taken up in these papers. The anonymous author of the 'Mémoire sur la colonie de Saint-Domingue', written during the latter part of 1801, suggested that he should be allowed to continue as governor but that his control over the armed forces should be taken away, so that 'military authority can promptly be returned to the white race, from whom it should never have been removed'. A common belief among his white critics (both in the colony and in France) was that Toussaint was weak of mind, and easily manipulated by those around him: the author of the 'Mémoire' was very much of this view, suggesting that 'since Toussaint Louverture is superstitious, like all negroes, we must make every effort to gain the confidence of his priest, and through him secure the governor's allegiance to France'.[80] An anonymous 'Notice sur Toussaint Louverture' was even more scathing, representing Toussaint as nothing but 'a very mediocre man' who had exploited the chaos of the revolutionary years to his advantage, largely thanks to British intrigue and the incompetence of successive French agents. Those who believed him capable of leading Saint-Domingue to independence 'gave him far too much credit'. The author recommended that the French government should hurry up and 'finish with' Toussaint, adding that this would not be too complicated as the unfortunate governor was incapable of logical thinking: 'his spoken French is poor, and he converses mainly in kreyol, and it is difficult for this tropical dialect to handle abstract ideas'.[81]

The belief that black people were incapable of conceptual reasoning because they did not speak French or any other European language was one of the enduring myths of white-settler racism, and was expounded at length in the 'Lettre d'un colon de Saint-Domingue au premier consul', written in early 1802. Its author, a planter who had lived through the revolutionary years, claimed that words such as 'citizenship, patriotism, human rights and liberty' were 'incomprehensible' to the average black inhabitant of the colony. The only freedom a negro labourer could appreciate was the leisure he enjoyed after a day's work in the fields, under 'the delicious shade of the banana tree by his hut'. The Enlightenment ideal of human perfectibility was not for him: 'no amount of education can improve his faculties, or moralize his being'. In this sense, even though he was denounced as a 'dark, perfidious and bloodthirsty usurper', Toussaint was seen merely as a symptom of a much deeper flaw in Saint-Domingue's political arrangements; it would be fixed only when the rights granted to black people by the revolution were abolished, and the proper hierarchy among races reinstated. This emphasis on restoring 'the natural order' of society was fully in line with the reactionary rhetoric Bonaparte was hearing from the colonial lobby in France.[82]

It was a goal also shared, though more elliptically, in 'Idées sur Saint-Domingue' (1801): here, human bondage was not mentioned by name, but the author observed that European power in the colony rested on moral force rather than on physical coercion, and that this authority had been irreversibly destroyed since the revolution – a common view among colonial whites, both *grands* and *petits*. In this text the portrayal of Toussaint was more conflicted: on the one hand, he was weak and subject to the influence of his European advisors, and perhaps of the British; on the other, he was a potent military figure whose power rested fundamentally on the might of his army. He was neither a monarchist nor a republican, but would 'adopt whatever system of government was most personally advantageous'. The author's proposed solution for the restoration of white order was the despatch of a European army of 24,000 men, who would land in the north, west and south and confront Toussaint's troops; those black soldiers who were not killed in combat should be 'transported back to Africa', so that there would be no armed black men left on the island. The remaining agricultural labourers would then be 'free' (by which he meant re-enslaved) to devote themselves fully to the plantations.[83]

An equally bleak portrait of the colony was sketched by the naturalist Michel-Étienne Descourtilz, who arrived in Saint-Domingue in April 1799, where he remained until 1803. As we have seen, Toussaint both facilitated his research and helped him recover the plantations owned by his French wife's relatives.[84] However he showed little gratitude towards his protector in his extensive memoir, which was only published in 1809, by which time his recollections were jaundiced by the French expulsion from Saint-Domingue (and hence his own personal losses). His account of his meetings with Toussaint provided some interesting glimpses of the leader's entourage and the deference with which he was treated by his civilian and military advisors. There were also entertaining passages about Toussaint's secret trysts with his mistresses – in one case, with the lady's husband obligingly guarding the entrance to the lovers' meeting room. Descourtilz noted, too, his appreciation of music (by 1800 he had a band of forty musicians), his typically obsessive oversight of all Church preparations before Sunday Mass, and his frequent and lengthy interjections during the priests' sermons. Yet, despite his poisonous tone, Descourtilz could not hide his admiration for Toussaint's intellectual powers, which were confirmed when he witnessed him dictating a series of letters simultaneously to his secretaries, and then correcting each text until every word carried his precise meaning. This 'literary penetration' overwhelmed Descourtilz, who declared him 'worthy of the genius announced by the philosopher Raynal'.[85]

These years were most intriguingly depicted in the writings of Jacques Périès, a senior French official in the colony's treasury department who arrived in 1800. Unlike most of the memorialists mentioned so far, Périès was an insider, occupying a position at the heart of the colonial administrative machinery; he also set up a small business in Cap, which involved him in Saint-Domingue's bustling commercial sphere. In March 1801 he was offered a position as tax collector with the Cap municipality. Here was a man who was exposed to a broad cross-section of Saint-Domingue's public life: he rubbed shoulders with the white civil, political and business elites, was on good terms with senior black military cadres, and crossed paths on numerous occasions with Toussaint. In an unpublished memoir written a few years later, he could not conceal his fascination: 'he was a figure who was one of a kind: an exceptional memory, an ardent desire to learn, a disproportionate sense of ambition, an inflexible but reasoned firmness, a boldness of imagination had made him a kind of phenomenon which was all the more remarkable given his physique and his colour'.[86]

Yet Périès rapidly became disillusioned. The main reason was that Toussaint excluded him from his 'white circle'.[87] Although they were on good terms, the ever-prudent governor kept him at a distance, suspecting – correctly, it turned out – that his loyalty was questionable; it appears Toussaint did not confirm his appointment with the Cap municipality.[88] There were other reasons for Périès' discontent: he had hoped to secure the lease of a sizeable portion of land in the former Spanish part of the colony, but his application was rejected;[89] and he experienced what he regarded as petty persecution from black military officials (in particular from Moyse's men), notably when he was asked to participate in the collective clearing-up of a ravine outside Cap. Deep down, he could not cope with the loss of status suffered by white officials in the new Saint-Domingue, for which he was neither intellectually nor emotionally prepared. By April 1801 he had become desperate to leave the colony, writing long letters to the Minister of Navy pleading for another posting in the French diplomatic service and confessing that he was 'suffering from cruel transes'.[90]

None of this was particularly unusual, and there were almost certainly other white officials who shared his predicament. What was striking was the way in which Périès chose to convey his dissatisfaction about Saint-Domingue to his superiors, and how quickly his views shifted to an extreme and aggressive form of racism. He railed against the 'utter disorganization' of the administration and asserted that commercial trade in Cap had 'collapsed' – which was patently false. In July 1800 he deliberately distorted the sufferings of the whites, who were initially portrayed as being 'constantly harassed and humiliated';[91] a month later he spoke of white critics of Toussaint being 'incarcerated and murdered in horrible prisons'; there was absolutely no evidence or suggestion of this, even in the other critical white memoirs sent to Paris in 1800–1801.[92] Indeed, in his March 1801 report the main British representative went out of his way to point out that whites were very well treated, and that all those who had returned to Saint-Domingue from Jamaica had had their properties returned to them.[93]

For Périès the real problem was the emergence of a new ruling class: he claimed that 'two-thirds' of Saint-Domingue's land was now in black hands, thanks to Toussaint's systematic policy of leasing émigré properties to his senior officials.[94] It is true that this caused some resentment among whites in the colony, as is shown in a letter from a settler who returned to Saint-Domingue after hearing about Toussaint's promise to return properties to their pre-revolutionary owners: despite his repeated attempts, his plantation was still sequestrated;[95] another letter sent to the French government also noted that 'the best farms have now been handed over to the generals, division chiefs and regional commanders'.[96] Périès, however, put it much more crudely, saying that 'black gangsters have instituted a reign of tyranny in this colony, they alone occupy all the key civil and military positions, and whites have now become debased, and they cannot even call themselves French, such is the hatred for this word among these vicious men'.[97]

The most remarkable aspect of Périès' alienation was the vicious rhetoric with which he described the black population, mirroring that of the most racist *colons*, in whose circles he clearly mingled. He echoed their claim that black people 'were not made for freedom', that 'their soul was truly as dark as their bodies' and they were naturally disposed only for 'pillage and plunder'.[98] Drawing on the writings of Moreau de Saint-Méry, he tried to provide a scientific basis for his racism by distinguishing the Kongo black inhabitants of the colony from those of the Côte d'Or; while the latter were peaceful and hard-working, the former (the majority in Saint-Domingue) were 'only capable of violence and criminality, which runs in their blood' – and this, he told the French Minister of Navy, was 'the same blood which charges through Toussaint's veins'.[99] After attending the Cap ceremony, where he feasted with the colony's leaders, he wrote that the new constitution had created 'an absolute despotism', and that law and order had completely broken down: 'thefts are now commonplace in towns as well as in the countryside'. He also alleged that five white *colons*, 'all good family men', had been locked up because they had dared criticize Toussaint's constitution. Tranquillity would only be guaranteed, he said, by a French military intervention and the deportation of 'all blacks wearing epaulettes, whatever their grade'[100] – uncannily similar language to that later used by Bonaparte in his instructions to his invading army.

All these fault lines in Toussaint's power – the doubts about his excessive concentration of executive authority, the resentment among Saint-Domingue's black plantation workers over his labour regime, the muffled contestation of his rule among a minority of whites, and the widening contrast between the moral values he promoted and the material aspirations of his officers and soldiers – came to a head in a series of rebellions which broke out during the latter half of October 1801 across the colony.

In mid October, Toussaint's schedule took him to Léogâne, Saint-Marc and Port-Républicain on various official engagements. It was mostly duty, but it was mingled with pleasure, too: he returned to Saint-Marc with his wife Suzanne to attend Dessalines' marriage to Claire-Heureuse, one of the glittering events of Saint-Domingue's social calendar. Accompanied by the groom, he then made his way to Verrettes, where he had been invited to attend a ceremony to bless the new parish church. It was there, on 22 October, that the two men were informed that there had been an uprising across the northern plantations and that massacres of white men, women and children had taken place; most of the killings occurred in Limbé, Acul, Port-Margot, Marmelade, Dondon and Grande-Rivière.[101] According to British consular sources, around 370 people lost their lives.[102] Toussaint acted quickly to pacify these areas, reducing the insurgents at Marmelade and pursuing them to Souffrière, where he dispersed them; he sent Dessalines to the north to attack all rebel positions. There had been an attempt to stage a major uprising at Cap, in which all the town's whites were to have been massacred; the plot had been promptly suppressed by Christophe. As Toussaint put it in a subsequent proclamation, all these incidents formed part of a more general insurrection 'against the government and the whites in the northern territories'. The conspirators had mobilized support by claiming that Toussaint had 'sold black citizens to the whites', and that Dessalines and Christophe were complicit in this arrangement; in Limbé the conspirators had even shown the local population the chains which were to be used to re-enslave them.[103]

That such lurid fabrications could gain traction across the colony, and in the very department named after Toussaint, was a huge embarrassment to him, and a measure of the volatility of the political climate in the later months of 1801. Rumours about divisions within his military leadership had begun to circulate; one report from a southern *colon* even predicted that 'great events prejudicial to Toussaint' would soon occur.[104] Some believed he personally instigated the October insurgency so that he could flush out his opponents in the army and smash any resistance to his rule among the plantation workers, while also reminding the white *colons* that he was their only effective saviour and protector.[105] These rumours travelled all the way to Roume in Philadelphia, where they were recycled in a feverish report to his minister in Paris. Roume, now an implacable enemy of Toussaint, concluded that the governor was the 'author and director' of the rebellion. All the circumstantial evidence pointed to him, wrote Roume: the mobilization of plantation workers and the threat to burn and pillage Cap had been one of Toussaint's main tactics against successive French agents, including himself; also suspicious was the absence of any trials and the summary execution of the plotters, carried out to prevent any compromising information from being revealed.[106]

Roume added that Toussaint had staged the insurrection because of his 'loathing' for the citizens of Cap, who were fierce republicans, unlike the 'anglophiles' of Port-Républicain, whose company he preferred; he had therefore wanted to destroy the town so that he could build a new capital 'to immortalize his name' in Gonaïves; the October 1801 rebellion was thus driven by Toussaint's 'despotic hatred and ambition'.[107] Of course, Roume supplied no evidence for any of these outlandish claims. And while Toussaint was certainly capable of Machiavellian acts, it is hard to see him deliberately destabilizing a political order which he had worked so hard to construct. The massacre of whites, in particular, was completely at odds with the entire political and economic strategy he had been pursuing up to that point, which was closely tied to reassuring the French authorities about his loyalty. But these tales about the restoration of slavery, though false, were politically meaningful: they showed the rising hatred of whites among the *cultivateurs*, as well as sections of the urban black population; the main slogan of the insurgents was 'death to the whites'.[108] Stoked by some of Toussaint's own local military commanders, some of whom led the rebellion, this violence was a crude response to the arrogance and increasingly uninhibited racism the black men and women were experiencing on the plantations at the hands of the old ruling class.

These fears of re-enslavement were also a reflection of Toussaint's declining support among some of his former core supporters; the wealth of his new black elite, combined with his draconian labour regulations and his refusal to allow plantation workers access to land ownership, all damaged his standing among black communities. As we noted earlier, there was a significant incidence of *marronage* in the northern plantations, and some of the rebel forces were drawn from these groups. But even among the plantation workforce, Toussaint's star had waned. During his months of enforced exile in Dondon (one of the main sites of the insurgency), Roume had seen this alienation for himself among the local citizens, both *bossale* and local-born: the French agent observed that 'the totality of black Africans and a considerable number of creoles' felt betrayed by the governor, and believed that he had used them 'as a stepping-stone to supreme power'; they were also 'furious' about the decision to import slave labour into the colony, which they viewed as a violation of the revolution's sacred promise – inscribed in Toussaint's own constitution – to end human bondage for ever on the island. Roume was of course not an unbiased observer, but there is little doubt that his impressions captured the unease among Saint-Domingue's plantation workers about the governor's policy.[109]

It soon emerged that the principal architect of the October 1801 revolt was none other than Moyse. In the reports received from his military officers, Toussaint was informed that the rebels had repeatedly cheered the name of the northern commander: at Plaisance, for example, they had chanted 'General Moyse is behind us', adding 'he is the one who supports us, he is our leader'.[110] Since the end of the war with Rigaud, Toussaint's abrasive young nephew – he was only twenty-eight years old – had become increasingly frustrated, making no secret of his opposition to his uncle's strategy. He had been critical of Toussaint's labour code for its harsh treatment of black workers in the plantations. He was also passionately committed to combating slavery: as one of the most ardent champions of black citizens sold into slavery in Santo Domingo,[111] he was hostile to Toussaint's plans to introduce indentured labour in the colony. He had challenged his uncle over this article of his constitution, and believed more generally that his vision of the common good had gone too far in protecting the interests of the *grands blancs*, whom he despised.

Moyse had told his supporters in Cap that their time would soon come: 'the French are no good in this country, and they are the only ones who are in our way; I will make their life so difficult that they will be compelled to leave and abandon their properties'.[112] Such views, accompanied by the regular intimidation of Cap's white residents by his militia, had made

Moyse immensely popular among the black communities in the north, and he was even credited with favouring wider popular access to land ownership – although this was more of a posture than a real commitment. Moyse was no egalitarian: he reserved the best lands in the northern department for his close military associates and enjoyed an opulent lifestyle; like Toussaint's other leading commanders, he had amassed a considerable personal fortune in land and properties; his annual income was estimated at 1.2 million *livres*.[113] All sorts of rumours circulated about his personal wealth; one story which did the rounds was that seven million *livres* in gold was found in his house when he was arrested.[114]

Toussaint easily overcame Moyse's attempted *coup de force*. Even though it had its roots in issues of principle, his insurrection was poorly planned and even more clumsily executed. Furthermore, there was plainly no appetite across the colony for an all-out racial war against the whites; so the political order the governor had established remained secure, at least for the moment. But the events shook Toussaint to the core: he confessed that the rebellion would 'never fade from his memory', and that his heart was 'broken with pain'[115] – especially as he would have known personally many of the whites who were killed, and because the insurgents were black citizens, led by a man who was not only one of the heroes of the revolution but an intimate relative whom Toussaint considered as an adoptive son.

But this was no time for regret. Toussaint promised that the spilling of innocent blood would be 'avenged', and that 'justice would be rendered in such a way as to deter even the boldest of scoundrels'.[116] He was true to his word. Moyse was arrested, taken to Port-de-Paix and tried by a specially appointed military commission, which heard testimonies against him by Toussaint and a number of his military officers. The accused was not allowed to defend himself, was found guilty of conspiracy, and was executed in the fort of Port-de-Paix. He died bravely, refusing to be blindfolded and commanding the firing squad himself. The white officer who presided over the commission, Brigadier-General François Pageot, was immediately deported from Saint-Domingue by Toussaint; he had tried to allow Moyse to testify (the governor, who missed and forgot nothing, also rebuked him for refusing to endorse the 1801 constitution). Although he did not doubt that Moyse was guilty, Pageot subsequently wrote that the judgment had been 'truncated' by Toussaint and published in a doctored form.[117]

Gone, too, were the days when Toussaint was more forgiving of sins committed by black people. The restoration of order across the northern region was carried out with extreme brutality. Dozens of *cultivateurs* were summarily executed, some merely for hailing from a locality which had been held by rebel commanders. When they recaptured Plaisance, for example, Dessalines and his soldiers butchered plantation workers with sabres and bayonets, and every prisoner captured during combat was stabbed to death. Not to be outdone by his lieutenant, Toussaint staged a gruesome scene in Cap in early November 1801, assembling the population for the execution of forty rebels who were chained to each other; among them was Joseph Flaville, one of the senior military commanders of the northern region, who had personally commanded the insurgents in his region of Limbé. Toussaint harangued the crowd menacingly and announced the impending execution of Moyse; he promised that anyone who threatened public order would meet the same fate, even if it was his own son. Three cannon were then lined up against the prisoners, who were blown to pieces; the crowd dispersed in terror.[118] The Place d'Armes – the scene of such joyful celebrations a few months earlier, when Toussaint proclaimed his constitution – was now drenched in blood.

The Moyse affair was a personal tragedy for Toussaint, and revealed the growing fault lines in his leadership. In the wake of the Rigaud insurrection, which had seen treachery from within the ranks of his senior officers, he had become increasingly reliant on his blood relatives – the three main commanders of the Santo Domingo invasion had been Moyse, Paul Louverture and Toussaint's nephew Charles Bélair. But it seemed he could be vulnerable even in this privileged group. It was also a matter of his style: like most self-made charismatic leaders, he became entirely self-reliant; in early 1801 he spoke of 'the entire island of Saint-Domingue united under my authority'.[119] He was extremely reluctant to communicate his intentions even to his leading military officers, or to share power with them in any meaningful way.

There were also emerging differences in strategy: Moyse's revolt was partly triggered by his belief that Toussaint's regime was too hard on its natural supporters, the black *cultivateurs*, and too soft on the whites. Christophe, for his part, thought that Toussaint's quest for autonomy from France was a dangerous mistake; from early 1801, the Cap commander began to send discreet signals to the French that he might prove a more pliable local ruler than the governor, were there to be a vacancy.[120] In this sense, Toussaint's new constitution, with its provision for designating his successor, had the paradoxical effect of destabilizing his leadership. And it was not just Christophe who was getting ideas above his station: Dessalines was not involved in the constitutional process at any stage, and in all probability took his exclusion as a sign that he would not be among the favourites in the line of succession.

Another potential source of instability for Toussaint was his delicate balancing act with the British authorities, which continued through much of 1801. He was frustrated with the slow progress of his discussions, and even the *loas* seemed to conspire against him: the vessel carrying his envoy Pennetier back from London to Jamaica was shipwrecked; for a while Toussaint refused to believe the news, and thought the British had abducted him (or, as he put it with typical quaintness, had 'made him invisible').[121] Trading on his characteristic combination of elusiveness and seduction, he courted the local British representatives and won them over to his cause. W. L. Whitfield, the sub-agent in Port-Républicain, vouched for Toussaint's good faith and stressed that had no plans to undermine the stability of Jamaica; his only interest was to consolidate his 'independence'.[122] The governor established a particularly strong rapport with Edward Corbet, who arrived in the colony in early 1801 to act as British agent in Port-Républicain. Corbet was a highly capable official, and his diplomatic reports were full of admiration for Toussaint's efficiency, his humane treatment of the white *colons* and his 'perfect despotism'; from the outset, he argued against any harassment of Toussaint's ships by the British.[123] Toussaint expressed his 'disappointment' that the British government was not more forthcoming in its dealings with him, and told Corbet that the 'only' friends of Saint-Domingue were the Americans – which of course produced the piqued reaction Toussaint intended. The governor also repeatedly affirmed that all he was doing in his dealings with the French was 'preserving appearances', and that he and his fellow officers had sworn 'to admit no other authority on this island but such as at present exists, which is in fact a black independent government'; were the French to attempt to send a new agent to the colony, he added, the official would 'not be received'. If the British treated him 'loyally' and with 'honour', Toussaint concluded alluringly, 'they could have the whole island under their influence'; he even allowed Corbet to raise the possibility of the British being allowed back in Môle Saint-Nicolas.[124]

The gambit paid off. Before he left Jamaica, Balcarres solemnly told his successor Nugent and his superiors in London that 'the good faith of the British is through me committed both to the United States of America and to the chieftain Toussaint'.[125] This was a remarkable statement from a man who three years earlier had denounced the black general as a 'brigand', and had to be persuaded by Maitland that reaching an accommodation with him was a 'necessary evil'. With the blessing of his government, Nugent eventually agreed an extension of the 1799 convention with Toussaint's envoy Bunel. The settlement, negotiated by Corbet on the British side,[126] was signed in mid November 1801: British vessels were to be allowed in Gonaïves, Jérémie, Les Cayes and Jacmel on the same terms as previously agreed for Cap and Port-Républicain, and Toussaint undertook to allow the British to appoint representatives in these locations. French émigré planters who had taken refuge in Jamaica during the 1790s would also be allowed to return to their properties in Saint-Domingue, the number and pace of these restitutions to be determined by the governor.[127]

Events were to overtake the implementation of this agreement, as we shall soon see. But the fact that it was signed was a measure of Toussaint's indisputable stature in the region. The fascination with Toussaint even spread to white Jamaican high society: having spent an evening hearing about his exploits from the British representative in Saint-Domingue, the new governor's wife Maria wrote enthusiastically in her diary: 'after dinner had a great conversation with Mr Corbet about General Toussaint L'Ouverture, which was particularly interesting. He must be a wonderful man, and I really do believe intended for very good purposes.'[128]

In Saint-Domingue, the immediate reaction among most ordinary residents of Cap after the crushing of the Moyse rebellion was, understandably, one of relief. Its American community issued a proclamation thanking the governor for restoring order 'with wisdom and energy',[129] while the municipal officers expressed their gratitude to Toussaint and Christophe for 'bringing the town back from the edge of the grave' – no doubt they had pictured themselves, too, on that chilling threshold. Saluting the 'just punishment of the criminals', they hailed the advent of 'a new dawn' for the colony.[130] A British trader from Gonaïves applauded the 'prompt and vigorous action' taken by Toussaint to quell the uprising, observing that Saint-Domingue's security would be 'seriously compromised' without his presence.[131]

For Toussaint, however, the immediate lesson of the Moyse rebellion was that further measures were needed to prevent any such recurrences. In his 10 November decree he rounded on the 'vagrants and bad subjects' of Cap who had taken to congregating there, posing 'a threat to public order and a menace to society as a whole'. Most of these vagrants had come from the plantations and taken refuge in the colony's towns because they no longer wished to work in the fields; however, Toussaint noted sternly, 'in a free country, liberty consists not in following one's whims, but in doing that for which one is destined'. He ordered each of the sections of Cap's National Guard to hold an immediate census of all the men, women and children above the age of twelve in their respective areas, to establish whether they were employed and had a fixed abode; those who were unable to satisfy these conditions were instantly to be sent back to the plantations. Any citizens who hid a vagrant in their house would incur a fine (of twenty-five *portugaises* if they were wealthy, ten if they were poor); those harbouring any 'disturber of the peace' or 'anyone known to be a bad subject' would be prosecuted and could face the death penalty.[132]

These were merely the preliminaries. Toussaint's full response to the Moyse rebellion came in the decree of 4 Frimaire (25 November 1801). Even though it built on many of his previous proclamations, it was an extraordinary document in all senses of the term: in its length (more than seven pages), in the sheer range of issues it addressed, in its often hectoring and accusatory tone, and in the scale of the repressive measures it proposed. It was remarkable, too, for its highly personal and emotional tone: it came four days after the execution of Moyse, which had obviously been a traumatic moment. Toussaint had been remembering the happier times, when Moyse was one of his brave warriors and used to liken himself to Toussaint's 'good child'.[133] Just a few months earlier, Moyse had written to Isaac and Placide in Paris and told them how proud the family was of their educational achievements.[134] Toussaint had been playing back in his mind his recent and past arguments with his nephew: he had reminded him 'a thousand times' that an army could not function without the virtues of discipline and obedience; he had preached to him, too, the 'saintly maxims of our religion and the duties of a Christian', and done 'everything in his power' to get him to 'change his vicious inclinations' and 'revert to the path of righteousness'. But in the end Moyse had obstinately refused to follow Toussaint's 'paternal' advice and 'perished miserably'.[135]

Significantly, Toussaint made no explicit mention of their arguments about the treatment of plantation workers, the rightful place of white *colons* in Saint-Domingue, or the emancipation of the colony from French rule. Instead, Moyse's rebellion served as an edifying example of the general decline in public and private ethics. Toussaint returned to the republican theme of the corruption of civic morals, which he had raised in his earlier proclamations. But this time he spared no one: he first attacked negligent parents, 'especially in towns', who indulged their children to grow up 'in idleness' and without any proper understanding of their duties to society; he noted that these young people were allowed to wear 'jewellery and earrings' from a very tender age, and acquired 'a taste for idleness and luxury'. He also chastised young women who ended up in prostitution, whose spirit of debauchery was a major source of social disorder; domestic servants, who needed to be watched so that they did not steal or fall into 'idleness' (a major vice in Toussaint's eyes); recently arrived foreigners, who sometimes expressed 'dangerous views' which could have unfortunate consequences; public servants and military commanders who did not respect their vows of marriage and had 'several concubines in their homes'; and 'a great number' of plantation workers, who allowed their children to lead lives of dissipation in towns, and whose laziness was potentially a 'menace' to society. Drawing again on his ideal of the common good, he asserted forcefully that 'this class of men must be compelled, even against its will, to play a socially useful role'.[136]

The decree ended with a raft of measures which showed a characteristically Louverturian mixture of efficiency, fierceness and eccentricity, ranging from the imperative duty of military commanders to combat 'sedition' to the issuing of security cards to all citizens, renewable every six months (when Toussaint visited Santo Domingo in early 1802, he ordered that every citizen must immediately be given these cards).[137] Sedition was defined in loose terms, including 'statements which might affect public tranquillity'; any 'creole' native of the colony found guilty of the crime would be sentenced to six months of hard labour ('with a chain on the foot'), while a 'foreigner' would be deported; this was the first time Toussaint distinguished the colony's population along these lines. The 'full' execution of the labour decree of October 1800 was further reaffirmed – but the lesson Toussaint took from the Moyse insurrection was that the measures he had then proposed were not draconian enough. So he now instructed his local military commanders to draw up precise lists of all the plantation workers in their areas and send them to the governor's office, to serve as a basis for 'fixing the *cultivateurs* to their plantations'. Tighter repression of *marronage* was announced, too: any worker who left his *habitation* without permission would be pursued by the military, brought back and deprived of his passport for three months. In a further attempt to protect the plantations from noxious external influences, no person who was not an employee could spend any length of time there, and even military personnel were allowed in only if they were visiting their parents.[138]

Amidst all these repressive measures, Toussaint had not abandoned his ambition to safeguard the marital bliss of Saint-Domingue's couples; and so, not content with requiring his soldiers, officers and plantation workers to obtain his personal permission before getting married, demanding the reconciliation of unhappy couples, and limiting the number of concubines per household, he now threatened grave sanctions against anyone who was 'known to have disrupted, or attempted to disrupt a marriage': unremittingly on the warpath, the moral crusader warned all the colony's seducers that they would be 'personally answerable to the governor'.[139]

11
The Tree of Black Liberty

After overcoming the Moyse rebellion and reasserting his authority across the territory through a vigorous show of force, Toussaint no doubt hoped that he had earned himself a breathing space. But the respite proved short-lived. The diplomatic landscape in Europe was shifting, and in early October 1801 France and Britain signed preliminaries which paved the way for peace between the hitherto uncompromising rivals. Toussaint immediately understood the potentially disastrous implications of such a Franco-British truce, were it to be confirmed, for Saint-Domingue. It would align the interests of Europe's main imperialist powers and undermine the incentive of Britain and her regional allies to maintain privileged relations with him. Worst of all, it would end the British naval blockade of the Atlantic and open the way for a French military expedition to overthrow his regime. By the time news of the agreement reached Saint-Domingue in early December, the colony was rife with rumours of an impending French invasion.[1]

Such apocalyptic tales had been circulating for a while, and were usually the product of the wishful thinking – and inebriated imaginings – of the more diehard *colons*. Yet this time Toussaint knew that there was more substance to them. Ominously, his negotiations with the British, which had been going so fruitfully, were abruptly terminated by Governor Nugent in late November 1801. The new Jamaican governor had been told by the British War Secretary, Lord Hobart, that the French were sending a large army to reconquer Saint-Domingue, and that his accommodating policy towards the colony was no longer to be pursued.[2] Nugent immediately notified Toussaint, and ordered all British agents and subjects in Saint-Domingue to withdraw to Jamaica.[3] Although Nugent did not explicitly mention a French invasion in his letter to Toussaint, there is little doubt that the latter fully understood its imminence; at a meeting in early December with the British representative Whitfield also attended by Dessalines, he complained that France and Britain were colluding in 'offensive measures' against him, and vowed that any invasion of Saint-Domingue would meet with 'resistance'; he added that he would never relinquish his command or allow his army to be 'disbanded'.[4] A week later Whitfield reported that Toussaint was 'daily recruiting his army, and buying up all the horses he can get', before concluding: 'I am afraid he means to try his strength with Bonaparte's legions.'[5]

Toussaint decided to issue a proclamation to prepare his people for the French attack. Printed on a large white poster and distributed across the colony, his 'Adresse' began by casting doubt on the rumour that French troops were on their way 'to destroy the colony and the freedoms it enjoyed'; such a story could only be spread by 'malicious' forces. Having confirmed the rumour by denying it, he then added that Bonaparte had rounded up 'all the blacks and persons of colour living in France' who were opposed to him and was sending them to fight against their own compatriots; that the French government was holding his two children 'as hostages', and was refusing to release them, despite their father's repeated demands for their return; and that the purpose of the invasion was to 'eliminate the soldiers and officers of the colonial army and bring them back into slavery'.

Describing his children as 'a possession which legitimately belongs to me',[6] Toussaint said that he was 'very irritated' by their continuing absence. He lamented the French government's treatment of his children as 'pawns', in breach of the principles of 'honour and equity'. It was 'inconceivable' – by which he meant extraordinary – that France should come to attack Saint-Domingue after its revolutionary citizens had selflessly given their lives to safeguard French interests against her internal and external enemies, and turned a 'chaotic colony' into a 'flourishing enterprise'. Such 'ingratitude', he observed pointedly, was unworthy of the French. In contrast to the hectoring tone of his recent proclamations, he now heaped praise on the people of Saint-Domingue, 'the great majority of whom [are] honest property-owners, decent folk and good fathers' who aspired to 'peace and prosperity'. He also appealed to the loyalty of the officers and soldiers of his army: 'obedience', he reminded them once more, was the 'highest military virtue', and he would show them 'the path to be followed'.

Midway through the proclamation, as he paused to reflect on what the future might hold, Toussaint's tone became sombre. Upon learning that France might send an invading force against him he had privately declared: 'France does not have the right to enslave us, our freedom does not belong to her. It is our right, and we will know how to defend it, or else perish.' As he now openly confronted the looming French aggression, Toussaint pronounced that an attack on Saint-Domingue would be a 'denatured act'. In an analogy drawn from his creole and Catholic values, he compared such an eventuality to an attempt by a father and mother to kill their own child. In such a 'monstrous' situation the ethical rules of filial obedience had to be suspended, and the child had a duty to defend himself and entrust his fate to the hands of God. He invited the citizens of Saint-Domingue to prepare to follow his example, and face their invaders with dignity and courage. 'If I have to die under these circumstances,' Toussaint concluded 'I will face death honourably, like a soldier who has led an exemplary life.'[7]

Toussaint had timed his proclamation well: six days before its publication, a large French military fleet had sailed from France heading for Saint-Domingue. Aboard were Isaac and Placide, the two children for whose safe return he had been long praying: they were coming back to their family, but accompanied by an invading army (including, as the rumour had surmised, a smattering of Saint-Domingue black and mixed-race dissidents, including his old foe André Rigaud). The long-awaited missive from Bonaparte was on its way too, but its emollient contents were no more than a sinister ruse: the French objective was to reoccupy the colony, restore white supremacy and eliminate the governor and the entire ruling group which had emerged under his leadership. Toussaint's moment of reckoning had arrived: how he responded to it would determine his personal fate, and that of the revolution he had so boldly championed over the previous decade.

Toussaint was often blamed for provoking Bonaparte by his intemperate actions during the final years of his rule, and more generally for not making enough of an effort to conciliate him. It is unlikely that Toussaint could ultimately have done anything to prevent the invasion, for reasons which will soon become apparent. But the specific charge of failing to cultivate Bonaparte is unfounded. As we saw, Toussaint wrote him a number of letters from 1800 onwards, all of which went unanswered. And the Bonapartes were in Toussaint's debt: Josephine's Martinique-based Beauharnais family had considerable financial interests in Saint-Domingue, notably a number of lucrative sugar plantations in Léogâne. Production had ground to a halt during the early revolutionary years but, hearing about Toussaint's restoration of order in the colony, Josephine wrote directly to him in 1798 pleading for his help; Bonaparte was away on his Egyptian campaign at the time. Toussaint immediately intervened to restore the plantations to working order, and soon Josephine was again receiving a healthy income from her Saint-Domingue estates.[8] She was so grateful that she invited Toussaint's sons several times to lunch and dinner at her

Parisian residences on Rue Chantereine and Rue de la Victoire, and praised the general effusively; she had a particular fondness for Placide.[9] Upon his return Bonaparte was no doubt informed by his wife of Toussaint's gracious intervention and was delighted by it. When he later met the commander-in-chief's children, he told them that their father 'was a great man, who had rendered eminent services to France'.[10]

Supporters of Toussaint in Paris, such as the parliamentarian Louis Rallier, urged Bonaparte to back him, arguing that he was by far the most effective defender of French interests in the colony.[11] This favourable view was reinforced by progressive figures in Bonaparte's entourage, notably Admiral Laurent Truguet, a former minister who was one of his principal naval advisors, and state councillor Daniel Lescallier, chief of the Colonial bureau and a specialist in the Antilles. Both were sincere admirers of Toussaint; they were also principled republicans who opposed slavery; Lescallier had been a member of the Amis des Noirs. In the early months of 1801, the First Consul seemed to have made up his mind to throw his weight behind Toussaint: he drafted a letter appointing him as 'capitaine-général' of the French part of the colony, and assuring him that he enjoyed the 'greatest trust' of the government in Paris.[12] Acknowledging receipt of all his previous letters, and saluting him as the 'principal representative of the republic', Bonaparte invited Toussaint to maintain peace and order, and continue to oversee the development of agriculture (particularly, one imagines, in the Léogâne area).[13] He appointed a new French envoy to Saint-Domingue, and in his detailed instructions urged him to 'give no umbrage' to Toussaint and to 'rally all the inhabitants to his leadership'. Clearly well briefed about Toussaint's religious beliefs, he even instructed this official to go to church regularly.[14]

But Bonaparte's letter was never sent, and by the end of March 1801 Toussaint was secretly struck off the register of French military officials. What had brought about such a dramatic reversal? Critics tend to attribute the First Consul's change of heart to specific actions by Toussaint, such as the internment of Roume and the promulgation of the constitution. But the timeline does not support this. By early 1801, Bonaparte already knew that Roume's relationship with Toussaint had broken down, which was precisely why he was despatching another official. The constitution was proclaimed only in July 1801 – and the news did not reach Paris until several months later. If there was a single event which undoubtedly provoked Bonaparte's anger it was Toussaint's takeover of the Spanish territory of Santo Domingo, of which he informed the French government in mid February 1801. The First Consul saw this as an act of insubordination; but it is implausible to claim, as many historians do, that this event alone decided Bonaparte to launch such a massive expedition against Toussaint. When informed about the takeover, the French Minister of Navy wrote back laconically to Toussaint: 'since the deed is done, let us now think about how to turn it to our advantage'. When the French invasion forces landed in Saint-Domingue they had no plans to return the territory to Spanish control.[15]

Bonaparte's shift on Saint-Domingue was more of a process than an event, and it began in the months immediately following his 18 Brumaire coup with a systematic policy of removing colonial officials believed to be too sympathetic to the black cause. In January 1800, plans for a fleet of French naval vessels to sail to Saint-Domingue were dropped; among the main reasons was that Lescallier, who was to become the colony's chief administrator, was too close to Toussaint and the black revolution.[16] Bonaparte also countermanded the Directory's appointment of Laveaux as the French agent in Guadeloupe, again because of his excessively pro-black affinities: when Toussaint's ally arrived in the colony to take up his position in March 1800 he was arrested by local officials, on Bonaparte's instructions, and sent back to France.[17] During a discussion of colonial affairs in the Council of State in August 1800, Bonaparte expressed his commitment to 're-establishing order and introducing discipline' in places like Saint-Domingue where slavery had been abolished.[18] His negative attitude towards Saint-Domingue was hardened by the steady flow of poisonous information the French government received from anti-Toussaint officials and private citizens in the colony, as seen earlier. The racial undertones in these writings were now overt. One of the most significant voices was that of the renegade French general Kerverseau, burning with resentment after his humiliating exit from Santo Domingo in January 1801. A few months later he wrote a long memorandum to the French government arguing for the immediate despatch of a military expedition in Saint-Domingue, which had been 'taken over by Africans'; the objective should be 'a political rehabilitation of the whites' and 'the expulsion from the colony all those who have usurped power' – meaning, of course, the black leadership.[19] Bonaparte included him in the French expedition, and Kerverseau's views manifestly shaped its political objectives.

Another key faction in this racial polarization was the reinvigorated colonial lobby in France, which became more prominent in Bonaparte's entourage in the course of 1801. Pro-invasion and pro-slavery sentiments were now back in fashion among French merchant and capitalist classes, and Bonaparte did not shy away from them – on the contrary. Such views were strongly represented among his new recruits into the Council of State. They included conservative figures such as former Navy

Minister Fleurieu; the colonial lawyer and planter advocate Moreau de Saint-Méry; the last *intendant* of the *ancien régime* in Saint-Domingue, Barbé de Marbois, who remained a vigorous defender of the slave trade;[20] and Pierre Victor Malouet, who had urged the British to invade the colony after 1793 to restore human bondage. In October 1801 Bonaparte appointed Denis Decrès as his Navy Minister, and he too shared Malouet's views on slavery, believing the Convention's 1794 abolition decree to have been a mistake.

By early October 1801 Bonaparte fully turned against Toussaint, ordering Decrès to prepare a major expeditionary force bound for Saint-Domingue. Later at Saint Helena, while acknowledging his mistake in ordering the invasion, Napoleon blamed the Council of State, Josephine and the 'shrieks of the colonial lobby' for poisoning his relations with Toussaint's regime.[21] But this was a classic piece of retrospective justification; in truth, the primary responsibility lay squarely with him. He did not even have the excuse of ignorance, as Toussaint's envoy Charles Vincent arrived in Paris in early October, just as he was finalizing his orders to invade Saint-Domingue. Vincent met with Bonaparte twice, and was ordered to assist the French plans by providing detailed maps of the island, as well as information about local military and administrative figures.[22] Despite denouncing Toussaint's 'loss of direction',[23] Vincent cautioned Bonaparte and his Navy Minister against the expedition and refused to take part in it. In a later memoir Vincent observed that the First Consul was entirely misguided, and that he would almost certainly have taken a different course of action had he 'personally seen and heard Toussaint, even for a moment'.[24]

In fact, Vincent predicted the sequence of events which would follow: the resistance of the majority of the black citizens; the strategic and logistical disadvantages the French army would face through lack of familiarity with the terrain, and the problems of resupply; the ravaging effects of the climate, and the onset of disease – all culminating in the loss of the colony itself. Bonaparte, confident in the power of his army and hoping to use Saint-Domingue as the lynchpin of a French economic empire which would include the Caribbean colonies, Guyana, Louisiana and Florida, blithely ignored these warnings.[25] His view of Saint-Domingue was by now fully infected by the racism of the colonial lobby: he told Vincent that he would 'not tolerate a single épaulette on the shoulders of these negroes', and ordered that black and mixed-race inhabitants from the colonies be banned from entering France.[26] In May 1802, when France restored the slave trade in Martinique, Tobago and Saint Lucia (soon followed by Guadeloupe and Guyana), Bonaparte was even more blunt in a conversation with Truguet: 'I am for the whites, because I am white; I have no other reason, and this one is good enough. How can we have given liberty to Africans, to men without any civilization, who had not the slightest idea as to what a colony, or for that matter France was? If the majority of the members of the Convention had understood what they were doing, and known about the colonies, would they have abolished slavery [in 1794]? I very much doubt it'.[27]

On 29 January 1802, the lead ships of the French fleet were sighted at Cape Samanà, on the north-eastern corner of the territory. Toussaint was visiting Santo Domingo at the time, as part of his reinforcement of coastal defences; he immediately rode to inspect the scene with his guard. He saw at least twenty-five French naval vessels already anchored, including ten ships of the line, the biggest carriers of the time: each could ferry 1,000 men. And as he gazed at the horizon, he could discern the silhouettes of dozens more warships heading for Saint-Domingue. He immediately realized the scale of the operation which Bonaparte had mounted. This was not an exercise in intimidation, or a tactical show of force as the prelude to a political negotiation: the French army had come to fight a war of extermination against him and his people. Turning to his officers, he declared: 'We must perish. All of France has come to Saint-Domingue. They have been deceived, and they have come to seek vengeance.'[28] He wrote to his brother Paul in Santo Domingo that it was time to resist to the death: 'spare no one, since we must conquer or die'.[29] Toussaint's final and most momentous struggle had begun.

Even though he was dismayed by the sheer size of Bonaparte's invading fleet, he had been preparing for the possibility for some time. In addition to strengthening coastal defences, he had diverted some of his customs revenues to import more weapons and ammunition from the United States;[30] these American shipments continued to arrive throughout 1801.[31] There are also suggestions that Toussaint had come to a mutually beneficial arrangement with Jamaica: according to a French report, quoting British sources on the island, he had established a 'lucrative trade in guns and munitions' with the Jamaican authorities. Once in Saint-Domingue, the material was crated in specially designed mahogany containers to prevent damage by the elements and moved inland to strategic locations on the mountains. These arms and munitions depots were carefully concealed in the uplands, and the roads leading to them were widened to enable the passage of artillery pieces.[32] A French military report estimated that there were 140,000 guns in Saint-Domingue by the end of 1801, of which at least 30,000 had been supplied to Toussaint by the Americans.[33]

A significant number of these weapons remained hidden, and would later play a major role in the war against the French.

Yet although arms – small arms at least – were relatively plentiful, Toussaint was aware that one of his weaknesses was his lack of manpower: by the end of 1801, having discharged thousands of former *cultivateurs* to work on restoring the plantation system, he was left with only around 20,000 combat-ready forces, a number he had hoped to raise considerably over the course of 1802.[34] The bulk of these troops (around 11,000) were in the southern and western divisions under Dessalines, while the rest were divided between the northern division commanded by Christophe and the eastern under Augustin Clervaux.[35] Toussaint's men faced a French expeditionary force whose first wave arrived from Brest, Rochefort and Lorient; a further batch landed from Toulon and Cádiz in mid February, bringing the total number of French troops to 20,000.[36] A significant portion came from the Army of the Rhine, an elite corps which included soldiers who had distinguished themselves in the revolutionary wars; among the officers were men who had seen action in Europe, the Caribbean (in Saint-Domingue, Guadeloupe and Martinique) as well as in Bonaparte's Egypt campaign.

With his battalions dispersed across the territory, Toussaint sent instructions to his lieutenants to prevent the French from disembarking and gaining access to the principal coastal towns, if necessary by fighting back; if their situation became untenable, they were to retreat inland after setting their positions alight.[37] The plan failed in Port-Républicain and Santo Domingo – in the latter case due to the incompetence of Toussaint's brother Paul, who was tricked into surrendering by Kerverseau.[38] Toussaint was particularly incensed about the loss of Port-Républicain, where the French laid their hands on three and a half million *livres* held in the treasury; the location of the locked chests was betrayed by Joseph Idlinger;[39] Toussaint demanded that the funds be returned to him.[40] The invaders took Fort-Liberté after a strong fight and massacred nearly all the 600 men who surrendered – the first of many war crimes.[41] However, General Jacques Maurepas, the military commander at Port-de-Paix, put up a spirited fight: he gathered a force made up of soldiers and local peasants, declaring that they were 'all ready to fight for their freedom' and that the invaders would be received with 'glowing red cannon balls'.[42] He was true to his word, and inflicted severe losses on the French forces sent to take the town. Maurepas then burned down Port-de-Paix, as instructed, and retreated to a fortified plantation nearby, from where he crushed the remains of the French unit; female skirmishers played an important role in this first defeat of the expeditionary army.[43]

The main prize for the invaders was Cap, and Toussaint raced there, arriving well before the enemy fleet. He first masterminded a diversion which took their ships to Port Margot, a landing point much further west than Acul bay. According to a number of witnesses, he then slipped into the city disguised as a Kongo peasant.[44] There, he directed Christophe to delay a request for a landing, sent via a French officer, telling him to reply that he was awaiting orders from the governor – who was listening to the conversation in the adjoining room. The breathing space was used to burn the city: after evacuating the inhabitants, boiling oil, sugar and heated barrels of rum were poured onto the streets and buildings, and the blaze soon caused the explosion of the arsenal. More than 90 per cent of the city was destroyed, including the granary – a devastating blow to the invaders even before they had set foot in Saint-Domingue.[45] An advance French party had tried to distribute a proclamation signed by Bonaparte, helpfully translated into kreyol. Invoking the republican principles of friendship and brotherhood, it promised to maintain liberty and peace in the colony, while urging the population of Saint-Domingue to pledge allegiance to the invading forces. Those who did not, the First Consul warned, would be considered 'traitors' and would be 'devoured by fire, like dried sugar cane'.[46] In the event, it was Bonaparte's parchment which went up in flames.

The First Consul may have hoped for better luck with another missive, addressed directly to Toussaint, in which he sought to rally him. It was adroitly written (probably with the assistance of Vincent), flattering Toussaint by describing him as 'one of the principal citizens of the greatest nation on earth', and 'the first of your colour to have attained such a position of eminence'. While it chided him for some aspects of his 1801 constitution, which were 'contrary to the dignity and sovereignty of the French people', it assured him of Bonaparte's 'unreserved esteem' and promised him 'consideration, honours and fortune'.[47] The letter was despatched with Toussaint's two children, accompanied by their tutor Coisnon. Isaac and Placide duly made their way to Ennery, where they were reunited with their mother and father, who had not seen them for six years. Even though he was moved beyond words to see his offspring, Toussaint immediately saw through Bonaparte's ruse and put the letter aside before he had finished reading it. He told his children and their tutor that if the First Consul truly wanted peace, he would not have sent a fleet of warships to Saint-Domingue.[48]

Toussaint was correct about Bonaparte's hostile intentions. In his secret instructions for the Saint-Domingue expedition, written in late October

1801, the First Consul had meticulously spelled out his plans for the restoration of French authority in the colony, which specifically included measures to eliminate the governor. In this extraordinary document, the extent of whose counter-revolutionary ambitions only become apparent when read in full, Bonaparte distinguished three intended 'periods' of French occupation: the first and second would see the securing of the major coastal areas and the elimination of any rebels who opposed the French forces. During these pacification phases, Toussaint and his supporters were to be 'heaped with kindness' if they co-operated, but court-martialled and executed 'within twenty-four hours' if they resisted. During the third period, which was meant to run on very quickly after the first two, Toussaint and his generals 'would not exist any more', and there was to be a massive purge of Saint-Domingue's revolutionary leadership. Toussaint would be captured and sent to France, while all those 'suspected' of sympathy with his regime were to be arrested and deported – 'whatever their colour';[49] among the first to be despatched to France were Bernard Borgella, Étienne Viard and André Collet, three of the white authors of Toussaint's 1801 constitution.

The reimposition of French order included a strong dose of cultural imperialism: the closing of all educational establishments, and the despatch of creole children to France; priests loyal to Toussaint were also to be returned to France, as were 'the white women who prostituted themselves to the blacks'. There was a pecking order in the destinations for the deportees: in addition to the women, France was reserved for the black collaborators of the invaders, Guyana for the whites who had compromised themselves with Toussaint, and Bonaparte's native Corsica became the dumping ground for the 'blacks and coloured men who had misbehaved'. Also to be thrown into forcible exile were 'all' individuals who had signed Toussaint's 1801 constitution (their destination was not specified, but it may also have been Corsica).[50] The colony's black soldiers were to be disarmed en masse and sent back to the plantations, and there was to be no black landowning class: all the properties leased under the Louverture regime were to be returned to their former white owners; 'no black above the rank of captain' was to remain in post. There was a brief reference to slavery in the document: the 'political goal' of French policy was to make the disarmed black citizens 'free farmers', while those of Santo Domingo were to be re-enslaved. This planned restoration of slavery in the eastern part of Hispaniola, a year after its abolition by Toussaint, was a striking illustration of the incoherence of Bonaparte's thinking: the idea that reintroducing slavery in one French territory would not have any effects on neighbouring ones was utterly delusional, as future events would prove.[51]

The officer entrusted with 'assuring for ever the ownership of the colony to France' was Bonaparte's brother-in-law, Victoire-Emmanuel Leclerc, the husband of his sister Pauline. It was a disastrous appointment. He was a greedy and vain man, completely unsuited to the task, with no experience of combat outside Europe and little understanding of the complexities of the colony's revolutionary culture. He had none of Bonaparte's genius and all of his defects – notably his belief in the innate superiority of white European forces, and that black people were 'cowards' who were 'afraid of war'.[52] Having been humiliated by the disastrous Cap landing (he finally entered the destroyed city on 6 February), and having failed to secure Toussaint's allegiance in response to the First Consul's letter, Leclerc declared the governor 'an outlaw' on 17 February.[53] Concealing his real objectives, he courted a number of the governor's senior black officers, a list of whom had been supplied by Bonaparte.[54] Many switched to the side of the invaders after receiving assurances that they would keep their positions (and properties): among the first to capitulate were Clervaux and Laplume, the commanders of the eastern and southern territories, soon followed by Maurepas; a number of local commanders in the northern region also sided with the French, notably in Port Margot, Acul and Plaisance.[55]

By mid February, once he had landed all his troops at Fort-Liberté, Cap, Port-de-Paix and Port-Républicain and secured control of the coastal areas, Leclerc planned to encircle Toussaint's army by sending five divisions to seize Gonaïves and Saint-Marc, converge in the interior, and defeat him in one blow. Led by Generals Hardÿ, Desfourneaux, Rochambeau, Debelle and Boudet, the French troops advanced swiftly, capturing Marmelade, Dondon, Vallière and Saint-Raphaël. Yet the forces of Christophe and Dessalines pushed back and broke through the attempt to encircle them, with Christophe successfully rallying the *cultivateurs* of the north to join the fight against the invaders.[56] Toussaint had no plan to capitulate, and despite the reduction of his forces by the defections – one historian who conducted extensive interviews with his former soldiers in Haiti estimates that he was down to just under 6,000 men by mid February[57] – he was brimming with confidence and energy. Toussaint was revitalized by the prospect of defending Saint-Domingue against the French: donning the outfit of national liberator again was a welcome return to the spirit of his heroic campaigns of the 1790s. His republican war instincts, which had been in abeyance during the later years of his rule, now firmly returned. Shortly after seeing the French fleet at Samanà he delivered a powerful harangue to his soldiers, reminding them of the 'torture and cruelty' their slave ancestors had suffered for the past three centuries and of their 'glorious conquest of liberty' during the previous decade. The French had come to Saint-Domingue not in the name of patriotism and freedom but to bring back slavery, in the service of the 'hatred and ambition of the Consul, who is my enemy because he is yours'. The fate of the invaders was already sealed: 'those who will be spared by our sword will receive death at the hands of our vengeful climate'.[58] In a similar vein, he instructed one of his loyal southern commanders, Dommage, to 'bring about a *levée en masse* of the plantation workers' and to warn them against the whites who had come from Europe, whose 'manifest objective is to enslave them'.[59]

And even though this southern uprising failed because of Laplume's treachery, Toussaint could still count on his bulldozer Dessalines, who as we saw earlier had predicted the French invasion and was fully prepared for it, both materially and emotionally. Toussaint's overall strategy, set out in a message to his general, was simple: until the arrival of the 'rainy season' in the middle of the year, which would 'rid the colony of its enemies', 'fire and destruction' were to be the main instruments of popular resistance to the French. He ordered Dessalines to send some of his best men to burn down Port-Républicain and then engage in a war of attrition, harassing the French positions on the plains. His instructions about the scorched-earth policy declared: 'it is imperative that the land which has been bathed by our sweat should provide not the slightest nourishment to the enemy. Tear up the roads with shot, and throw the carcasses of dead horses into the springs; destroy and burn everything, so that those who come to re-enslave us always have before their eyes the image of hell they deserve'.[60]

This letter was intercepted, but Dessalines had already anticipated it. He raced off to the south, where his columns burned and destroyed whatever came their way. The town of Léogâne was reduced to ashes after his arrival on 9 February, including Josephine's lovingly restored colonial properties; after visiting the scene, a French officer observed that these destructions had been carried out 'with a particular decorum and even solemnity'.[61] Saint-Marc suffered the same fate, with Dessalines personally setting alight his own palace, which had just been completed. Hundreds of whites who had joyfully welcomed the French invasion were massacred and their burial was forbidden: their rotting corpses were intended to strike terror among the French forces. Wherever he went, Dessalines spread Toussaint's message of mass resistance to local soldiers and peasants. At Saint-Michel, according to a local military commander, he assembled the black troops and told them that the 'enemy had arrived in Cap and was planning to restore the *ancien régime* in the colony, and to take away our freedoms which cost us such sacrifices, in order to plunge us back into a horrifying slavery'. Dessalines then reminded them of the early moments of the slave rebellion in 1791, when they had no weapons: the situation was different now, and he urged them to mobilize against the invaders, telling those who had no arms 'to use their knives and any other lethal weapons they might find'.[62] The naturalist Michel-Étienne Descourtilz, who survived thanks to the intervention of Claire-Heureuse Dessalines, who hid him under her bed, heard Dessalines echo Toussaint's prophecy about the long-term inability of the occupying forces to survive: 'be brave of heart, the French will start off well, but soon they will become ill, and they will die like flies'.[63]

The spring campaign of 1802, which lasted seventy-two days, was Toussaint's last stand, and his greatest. Pushing himself and his men to their physical limits, and ably seconded by commanders such as André Vernet and Charles Bélair,[64] he drew upon his wealth of military knowledge and experience, combining the resources of conventional warfare with the techniques of guerilla combat. Constantly on the move, and sleeping on a plank for a few hours every night, he sent the French on long and exhausting marches to chase him across the mountains but remained out of reach, despite their frequent and increasingly desperate efforts to track him down.[65] After burning Gonaïves, he retreated to the Cahos

This depiction of a battle scene in the early months of the French invasion of Saint-Domingue in 1802 shows Leclerc's troops (on the left, in uniform) fighting Toussaint's colonial forces.

mountains to retrieve his concealed caches of weapons, and mercilessly harassed the French positions. Starving the invaders of rest and supplies, he lethally ambushed their troops: one French commander reported that he was 'losing a lot of men to the rebels, who are dispersed in the woods and mountains; they kill all the stragglers on the roads, and attack our columns, and then retreat swiftly thanks to their perfect familiarity with the local areas'.[66] Toussaint knew exactly when and where to launch these attacks because of his network of messengers. Travelling into the treacherous maze of forests, ravines and mountains in the inland regions with Leclerc, Norvins, his secretary, could not conceal his admiration at the efficiency of Toussaint's informants:

> pressed against the rocks and hidden in trees at our arrival and departure, these men followed and preceded our marches across the woods, where they could guide themselves through tracks which only they knew of, and were able to find even in the darkest of nights by relying on natural starlight. Toussaint would send his orders to his combatants at the most unexpected of moments through these men. They never betrayed his secrets, and his orders were always scrupulously executed, no matter what they were – as if he were present.[67]

How damaging were the attacks carried out by Toussaint and his forces? The concept of 'success' takes on a broader meaning in a war which was mostly irregular: from Toussaint's perspective it was also about establishing that his men were equally valorous combatants, unsettling the French and undermining any sense they might have that their campaign was making progress. He clearly achieved these objectives, as one senior French officer later acknowledged: 'the enemy was like a hydra with a thousand heads: it would be reborn after every blow we struck. An order from Toussaint Louverture would suffice to make his men reappear, and cover the entire territory in front of us.'[68] And even by conventional standards, it was soon obvious that the war was not going according to Bonaparte's masterplan: a month after landing, Leclerc was still very much stuck in the 'first period', and its end seemed nowhere in sight. By late February 1802 the French were, by their own admission, seriously weakened: the various engagements with Toussaint's forces had cost Leclerc over 4,000 men through death, injury and disease – on 27 February he wrote to the Minister of Navy asking for urgent reinforcements of 12,000 soldiers 'in order to save the colony'.[69] A month later Leclerc was so demoralized that he wrote to Bonaparte asking to be recalled to France.[70] By late April, despite repeated French efforts to track him down and defeat him, Toussaint still commanded a force of 4,000 men and 'a very considerable number of armed labourers', and retained overall control of the mountainous regions of the north and west.[71]

The effectiveness of Toussaint's campaign was undoubtedly strengthened by the inclusivity of his combatants – his 'children', as he called them. Even though he was abandoned by his chief of staff, General Agé, who surrendered to French forces in Port-Républicain, several white French officers remained loyal to him, such as Barada, the former military commander of Cap; they joined him in battle, some losing their lives; Dessalines' division also included some white soldiers. Toussaint recruited auxiliaries among fiercely independent bands of *marron* fighters, such as Petit-Noël Prieur in Dondon, Macaya in Limbé and Acul, Sylla at Mapou (near his own base in Ennery), and his old comrade Sans-Souci in Grande-Rivière. By the early 1800s Sans-Souci had become the most powerful military leader of the northern region; after initially supporting the French he joined the uprising and held the rank of colonel in Toussaint's forces; he ably seconded the governor's frequent skirmishes against Leclerc's forces stationed in Cap.[72] As he moved across the mountainous regions, Toussaint also drafted farm labourers into his army, a significant number of whom were African-born women.[73] Toussaint had come full circle: women fighters had played a major role in the early months of the 1791 slave insurrection, too.

Alongside these white, creole, *bossale* and women fighters were Toussaint's flamboyant mixed-race combatants, such as Bazelais, Larose, Morisset and Gabart (the future hero of the decisive Battle of Vertières in November 1803); one of the most dashing was Louis-Daure Lamartinière.[74] This illegitimate son of a white southern planter from Léogâne was a brigadier in Toussaint's army and was fiercely patriotic; he had unsuccessfully tried to oppose the French landing at Port-Républicain by shooting a fellow officer who called for surrender. Toussaint appointed Lamartinière as one of the commanders of the fort of Crête-à-Pierrot, a strategic location in the mountains bordering the River Artibonite which was defended by around 1,200 soldiers, nine cannon and trenches fifteen feet deep. In early March the French attacked it, and the ensuing siege was the most sustained military encounter of the spring campaign. The French were initially driven back by Dessalines; a counter-attack by Toussaint's cavalry, headed by Morisset, routed them and seriously wounded the French commander, Debelle. Two more French charges followed, in which Leclerc, his chief of staff Dugua and Rochambeau were involved. These assaults also failed, and Leclerc was injured in the groin. Toussaint now instructed the erection of a second fortification on a nearby hill, which helped strengthen his men's position; Lamartinière was given its command.[75] Although Toussaint's troops lost nearly half of their strength, the total French deaths amounted to 1,500 – a greater number than were actually guarding the fort. Despite being surrounded by 12,000 French soldiers, Lamartinière staged a daring nocturnal escape and managed to crawl through enemy lines with most of his surviving fighters. They nearly captured Rochambeau on their way out; the French general only saved his neck by fleeing into the nearby woods. One of the fort's most valiant defenders was Lamartinière's wife Marie-Jeanne, who was dressed in a Mamluk outfit and continuously resupplied the defenders with ammunition and gunpowder; she also frequently shot at the French herself.[76]

Toussaint not only fought defensively: in early March 1802 he launched a sustained counter-attack on French positions, and succeeded in retaking Saint-Michel, Marmelade, Saint-Raphaël and Dondon, nearly cutting off Leclerc completely in Cap; he even hoped to use the siege at Crête-à-Pierrot to launch a surprise attack on Cap, capture the French commander and his senior staff, and send him back to France.[77] Nor did he leave the struggle to his subordinates: as with his campaigns against the Spaniards and the British, he put himself directly in the front line. For example, when an encounter with Rochambeau's forces on 23 February at Ravine-à-Couleuvres, near Ennery, turned into desperate hand-to-hand combat, Toussaint stood alongside his force of 3,000 men, encouraging them and driving them back to battle on several occasions when it seemed the French were gaining the advantage; he 'risked a thousand deaths' during this six-hour encounter.[78] Toussaint's charisma was evident as he galvanized his troops; perhaps the most remarkable moment came when he realized that the French force contained troops from his own 9th regiment, latterly commanded by Maurepas, who had just defected to the French side. Walking up boldly to the men, he asked them if they were prepared to kill their 'father' and their own 'brothers'; even though one officer fired at him, most of the regiment lowered their weapons at the sight of their former commander, and many fell on their knees and begged Toussaint for forgiveness.[79]

Toussaint was in his element. He toyed with his adversaries, issuing a proclamation on 1 March 1802 in which he responded to Leclerc's earlier decree pronouncing him an outlaw. Toussaint refuted the French commander point by point, declaring that it was he and his generals who were the real outlaws. He ridiculed Leclerc's 'perfidious' assertion that he had come in peace, claiming that if that had been the case, his ships would have been laden with merchandise, not soldiers. He added that he had been ready to receive Bonaparte's 'benevolent views' – a generous interpretation of the First Consul's letter; Toussaint was careful not to attack him directly in writing. But Leclerc had not given him time to respond. In fact, it was all Leclerc's fault: he was incompetent and had chosen to bring 'death and desolation' to the colony; even the burning of Cap was his responsibility (a blatant lie, but one Toussaint knew he could get away with). At the same time, he reaffirmed his position as the legitimate ruler of Saint-Domingue by virtue of the 1801 constitution, and lambasted the senior officers who had come with the invading army, such as the traitor Kerverseau. He prophetically described the brutal Rochambeau, who would succeed Leclerc, as the 'destroyer of blacks and men of colour'. As for the French promise to bless the inhabitants of the colony with 'freedom', Toussaint's retort was crisply sarcastic: 'one cannot provide someone with something they already have'. Tellingly, the proclamation ended by observing that Saint-Domingue owed its freedom not to France, but to 'God' and 'the struggle of its people against tyranny'.[80]

In the last week of March 1802, Toussaint began to sound out the French about the possibility of a truce. Such a move was not, in itself, surprising. Throughout his career he had been true to his name, and had engaged with his enemies for all sorts of sensible tactical reasons – to buy time, to play his foes off against each other, to strengthen his existing options and open new ones. Even though the retreat from Crête-à-Pierrot had been a *défaite glorieuse* for his army, it was still a setback; he now needed to see whether he could offset it with a shrewd negotiating manoeuvre. This too was exactly what he had pulled off many times before: forging elements of freedom even in the most constrained of circumstances.

He decided to approach General Jean Boudet, one of Leclerc's senior officers. It was a sensible choice. Boudet was a comrade-in-arms of Bonaparte's, having been at his side at the Battle of Marengo. He had none of the murderous tendencies of some of his fellow French officers, and understood that the revolution had transformed social life in the Caribbean (he had fought and helped expel the British from Guadeloupe during the 1794–5 campaign led by Victor Hugues). Boudet had also been injured at Crête-à-Pierrot, and was forced to abandon his command: Toussaint therefore knew that he had first-hand experience of the valour of his men. He loudly professed his republican beliefs, but rumour had it that he had helped himself generously from the public coffers after the French capture of Port-Républicain.[81] Toussaint's first letter to Boudet has been lost, but we can guess its contents from the French general's reply, dated 1 April 1802. Toussaint was trying to communicate directly with Bonaparte through him, bypassing Leclerc. Boudet was not so easily manipulated, and reminded him that Leclerc was not only his commander, but

Bonaparte's brother-in-law: trying to go behind his back was futile. He went on to chastise Toussaint for his constitution, which had 'raised the banner of independence' in the colony and appeared to open the door to a hereditary monarchy, which was incompatible with republican principles (though this did not stop the same Boudet from swearing allegiance to Napoleon's hereditary empire two years later). After making it clear that he was speaking with his commander's approval, Boudet ended his letter with a plea to Toussaint to end the 'spilling of French blood'.[82]

Toussaint responded ten days later. He was willing to open discussions, provided he was treated with 'frankness and loyalty'; this was the way Laveaux had dealt with him in the past, and in return had always received his 'absolute obedience'. Toussaint's lengthy reply covered a wide range of political questions, which offer a glimpse of the conflicting pressures he felt as he weighed his options. He began by dwelling again on his loyal record in Saint-Domingue. As the leader who had restored order and good government in the colony, he was frustrated that the French had chosen to attack him so soon after he and his forces had put down the 'perverse and criminal' rebellion of November 1801 (unbeknownst to Toussaint, Bonaparte's secret instructions had identified Moyse as one of the main black leaders to be eliminated). Toussaint reaffirmed his allegiance to France, mentioning that he had been approached by 'foreign powers' on a number of occasions but had always spurned them in favour of France, because 'she alone had proclaimed the freedom of the blacks'; here he could not resist another poke at Leclerc, accusing him of refusing to negotiate with him 'because he was a black man'.[83]

Yet Toussaint also went to considerable lengths to defend his 1801 constitution. He dismissed the accusation that he had tried to break away from France ('if the inhabitants of the colony had wanted it, they would have become independent a long time ago'), and offered the jacobin French general a lecture in the virtues of constitutional decentralization: 'experience demonstrates that the legislative system of a country must necessarily be adapted to its climate, to the nature of its agriculture, and to the values and customs of its peoples'. Indignantly responding to Boudet's charge that he was trying to establish a monarchy in the colony, Toussaint affirmed that he had always been 'the best friend of the republic' and would stand by his 'immense people', who still had full confidence in him and counted on him to defend them against the French invasion. In fact, he had been planning to retire from the governorship once agricultural production had been fully restored; he knew by 'solid common sense' that he could not rule for ever, and that 'the powerful man of today is impotent tomorrow'. In any event, he added, he had neither the inclination nor the capacity to make his rule hereditary: his successor would gain his investiture through an orderly transition.[84]

The letter to Boudet sheds important light on Toussaint's frame of mind as he approached his discussions with the French. He was neither bowed nor defeated, and his experiences in battle had reconnected him with the fighting spirit of his people: indeed, he had been energized by the determination they had shown throughout the spring campaign. But he also knew that he did not have the necessary military resources to defeat the French at this point and needed more time; hence his attempt to explore the possibility of a political solution which would safeguard the essential gains of his revolution, as enshrined in his constitution, while waiting for disease to take its inevitable toll on the invading army.[85] In the end, the main factor which tipped the scales towards compromise was the strategic situation on the ground, which had reached an awkward stalemate by the end of April 1802. The French retained control of the major coastal areas, even though their authority was tenuous and their army seriously weakened: by this point, half the army which had arrived with Leclerc was dead, injured or infected with yellow fever.

Yet even though Toussaint's forces still held a significant swathe of territories (Marmelade, part of upper Plaisance, Saint-Raphaël, Mirebalais, Petit and Grand Cahos, as well as some positions on the Artibonite plain), he did not have enough men to land a decisive blow upon the invaders; one of his local commanders reported that he could not supply more than a handful of guides because the rest were 'in a pitiful condition' and most of his horses were injured.[86] He also struggled to find volunteers to help as nurses and washerwomen in military hospitals: 'members of the community are invited to use their moral influence on those individuals who stay at home and live in indolence, to compel them to apply for these positions which are being made available'.[87] Many of his own lieutenants had defected; the last to do so was Christophe (on 26 April) – a significant setback, especially as he went over with his 5,000 men. Toussaint had pleaded in vain with him to work out a common strategy for dealing with Leclerc, in order to prepare for a second major offensive.[88] Treachery was lurking even in his close entourage: among those now working to undermine him was his former secretary Pascal, who had been dismissed in November 1801. By this time, Pascal had become a French agent who had been writing letters to Paris about his 'dangerous situation'; he briefed the French extensively about his master when they landed.[89]

There was perhaps also a deeper reason: Toussaint could not bring himself to break decisively with France. Unlike those in his camp such as Dessalines, who were beginning to think seriously about independence, the governor still believed, somehow, that only a French Saint-Domingue could guarantee the colony's long-term security and prosperity. Even if Bonaparte and Leclerc were evil, there had been, and would again be, other virtuous Frenchmen like 'Papa' Laveaux, and like those valiant *sans-culottes* who had defended their nation against imperial attack at Valmy. Toussaint's admiration for the French defensive republican war tradition was intact, reflected in the fact that he showed no personal animosity towards the soldiers of the invading army and treated those he captured with humanity, according to the principles of the *droit des gens*, as did many of his commanders (notably Maurepas).[90] This ongoing identification with French revolutionary mythology was shared by Toussaint's men – at the height of one of the battles at Crête à Pierrot, his black soldiers had spontaneously burst into a full-throated 'Marseillaise' as they repelled a French attack. Toussaint put it simply in one of his letters to Leclerc: 'we have never stopped being French'.[91]

The commander of the expeditionary force was only too happy to hear such sentiments. The two men met at Cap in early May, and reached an agreement on the immediate cessation of hostilities and the disarmament of the *cultivateurs* who had joined the struggle against the invaders. Toussaint was greeted with military honours, and with the 'most profound respect' of the inhabitants.[92] The governor demanded something he knew Leclerc would not accept – his appointment as 'lieutenant-général' of the colony – so that he could achieve what he actually wanted: the amnesty and integration of all his officers and soldiers into the French army; he specifically insisted that the deal should include Dessalines, the terror of the whites. Leclerc agreed, but only because he hoped to turn Dessalines against his commander. On 7 May Leclerc hosted a lavish reconciliation lunch, attended by senior officers from both sides; among the guests were four future leaders of Haïti: Dessalines and Christophe, who had been fighting with Toussaint, and Alexandre Pétion and Jean-Pierre Boyer, who had travelled to Saint-Domingue on board the invading fleet. Still wary of the French, Toussaint only ate a slice of Gruyère.[93] But he had lost none of his impertinence: when Leclerc asked him where he would have found the weapons and ammunition to keep fighting had he chosen to continue the war, he replied smoothly: 'I would have taken them from your stores.'[94]

Toussaint was acclaimed by his soldiers when he returned to his headquarters at Marmelade. He bade an emotional farewell to his chief of staff, Jean-Pierre Fontaine, and his intrepid cavalrymen, some of whom had fought by his side since the epic campaigns of the early 1790s. According to the terms of the agreement with Leclerc, his guard was redeployed in

Cap and Plaisance, and he was only allowed to keep a symbolic retinue of soldiers.[95] He then departed for one of his estates in Ennery, Habitation Sancey, where he promised to help send the insurgent *cultivateurs* of the Gonaïves region back to their plantations.[96] As he spent time on the four coffee plantations he owned in the area, he began to glimpse the quiet life he had so often yearned for: surrounded by his family, he received local military, civilian and religious dignitaries and went on daily horse rides. The pace, though, was anything but genteel: old habits died hard.[97]

Still smarting from the terms of the agreement with Toussaint, which were widely seen as a personal humiliation, Leclerc was determined to show Bonaparte that he had not lost control of the situation. In March 1802 the First Consul had written reminding him of his secret instructions, specifically asking for the 'principal brigands' to be deported to France as soon as the black citizens had been disarmed.[98] Unable to do that, Leclerc decided to move on Toussaint himself. He began by sending some troops to harass local peasants in the area surrounding Ennery and drive them away from his plantations. Toussaint complained to the local commander in Gonaïves about this 'insulting behaviour',[99] and then, when the disorder continued, wrote to Leclerc's chief of staff.[100] Furthermore, Toussaint's ally Sylla had refused to lay down his arms, and the French pinned the blame on Toussaint for encouraging his continuing resistance. It turned out that the main source of this provocative information was Dessalines, who was now actively working against his former leader.[101] It was said that soon after the landing of Leclerc's expedition, Toussaint consulted a *vodou* soothsayer, who foretold that he would be betrayed by his principal lieutenant; the prophecy turned out to be accurate.[102]

On 7 June the French sprang a trap for Toussaint, inviting him to a meeting at the Georges plantation with one of their local commanders, General Jean-Baptiste Brunet. Purporting to be his 'sincere friend', Brunet wrote to ask for his assistance in protecting the local area from 'brigands' and getting peasants back to work. Toussaint replied in what was his last letter as a free man: he reaffirmed his commitment to the public good and expressed his willingness to help, provided he was treated with 'honour'.[103] Honour was the last thing on the mind of Leclerc: an hour after Toussaint entered the house where the meeting was scheduled, he was arrested by Brunet's men and put on a ship which immediately headed for Cap. His servant, wife, niece and sons were also detained, and French troops went on a looting rampage at his property at Ennery, stealing money, clothing, furniture and works of art; under the pretence of looking for Toussaint's papers, Brunet's aide-de-camp, Grand-Seigne, stuffed his pockets with all the jewellery he could find.[104]

Leclerc justified Toussaint's arrest by claiming he had been plotting against the French since the truce. He issued a proclamation accusing him of inciting the continuing insubordination of Dessalines (who had reported this to Leclerc) and Sylla (who had retreated from Mapou and was still on the run).[105] The French commander also produced a letter allegedly written by Toussaint and addressed to his former chief of staff Fontaine, who was now part of Leclerc's staff. Toussaint apparently asked Fontaine to spread the rumour that the *cultivateurs* in his region were no longer willing to work; he also instructed him to tell the military commander of Borgne, the wonderfully named Gingembre Trop Fort, to get the peasants in his area to drag their feet.[106] In addition to promoting this campaign of passive resistance, Toussaint allegedly enquired about Leclerc's health and joked about the outbreak of yellow fever, whose first victims were being treated at the Providence hospital at Cap. 'Providence', he claimed, 'has come to save us.'[107]

This *bon mot* sounded authentically Louverturian, and there was little doubt that Toussaint believed that the French would eventually be destroyed by disease; he had said as much in his letter of 8 February to Dessalines, and many times thereafter in his speeches to his troops and auxiliary forces; this was why he was rightly confident that the French occupation could not succeed in the long run. The quiet encouragement of subversive activities by others while maintaining his own deniability was a classic trick, too. That said, Toussaint knew better than to pass on such potentially incriminating instructions in writing: these sorts of messages were sent by word of mouth, by men who (as Norvins noted earlier) would rather have died than reveal their secrets. All his correspondence in the aftermath of his submission to Leclerc shows that Toussaint painstakingly respected the military arrangements he had entered into, even to the extent of sending all the munitions in his possession to the bemused local French commander in Gonaïves. This was hardly the behaviour of a man who was expecting to resume combat any time soon.[108]

Whether Toussaint wrote any or all of this is almost beside the point. Bonaparte had reiterated his order to take the commander-in-chief, and sooner or later Leclerc would have come after him. The real question is why a man who had avoided dozens of ambushes throughout his career allowed himself to be captured so easily. When he met Leclerc in Cap just a month earlier he arrived a day early, surrounded by 300 soldiers and a retinue of his guards who kept their sabres drawn at all times. A French military officer who spoke to him in mid May found him 'extremely wary'.[109] As late as 5 June, in his response to Brunet, he was still complaining about Leclerc, making it clear that he did not regard his behaviour as 'honourable'. Yet even though he had been warned that the Brunet meeting was a trap, he went with one aide-de-camp and a single domestic servant.[110] Perhaps he had become over-confident, thinking that he had managed to contain the French challenge to his position, at least for the moment, and held the strategic advantage. He also underestimated the scale of the treachery around him: correspondence between Brunet and Leclerc in the aftermath of Toussaint's arrest indicates that some members of his inner circle had been bribed and were supplying the French with information.[111]

There may have been another factor. Toussaint's succession was now on the horizon: his constitution had put in place a clear system to allow him to appoint the next governor, as he had mentioned – rather imprudently – in his letter to Boudet. This prospect accentuated the conflicts among his subordinates, which the French were quick to exploit; in particular, they played on Dessalines' growing resentment of his commander. Dessalines was in close touch with Brunet before Toussaint's capture, and in one of their conversations complained bitterly that the governor took him for granted and had not involved him in the drafting of the constitution. This example was not accidental: Dessalines had apparently realized that he was unlikely to be chosen in the event of a formal succession. He gave his tacit support to Brunet's operation, thus sealing Toussaint's fate.

The prisoner reached Brest on 9 July. It was his first time on a ship. He was confined to his cabin throughout the crossing and was allowed no contact with the members of his family who were on board. Indeed, once in France he was separated from them and was never to see them again. He wrote a letter of protest to Bonaparte, pleading with him to spare his wife Suzanne, 'a mother who deserves the indulgence and goodwill of a generous and liberal nation'.[112] Placide, who had taken up arms against the French, was detained separately in the citadel of Belle-Île, and the rest of family (Suzanne, her other two sons Isaac and Saint-Jean, her daughter-in-law Victoire, her niece Louise Chancy and her maid Justine) were sent to Bayonne.[113] They were later moved to Agen, and were kept under close surveillance throughout Napoleon's reign. After being held in a castle in Brest for a month, Toussaint and his devoted mixed-race servant Mars Plaisir were transferred to Fort de Joux, where they were interned on 24 August 1802. Toussaint's final ordeal had begun.[114]

The authorities did everything in their power to break him, both physically and psychologically. He received no communications from his family, and was not told where they were being held; he only managed to

Toussaint was moved to this prison in the Jura mountains in eastern France in late August 1802. The Fort de Joux was a medieval fortress, deliberately chosen for its cold weather and its remoteness from the sea. Toussaint remained there until his death in April 1803.

send one letter to Suzanne, a month after his arrival. The medieval fortress in which he was imprisoned was deep in eastern France, in the Jura mountains, the austere location deliberately chosen for its cold weather and its remoteness from the sea – Leclerc was terrified that he might escape and return to Saint-Domingue ('his mere presence would set the colony alight').[115] Even with the help of Makandal's spirit such a flight would have been impossible: he was held in the high-security section on the top floor of the prison. He was kept in his cell, allowed no reading material or visitors, and even his intake of sugar – which he mixed into all his drinks, as his only luxury – was rationed, as was the wood to heat his cell.[116] Despite his repeated demands to be put on trial, he was held without charge. Very soon, as Bonaparte felt he was not being sufficiently co-operative, the petty humiliations began: first, Mars Plaisir, who was his only real companion, was removed from Fort de Joux and sent to Nantes.[117] He then had all his personal effects seized, including his watch, his spurs, his hat and even his razor. Finally, in late October 1802, further instructions were received from the French government: his cell was thoroughly searched for money and items of jewellery, and he was denied any paper. His military uniform was taken away and the prison governor was instructed to refer to him only as 'Toussaint'.[118]

Toussaint Louverture remained unbowed. He faced up to this degrading treatment with dignity and defiance; according to the later testimony of one of his guards, when he removed his military outfit he flung it at the officer and told him: 'take this to your master'.[119] In September 1802 Bonaparte sent one of his aides-de-camp, General Caffarelli, to question the captive, both to get him to admit to his treacherous actions and reveal the whereabouts of his hidden booty: this had become an obsession for the First Consul, who even had Mars Plaisir interrogated on the subject.[120] The ever-mercenary British also came to believe that Toussaint had amassed an 'immense treasure'.[121] According to the rumour, which was spread widely in the invading army, Toussaint was believed to have ordered six of his subordinates to conceal his riches in Saint-Domingue's Cahos mountains and then had them executed to protect his secret.[122] Despite the logical absurdity of the story (Toussaint would have had to kill those who killed the six men, and so on), Caffarelli repeated the tale to Toussaint, who rejected it scornfully. In fact, he denied everything: that he had colluded with the British and Americans, that his constitution was seditious and that he had stashed away funds in Jamaica, America, or England. He added that he had never been affluent; all his assets were in his properties. This was true, but he also allowed himself to play with his interrogator: when asked how he had purchased these assets, he replied: 'my wife is wealthy'.[123]

After meeting Toussaint seven times and being exposed to his lengthy monologues, Caffarelli was forced to admit to Bonaparte that his mission had failed, and that the 'self-possessed, cunning and skilful' prisoner had stonewalled him.[124]

Toussaint even managed to enlist Caffarelli to act as his messenger, and take back to Paris what he described as his 'report' to the First Consul.[125] This, his last piece of prose, was dictated to Jeannin, the secretary of Fort de Joux, during the first month of his imprisonment and has come to be known as his *Memoir*.[126] It is often dismissed as yet another attempt at self-justification, or at best a futile appeal to Bonaparte's magnanimity. But it represents something much more profound. By September 1802 Toussaint was under no illusion that he would ever leave Fort de Joux alive. This was not only because he had taken the full measure of Bonaparte's vindictiveness, but also because he sensed that his own health was beginning to fail. The *Memoir* was in this respect also written for posterity, and was both an overt display of respect mingled with a touch of contrition and a subtle but powerful message of revolutionary defiance. It was to be read as an edifying tale of the struggle between republican virtue and corruption or, as he put it in one of his favourite metaphors, between 'light and darkness'.[127]

He dwelled on his services to the republic from 1794, noting with undiminished self-confidence that it would require 'several volumes' to list all his military accomplishments alone. He stressed his patriotism, adding that he had risked his life for France on countless occasions and had 'spilled his blood' for his fatherland; among the injuries he had sustained was a bullet which was still lodged in his right hip (he could also, of course, have mentioned the loss of most of his front teeth).[128] And yet his reward for all of these sacrifices had been his arrest and deportation as a 'vulgar criminal'. Toussaint here opened up the issue of his race, observing that such treatment would certainly not have been meted out to a 'white general' and that these indignities were undoubtedly linked to his colour. He then stood the racist argument on its head: 'but my colour . . . did my colour prevent me from serving my country with zeal and loyalty? Does the colour of my skin get in the way of my honour and my bravery?'[129]

As an administrator, Toussaint had dedicated himself fully to the colony and imbued in his compatriots a sense of public-spiritedness. He offered a robustly republican defence of his controversial labour policy: 'if I made my people work, it was to make them appreciate the real value of freedom, which is different from mere licentiousness; it was to prevent civic corruption; it was for the general happiness of the colony, and for the interest of the republic'.[130] His record was one of impeccable service to the republic, with 'honour, faithfulness and probity'. He had managed the colony's finances 'soundly and in the public interest', and pointed out – accurately – that when Leclerc landed, he had found millions in the colony's public coffers all over the territory.[131] The French commander had destroyed this peaceful order by arriving unannounced, and attacking the hard-working inhabitants of the colony: he was the 'source of the evil'. Toussaint here kept to his strategy of blaming Leclerc while sparing Bonaparte, but no reader could miss his argument: it was the French who, by their unprovoked aggression, had shattered the harmony of Saint-Domingue.[132]

The 1801 constitution, too, was turned into a contrast between purity and decadence. The French had viewed this document as evidence of his 'criminal' intentions. Robustly rejecting this accusation, Toussaint insisted on the integrity of his motives: he had been trying to deal with the 'urgency' provoked by the absence of appropriate laws for the colony. The process had been exemplary, with the appointment of constitutional delegates by local assemblies, the production of a draft by these representatives, and the despatch of this text to the French government. Above all, the outcome was a perfect example of republican constitutionalism, for the text was based on 'the character and habits of the inhabitants of the colony'[133] – this was a veiled but pointed reference to the abolition of slavery, which had been enshrined in the constitution to protect Saint-Domingue from any French attempt to restore it. This specific point was not mentioned in the *Memoir*. But Toussaint again left his readers in no doubt by littering his text with metaphors drawn from slavery: at one point he compared himself to someone whose 'leg and tongue had been cut off', and who had been 'buried alive'.[134]

As we have seen, underlying Toussaint's ethical values was a strong belief in the harmony of nature. The behaviour of Leclerc's troops as they laid waste the colony allowed him to introduce another devastating contrast in his narrative: between the innocent and bucolic purity of the native citizens of Saint-Domingue and the rapaciousness of the invaders, which he illustrated by first noting that General Hardÿ's troops had raided one of his plantations and stolen all his animals, including his horse Bel Argent.[135] This had occurred in late March 1802, while the war was still going on, but even after the truce his plantations in Ennery had been systematically plundered by French soldiers. For three weeks they seized the belongings of the local peasants, and even came to cut bananas from his own doorstep; he also once noticed that the fruits they were carrying away 'were not even ripe'; the point here was to contrast the alleged 'civilization' of the French invaders with their actual barbaric practices.[136]

Through this account of his own experience, Toussaint was pointing more generally, with an obvious nod to Raynal and Diderot's *Histoire philosophique*, to the savage brutality of the French invading army towards the local populations of the colony – of all colours. This too was entirely accurate. On their way across the Atlantic to Saint-Domingue, where they had been told they would find untold riches, French soldiers prepared special pouches in their belts in which they hoped to store their gold.[137] In fact, within a year of the arrival of the French fleet the colony had become the theatre of corruption and embezzlement on a gargantuan scale. Some whites soon began to regret the passing of the good old days of Toussaint's rule: one Cap resident, complaining about the 'extortion' of businesses by French military officials, noted: 'the men who are here only want money, money and then more money'.[138]

The captive wrote to Bonaparte in early October 1802, in what proved to be his final appeal to the First Consul's 'humanity'. He acknowledged that he may have made some 'mistakes', but claimed that the French government had been 'entirely deceived about Toussaint Louverture', and that since the revolution he had always served France with 'fidelity, probity, zeal and courage', and worked for the nation's 'honour and glory'. Remembering that Bonaparte was a family man, he evoked Pierre-Baptiste, whom he referred to as his 'father' and who had shown him 'the path to virtue'; he hoped that Bonaparte's heart would be 'touched' by his suffering, and that he would 'grant him his freedom'.[139] Predictably, he received no reply, and soon the final stages of his martyrdom unfolded. Harassment by the prison authorities intensified, with regular night searches of his cell. As the winter of 1802–1803 set in, his health deteriorated rapidly: he lost weight, began to suffer from a chronic cough, and complained of constant headaches and stomach pains. He was given little medical assistance, and on 7 April 1803 the prison governor found him dead in his cell, slumped by the fireside. His body was buried in the fort chapel.[140] Contrary to the myth that he had forsaken his faith in captivity, Toussaint died a Catholic: he twice referred to God in his last letter, and described himself as 'crowned with thorns'.[141]

By the time of Toussaint's death, the military advantage in Saint-Domingue had decisively swung away from the occupying forces. Bonaparte's three-period plan for the reconquest of the colony was a distant memory, and the man charged with executing it died of yellow fever in November 1802. Months before his death, Leclerc knew that the game was over. It was the insurgent advance that now fell into three periods. The first began with the French decision to restore slavery in neighbouring Guadeloupe; when the news reached Saint-Domingue in early August

1802, shortly after Toussaint's capture, it provoked widespread revolts across the colony and destroyed all efforts to disarm the *cultivateurs*. By October 1802 the second period began, when all the black and mixed-race generals who had been serving the French up to that point (Christophe, Dessalines, Pétion and Clervaux) joined the rebellion – which had by now become a general insurrection. This phase would culminate in the Arcahaie agreement of May 1803, in which all the local generals swore allegiance to Dessalines, who was appointed commander-in-chief of the insurgency; it was at this point that Dessalines created the future blue and red Haitian national flag by ripping out the white strip from the French tricolour. The final period saw the sale of Louisiana to the United States in April 1803, marking the end of Bonaparte's dream of a western empire, and the defeat of French forces at the Battle of Vertières in November 1803, followed by the evacuation of occupying troops from the French part of the territory. On 1 January 1804 Dessalines proclaimed the independence of the new state of Haiti.[142]

What has become known as the Haitian War of Independence is sometimes portrayed as the second death of Toussaint Louverture. He did not want to break free from France, and until the very end he held on to the belief that the French would realize that their objectives could not be achieved by military force, and that a mutually beneficial arrangement with Saint-Domingue's revolutionary leaders could be reached. This was not entirely unrealistic: Bonaparte himself later acknowledged at Saint Helena that the Saint-Domingue expedition had been a catastrophic mistake, one of the greatest he ever committed, and that he should have 'struck a deal with Toussaint, and made him viceroy'.[143] However, the War of Independence saw the comprehensive mobilization of the rural masses, which Toussaint had been unable to achieve during his spring campaign and was seen through in the end by the very generals who had betrayed him, after owing him everything. When it was done, Dessalines systematically eliminated Toussaint's supporters and allies, both white and black. The regime which emerged after independence, which explicitly rejected the colony's European heritage, appeared to be the antithesis of Toussaint's dream of a multiracial republic. It was as if, even though he had failed in every other respect, Bonaparte had at least achieved his goal of making Toussaint 'no longer exist'.

Yet such a conclusion would be hasty. Toussaint was the first to understand the real nature of the conflict. From the moment he saw the French fleet at Samanà bay, he realized that the invaders would succeed in their project of retaking Saint-Domingue only if they restored slavery. He came to this conclusion even before Bonaparte himself did; eventually the First

Consul conceded to Leclerc through his Navy Minister in June 1802 that the black population of the colony would eventually have to 'revert back to their original condition, from which it has been so unfortunate to have removed them'.[144] Although Leclerc refused to carry out this instruction and is often praised for his humanity, his views about restoring the white order in the colony were no less extreme. A month before his death he told Bonaparte that the only way to preserve French rule on the colony would be 'to destroy all the negroes of the mountains, men and women, and keep only the children below twelve years of age, to destroy half of the blacks living on the plains and not to leave on the colony a single man of colour who has worn an épaulette'.[145]

Leclerc's successor Rochambeau carried out these genocidal instructions to the letter: under his gruesome reign mass executions proliferated, and thousands of men, women and children were killed in a campaign of terror. The means of execution included shooting, hanging, beheading, burning and drowning; Rochambeau also introduced hunting dogs from Cuba.[146] Among those murdered were Pierre-Baptiste, Toussaint's stepfather, to whom the prisoner had paid homage in his *Memoir* and whose son Simon he had written to in late January 1802;[147] although he was over 100 years old and blind, the Haut-du-Cap patriarch was taken by French soldiers from his home and drowned at sea, for no apparent reason other than his family ties with Toussaint. In April 1803 Rochambeau wrote to Bonaparte asking for Toussaint to be sent back to Saint-Domingue, so that he could be hanged 'with the greatest decorum'. He also advised that slavery should be restored, as in Guadeloupe, and that the *Code Noir* be made 'more severe', with white planters being given 'the right of life and death' over their slaves.[148]

Toussaint not only anticipated the nature of the war of liberation: he also devised the strategy successfully pursued by the insurgents. The meticulous concealment of weapons, the scorched-earth policy, the systematic destruction of the economic apparatus of the colony (sugar production ground to a complete halt by the end of 1802), the retrenchment of rebel forces on higher ground and the appeal to the *levée en masse* – all these were his ideas;[149] in early 1802 a senior French officer admitted that the war was being conducted 'entirely on Toussaint's terms'.[150] Christophe later referred to the strategy as 'Toussaint's system', regretting that he and other generals had not understood him and not fully backed him in implementing it.[151] Toussaint was right, too, in his prediction of the devastation of the French army: by mid 1804, out of a total of 44,000 troops which had arrived in Saint-Domingue in successive waves, the French had lost around 85 per cent to death, injury or disease (a very similar proportion to that suffered by the British earlier). Above all, the unification of the resistance under a single central command, which was achieved in May 1803, was a fundamental principle of Toussaint's. There is little doubt that, had he still been in Saint-Domingue after June 1802, he would have led the insurrection with the same panache he had demonstrated in the spring campaign; and he would probably have done so without the bloodletting which saw the elimination of brilliant black commanders such as Charles Bélair, Sylla, Sans-Souci and Macaya.

Toussaint Louverture decisively shaped the course of the Haitian War of Independence. But fighting it had brought him back to his republican self and reminded him of the extraordinary qualities of the 'immense people' whose destinies he had steered from the mid 1790s. By the time of the French invasion, the people of Saint-Domingue understood, largely due to Toussaint, that their freedom was not a quality bestowed upon them by a benevolent authority but a right which they had seized through struggle; during his military reviews he often used to seize a rifle, brandish it in the air and shout: 'this is our freedom'. The people knew, too, that this right would be taken away from them if they allowed themselves to be disarmed, and that their strength lay in their collective force. This was another legacy of Toussaint's: as he boarded the ship that would take him away from Gonaïves, he made the point to his captors – 'by striking me, you have cut the tree of black liberty in Saint-Domingue. But it will spring back up from its roots, for they are many and deep.'[152]

12
A Universal Hero

In the immediate aftermath of the Haitian Revolution, Toussaint and his comrades receded from Western historical consciousness. But it did not mean that his popular fame disappeared with him in the Jura mountains – on the contrary. In the course of the nineteenth and twentieth centuries he became an iconic figure, not just in the newly independent state of Haiti but across the Atlantic area – a legend who symbolized the bracing power of the Saint-Domingue revolution and emboldened those fighting for slave emancipation and universal brotherhood, as well as radical political change within their own societies. Jailed for his attack on the Moncada barracks, Fidel Castro reflected in 1954 from his prison cell that the historical episode which was driving him to 'revolutionize Cuba from top to bottom' was 'the insurrection of black slaves in Haiti', adding: 'at a time when Napoleon was imitating Caesar, and France resembled Rome, the soul of Spartacus was reborn in Toussaint Louverture'.[1]

This inspirational quality was already evident in the final years of Toussaint's rule in Saint-Domingue, which established his international reputation as a liberating hero for all those who sought to challenge the slave-owning ruling classes – and as a terrifying ogre for slavery's defenders.[2] The late eighteenth and early nineteenth centuries saw a surge in slave rebellions of a new type across the Caribbean and the Americas, with a shift from individual revolts to conscious efforts to overthrow slavery as a system.[3] It was against this backdrop that the Saint-Domingue revolutionaries captured the collective imagination of their era – a phenomenon all the more remarkable that Toussaint himself did little actively to export his revolution to other territories. Yet a spontaneous Louverturian cult became plainly visible – and audible: in the region's popular-musical repertoire, Toussaint was hailed for his achievement of racial equality and for Saint-Domingue's ability to govern itself in an orderly way. One of the many songs composed by Jamaican slaves in its honour, and frequently heard on the streets of Kingston in 1799, went 'black, white and brown

[were] all de same'. Toussaint was cheered on, too, as a martial counterforce to the might of the colonial and imperial powers: shortly after he wrestled Santo Domingo from Spanish control, freemen and slaves in the hills above Coro in western Venezuela, who had already revolted in 1795, were reported to be openly rejoicing at the victory of their idol, whom they referred to as 'the firebrand', before ending with a menacing chorus directed at the authorities: 'they had better watch out!'[4]

Legendary figures can embody contrasting characteristics, and so, alongside the harmonious ideals of good governance and racial equality, these popular idealizations also nourished the subversive myth of black power. In the Dutch colony of Curaçao in the southern Caribbean, a slave uprising in 1795 was inspired not only by Saint-Domingue's abolitionism but also by its charismatic leaders, who were republican exemplars to their fellow slaves: one of the rebels executed by the Dutch authorities called himself 'Toussaint', and many black parents began to name their children after him.[5] Such was the potency of this combative strand of his legend that it helped instigate revolts in late 1797 even in republican Guadeloupe, where slavery had been formally abolished: first in the dependency of Marie-Galante, then in the town of Lamentin, insurgents called on local plantation workers violently to overthrow the economic power of the whites. Their rhetoric appealed explicitly to the example of Saint-Domingue, where, they claimed, 'everyone does what they please, and all those in command are black', and 'white women go with the blacks'. Local French officials believed that the trigger for these insurrections had been Toussaint's removal of Sonthonax from the colony.[6]

Likewise, when a conspiracy by black and mixed-race people in the Venezuelan coastal city of Maracaibo was suppressed in May 1799, the authorities discovered that its aim had been to introduce 'the same system of freedom and equality' in the locality as in Saint-Domingue;[7] similar plots were uncovered in Brazil and Uruguay, where Louverturian principles were disseminated by slaves and free men of colour.[8] This ideal of black power often crystallized around stories, material objects and rumours relating to Toussaint's republican army. After his expulsion of the British from Saint-Domingue in 1798, tales began to fly around the region about Toussaint's 'secret plans' to attack Spanish-controlled Santo Domingo (which he of course did), but also to send expeditionary forces into Cuba, Jamaica, Saint Lucia, Tobago, Puerto Rico, Mexico and the United States.[9] In July 1798 white Virginians became alarmed by persistent rumours that a 'number of vessels' from Saint-Domingue were heading towards the Chesapeake bay 'loaded with armed negroes'.[10] Two years later, the 'distant figure of Toussaint' loomed over Gabriel Prosser's slave conspiracy in Virginia.[11]

There were no geographical limits: one story which reached the Cuban authorities in 1800 even suggested that Toussaint had set his sights on taking control of 'the whole globe'.[12] Yet these fantastic tales also came in very specific variants: a Baltimore newspaper alleged that while Toussaint was keen to implement his plans for world domination, he lacked the funds to finance his operations. His solution was effectively to blackmail the Jamaican authorities, threatening to attack the island unless they paid him 200,000 *gourdes* every three months – proof that the myth of Toussaint's omnipotence could also accommodate his fastidious attention to detail.[13]

Toussaint Louverture was the first black superhero of the modern age. The main elements of his legend were already in place by the time he left the political stage at the beginning of the nineteenth century: he was seen as a saviour, a military hero and martial emblem of masculinity, a lawgiver (his 1801 constitution was a particularly important landmark), a symbol of emancipated blackness and, as William Wordsworth put it in his 1802 poem 'To Toussaint Louverture', of 'man's unconquerable mind'. In keeping with the *vodou* practice of deification of powerful ancestors, and despite his own efforts to suppress Saint-Domingue's popular religion during the final years of his rule, Toussaint also eventually took his place, with Dessalines, among Haiti's *loas*;[14] according to Haitian tradition, his principal decisions were informed by Ogoun-Fer, the warrior god.[15] A traditional *vodou* song paid tribute to both men in the struggle for Haitian independence: Toussaint, 'not afraid to die badly', and Dessalines, the 'Bull of Haïti'.[16]

As we have seen, Toussaint's legend was initially forged through popular oral stories about the exploits of Saint-Domingue's revolutionaries which became part of Haitian collective memory and folklore, and were then reappropriated by slave, free black and mixed-race communities in the Atlantic region. These tales, like their subject, travelled at extraordinary speed: they had already begun to circulate in the aftermath of the 1791 insurrection and Toussaint's first string of military victories against the Spanish in 1794–5. A letter from a concerned white planter in the British colony of Tobago in 1794 noted that many slaves had become imbued with ideas of 'fraternity' and now believed themselves 'equal to their masters'; he feared they would soon come together to 'exterminate the proprietors in the colonies'.[17] Such revolutionary ideas were later spread by newspapers, pamphlets and cheap prints, as well as artefacts such as buttons, military jackets and necklaces bearing the portraits of revolutionary leaders, which were passed on by travellers to and from Haiti. Black sailors played a crucial role in this international communication network which flourished around Atlantic ports, in Masonic lodges, pubs, boarding houses, pawnshops, chapels and coffee houses.[18] In 1805, a year after Haitian independence, black officers of the Rio de Janeiro militia were found wearing miniature portraits of Dessalines around their necks.[19] These Saint-Domingue stories interacted creatively with local political mobilizations, helping to forge a transnational arena for the development of radical anti-slavery ideas.[20]

Saint-Domingue's myths populated this Atlantic revolutionary imagination in a wide variety of ways. A year after Haitian independence, when enslaved Africans in Trinidad planned a revolt against French-owned plantations, they came together in a ritual which directly echoed the 1791 Bois-Caïman ceremony, chanting, 'Hey Saint-Domingue, remember Saint-Domingue!'[21] Toussaint and his comrades were here invoked in a quasi-religious setting. The solidarity shown by United Irishmen in 1798 towards their black brethren in Saint-Domingue was more overtly ideological. Irish republicans, whose rebellion was brutally suppressed, frequently compared their own predicament under British rule to a form of slavery. When he learned of the French invasion of Saint-Domingue, the Irish republican leader James Napper Tandy expressed his solidarity with Toussaint, noting that 'we are all of the same family, black and white, the work of the same creator'. A few years later another United Irishman, John Swiney, named one of his sons Toussaint – a practice widely followed among Atlantic progressives during the nineteenth century. On a more elegiac note, the Irish anti-slavery poet James Orr published his 'Toussaint's Farewell to St Domingo' in 1805: in its evocation of grief, devastation and usurpation, as well as the enslavement of small nations by great ones, it delicately wove together the fates and aspirations of Saint-Domingue and Ireland.[22]

Because the authors of slave rebellions in the Caribbean or the Americas were rarely as literate as these Irish republicans, few documentary traces of their activities have survived in the archives, and so we have little direct evidence of the precise ways in which Saint-Domingue's heroic traditions were appropriated in these local settings. A remarkable exception was the neighbouring island of Cuba, which became one of the most active sites of rebellion in the region, partly as a consequence of the tripling of the slave population at the time of the Haitian Revolution: between 1795 and 1812 there were nineteen significant conspiracies or insurrections in Cuba, notably in Havana but also in Puerto Príncipe, Bayamo, Santa Cruz and Güines. There was a great deal of testimony from captured insurgents, which was transcribed and held in the Spanish colonial archives and highlighted the extent to which the leaders, images and values associated with Saint-Domingue influenced the political consciousness of Cuban slaves and freedmen at this time.[23]

So fascinated were these men and women with the transformation taking place in Saint-Domingue that Toussaint Louverture and his comrades became household names; one Cuban newspaper asserted that locals knew of the events of the Haitian Revolution 'as if by memory'.[24] This was no exaggeration. Toussaint's name, along with those of his fellow revolutionary leaders, frequently featured in the responses given by slaves when interrogated about their participation in Cuban rebellions. Even when they denied being involved in conspiratorial activities, prisoners testified that figures such as Toussaint were often the subject of conversation among Cuban slaves. In a number of instances his name was deliberately used as a means of recruitment: slaves were promised that they would serve as military commanders in future rebellions, in a capacity similar to Toussaint's in Saint-Domingue. There was clearly a widely shared understanding of his role as a fighter and liberator among local Cuban slave communities.[25]

The 1806 conspiracy in the region of Güines, an area of intensive sugar cultivation where the slave regime was especially brutal, demonstrated how the Haitian myth could serve both as a model of 'absolute freedom' for individual rebels and (as in Toussaint's Saint-Domingue) an intellectual framework for a variety of revolutionary aspirations. Its three ringleaders who were arrested and interrogated by the authorities were Mariano Congo, an African-born slave, Francisco Fuertes, a creole from Cuba, and Estanislao, a 'French' slave who had earlier taken part in the Saint-Domingue revolution; the trio appealed at the same time to African, European and Caribbean ideals. Slave insurgents here combined classical republican principles with royalist values, while also engaging in traditional ritual dances and pig sacrifices. But the common denominator, and key mobilizing agent, was Saint-Domingue, whose hardy rebels such as Toussaint were admired for having had the 'balls' to take their destiny into their own hands. When he went to rouse the slaves in a local plantation, Fuertes engaged in a 'prolonged discussion' about Haiti and its feats: he extolled the martial qualities of its leaders, and their achievement of freedom, which had made them 'the absolute masters' of their country.[26] The ideal of black empowerment was at the heart of Toussaint's legend.

Saint-Domingue was just as present in the minds of Cuban revolutionaries active in the towns. In 1812, after a series of insurrections were initiated or planned in a number of provincial towns, authorities arrested José Antonio Aponte, a free black artist and craftsman who resided on the outskirts of Havana. Aponte was a former captain in the local militia, and a leading member of an African fraternal society; his network included literate artisans, *cabildo* heads and militia members, as well as black slaves.[27] During the interrogation of Aponte and his fellow rebels, ambitious plans for a general uprising to emancipate Cuban slaves emerged, as did the rumour (spread by them) that the Haitian authorities had despatched two officers and 5,000 armed men, who were waiting in the hills outside Havana to join the Cuban rebellion. Among the objects found in the search of Aponte's house was a blue military jacket (the outfit of the revolutionary army since Toussaint's days), which he probably wore to lend credence to the stories of Haitian involvement.[28]

The most intriguing object uncovered in Aponte's library was a book of drawings of distinguished international heroes: it included an image of George Washington, portraits of Greek and Roman deities and Abyssinian kings, all mingled with the Haitian revolutionaries, including Christophe, Dessalines and Toussaint Louverture. The book, about which Aponte was interrogated for three days, was put together from images which he had collected over several years among black dock workers in the Cuban capital; like thousands of men and women in Saint-Domingue, they kept these portraits in their homes as precious relics. Aponte had made copies of them and had been using them as props during revolutionary meetings held in his house. We have no record of what he said specifically about Toussaint, but we can imagine that the black general would have been a perfect exemplar of Aponte's eclectic ideal of republican emancipation.[29]

In 1824, the Haitian mixed-race writer and parliamentarian Hérard Dumesle published his *Voyage dans le nord d'Hayti*. Born in the southern town of Les Cayes, as whose elected representative he served, Dumesle offered a poetic evocation of his country's tumultuous history after independence. The first ruler of the new state, Dessalines, vowed in April 1804 that henceforth 'no colonist or European' would set foot in Haiti 'as a master or proprietor'; almost all the white settlers remaining in the territory were killed.[30] Dessalines proclaimed himself emperor in October 1804 but his reign proved short-lived, as he was assassinated two years later. His death was followed by the effective division of the territory into a northern kingdom ruled by Christophe from 1807 to 1820, and a southern republic governed between 1807 and 1818 by the mixed-race leader Alexandre Pétion, another hero of the Haitian War of Independence, whom Dumesle greatly admired. In the course of his journeys, Dumesle gathered testimony from locals and visited revolutionary sites of historical significance – hence the work's subtitle: *Révélations des lieux et des monuments historiques*. Thanks to the information he put together from these various sources, Dumesle was able to provide a detailed account of the

1791 Bois-Caïman ceremony; his was among the first works written in Haiti clearly to celebrate the revolutionary contributions of Saint-Domingue's black slaves.[31]

One of the most striking moments occurred during the author's visit to the villa built by Pétion at Volant-le-Thor, in the north-east of Haiti. As he stepped into the magnificent salon, Dumesle found that it had been designed by Pétion as a tribute to universal heroism. As in Aponte's intimate gallery, there were representations of distinguished Europeans who had fought to liberate humankind from the scourge of slavery, including Raynal, Grégoire and William Wilberforce, who had played a leading role in securing the banning of the slave trade by Britain in 1807. The room also featured portraits of 'great conquerors of antiquity' such as Alexander, Hannibal and Caesar. What particularly caught Dumesle's eye, though, was a list of eight Haitian names, positioned alongside these luminaries and inscribed in gold letters: seven were persons of colour, including the eminent martyrs Ogé and Chavannes. The only black name, placed right next to that of his old foe Rigaud, was Toussaint Louverture.[32]

Dumesle was unsettled by the sight of this homage to Toussaint: earlier in his *Voyage* he had described him as a man 'devoured by a thirst for domination' and a 'bloodthirsty tyrant' responsible for terrible atrocities during the southern war;[33] this was the common view among mixed-race intellectuals in Haiti during the first half of the nineteenth century.[34] Yet he could not help but reflect that, despite his flaws, Toussaint was an exceptional figure. In fact, the presentation in Pétion's living room was symptomatic of Toussaint's posthumous fate in his native land. Mixed-race historians sharply criticized him, and he was officially spurned by black leaders such as Dessalines and Christophe who had been his subordinates. Yet Toussaint would not go away. He remained a magnetic presence in the minds and memories of his compatriots; the veterans who fought in his army continued to revere him, and kept images and relics of him; they would later recount their tales to the historian Thomas Madiou, whose accounts of the military engagements of the revolutionary era were largely based on testimonies from former combatants.[35] To his credit, Pétion eventually accepted their view of his nation's eminent heroes. Although he had been an implacable adversary of Toussaint's before 1802 (he sided with Rigaud during the southern war, and came back to fight him with Leclerc's invading army), he recognized his essential role in shaping the destiny of the Haitian people and promoting the ideal of slave emancipation in the Atlantic world. This republican heritage was no doubt in Pétion's mind when he offered asylum to Simón Bolívar in late 1815, just as the villa at Volant was being completed, and went on to provide crucial assistance to the liberator's campaign for South American independence.[36]

Toussaint made his first appearance in the official iconography of the Haitian state in the early 1820s, when the mixed-race President Jean-Pierre Boyer commissioned a series of prints to commemorate the nation's great men. After the deaths of Christophe and Pétion, Boyer's forces invaded the north and brought back a unified government in Haiti in 1820, and his inclusion of Toussaint reflected his personal admiration. He had met Toussaint as a young officer, when the commander-in-chief charged him with forming a cavalry regiment in the west.[37] But it was principally a political gesture, destined to find a consensual symbol of the country's 'newfound unity', and in particular one who would appeal to the black populations of the north.[38] In the early 1820s, Haiti was still widely regarded as a pariah state – still unrecognized by the major powers and threatened militarily by them. Following exactly in Toussaint's footsteps, in 1822 Boyer reinvaded Santo Domingo, which had reverted to Spanish rule, where he again abolished slavery. As the price of recognition by France, Boyer was eventually forced to agree to pay a ruinous indemnity of 150 million francs as compensation for the loss of her colony.[39] In such troubled times, Toussaint Louverture could serve as a fitting icon of Haitian nationalism.[40]

The four Boyer prints, which were intended for public circulation, were produced in France, with the Haitian authorities carefully overseeing the selection of each historical episode and the precise wording of the illustrative texts. They were drawn by at least two different artists and, in keeping with the aesthetic sensibilities of Haiti's mixed-race leaders, Toussaint's features were somewhat Europeanized – in contrast with the 'negroid' look which characterized his depictions more generally during the first half of the nineteenth century.[41] The first image was entitled 'Meeting of Toussaint Louverture and General Maitland'. Toussaint was seen showing the British officer some documents, and the lengthy caption beneath explained that he had been ordered to arrest Maitland – but that the commander-in-chief had refused, stating that he would be 'dishonoured' to follow such an order, as Maitland had come to him in good faith.[42] This incident took place, as we saw in Chapter 7, at the time of Toussaint's negotiations leading up to the Maitland Convention in 1799: the point here was to underscore Toussaint's true republican spirit; to highlight, through his sense of integrity, the absolute trustworthiness of the Haitian government; and to celebrate this landmark moment in the achievement of the nation's sovereignty.

Indeed, the second print, 'Toussaint Louverture proclaims the 1801 Constitution', showed the governor holding up the sacred document in the presence of the 'legally assembled delegates of the people': an important endorsement of the point consistently made by Toussaint that the text had been produced lawfully; a young child, clasped by her mother, symbolized the ending of slavery 'for ever'. The presence of a priest in the foreground, and the benevolent gaze of the Almighty, watching from above, added a powerful tone of religiosity to the image, whose composition was very similar in style to Guillaume Guillon-Lerthière's classic painting *The Oath of the Ancestors* (1822), showing Dessalines and Pétion swearing the oath of independence (see Plate 10). The connection between Toussaint's constitution and the 1804 declaration was made explicit in the caption, which stated that 'the constitution of the Republic of Hayti'[43] had been proclaimed in 1801 – an elegant anachronism, but one which achieved the deeper truth of reclaiming Toussaint as one of the nation's founding fathers.

The next image was more intimate, recreating the heart-rending moment in early 1802 when, in the wake of Leclerc's invasion, Toussaint's children were brought back to their father by their tutor Coisnon in a bid to buy his allegiance. The governor was represented in a posture of noble defiance, refusing to be swayed by Napoleon's envoy, despite the pleas from his wife and children. The caption had Toussaint inviting Coisnon to 'take back' Isaac and Placide, as he wished to be 'faithful to his brothers and to his God'.[44] This was again an oversimplification: at the time, it was only Isaac who had urged his father to accept Napoleon's terms, and he too soon changed his mind. But it was a perfectly accurate depiction of Toussaint's conception of fraternity, grounded both in his republicanism and in his Christian faith. The image also held up his patriotism as an example of civic behaviour – hence his willingness to sacrifice even his family so as to preserve his people from enslavement.

In keeping with the conventions of the heroic genre, the final image in the Boyer series was Toussaint's death. He was shown expiring in the arms of his faithful servant Mars Plaisir, who had actually long been removed from Fort de Joux by the time of his master's passing. The prisoner appeared in the classic posture of Christian martyrdom, arms stretched, with a halo of light shining on him through the window of his prison cell, symbolizing his ascent to Heaven; David's *Death of Marat* was an obvious inspiration for this drawing. The key theme here again was Toussaint's republican virtue, as made clear by the caption: 'thus ended the life of a great man. His talents and qualities earned him the gratitude of his countrymen; posterity will place his name among those of the most virtuous and patriotic

The first in the series of prints commissioned by the Haitian President Boyer. It depicts Toussaint meeting Maitland and showing him two letters: Roume's demand that he should arrest Maitland, and his own reply that such an action would be dishonourable.

The second Boyer print shows the governor holding up the constitution before the 'legally assembled delegates of the people'; a young child, clasped by her mother, symbolizes the ending of slavery. The presence of a priest in the foreground and the benevolent gaze of the Almighty add a powerful tone of religiosity to the image.

The third print re-creates the moment in early 1802 when, in the wake of Leclerc's invasion, Toussaint's children were brought back to their father by their tutor, Coisnon, in a bid to buy his allegiance. The governor defiantly invites Coisnon to 'take back' Isaac and Placide, as he wishes to be 'faithful to his brothers and to his God'.

The final image in the Boyer series represents Toussaint's death. The prisoner appears in the classic posture of Christian martyrdom, arms stretched, with a halo of light shining on him through the window of his prison cell, symbolizing his ascent to Heaven.

legislators.'[45] Such was the force of his popular appeal that Boyer commissioned a double portrait shortly afterwards in which he had himself represented alongside Toussaint.[46] These four prints spoke, above all, of Toussaint's ability to embody the experiences of his people during their long struggle for freedom and to capture their collective imagination; in the subsequent words of an eminent Haitian ethnologist, the life of Toussaint inspired 'many a tale and legend' in the nation's popular culture, as well as some of its 'most enduring superstitions'.[47]

With this entry into the Haitian pantheon, Toussaint's posthumous rebirth was complete. His legend had travelled considerable distances, in both time and space, before this spectacular return to his native land. Two decades after his forcible exit from Saint-Domingue, Toussaint re-emerged as the only figure who could credibly symbolize the different traditions of the Haitian nation and hold them together in the face of an aggressive and hostile world. In the verses of *The Haïtiade*, the most sophisticated epic poem devoted to the revolution during the post-independence era, Toussaint was hailed as 'the very base on which the Haitian race was founded'.[48] His compatriots celebrated his memory throughout the nineteenth century, and in 1903 a journalist visiting Haiti found an aged mixed-race woman who was over 100 years old and who claimed that she was Toussaint's god-daughter.[49]

The Saint-Domingue epic was emblazoned in the hearts and minds of Haitians and Atlantic progressives, but nothing quite matched the fervour with which it was embraced by African Americans.[50] From its very outset, black men and women in the United States watched the unfolding of the Haitian Revolution with profound fascination. The sense of closeness, both physical and intellectual, was accentuated by the presence in America of scores of refugees of all races from Saint-Domingue from the early 1790s onwards, and the frequency of travel in the opposite direction. A large number of sailors who worked on American ships were African American, and the stories they brought back after their Caribbean journeys gave an almost transcendental aura to the revolutionary events and their leaders.[51] This mystique drove slave conspirators such as Denmark Vesey and Nat Turner to action, but over time the legend of Saint-Domingue also inspired speeches, demonstrations, commemorations, songs and the naming of institutions in the United States. At specific junctures, the revolution also provoked a significant population exodus: for example, around 10,000 African Americans moved to Haiti in the 1820s.[52] The newly created state symbolized black military power and racial equality: in his *Appeal to the Coloured Citizens of the World* (1829), the abolitionist writer David Walker called Haiti 'the glory of the blacks and terror of tyrants'.[53]

At the same time, heroic tales about Saint-Domingue and the Haitian Revolution stimulated new and creative ways of imagining African American blackness. These played an important role in the emergence of black nationalist consciousness in the United States, while also promoting a shared sense of belonging with communities of African descent elsewhere. In 1855 an article in the *Anti-Slavery Bugle*, published in New Lisbon (Ohio), hailed Toussaint as the 'hero of Saint-Domingue', and expressed the hope that the story of his life could help destroy 'that bitter prejudice of colour which denies the blacks the rights of citizens'.[54] Just before the outbreak of the Civil War, a chaplain in South Carolina noted that in the American South, where there were four million slaves by 1860, 'the name of Toussaint Louverture has been passed from mouth to mouth until it has become a secret household word' which symbolized 'the universal love of liberty'.[55] Free blacks contrasted the rights enjoyed by Haitians with the violence, racism and political disenfranchisement they often experienced in the North.[56] And because of his singular combination of political radicalism and religiosity, Toussaint also acted as a conduit between two strands in nineteenth-century African American political thought about the abolition of slavery: the revolutionary, which took its inspiration from Haiti's struggle for self-determination, and the religious, which framed the battle for slave emancipation around a renewed version of Christian evangelism.[57]

Toussaint's magnetic presence was powerfully illustrated in *Freedom's Journal*, the first ever African American newspaper. Published in New York between 1827 and 1829, it sought to develop a sense of solidarity among black people in the United States, while also linking their destinies to the African diaspora across the world. There were numerous columns devoted to Haiti and the 'extraordinary men' it had produced.[58] In May 1827 the paper ran a three-part biographical account of Toussaint. The point of this flamboyant portrayal of the 'Black Spartacus', as he was explicitly termed, was to hold him up as an ideal for emulation – a vivid demonstration that black people were 'not wanting in the higher qualifications of the mind', and could be 'pregnant with heroic energies, capable of wielding the sword of war, and swaying the rod of empire'.[59] The article described Louverturian Saint-Domingue as a golden age, 'advancing as if by enchantment towards its ancient splendour' under the rule of its 'guardian angel', who was hailed by black and white people alike with 'universal joy'.[60] Toussaint's charismatic leadership was marked by his sense of integrity, his dedication to 'order and regularity' and his refusal to yield to corruption: he was thus a fitting incarnation of the virtues.[61] Particular note was taken, too, of the 'strict sobriety' of his personal life and his endeavours to reform the 'loose and licentious manners' of white women; 'his maxim', the article stated approvingly, 'was that women should always appear in public as if they were going to church'.[62]

Although appealing here to a traditional conception of masculinity, the events of the Haitian Revolution, and Toussaint's memory specifically, were also called upon to honour female empowerment. A four-part fictional narrative entitled 'Theresa – a Haytien Tale', published in *Freedom's Journal* in 1828, depicted the active engagement of a young black woman in Saint-Domingue at the time of the war of liberation against Leclerc's invading army. Uncovering crucial information about imminent French plans to attack Toussaint's positions, the heroine, Theresa, faced an agonizing choice between protecting her country and compromising the safety of her mother Paulina and sister Amanda. The 'dauntless' young woman chose the patriotic course, and successfully conveyed the vital intelligence to the governor in his nearby military camp. The 'kind and fatherly' Toussaint received her with gratitude and afforded her 'all the distinctions due her exalted virtue'.[63]

The New-York-based American Anti-Slavery Society held up Toussaint as a model citizen. One of the first issues of the society's periodical in 1835 carried an image of Toussaint on its front page, depicting the scene where he rejected Napoleon's attempt to bribe him into submission in 1802 by returning his two children. The caption beneath quoted Toussaint as saying: 'Take them back, since it must be so; I am determined to be faithful to my brethren and to my God.' It described Toussaint as 'the George Washington of St Domingo', who gave 'union, energy and a wise constitution to his countrymen, and by his bravery repelled every foe, and put an end to civil and insurrectionary wars'. Noting that his life was powerful evidence of the equality of black people, the piece concluded: 'the world may safely be challenged to produce a nobler character than that of Toussaint L'Ouverture'.[64]

Toussaint also became a star attraction on the African American lecture circuit, particularly for those speakers who sought to focus attention away from the more violent aspects of the Haitian Revolution, symbolized by figures such as Dessalines, emphasizing instead its harmonious, orderly and regenerative characteristics; these qualities were often framed around Toussaint's religiosity. At a public lecture given in February 1841, the community leader James McCune Smith stressed that Toussaint was above all a 'peacemaker', a 'Christian man' with a 'soul uncontaminated by the degradation which surrounded him'. Adopting the widespread comparison of Toussaint

THE

ANTI-SLAVERY RECORD.

VOL. I. APRIL, 1835. NO. 4.

"Take them back, since it must be so; I am determined to be faithful to my brethren and to my God."

TOUSSAINT L'OUVERTURE.

The friends of the enslaved are continually told that the Africans are an *inferior race.* If this were true, it would be no good reason for enslaving them. But it is not. The world may safely be challenged to produce a nobler character than that of Toussaint L'Ouverture—the George Washington of St. Domingo. Calumny has striven to paint him a monster.—She has brought the printing presses of both continents to her aid—but in vain.

Toussaint Louverture was one of the iconic figures of the American anti-slavery movement during the nineteenth century. Here he is described as the 'George Washington of St Domingo', and the image, copied from the Boyer print (see p. 338), shows the scene where he rejects Napoleon's attempt to bribe him into submission in 1802 by returning his two sons.

with Raynal's 'avenger of the black race', Smith affirmed that the black revolutionary chose to 'avenge those injuries by forgiveness'. Indeed, according to Smith, once Toussaint acceded to supreme power he turned his mind away completely from thoughts of war and conquest, even though he could 'easily have revolutionized the entire Archipelago of the west'. As Saint-Domingue's ruler, his absolute priority was to demonstrate that the black race was 'entirely capable of achieving liberty and self-government'; such was the extraordinary legacy of this 'benefactor of mankind'.[65]

This emphasis on Toussaint's genius and Christian elevation of spirit could be heard in the 1850s and early 1860s. It drew upon European works on Toussaint by evangelist abolitionists, most notably in *The Hour and the Man* (1841), a novel by the English writer Harriet Martineau in which Toussaint was the central character. Martineau's writings were widely circulated among American abolitionists; she portrayed her hero as a family-oriented figure who embodied the stoic virtues of forbearance and mercy, and demonstrated through his leadership that black people were fit to govern.[66] An edition of a Louverture biography by the English writer John Relly Beard was published in the United States in 1863 and widely promoted among Americans of African descent; it concluded that, for Toussaint, 'God was the sole reality and the sovereign good.'[67] Demand for the book was so high in the mid 1860s that suppliers frequently ran out of stock.[68]

In a series of lectures delivered by the African American priest James Theodore Holly, Toussaint was described as 'an unswerving friend and servant of God and humanity'; his record as 'hero and statesman' was also taken as irrefutable evidence of the black capacity for self-government. The revolutionary leader's only flaw – and Holly was not just alluding to Saint-Domingue here – was his 'too great confidence in the word of the white man'.[69] Speaking in Virginia about her escape from slavery, Eliza Wood concluded with a glowing tribute to the 'Negro statesman and martyr' Toussaint Louverture.[70] The most eminent publicist of the Haitian hero was the Harvard-educated abolitionist Wendell Phillips, whose lectures on the great man, published as a pamphlet in 1861, dwelled on his human qualities, his trustworthiness and his sense of Christian mercy: this was someone who 'never broke his word' and whose motto was 'no retaliation'. Taking some liberty with the historical record, Phillips even claimed that after his capture Toussaint had instructed his son to 'forget' what the French had done to him; he was the model of the 'soldier, statesman, and martyr'.[71] One of the major influences on Phillips was Martineau's novel, which he carried with him on his speaking engagements.[72] In 1862 he delivered his lecture on Toussaint at the Smithsonian in Washington, in the presence of President Abraham Lincoln;[73] his speech became a classic, which was frequently reproduced in the American press[74] and inspired several generations of successful high-school orators; excerpts from the text continued to be read out at African American civic meetings well into the twentieth century.

Yet, in this torrent of religious fervour, Toussaint's revolutionary image was not swept away: his masculine heroism resurfaced powerfully during the era of the American Civil War. Efforts to increase the number of black volunteers in the Union army after 1861 appealed to the memory of the Haitian Revolution, with frequent and explicit references to Toussaint. One call for black recruits in Massachusetts suggested that joining the army would provide the African American with 'the opportunity to display those qualities which the experience of this war, as well as the history of Toussaint's Battles, has shown him to possess'. Another call strikingly referred to African American military recruits as 'black Toussaints', whose 'superior talents and principles' would advance not just the cause of slave emancipation but also the broader integration of black people in American society.[75]

The 54th Massachusetts Regiment was the home of many of these African American fighters. During one of their most famous engagements, the attack on Fort Wagner in South Carolina in July 1863, a company from the 54th took the name of 'Toussaint's guards'; among its hardy combatants was Toussaint L'Ouverture Delany, the son of African American writer and abolitionist Martin Delany; as in other parts of the Atlantic, the naming of African American children after the hero of the Haitian Revolution had by now become common in the United States. Toussaint's medical skills were also celebrated, with his memory being associated with the provision of care for soldiers: when a medical facility was established by black freedmen in Alexandria, Virginia in 1863 to provide assistance to injured black soldiers, it was named the 'L'Ouverture Branch Hospital'.[76] In his later chronicle of the role of black soldiers in the civil war, George Washington Williams argued for a central connection between the Haitian Revolution and the American Civil War: both had been fought to end slavery, and he saw the achievement of emancipation in the United States as a continuation of Toussaint's work.[77]

By the end of the nineteenth century, Toussaint and the Haitian Revolution had become powerful symbols of collective emancipation, inspiring men and women far and wide, from the Atlantic right across to Māori communities in New Zealand: in 1863 one of their newspapers likened the Māori struggle to reclaim their rights from European settlers to that of the Haitian revolutionaries during their War of Independence.[78] During the Cuban War of Independence (1895–8) Toussaint's example was often invoked, and he was specifically compared to one of its heroic figures, Antonio Maceo, who became known in the United States as the 'Cuban Toussaint Louverture'.[79] At the same time, the events in Saint-Domingue stood as shining historical reference points for progressives seeking to reflect on (and reimagine) the international system, and for black intellectuals increasingly contesting the racial ordering of the world.[80] Rebutting Arthur de Gobineau's influential pamphlet about the superiority of the white race, the positivist Haitian intellectual Anténor Firmin championed Toussaint Louverture's life and achievements as irrefutable evidence of the principle of racial equality.[81]

As the norm of white racial supremacy became more openly entrenched in the later decades of the nineteenth century, critical voices also drew on Toussaint's legend to celebrate black contributions to global civilization. There were few more eloquent exponents of this counter-narrative than the African American abolitionist and civil rights leader Frederick Douglass. One of the greatest orators of his generation, Douglass was especially well placed to comment on Haiti's world-historical significance. The Saint-Domingue epic captivated his imagination throughout his life, and he remained to the end a passionate champion of Toussaint Louverture. He served as the resident American consul-general in Haiti between 1889 and 1891, and was then appointed by the Haitian government to act as the commissioner for its pavilion at the Chicago World's Fair in 1893 – which featured, among other objects, a prominent bust of Toussaint.[82]

In his speeches, Douglass reminded his audiences that at the time of Saint-Domingue's revolution, 'all the neighbouring islands were slaveholding', and that 'her hand was against the Christian world, and the hand of the Christian world was against her'. The freedom of Haiti was not 'given as a boon', but 'conquered as a right' – notably against the 'brave and skilful warriors' sent by Napoleon.[83] Engaging directly with the erasure of the Haitian story in the Western world, Douglass noted that the standards by which revolutions were judged internationally were strongly influenced by racial considerations. Hence George Washington's struggle for freedom was universally praised, while Saint-Domingue's was passed over in silence – or, worse, condemned as barbaric. The absence of 'monuments of marble' to commemorate black revolutionaries was not fortuitous: 'colour and race make all the difference'. Douglass observed many 'busts and portraits' of Toussaint in Haiti, and confirmed that he was a 'full-blooded negro'; but he noticed that Toussaint's standing even among Haiti's elites was not as high as it should have been. They blamed him for being 'too French', despite their own adoption of French mannerisms and cultural habits – a classic example of the kind of neocolonial alienation that Frantz Fanon would later call 'turning white'.[84]

The majesty of the Haitian Revolution, in Douglass's account, centred around Toussaint – a 'unique figure' who stood alone and was 'without example' (at the first mention of his name, the stenographer at his Chicago speech noted that there was 'prolonged applause'). By his extraordinary leadership, he had transformed the black slaves of the colony into fearsome warriors. He did so just by the sheer force of his personality: 'the fire and fortitude of his soldiers proceeded from himself'. This ability to make his people believe in themselves and in the great cause of liberty, despite his own slave origins, also attested to his greatness. Toussaint was a model, too, because in the midst of all the horrors of the revolution he remained devoted to the ideal of 'mercy', and focused his energies on the effective administration and organization of the colony. Above all, Toussaint's life and achievements were driven by a 'mission to the whole white world': to bring about a universal realization of the moral imperative of emancipation. 'The slavery of the Christian world was more disturbed by him than by any man prior to him.'[85]

This allowed Douglass to move on to the more general Haitian contribution to global civilization. Even though she had not enjoyed much prosperity during the nineteenth century, and remained plagued by political division and social misery, the infant Haitian state had nonetheless had a transformative impact on world affairs. Greeks had brought philosophical beauty to humankind, and Rome a love of laws; Britannia's commercial spirit had ruled the waves, while Germans had taught the world to think; America had established the ideal of modern democratic rule (there was, evidently, no room for the French in this hit parade of world-historical glory). Haiti's seminal contribution had been to 'serve the cause of universal liberty'. For the revolutionaries of Saint-Domingue had fought not just for themselves: 'interlinked with their race, and striking for their freedom, they struck for the freedom of every black man in the world'. The Haitian Revolution had acted as 'the original pioneer emancipator of the nineteenth century'.[86]

Thanks to the efforts of Douglass, and also those of successive generations of writers, journalists, publicists and preachers, the resonance of Toussaint Louverture's legend in African American culture was prodigious: he was acclaimed as a role model exemplifying the qualities of 'leadership, independence, and sacrifice'.[87] The press played a key role in the dissemination of this ideal. From the mid nineteenth century onwards, black and progressive newspapers in Washington, New York, San Francisco and

Chicago, but also in small towns in Ohio, the Carolinas, Oregon, Indiana, Utah, Kentucky, Louisiana, Minnesota and Montana celebrated the 'Black Spartacus'[88] and cited his name in general chronologies of modern world history, taking due note of the seminal nature of the Haitian Revolution. Articles carried quotations by him, especially his 'tree of liberty' statement (which appeared with some variations),[89] and recounted stories about his exploits, ranging from summaries of his revolutionary acts to serializations of his life and achievements.[90] His name (spelled with an apostrophe) was given to African American children and was considered to symbolize 'the quintessence of reliability', as in the case of Toussaint L'Ouverture Lambert, an employee of the Detroit mail service who 'had never missed a day from service in fifty years'.[91] The Toussaint title was also taken by a range of American political, artistic and cultural associations; one of them, the Toussaint Louverture Literary Society in St Paul, Minnesota, was an Irish fraternity which celebrated the historic links between the Irish and Haitian Revolutions;[92] in a similar spirit, a Washington-based organization called 'The Knights of Toussaint Louverture' held a rally in 1915 to protest against the adoption of segregation laws in the District of Columbia.[93] A film about Toussaint, the 'Abraham Lincoln of Haiti', was written, produced and directed in 1920 by Clarence E. Muse, who went on to become one of the leading African American movie stars of his generation.[94] Images of Toussaint proliferated across the United States: prints of him were sold, displayed prominently during commemorative events and used by commercial companies to market newspapers, books, watches, insurance products and even beer: in 1940 the Michigan-based Pfeiffer brewery ran a large advertisement in the *Detroit Tribune* celebrating Toussaint as an 'inspiring name in Negro history'; it included a handsome drawing of him, and beneath it the Wendell Phillips caption, 'soldier, statesman, martyr'.[95]

During his spell as consul, Douglass directly witnessed aggressive attempts to promote American military and economic interests in Haiti, and warned against those of his compatriots who were trying to turn the country into an American 'protectorate'. Advocates of this neo-imperial policy eventually prevailed, and in 1915 President Woodrow Wilson ordered the invasion of Haiti, initiating a brutal occupation which lasted nearly two decades and which blatantly contradicted Wilson's lofty liberal rhetoric about the right of national self-determination. During these years Haiti effectively became a vassal state, losing her economic and political sovereignty: her legislature was disbanded, and a new constitution, which for the first time allowed foreigners to own land, was forcibly imposed; US-style racial segregation was introduced and popular protest violently suppressed.[96]

As opposition to the American military occupation gradually built up both in the United States and in Haiti, it often coalesced around Toussaint's memory. The radical internationalist Hubert Harrison denounced the invasion in the *Negro World* in 1920, and urged fellow black people not to allow 'the land of L'Ouverture to lie like a fallen flower beneath the feet of the swine'.[97] In Haiti, resistance to the American presence directly inspired the formation in December 1923 of the *Societé d'Histoire et de Géographie Haïtienne*, which brought together the nation's intellectuals in a bid to reaffirm Haiti's distinct cultural heritage, rooted in its African origins; among the founders were Jean Price-Mars, Dantès Bellegarde and Alfred Nemours.[98] Significantly, its first president was Horace Pauleus Sannon, Haiti's leading Toussaint Louverture scholar; at the society's first meeting in March 1924 Sannon explicitly linked the study of past heroes to the inspiration for collective resistance against American occupation: 'in times of crisis, all peoples instinctively look back to find lessons of collective patriotism in their history'.[99] The third volume of Sannon's biography of Toussaint, published in 1933 at the height of the American occupation, dealt with the French invasion of Saint-Domingue and ended with the proclamation of Haitian independence – a pointed reminder of what his people could do in the face of a 'bloody and odious oppression'.[100]

The teaching of history as a means of releasing black communities from the 'servility of the mind' was also at the heart of the work of the Jamaican pan-Africanist leader Marcus Garvey. In his efforts to kindle a sense of pride among men and women of African descent he celebrated the greatness of Ethiopian rulers and Zulu warriors, as well as the revolts of dissident slaves; in 1920 Garvey stated that the next global conflict would be a racial war, which would be led by a 'new Toussaint Louverture of the negro race', heading an army '400 million strong to carve an African imperialism and an African nationalism'.[101] Garvey always reserved a special place in his pantheon for Toussaint, whose 'brilliancy as a soldier and statesman outshone that of a Cromwell, Napoleon and Washington'.[102] As the international communist movement developed in the inter-war period, the Saint-Domingue revolutionary was also appropriated by Marxist intellectuals in order to embody a radically different ideal of heroism. In 1929, the black West Indian radical Cyril Briggs claimed that Toussaint belonged to a historical lineage of 'martyrs of the world proletariat', and served as an inspiration for 'the present struggle against the master class'.[103]

A year later, a young African American named Jacob Lawrence arrived with his family in Harlem. He was thirteen years old, and cherished the

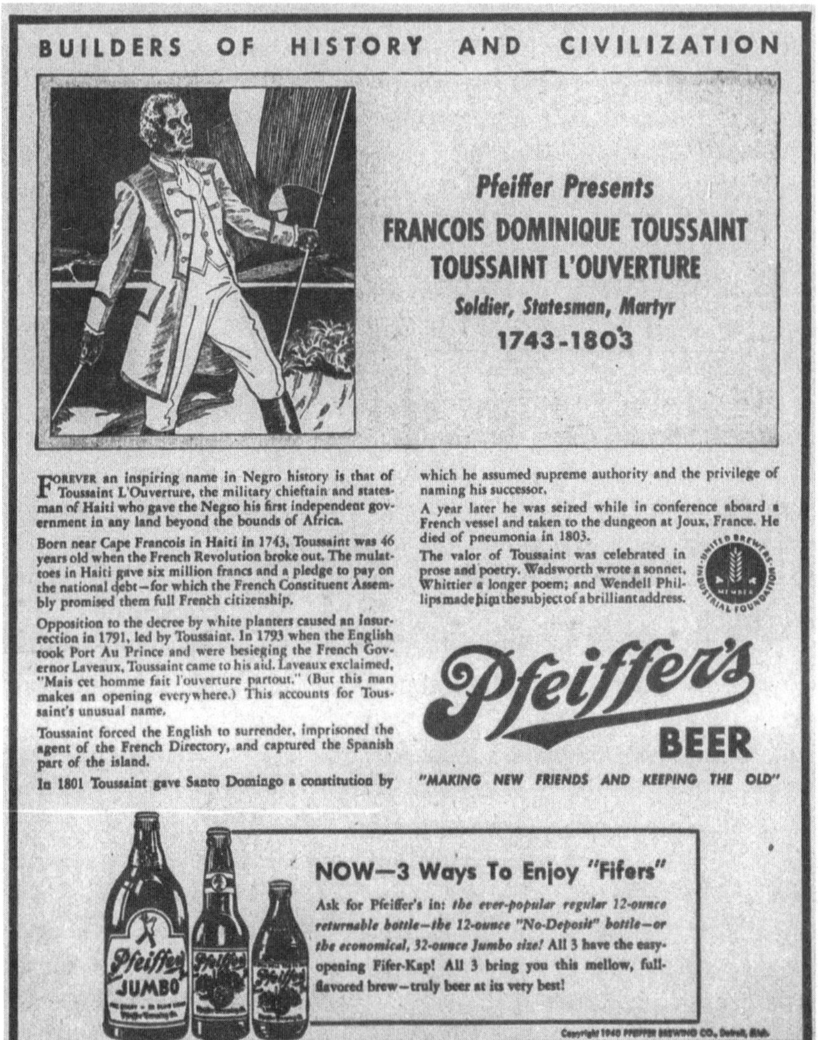

In 1940 the Michigan-based Pfeiffer brewery ran a large advertisement celebrating Toussaint's inspiring role in leading the Haitian people towards independence. It included a handsome drawing of him, and beneath it the Wendell Phillips caption: 'soldier, statesman, martyr'.

dream of becoming an artist; as a young adolescent he heard orators recounting the exploits of eminent black heroes in the churches, schools, clubs and streets of his neighbourhood. Through this popular education, he came to learn about the lives of Nat Turner, Denmark Vesey, Frederick Douglass, W. E. B. Du Bois and Marcus Garvey, and they became his icons too. But the figure who most captivated Lawrence's imagination was Toussaint Louverture, whose story he first heard about at a lecture at the Harlem YMCA – so much so that he dedicated his first major work to him. First exhibited in Baltimore in 1939, Lawrence's forty-one narrative paintings of Toussaint and the Saint-Domingue revolution have become one of the monuments of modern political iconography. Each image was given a brief caption, telling the story of the Haitian Revolution from the imposition of slavery to Toussaint's military and political achievements, and the subsequent Haitian War of Independence. The overall aim, as Lawrence later declared, was to use the example of the Haitian Revolution to challenge the 'economic and racial slavery' of modern times.[104]

With their arresting modernity, simple lines, dynamic colours and powerful representation of the revolution's raw energy – notably in the six equestrian portraits of Toussaint – Lawrence's paintings in one sense marked the culmination of the heroic Louverturian legend. Lawrence's genius lay in his ability to allow us to glimpse how Toussaint was visualized by generations of black men and women across the Atlantic from the early nineteenth century onwards. At the same time, the paintings and their captions integrated Toussaint within the emerging emancipatory traditions of Pan-African politics. Lawrence's Toussaint was a son of Haiti to the core, but also a Caribbean internationalist who was inspired by the transformations in America and in France; a man of action but also a thinker, who carefully planned the different stages of his political interventions; an exceptional genius, but also a commander who knew how to use the abilities of his subordinates; a solitary figure, but also a chief who drew his strength from the collective force of Saint-Domingue's people; a fierce warrior, but also a tolerant and humane leader. The caption beneath the final, imposing image of Dessalines drew an unfavourable contrast between his dictatorial style and the 'more liberal leadership' embodied by Toussaint.[105]

Lawrence's Toussaint series stood at the cusp of another major historical moment: the heightening of anti-imperial consciousness, and the emergence of popular movements for self-determination across the colonial world. As this struggle began to gather pace in the 1930s, Toussaint and the Haitian Revolution helped to counter ongoing claims that colonial subjects lacked the capacity for self-government. These heroic figures were also deployed to contest what had by then become the conventional view in the Western world about the abolition of slavery: that it had essentially been the outcome of European humanitarian benevolence. The case of Haiti was used to show that emancipation was achieved through the efforts of the slaves themselves – an example which had obvious implications for colonized peoples' pursuit of self-determination and collective empowerment.

All these dimensions of anti-colonialism came together in the work of the Marxist Trinidadian intellectual C. L. R. James. In an article written in 1933, James denounced the continuing existence of slavery in parts of the British Empire, a century after the formal Abolition Act passed by the House of Commons.[106] A few years before the publication of *The Black Jacobins*, his seminal political biography of Toussaint Louverture, James wrote a play in three acts about him. It was staged at London's Westminster Theatre in 1936, with his friend the radical African American actor and singer Paul Robeson, who had admired Toussaint since high school, cast in the leading role.[107] While it questioned the more authoritarian aspects of Tousaint's rule and his reluctance to break with France, the play was a tribute to him and the dauntless spirit of his people, summed up by the words James put in Toussaint's mouth as he confronted his French jailers: 'you can defeat an army, but you cannot defeat a people in arms'.[108] The play thus distilled ongoing debates about black liberation and anti-colonialism among Caribbean, African American and pan-African progressives.

Toussaint's appeal to the anti-colonial imagination grew in the aftermath of the Second World War. Robeson was a notable example, campaigning for African American civil rights and supporting wars of national liberation against European imperial powers. In 1954 – just as Fidel Castro was likening Toussaint to a modern Spartacus in Cuba – Robeson made an explicit comparison between the Haitian and Vietnamese struggles: in the wake of the defeat of the French colonial army by Vietnamese forces at the Battle of Dien Bien Phu, he described the revolutionary leader Ho Chi Minh as 'the Toussaint of Vietnam'. Warning prophetically against American intervention, Robeson appealed to African Americans not to support the cause of 'white imperialism'.[109] At around the same time, the communist Chilean poet Pablo Neruda included Toussaint Louverture in his epic homage to Latin American liberators in his *Canto General*: depicting Toussaint as a 'natural monarch [who] attacks, blocks the way, rises, commands, repels, defies', he saluted his scorching revolutionary legacy, thanks to which 'the cliffs burn, hidden branches speak, and hopes are transmitted'.[110]

Toussaint and the Haitian Revolution also featured in the works of early African anti-colonial writers, such the Angolan poet Viriato da Cruz, whose poem 'Mamã Negra' featured Toussaint as a global symbol of resistance and rebellion, alongside Cuban slaves and jazz musicians. This presence was even more pronounced in the anti-colonial pan-Africanist cultural movement known as *négritude*, which developed among francophone thinkers and political figures from the 1930s onwards and which took different, often contrasting forms: for example, Léopold Sédar Senghor, one of the intellectual founders of *négritude*, rarely mentioned Saint-Domingue in his works, although his 1948 'Prayer for Peace' strikingly represented as the heart of the colonized pan-African world 'the beloved Haiti, which dared to proclaim Humankind in the face of the Tyrant'.[111] For the writer René Depestre, one of the founders of the Haitian Communist Party, Toussaint Louverture symbolized the struggle to restore a 'free, prosperous and independent Haïti' in the face of the brutal dictatorship of François Duvalier, better known as 'Papa Doc', who governed the country despotically between 1957 and 1971.[112]

Some writers in the *négritude* tradition drew upon Toussaint to reflect on the political and cultural tensions of colonial emancipation. In his play *Monsieur Toussaint*, first performed in 1961 at the height of the Algerian War of Independence, the Martiniquais poet Édouard Glissant imagined Toussaint in his French prison cell, engaging in a dialogue across space and time with figures he had encountered during his lifetime, from Makandal and Bayon de Libertat to Laveaux, Rigaud, Moyse and his own successor, Dessalines. By removing the physical frontier between France and Saint-Domingue, Glissant liberated the prisoner from the confines of his cell; his conversations with the dead also reconnected him to one of Haiti's long-standing cultural traditions, and hence to his creole and African roots. This 'prophetic vision of the past' was at the heart of Glissant's ideal of *négritude* as an exercise in intellectual liberation, in which lost or forgotten histories were creatively revived by colonial subjects.[113]

Yet, for Glissant's Toussaint at least, this homeward journey only opened up a deeper paradox, as the tragic hero, though liberated from his cell, remained trapped by the conflict between his loyalty to France and the defence of his own people's interests. This existential contradiction was highlighted even more acutely in the Ivorian playwright Bernard Dadié's *Îles de Tempête* (1973), which began with a sympathetic portrayal of Toussaint but went on openly to lampoon him for his material and intellectual dependence on France. The ultimate heroes of the Haitian Revolution, for Dadié, were Dessalines and Moyse, who both argued that Toussaint's reliance on white settlers, and his insistence on retaining close colonial ties with France, could lead only to disaster. At one point in the play Moyse berated his uncle, in a question which vividly captured the post-colonial predicament: 'when shall we ever stop living with our eyes permanently fixed on Europe?'[114]

This charge of excessive – and naïve – Europhilia was commonly levelled at Toussaint by some of his black critics, both in the diaspora and in Haiti. The figure who defended him most vigorously from such claims was, fittingly, the thinker who originally invented the concept of *négritude*: the radical Martiniquais poet Aimé Césaire. Saint-Domingue's revolution was, for him, the defining moment in the modern history of the Caribbean, and he constantly evoked it in his plays, essays and poems – notably in his *Cahier d'un retour au pays natal* (1939), where he described Haiti as the site where 'negritude stood up for the first time and affirmed its belief in its humanity'.[115] In one of the poem's most famous passages, he poignantly depicted Toussaint alone in his prison cell, 'imprisoned by whiteness', but at the same time defying the 'white screams of a white death'.[116] Toussaint guided Césaire in his intellectual awakening about the brutal realities of French colonial racism and in the decisive moments of his political life, notably when he formed his Progressive Party in Martinique in 1945: he later noted that he had not wished to enter the political arena but felt, like Toussaint in the early 1790s, that events left him with no choice.[117]

Toussaint and the Haitian Revolution lurked in the background in Césaire's *Discours sur le colonialisme* (1950), one of the first comprehensive modern critiques of colonialism, which anticipated many of the key themes later developed by post-colonial thinkers such as Frantz Fanon and Edward Said – notably the 'decivilizing' effect of colonialism on indigenous populations. Césaire brought all these historical, personal and philosophical elements together in his essay on Toussaint and the Haitian Revolution, first published in 1960. This sweeping account was a rejoinder to C. L. R. James's *Black Jacobins*, which had portrayed the Haitian Revolution as largely derivative of its French counterpart. For Césaire, however, while it was originally influenced by French events, Saint-Domingue's revolution took place 'according to its laws and with its own objectives'; it was a 'colonial type of revolution'.[118] This distinctness was a consequence of its racial dimension, which Césaire analysed thoroughly, underscoring the contradictory and hypocritical approach of the French revolutionaries (including Robespierre and the Montagnards) towards black emancipation; he was especially scathing about the elaboration of a 'republican' version of the *Code Noir* in 1793, which he sarcastically noted 'made for very interesting reading'.[119]

Even though he was critical of some aspects of Toussaint's leadership, such as his militarization of politics, Césaire's tribute to him was fulsome. He represented him as the founding father of Haitian independence, who had prepared the ground for Dessalines; a nation-builder who had awakened the spiritual consciousness of his people; and a martyr who knowingly sacrificed himself for the greater good: his 'greatness' resided in his single-minded devotion to the emancipation of his people – all races and ethnicities combined.[120] Having successfully destroyed the 'ontology' of colonialism – the idea of the whites' natural entitlement to rule, and the inherent inferiority of black people – Louverture was 'the first great anti-colonialist leader the world has ever seen'.[121]

Césaire also dealt crisply with the criticism that Toussaint had remained too close to the French (an accusation which was frequently levelled at Césaire himself, who did not campaign for Martinique's independence). As a leader, Toussaint had 'interiorized' the principles of liberty and equality, and skilfully deployed the cultural resources available to him to win the slaves over to the revolutionary cause – hence his appeal to Caribbean and monarchical ideals, which Césaire vigorously defended.[122] True, his 1801 constitution had not contained the 'magic' word of independence, but this was an ingenious attempt to fend off a French military invasion – and was not based on 'some black fondness for dictatorship', as Toussaint's opponents had often alleged. In fact, his constitution was a 'precious contribution to modern political science', as it was the first attempt to frame a theory of imperial dominion which could allow colonies to develop their own laws and institutions while retaining their formal ties to France. Toussaint's 'brilliant intuition' thus anticipated the idea of a 'French Commonwealth', in which colonies could organically and peacefully evolve towards self-government; its only drawback was that it had been ahead of its time by 150 years. Toussaint was – and this was a fitting epitaph – a 'precursor' of modern emancipatory politics.[123]

Slaves and freedmen, artists and statesmen, dock workers and public intellectuals, black nationalists and pan-Africans, devout Christians and uncompromising materialists, utopian rebels and order-loving conservatives, feisty Cuban labourers and misty-eyed Irish poets: Toussaint Louverture's legend played to a dizzyingly broad gallery, reverberating throughout the Atlantic world and beyond, and prompted new ways of political thinking, while interacting in myriad ways with local struggles for emancipation. In more domestic settings, the story of Toussaint also served as an education in the virtues. Evoking her childhood in the United States in the 1940s and 1950s as the daughter of *engagé* Jewish intellectuals, the literary theorist Cora Kaplan remembered the 'household gods' who were revered as secular family heroes; this eclectic list brought together William Shakespeare, Ludwig van Beethoven, Tom Paine, Karl Marx, Frederick Douglass, Eleanor Roosevelt – and Toussaint Louverture.[124]

In its robustness, its plasticity and its constant ability to renew itself, Toussaint's legend manifested the classic traits of modern political heroism. He epitomized the figures of the great captain, providential leader, founding father, sage (with more than a whiff of Caribbean supernaturalism), national liberator and saintly martyr. Ironically, his legend most resembled that of his nemesis, Napoleon Bonaparte: in the early nineteenth century the two men were often compared, and Denis Volozan's neoclassical painting of Louverture on horseback was very similar in style to Jacques-Louis David's depiction of Napoleon crossing the Alps. There was considerable overlap, too, in their insular origins, in their depictions as saviours and their lurid, racist and ogre-like demonizations, and in their tragic final fates, banished in equally desolate locations – with the added poetic justice that Napoleon's humiliating treatment by the British mirrored his own callousness towards Toussaint, right down to the instructions that he should not be addressed by his proper title.[125]

There were also compelling similarities between the two men's posthumous resurrection and subsequent global appeal, as well as their unresolved relationship with their respective homelands, with some Haitians and Corsicans believing that Toussaint and Napoleon strayed too far away from their native roots. Yet a more fine-grained comparison reveals three major differences, which pinpoint the singularities of Toussaint's legend. First, Napoleon's myth was grounded in his own radical reinvention in the *Mémorial de Sainte-Hélène*, where he used his conversations with Las Cases, its author, to turn himself into a faithful disciple of the French Revolution, a father of modern nationalism and (most improbably) a man of peace. Toussaint's legend was not originally based on any authoritative self-narrative, or for that matter any set of primary texts; even his *Memoir*, discovered in the French archives by the Haitian historian Saint-Rémy and first published in 1853, occupied a relatively marginal place in the posthumous laudatory narratives surrounding his name.[126]

Furthermore, there is a much greater visual component to Napoleon's myth than to Toussaint's, with busts, portraits, images and (eventually) statues playing a major role in the diffusion of his legend in the nineteenth century, which reached its zenith in the solemn official ceremony which accompanied the return of his ashes to the Invalides in 1840. In contrast, Toussaint's legend was conveyed primarily through oral popular traditions, and – notwithstanding the prints commissioned by President

Boyer – with relatively little support from official state institutions or organized political groups. Last, but not least, while military prowess was at the heart of the Napoleon and Toussaint myths, the emperor's was essentially that of an expansive conqueror, in the imperial traditions of Alexander, Caesar and Charlemagne, while Toussaint symbolized, and was one of the founders of, the defensive just-war tradition of popular resistance to empire.[127]

Political legends are powerful bearers of collective ideals and values, and in this respect too Toussaint's legacy was highly influential. It helped maintain, and over time bring to the fore, the central issue of race in global politics. It did so initially through its association with collective struggles for slave emancipation across the nineteenth century (slavery was formally abolished in Cuba only in 1886), and the later battle to confront an international order which legitimized imperial and settler colonial rule and rejected the principle of racial equality until at least the mid twentieth century. In the process, Toussaint inspired the world's first black champion, immortalized in Ralph Ellison's short story 'Mister Toussan' (1941), where the young Riley evoked 'one of the African guys named Toussan' who 'whipped Napoleon', 'shot down his peckerwood soldiers' from his mountain retreat and 'scared them white folks almost to death'.[128]

But while it is often said that Toussaint's legend embodied martial ideals, this masculinity was not limited to his swashbuckling victories on the battlefield. It also challenged entrenched racist stereotypes in the Western world, helping to associate blackness with notions of rationality, good governance, sobriety and forgiveness. His legacy also offered a bridge between different, and at times competing, visions of blackness in the modern era: the reformist and the revolutionary; the separatist and the transnationalist; the Caribbean and the African; the Catholic and the *vodou*; the religious and the secular; and the Marxist and the anti-imperial. Toussaint's charismatic personality, and his capacity to straddle divides across the ideological spectrum, also explain why he resonates so powerfully in the imagination of the modern global South: there was something unmistakably Louverturian in Frantz Fanon's single-minded pursuit of revolution; in Fidel Castro's indomitable physical and discursive energy; in Ho Chi Minh's and Yasser Arafat's strategic artfulness and ability to transform material weakness into political strength; and in Nelson Mandela's generous spirit of reconciliation.

Above all, Toussaint's legacy provided the historical mythology for a form of anti-slavery republicanism, which grew out of the Saint-Domingue revolution in the late eighteenth century and spread across the Atlantic. Rooted in communities of African descent and in the concept of fraternity, it was a way of thinking that was ideologically distinct from its American and French variants. This republicanism, whose history is only beginning to be excavated, underpinned the struggles for slave emancipation in the nineteenth century, as well as the battle for civil rights in America. It later inspired a strand of anti-colonialism which emphasized shared ideals of justice and a vision of citizenship based on common political values rather than ethnicity, and which reaffirmed the classic republican opposition to imperial conquest and military occupation.[129]

Conclusion

An Inspiration for Our Times

In 1975, the black writer Ntozake Shange completed her verse play *for colored girls who have considered suicide/when the rainbow is enuf*. In this work, which has become one of the classics of the modern feminist dramatic repertoire, seven African American women discussed their experiences of racism and sexism in society, and the creative strategies they devised to counter them. One of the characters, the 'Lady in Brown', spoke of her mind-blowing discovery of Toussaint Louverture as an eight-year-old child from St Louis. After entering a reading contest in her local library, she was swept away by how Toussaint had freed Haiti from slavery 'wid the spirits of ol dead africans from outta the ground'. Because she had found the book about Toussaint in the 'adult reading room', however, she was disqualified from the competition. The disappointment only compounded her fixation with her hero: 'he waz dead & livin to me'. He became her 'secret lover' and confidant, advising her on 'how to remove white girls' from her 'hop-scotch games'. Frustrated with her situation, she decided to run away to Haiti, but then met a young boy who proved to be a more than adequate substitution – all the more so that his name was 'Toussaint Jones'.[1]

Shange's sparkling evocation highlighted not just the enduring quality of Toussaint's legend, but also its delightful capacity for reinvention. Once symbolizing black masculinity, the Saint-Domingue revolutionary was now inspiring a second-wave feminist to unsettle traditional notions of political and cultural authority. While restricted library access to Toussaint reflected efforts by Establishment forces to preserve their power, the narrator's exuberant appropriation of her hero celebrated the transgressive joys of rebellion. Indeed, this identification produced a Toussaint who was himself liberated from the somewhat leaden image constructed by previous generations of men – here was a Toussaint who was young, playful, maliciously subversive and fully immersed in Saint-Domingue's African and *vodou* traditions. Shange's Toussaint was a call to challenge stereotypical representations of blackness, expressed in the 'monolithic idea that everybody is the same'. He was also a prompt to reject intellectual conformism and take charge of one's destiny, not 'sit around waiting for the powers that be' – whether they were white or black.[2]

From the final decades of the twentieth century, Toussaint's myth soared to new heights. As with Shange's play, novelists, poets, playwrights, painters and musicians drew on his life to explore a wide range of personal and even intimate issues. At the same time, he was formally canonized as a global icon by public institutions. He remained, of course, a potent emblem of Haitian nationalism and the promise of a better future: when the Catholic priest and liberation theologian Jean-Bertrand Aristide won the 1990 Haitian presidential election, mural portraits of Toussaint (whose achievements Aristide celebrated) appeared across the country.[3] He was also depicted full of youthful vigour in a statue erected in Haut-du-Cap, near his birthplace on the Bréda plantation, and the bicentenary of his 1801 constitution was widely commemorated, with his face portrayed on a new 20-*gourde* banknote.[4] In a similar spirit, busts honouring his memory appeared in Miami and Montreal, two cities with large and long-established Haitian communities. Just as he was being feted by the American diasporas, a towering statue of Toussaint sought to reclaim the revolutionary leader's pan-African heritage in the town of Allada in Benin, where there is also a project to build a museum in his honour (see Plates 14 and 16).[5] His progressive ideals were not forgotten: a bust hails his role as an emancipator and liberator in Santiago de Cuba. A shining effigy sprung up in the new National Museum of African American History and Culture in Washington, where a full-length Toussaint, armed with a copy of his constitution, looms near Jefferson and a pile of bricks representing his slaves; likewise, in South Africa Toussaint has been chosen for inclusion in the Gallery of Leaders in Freedom Park, the official memorial to the struggle against apartheid.[6]

Perhaps the most spectacular sign of Toussaint's Olympian status was his symbolic entry in April 1998 into the Panthéon, the sacred Parisian abode of France's eminent leaders. The former pariah of Saint-Domingue was now officially anointed as one of the republic's *grands hommes*. The commemorative inscription lauded him as a 'freedom fighter, architect of the abolition of slavery, and Haitian hero' – a gracious homage, but one which might have been enlivened with the zest of Shange: 'TOUSSAINT led they army of zombies / walkin cannon ball shootin spirits to free Haiti'.[7]

The later twentieth century was also a milestone in Toussaint's literary representations. For a long time, creative writing about the Haitian Revolution was dominated by theatrical and poetic productions: between the late 1790s and 1975, there were no fewer than sixty-three plays about Saint-Domingue by playwrights from Africa, the Caribbean, Europe, Scandinavia and the United States.[8] At their best, these works were rich, complex and striking in dramatic terms, and offered contrasting ideological representations of Toussaint, typically dividing between revolutionary and conservative visions.[9] But they tended to view the Saint-Domingue epic from an external standpoint. In particular, they made little effort sympathetically to imagine the events from the perspectives of the agents themselves – a literary echo of the 'erasure' which Michel-Rolph Trouillot noted as the defining characteristic of the revolution's historiography.[10]

Two examples, a century apart, illustrate the point. Despite its title, Alphonse de Lamartine's drama *Toussaint Louverture* (1850) had little to say about his military and political leadership, let alone the social transformations which took place in Saint-Domingue during the 1790s. Indeed, even though the play superficially defended the idea of racial equality, it stuck to the mid-nineteenth-century republican colonial mantra that the slaves of Saint-Domingue owed their liberty to the intervention of French authorities rather than their own actions – the play was written two years after the abolition of slavery by the Second Republic in 1848. Furthermore, the text was suffused with paternalistic undertones about European aesthetic and intellectual superiority. Lamartine's Toussaint was physically ugly and loathed his own body; the qualities he admired – intelligence, courage, decisiveness and patriotism – were all defined by the French; and he appeared fixated with Napoleon, with whom he obsessively compared himself: 'he the first of the whites, me, the first of the blacks'.[11]

A different but equally depreciative perspective was at work in Alejo Carpentier's *The Kingdom of this World* (1949), one of the most famous modern novels about the Haitian Revolution. In contrast with Lamartine, Carpentier set out to narrate the events through the eyes of a black slave, Ti Noël. With the exception of Christophe and (briefly) Dessalines, Saint-Domingue's great leaders barely featured in the novel; Toussaint was completely absent. Yet Ti Noël's relationship with the revolution was largely passive, and in the end his story served essentially to highlight its futility. Carpentier engaged explicitly with the spiritual dimension of the Haitian Revolution, with some eloquent passages about Makandal, the 'Lord of Poison' who was 'invested with superhuman powers'. Ti Noël was one of his followers, and as an adept of *vodou* he later attended the Bois-Caïman ceremony. For all its emphasis on its marvellous aspects, Carpentier's overall depiction of Saint-Domingue's slave religion was nihilistic: it came across not as an empowering ideal, or even a soothing balm on the scars of slavery, but as a savage, destructive force. So, even though Dessalines' victory over the French was credited to the 'deities of powder and fire', the *vodou*-inspired orgy of violence and racial hatred ended up consuming the revolution itself, with Ti Noël left to contemplate a devastated land 'invaded by cactus and brush'.[12]

The prospect of the bicentennial of the Haitian Revolution in 2004 acted as a catalyst for more complex literary works. The movement was largely driven by writers of Caribbean origin, and it was no coincidence that it coincided with a return to centre stage of the revolution's iconic figure. Among the most eminent contributors to this Toussaint renaissance was the St Lucian poet and playwright Derek Walcott. His drama on the revolution, *The Haitian Earth*, was first produced in 1984; it marked the culmination of a lifelong engagement with the Saint-Domingue epic, which began with his play *Henri Christophe* (1950) and his historical pageant *Drums and Colours* (1961). Heroism and its popular archetypes were a central concern for Walcott, and in *The Haitian Earth* they were embodied by Yette, a young mixed-race woman, and Pompey, a black slave-driver; their tragic and ultimately doomed love affair symbolized Toussaint's republican dream of a multiracial society in Saint-Domingue. Walcott repeatedly contrasted the noble ambitions of the 'good doctor Toussaint' with the narcissistic weaknesses of Dessalines and Christophe (who, in the play, ordered the execution of Yette for attempting to place a curse on him).[13] Brave, compassionate and humane in his leadership, Toussaint was the true patriot of the Haitian Revolution, and his betrayal and exile appeared as its greatest tragedy.[14]

There were also critical explorations of his more contentious policies. This was notably the case in Maryse Condé's *In the Time of the Revolution*, a play about the struggle against slavery in Guadeloupe and Saint-Domingue which was first staged in 1989, the bicentenary year of the French Revolution. Condé saluted the 'extraordinary story' of Toussaint, the 'Black Spartacus' who understood that 'he had to play his own cards, the black man's cards'. Yet Condé severely censored his refusal to divide the land among the peasantry and his harsh regime on the plantations: the drama's storyteller described him as a 'frightening' leader, and condemned his brutal disciplinary methods. That said, when Toussaint was captured by Leclerc's troops and deported in 1802, and the French restored slavery in Guadeloupe, Condé credited the Louverturian spirit with igniting the popular resistance; one of the rebel commanders summed up his inspiring role by commenting: 'the whites took Toussaint. But there are thousands of Toussaints in Saint-Domingue!'[15]

Among the most subtle and original literary evocations was Fabienne Pasquet's novel *La deuxième mort de Toussaint Louverture* (2001), where the revolutionary hero returned in a *loa*-like capacity to his cell in Fort de Joux in 1807, now occupied by the Prussian poet and dramatist Heinrich von Kleist. Pasquet, whose father was Haitian, sketched a Toussaint who was magnificent in his virility and his cultural eclecticism, using his knowledge of medicinal herbs to cure the prisoner's knee injury, drawing on *vodou*, native American and African myths to celebrate nature's healing properties, and embarking on a captivating philosophical dialogue with Kleist about the meaning of life, in which he dampened Kleist's romantic and grandiloquent fantasies. In a notable reversal of the traditional hierarchical relationship between the European Enlightenment and its colonial subjects, it was Toussaint-the-sage who performed a cathartic role, drawing out Kleist's Jungian 'shadow', his suppressed (and better) self. He brought Kleist to embrace an absolute love of life, and educated him in the ideals of patriotic resistance, universal freedom and progressive transformation; comparing a revolution to a wildfire, he observed: 'so that this fire can become a flame of liberty, it has to be contained and controlled, fanned in some places, reduced in others'.[16]

Fort de Joux– an unfailingly popular site of Louverturian memory – also served as the backdrop to the Haitian novelist Jean-Claude Fignolé's fictional autobiography *Moi Toussaint Louverture* (2004). Here too Toussaint was cast in the role of the oracle, projecting himself forward in time to compare himself to fellow providential leaders such as Bismarck, Mao and de Gaulle. But this was a sombre hero, assailed by regrets as he revisited his career and contemplated the troubled history of his native land over the course of the nineteenth and twentieth centuries. Fignolé's Toussaint was at his most provocative in his comments about contemporary Haiti. He distanced himself from the country, claiming that he was a 'French general'; he ridiculed the notion that Haitians were part of a wider community of African descent (both of these could be read as critical commentaries by Fignolé on elitist social attitudes in Haiti, rather than first-order beliefs the author was ascribing to Toussaint). The revolutionary hero acknowledged some of his own mistakes – in particular that of succumbing to the vice of 'caesarism', and allowing his legacy to be appropriated by brutal dictators such as the Duvaliers: after the dictatorship of François, his son Jean-Claude ruled Haiti despotically from 1971 to 1986. Most dramatically, he lamented the civic and moral disintegration of Haitian society, noting that the descendants of Saint-Domingue's revolution had become a 'people of shadows'. But this prophet of doom had not completely lost his sense of humour, complaining that he had not been invited to the inauguration of his statue in Benin.[17]

Fignolé's absorbing novel demonstrated the contemporary resonance of Toussaint's legend, further reflected in Madison Smartt Bell's fictional trilogy about the Haitian Revolution.[18] Indeed, the Toussaint myth has become, to borrow Sartre's expression, the 'horizon indépassable' of the contemporary Haitian literary imagination. For his Caribbean admirers, Toussaint's fundamental role was to act as a symbolic repository, welding together (along with Dessalines) the different elements of the Haitian revolutionary tradition[19] while also standing as one of the precursors of the ideal of *négritude*.[20] This synthesis was most powerfully conjured in the oeuvre of the Haitian novelist Jean Métellus, most notably in his *Toussaint Louverture, le précurseur*, which first appeared in 2004 and was republished after his death in 2014. Métellus offered an exalted defence of Toussaint's heritage, which stood as an exemplar not just for the history of anti-colonialism but also for contemporary struggles against injustice and racism in the global South. Echoing a widespread view among Haitians, the novel insisted on Toussaint's intellectual originality and his seamless ability to combine European, African and Caribbean influences. Métellus dwelled on Toussaint's medicinal powers, which were grounded in his cult of nature and expressed his own highly personal form of spirituality – one which was indebted to, but at the same time distinct from, *vodou* faith and Catholic values. In the concluding section of the novel – inevitably, in the Fort de Joux cell – Métellus brought Toussaint back to this theme with a vividly tropical rendering of his Machiavellianism: 'in order to achieve this liberty which we were always denied, I deployed all the ruses of the animal kingdom: that of the spider which eventually traps its prey, that of the fox which hypnotizes its victims, and that of the serpent which paralyses its aggressor'.[21]

Just as Toussaint's status as one of the modern giants of the Caribbean was being confirmed, his public renown in France, too, was rising to new heights. His entry into the Panthéon in 1998 was a symbolic landmark in a broader historical turn in France, which witnessed the start of collective debates about the significance of slavery in modern French history. This process notably saw the passing of the Taubira law by the French National Assembly in May 2001 recognizing the slave trade and slavery as crimes against humanity. This was followed by the official designation of a specific day in the annual calendar (10 May) for the commemoration of slavery and its abolition. Since 2006, this 'journée nationale' has been marked by formal ceremonies at designated sites of memory across France, as well as initiatives by educational institutions and cultural associations to promote greater awareness of the history of slavery.[22]

New public memorializations of Saint-Domingue's icon have been a central feature of this French effort critically to revisit its slave history. Toussaint's name was given to schools, streets, squares, theatres and even car parks in numerous locations, including Paris, Bobigny, Saint-Denis, Angers, Poitiers, Montpellier, Clermont-Ferrand, Narbonne and Niort; in the château of l'Isle-de-Noé (Gers), formerly the seat of the Noé clan, the owners of the Bréda plantation, there is now an 'allée Toussaint Louverture', and the village dedicated a monument to him in 2003; the Noé family also donated what they claimed was Toussaint Louverture's walking stick to the neighbouring Musée des Beaux-Arts in Mirande.[23] In the same year, the municipality of Bordeaux unveiled a plaque on the house formerly inhabited by Isaac Louverture, who died in exile there in 1854, and also created – perhaps infelicitously – an 'Impasse Toussaint Louverture' in the city. In the Château de Cormatin in Burgundy, where Étienne Laveaux lived from 1809 until his death in 1828, a plaque commemorates Laveaux's friendship with Toussaint Louverture, the 'leader of the slave insurrection'. The city of Nantes, once France's largest slave-trading port, built a Memorial to the Abolition of Slavery and named a square after Toussaint. Monuments in his honour appeared in all corners of metropolitan France: in the Parisian region, the town of Massy put up a bronze statue of him in one of its main public squares; in May 2005 the municipality of Grenoble inaugurated a Louverture plaque on the city-hall building, and in the same year a bust of Toussaint was erected on the bank of the River Garonne in Bordeaux, where thousands of slaves were also bought and sold; since 2009, the city's Musée d'Aquitaine has dedicated several permanent exhibits to the history of Atlantic slavery. In the Jura, Toussaint's denuded former cell in Fort de Joux was enhanced with a bust of the great man, as well as a commemorative plaque (both donated by the Haitian government). The most arresting monument to emerge in France was a full-length bronze statue by the Senegalese sculptor Ousmane Sow, who had earlier produced a highly praised sculpture, 'Toussaint L'Ouverture and the elderly slave'. Inaugurated in May 2015 in the western coastal city of La Rochelle, another of France's principal slave-trading ports, Sow's work depicted an engrossed Toussaint scrolling through a copy of his 1801 constitution (see Plate 16).

Sow's statue, a fine symbiosis of European, Caribbean and African motifs, seemed a serene illustration of France's reconciliation with the revolutionary hero of Saint-Domingue, and its willingness squarely to engage with its colonial history since the early twenty-first century. Yet a closer inspection revealed ongoing tensions. Even though Toussaint's entry into the Panthéon was a considerable gesture by the French state, it was a belated one, coming after more than a decade of campaigning by anti-slavery associations. To make the same point differently, white abolitionism was easier – and much less troubling – to honour than black resistance to

DANS CE CHÂTEAU VÉCUT DE 1809 À SA MORT
LE GÉNÉRAL ETIENNE MAYNAUD DE LAVAUX
1751 · 1828
GOUVERNEUR DE ST DOMINGUE (1793·96), IL FUT L'ALLIÉ
ET L'AMI DE TOUSSAINT LOUVERTURE,
CHEF DES ESCLAVES RÉVOLTÉS.
IL REÇUT A.DE LAMARTINE AU CHÂTEAU DE CORMATIN
ET LUI TRANSMIT SES CONVICTIONS ANTI - ESCLAVAGISTES.
SON ACTION ET SES ÉCRITS INSPIRÈRENT
LA LOI D'ABOLITION DE 1848.

In the Château de Cormatin in Burgundy, where the Saint-Domingue governor Étienne Laveaux lived from 1809 onwards, this plaque commemorates his friendship with Toussaint Louverture, the 'leader of slave insurrection'. It also celebrates Laveaux's influence on Lamartine, who later played a key role in the abolition of slavery by the Second Republic.

slavery: Victor Schoelcher, the republican leader (and Toussaint biographer) who oversaw the definitive ending of slavery, entered the Panthéon in 1948. The locations chosen for some of the Toussaint monuments seemed to betray a lingering unease on the part of French local authorities: this was notably the case with the Bordeaux bust, placed well away from the city centre. Likewise, Sow's statue was put on display in the courtyard of the Musée du Nouveau Monde, and so out of immediate public reach. This museum happened to be in a building (the Hôtel Fleuriot) named after one of La Rochelle's principal slave-traders – an inelegant juxtaposition, to say the least.

Confirmation of Toussaint's unsettling presence in French collective memory could be found in the contrasting ways he was described in the different public monuments. The Panthéon inscription noted that he died 'in exile' ('déporté') in Fort de Joux – an oddly inappropriate expression, given that he was French at the time of his death and died in France. In Sow's statue, in contrast, he was wearing the outfit of a French governor. The Grenoble plaque wisely sidestepped the issue of his nationality by celebrating him as a republican abolitionist – but illustrated this with his 'tree of liberty' quotation, which he uttered after he was taken by Leclerc's men; the statement anticipated Saint-Domingue's independence struggle. None of the inscriptions explained why Toussaint was captured, or that he was taken treacherously by the French army, or that the men who arrested him were sent by Bonaparte to restore slavery in the Caribbean. These evasions and contradictions reflected the inability of the French republican tradition to go beyond its self-serving accounts of slavery and its abolition, and engage with the 1789 revolution's faltering attitude towards racial equality. Toussaint's official memorialization showed up France's reluctance to stray too far away from its 'sweet colonial utopia' about its imperial history – namely that slavery was a product of the *ancien régime*, which was excised from the body politic by the revolution; that this outcome was the result of enlightened French intervention, rather than revolutionary action by the black slaves themselves; and that colonial authorities genially acted in the best interests of the black populations living under imperial dominion.[24]

These ambivalences were played out in a two-part drama on Toussaint broadcast on French television in 2012. Directed by the Franco-Senegalese film-maker Philippe Niang, *Toussaint Louverture* cast the Haitian-American actor Jimmy Jean-Louis in the lead role. That such a film was even made was remarkable, given the absence of any significant cinematic treatment of the Haitian Revolution either in Europe or in the United States;[25] and Toussaint's personal qualities (his dignity, bravery, love for his family and aspiration for a better life for black people) were sympathetically portrayed. But the overall depiction of him and of late-eighteenth-century Saint-Domingue was caricatural in the extreme. Slavery was sugar-coated so as not to offend French sensibilities: the impression was given that it was a peaceful, consensual labour system, where plantation workers shared in the profits. Indeed, Niang's Toussaint declared himself to have been a 'happy' slave until his eyes were opened by Raynal and Diderot's *Histoire philosophique*. The French military invasion, too, was treated positively, with a dashing Leclerc shown as a morally scrupulous officer who reluctantly resorted to force in the face of Toussaint's insubordination. Taking its cue from neo-imperial orthodoxy, the film effectively blamed the war on Toussaint, in particular his 1801 constitution, which was presented as an act of wanton stubbornness. There was no allusion to French plans to restore slavery in the Caribbean or the ferocious brutality of Rochambeau's forces; all the atrocities seen on screen were committed by the rampaging black insurgents, driven to 'kill the whites' by their primitive *vodou* religion. Through its nostalgic vision of white plantations, its paternalistic portrait of Toussaint and its stigmatization of black Haitian revolutionaries, Niang's film illustrated the resilience of French colonialist *roman national* (see Plate 15).[26]

Toussaint's French resurgence indicated that, even though his legend was highly elastic, it did not sit comfortably with simplistic interpretations. In this sense, his French memorializations (and their limits) reflected ongoing conversations in former slave-owning and colonial states about creating more inclusive public spaces in which figures who resisted slavery could be honoured, and buildings and public monuments associated with the defence of white supremacist views removed or renamed. In France, for example, a local debate has begun about the statue of General Leclerc in the town of Pontoise, with some citizens saying that it is inappropriate for such a 'war criminal' still to be honoured.[27] In Britain, discussions about the active legacies of colonialism have so far had a limited outcome, as reflected in the unsuccessful campaign to remove an Oxford statue of the British imperialist Cecil Rhodes.[28] The United States has been much more forthright in both respects, with notably the erection of a statue honouring Denmark Vesey in Charleston and the dismantling of several major Confederate monuments – although more than 700 remain across the United States, mostly in the South. In 2017 the New York activist Glenn Cantave sparked a lively discussion when he suggested that the statue of Columbus in New York should be replaced with one of Toussaint Louverture.[29]

The real essence of the Louverture legend, as championed by creative artists, writers and educationalists, is vigorously dissenting – and universalist. The Haitian-American painter Jean-Michel Basquiat caught its combative spirit in his *Toussaint L'Ouverture v. Savonarola*, a neo-expressionist work which celebrated Toussaint's timeless humanity by placing him alongside the Florentine scourge of Papal corruption and despotism.[30] The Afro-Guyanese poet John Agard, likewise, penned an 'acknowledgement' by Toussaint of Wordsworth's poem in his honour: even though he had never set foot in Britain, Agard's Toussaint spoke of his 'tongue' which reached out from 'Europe to Dahomey', and saluted his Cumbrian 'brother' in their shared devotion to the 'sweet smell of liberty'.[31] The former French World Cup-winning footballer Lilian Thuram, a major international campaigner against racism, held up Toussaint as one of his 'black stars', a beacon of fraternity who could help teach younger generations about the achievements of men and women of African descent.[32] The comic-strip book series *Jour J*, centred around historical counterfactuals, portrayed Toussaint being released from French captivity in 1802 by an Irish freedom fighter and being given a 'second chance', which he promptly used to secure the liberation of his American brothers from slavery.[33] This ambitious vision also featured in the mission statement of the Lycée Toussaint Louverture in Pontarlier (Doubs), which hailed Toussaint as the 'precursor' of the global struggle for racial equality, and the founder of a tradition of revolutionary internationalism whose modern incarnations included Martin Luther King and Nelson Mandela.[34] This image was amplified on a 2016 West Belfast republican street mural in homage to Frederick Douglass, which showed Toussaint on horseback alongside Mandela and King, and in the company of such legends of black emancipation as Abraham Lincoln, Rosa Parks, Paul Robeson, Muhammad Ali, Bob Marley, Steve Biko and Angela Davis.[35]

Seen in this light, Toussaint is much more than a glorious relic of the past, to be wheeled out at official anniversaries. The Louverturian struggle remains a vital source of intellectual inspiration and progressive renewal – especially in the current age of populism – and serves as a reminder that the global injustices of today, within and across societies, have deep historical roots. Toussaint's life also stands as an example of classic republican ideals and virtues – the equal dignity of all humans, irrespective of their race, creed or colour; steadfastness and courage, even in the face of overwhelmingly superior enemy forces; integrity and refusal to compromise on one's fundamental values; coexistence and forgiveness, rather than separation and hatred; and above all the audacity to envision a world organized around radically different principles. This ethic can serve as an effective basis for bringing back a politics of hope rather than fear, and promoting a robust internationalism which challenges the false idols of ethno-nationalism and 'identity politics', while at the same time avoiding the self-pitying negativity which often corrodes post-colonial narratives.

Music is the art form which best captures the universalist spirit of this Louverturian promise, and it provides a fitting coda for our odyssey. Toussaint himself was a great music lover, as has been depicted in some of the more recent literary works: for example, Métellus visualized him performing on the *banza*, a four-string violin which was much used in slave dances in late-colonial Saint-Domingue. In fact, every musical generation has found inspiration in Toussaint's life: from the feisty songs of Caribbean and African American slaves and freedmen in the nineteenth century to the members of the Toussaint Louverture musical club in Wilmington, Delaware[36] and the classical composer Samuel Coleridge-Taylor's pan-African symphonic poem *Toussaint L'Ouverture* (1901), through to the tribute to the Haitian Revolution by the Black Swan record company, whose phonographs included a 'L'Ouverture' model,[37] and the creations of later jazz legends Duke Ellington and Charles Mingus, and the New York jazz trumpeter and bandleader Donald Toussaint Louverture Byrd.[38] In September 1977, the composer

David Blake premiered his opera *Toussaint* at the Coliseum in London, a sweepingly lyrical evocation of the last seven years of the life of the liberator, who spoke in biblical terminology and was inspired as much by *vodou* as by the serene presence of his wife Suzanne.[39]

In a 'musical tale' first released as a compact disc in 2012, Jérôme Brie imagined the final days of Toussaint, 'the black star who shed his singular light on the world around him'.[40] Modern rock music, too, has feted Toussaint, with an acclaimed composition in his honour by the Mexican-American guitarist Carlos Santana in 1970, and a suitably eccentric more recent opus entitled 'Bring The Sun/Toussaint Louverture' by the experimental American group Swans; the thirty-four-minute piece featured bloody incantations against a backdrop of deep horn blasts and galloping horses. Asked about the song, the composer Michael Gira disclosed that it was his 'metaphysical' homage to the Haitian Revolution, and that 'it grew out of playing music and needing some fucking words. I started screaming "Toussaint!" and I came up with words that fit the phenomenon.'[41]

Gira was not the only artist to be possessed by the Louverturian spirit. In his album *From the Hut, to the Projects, to the Mansion*, the Haitian rapper Wyclef Jean turned himself into 'Toussaint St Jean', a figure from the hood who 'will not tolerate disrespect', while his British comrade Akala applauded Toussaint's 'bulletproof' ideas. Not to be outdone, the Haitian band Chouk Bwa (Tree Stump), which completed its first British tour in 2018, took its name from the famous Toussaint quote about the 'tree of liberty'. Originating from the great man's beloved Gonaïves, the band proudly promoted an altogether different strand of his heritage by performing highly percussive pieces infused with a *vodou* sensibility. Its song 'Neg Ayisyen' (Haitian Man) invoked Makandal, Toussaint and Dessalines, and serenaded the Haitian people as 'the children of Nago, Kongo and Dahomey'. Singer Edele Joseph crisply summarized the band's upbeat Louverturian message: 'the mission is to bring positive energy to people . . . this energy has no borders'.[42]

Notes

ABBREVIATIONS

AGI	General archives of the Indies
AGS	General archives of Simancas
AN	Archives Nationales, Paris
ANOM	Archives Nationales d'Outre-Mer, Aix-en-Provence
BNF	Bibliothèque Nationale de France
NAM	Templar Study Centre and Archive, the National Army Museum, London

INTRODUCTION – THE ORIGINALITY OF TOUSSAINT LOUVERTURE

1. Toussaint proclamation, 25 August 1793. AN AE II 1375. 2. For an overview of the key events in Saint-Domingue from the late eighteenth century to the declaration of Haitian independence see Jeremy Popkin, *A Concise History of the Haitian Revolution* (Oxford: Wiley-Blackwell, 2012), and David Geggus, *The Haitian Revolution: A Documentary History* (Indianapolis: Hackett Publishing Company, 2014). 3. See David Armitage and Sanjay Subrahmanyam (eds), *The Age of Revolutions in Global Contexts* (Basingstoke: Palgrave Macmillan, 2009); and Rafe Blaufarb, *The Revolutionary Atlantic: Republican Visions 1760–1830* (New York: Oxford University Press, 2017). 4. Toussaint to Minister of Navy, 9 Prairial an V (28 May 1797). AN AFIII 210. 5. For further discussion of the wider context of the Haitian Revolution see Robin Blackburn, 'Haiti, slavery, and the age of democratic revolution', *The William and Mary Quarterly* vol. 63, no. 4 (October 2006). 6. Speech at festival of general liberty, Môle Saint-Nicolas, 16 Pluviôse an VIII (5 February 1800). ANOM CC9B 9. 7. Quoted in James Alexander Dun, *Dangerous Neighbours: Making the Haitian Revolution in Early America* (Philadelphia: University of Pennsylvania Press, 2016), p. 149. 8. *London Gazette*, 12 December 1798. 9. Quoted in Grégory Pierrot, '"Our hero": Toussaint Louverture in British representations', *Criticism* vol. 50–54 (Fall 2008), p. 598. 10. See Susan Buck-Morss, *Hegel, Haiti and Universal History* (Pittsburgh: University of Pittsburgh Press, 2009). 11. Quoted in Donald Hickey, 'America's response to the slave revolt in Haiti, 1791–1806', *Journal of the Early Republic* vol. 2, no. 4 (Winter 1982), p. 368. 12. Hobart to Nugent, Downing Street, London, 18 November 1801. National Archives, Kew, CO 137/106. 13. Quoted in Christer Petley, *White Fury: A Jamaican Slave-holder and the Age of Revolution* (Oxford: Oxford University Press, 2018), pp. 176–7. 14. See, from 1798 onwards, the *Gazette of the United States and Daily Advertiser* (Philadelphia) and *National Intelligencer and Washington Advertiser* (Washington). Library of Congress, Historic American Newspapers. 15. On this wider pattern of

slave empowerment see in particular Eugene Genovese, *From Rebellion to Revolution: Afro-American Slave Revolts in the Making of the Modern World* (Baton Rouge: Louisiana State University Press, 1979); on the revolution as a source of terror and inspiration in the United States see Ashli White, *Encountering Revolution: Haiti and the Making of the Early Republic* (Baltimore: Johns Hopkins University Press, 2010), and Elizabeth Maddock Dillon and Michael Drexler (eds), *The Haitian Revolution and the Early United States* (Philadelphia: University of Pennsylvania Press, 2016). **16.** The annual subscription to the paper, which cost $2.50 for a year, came with the gift of 'a fine photograph of either Frederick Douglass, Esq. or Toussaint L'Ouverture'. *New National Era*, 16 April 1874. Library of Congress, Historic American Newspapers. **17.** Médéric Louis Élie Moreau de Saint-Méry, *Description topographique, physique, civile, politique et historique de la partie française de l'isle Saint-Domingue* (Paris, 1797), vol. 1, p. 105. **18.** On the history of the capital see Roland Devauges, 'Une capitale antillaise: Port-au-Prince (Haïti)', *Les Cahiers d'Outre-Mer* (1954), pp. 7–26. On the coastal towns see David Geggus, 'The major port towns of Saint-Domingue in the late eighteenth century', in P. Liss and F. Knight (eds), *Atlantic Port Cities* (Knoxville: University of Tennessee Press, 1991). **19.** Jean Saint-Vil, 'Villes et bourgs de Saint-Domingue au XVIIIe siècle (essai de géographie historique)', *Les Cahiers d'Outre-Mer* (1978), p. 251. **20.** In the final years of the eighteenth century, in alignment with the territorial changes introduced by the French Revolution, the provinces became departments. **21.** François Girod, *La vie quotidienne de la société créole (Saint-Domingue au 18e siècle)* (Paris: Hachette, 1972), pp. 71–2. **22.** Laurent Dubois, *Avengers of the New World* (Cambridge, Mass. and London: Harvard University Press, 2004), p. 26. **23.** Alexandre de Laujon, *Souvenirs et voyages* (Paris, 1835), p. 124. **24.** See M.-A. Menier and G. Debien, 'Journaux de Saint-Domingue', *Revue d'Histoire des Colonies*, 36 (1949), and Jean Fouchard, 'Les joies de la lecture à Saint-Domingue', *Revue d'Histoire des Colonies*, 41 (1954); see also Fouchard's classic *Le Théâtre à Saint-Domingue* (Port-au-Prince: Imprimerie de l'État, 1955). **25.** For further analysis of the Cercle, and of scientific life in pre-revolutionary Saint-Domingue more generally, see James McClellan III, *Colonialism and Science: Saint-Domingue in the Old Regime* (Baltimore and London: Johns Hopkins University Press, 1992). **26.** Julius Scott, *The Common Wind: Afro-American Currents in the Age of the Haitian Revolution* (London: Verso, 2018), p. 115. **27.** The classic work on the subject is Charles Frostin's *Les révoltes blanches à Saint-Domingue au XVIIe et XVIIIe siècles* (1975; Rennes: Presses Universitaires de Rennes, 2008). **28.** Henri-Baptiste Grégoire, *Mémoire en faveur des gens de couleur ou sang-mêlés de Saint-Domingue* (Paris, 1789), pp. 7–8. **29.** *Ordonnance du Roi, concernant les procureurs & économes-gérans des habitations situées aux Isles sous le Vent, du 17 Décembre 1784* (Paris, 1785), p. 5. **30.** Quoted in Girod, *La vie quotidienne de la société créole*, p. 189. **31.** Conversation with Edward Corbet, reported in Corbet letter, Port-Républicain, 21 July 1801. National Archives, Kew, CO 137/105. **32.** See Fritz Daguillard, *Toussaint Louverture: mystérieux dans la gloire* (Port-au-Prince: Musée du Panthéon National Haïtien, 2003), pp. 11–15. **33.** Jacques de Norvins, *Souvenirs d'un historien de Napoléon* (Paris, 1896), vol. 2, p. 362. **34.** George E. Simpson and J. B. Cinéas, 'Folk tales of Haitian heroes', *Journal of American Folklore* vol. 54, no. 213/14 (July–December 1941), p. 184. **35.** Louis Dubroca, *Vie de Toussaint Louverture, chef des noirs insurgés* (Paris, 1802), p. 53; Thomas-Prosper Gragnon-Lacoste, *Toussaint Louverture* (Paris, 1877), p. 1. **36.** For a summary of this mixed-race historical account see David Nicholls, *From Dessalines to Duvalier: Race, Colour and National Independence in Haiti* (Cambridge: Cambridge University Press, 1979), pp. 90–91, 95 and 97. **37.** Victor Schoelcher, *Vie de Toussaint Louverture* (1889; Paris: Karthala, 1982). **38.** Horace Pauléus Sannon, *Histoire de Toussaint Louverture*, 3 vols (Port-au-Prince: Imprimerie Héraux, 1920–33). **39.** For a comprehensive assessment of James's biography of Toussaint see the collection edited by Charles Forsdick and Christian Høgsbjerg, *The Black Jacobins Reader* (Durham, NC and London: Duke University Press, 2017). **40.** See Richard Drayton and David Motadel, 'Discussion: the futures of global history', *Journal of Global History* vol. 13, issue 1 (2018), p. 7. **41.** See notably Alyssa Goldstein Sepinwall (ed.), *Haitian History: New Perspectives* (New York and London: Routledge, 2013); and her article 'Beyond "*The*

Black Jacobins": Haitian Revolutionary historiography comes of age', *Journal of Haitian Studies* vol. 23, no. 1 (Spring 2017). **42.** Jean Fouchard, *Les marrons de la liberté* (Paris: Éditions de l'École, 1972; English translation *The Haitian Maroons*, New York: Blyden Press, 1981); Carolyn Fick, *The Making of Haiti: The Saint-Domingue Revolution from Below* (Knoxville: University of Tennessee Press, 1990). **43.** See especially Ada Ferrer, *Freedom's Mirror: Cuba and Haiti in the Age of Revolution* (New York: Cambridge University Press, 2014). **44.** Mimi Sheller, 'Sword-bearing citizens: militarism and manhood in nineteenth-century Haiti', in Sepinwall (ed.), *Haitian History*, p. 157. **45.** Michael O. West and William G. Martin, 'Haiti, I'm sorry: the Haitian Revolution and the forging of the black international', in Michael O. West, William G. Martin and Fanon Che Wilkins (eds), *From Toussaint to Tupac: The Black International Since the Age of Revolution* (Chapel Hill: University of North Carolina Press, 2009), p. 76. **46.** Pierre Pluchon, *Toussaint Louverture, un révolutionnaire noir d'Ancien Régime* (Paris: Fayard, 1989). **47.** Philippe Girard, *Toussaint Louverture: A Revolutionary Life* (New York: Basic Books, 2016), pp. 4–5. **48.** Philippe Girard, *The Slaves Who Defeated Napoleon: Toussaint Louverture and the Haitian War of Independence 1801–1804* (Tuscaloosa, AL: University of Alabama Press, 2011), pp. 9–10 and 43. **49.** David Scott, *Conscripts of Modernity: The Tragedy of Colonial Enlightenment* (London and Durham, NC: Duke University Press, 2004), p. 210. **50.** Celeste-Marie Bernier, *Characters of Blood: Black Heroism in the Transatlantic Imagination* (Charlottesville: University of Virginia Press, 2012), p. 7. **51.** See for example his official report on 'the re-establishment of order in the mountains of Port-de-Paix', 7 Brumaire an V (28 October 1796). ANOM CC9A 13. **52.** Gordon K. Lewis, *Main Currents in Caribbean Thought: The Historical Evolution of Caribbean Society in its Ideological Aspects, 1492–1900* (Baltimore: Johns Hopkins University Press, 1987), p. 27. **53.** See Laurent Dubois, 'An enslaved Enlightenment: rethinking the intellectual history of the French Atlantic', *Social History* vol. 31, no. 1 (February 2006), p. 12; on the notion of a hybrid diasporic culture more generally see the classic work by Paul Gilroy, *The Black Atlantic* (London: Verso, 1993). **54.** Nick Nesbitt, 'Turning the tide: the problem of popular insurgency in the historiography of the Haitian Revolution', *Small Axe*, 27 (October 2008), p. 31; on this theme see also the excellent article by Adom Getachew, 'Universalism after the post-colonial turn: interpreting the Haitian Revolution', *Political Theory* vol. 44, no. 6 (2016), pp. 821–45. **55.** Leclerc, 'Campagne du Limbé, et détail de quelques événements qui ont eu lieu dans ce quartier, jusqu'au 20 juin 1793', n.d. [1793]. ANOM CC9A 8. **56.** Report of French agent Roume, 15 Messidor an VII (3 July 1799). National Archives, Kew, CO 137/104. **57.** Toussaint to Pascal, 26 Germinal an VII (15 April 1799). National Archives, Kew, CO 245/2. **58.** See for example Toussaint's letter to the citizens of Petite-Montagne, 29 Nivôse an IV (19 January 1796). BNF NAF 12104. **59.** See Quentin Skinner, *Liberty Before Liberalism* (Cambridge: Cambridge University Press, 1998). **60.** See notably Toussaint, 'Address to the citizens capable of bearing arms', Cap, 15 Pluviôse an V (3 February 1797), *Bulletin Officiel de Saint-Domingue*, 12 February 1797. **61.** On this theme see Chapter 3 in Michel-Rolph Trouillot, *Silencing the Past* (Boston, Mass.: Beacon Press, 1995). **62.** On this point see Charles Forsdick and Christian Høgsbjerg, *Toussaint Louverture: A Black Jacobin in the Age of Revolutions* (London: Pluto Press, 2017), p. 147. **63.** Yanick Lahens, 'Le 19e siècle, ce grand inconnu', Collège de France lecture, 1 April 2019. **64.** 'Toussaint Louverture: A finding list of his letters and documents in archives and collections (public and private) of Europe and America'. Joseph Boromé Papers, Sc MG 714, Box 2, New York Public Library. **65.** Patrice Gueniffey, *Bonaparte* (Paris: Gallimard, 2013), p. 595. **66.** Joseph Boromé, 'Some desiderata in Caribbean biography', *Caribbean Quarterly* vol. 19, no. 4 (December 1973), p. 29. **67.** Hippolyte de Saint-Anthoine, *Notice sur Toussaint Louverture* (Paris, 1842), p. 30. **68.** Toussaint to Hédouville, 7 Thermidor an VI (25 July 1798). ANOM CC9 B6. **69.** Toussaint to Lescallier, 21 Prairial an VI (9 June 1798). ANOM CC9A 14. **70.** Toussaint to Charles-François Liot, commercial consul, Philadelphia, Cap, 3 July 1801. Archives of French Foreign Ministry, CCC, Philadelphia V. **71.** Stuart Hall, 'Cultural identity and diaspora', in P. Williams and L. Chrisman (eds), *Colonial Discourse and Postcolonial Theory: A Reader* (London and New York: Routledge, 1994), p. 235. **72.** 'perfidious and misleading scoundrel'. Toussaint to Antoine Chanlatte (a colonel in the French republican army), 27 August 1793. ANOM CC9A 8. 73. Jean Fouchard, 'Toussaint Louverture', *Revue de la Société haïtienne d'histoire et de géographie* no. 164 (September–December 1989), p. 41. 74. Toussaint to Renne de Saba, 28 Germinal VII (17 April 1799). Library of Congress, Manuscript Division, Papers of Toussaint Louverture. 75. Letter from Madame Louverture to Toussaint, 24 July 1794. Archives Départementales de la Gironde, Collection Marcel Chatillon, 61 J 18. 76. Toussaint to Laveaux, 16 September 1795. BNF NAF 12103. Toussaint note dated 30 Nivôse an X (20 January 1802). Edmond Mangonès collection, University of Florida, cited in Boromé, 'A finding list'. 77. Toussaint to Minister of Navy, 24 Germinal an VII (13 April 1799), quoted in *Testament politique de Toussaint Louverture* (Paris, 1855), p. 5.

1: THE SOUL OF A FREE MAN

1. 'Né dans l'esclavage, mais ayant reçu de la nature l'âme d'un homme libre'. Toussaint report to Directory, 18 Fructidor an V (4 September 1797). AN AFIII 210. 2. Anna Julia Cooper, *Slavery and the French and Haitian Revolutionists* (Lanham, MD: Rowman and Littlefield, 2006), p. 102. 3. These consist mainly of annual accounts, slave listings, labour reports and management instructions. For a full description of these sources see Gabriel Debien, *Les esclaves aux Antilles françaises, XVII–XVIIIe siècles* (Basse Terre: Société d'histoire de la Guadeloupe, and Fort-de-France: Société d'histoire de la Martinique, 1974), pp. 9–38. 4. Isaac Louverture, *Notes sur la vie de Toussaint Louverture*, p. 325. BNF NAF 6864. 5. Charles Vincent, *Notice sur Dominique Toussaint Louverture*, n.d. Archives Diplomatiques Paris-La Courneuve, 23MD/2 (mémoires et documents, Haïti). 6. On Toussaint's family see Alfred Nemours, *Histoire de la famille et de la descendance de Toussaint Louverture* (Port-au-Prince: Imprimerie de l'État, 1941). 7. See the PhD dissertation by Christian Frances Mobley, 'The Kongolese Atlantic: Central African Slavery & Culture from Mayombe to Haïti' (Duke University, 2015). 8. The classic article on the subject is by John Thornton, '"I am the subject of the King of the Congo": African political ideology and the Haitian Revolution', *Journal of World History* vol. 4, no. 2 (Fall 1993). 9. On the estate owners see Jean-Louis Donnadieu, *Un grand seigneur et ses esclaves. Le comte de Noé entre Antilles et Gascogne* (Toulouse: Presses Universitaires du Mirail, 2009). 10. Article XI stated that 'children born from a marriage between slaves will be slaves'. *Le Code Noir* (Paris, 1685), p. 5. 11. David Geggus, 'Toussaint Louverture and the slaves of the Bréda plantations', *Journal of Caribbean History* vol. 20, no. 1 (1985–6), p. 36. 12. 'Fatras' was commonly used to refer to slaves who were injured or disabled. 13. Saint-Rémy, *Vie de Toussaint* (Paris: Moquet, 1850), p. 8. 14. Vincent, *Notice sur Dominique Toussaint Louverture*. 15. Isaac Louverture, *Notes historiques sur Toussaint Louverture*. BNF NAF 6864. 16. Antoine Métral, *Histoire de l'insurrection des esclaves dans les nord de Saint-Domingue* (Paris, 1818), p. 53. 17. *Code Noir*, p. 8. 18. Fick, *The Making of Haiti*, p. 21. 19. Isaac Louverture, *Notes historiques*. BNF NAF 12409. 20. François Cliquot, 'Nouvelle description de l'île d'Haïti', unpublished MS, 1843. Archives Diplomatiques Paris-La Courneuve, 23MD/2 (mémoires et documents, Haïti). 21. Debien, *Les esclaves aux Antilles françaises*, p. 285. 22. Ibid., p. 287. 23. Charles Frostin, 'Méthodologie missionnaire et sentiment religieux en Amérique française au 17e et 18e siècles: le cas de Saint-Domingue', in *Cahiers d'Histoire* (Universities of Clermont, Lyon and Grenoble, 1979), vol. 24, no 1, p. 24. See more generally François Kawas, *Sources documentaires de l'histoire des jésuites en Haïti aux XVIIIe et XXe siècles* (Paris: L'Harmattan, 2006). 24. In a letter to Grégoire dated 9 April 1799 a local priest, Father Constantin de Luxembourg, claimed to have been served dinner by 'Toussaint, slave at the hospital of the Brothers of Charity'; cited in Adolphe Cabon, *Notes sur l'histoire religieuse d'Haïti* (Port-au-Prince: Petit Séminaire Collège Saint-Martial, 1933), p. 44. 25. John Thornton, *Africa and Africans in the Making of the Atlantic World* (Cambridge: Cambridge University Press, 1998), p. 319. 26. See David Richardson, 'Slave exports from West and Central Africa, 1700–1810: new estimates of volume and

distribution', *Journal of African History* vol. 30 (1989), pp. 10–14. **27.** Phillipe Girard and Jean-Louis Donnadieu, 'Toussaint before Louverture: new archival findings on the early life of Toussaint Louverture', *William and Mary Quarterly* vol. 70, no. 1 (January 2013), p. 46. **28.** Dubois, *Avengers*, p. 42; see more generally Gérard Barthélémy, *Créoles–Bossales: conflit en Haïti* (Petit-Bourg, Guadeloupe: Ibis Rouge, 2000). **29.** Quoted in Debien, *Les esclaves aux Antilles françaises*, p. 321. **30.** 'Unhappy is the man who has negroes, and even more unhappy is the man who does not.' Regnaud de Beaumond to his mother, Saint-Marc, 6 April 1785, quoted in Gabriel Debien, 'À Saint-Domingue avec deux jeunes économes de plantation', *Revue de la société d'histoire et de géographie d'Haïti* vol. 16, no. 58 (July 1945), p. 61. **31.** Hilliard d'Auberteuil, *Considérations sur l'état présent de la colonie française de Saint-Domingue* (Paris, 1776), vol. 2, p. 68. **32.** Frantz Fanon, *The Wretched of the Earth* (London: Penguin, 2001), p. 32. **33.** Moreau de Saint-Méry, *Description topographique*, vol. 1, p. 29. **34.** The largest group were the Kongos. See David Geggus, 'Sex ratio, age and ethnicity in the Atlantic slave trade', *Journal of African History* vol. 30, no. 1 (1989); Debien, *Les esclaves aux Antilles françaises*, p. 48. **35.** Bernard Gainot, *La révolution des esclaves: Haïti, 1763–1803* (Paris: Vendémiaire, 2017), p. 50. **36.** Gragnon-Lacoste, *Toussaint Louverture*, pp. 3–4. **37.** See Baron Alexandre-Stanislas de Wimpffen, *Saint-Domingue à la veille de la Révolution* (Paris: L. Michaud, 1911), p. 90. **38.** Rachel Beauvoir Dominique, 'La valeur sociale du vaudou à travers l'histoire', *Museum International* vol. 62, no. 4 (2010), p. 108. **39.** On the general characteristics of Haitian *vodou* during the later eighteenth century see Michel Laguerre, *Voodoo and Politics in Haiti* (Houndmills and London: Palgrave Macmillan, 1989), pp. 32–3. **40.** Patrick Bellegarde-Smith, 'Resisting freedom: cultural factors in democracy: the case for Haiti', in Claudine Michel and Patrick Bellegarde-Smith (eds), *Vodou in Haitian Life and Culture* (New York: Palgrave Macmillan, 2006), p. 101. **41.** Robbie Shilliam, 'Race and revolution at Bwa Kayiman', *Millenium* vol. 45, no. 3 (2017), p. 280. **42.** Alfred Métraux, *Le vaudou haïtien* (Paris: Gallimard, 1958), p. 40. **43.** Stephen Alexis, *Black Liberator: The Life of Toussaint Louverture* (London: E. Benn, 1949), p. 12. **44.** For further discussion of these techniques see Karol Weaver, *Medical Revolutionaries: The Enslaved Healers of Eighteenth-Century Saint-Domingue* (Urbana and Chicago: University of Illinois Press, 2006), pp. 69–75. **45.** Saint-Rémy, *Vie de Toussaint*, p. 8. AN 18 AP 3, Papiers Bréda; letter of 3 February 1785. **46.** Isaac Louverture, *Notes sur la vie de Toussaint Louverture*, pp. 336–7. **47.** Isaac Louverture, *Notes historiques*. BNF NAF 12409. **48.** Toussaint, *Réfutation de quelques assertions d'un discours prononcé au Corps Législatif le 10 Prairial an cinq par Viénot Vaublanc*, Cap, 8 Brumaire an VI (29 October 1797), pp. 18–19. **49.** *Code Noir*, articles XI, XV, XXVIII and XXXI; for further discussion see Frédéric Régent, *La France et ses esclaves* (Paris: Grasset, 2007), pp. 66–87. **50.** de Wimpffen, *Saint-Domingue à la veille de la Révolution*, pp. 63–4, n.2; for a more detailed analysis of cruelty towards slaves in the colony see Fouchard, *Marrons de la liberté*, pp. 103–29. **51.** Geggus, 'Toussaint Louverture and the slaves of the Bréda plantations', pp. 36–7. **52.** Gragnon-Lacoste, *Toussaint Louverture*, pp. 6–7. **53.** Jacques de Cauna, 'La famille et la descendance de Toussaint Louverture', in J. de Cauna (ed.), *Toussaint Louverture et l'indépendance d'Haïti* (Paris: Karthala, 2004), p. 183. **54.** Vincent, *Notice sur Dominique Toussaint Louverture*. **55.** Ibid. **56.** Gragnon-Lacoste, *Toussaint Louverture*, pp. 14–15. **57.** See Jean-Louis Donnadieu, 'La famille oubliée de Toussaint Louverture', *Bulletin de la Société Archéologique et Historique du Gers* no. 401 (2011). **58.** Ibid., p. 359. **59.** Karen McCarthy Brown, 'Afro-Caribbean spirituality: a Haitian case study', in Michel and Bellegarde-Smith (eds), *Vodou in Haitian Life and Culture*, p. 6. **60.** François de Kerverseau, report to French government, 1 Germinal an IX (22 March 1801). ANOM CC9B 23. **61.** AN 18 AP 3, Papiers Bréda; correspondence of Bayon de Libertat. **62.** 'Toussaint Louverture', *Le Moniteur Universel*, 9 January 1799. **63.** See for example Schoelcher, *Vie de Toussaint Louverture*, p. 387. **64.** Toussaint to Directory, 30 Messidor an V (18 July 1797). AN F7 7321. **65.** His emancipation was an extraordinary individual accomplishment, especially considering that most manumissions in the late-colonial era were granted either to women or to men who had been on military service. Moreover, even the latter numbers declined sharply towards the end of the eighteenth century: in the year 1789, out of a regional population of over 190,000, only seven black males were freed in the whole of northern Saint-Domingue. See David Geggus, 'Saint-Domingue on the eve of the Haitian Revolution', in D. Geggus and N. Fiering (eds), *The World of the Haitian Revolution* (Bloomington: Indiana University Press, 2009), p. 9. **66.** Marie-Antoinette Menier, Gabriel Debien and Jean Fouchard, 'Toussaint Louverture avant 1789. Légendes et réalités', *Conjonction* no. 143 (1977). **67.** Lease agreement between Philippe-Jasmin Désir and Toussaint Bréda, Cap, 17 August 1779. ANOM G3 527. The agreement was cancelled, by mutual consent, in July 1781. **68.** AN 18 AP 3, Papiers Bréda. **69.** Jacques de Cauna and Jean-Louis Donnadieu, 'Quand le Comte de Noé écrit à Toussaint Louverture', *Outre-Mers. Revue d'Histoire* no. 358–9 (2008), p. 297. **70.** Girard and Donnadieu, 'Toussaint before Louverture', pp. 68–9. **71.** Isaac Louverture, *Notes historiques*. BNF NAF 6864. **72.** 'Toussaint Louverture, l'Aquitaine, et les Gascons', in de Cauna (ed.), *Toussaint Louverture et l'indépendance d'Haïti*, p. 190. **73.** Letter of Bayon descendant to Rose Louverture, 19 December 1878, cited in Alfred Nemours, 'Lieux et dates de la naissance et de la mort de Toussaint Louverture', in *Toussaint Louverture fonde à Saint-Domingue la liberté et l'égalité* (Port-au-Prince: Imprimerie du Collège Vertières, 1945), p. 13. **74.** AN 18 AP 3, Papiers Bréda; Bayon accounts for the year 1788. **75.** Debien, *Les esclaves aux Antilles françaises*, pp. 318–19. **76.** See table in Régent, *La France et ses esclaves*, p. 189. **77.** Gabriel Debien, 'A propos du trésor de Toussaint Louverture', *Revue de la société d'histoire et de géographie d'Haïti* vol.17, no. 62 (July 1946), p. 35. **78.** Sue Peabody, 'Négresse, mulâtresse, citoyenne: gender and emancipation in the French Caribbean', in Pamela Scully and Diana Paton (eds), *Gender and Slave Emancipation in the Atlantic World* (Durham, NC and London: Duke University Press, 2005), pp. 61–2. **79.** Register of slaves on Bréda plantation, December 1785, reproduced in Jean-Louis Donnadieu, 'Nouveaux documents sur la vie de Toussaint Louverture', *Bulletin de la Société d'Histoire de la Guadeloupe* vol. 166–7 (2013), p. 133. **80.** Ibid., p. 136. **81.** Ibid., p. 129. **82.** Ibid., p. 136. **83.** Guillaume-Thomas Raynal and Denis Diderot, *Histoire philosophique des Deux Indes* (Geneva, 1780 edn), vol. 1, p. 545. **84.** Michel-Rolph Trouillot, 'An unthinkable history: the Haitian Revolution as a non-event', in Sepinwall (ed.), *Haitian History*, p. 40. **85.** Louis Sala-Molins, *Dark Side of the Light: Slavery and the French Enlightenment* (Minneapolis: University of Minnesota Press, 2006), p. 124. **86.** Guillaume-Thomas Raynal, *Essai sur l'administration de Saint-Domingue* (Paris, 1785), pp. 14–15. **87.** Dantès Bellegarde, *Histoire du peuple Haïtien* (Port-au-Prince, 1953), p. 59. **88.** Fouchard, *Les marrons de la liberté*, p. 388. **89.** Moreau de Saint-Méry, *Description topographique*, vol. 1, p. 653. **90.** For a more sceptical view, which suggests that the whole Makandal 'conspiracy' was the product of the fervid paranoia of white planters, see Trevor Burnard and John Garrigus, *The Plantation Machine: Atlantic Capitalism in French Saint-Domingue and British Jamaica* (Philadelphia: University of Pennsylvania Press, 2016). **91.** On Makandal and his legend in Saint-Domingue during the second half of the eighteenth century see the third section in Pierre Pluchon, *Vaudou, sorciers, empoisonneurs. De Saint-Domingue à Haïti* (Paris: Karthala, 1987). **92.** Jason Daniels, 'Recovering the fugitive history of *marronage* in Saint-Domingue, 1770–1791', in *Journal of Caribbean History* vol. 46, no. 2 (2012), p. 131. **93.** Girard and Donnadieu, 'Toussaint before Louverture', pp. 64 and 66. **94.** Advertisement in *Affiches Américaines* newspaper, 7 April 1784, sourced in *Le marronage à Saint-Domingue*, http://www.marronnage.info/. **95.** December 1785 report cited in Donnadieu, 'Nouveaux documents sur la vie de Toussaint Louverture', p. 126; for further reports on *marronage* on the Bréda plantation in 1790 see Debien, *Les esclaves aux Antilles françaises*, p. 458. **96.** On the fusion of African ritual and Catholic practice in *vodou* see Métraux, *Le vaudou haïtien*, p. 288. **97.** 'respecté par les Africains comme une espèce de *Macanda* [*sic*]', emphasis in text. Kerverseau report to French government, 1 Germinal an IX (22 March 1801). ANOM CC9B 23. **98.** Frederick Douglass, 'Toussaint Louverture', undated MS. Frederick Douglass Papers, Library of Congress. **99.** Roger Dorsinville, *Toussaint Louverture ou la vocation de la liberté* (Paris: Julliard, 1965), p. 94. **100.** Toussaint speech in kreyol in southern Saint-Domingue, 1799, cited in Pélage-Marie Duboys, *Précis historique des Annales de la Révolution à Saint-Domingue*, vol. 2, p. 80. BNF NAF

14879. **101.** Bayon accounts, cited in Debien, *Les esclaves aux Antilles françaises*, p. 242. **102.** Gérard Barthélémy, 'Toussaint Louverture, noir libre', *Revue de la Société haïtienne d'histoire et de géographie* vol. 83, no. 236 (January–June 2009), pp. 23–78. **103.** Vincent, *Notice sur Dominique Toussaint Louverture*; this information almost certainly came from Pierre-Baptiste, whom Vincent met in 1801. **104.** Scott, *The Common Wind*, p. 28. **105.** Donnadieu, 'Nouveaux documents sur la vie de Toussaint Louverture', p. 127. **106.** Girard and Donnadieu, 'Toussaint before Louverture', p. 55. **107.** On the infamous case of 1788, in which the planter Nicolas Lejeune was acquitted of torture despite overwhelming evidence against him, see Malick Ghachem, 'Prosecuting torture: the strategic ethics of slavery in pre-revolutionary Saint-Domingue', *Law and History Review* vol. 29, no. 4 (November 2011). See also Ghachem's study of legal debates in late-colonial Saint-Domingue, *The Old Regime and the Haitian Revolution* (New York: Cambridge University Press, 2012). **108.** I am grateful to Robbie Shilliam for this insightful suggestion. **109.** Franklin Midy, 'L'exception Haïtienne', in Marcel Dorigny (ed.), *Haïti, première république noire*, special issue of *Outre-Mers. Revue d'histoire*, XC (2003), pp. 133 and 135. **110.** Charles Malenfant, *Des colonies et particulièrement de celle de Saint-Domingue* (Paris, 1814), pp. 93–4, n.1. **111.** Nemours, *Toussaint Louverture fonde à Saint-Domingue la liberté et l'égalité*, p. 19; Bellegarde-Smith, 'Resisting freedom', pp. 102–3.

2: THE GATES OF DESTINY

1. Toussaint, Camp Turel proclamation, 29 August 1793. AN AA 53. **2.** Dubois, *Avengers*, p. 176. **3.** Toussaint, Camp Turel proclamation. **4.** Testimony of Guillaume Moulinet, 24 December 1791. AN D/XXV/63, dossier 635. **5.** 'That fellow is making openings for himself everywhere!' Isaac Louverture, *Notes historiques*. BNF NAF 6864. **6.** 'Papa Legba, open the gate for me!' Cited in Ralph Korngold, *Citizen Toussaint* (London: Victor Gollancz, 1945), p. 86. **7.** Minutes of 8 April 1788 meeting, quoted in Jean-Pierre Barlier, *La Société des Amis des Noirs 1788–1791* (Paris: Éditions de l'Amandier, 2010), p. 94. **8.** For the study of one case see Elodie Lambert, 'L'intervention des habitants de Champagney pour l'abolition de l'esclavage des noirs dans leur cahier de doléances (1789)', *Bulletin de la Société d'Histoire de la Guadeloupe* no. 172 (September–December 2015). **9.** See Gabriel Debien, *Les colons de Saint-Domingue et la Révolution. Essai sur le Club Massiac* (Paris: A. Colin, 1953); and Déborah Liébart, 'Un groupe de pression contre-révolutionnaire: le club Massiac sous la Constituante', *Annales Historiques de la Révolution française* no. 354 (October–December 2008). **10.** Assemblée Nationale, *Décret du 15 mai 1791*, p. 4. AN D/XXV/3. **11.** Henri-Baptiste Grégoire, *Lettre aux citoyens de couleur et nègres libres* (Paris, 1791), p. 12. **12.** Raimond letter, quoted in Geggus, *The Haitian Revolution*, p. 44. **13.** David Geggus, *Slavery, War, and Revolution: The British Occupation of Saint-Domingue 1793–1798* (New York: Oxford University Press, 1982), pp. 34–5. **14.** Garran Coulon, *Rapport sur les troubles de Saint-Domingue, fait au nom de la Commission des Colonies*, vol. 1 (Paris, 1797), pp. 170–71. **15.** *Convocation de l'Assemblée coloniale* (Port-au-Prince, 1790), pp. 2–3. **16.** *Doutes proposés à l'Assemblée Nationale, par un membre de l'Assemblée générale de la partie française de Saint-Domingue* (Paris, 1790). **17.** Tanguy de la Boissière, *Réflexions impartiales d'un citoyen sur les affaires de Saint-Domingue* (Port-au-Prince, 1789). **18.** Petition of free coloureds to assembly of north province, 10 November 1789. Archives départementales de la Gironde 61 J 15. **19.** Schoelcher, *Vie de Toussaint Louverture*, p. 5; Dubois, *Avengers*, p. 64. **20.** Ogé message to assembly of north province, 29 October 1790, quoted in Geggus, *The Haitian Revolution*, p. 63. **21.** John Garrigus, 'Vincent Ogé "jeune" (1757–91): social class and free colored mobilisation on the eve of the Haitian Revolution', *The Americas* vol. 68, no. 1 (July 2011), p. 34. **22.** Letter from Henry, visiting captain of French ship, Cap, 27 September 1791. AN D/XXV/78. **23.** Scott, *The Common Wind*, pp. 111–17. **24.** Félix Carteaux, *Soirées bermudiennes* (Bordeaux, 1802), pp. 76–7. **25.** Cited in Fick, *The Making of Haiti*, p. 86. **26.** Wimpffen, *Saint-Domingue* *à la veille de la Révolution*, entry for July 1790, p. 186. **27.** See for example the testimony of the slave Antoine, January 1791, in Fick, *The Making of Haiti*, appendix C, pp. 267–9. **28.** François Barbé-Marbois report, 10 October 1789, quoted in Geggus, *The Haitian Revolution*, p. 76. **29.** 'Mon Odyssée', quoted in Jeremy Popkin, *Facing Racial Revolution: Eyewitness Accounts of the Haitian Insurrection* (Chicago: University of Chicago Press), p. 79. **30.** Hence the local expression 'heureux comme les esclaves à Gallifet'. **31.** Letter, 25 September 1791. AN D/XXV/78. **32.** Garran Coulon, *Rapport sur les troubles de Saint-Domingue*, vol. 2 (Paris, 1798), p. 214. **33.** Anon, 'La Révolution de Saint-Domingue', cited in Popkin, *Eyewitness Accounts*, pp. 50, 53. **34.** For further discussion see Kate Ramsey, *The Spirits and the Law: Vodou and Power in Haiti* (Chicago: University of Chicago Press, 2011), pp. 42–4. **35.** Fick, *The Making of Haiti*, p. 95; on the continuing resonance of Bois-Caïman in contemporary Haitian collective memory see Rachel Beauvoir-Dominique and Eddy Lubin, *Investigations autour du site historique du Bois-Caïman* (Cap-Haïtien: ISPAN, 2000). **36.** Schoelcher, *Vie de Toussaint Louverture*, p. 89. **37.** C. L. R. James, *The Black Jacobins: Toussaint L'Ouverture and the San Domingo Revolution* (New York: Vintage Books, 1989), p. 90. **38.** Sannon, *Histoire de Toussaint Louverture*, vol. 1, p. 9. **39.** See for example Roume, 'Précis historique de la Révolution de Saint-Domingue', Paris, 3 Brumaire an III (24 October 1794). AN D/XXV/3. **40.** Quoted in Beaubrun Ardouin, *Études sur l'histoire d'Haïti* (Paris, 1854), vol. 1, p. 228. **41.** Letter dated 15 April 1790, marked 'received 20 June'. ANOM CC9A 4 (correspondence of governors general, 1789–90). **42.** 'Certificate of Toussaint Louverture, general at Dondon', Dondon, 15 July 1793. Archivo General de Simancas (ARGS), Guerra Moderna 7157; quoted in Boromé, 'A finding list'. **43.** Toussaint to Rallier, 26 Germinal an VII (15 April 1799). National Archives, Kew, CO 245/2. **44.** Dubois, 'An enslaved Enlightenment', p. 11. **45.** On Lahaye see Chris Bongie, 'A flexible quill: Abbé de Lahaye's role in late colonial Saint-Domingue', *Atlantic Studies* vol. 15, no. 4 (2018), pp. 476–503. On the clergy's support for slave rebellion see more generally Laënnec Hurbon, 'Le clergé catholique et l'insurrection', in Laënnec Hurbon (ed.), *L'insurrection des esclaves de Saint-Domingue* (Paris: Karthala, 2000), p. 32; see also Chapter 1 in Erica R. Johnson, *Philanthropy and Race in the Haitian Revolution* (New York: Palgrave Macmillan, 2018). **46.** Kerverseau, report to French government, 1 Germinal an IX (22 March 1801). ANOM CC9B 23. **47.** Joubert, 'Renseignements sur la position actuelle du Limbé, et depuis le commencement de la Révolte', n.d. [late 1791]. AN D/XXV/78. **48.** Jacques de Cauna, 'Toussaint Louverture et le déclenchement de l'insurrection des esclaves du Nord en 1791', in Alain Yacou (ed.), *Saint-Domingue espagnol et la révolution nègre d'Haïti* (Paris: Karthala, 2007), pp. 152–3. **49.** See *Discours de M. de Cambefort, commandant particulier de la ville du Cap, à l'Assemblée provinciale du Nord, dans la séance du 10 Novembre 1791* (Cap, 1791). **50.** Fouchard, *Marrons de la liberté*, p. 532. **51.** Some historians maintain that these letters were written not by Toussaint but by Jeannot, which is possible but unlikely. **52.** See Antonio del Monte y Tejada, *Historia de Santo Domingo* (Santo Domingo, 1890), vol. 3, pp. 154–5. **53.** 'Lettre signée Médecin Général, datée de Grande-Rivière, 15 octobre 1791', in ibid., p. 155. **54.** Letter to the civil commissioners, 12 December 1791, signed by Generals Jean-François and Biassou and commissioners Manzau, Aubert and Toussaint. AN DXXV/1/1. **55.** Testimonies of René Guillemeton and René Cossait, 24 December 1791. AN D/XXV/63 (635). **56.** Gabriel Le Gros, *Récit historique sur les événemens qui se sont succédés dans les camps de la Grande-Rivière, du Dondon, de Sainte-Suzanne & autres, depuis le 26 octobre 1791, jusqu'au 24 décembre de la même année* (Paris, 1793), p. 7. **57.** Ibid., p. 17. **58.** Popkin, *Facing Racial Revolution*, p. 57. **59.** Gros, *Récit historique*, pp. 26–7. **60.** Testimonies of prisoners, 24 December 1791. AN D/XXV/63, dossier 635. **61.** Guy Lemarchand, 'A propos des révoltes et des révolutions de la fin du XVIIIe siècle', *Annales Historiques de la Révolution Française* no. 340 (April–June 2005), p. 164. **62.** Fick, *The Making of Haiti*, p. 162. **63.** 24 September proclamation, quoted in Geggus, *The Haitian Revolution*, p. 82. **64.** 'An end to the whites'. **65.** Gros, *Récit historique*, p. 17. **66.** Tousard letter, 27 November 1791, quoted in Geggus, *The Haitian Revolution*, p. 87. **67.** Dorigny, in Hurbon (ed.), *L'insurrection des esclaves de Saint-Domingue*, p. 108. **68.** For the full text of the *Lettre* see Nathalie

Piquionne, 'Lettre de Jean-François, Biassou et Belair', *Annales Historiques de la Révolution Française* no. 311 (1998), pp. 132–5. **69.** On the writings of Milscent more generally see Alexandra Tolin Schultz, 'The *Créole Patriote*: the journalism of Claude Milscent', *Atlantic Studies* vol. 11, no. 2 (2014). **70.** For example, Nathalie Piquionne, in 'Lettre de Jean-François, Biassou et Belair', p. 137. **71.** Biassou to Delahaye, *curé* of Dondon, n.d. [1792]. ANOM CC9A 7. **72.** See notably the correspondence of Biassou and Jean-François (1792–3). AN D/XXV/12. **73.** Not to be confused with Charles Bélair, Toussaint's nephew and a future general in the revolutionary army. **74.** See Bongie, 'A flexible quill', pp. 493–6. **75.** See Scott, *The Common Wind*, pp. xv–xvi. **76.** Piquionne, 'Lettre de Jean-François, Biassou et Belair'. **77.** Biassou convocation, 24 August 1792. AN D/XX/12. **78.** Letter from Matias de Armona to Governor García, 20 and 30 August 1793, quoted in Geggus, *The Haitian Revolution*, p. 110. **79.** Biassou to Delahaye, *curé* of Dondon, 28 October 1792. ANOM CC9A 7. **80.** See for example Biassou's proclamation 14 August 1793. AN D/XXV/12 (correspondence of Biassou and Jean-François). **81.** Testimonies of white prisoners, 24 December 1791; and interrogation of slave prisoner, 2 April 1792. AN D/XXV/63, dossier 635. **82.** Alain Yacou, 'La stratégie d'éradication de Saint-Domingue', in Yacou (ed.), *Saint-Domingue espagnol*, p. 180. **83.** Ibid., p. 141. **84.** Report of 3 January 1794, Santo Domingo. AGI, quoted in Gérard Laurent, *Trois mois aux archives d'Espagne* (Port-au-Prince: Imprimerie Les Presses Libres, 1956), p. 45. **85.** AGS, report dated 22 July 1793, Santo Domingo; quoted in Antonio Jesús Pinto Tortosa, *Santo Domingo: Una colonia en la encrucijada 1790–1820* (Madrid: FEHME, 2017), p. 85. **86.** Toussaint reply to French commander of western sector, Camp Bassin-Cayman, 25 June 1793. AN D/XXV/20. **87.** See for example the document dated 1 September 1793, awarding the commission of captain to Talamon. AN AA55/1511. **88.** Saint-Rémy, *Vie de Toussaint*, p. 85. **89.** Thomas Madiou, *Histoire d'Haïti* (Port-au-Prince: Imprimerie Courtois, 1847), vol. 1, p. 164. **90.** García to Toussaint, Bayaja, 16 February 1794. AGI, quoted in Laurent, *Trois mois aux archives d'Espagne*, p. 53. **91.** Sonthonax proclamation, Cap, 30 December 1792. **92.** Sonthonax article in *Révolutions de Paris* no. 63 (25 September 1790), quoted in Geggus, *The Haitian Revolution*, p. 102. **93.** The correspondence was denounced by Jean-François in a letter to the Spanish authorities, 17 September 1793. AGS, quoted in Tortosa, *Santo Domingo*, p. 88. **94.** Étienne Polverel, Jean-Antoine Ailhaud and Léger-Félicité Sonthonax, 'Proclamation au nom de la nation aux hommes libres de Saint-Domingue', Cap, 24 September 1792. **95.** For a detailed study of the events of 1793 see Jeremy Popkin, *You Are All Free: The Haitian Revolution and the Abolition of Slavery* (Cambridge: Cambridge University Press, 2010). **96.** James, *The Black Jacobins*, p. 124. **97.** Toussaint proclamation, 8 August 1793. AN AA55/1511. **98.** One such meeting, arranged for 10 August, was mentioned in a 1793 letter by the republican officer Antoine Chanlatte, cited by Gérard Laurent, *Erreurs et vérités dans l'histoire d'Haïti* (Port-au-Prince: Imprimerie Tehomme, 1945), p. 364. **99.** Toussaint proclamation, 25 August 1793. AN AEII 1375. **100.** See Georges Corvington, *Port-au-Prince au cours des ans*, vol. 2 (Port-au-Prince: Imprimerie Henri Deschamps, 1992), p. 150. The British occupation will be discussed in greater detail in Chapter 3. **101.** Tortosa, *Santo Domingo*, p. 92. **102.** Isaac Louverture, *Notes historiques*. BNF NAF 12409. **103.** Toussaint to Don García, 20 March 1794, cited in Ardouin, *Études sur l'histoire d'Haïti*, vol. 2, p. 420. **104.** Toussaint to Don García, 27 March 1794, cited in ibid., vol. 2, pp. 423–6. **105.** Ibid. In his *Notes historiques*, Isaac Louverture observes: 'Biassou had stained the cause for which he was fighting by selling blacks to the Spaniards.' BNF NAF 12409. **106.** See Carlos Esteban Deive, *Los refugiados franceses en Santo Domingo* (Santo Domingo: Universidad Nacional Pedro Henríquez Ureña, 1984), pp. 110–19. **107.** Letter of Laplace to Don García, Fort-Dauphin, 4 April 1794. BNF NAF 12102. **108.** Memorandum signed by Biassou, Jean-François and Toussaint, Saint-Raphaël, 16 November 1793. AGI, quoted in Laurent, *Trois mois aux archives d'Espagne*, pp. 46–7. **109.** Toussaint letters of 20 and 27 March 1794, quoted in Ardouin, *Études sur l'histoire d'Haïti*, vol. 2, pp. 422 and 426. **110.** Ibid., p. 425. **111.** See David Geggus, 'From his most Catholic Majesty to the godless Republic: the "volte-face" of Toussaint Louverture and the ending of slavery in Saint-Domingue', *Outre-Mers. Revue d'histoire* no. 241 (1978), pp. 481–99. 112. Ibid., appendix. 113. See the 1795 dossier, in which Lleonart justified his conduct over the losses of Spanish-controlled territories to Toussaint. Archivo General de Simancas, SGU, LEG, 6855, 51. 114. See the chapter (based on Spanish archival sources) by Carlos Esteban Deive, 'Les débuts de la révolution nègre: Toussaint Louverture change de camp, d'après des documents inédits', in Yacou (ed.), *Saint-Domingue espagnol*, pp. 187–201. 115. García letter, 6 August 1796, quoted in Tortosa, *Santo Domingo*, p. 116. 116. Report of local French officer to Laveaux, Plaisance, 10 August 1793. BNF NAF 12012. 117. See full report by Laveaux on this early 1793 campaign, April 1793. AN D/XXV/50, correspondence Laveaux. 118. Laurent, *Erreurs et vérités dans l'histoire d'Haïti*, p. 364. 119. Toussaint to Laveaux, 18 May 1794. BNF NAF 12102. 120. Toussaint to Laveaux, 7 July 1794. BNF NAF 12102. 121. 'Mauvais sujets'. Laveaux report to Convention, Port-de-Paix, 1 Vendémiaire an III (22 September 1794). ANOM CC9A 9. 122. Laveaux report, Port-de-Paix, 25 March 1795. ANOM CC9A 10.

3: BRAVE REPUBLICAN WARRIORS

1. Toussaint letter to military chiefs of Petite-Rivière, 29 Nivôse an III (18 January 1795). BNF NAF 12103. 2. Michael Duffy, 'World-wide war, 1793–1815', in P. J. Marshall (ed.), *The Oxford History of the British Empire*, vol. 2 (Oxford: Oxford University Press, 1998), p. 186. 3. 'My Odyssey', quoted in Popkin, *Facing Racial Revolution*, p. 266. 4. Geggus, *Slavery, War, and Revolution*, p. 68. 5. Toussaint to Laveaux, 31 January 1795, in Toussaint Louverture, *Lettres à la France* (Bruyères-le-Châtel: Nouvelle Cité, 2011); this is a published version of the Toussaint correspondence with Laveaux which forms an important part of the BNF NAF 12102-12103-12104 documents, and all the letters to Laveaux cited in this chapter and the next refer to this edition. 6. The exact date of the transfer was not specified, and Santo Domingo remained under Spanish control until 1801, when Toussaint's army invaded the territory. See Chapter 8. 7. Adolphe Thiers, *Histoire du Consulat et de l'Empire* (Paris, 1865), vol. 4, p. 173. For similarly dismissive views see Pluchon, *Toussaint Louverture*, p. 563. 8. Fick, *The Making of Haiti*. 9. Karma Nabulsi, *Traditions of War: Occupation, Resistance, and the Law* (Oxford: Oxford University Press, 1999). 10. Letter of Toussaint to Generals Beauvais and Laplume, 29 Floréal an VI (2 June 1798). ANOM CC9A 19. 11. Laveaux report to Marine and Colonial Commission of Convention Nationale, 25 March 1795. ANOM CC9A 10. 12. Toussaint to Laveaux, 20 October 1795. 13. Toussaint to Laveaux, 18 March 1796. 14. Bernard Gainot, 'Le général Laveaux, gouverneur de Saint-Domingue, député néo-jacobin', *Annales Historiques de la Révolution Française* no. 278 (1989), pp. 436 and 452. 15. Laveaux report, 1794. ANOM CC9A 8, correspondance du général Laveaux. 16. See Carolyn Fick, 'The Haitian Revolution and the limits of freedom', *Social History* vol. 32, no. 4 (November 2007), p. 400. 17. Laveaux report, 6 February 1794. ANOM CC9A 8. 18. Toussaint to Laveaux, 31 August 1796. 19. Laveaux letter, 9 September 1795, in Girard Papers, American Philosophical Society, Philadelphia, quoted in White, *Encountering Revolution*, p. 148. 20. Undated Toussaint letter to Laveaux (probably late 1798 or early 1799). BNF NAF 12104, f. 417. 21. Toussaint proclamation, 18 February 1795. BNF NAF 12103. 22. The 'Carmagnole' was sung by French republican armies as a rallying cry; it was also intoned to mock those who supported the monarchy. 23. Vincent, *Notice sur Dominique Toussaint Louverture*. 24. Saint-Anthoine, *Notice sur Toussaint Louverture*, pp. 26–7 and 30. 25. Michel and Bellegarde-Smith (eds), *Vodou in Haitian Life and Culture*, p. 205. 26. Laguerre, *Voodoo and Politics in Haiti*, p. 65. 27. Thomas Madiou, *Histoire d'Haïti* (Port-au-Prince, 1847), vol. 1, p. 199; see also Toussaint to Laveaux, 21 October 1794. 28. Toussaint to Laveaux, 6 August 1795. 29. Toussaint to Laveaux, 7 July 1794. 30. Madiou, *Histoire d'Haïti*, p. 211. 31. Ibid. 32. Isaac Louverture, *Notes historiques*. BNF NAF 12409. 33. Toussaint to Laveaux, 30 September 1795. 34. Madiou, *Histoire d'Haïti*, p. 210. 35. Toussaint to Laveaux, 5 December 1795. 36. Letter of French commissioner Sonthonax to Toussaint, Cap, 24 Floréal an V (13 May 1797). BNF NAF 8987, Papiers Sonthonax. 37. Letter to

General Pierre Michel, 13 July 1796. BNF NAF 12103. **38.** Madiou, *Histoire d'Haïti*, p. 202; Isaac Louverture, *Réfutation des assertions avancées dans l'Histoire du Consulat et de l'Empire par M. Thiers, concernant le général Toussaint Louverture, par Isaac Louverture*, Bordeaux, 18 August 1845. BNF NAF 6864. **39.** Toussaint to Laveaux, 17 August 1796. **40.** Toussaint report, 26 Nivôse an VII (15 January 1799). National Archives, Kew, CO 245/2. **41.** Madiou, *Histoire d'Haïti*, p. 279. **42.** Toussaint to Laveaux, 31 August 1794. **43.** Isaac Louverture, *Notes historiques*. BNF NAF 12409. **44.** Marcus Rainsford, *An Historical Account of the Black Empire of Hayti* (London, 1805), p. 244. **45.** Toussaint to Laveaux, 14 August 1794. **46.** Toussaint to Laveaux, 30 September 1795. **47.** Rainsford, *An Historical Account*, p. 283. **48.** Ibid., p. 218. **49.** Fick, *The Making of Haiti*, p. 111. **50.** Toussaint to Laveaux, 4 October 1794; Madiou, *Histoire d'Haïti*, pp. 200–201; Geggus, *Slavery, War, and Revolution*, p. 128. Brisbane was shot in the neck during a cavalry charge by Toussaint in February of the following year and died from his wound. **51.** Toussaint to Laveaux, 25 January 1795. **52.** Toussaint to Laveaux, 19 January 1796. **53.** Toussaint to Generals Beauvais and Laplume, 8 Pluviôse an VI (27 January 1798). ANOM CC9A 19. **54.** Toussaint to Laveaux, 19 July 1794. **55.** *The Haitian Journal of Lieutenant Howard* (Knoxville: University of Tennessee Press, 1985), p. 39. **56.** Ibid., p. 59. **57.** Henry de Poyen-Bellisle, *Histoire militaire de la révolution de Saint-Domingue* (Paris, 1899), p. 54. **58.** Toussaint to Laveaux, 14 September 1795. **59.** Howard, p. 60. **60.** M. Grouvel, *Faits historiques sur Saint-Domingue* (Paris, 1814), pp. 93, 97–8. **61.** Howard, p. 81. **62.** Toussaint gave a list of the territories he captured for the republic from 1794 onwards in his letter to Rallier, 26 Germinal an VII (15 April 1799). National Archives, Kew, CO 245/2. **63.** Geggus, *Slavery, War, and Revolution*, p. 157. **64.** Toussaint to Laveaux, 13 August 1796. **65.** 'Procès-verbal de l'expédition du général divisionnaire Toussaint Louverture sur le Mirebalais et sa dépendance', 20 Germinal an V (9 April 1797). Archives Départementales de la Gironde, Collection Marcel Chatillon, 61 J 18. **66.** Ibid. **67.** Toussaint proclamation, Mirebalais, 22 Germinal an V (11 April 1797). ANOM CC9A 12. **68.** Madiou, *Histoire d'Haïti*, p. 279. **69.** 'Procès-verbal de l'expédition du général divisionnaire Toussaint Louverture sur le Mirebalais et sa dépendance'. **70.** 'Nus comme des vers de terre'. Toussaint to Laveaux, 5 and 7 December 1795. **71.** Petition of officers of the 5th regiment to Toussaint, 31 January 1796. BNF NAF 12104. **72.** Letter from Dubuisson, commander of Fort Louverture, to Toussaint, 18 April 1796. BNF NAF 12104. **73.** Toussaint to Laveaux, 7 July 1796. **74.** Toussaint report, Port-de-Paix, 9 Ventôse an V (27 February 1797). ANOM CC9A 12. **75.** Toussaint military report, 1 July 1798. ANOM CC9A 23. **76.** Toussaint to Hédouville, 9 August 1798. ANOM CC9A 23. **77.** This complaint is mentioned in a letter from Sonthonax to Toussaint, 15 Brumaire an V (5 November 1796). BNF NAF 8986, Papiers Sonthonax. **78.** Toussaint to Laveaux, 18 May 1794; 4 October 1794; and 24 April 1796. **79.** Toussaint to Laveaux, 5 February 1795 and 18 July 1796. **80.** Toussaint to Laveaux, 23 December 1795. **81.** Toussaint to Generals Beauvais and Laplume, 29 Floréal an VI (2 June 1798). ANOM CC9A 19. **82.** Madiou, *Histoire d'Haïti*, p. 212. **83.** Geggus, *Slavery, War, and Revolution*, pp. 224 and 318. **84.** Toussaint, 'Procès-verbal de la campagne ouverte le 13 Pluviôse an VI contre les ennemis de la République', 29 Floréal an VI (18 May 1798). ANOM CC9A 19. **85.** Toussaint to Laveaux, 9 December 1794. **86.** Toussaint to Laveaux, 15 October 1795. **87.** 'Réponse à l'adresse faite par Jean-François à ses soi-disants frères du Dondon', 13 June 1795. BNF NAF 12103. **88.** Pamphile de Lacroix, *La Révolution de Haïti* (Paris: Karthala, 1995), p. 214. **89.** Toussaint report to Minister of Navy, 4 Germinal an VII (24 March 1799). National Archives, Kew, CO 245/2. **90.** 'Procès-verbal de l'expédition du général divisionnaire Toussaint Louverture sur le Mirebalais et sa dépendance'. **91.** For an account of one such operation see Dessalines' letter to Toussaint, 11 May 1796. BNF NAF 12103. **92.** See for example the report by Toussaint on Dessalines' intervention in Petite-Rivière, 13 Germinal an VII (2 April 1799). National Archives, Kew, CO 245/2. **93.** Jacques de Cauna, 'L'entourage, la famille, et la descendance', in de Cauna (ed.), *Toussaint Louverture et l'indépendance d'Haïti*, pp. 183–6. **94.** Isaac Louverture, *Notes historiques sur Toussaint Louverture*. BNF NAF 12409. **95.** See Claude B. Auguste, 'Les Congos dans la Révolution Haïtienne', *Revue de la Société* *haïtienne d'histoire et de géographie* vol. 46, no. 168 (December 1990). **96.** On the Dieudonné incident see Toussaint to Laveaux, 24 February 1796. **97.** Isaac Louverture, *Notes historiques sur Toussaint Louverture*. BNF NAF 12409. **98.** 'une morale véhémente', 9 December 1794. **99.** Vincent, *Notice sur Dominique Toussaint Louverture*. **100.** Petition to Toussaint by second battalion of 141st half-brigade (1798). ANOM CC9A 18. **101.** Toussaint to Generals Beauvais and Laplume, 8 Pluviôse an VI (27 January 1798). ANOM CC9A 19. **102.** Toussaint, 'Ordre de marche donné au général Dessalines', Petite-Rivière, 15 Pluviôse an VI (3 February 1798). ANOM CC9A 19. **103.** Toussaint to Christophe, Camp Maugé, 28 Pluviôse an VI (16 February 1798). Boromé, 'A finding list', p. 100. **104.** 'Ordre de marche donné au général Dessalines'. **105.** 'S'amuser à tirailler', ibid. **106.** Toussaint letter of defence of Captain Mayandon, 24 Frimaire an VI (14 December 1797). Rochambeau Papers, University of Florida. **107.** Toussaint to military chiefs of Petite-Rivière, 29 Nivôse an III (18 January 1795). BNF NAF 12103. **108.** Toussaint, 'Adresse aux officiers, sous-officiers, et soldats composant l'armée en marche', 4 Pluviôse an VI (23 January 1798). ANOM CC9A 19. **109.** Vincent, *Notice sur Dominique Toussaint Louverture*. **110.** Toussaint, 'Procès-verbal de la campagne ouverte le 13 Pluviôse an VI contre les ennemis de la République'. **111.** Toussaint to Hédouville, 6 Floréal an VI (25 April 1798). ANOM CC9A 23. **112.** Toussaint, 'Adresse aux officiers'. **113.** Ibid. **114.** Toussaint to Morin, 28 Germinal an III (17 April 1795), cited in *Mémoires du citoyen Morin, commandant militaire au quartier des Verrettes* (Port-de-Paix, n.d.), p. 23. **115.** Toussaint, 'Adresse aux généraux de brigade et aux chefs des colonnes', 24 Ventôse an VI (14 March 1798). ANOM CC9A 19. **116.** Toussaint, 'Adresse aux officiers'. **117.** Schoelcher, *Vie de Toussaint Louverture*, p. 391. **118.** Isaac Louverture, *Notes historiques sur Toussaint Louverture*. BNF NAF 12409. **119.** Madiou, *Histoire d'Haïti*, p. 236; this episode will be further discussed at the beginning of Chapter 4. **120.** See Toussaint letter to Huin, 13 Floréal an VI (2 May 1798). ANOM CC9A 18. **121.** Toussaint to Hédouville, Port-Républicain, 17 Floréal an VI (6 May 1798). ANOM CC9A 23. **122.** Speech by the mayor of Saint-Marc, 20 Floréal an VI (9 May 1798). ANOM CC9A 19. **123.** BNF NAF 14878, cited in Geggus, *The Haitian Revolution*, p. 133. **124.** Corvington, *Port-au-Prince au cours des ans*, vol. 2, pp. 143–4. **125.** Toussaint to Laveaux, 21 October 1794. **126.** Toussaint to Laveaux, 30 September 1795. **127.** Toussaint to Laveaux, 14 July 1795. **128.** Letter of Cordon commander to Toussaint, 15 September 1795. BNF NAF 12103. **129.** Report, Santo Domingo, 29 August 1796. AGI, cited in Tortosa, *Santo Domingo*, pp. 143–4. **130.** Toussaint proclamation, 25 Pluviôse an VI (13 February 1798). ANOM CC9A 19. **131.** Toussaint report, 9 Prairial an V (28 May 1797). ANOM CC9A 13. **132.** See for example the local British military reports for the early months of 1798. National Archives, Kew, WO 1/68 and WO 1/69. **133.** Madiou, *Histoire d'Haïti*, p. 279. **134.** Toussaint to Laveaux, 14 September 1795. **135.** Isaac Louverture, *Notes historiques sur Toussaint Louverture*. BNF NAF 12409. **136.** Rainsford, *An Historical Account*, pp. 248–9. **137.** Letter of British prisoner-of-war commissioner to Toussaint, 7 November 1795. BNF NAF 12103. **138.** On black prisoners see Toussaint letter to Whyte, 13 Germinal an VI (2 April 1798), ANOM CC9A 18; also the exchange of letters between Toussaint and Maitland, 29 Prairial an VI (17 June 1798), ANOM CC9A 23. **139.** Toussaint, 'Procès-verbal de la campagne ouverte le 13 Pluviôse an VI contre les ennemis de la République'. **140.** Lettre s.d. de Jean-Baptiste Lapointe, commandant pour sa majesté britannique aux Arcahayes, trouvée lors de la prise du camp Dubourg. ANOM CC9A 19. **141.** On Lapointe's career see Placide David, 'Un terroriste: Jean-Baptiste Lapointe', in *Sur les rives du passé* (Montreal: Éditions Leméac, 1972), pp. 155–80. **142.** Toussaint to John Whyte, n.d. ANOM CC9A 19. **143.** Roume to Minister of Navy, Santo Domingo, 2 Frimaire an VII (22 November 1798). ANOM CC9A 18. **144.** Sannon, *Histoire de Toussaint Louverture*, vol. 2, pp. 60–61. **145.** 'Morin, chef de brigade, au Directoire Exécutif, Paris', 28 Nivôse an VII (17 January 1799). ANOM CC9A 23. **146.** On the work of these military hospitals see 'Précis des services de Joseph Antoine Idlinger, commissaire ordonnateur à Saint-Domingue'. Archives de la Seine, Paris, DQ10-1418, dossier Joseph Idlinger. **147.** Toussaint to Flaville, 26 June 1795. BNF NAF 12103. **148.** Toussaint to Laveaux, 19 July 1794. **149.** 'honnête homme'. Toussaint address to the population of Arcahaie, 22 Ventôse an VI (12 March 1798). ANOM CC9A 19. 150. Toussaint to Laveaux, 4 October 1794. 151. Isaac Louverture, *Réfutation*. 152. Toussaint to Laveaux, 7 July 1795. 153. Saint-Rémy, *Vie de Toussaint Louverture*, p. 187, fn.1. 154. Laveaux, 'Résumé des observations et réflexions sur la colonie', 1 Vendémiaire an III (22 September 1794). ANOM CC9A 9. 155. In a letter dated 23 May 1796, the French Assembly member Dufay wrote to Laveaux: 'I fully support your view that we need to have an *imposing* force of European troops in Saint-Domingue'; emphasis in text. 156. 'Les officiers et les soldats de l'armée sous les ordres de Toussaint Louverture, général de brigade des armées de la République, à la Convention Nationale'. Cordon de l'Ouest, Saint-Domingue, 14 Frimaire an IV (5 December 1795). ANOM CC9A 12. 157. 'you whites cannot wage war against the blacks'; cited in Charles Malenfant, 'Observations sur Saint-Domingue', 23 Pluviôse an VI (11 February 1798). ANOM CC9A 19. 158. Toussaint to Hédouville, 22 Germinal an VI (11 April 1798). ANOM CC9A 23. 159. Toussaint, 'Procès-verbal de la campagne ouverte le 13 Pluviôse an VI contre les ennemis de la République'. 160. Ibid. 161. Vincent, *Notice sur Dominique Toussaint Louverture*. 162. Toussaint, 'Procès-verbal de la campagne ouverte le 13 Pluviôse an VI contre les ennemis de la République'.

4: A SINGLE FAMILY OF FRIENDS AND BROTHERS

1. Laveaux report to Minister of Navy, Cap, 8 Thermidor an IV (26 July 1796). ANOM CC9A 12. 2. Quoted in Schoelcher, *Vie de Toussaint Louverture*, p. 172. 3. Pamphile de Lacroix, *La Révolution de Haïti*, p. 194. 4. Madiou, *Histoire d'Haïti*, p. 237. 5. James, *The Black Jacobins*, p. 173. 6. Michel-Étienne Descourtilz, *Voyages d'un naturaliste* (Paris, 1809), vol. 3, p. 246. 7. Henry Perroud, *Précis des derniers troubles qui ont eu lieu dans la partie du nord de Saint-Domingue* (Cap-Français, 1796). 8. Toussaint to Vincent, 30 Vendémiaire an VI (21 October 1797). Archives of Smithsonian Museum of African American History and Culture, Washington DC. 9. Toussaint to Vincent, Port-de-Paix, 29 Thermidor an VII (16 August 1799). Lettres inédites de Toussaint Louverture, Archives Diplomatiques Paris-La Courneuve, 23MD/2 (mémoires et documents, Haïti). 10. Toussaint to Laveaux, Gonaïves, 23 May 1797. BNF NAF 12104. 11. Madiou, *Histoire d'Haïti*, pp. 193–4. 12. On Rigaud's praise for his 'brave and intrepid friend' Villatte see Rigaud letter to Laveaux, Les Cayes, 20 Thermidor an II (7 August 1794). AN AFIII 209. 13. Madiou, *Histoire d'Haïti*, pp. 76–7. 14. 'Slippery customer'. 15. Toussaint to Laveaux, 21 April 1796. 16. Juste Chanlatte, *Réflexions politiques sur les troubles et la situation de la partie françoise de Saint-Domingue* (Paris, 1792), p. 17. 17. Vincent, *Notice sur Dominique Toussaint Louverture*. 18. See for example 'Rapport au Directoire Exécutif', Paris, 30 Thermidor an IV (17 August 1796). ANOM CC9A 12. 19. Toussaint to Laveaux, 4 October 1794. 20. Toussaint to Laveaux, 25 January 1795. 21. Toussaint to Laveaux, 31 January 1795. 22. Toussaint to Laveaux, 6 February 1795. 23. Toussaint to Laveaux, 14 April 1796. 24. Toussaint to Laveaux, 5 June 1796. 25. Toussaint to Laveaux, 12 March 1796. 26. Toussaint proclamation to citizens of Gros-Morne, 30 Germinal an IV (19 April 1796). *Courrier Français*, 19 July 1796. 27. Laveaux report to Minister of Navy, Cap, 24 Pluviôse an IV (13 February 1796). ANOM CC9A 11. 28. Ibid. 29. Schoelcher, *Vie de Toussaint Louverture*, p. 172. 30. Toussaint to Laveaux, 5 December 1795. 31. Toussaint to Laveaux, 7 July 1795. 32. Toussaint to Laveaux, 21 July 1795. 33. Toussaint to Laveaux, 4 October 1794. A *portugaise* was a half-ounce of gold; it was worth eight *gourdes*. 34. Toussaint to Laveaux, 15 January 1796. 35. Toussaint to Laveaux, 11 May 1796. 36. Toussaint to Laveaux, 25 Pluviôse an IV (14 February 1796). Archives Départementales de la Gironde, Collection Marcel Chatillon, 61 J 18. 37. Toussaint, 'Rapport sur le rétablissement de l'ordre dans la montagne du Port-de-Paix', Vendémiaire–Brumaire an V (September–October 1796). ANOM CC9A 13. 38. Raimond report to Minister of Navy, 18 Brumaire an V (8 November 1796). ANOM CC9A 12. 39. 'He who has to walk barefoot must check that there are no thorns on the road.' Quoted in Vincent, *Notice sur Dominique Toussaint Louverture*. 40. Toussaint to Laveaux, 10 July

1795. **41.** Toussaint to Dieudonné, 12 February 1796. BNF NAF 12104. **42.** Toussaint to Laveaux, 5 April 1796. **43.** Quoted in Delatte, 'Mémoire sur les évènements de Fort-Liberté', 16 Frimaire an VII (6 December 1798). ANOM CC9A 22. **44.** Toussaint to Laveaux, 20 February 1796. BNF NAF 12104. **45.** Ibid. **46.** Toussaint to Laveaux, 6 February and 31 October 1795. **47.** Toussaint to Laveaux, 26 June 1795. **48.** Toussaint to Laveaux, 15 April 1796. **49.** Toussaint to Laveaux, 19 April 1796. **50.** Toussaint to Laveaux, 17 June 1795. **51.** Madiou, *Histoire d'Haïti*, p. 181. **52.** See for example Pluchon, *Vaudou*, pp. 138–9. **53.** 'Hear reason'. See for example Toussaint to Laveaux, 15 June 1794 and 10 August 1794. **54.** Toussaint to Laveaux, 6 March 1796. **55.** Toussaint proclamation, Gonaïves, 10 Fructidor an IV (27 August 1796). Library of Congress, Toussaint Louverture Papers. **56.** Toussaint to Laveaux, 6 March 1796. **57.** Toussaint to Laveaux, 21 July 1795. **58.** Toussaint to Laveaux, 14 September 1795. **59.** Toussaint to Laveaux, 22 February 1796. **60.** Dubois, *Avengers*, pp. 201–2. **61.** Thornton, *Africa and Africans*, pp. 207, 208 and 213. **62.** Toussaint proclamation of 25 April 1796, cited in Schoelcher, *Vie de Toussaint Louverture*, p. 175. **63.** The Conseil des Cinq Cents was established in the wake of the constitution of an III, and was first convened in October 1795. It was dissolved in 1799 after the *coup d'état* of 18 Brumaire. **64.** Toussaint to Laveaux, 17 August 1796. BNF NAF 12103. **65.** On Laveaux's departure and his role in the French Assembly see Gainot, 'Le général Laveaux', pp. 444–5. **66.** Marcel Dorigny and Bernard Gainot, *La Société des Amis des Noirs 1788–1799* (Paris: EDICEF, 1998), pp. 317–19. **67.** In a letter to Domergue jeune, shortly after his return to the colony, Sonthonax referred to himself as the 'founder of liberty in Saint-Domingue'; letter of 19 Prairial an IV (7 June 1796). BNF NAF 8986, Papiers Sonthonax. **68.** Letter of 20 June 1796, quoted in Robert Louis Stein, *Léger Félicité Sonthonax: The Lost Sentinel of the Republic* (Cranbury, NJ: Fairleigh Dickinson University Press,1985), p. 138. **69.** Toussaint to Directory, 13 Pluviôse an V (1 February 1797). AN AFIII 210. **70.** See Sonthonax to Toussaint, 13 Messidor an IV (trumpet, 1 July 1796), and his thanks to Toussaint for the horse, 7 Pluviôse an V (26 January 1797). BNF NAF 8986 and 8987, Papiers Sonthonax. **71.** Letter of 14 June 1796, Stein, *Léger Félicité Sonthonax*, p. 159. **72.** Sonthonax report to Minister of Navy, 26 Floréal an V (15 May 1797). ANOM CC9A 13. **73.** Sonthonax to Toussaint, 11 and 29 Brumaire an V (1 and 19 November 1796). BNF NAF 8986, Papiers Sonthonax. **74.** Toussaint to Sonthonax, n.d. BNF NAF 12104. Sonthonax to Toussaint, 24 Prairial an IV (12 June 1796), and to Madame Louverture, 19 Messidor an IV (7 July 1796). BNF NAF 8986, Papiers Sonthonax. **75.** See Michel Roussier, 'L'Éducation en France des enfants de Toussaint Louverture', *Revue Française d'Histoire d'Outre-Mer* no. 236 (1977), pp. 308–49. **76.** Stein, *Léger Félicité Sonthonax*, p. 129. **77.** Toussaint to Laveaux, 5 June 1798. **78.** 'sa bouche n'a pas de dimanche'. **79.** Toussaint to Chanlatte, 27 August 1793. ANOM CC9A 8. **80.** Sonthonax to Directory, 8 Pluviôse an VI (27 January 1798). AN AFIII 210. **81.** Quoted in François de Kerverseau, report to French government, 1 Germinal an IX (22 March 1801). ANOM CC9B 23. **82.** Sonthonax to Toussaint, Cap, 27 Floréal an V (16 May 1797). BNF NAF 8987, Papiers Sonthonax. **83.** Sonthonax to Toussaint, 14 Fructidor an IV (31 August 1796). BNF NAF 8986, Papiers Sonthonax. **84.** Vincent, *Notice sur Dominique Toussaint Louverture.* **85.** Toussaint to Philippe-André-Joseph Létombe, French consul-general, Cap, 9 Nivôse an VI (29 December 1797). French Ministry of Foreign Affairs archives. **86.** Toussaint to Directory, 30 Messidor an V (18 July 1797). AN F7 7321, dossier B4/5915. **87.** See decree of Saint-Domingue commissioners, Cap, 28 Brumaire an V (18 November 1796); it noted that he had arrived in the colony and was 'gravement prévenu d'émigration', and ordered his immediate arrest and deportation to France to face criminal charges. BNF NAF 6847, Papiers Sonthonax. **88.** Sonthonax to Toussaint, 7 Frimaire an V (27 November 1796). BNF NAF 8986, Papiers Sonthonax. **89.** Sonthonax to Toussaint, 6 Floréal and 16 Messidor an V (25 April and 4 July 1797). BNF NAF 8987 and 8988, Papiers Sonthonax; see also François Bléchet, 'La seconde mission de Sonthonax à Saint-Domingue', *Revue Française d'Histoire d'Outre-Mer* vol. 84, no. 316 (1997), p. 82. **90.** Vincent, *Notice sur Dominique Toussaint Louverture.* **91.** Citoyen B*** (François Marie Bottu), *La liberté générale ou les colons à Paris* (Cap, 1796). **92.** Madiou, *Histoire d'Haïti*,

p. 250. **93.** See for example Toussaint's exchanges with Sonthonax about who was in overall charge of military operations, in Sonthonax letter to Toussaint, 21 Messidor an IV (9 July 1796). BNF FR 8986, Papiers Sonthonax. **94.** Sonthonax to Toussaint, 6 Messidor an IV (24 June 1796). BNF NAF 8986, Papiers Sonthonax. **95.** Sonthonax to Toussaint, 3 and 7 Thermidor an V (21 and 25 July 1797). BNF NAF 8988, Papiers Sonthonax. **96.** Sonthonax to Toussaint, 22 Fructidor an IV (8 September 1796). BNF NAF 8986, Papiers Sonthonax. **97.** Moyse wrote that Sonthonax's departure would provoke 'disunity among the people', 19 Floréal an V (8 May 1797). AN D XXV/13. **98.** Proclamation of municipality of Gonaïves, 25 Floréal an V (14 May 1797). BNF NAF 6847, Papiers Sonthonax. **99.** Télémaque to Sonthonax, Cap, 4 Fructidor an V (21 August 1797). BNF NAF 6846, Papiers Sonthonax. **100.** Gérard Laurent, *Le Commissaire Sonthonax à Saint-Domingue* (Port-au-Prince: La Phalange, 1965), vol. 2, p. 148. **101.** Toussaint to Sonthonax, 3 Fructidor an V (20 August 1797). AN AFIII 210. **102.** Extraordinary session of Cap municipality, 19 Floréal an V (8 May 1797). BNF NAF 6847, Papiers Sonthonax. **103.** Toussaint, 'Aux citoyens composant l'administration municipale de la ville du Cap', 5 Fructidor an V (22 August 1797). AN AFIII 210. **104.** Toussaint to Julien Raimond, Petite Anse, 3 Fructidor an V (20 August 1797). ANOM CC9A 14. See also Julien Raimond reports to Directory, 18 Fructidor an V (ANOM CC9A 14) and 24 Fructidor an V (4 and 10 September 1797). AN AFIII 210. **105.** Proclamation addressed to Sonthonax by Toussaint and his military staff, 3 Fructidor an V (20 August 1797). Service Historique de la Défense, Vincennes, B7 carton 1, correspondance Toussaint Louverture. **106.** Toussaint to Maurepas, Petite Anse, 8 Fructidor an V (25 August 1797). AN AFIII 210. **107.** Toussaint proclamation, Cap, 12 Fructidor an V (29 August 1797). AN AFIII 210. **108.** Toussaint to Laveaux, 1 June 1798. **109.** Letter of 15 June 1796, cited in Stein, *Léger Félicité Sonthonax*, p. 154. **110.** Sonthonax to Minister of Navy, Paris, 17 Frimaire an VIII (8 December 1799). ANOM CC9A 23. **111.** 'A pig that has eaten a chicken always tries to eat another one if it comes within its reach, even if you cover one or both of its eyes.' **112.** All quotations taken from Toussaint, 'Rapport au Directoire Exécutif', Cap-Français, 18 Fructidor an V (4 September 1797). AN AFIV 1213. **113.** Toussaint, 'Extrait du rapport adressé au Directoire Exécutif', Cap, September 1797. **114.** Proclamation of municipality of Jean-Rabel, 20 Vendémiaire an VI (11 October 1797). AN AFIII 210. **115.** Proclamation of municipality of Petite-Rivière, 28 Vendémiaire an VI (19 October 1797). AN AFIII 210. **116.** Letter of JP Lamontagne, 24 Vendémiaire an VI (15 October 1797). AN AFIII 210. **117.** Minister of Navy Truguet took out subscriptions to the main newspapers for Toussaint. See Sonthonax letter to Toussaint, 10 Thermidor an IV (28 July 1796). BNF NAF 8986, Papiers Sonthonax. **118.** *Discours de Villaret-Joyeuse au Conseil des Cinq Cents, 12 Prairial an V* (31 May 1797) (Paris, 1797), pp. 4 and 6–7. **119.** Gros, *De l'affranchissement des noirs* (Paris, 1797), p. 2; see also *De la nécessité d'adopter l'esclavage en France* (Paris, 1797). For further discussion of the debates within the colonial lobby at this time see Baptiste Biancardini, 'L'opinion coloniale et la question de la relance de Saint-Domingue 1795–1802', *Annales historiques de la Révolution Française* 382 (October–December 2015). See more generally Yves Benot, *La Révolution Française et la fin des colonies* (Paris: La Découverte, 1989), and Claude Wanquet, *La France et la première abolition de l'esclavage* (Paris: Karthala, 1998). **120.** Toussaint to Directory, Cap, 8 Brumaire an VI (29 October 1797). ANOM CC9A 14. On Moreau's bookshop in Philadelphia see Sara. E. Johnson, 'Moreau de Saint-Méry: itinerant bibliophile', *Library and Information History* vol. 31, no. 3 (2015), pp. 171–97. **121.** *Discours sur l'état de Saint-Domingue et sur la conduite des agens du Directoire, prononcé par Viénot-Vaublanc, séance du 10 Prairial an V* (29 May 1797) (Paris, 1797). **122.** Raimond report to Minister of Navy, 28 Vendémiaire an VI (19 October 1797). ANOM CC9A 13. **123.** See Bernard Gainot, 'La députation de Saint-Domingue au Corps Législatif du Directoire', *Outre-Mers. Revue d'Histoire* no. 316 (1997), pp. 95–110. **124.** *Réponse d'Étienne Laveaux, général de division, ex-gouverneur de St-Domingue, aux calomnies que le citoyen Viénot-Vaublanc, colon de St-Domingue et membre du Conseil des Cinq-Cents, s'est permis de mettre dans son discours prononcé à la séance du 10 Prairial dernier* (Paris, 1797), p. 15. **125.** Toussaint to Minister of Navy, 29 Vendémiaire an VI

(20 October 1797). ANOM CC9A 14. **126.** Toussaint to Directory, Cap, 8 Brumaire an VI (29 October 1797). ANOM CC9A 14. **127.** *Discours sur l'état de Saint-Domingue*, p. 12. **128.** Toussaint, *Réfutation*. **129.** Ibid., p. 5. **130.** Ibid., pp. 9–10 and 14. **131.** Ibid., pp. 12–13. **132.** Ibid., p. 10. **133.** Ibid., pp. 22–3. **134.** Ibid., p. 6. **135.** Ibid., p. 10. **136.** Ibid., pp. 18–19. **137.** 'Vrais français', ibid., p. 15. **138.** See Chapter 2. **139.** Toussaint, *Réfutation*, pp. 18 and 32. **140.** Toussaint to Directory, 14 Brumaire an VI (4 November 1797). AN AFIII 210. **141.** Toussaint to Vincent and Desfontaines, Cap, 10 Brumaire an VI (31 October 1797). Lettres inédites de Toussaint Louverture, Archives Diplomatiques Paris-La Courneuve, 23MD/2 (mémoires et documents, Haïti). **142.** Toussaint to Lescallier, 21 Prairial an VI (9 June 1798). ANOM CC9A 14. **143.** Toussaint, *Réfutation*, pp. 28–9. **144.** 'une chose accidentelle'; Isaac Louverture, *Réfutation*. **145.** Noé to Toussaint, London, 6 April 1799. National Archives, Kew, CO 137/50. This correspondence is also mentioned in a letter from the governor of Jamaica, Balcarres, to the Duke of Portland, 21 March 1800. National Archives, Kew, CO 137/104. **146.** Saint-Anthoine, *Notice sur Toussaint Louverture*, p. 23. **147.** Toussaint to Laveaux, Cap, 1 June 1798. BNF NAF 12104. **148.** Toussaint to Rallier, 26 Germinal an VII (15 April 1799). National Archives, Kew, CO 245/2. **149.** On the 'impossible abstraction' of French colonial citizenship see Silyane Larcher, *L'autre citoyen: l'idéal républicain et les Antilles après l'esclavage* (Paris, 2014). **150.** Toussaint, *Réfutation*, p. 32.

5: THE AGENT IS UNWELL

1. Balcarres to Maitland, Kingston, Jamaica, 4 July 1798. NAM, 6807/183/1, ff. 39–43. **2.** Dorigny and Gainot, *La Société des Amis des Noirs*, p. 307. **3.** *Observations du général du génie Vincent* (Paris, 1824), pp. 9–10. **4.** *Déclaration du citoyen Baud* (1797), quoted in Christian Schneider, 'Le Colonel Vincent, officier de génie à Saint-Domingue', *Annales historiques de la Révolution française* no. 329 (2002), p. 107. **5.** For more biographical details on Hédouville see Antoine Michel, *La mission du général Hédouville à Saint-Domingue* (Port-au-Prince: Imprimerie La Presse, 1929). **6.** 'susceptible de bien deviner les personnes avec lesquelles il a affaire'; letter in private Haitian collection, quoted in Faine Scharon, *Toussaint Louverture et la révolution de Saint-Domingue* (Port-au-Prince: Imprimerie de l'État, 1957), vol. 2, p. 129. **7.** Toussaint to Minister of Navy, 19 Prairial an VI (7 June 1798). AN EE 1991. **8.** Toussaint to Lescallier, 21 Prairial an VI (9 June 1798). ANOM CC9A 14. **9.** Toussaint to Hédouville, 22 Germinal an VI (11 April 1798). ANOM CC9A 23. **10.** Toussaint to Hédouville, Camp du Gros-Morne, 15 Floréal an VI (4 May 1798). ANOM CC9A 23. **11.** Toussaint to Hédouville, 18 Germinal an VI (7 April 1798). ANOM CC9B 6. **12.** Toussaint to Hédouville, 22 Germinal an VI (11 April 1798). ANOM CC9A 23. **13.** Toussaint to Hédouville, 6 Floréal an VI (25 April 1798). ANOM CC9B 6. **14.** Hédouville to Toussaint, 3 Prairial an VI (22 May 1798). ANOM CC9A 23. **15.** Toussaint to Hédouville, 18 Floréal, 8 and 11 Prairial an VI (7, 27 and 30 May 1798). ANOM CC9B 6. **16.** Quoted in *Mémoire abrégé des événements de l'île de Saint-Domingue, 1789–1807*, in de Cauna (ed.), *Toussaint Louverture et l'indépendance d'Haïti*, p. 94, fn. 138. **17.** Toussaint speech at fête des victoires, Cap, 20 Prairial an VI (8 June 1798). ANOM CC9B 6. **18.** Toussaint to Hédouville, 14 Prairial an VI (2 June 1798). ANOM CC9B 6. **19.** Hédouville to Toussaint, 6 Messidor an VI (24 June 1798). ANOM CC9A 23. **20.** Toussaint to Hédouville, 22 Messidor an VI (10 July 1798). ANOM CC9A 23. **21.** See for example Toussaint to Hédouville, 24 Floréal an VI (31 May 1798). ANOM CC9B 6. **22.** Dessalines to Hédouville, 17 Messidor an VI; Toussaint to Hédouville, 21 Messidor an VI (5 and 9 July 1798). ANOM CC9A 23. **23.** Toussaint speech at Port-Républicain, 21 Messidor an VI (9 July 1798). ANOM CC9A 23. **24.** Hédouville report to Directory, undated (an VI). ANOM CC9A 19. **25.** Hédouville to Toussaint, 7 Messidor an VI (25 June 1798). ANOM CC9A 23. **26.** Hédouville to Toussaint, 23 Messidor an VI (11 July 1798). ANOM CC9A 23. **27.** 'An expected misfortune'; Toussaint to Hédouville, 29 Messidor an VI (17 July 1798). ANOM CC9B 6. **28.** Toussaint to Hédouville,

1 Fructidor an VI (18 August 1798). ANOM CC9B 6. **29.** Toussaint to Hédouville, n.d. [early–mid July 1798]. ANOM CC9A 23. **30.** Hédouville to Toussaint, 5 Vendémiaire an VII (26 September 1798). ANOM CC9A 23. **31.** Maitland to Dundas, 18 March 1798. National Archives, Kew, WO 1/69. **32.** Hédouville to Toussaint, Cap, 9 Messidor an VI (27 June 1798). ANOM CC9A 23. **33.** Toussaint to Maitland, 8 Floréal an VI (27 April 1798), and to Huin, 9 Floréal an VI (28 April 1798). ANOM CC9A 18. **34.** Story recounted in 'Character of Toussaint Louverture', *The National Intelligencer and Washington Advertiser*, 17 August 1801. **35.** Maitland to Dundas, 10 May 1798. National Archives, Kew, WO 1/69. **36.** Toussaint to Charles Vincent, Cap, 10 Nivôse an VII (30 December 1798). Lettres inédites de Toussaint Louverture, Archives Diplomatiques Paris-La Courneuve, 23MD/2 (mémoires et documents, Haïti). **37.** 'Conventions secrètes', Camp de la Pointe Bourgeoise, 31 August 1798. National Archives, Kew, WO 1/70. **38.** Maitland to Balcarres, 31 August 1798. National Archives, Kew, WO 1/70. **39.** *Mémoire abrégé des événements de l'île de Saint-Domingue, 1789–1807*, pp. 96–7. **40.** Toussaint to Hédouville, 16 Fructidor an VI (2 September 1798). ANOM CC9A 23. **41.** Toussaint's letter thanking Maitland for the gift was dated 27 Floréal an VI (16 May 1798). ANOM CC9A 18. **42.** Toussaint to Hédouville, 29 Fructidor an VI (15 September 1798). ANOM CC9A 23. Despite Toussaint's efforts, some of the slaves in British-occupied areas were shipped out to Jamaica; a document in the British archives from 1799 provides a listing of 515 'nègres cultivateurs français réfugiés en Jamaïque'. National Archives, Kew, CO 137/102. **43.** Hédouville to Toussaint, 9 and 16 Floréal an VI (28 April and 5 May 1798). ANOM CC9A 23. **44.** Hédouville to Toussaint, 23 Fructidor an VI (9 September 1798). ANOM CC9A 23. 'Proclamation portant amnistie en faveur des habitants de Jérémie et du Môle, par le général de division Hédouville', Cap, 28 Thermidor an VI (15 August 1798). University of Florida, Documents originating in Saint-Domingue 1789–1802, reel 9 n.40. **45.** Duboys, *Précis historique*, vol. 2, p. 19. **46.** Toussaint to Hédouville, 29 Fructidor an VI (15 September 1798). ANOM CC9A 23. **47.** Hédouville to Toussaint, 12 Thermidor an VI (30 July 1798). ANOM CC9A 20. **48.** Toussaint to Hédouville, 1 Vendémiaire an VII (22 September 1798). ANOM CC9 B6. **49.** Ibid. **50.** Hédouville to Toussaint, 1er jour complémentaire an VI (17 September 1798). ANOM CC9A 23. **51.** Hédouville proclamation, 1 Brumaire an VII (22 October 1798). ANOM CC9A 23. **52.** See for example his letter of 16 Prairial an VI (4 June 1798) to *citoyennes* Fontanges and Emilie and Pauline Descahaux in Paris, reminding them of his generous amnesty policy in areas liberated from British control. Toussaint Louverture manuscripts, Bibliothèque Municipale, Nantes. **53.** *Le Citoyen véridique, ou gazette du Port-Républicain*, 26 September 1798. ANOM CC9B 8. **54.** Boerner to Hédouville, 10 Fructidor an VI (27 August 1798). ANOM CC9A 23. **55.** Hédouville report to Directory, n.d. AN AFIII 210. **56.** Military commander of Saint-Louis du Nord to Hédouville, 23 Fructidor an VI (9 September 1798). ANOM CC9A 23. **57.** See Hédouville letter to Boerner, 20 Messidor an VI (8 July 1798). ANOM CC9A 23. **58.** Hédouville to Toussaint, 24 Messidor an VI (12 July 1798). ANOM CC9A 23. **59.** Toussaint to Hédouville, 22 Messidor an VI (10 July 1798). ANOM CC9 B6. **60.** Toussaint to Hédouville, 19 Floréal an VI (8 May 1798). ANOM CC9 B6. **61.** Hédouville to Toussaint, 23 Fructidor an VI (9 September 1798), ANOM CC9A 23; 'eight ounces', Toussaint to Hédouville, 13 Messidor an VI (1 July 1798), ANOM CC9 B6. **62.** Hédouville to Toussaint, 3 Messidor an VI (21 June 1798), ANOM CC9A 20; Boerner to Dessalines, 25 Messidor an VI (13 July 1798), ANOM CC9A 23. **63.** Toussaint to Hédouville, 13 Messidor an VI (1 July 1798). ANOM CC9 B6. **64.** Dessalines to Hédouville, 25 Messidor an VI (13 July 1798). ANOM CC9A 23. **65.** Hédouville to Toussaint, 1er jour complémentaire an VI (17 September 1798). ANOM CC9A 23. **66.** Toussaint to Hédouville, 27 Floréal; Hédouville to Toussaint, 3 Prairial an VI (16 and 22 May 1798), ANOM CC9A 20; Toussaint to Hédouville ('je suis fâché'), 11 Prairial an VI (30 May 1798), ANOM CC9B 6. **67.** Toussaint to Hédouville, 1 Fructidor an VI (18 August 1798). ANOM CC9 B6. **68.** Hédouville to Toussaint, 6 Fructidor an VI (23 August 1798). ANOM CC9A 23. **69.** Toussaint to Hédouville, 13 Thermidor an VI (31 July 1798). ANOM CC9A 23. **70.** Toussaint to Hédouville, 5 Fructidor an VI (22 August 1798). ANOM CC9A 23. **71.** Toussaint to Hédouville, 15

Vendémiaire an VII (6 October 1798). ANOM CC9A 23. **72.** Toussaint to Hédouville, 26 Vendémiaire an VII (17 October 1798). ANOM CC9A 23. **73.** Toussaint to Hédouville, 1 Vendémiaire an VII (22 September 1798). ANOM CC9A 23. **74.** Hédouville report to Directory, n.d. AN AFIII 210. **75.** 'your ship is not big enough to take General Toussaint to France'; quoted in Vincent, *Notice sur Dominique Toussaint Louverture*; see also Scharon, *Toussaint Louverture*, p. 175. **76.** Toussaint to Hédouville, n.d. [1798]. AN AFIV 1213. **77.** 'Discours du général Hédouville, agent particulier du Directoire Exécutif, prononcé le 1er Vendémiaire an VII' (22 September 1798), Cap, 1798, p. 3. **78.** Toussaint to Hédouville, 5 and 16 Fructidor an VI (22 August and 2 September 1798); 1 and 4 Vendémiaire an VII (22 and 25 September 1798). ANOM CC9B 6. **79.** Toussaint to Hédouville, Arcahaie, 17 Thermidor an VI (4 August 1798), ANOM CC9B 6; and Port-Républicain, 21 Thermidor an VI (8 August 1798), ANOM CC9A 23. **80.** Hédouville to Toussaint, Cap, 21 Thermidor an VI (8 August 1798). ANOM CC9A 23. **81.** *Arrêté concernant la police des habitations, et les obligations réciproques des propriétaires ou fermiers et des cultivateurs*, Cap, 6 Thermidor an VI (24 July 1798). ANOM CC9B 9. **82.** Hédouville to Toussaint, 1er jour complémentaire an VI (17 September 1798). ANOM CC9A 23. **83.** Toussaint circular letter to all military commanders, 2 Vendémiaire an VII (23 September 1798), ANOM CC9B 8; Toussaint to Hédouville, 1 Vendémiaire an VII (22 September 1798), ANOM CC9A 23. **84.** Report by Brigadier Jaubert to Toussaint, 5ème jour complémentaire an VI (21 September 1798). ANOM CC9A 23. **85.** Municipality of Petit-Goâve to Toussaint, 1 Vendémiaire an VII (22 September 1798). ANOM CC9A 23. **86.** Boerner to Hédouville, 16 Fructidor an VI (2 September 1798). ANOM CC9A 23. **87.** Hédouville to Moyse, 14 Vendémiaire an VII (5 October 1798). ANOM CC9A 23. **88.** Claude B. Auguste, 'Les Congos dans la Révolution Haïtienne', *Revue de la Société haïtienne d'histoire et de géographie* vol. 46, no. 168 (December 1990), p. 25. **89.** Toussaint to Minister of Navy, 4 Germinal an VII (24 March 1799). National Archives, Kew, CO 245/2. **90.** Recounted in Godard, 'Rapport sur la situation morale et politique de Saint-Domingue', 17 Thermidor an VII (4 August 1799). ANOM CC9A 22. **91.** Quoted in *Mémoire abrégé des événements de l'île de Saint-Domingue, 1789–1807*, p. 98. **92.** Hédouville report to Directory, n.d. AN AFIII 210. **93.** Proclamation of municipal administration of Cap, 7 Brumaire an VII (28 October 1798). AN AFIV 1213. **94.** Toussaint, 'Aux citoyens Président et membres de la commune du Cap', 3 Brumaire an VII (24 October 1798). AN AFIV 1213. **95.** Proclamation of municipal administration of Cap, 7 Brumaire an VII (28 October 1798). AN AFIV 1213. **96.** Toussaint to Dessalines, October 1798, cited in Deborah Jenson, 'Toussaint Louverture, spin doctor?', in Doris Garraway (ed.), *Tree of Liberty: Cultural Legacies of the Haitian Revolution in the Atlantic World* (Charlottesville: University of Virginia Press, 2008), pp. 52–5. **97.** Proclamation of municipality of Gonaïves, 6 Brumaire an VII (27 October 1798). AN AFIII 210. **98.** Proclamation of municipality of Petite-Rivière, 8 Brumaire an VII (29 October 1798). AN AFIII 210. **99.** Proclamation of municipality of Plaisance, 2 Brumaire an VII (23 October 1798). AN AFIII 210. **100.** Proclamation of municipality of Marmelade, 2 Brumaire an VII (23 October 1798). AN AFIII 210. **101.** Proclamation of municipality of Gros-Morne, 8 Brumaire an VII (29 October 1798). AN AFIII 210. **102.** Proclamation of municipality of Gonaïves, 6 Brumaire an VII (27 October 1798). AN AFIII 210. **103.** Proclamation of municipality of Port-à-Piment and Terre-Neuve, 2 Brumaire an VII (23 October 1798). AN AFIII 210. **104.** Proclamation of municipality of Toussaint Louverture, 3 Brumaire an VII (24 October 1798). AN AFIII 210. **105.** Ibid. **106.** 'Lettre du citoyen Ignace, commandant militaire, au conseil municipal de Port-à-Piment et Terre-Neuve', 8 Brumaire an VII (29 October 1798). AN AFIII 210. **107.** Proclamation of municipality of Petite-Rivière, 8 Brumaire an VII (29 October 1798). AN AFIII 210. **108.** Petition of citizens of Toussaint Louverture to general-in-chief, Brumaire an VII (October 1798). AN AFIII 210. **109.** 'We are not happy with him, for one thing, he is not able to maintain order in our country, indeed he seems capable only of provoking disorder.' Petite-Rivière petition, 8 Brumaire an VII (29 October 1798). AN AFIII 210. **110.** Undated Hédouville letter to Minister of Navy. ANOM CC9A 23. **111.** Hédouville report to Directory, n.d. AN AFIII 210. **112.** Roume report to Minister of

Navy, Santo Domingo, 2 Frimaire an VII (22 November 1798). ANOM CC9A 18. **113.** Hédouville proclamation, 1 Brumaire an VII (22 October 1798). ANOM CC9A 23. **114.** Hédouville to Rigaud, 1 Brumaire an VII (22 October 1798). ANOM CC9A 20; this conflict will be discussed in Chapter 7. **115.** Quoted in Delatte, 'Mémoire sur les événements de Fort-Liberté', 16 Frimaire an VII (6 December 1798). ANOM CC9A 22. **116.** Maitland to Dundas, London, 26 December 1798. National Archives, Kew, WO 1/70. **117.** Harcourt to Toussaint, Gonaïves, 20 April 1799. Service Historique de la Défense, Vincennes, B7 carton 1, correspondance Toussaint Louverture. **118.** *London Gazette*, 12 December 1798. **119.** Hédouville report to Directory, n.d. AN AFIII 210. **120.** 'Li aurait mieux fait de baisser pour hausser que hausser pour baisser'. Quoted in 'Rapport anonyme sur les causes et les suites du depart d'Hédouville', Frimaire an VII (November 1798). ANOM CC9A 19. **121.** Toussaint, report to Directory, Cap, 22 Brumaire an VII (12 November 1798). AN AFIV 1213. **122.** Toussaint, 'Aux citoyens Président et membres de la commune du Cap'. **123.** Toussaint to Perodin, 28 Germinal an VII (17 April 1799). National Archives, Kew, CO 245/2. **124.** Proclamation of municipality of Marmelade. **125.** 'Rapport anonyme sur la situation à Saint-Domingue', Nivôse an VIII (December 1799). ANOM CC9A 18.

6: VIRTUOUS CITIZENS

1. Juin and d'Hébécourt to Minister of Navy, 10 Brumaire an IX (1 November 1800). ANOM CC9A 21. **2.** Administrative report, 28 Germinal an VII (17 April 1799). National Archives, Kew, CO 245/2. **3.** Reported in *The Sumter Banner* (Sumterville, SC), 25 April 1849. Library of Congress, Historic American Newspapers. **4.** Pamphile de Lacroix, *La Révolution de Haïti*, p. 244. **5.** Malenfant, *Des colonies*, p. 93. **6.** Isaac Louverture, *Réfutation*. **7.** 'Après Bon Dieu, c'est François Makandal', quoted in Franklin Midy, 'Vers l'indépendence des colonies à esclaves d'Amérique: l'exception Haïtienne', *Outre-Mers. Revue Historique* no. 340–41 (2003), p. 132. **8.** 'Slowly does it.' **9.** Alain Le Bihan, *Loges et chapitres de la Grande Loge et du Grand Orient de France (2e moitié du XVIIIe siècle)* (Paris: Bibliothèque Nationale, 1967), pp. 389–95. **10.** *Tableau des FF. qui composent la R.L. de S.J. de J.em* (Port-Républicain, 1800). BNF Gallica NUMM-316971. **11.** On the Masonic connections in Toussaint's entourage see Jacques de Cauna, 'Toussaint Louverture, l'Aquitaine, et les Gascons', in de Cauna (ed.), *Toussaint Louverture et l'indépendance d'Haïti*, pp. 197–9. **12.** François de Kerverseau, report to French government, 1 Germinal an IX (22 March 1801). ANOM CC9B 23. **13.** On Gonaïves municipal matters see the letter from Roume to Toussaint, 15 Germinal an VII (4 April 1799), National Archives, Kew, CO 245/2. On Cazes see de Cauna, 'Toussaint Louverture, l'Aquitaine, et les Gascons', p. 200. **14.** Jean Fouchard, 'Toussaint Louverture', *Revue de la Société haïtienne d'histoire et de géographie* no. 164 (September–December 1989), p. 41. **15.** See Toussaint letter to Perroud on the delivery of a sugar mill in Acul; Gonaïves, 10 Brumaire an IV (1 November 1795). Archives municipales, Reims, Tarbé collection, XXI–105. **16.** Saint-Anthoine, *Notice sur Toussaint Louverture*, p. 26. **17.** Isaac Louverture, *Notes historiques sur Toussaint Louverture*. BNF NAF 12409. **18.** Rainsford, *An Historical Account*, p. 252. **19.** See for example the letter from Sonthonax to Toussaint, 7 Vendémiaire an IV (29 September 1795), on the (successful) appointment of his candidate Chenaux as justice of the peace in Petite-Rivière. BNF NAF 8986, Papiers Sonthonax. **20.** Toussaint to Isaac and Placide Louverture, Cap, 25 Germinal an VII (14 April 1799). Toussaint Louverture manuscripts, Bibliothèque Municipale, Nantes. **21.** Toussaint to Minister of Navy, 25 Germinal an VII (14 April 1799). National Archives, Kew, CO 245/2. **22.** Toussaint to Monginot and citoyenne Flanet, 20 Ventôse an VI (10 March 1798). ANOM CC9A 18. **23.** Report to Directory, 23 Pluviôse an VII (11 February 1799). AN AFIII 210. **24.** Isaac Louverture, *Notes historiques*. BNF NAF 12409. **25.** See Toussaint's letter to Grégoire, Cap, 23 Brumaire an VII (13 November 1798); quoted in *Annales de la religion* 8 (1799). **26.** Isaac Louverture, *Notes historiques*. BNF NAF 12409. **27.** On Toussaint's religious entourage see Jean Fritzner Étienne, 'L'Église et la révolution des esclaves à Saint-Domingue (1791–1804)', *Histoire, monde et* *cultures religieuses* no. 29 (2014-1), pp. 27–8. **28.** Isaac Louverture, *Notes historiques*. BNF NAF 12409. **29.** Jean Fouchard, 'Toussaint Louverture', *Revue de la Société haïtienne d'histoire et de géographie* no. 164 (September–December 1989), p. 41. **30.** Jacques Périès, *La révolution de Saint-Domingue*. British Library MS 38074, f. 20. **31.** Madiou, *Histoire d'Haïti*, vol. 2, p. 91. **32.** One of these prayers is cited in Duboys, *Précis historique*, vol. 2, p. 172. **33.** Toussaint, 'Adresse à tous les militaires', 22 Floréal an V (11 May 1797). AN FIII/201. **34.** Toussaint, 'Adresse à tous les militaires composant l'armée de Saint-Domingue', 19 Vendémiaire an VII (10 October 1798). ANOM CC9A 23. **35.** See for example his letter to the municipality of Port-Républicain, 30 Messidor an VI (18 July 1798). ANOM CC9 B6. **36.** Toussaint, 'Proclamation aux soldats de l'Armée', Cap, 1796. **37.** Toussaint, 'Adresse à tous les militaires'. **38.** Isaac Louverture, *Notes historiques*. BNF NAF 12409. **39.** Toussaint, 'Adresse à tous les militaires'. **40.** Toussaint, *Aux citoyens Président et membres de la Commune du Cap*, 3 Brumaire an VII (24 October 1798). AN AFIII 210. **41.** Toussaint speech at Môle Saint-Nicolas tree of liberty ceremony, 15 Vendémiaire an VII (6 October 1798). ANOM CC9B 9. **42.** Ibid. **43.** Toussaint to Laveaux, 14 September 1795 BNF NAF 12103. See also Laveaux correspondence with Toussaint on convocation of local assemblies, an V. AN D/XXV/50. **44.** Duboys, *Précis historique*, vol. 2, p. 37. **45.** Desfontaines was sent to France to explain Toussaint's expulsion of Sonthonax to the French government; see his letter to Minister of Navy, 11 Brumaire an V (1 November 1796). ANOM CC9A 13. See also Toussaint letter to state councillor Lescallier, 21 Prairial an VI (9 June 1798). ANOM CC9A 14. **46.** See for example the report by Laplume to Toussaint about the assemblies of Léogâne, Grand-Goâve and Petit-Goâve, 10 Germinal an VII (30 March 1799). ANOM CC9A 22. **47.** *Aux administrateurs municipaux des divers départements de Saint-Domingue*, Port-Républicain, 19 Frimaire an VII (9 December 1798). University of Florida, Documents originating in Saint-Domingue 1789–1802, reel 9 n.42. The proclamation was signed by Dessalines, Clervaux, Laplume, Christophe and more than thirty regional commanders. **48.** Toussaint to the municipal administration of Cap, Gonaïves, 1 Germinal an IV (21 March 1796). BNF NAF 12104. **49.** See Sonthonax letter to Toussaint on the matter, 19 Messidor an IV (7 July 1796). BNF NAF 8986, Papiers Sonthonax. **50.** This occurred on 1 December 1800 and is mentioned in Duboys, *Précis historique*, vol. 2, p. 178. **51.** See for example his (negative) response to the municipality of Môle, 16 Germinal an IX (6 April 1801). ANOM CC9A 28. **52.** 'Ordonnance du général Toussaint Louverture', 13 December 1794. BNF NAF 12102. **53.** 'Proclamation de Toussaint Louverture aux administrations municipales de la colonie, et à ses concitoyens', 16 Pluviôse an IX (5 February 1801). ANOM CC9B 9. **54.** Toussaint, *arrêté*, 22 Pluviôse an IX (11 February 1801). ANOM CC9B 9. **55.** Isaac Louverture, *Notes historiques sur Toussaint Louverture*. BNF NAF 12409. **56.** Sonthonax to Toussaint, Cap, 8 Prairial an V (27 May 1797). BNF NAF 8988, Papiers Sonthonax. **57.** Toussaint, *ordonnance*, 17 Thermidor an IX (5 August 1801). ANOM CC9B 9. **58.** Isaac Louverture, *Notes historiques*. BNF NAF 12409. **59.** Report to Ministry of Navy, Floréal an V (April 1797). ANOM CC9A 13. **60.** Report to Ministry of Navy, Germinal an VII (March 1799), quoted in Geggus, *The Haitian Revolution*, p. 158. **61.** Toussaint, 'Lettre de service du général de brigade Maurepas', 14 Floréal an IX (14 May 1801). ANOM CC9B 9. **62.** Toussaint, *Pour le soulagement de l'humanité souffrante*, 2 Nivôse an VIII (23 December 1799). ANOM CC9B 9. **63.** Letter of municipality of Môle Saint-Nicolas to Toussaint, 27 Ventôse an IX (18 March 1801). ANOM CC9B 9. Toussaint granted them the exemption. **64.** Toussaint, 'Proclamation à tous les Français qui sont au Môle', Camp de la Pointe Bourgeoise, 9 Vendémiaire an VII (30 September 1798). Archives de la Seine, Paris, DQ10-1418, dossier Joseph Idlinger. **65.** See Geggus, *Slavery, War, and Revolution*, p. 140. **66.** 'Liste des personnes les plus capables de gérer les affaires communales', Môle Saint-Nicolas, 11 Brumaire an IX (2 November 1800). ANOM CC9B 9. **67.** Declaration of Môle municipal council, 4 Brumaire an X (26 October 1801). ANOM CC9B 9; see Chapter 10. **68.** 'Adresse de l'administration municipale du Môle au citoyen Ministre de la Marine', 10 Fructidor an VIII (28 August 1800). ANOM CC9B 9. **69.** Proclamation of the municipality of Môle Saint-Nicolas, 10 Pluviôse an VIII (30 January 1800). ANOM CC9B 9. **70.** 'Discours de l'administration municipale du Môle', 16 Pluviôse an VII (4 February 1799). ANOM CC9A 21. **71.** All Rochefort's citations are taken from his two speeches, fully transcribed in Môle Saint-Nicolas municipal reports on the celebration of the fête de la liberté générale, 16 Pluviôse an VIII and an IX (5 February 1800 and 1801). ANOM CC9B 9. **72.** Speech at National Guard ceremony, Môle Saint-Nicolas, 10 Frimaire an VII (30 November 1798). ANOM CC9B 9. **73.** Municipal proclamation, Môle Saint-Nicolas, 12 Pluviôse an VIII (1 February 1800). ANOM CC9B 9. **74.** Municipal proclamation, Môle Saint-Nicolas, 26 Vendémiaire an VII (17 October 1798). ANOM CC9B 9. **75.** Municipal proclamation, Môle Saint-Nicolas, 1 Floréal an X (21 April 1802). ANOM CC9B 9. **76.** See for example the municipal proclamation, Môle Saint-Nicolas, 28 Vendémiaire an VII (19 October 1798). ANOM CC9B 9. **77.** Municipal proclamation, Môle Saint-Nicolas, 15 Vendémiaire an X (7 October 1801). ANOM CC9B 9. **78.** Toussaint proclamation, Cap, 7 Floréal an VIII (27 April 1800). ANOM CC9B 18. **79.** Municipal proclamation, Môle Saint-Nicolas, 4 Brumaire an VII (25 October 1798). ANOM CC9B 9. **80.** Municipal proclamation, Môle Saint-Nicolas, 3 Brumaire an VII (24 October 1798). ANOM CC9B 9. **81.** Municipal proclamation, Môle Saint-Nicolas, 9 Prairial an VIII (29 May 1800). ANOM CC9B 9. **82.** Municipal proclamation, Môle Saint-Nicolas, 18 Vendémiaire an VIII (10 October 1799). ANOM CC9B 9. **83.** Municipal proclamation, Môle Saint-Nicolas, 27 Vendémiaire an VII (18 October 1798). ANOM CC9B 9. **84.** Municipal proclamation, Môle Saint-Nicolas, 28 Vendémiaire an VII (19 October 1798). ANOM CC9B 9. **85.** Municipal proclamation, Môle Saint-Nicolas, 5 Ventôse an VII (23 February 1799). ANOM CC9B 9. **86.** Municipal proclamation, Môle Saint-Nicolas, 6 Ventôse an IX (25 February 1801). ANOM CC9B 9. **87.** Toussaint to Roume, 14 Nivôse an VIII (4 January 1800). ANOM CC9B 1. **88.** Toussaint to Christophe, Verrettes, 3 April 1798. Nemours Papers, University of Puerto Rico; quoted in Boromé, 'A finding list'. **89.** Isaac Louverture, *Notes historiques*. BNF NAF 12409. **90.** Jujardy speech for anniversary of foundation of French Republic, Môle Saint-Nicolas, 1 Vendémiaire an VIII (23 September 1799). ANOM CC9A 23. **91.** Rainsford, *An Historical Account*, p. 255. **92.** Placide David, 'Vie amoureuse de Toussaint Louverture', in *Sur les rives du passé*, p. 101. **93.** Report of British representative Hugh Cathcart, Port-Républicain, 26 November 1799. National Archives, Kew, CO 245/1. **94.** Roume report to Directory, 23 Pluviôse an VII (11 February 1799). AN AFIII 210. **95.** Proclamation of municipality of Saint-Marc, addressed to French Minister of Navy, 12 Germinal an VIII (2 April 1800). ANOM CC9B 17. **96.** Proclamation of municipality of Ennery, 19 Floréal an V (8 May 1797). AN AFIII 210. **97.** Descourtilz, *Voyages d'un naturaliste*, vol. 2, p. 121. **98.** Proclamation of municipality of Arcahaie, 22 Germinal an VIII (12 April 1800). ANOM CC9B 17. **99.** Proclamation of municipality of Terre-Neuve, 22 Pluviôse an VII (10 February 1799). ANOM CC9A 21. **100.** Proclamation of municipality of Terre-Neuve, 1 Floréal an VIII (21 April 1800). ANOM CC9B 17. **101.** Roume reports to Minister of Navy, Port-Républicain, 1 Pluviôse and 29 Germinal an VII (20 January and 18 April 1799). National Archives, Kew, CO 245/2. **102.** Marin-Gallon, 'Bouquet à l'armée victorieuse, commandée par le général Toussaint Louverture', *Le Citoyen véridique, ou gazette du Port-Républicain*, 30 Ventôse an VIII (21 March 1800). ANOM CC9A 24. **103.** Deliberation of municipality of Port-Républicain, 13 Germinal an VIII (3 April 1800), addressed to French Minister of Navy. ANOM CC9B 17. **104.** Proclamation of municipality of Gonaïves, 22 Vendémiaire an VI (13 October 1797). AN AFIII 210. **105.** Proclamation of municipality of Gonaïves, addressed to French Minister of Navy, 19 Germinal an VIII (9 April 1800). ANOM CC9B 17. **106.** Municipality of Cap to Ministry of Navy, Prairial an VIII (May 1800). ANOM CC9B 2. **107.** Jacques Périès, *La révolution de Saint-Domingue*. British Library MS 38074, f. 15.

7: GREAT LATITUDE

1. Toussaint report to Minister of Navy, 4 Vendémiaire an VII (25 September 1798). ANOM CC9A20. **2.** Mats Lundahl, 'Toussaint Louverture and the war economy of

Saint-Domingue, 1796–1802', *Slavery and Abolition* vol. 6, no. 2 (1985), pp. 125–6. 3. *Observations sur la situation actuelle de la colonie de Saint-Domingue, par Rallier, député d'Ille et Vilaine*, Paris, 16 Frimaire an VIII (7 December 1799). ANOM CC9A 23. 4. Someruelos to Urquijo, Havana, 6 August 1799, AGI, quoted in Scott, *The Common Wind*, p. 208; on the slave regime in Cuba see Ferrer, *Freedom's Mirror*. 5. Toussaint's missive is mentioned in an exchange of letters between Spanish officials in Cuba, April 1800, and is cited in Ada Ferrer, 'Talk about Haiti', in Sepinwall (ed.), *Haitian History*, p. 141. 6. Hyde Parker to Lord Spencer, 19 May 1799, quoted in Scott, *The Common Wind*, p. 205. 7. 'offres séduisantes'; Toussaint to Roume, 12 Prairial an VII (31 May 1799). National Archives, Kew, CO 137/104. 8. See for example the report on Toussaint's successful campaign against the British in *Gazette of the United States and Daily Advertiser* (Philadelphia), 1 May 1798. 9. For further discussion see Ashli White, 'The politics of "French negroes" in the United States', in Sepinwall (ed.), *Haitian History*. 10. An expression which could loosely be translated as 'showing great political dexterity'. Toussaint letter, 22 Fructidor an VII (8 September 1799). ANOM CC9A 26. 11. See his *Rapport de Philippe-Rose Roume sur sa mission à Saint-Domingue* (Paris, 1793). 12. 'Acte de naissance de Rose-Marie-Gabrielle ROUME, fille de Philippe-Rose ROUME, agent du Directoire exécutif de la colonie de Saint-Domingue, habitant à Port-Républicain, et de Marie-Anne-Élisabeth ROCHARD-L'EPINE, née le 28 Brumaire an VIII (19 November 1799)'. AN MC/ET/XXXI/703. 13. 'courses trop violentes'; Roume to Toussaint, 22 Frimaire, 22 Nivôse and 9 Germinal an VII (12 December 1798, 11 January and 29 March 1799). National Archives, Kew, CO 245/2. 14. In his *Vie de Toussaint Louverture* (1850), Saint-Rémy noted that this portrait was 'religiously preserved by the family of Roume' in Paris. 15. Toussaint to Roume, 10 Brumaire an VII (31 October 1798). ANOM CC9A 18. 16. Letter of Cap municipality to Roume, 12 Brumaire an VII (2 November 1798). ANOM CC9A 18. 17. Toussaint to Roume, 5 Frimaire an VII (25 November 1798). National Archives, Kew, CO 245/2. 18. Toussaint to Roume, 17 Ventôse an VII (7 March 1799). National Archives, Kew, CO 245/2. 19. Roume to Toussaint, 23 Frimaire and 30 Ventôse an VII (13 December 1798 and 20 March 1799). ANOM CC9A 20. 20. Roume to Toussaint, 4 Pluviôse an VIII (24 January 1800). ANOM CC9B 1. 21. Roume to Toussaint, 21 Vendémiaire an VIII (13 October 1799). ANOM CC9A 26. 22. Roume to Toussaint, 15 Pluviôse an VIII (4 February 1800). ANOM CC9B 1. 23. Roume to Toussaint, 16 Nivôse an VIII (6 January 1800). ANOM CC9B 17. 24. 'Précis des services de Joseph Antoine Idlinger, commissaire ordonnateur à Saint-Domingue'. Archives de la Seine, Paris, DQ10-1418, dossier Joseph Idlinger. 25. Alexander DeConde, *The Quasi-War: The Politics and Diplomacy of the Undeclared War with France, 1797–1801* (New York: Scribner, 1966), p. 140. 26. Toussaint's letter was written in November 1798. On the remarkable life and career of the Bunel couple see Philippe Girard, 'Trading races: Joseph and Marie Bunel, a diplomat and a merchant in revolutionary Saint-Domingue and Philadelphia', *Journal of the Early Republic* vol. 30, no. 3 (Fall 2010), pp. 351–76. 27. Toussaint to Adams, 6 November 1798, quoted in 'Letters of Toussaint Louverture and Edward Stevens', *American Historical Review*, October 1910, pp. 66–7; see also Toussaint letter to Bunel, Cap, 17 Nivôse an VII (6 January 1799), cited in Boromé, 'A finding list'. 28. Stevens to Pickering, Cap, 3 May 1799, in 'Letters of Toussaint Louverture and Edward Stevens'. 29. White, *Encountering Revolution*, p. 157. 30. Ibid. 31. Roume to Toussaint, 2 Brumaire an VIII (24 October 1799). ANOM CC9A 26. 32. Roume speech on the anniversary of the *fête de la liberté générale*, 20 Pluviôse an VIII (9 February 1800). ANOM CC9B 1. 33. Roume to Toussaint, 15 Thermidor an VII (2 August 1799). ANOM CC9A 25. 34. Roume to Minister of Navy, 27 Thermidor an VII (14 August 1799), National Archives, Kew, CO 137/104; the information was confirmed in a report by Douglas to Balcarres, Port-Républicain, 21 August 1799, National Archives, Kew, CO 137/102. 35. *Mémoire abrégé des évènements de l'île de Saint-Domingue, 1789–1807*, pp. 100–101. 36. Philippe Girard, 'Black Talleyrand: Toussaint Louverture's diplomacy, 1798–1802', *William and Mary Quarterly* vol. 66, no. 1 (January 2009), p. 110. 37. 'État sommaire des denrées coloniales exportées du Cap Français depuis le 1er Vendémiaire an 8 jusqu'au 20 Fructidor, Cap, 25 Fructidor an VIII' (12 September 1800). Archives de la Seine,

Paris, DQ10-1418, dossier Joseph Idlinger. **38.** Roume to Toussaint, 12 Brumaire an VIII (3 November 1799). ANOM CC9A 26. **39.** Toussaint to Roume, 5 Floréal an VIII (25 April 1800). ANOM CC9 B 2. **40.** Toussaint to Roume, 5 Frimaire an VIII (26 November 1799). ANOM CC9 A 26. **41.** Quoted in Dun, *Dangerous Neighbours*, p. 153. **42.** Placide Justin, *Histoire politique et statistique de l'île d'Hayti* (Paris, 1826), pp. 331–2. **43.** Ronald Angelo Johnson, *Diplomacy in Black and White: John Adams, Toussaint Louverture and their Atlantic World Alliance* (Athens, GA: University of Georgia Press, 2014), p. 101. **44.** Stevens to Pickering, 26 October 1799, in 'Letters of Toussaint Louverture and Edward Stevens'. **45.** Stevens to Pickering, 24 June 1799, ibid. **46.** Ibid. **47.** Ibid. **48.** Stevens to Pickering, 13 February 1800, ibid. **49.** Roume to Toussaint, 9 Frimaire an VIII (30 November 1799). ANOM CC9A 26. **50.** Maitland to Toussaint, London, 15 January 1799. Service Historique de la Défense, Vincennes, B7 carton 1, correspondance Toussaint Louverture. **51.** Maitland to Toussaint, Cap harbour, 14 May 1799. Service Historique de la Défense, Vincennes, B7 carton 1, correspondance Toussaint Louverture. **52.** Maitland to Toussaint, bay of Gonaïves, 20 May 1799. Service Historique de la Défense, Vincennes, B7 carton 1, correspondance Toussaint Louverture. **53.** Toussaint to Roume, 12 Prairial an VII (31 May 1799). National Archives, Kew, CO 137/104. **54.** 'Propositions du général en chef de l'armée de Saint-Domingue à son excellence l'honorable brigadier-général Maitland', n.d. [May 1799]. Service Historique de la Défense, Vincennes, B7 carton 1, correspondance Toussaint Louverture. **55.** 'Convention secrette [*sic*] arrêtée entre l'Honorable Brigadier General Maitland et le général en chef de Saint-Domingue Toussaint L'Ouverture [*sic*], Arcahaye, 25 Prairial an VII' (13 June 1799). Service Historique de la Défense, Vincennes, B7 carton 1, correspondance Toussaint Louverture. See also Alfred Nemours, *Histoire des Relations internationales de Toussaint Louverture* (Port-au-Prince: Imprimerie du Collège Vertières, 1945), pp. 185–90. **56.** Balcarres to Portland, Kingston, Jamaica, 7 December 1799. NAM, 6807/183/1, ff. 121–6. See also Stevens to Maitland, 23 May 1799, in 'Letters of Toussaint Louverture and Edward Stevens'. **57.** His ships were prohibited from sailing outside a radius of fifteen miles from the Saint-Domingue coast; there were also restrictions on tonnage and size of crews. See Maitland to Hyde Parker, 31 May 1799. National Archives, Kew, CO 137/102. **58.** Maitland to Stevens, 23 May 1799. Ibid., p. 237. **59.** Maitland to Balcarres, on board HMS *Camilla*, 17 June 1799. NAM, 6807/183/1, ff. 143–53. **60.** Balcarres to Portland, 14 July 1799. National Archives, Kew, CO 137/102. **61.** Sasportas to Roume, 22 Germinal an VII (11 April 1799). ANOM CC9 B17. **62.** Roume to Sasportas, 1 Thermidor an VII (19 July 1799). ANOM CC9 B17. **63.** Roume, *arrêté*, 13 Fructidor an VII (30 August 1799). ANOM CC9 B17. **64.** See Toussaint's two letters to Roume, both dated 2 Brumaire an VIII (24 October 1799). ANOM CC9A 26. **65.** Roume summarized the preparations for the Jamaica invasion (including his conversations with Toussaint) in a letter to Pons, 2 Pluviôse an VIII (22 January 1800). ANOM CC9 B 1. **66.** Toussaint to Charles Vincent, Cap, 10 Nivôse an VII (30 December 1798). Lettres inédites de Toussaint Louverture, Archives Diplomatiques Paris-La Courneuve, 23MD/2 (mémoires et documents, Haïti). **67.** Raimond's letter was addressed to Christophe and is cited in Stevens's letter to Pickering, 30 September 1799, in 'Letters of Toussaint Louverture and Edward Stevens'. **68.** Balcarres to Portland, Jamaica, 28 October 1799. National Archives, Kew, CO 137/103; a copy of Besse's presentation was attached to the letter. **69.** Stevens to Pickering, 30 September 1799, in 'Letters of Toussaint Louverture and Edward Stevens'. **70.** For details of the capture, interrogation and trial of Sasportas see Balcarres report to Portland, 31 December 1799 and 1 January 1800. National Archives, Kew, CO 137/103. **71.** See notably Gabriel Debien and Pierre Pluchon, 'Un plan d'invasion de la Jamaïque en 1799 et la politique anglo-américaine de Toussaint Louverture', *Revue de la Société haïtienne d'histoire, de géographie et de géologie* vol. 36, no. 119 (July 1978), pp. 36–7; Girard, 'Black Talleyrand', pp. 106–7. **72.** Balcarres to Stevens, Jamaica, 29 October 1799. National Archives, Kew, CO 137/105. **73.** Balcarres to Portland, Kingston, Jamaica, 7 December 1799. NAM, 6807/183/1, ff. 121–6. **74.** Toussaint to Balcarres, 8 October 1799; Balcarres reply, 24 October 1799. National Archives, Kew, CO 137/103. **75.** The ships were carrying a total of fifty-four cannon and over 400 men. See report from Jamaica, 20 December 1799. National

Archives, Kew, WO 1/74. **76.** Scott, *The Common Wind*, p. 207. **77.** Toussaint to Cathcart, 19 December 1799. National Archives, Kew, CO 245/1. **78.** See Douglas to Toussaint, 24 September and 12 October 1799. National Archives, Kew, CO 137/103. **79.** Toussaint to Balcarres, 21 December 1799. National Archives, Kew, WO 1/74. **80.** Toussaint first wrote to Parker in September asking that his cruisers 'not be molested' in the south of Saint-Domingue; see Parker to Toussaint, 10 September 1799, National Archives, Kew, WO 1/74. Then in early November he wrote specifically about his planned operation against Rigaud, asking for British naval support; see Toussaint to Parker, Port-Républicain, 10 November 1799, Jamaica Archives; cited in Boromé, 'A finding list'. **81.** Toussaint to Roume, Jacmel, 8 Pluviôse an VIII (28 January 1800). ANOM CC9B 1. **82.** Quotes from Toussaint in report by British sub-agent Robinson, 29 January 1800. National Archives, Kew, WO 1/74. **83.** Roume to Toussaint, 2 Nivôse an VIII (23 December 1799). ANOM CC9A 26. **84.** Toussaint to Roume, 23 Nivôse an VIII (13 February 1800). ANOM CC9 B1. **85.** Toussaint to Roume, 27 Nivôse and 3 Pluviôse an VIII (17 and 23 January 1800). ANOM CC9 B1. **86.** Roume to Toussaint, 3 Pluviôse an VIII (23 January 1800). ANOM CC9 B1. **87.** Toussaint to Roume, 8 Pluviôse an VIII (28 January 1800). ANOM CC9B 1. **88.** Toussaint to Roume, 8 Floréal an VIII (28 April 1800). ANOM CC9 B1. **89.** Arambarri to Someruelos, 19 February 1800, quoted in Matt Childs, '"A French black general arrived to conquer the island": images of the Haitian revolution in Cuba's 1812 Aponte rebellion', in David Geggus (ed.), *The Impact of the Haitian Revolution in the Atlantic World* (Columbia: University of South Carolina Press, 2001), p. 139. **90.** 'Le salut de mon pays'; Toussaint to Roume, 22 Fructidor an VII (8 September 1799). ANOM CC9A 26; emphasis added. **91.** Toussaint to Roume, 23 Nivôse an VIII (13 January 1800). ANOM CC9 B1. **92.** Roume to Toussaint, 3 Pluviôse an VIII (23 January 1800). ANOM CC9 B1. **93.** Roume proclamation, Cap, 14 Ventôse an VIII (5 March 1800). ANOM CC9 B1. **94.** Toussaint to Roume, 18 Ventôse an VIII (9 March 1800). ANOM CC9 B1. **95.** See Roume letter to Rigaud, 2 Ventôse an VII (20 February 1799); see also Laplume report to Toussaint, 16 Floréal an VII (5 May 1799). ANOM CC9A 22. **96.** Rigaud proclamation, Les Cayes, 14 Prairial an VII (2 June 1799). ANOM CC9A 25. **97.** Roume to Toussaint, 29 Messidor an VII (17 July 1799). ANOM CC9A 25. **98.** *Réponse du citoyen Toussaint Louverture aux calomnies et aux écrits mensongers du général de brigade Rigaud*, Gonaïves, 30 Floréal an VII (19 May 1799); also published in *Bulletin Officiel de Saint-Domingue* nos 24 and 25, 19 and 24 Prairial an VII (7 and 12 June 1799). **99.** Toussaint to Roume, 6 Fructidor an VII (23 August 1799). ANOM CC9A 25. **100.** Lieutenant Lacroix to Toussaint, 23 Vendémiaire an VIII (15 October 1799). ANOM CC9A 23. **101.** Toussaint to Vincent, Port-de-Paix, 29 Thermidor an VII (16 August 1799). Lettres inédites de Toussaint Louverture, Archives Diplomatiques Paris-La Courneuve, 23MD/2 (mémoires et documents, Haïti). **102.** Toussaint to Vincent, Port-de-Paix, 3 Fructidor an VII (20 August 1799). Lettres inédites de Toussaint Louverture, Archives Diplomatiques Paris-La Courneuve, 23MD/2 (mémoires et documents, Haïti). **103.** *Toussaint Louverture, général en chef de l'Armée de Saint-Domingue aux cultivateurs et aux hommes de couleur égarés*, Port-de-Paix, 12 Thermidor an VII (30 July 1799). University of Florida, Saint-Domingue collection (A, 45). **104.** Cited in Corvington, *Port-au-Prince au cours des ans*, vol. 2, p.178. **105.** According to Vincent's version, Toussaint warned people of colour that they were 'on the path to self-destruction', and that he held them in the 'palm of his hand'; if he moved just one of his fingers they would all be 'crushed'. Vincent, *Notice sur Dominique Toussaint Louverture*. **106.** Toussaint to Roume, 13 Thermidor an VII (31 July 1799). ANOM CC9A 25. **107.** Toussaint proclamation, 8 Fructidor an VII (25 August 1799). ANOM CC9 B9. **108.** Toussaint to Roume, 10 Thermidor an VII (28 July 1799). ANOM CC9A 25. **109.** Toussaint report to Minister of Navy, 4 Germinal an VII (24 March 1799). National Archives, Kew, CO 245/2. **110.** Toussaint to Roume, 4 Thermidor an VII (22 July 1799). ANOM CC9A 25. **111.** Toussaint to Roume, 10 Thermidor an VII (28 July 1799). ANOM CC9A 25. **112.** Douglas report to Balcarres, Port-au-Prince, 15 August 1799. National Archives, Kew, CO 137/102. **113.** Toussaint to Roume, 13 Germinal and 12 Thermidor an VII (2 April and 30 July 1799). ANOM CC9A 25. **114.** Story reported by Toussaint in letter to Roume, 25 Thermidor an VII (12 August 1799). ANOM CC9A 25. **115.** Letter from Admiral Hyde Parker, commander of British Caribbean naval fleet, to Spencer, First Lord of the Admiralty, quoted in Michael Palmer, *Stoddert's War: Naval Operations during the Quasi-War with France 1798–1801* (Columbia, SC: University of South Carolina Press, 1987), p. 161. **116.** Maitland to Balcarres, 17 June 1799, on board HMS *Camilla*. NAM, 6807/183/1, ff. 143–53. **117.** Roume report to Minister of Navy, 27 Thermidor an VII (14 August 1799). ANOM CC9A 25. **118.** For further details of such incidents see Toussaint letter to Roume, 21 Messidor an VII (9 July 1799). ANOM CC9A 25. **119.** Toussaint to Roume, 20 Thermidor an VII (7 August 1799). ANOM CC9 A 25. **120.** Toussaint, 'Aux citoyens composant la garnison du Môle', 1 Thermidor an VII (19 July 1799). ANOM CC9A 21. **121.** Toussaint to Roume, 25 Thermidor an VII (12 August 1799). ANOM CC9A 25. **122.** Proclamation of Roux, mayor of Saint-Louis-du-Nord, 24 Messidor an VII (12 July 1799). ANOM CC9A 25. **123.** Toussaint to Roume, 10 Thermidor an VII (28 July 1799). ANOM CC9A 25. **124.** Toussaint to Roume, 4 Thermidor an VII (22 July 1799). ANOM CC9A 25. **125.** Toussaint to Roume, 21 Fructidor an VII (7 September 1799). ANOM CC9A 26. **126.** Toussaint to Roume, 6 Fructidor an VII (23 August 1799). ANOM CC9A 25. **127.** Dessalines report to Toussaint, 21 Vendémiaire an VIII (13 October 1799). ANOM CC9A 26. **128.** Toussaint to Roume, 2e jour complémentaire an VII (18 September 1799). ANOM CC9A 26. **129.** See for example the report by National Guard commander Latour on the assassinations carried out by Rigaud's men in Mirebalais, 1 Fructidor an VII (18 August 1799). ANOM CC9A 22. **130.** 'anéantir'; Roume to Toussaint, 29 Messidor an VII (17 July 1799). ANOM CC9A 25. **131.** Duboys, *Précis historique*, vol. 2, p. 92. **132.** Sanon Desfontaines to Roume, Gonaïves, 2 Thermidor an VII (20 July 1799). ANOM CC9A 25. **133.** Letter of Pierre Lyonnet (former forestry official in Saint-Domingue) to Minister of Navy, 1 Vendémiaire an IX (23 September 1800), ANOM CC9A 26; for a specific account of atrocities in Port-Républicain see Cathcart report to Maitland, 31 October 1799, National Archives, Kew, CO 245/1. **134.** Letter of François Dubois and Germain Crespin to Minister of Navy, Havana, 26 Prairial an VIII (15 June 1800). ANOM CC9B 17. **135.** Toussaint proclamation, in *Bulletin officiel de Saint-Domingue* no. 12, 29 Frimaire an VIII (20 December 1799). **136.** Vincent, 'Considérations sur les moyens de faire cesser la guerre civile à Saint-Domingue', 6 Floréal an VIII (26 April 1800). ANOM CC9B 17. **137.** 'I told you to prune (the tree), not uproot it.' **138.** 'Whatever is outside gets wet.' **139.** Toussaint proclamation, 20 Messidor an VIII (9 July 1800). Lettres inédites de Toussaint Louverture, Archives Diplomatiques Paris-La Courneuve, 23MD/2 (mémoires et documents, Haïti). **140.** Toussaint proclamation, 30 Messidor an VIII (19 July 1800). ANOM CC9B 9. **141.** Toussaint proclamation, 26 Frimaire an VIII (17 December 1799). ANOM CC9B 1. **142.** Toussaint to Roume, 22 Nivôse an VIII (12 January 1800). ANOM CC9B 1. **143.** Stevens to Pickering, 16 March 1800, in 'Letters of Toussaint Louverture and Edward Stevens'. **144.** Roume to Toussaint, 4 Frimaire an VIII (25 November 1799). ANOM CC9A 26. **145.** Stevens to Pickering, 24 June 1799, in 'Letters of Toussaint Louverture and Edward Stevens'. **146.** For a description of one such confrontation see Stevens's letter to Pickering, 16 January 1800. **147.** Toussaint to Commander Silas Talbot, Port-Républicain, 26 Germinal an VIII (16 April 1800), in *Revue de la société haïtienne d'histoire et de géographie* vol. 18, no. 66 (July 1947), pp. 64–6. **148.** Johnson, *Diplomacy in Black and White*, p. 123. **149.** Toussaint circular to civil and military authorities, Les Cayes, 17 Thermidor an VIII (5 August 1800). ANOM CC9B 9. **150.** Toussaint decree, Les Cayes, 30 Thermidor an VIII (18 August 1800). Service Historique de la Défense, Vincennes, B7 carton 1, correspondance Toussaint Louverture. **151.** Toussaint proclamation to the army, 12 Fructidor an VIII (30 August 1800). ANOM CC9B 9. **152.** Duboys, *Précis historique*, vol. 2, pp. 197–8. **153.** 'Sans son appui, l'ouvrage des hommes est périssable, et ses desseins sont plus mobiles que les flots agités de la mer', Toussaint proclamation, Les Cayes, 18 Thermidor an VIII (6 August 1800). ANOM CC9B 2. **154.** Toussaint to municipal administration of Cap, 12 Germinal an VIII (2 April 1800); cited in Duboys, *Précis historique*, vol. 2, p. 151. See also Toussaint decree 10 Frimaire an IX (1 December 1800). ANOM CC9B 9. **155.** See Toussaint to Vollée, 21 Nivôse an VIII (11 January 1800), in which he instructs his official not to issue any further leases without his permission. ANOM CC9B 1. **156.** 'Pas un sou'; Toussaint note to Idlinger, Léogâne, 27 Nivôse an VIII (17 January 1800). ANOM CC9B 1. **157.** Report of British representatives' meetings with Toussaint, 29 January 1800. National Archives, Kew, WO 1/74. **158.** Toussaint to Vincent, Port-Républicain, 19 Messidor an VII (7 July 1799). Lettres inédites de Toussaint Louverture, Archives Diplomatiques Paris-La Courneuve, 23MD/2 (mémoires et documents, Haïti). **159.** Isaac Louverture, *Notes historiques sur Toussaint Louverture*. BNF NAF 12409. **160.** Balcarres to Hyde Parker, 5 February 1800; and to Portland, 23 March 1800. National Archives, Kew, CO 137/105 and CO 137/104. **161.** Toussaint to Portland, 30 Ventôse an VIII (21 March 1800). National Archives, Kew, WO 1/74. **162.** Pennetier was fluent in English, and Toussaint had used him as an interpreter at Port-Républicain. See Toussaint to Roume, 28 Frimaire an VIII (19 December 1799). ANOM CC9A 26. **163.** Toussaint to Maitland, 11 March 1800. National Archives, Kew, WO 1/74. **164.** Toussaint to Portland, 11 March 1800. National Archives, Kew, WO 1/74. **165.** Portland to Balcarres, London, 19 March 1801. NAM, 6807/183/1, ff. 273–83. **166.** Harcourt to Balcarres, 11 April and 8 May 1799. National Archives, Kew, CO 137/102. **167.** Whitfield report to Corbet, 21 January 1801. National Archives, Kew, CO 245/1. **168.** Cathcart report to Maitland, Port-Républicain, 26 November 1799. National Archives, Kew, CO 245/1. **169.** Graham T. Nessler, *An Islandwide Struggle for Freedom: Revolution, Emancipation and Re-Enslavement in Hispaniola, 1789–1809* (Chapel Hill: University of North Carolina Press, 2016), p. 99. **170.** Quoted in Donald Hickey, 'America's response to the slave revolt in Haiti, 1791–1806', *Journal of the Early Republic* vol. 2, no. 4 (Winter 1982), p. 367. **171.** See W. Jeffrey Bolster, *Black Jacks: African American Seamen in the Age of Sail* (Cambridge, Mass.: Harvard University Press, 1997). **172.** 'Character of Toussaint Louverture', *National Intelligencer and Washington Advertiser*, 17 August 1801. **173.** On the Les Cayes meeting between Toussaint and Geneviève see Ardouin, *Études sur l'histoire d'Haiti*, vol. 5, p. 198.

8: NO TIME TO LOSE

1. Constitution of 22 Frimaire an VIII (13 December 1799), in A. C. Bouyer (ed.), *Constitutions Françaises* (Paris, 1848), p. 142. **2.** Quoted in Pluchon, *Toussaint Louverture*, p. 322. **3.** All the citations in this section are drawn from three Vincent letters, addressed to state councillor Lescallier on 4 Floréal, 7 Messidor and 16 Messidor an VIII (24 April, 26 June and 5 July 1800). ANOM CC9B 17. **4.** One hundred and twenty miles. **5.** On this point see also Madiou, *Histoire d'Haïti*, vol. 2, p. 106. **6.** 'Ne perdons pas notre temps.' **7.** Harcourt to Balcarres, 8 May 1799. National Archives, Kew, CO 137/102, emphasis in text. **8.** Balcarres to Portland, 14 September 1800. National Archives, Kew, CO 137/104. **9.** Chanlatte report to Minister of Navy, 13 August 1800. ANOM CC9B 18. **10.** Minister of Navy to Toussaint, Brumaire an IX (October 1800). ANOM CC9B 18. **11.** Report by Godard to Minister of Navy, 17 Thermidor an VII (4 August 1799). ANOM CC9A 22. **12.** Letter to Minister of Navy, 19 Prairial an VIII (8 June 1800). ANOM CC9A 27. **13.** Toussaint to Roume, 25 Thermidor an VII (12 August 1799), quoted in Ardouin, *Études sur l'histoire d'Haiti*, vol. 4, p. 35. **14.** Toussaint to Roume, 13 Ventôse an VIII (4 March 1800). ANOM CC9B 1. **15.** Toussaint to Roume, 27 Nivôse an VIII (17 January 1800). ANOM CC9B 1. **16.** Declaration by Michel Pérèz, 12 January 1800. ANOM CC9B 1. **17.** Roume to Toussaint, 24 Pluviôse an VIII (13 February 1800). ANOM CC9B 1. **18.** Toussaint to Roume, 28 Nivôse an VIII (18 January 1800). ANOM CC9B 1. **19.** See for example Girard, who, on the basis of the denials of the Spanish authorities in Santo Domingo, argues that slavery was 'not even a secondary motive' for Toussaint's actions. 'Black Talleyrand', pp. 111–12. **20.** Toussaint to Laveaux, 29 Frimaire an IV (20 December 1795). BNF NAF 12103. **21.** Toussaint's own forces were treacherously attacked when they took control of the town of Lascahobas. On the 'atrocious perfidiousness' of the Spanish at this time see Sonthonax reports, 25 and 27 Thermidor an IV (12 and 14 August 1796). BNF 8986, Papiers Sonthonax. **22.** Roume to Moyse, 26

Vendémiaire an VIII (18 October 1799). ANOM CC9A 26. **23.** Toussaint to Roume, 28 Nivôse an VIII (18 January 1800). ANOM CC9B 1. **24.** Roume to Toussaint, 4 Pluviôse an VIII (24 January 1800). ANOM CC9B 1. **25.** Toussaint to Roume, 8 Ventôse an VIII (27 February 1800). ANOM CC9 B 1. **26.** All the details in this passage are drawn from Roume's diary, entitled 'Journal du transport de l'agent du gouvernement au Haut du Cap', dated 5 Floréal an VIII (25 April 1800). ANOM CC9B 2. **27.** Proclamation of municipality of Gros-Morne, 20 Germinal an VIII (10 April 1800). ANOM CC9B 2. **28.** Proclamation of municipality of Dondon, 20 Germinal an VIII (10 April 1800). ANOM CC9B 2. **29.** Roume, 'Journal'. **30.** Roume report to Minister of Navy, 27 Prairial an VIII (16 June 1800). ANOM CC9B 1. **31.** Roume to Toussaint, 13 Floréal an VIII (3 May 1800). ANOM CC9B 2. **32.** Roume report to Minister of Navy, 19 Prairial an VIII (8 June 1800). ANOM CC9B 2. **33.** Toussaint letter, 7 Floréal an VIII (27 April 1800). ANOM CC9B 1. **34.** See Chapter 2. **35.** García to Roume, 24 Floréal an VIII (14 May 1800). ANOM CC9B 1. **36.** García letter, 27 April 1800, quoted in Itamar Olivares, 'La cession de Santo Domingo à la France', *Mélanges de la Casa de Velázquez* vol. 30, no. 2 (1994), p. 67. **37.** Petition of Santo Domingo notables to Bonaparte, 28 April 1800. ANOM CC9B 17. **38.** Petition of the inhabitants of Santo Domingo, 16 May 1800. ANOM CC9B 1. **39.** García proclamation, 21 May 1800, cited in Tortosa, *Santo Domingo*, p. 185. **40.** Roume to Toussaint, 24 Prairial an VIII (13 June 1800). ANOM CC9B 1. **41.** Roume to Toussaint, 18 Prairial an VIII (7 June 1800). ANOM CC9B 1. **42.** Roume to Toussaint, 27 Prairial an VIII (16 June 1800). ANOM CC9B 1. **43.** Roume decree, 27 Prairial an VIII (16 June 1800). ANOM CC9B 1. **44.** Toussaint to Roume, 18 Prairial an VIII (7 June 1800). ANOM CC9B 1. **45.** See for example Toussaint's letter to Joseph Idlinger, 28 Vendémiaire an VIII (20 October 1799). Boromé, 'A finding list'. **46.** Toussaint to Roume, 9 Messidor an VIII (28 June 1800). ANOM CC9B 1. **47.** Roume, *Moyens proposés au gouvernement français par son agent à Saint-Domingue pour la réorganisation de cette colonie, sans recourir aux voies de rigueur*, Cap, 22 Prairial an VIII (11 June 1800). ANOM CC9B 2. **48.** Ibid. **49.** Ibid. **50.** Ibid. **51.** 'réformé de toutes ses idées coloniales', ibid. **52.** *Compte-rendu sur Saint-Domingue par le citoyen Michel, général de division*, Paris, an IX (1800). AN AFIV 1213. **53.** Ibid. **54.** Ibid. **55.** 'Forfait' means 'default' or 'misdeed'. **56.** 'Métal corrupteur'. **57.** Toussaint to Bonaparte, n.d. [June 1800]. AN AFIV 1213. **58.** Nemours, *Histoire de la famille et de la descendance de Toussaint-Louverture*, pp. 149–54; the mission failed because the French authorities found out about it, and kept Toussaint's agents under close surveillance. **59.** Quoted in *Observations du général du génie Vincent*, p. 11. Slavery was abolished in the aftermath of the French Revolution in Saint-Domingue, Guadeloupe and Guyana, but in Bourbon (Réunion) island it remained in force, as local *colons* refused to accept the 1794 abolition decree. In 1802, slavery was formally restored in Bourbon island. **60.** Full details of the incident were related in a report to Roume by a French officer who was travelling alongside Michel. See report by Brigadier-General Pageot, 20 Prairial an VIII (9 June 1800); Pageot observed that this was not an isolated incident: 'il se vendait souvent des noirs français que des voleurs enlevaient'. ANOM CC9B 1. **61.** Toussaint, *Règlement relatif à la culture*, 20 Vendémiaire an IX (12 October 1800). ANOM CC9B 9. **62.** Vincent to Minister of Navy, 27 Floréal an IX (17 May 1801). ANOM CC9A 28. **63.** Sannon, *Histoire de Toussaint Louverture*, vol. 2, pp. 213–14. **64.** Lear to Douglas, Cap, 28 August 1801. National Archives, Kew, CO 137/106. **65.** Toussaint to Roume, 5 Frimaire an IX (26 November 1800). ANOM CC9B 2. **66.** Toussaint proclamation, Cap, 5 Frimaire an IX (26 November 1800). ANOM CC9B 2. **67.** Cited in Sannon, *Histoire de Toussaint Louverture*, vol. 2, pp. 216–17. **68.** Toussaint proclamation, San Jean de la Maguana, 14 Nivôse an IX (4 January 1801). ANOM CC9B 9. **69.** Emilio Cordero Michel, *La revolución haitiana y Santo Domingo* (Santo Domingo: Universidad Abierta para Adultos, 2000), p. 252. **70.** The details which follow are largely drawn from Toussaint, *Procès-verbal de la prise de possession de la partie espagnole de Saint-Domingue, Santo Domingo*, 12 Ventôse an IX (3 February 1801). BNF LK12-1277. **71.** Tortosa, *Santo Domingo*, p. 191. **72.** Toussaint, *Proclamation aux concitoyens de la partie française de*

Saint-Domingue, 13 Pluviôse an IX (2 February 1801). National Archives, Kew, CO 137/105. **73.** Chanlatte, *Précis historique des faits qui ont précédé l'invasion du territoire de la partie ci-devant Espagnole de Saint-Domingue par Toussaint Louverture*, Paris, 8 Prairial an IX (28 May 1801). ANOM CC9B 18. **74.** On the reception of these men by the local authorities, and the reaction in Venezuela to the events in Santo Domingo, see Jean-Pierre Tardieu, 'La province du Venezuela et l'insurrection de Saint-Domingue', *Annales historiques de la Révolution Française* 390 (2017), pp. 129–54. **75.** Isaac Louverture, *Notes historiques*. **76.** Quoted in Vincent, *Notice sur Dominique Toussaint Louverture*. **77.** Gilbert Guillermin, *Journal historique de la révolution de la partie est de Saint-Domingue* (Philadelphia, 1810), pp. 313–14. The author was a French officer and he witnessed the events described. **78.** Ibid., p. v. **79.** Toussaint to García, 26 Pluviôse an IX (15 February 1801), cited in Ardouin, *Études sur l'histoire d'Haiti*, vol. 4, p. 66. According to Périès, Toussaint told him that there were 900,000 *gourdes* in the Santo Domingo coffers at the time of his takeover of the Spanish territory, but that García had managed to get the bulk of the funds out. Jacques Périès, *La révolution de Saint-Domingue*. British Library MS 38074, f. 17, n.17. **80.** Diplomatic reports, late January and early February 1801, quoted in Tortosa, *Santo Domingo*, p. 189. **81.** Toussaint to Bonaparte, 23 Pluviôse an IX (12 February 1801), Santo Domingo. Archives Nationales d'Haïti (online document). **82.** Toussaint to Bonaparte, 23 Pluviôse an IX (12 February 1801). AN AB XIX 5002, Papiers Leclerc. **83.** Vincent, *Notice sur Dominique Toussaint Louverture*. **84.** Toussaint to Roume, 2 Floréal an IX (22 April 1801). ANOM CC9B 2. **85.** Toussaint to Cap municipality, 11 Fructidor an IX (29 August 1801). ANOM CC9B 2. Roume embarked on 16 Fructidor (3 September), and arrived in New York on 1 Vendémiaire an X (23 September 1801). See his letter to French consul-general Pichon, same date. Archives Diplomatiques Paris-La Courneuve, 40CP/37. **86.** Quoted in Sannon, *Histoire de Toussaint Louverture*, p. 223. **87.** Ardouin, *Études sur l'histoire d'Haïti*, vol. 4, p. 303. **88.** Tortosa, *Santo Domingo*, pp. 201 and 203. **89.** See José Luis Saez, *La iglesia y el negro esclavo en Santo Domingo: una historia de tres siglos* (Santo Domingo: Ciudad Colonial de Santo Domingo, 1994), p. 561. **90.** Nessler, *An Islandwide Struggle for Freedom*, p. 131. **91.** Memoirs of Gaspar Arredondo y Pichardo, quoted in Emilio Cordero Michel, 'Toussaint en Saint-Domingue espagnol', in Yacou (ed.), *Saint-Domingue espagnol*, p. 256. **92.** Michel, ibid., p. 255. **93.** Toussaint proclamation, Santo Domingo, 19 Pluviôse an IX (8 February 1801). ANOM CC9B 18. **94.** Toussaint proclamation, Santo Domingo, 19 Pluviôse an IX (8 February 1801). ANOM CC9B 9; emphasis added. This would also explain why Toussaint did not feel the need to proclaim the abolition of slavery in Santo Domingo: if the territory came under French law, it automatically meant that human bondage was not permitted. **95.** Pamphile de Lacroix, *La Révolution de Haïti*, pp. 258–9. **96.** Toussaint to García, Santo Domingo, 27 Pluviôse an IX (16 February 1801). Boromé, 'A finding list'. **97.** Toussaint proclamation, Santo Domingo, 23 Pluviôse an IX (12 February 1801). ANOM CC9B 9. **98.** Toussaint proclamation, Santo Domingo, 18 Pluviôse an IX (7 February 1801). ANOM CC9B 9. **99.** Pierre Lyonnet, *Statistique de la partie espagnole de Saint-Domingue* (Paris, 1800). **100.** See Descourtilz, *Voyages d'un naturaliste*, vol. 2, p. 448. **101.** Toussaint proclamation, Santo Domingo, 19 Pluviôse an IX (8 February 1801). ANOM CC9B 9. **102.** Toussaint proclamation, Santo Domingo, 12 Ventôse an IX (3 March 1801). ANOM CC9B 9. **103.** Toussaint to Dupré, Azua, 11 Pluviôse an X (31 January 1801); quoted in Dupré, *Mémoire*, 6 Vendémiaire an XI (28 September 1802). ANOM CC9A 32. **104.** Toussaint proclamation, Azua, 21 Nivôse an IX (11 January 1801). ANOM CC9B 18. **105.** Isaac Louverture, *Notes historiques*. **106.** Toussaint proclamation, Santo Domingo, 26 Ventôse an IX (17 March 1801). ANOM CC9B 9. **107.** Toussaint proclamation, Santo Domingo, 23 Fructidor an IX (10 September 1801). ANOM CC9B 9. **108.** Quoted in Tortosa, *Santo Domingo*, p. 196, n.258. **109.** Madiou, *Histoire d'Haïti*, vol. 2, p. 86. **110.** Emilio Cordero Michel, *La revolución haitiana y Santo Domingo*, p. 256. **111.** Fernando Pérez Memén, *La politica religiosa de Toussaint L'Ouverture en Santo Domingo* (Santo Domingo: Museo del Hombre Dominicano, 1984), p. 20. **112.** Letter of Doña Francisca Valerio, Santiago, January 1802, quoted in Michel, 'Toussaint en

Saint-Domingue espagnol', p. 255. **113.** 'Diario de lo ocurrido en Santo Domingo desde el 1° de enero de 1801 hasta el 20 del mismo', AGI, quoted in Boromé, 'A finding list'. **114.** Toussaint proclamation, Santo Domingo, 15 Nivôse an X (5 January 1802). ANOM CC9B 9.

9: IN THE REGION OF EAGLES

1. Toussaint proclamation, Santo Domingo, 16 Pluviôse an IX (5 February 1801). ANOM CC9B 9. **2.** Quoted in Sannon, *Histoire de Toussaint Louverture*, vol. 3, p. 4. **3.** Louis Dubroca, *La Vie de Toussaint-Louverture, chef des noirs insurgés de Saint-Domingue* (Paris, 1802), p. 43. **4.** James, *The Black Jacobins*, p. 266. **5.** Madiou, *Histoire d'Haïti*, vol. 2, p. 96. **6.** See most notably Julia Gaffield, 'Complexities of imagining Haiti: a study of national constitutions 1801–1807', *Journal of Social History* vol. 41, no. 1 (Fall 2007); Nick Nesbitt, *Universal Emancipation: The Haitian Revolution and the Radical Enlightenment* (Charlottesville: University of Virginia Press, 2008); Lorelle D. Semley, '"To Live and Die, Free and French": Toussaint Louverture's 1801 Constitution and the original challenge of black citizenship', *Radical History Review* vol. 115 (2013); Philip Kaisary, 'Hercules, the Hydra, and the 1801 Constitution of Toussaint Louverture', *Atlantic Studies*, September 2015; and Sibylle Fischer, 'Inhabiting rights', *L'esprit créateur* vol. 56, no. 1 (Spring 2016). **7.** Dorigny and Gainot, *La Société des Amis des Noirs*, pp. 324–5. **8.** For an illuminating discussion of the question see Sibylle Fischer, *Modernity Diasavowed: Haiti and the Cultures of Slavery in the Age of Revolution* (Durham, NC: Duke University Press, 2004), pp. 265–6. **9.** Toussaint to Minister of Navy, Santo Domingo, 23 Pluviôse an IX (12 February 1801). Archives Départementales de la Gironde, Collection Marcel Chatillon, 61 J 18. **10.** *Constitution républicaine des colonies française [sic] de Saint-Domingue en soixante-dix-sept articles, concernant la liberté des nègres, des gens de couleurs et des blancs*, Port-Républicain, 19 Floréal an IX (9 May 1801). BNF LK12-554. **11.** Cited in Placide Justin, *Histoire d'Hayti*, p. 340. **12.** *The Papers of Alexander Hamilton* (New York: Columbia University Press, 1975), vol. 22, pp. 492–3. **13.** Jean-Baptiste Lapointe to British government, London, May 1800. National Archives, Kew, WO 1/73. **14.** Report by Governor Manuel Guevara Vasconcelos, Caracas, 29 January 1801. Archivo General de Indias, Estado 59, n.17. **15.** Toussaint wrote of the 'sotte crédulité' of the British in a letter to the French Minister of Navy, 25 Thermidor an VII (12 August 1799). National Archives, Kew, CO 137/104. **16.** Corbet report of his conversations with Toussaint, Port-Républicain, 21 July 1801. National Archives, Kew, CO 137/105. **17.** Raimond report to Bonaparte, n.d. [1800]. ANOM CC9 B 2. For a more general evaluation of Raimond see John D. Garrigus, 'Opportunist or Patriot? Julien Raimond (1744–1801) and the Haitian Revolution', *Slavery and Abolition* vol. 28, no. 1 (2007). **18.** Jacques Périès, *La révolution de Saint-Domingue.* British Library MS 38074, ff. 24–5. **19.** Placide Justin, *Histoire d'Hayti*, p. 341. **20.** Sannon, *Histoire de Toussaint Louverture*, vol. 3, p. 5. **21.** Laurent Dubois, *Haiti: The Aftershocks of History* (New York, 2012), p. 34. **22.** For obvious reasons, no reports of the discussions were sent to France, but a copy of the minutes of the opening session rather mysteriously ended up in the British archives; see the following note. **23.** 'Extract from the records of the Central Assembly of Saint-Domingue', Port-Républicain, 28 March 1801. National Archives, Kew, CO 137/106. **24.** Article 34, ibid. **25.** 'Extract from the records of the Central Assembly of Saint-Domingue'. **26.** *Constitution républicaine.* **27.** Gaston de Nogérée, untitled recollections of his time in Saint-Domingue. Nogérée Papers, AN AB/XIX/5002. **28.** Ibid. **29.** Ibid. **30.** Toussaint to Minister of Navy, 6 Fructidor an IX (24 August 1801). AN AFIV 1213. **31.** Article 15, *Constitution républicaine.* **32.** Nogérée, recollections. **33.** 'Extract from the records of the Central Assembly of Saint-Domingue'. **34.** Nogérée, recollections. **35.** 'There must be a collective uprising of the people, men as well as women', ibid. This Dessalines speech was frequently cited in *colon* memoirs of the period; see for example *Considérations politiques sur la révolution des colonies françaises, mais particulièrement sur celle de Saint-Domingue, par Guillaume-Thomas DUFRESNE, colon de cette isle* (1805). BNF NAF 4372, f. 291. **36.** See for example Henry Perroud, *Projet* *d'une nouvelle organisation de la colonie de Saint-Domingue*, 1 Germinal an IX (22 March 1801). ANOM CC9A 28. **37.** *Faits historiques sur la colonie de Saint-Domingue*, 1800. AN AB XIX 3226. **38.** Letter from Roux, former inhabitant of Saint-Domingue, 1 Prairial an VIII (21 May 1800). ANOM CC9B 2. **39.** Proclamation of municipality of Gros-Morne, 20 Germinal an VIII (10 April 1800). ANOM CC9B 2. **40.** Proclamation of municipality of La Croix des Bouquets, 27 Germinal an VIII (17 April 1800). ANOM CC9B 17. **41.** Cited in Madiou, *Histoire d'Haïti*, vol. 2, p. 98. **42.** Toussaint, *Programme de la cérémonie qui aura lieu le 18 Messidor*, Cap, 15 Messidor an IX (4 July 1801). ANOM CC9B 18. **43.** *Procès-verbal de la cérémonie qui a eu lieu, au Cap-Français, le 18 Messidor, l'an neuvième de la République Française, une et indivisible, jour de la proclamation de la Constitution*. ANOM CC9B 18; all subsequent citations are from this source. **44.** Ibid., pp. 3–4. **45.** Ibid., pp. 7–9. **46.** Ibid., pp. 5–6. **47.** Ibid., p. 6 **48.** Article 76, *Constitution républicaine*. **49.** Jacques Périès, *La révolution de Saint-Domingue*. British Library MS 38074, f. 27. **50.** *Procès-verbal de la cérémonie qui a eu lieu, au Cap-Français, le 18 Messidor, l'an neuvième de la République Française, une et indivisible, jour de la proclamation de la Constitution*, pp. 11–12. **51.** Charles Vincent, 'Précis de mon dernier voyage à Saint-Domingue', Paris, 20 Pluviôse an X (9 February 1802). AN AFIV 1212. **52.** Vincent to Minister of Navy, 29 Prairial an VIII (18 June 1800). ANOM CC9A 28. **53.** Vincent, 'Précis de mon dernier voyage'. **54.** Ibid. **55.** Ibid. **56.** Toussaint letter, 27 Messidor an IX (16 July 1801). At around this time, Pichon had already written to Toussaint, informing him of rumours that he was about to declare his independence from France and make his rule a 'hereditary' position. See Pichon to Toussaint, 4 Thermidor an IX (23 July 1801). Archives Diplomatiques Paris-La Courneuve, 40CP/37. **57.** Pascal also made the same recommendation to the French commissioner in Philadelphia; see his letter to Pichon, 2 Thermidor an IX (21 July 1801). ANOM CC9A 28. **58.** 'He who can plant potatoes must also eat them'; quoted in Vincent, *Notice sur Dominique Toussaint Louverture*. **59.** Vincent, 'Précis de mon dernier voyage'. **60.** Vincent to Toussaint, Cap, 29 Messidor an IX (18 July 1801). AN AFIV 1212. **61.** The text was published in the *National Intelligencer* (Washington DC) on 12 August 1801, and then by several other American papers, notably in Philadelphia. **62.** Pichon to Toussaint, Georgetown, 5 Fructidor an IX (23 August 1801). Archives Diplomatiques Paris-La Courneuve, 40CP/37. By the early nineteenth century Algiers, although formally part of the Ottoman Empire, had become one of the centres of Barbary piracy, and its ships were frequently involved in attacks against European and American vessels. **63.** Pichon to Toussaint, Georgetown, 9 Fructidor an IX (27 August 1801). Archives Diplomatiques Paris-La Courneuve, 40CP/37. **64.** Vincent to Toussaint, Philadelphia, Fructidor an IX (August 1801). AN AFIV 1212. **65.** Article 40, *Constitution républicaine*. **66.** Vincent to Toussaint, Fructidor an IX (August 1801). AN AFIV 1212. **67.** Ibid. **68.** Pichon to French Minister of Navy, 18 Fructidor an IX (5 September 1801). ANOM CC9A 28. **69.** Vincent to Toussaint, Fructidor an IX (August 1801). AN AFIV 1212. **70.** Toussaint to Bonaparte, 27 Messidor an IX (16 July 1801). AN AFIV 1213. **71.** Toussaint to Bonaparte, 6 Fructidor an IX (24 August 1801). AN AFIV 1213. **72.** Pichon's source for this information was Edward Stevens, who had been secretly providing assistance to Roume throughout his ordeal in Dondon. Pichon mentioned Roume specifically in at least four letters to Toussaint: 4 Prairial, 4 Thermidor, 5 and 9 Fructidor an IX (24 May, 23 July, 23 and 27 August 1801). When Roume was released and finally reached the United States, Pichon thanked Toussaint (letter of 8 Vendémiaire [30 September]) while also complaining about his treatment of Roume, and noting that Agency funds amounting to 22,000 *livres* in cash (and as much in precious stones) he had left for safekeeping in the hands of the president of the Cap municipality had been 'appropriated'. Archives Diplomatiques Paris-La Courneuve, 40CP/37. **73.** Toussaint to Minister of Navy, 27 Messidor an IX (16 July 1801). AN AFIV 1213. **74.** Toussaint to Minister of Navy, 10 Fructidor an IX (28 August 1801). AN AFIV 1213. **75.** Toussaint to Bonaparte, 7 Fructidor an IX (25 August 1801). AN AFIV 1213. **76.** Periès report to Minister of Navy, 10 Fructidor an IX (28 August 1801). ANOM CC9B 18. But his death was in some sense a blessing, as Raimond's name was high on the list of Toussaint's supporters who were designated for elimination by the French invading army in 1802. **77.** *Anecdotes de la révolution de Saint-Domingue, racontées par Guillaume Mauviel, évêque de la colonie (1799–1804)* (Saint-Lô, 1885), p. 39. **78.** Bonaparte to Toussaint, 27 Brumaire an X (18 November 1801), in T. Lentz (ed.), *Napoléon Bonaparte: Correspondance générale* (Paris: Fayard, 2006), vol. 3, p. 853. **79.** *Constitution républicaine*, emphasis added. **80.** In his letter of 4 Thermidor an IX to Toussaint, Pichon mentions his letter to Pascal and dates it as 27 Messidor (16 July 1801). Archives Diplomatiques Paris-La Courneuve, 40CP/37. **81.** Pascal to Pichon, Cap, 20 Fructidor an IX (7 September 1801). ANOM CC9B 18. **82.** On this wider republican constitutional tradition see Nabulsi, *Traditions of War.* **83.** For further details see Charles Vincent, 'Notice sur un grand nombre d'hommes civils et militaires actuellement dans la colonie de Saint-Domingue' (1802). ANOM Collection Moreau de Saint-Méry F3 59. **84.** *Lois de la colonie française de Saint-Domingue* (Cap, 1801). **85.** *Loi sur les costumes*, 24 Thermidor an IX (12 August 1801), ibid., pp. 102–4. **86.** Article 30, *Constitution républicaine.* **87.** See for example Claude Moïse, *Le projet national de Toussaint Louverture* (Port-au-Prince, 2001), p. 33; see also the chapter on 'presidential monarchism' in Robert Fatton Jr, *The Roots of Haitian Despotism* (Boulder, CO: Lynne Rienner, 2007), pp. 81–130. **88.** The governor was tasked with 'overseeing the respect of the obligations or other commitments made by planters and their representatives to the labourers and workers'. Article 35, *Constitution républicaine.* **89.** See in particular article 33 of the constitution, which entrusts oversight of the proper functioning of the executive succession to the highest-ranking military officer. *Constitution républicaine.*

10: RAPID AND UNCERTAIN MOVEMENTS

1. *Loi sur la division du territoire de la colonie française de Saint-Domingue*, 14 Messidor an IX (3 July 1801). **2.** *Arrêté de Toussaint Louverture, gouverneur de Saint-Domingue, aux citoyens du département Louverture*, Cap-Français, 25 Messidor an IX (14 July 1801). ANOM CC9B 9. **3.** *Bulletin officiel de Saint-Domingue*, 19 Messidor an IX (8 July 1801). **4.** For a vivid description of social life in late-colonial Saint-Domingue see Rainsford, *An Historical Account*, pp. 220–28. **5.** See for example Toussaint's letter to Idlinger asking him to prepare a batch of letters for him to sign, Quartier Général d'Héricourt, 12 Brumaire an X (3 November 1801). Rochambeau Papers, University of Florida. **6.** Bunel to Nugent, Jamaica, September 1801. National Archives, Kew, CO 137/106. **7.** Pichon to Toussaint, Georgetown, 26 Germinal and 5 Floréal an IX (16 and 25 April 1801); Toussaint to Pichon, Cap, 14 Messidor an IX (3 July 1801). Archives Diplomatiques Paris-La Courneuve, 40CP/37. **8.** Report to French Minister of Navy, New York, 14 Prairial an IX (3 June 1801). ANOM CC9A 28. **9.** Tobias Lear to James Madison, Cap, 20 July 1801. Madison Papers, National Archives, Washington DC. **10.** Lear to Madison, Cap, 30 August 1801. Madison Papers, National Archives, Washington DC. **11.** Toussaint to Lear, 25 November 1801. Toussaint Louverture collection, Smithsonian Institution, Washington DC. **12.** 'activité dévorante': Pascal to Pichon, Cap, 20 Fructidor an IX (7 September 1801). ANOM CC9B 18. **13.** Toussaint, *Instructions aux fonctionnaires publics, civils et militaires*, 24 Floréal an IX (14 May 1801). ANOM CC9A 28. **14.** Ibid. **15.** Quoted in Vincent, *Notice sur Dominique Toussaint Louverture.* **16.** Toussaint to Julien Raimond, Cap, 6 Prairial an IX (26 May 1801). New York Public Library, digital collections. **17.** See Chapter 6. **18.** Toussaint to Pichon, Cap, 1 Thermidor an IX (20 July 1801); Pichon to Toussaint, Georgetown, 9 Fructidor an IX (27 August 1801). Archives Diplomatiques Paris-La Courneuve, 40CP/37. **19.** Toussaint, *arrêté*, 14 Thermidor an IX (2 August 1801). ANOM CC9B 18. **20.** Corbet report to Balcarres, Port-Républicain, 31 March 1801. NAM, 6807/183/1, ff. 285–291. **21.** Toussaint, *Règlement relatif à la culture*, 18 Floréal an IX (8 May 1801). ANOM CC9B 18. **22.** Sannon, *Histoire de Toussaint Louverture* vol. 3, p. 13. **23.** Toussaint, *arrêté*, 22 Messidor an IX (11 July 1801). ANOM CC9B 18. **24.** Madiou, *Histoire d'Haïti*, vol. 2, p. 117. **25.** 'maîtres voleurs'; Toussaint, *Avis*, 9 Thermidor an IX (28 July 1801). ANOM CC9B 18. **26.** *Instructions aux fonctionnaires publics.* **27.** See Whitfield report to Corbet, 8 May 1801. National Archives, Kew, CO 137/105. **28.** This will be discussed more fully in the next chapter. **29.** Robinson to Balcarres, Port-Républicain, 13 September 1800. National Archives, Kew, CO 137/105. **30.** Toussaint to Corbet, Port-Républicain, 11 Germinal an IX (1 April 1801). NAM, 6807/183/1, ff. 302–20. **31.** Corbet report to Balcarres, 31 March 1801. National Archives, Kew, CO 137/105. **32.** Toussaint proclamation, 16 Germinal an IX (6 April 1801). ANOM CC9B 18. **33.** Toussaint proclamation, 9 Floréal an IX (29 April 1801). NAM, 6807/183/1, f. 345. **34.** *Adresse de Toussaint Louverture général en chef de l'armée de Saint-Domingue aux militaires de tout grade*, Cap, 6 Floréal an IX. *Bulletin Officiel du Port-Républicain*, 29 Floréal an IX (19 May 1801). NAM, 6807/183/1, f. 344. **35.** Madiou, *Histoire d'Haïti*, vol. 2, p. 105. **36.** *Loi sur la religion catholique, apostolique et romaine*, 16 Messidor an IX (5 July 1801). **37.** Report to French Minister of Navy, New York, 14 Prairial an IX (3 June 1801). ANOM CC9A 28. **38.** Fritzner Étienne, 'L'Eglise et la révolution des esclaves', p. 19. **39.** *Profession de foi des ministres du culte catholique du département du Nord*, Cap, 11 Germinal an IX (1 April 1801). ANOM CC9B 18. **40.** Guillaume Mauviel, 'Mémoire sur la colonie de Saint-Domingue', unpublished MS, 1805. AN FIV 1212. On Mauviel see more generally Gabriel Debien, *Guillaume Mauviel, evêque constitutionnel de Saint-Domingue* (Basse-Terre, Guadeloupe: Société d'histoire de la Guadeloupe, 1981). **41.** Toussaint, *arrêté*, 19 Floréal an IX (9 May 1801). ANOM CC9B 9. **42.** Toussaint, ordinance, Port-Républicain, 14 Nivôse an VIII (4 January 1800). ANOM CC9B 9. **43.** Ramsey, *The Spirits and the Law*, p. 48. Article 3 of the *Loi sur la religion* stipulated that no religious ceremony could take place 'before sunrise or after sunset'. **44.** Toussaint proclamation, 24 Vendémiaire an X (16 October 1801). ANOM CC9B 18. **45.** *Instructions aux fonctionnaires publics*. **46.** Madiou, *Histoire d'Haïti*, vol. 2, p. 109. **47.** Pichon to Minister of Navy, 18 Fructidor an IX (5 September 1802). ANOM CC9A 28. **48.** See L. Darondel, 'La fortune de Toussaint Louverture et Stephen Girard', *Revue de la Société d'histoire et de géographie d'Haïti* (July 1943); and Gabriel Debien, 'À propos du trésor de Toussaint Louverture', *Revue de la société d'Histoire et de Géographie d'Haïti* (July 1946); the alleged sums ranged between two million and forty million dollars. **49.** Toussaint, *Règlement relatif à la culture*, 20 Vendémiaire an IX (12 October 1801). ANOM CC9B 9. **50.** See Dessalines proclamation, Port-Républicain, in *Bulletin Officiel du Port-Républicain*, 29 Floréal an IX (19 May 1801). **51.** Toussaint, 'Ordonnance sur la répression des propos incendiaires', 5 Brumaire an IX (27 October 1800). ANOM CC9B 9. **52.** Gabriel Debien, *Plantations et esclaves à Saint-Domingue* (Dakar: University of Dakar, 1962), p. 161. **53.** Nugent to Portland, Jamaica, 5 September 1801. National Archives, Kew, CO 137/106. **54.** Mauviel, 'Mémoire sur la colonie de Saint-Domingue'. **55.** Toussaint, memorandum to civil and military officials, 28 Fructidor an IX (15 September 1801). ANOM CC9B 18. **56.** Toussaint to Pichon, 14 Messidor and 23 Thermidor an IX (3 July and 11 August 1801). Archives Diplomatiques Paris-La Courneuve, 40CP/37. **57.** Toussaint proclamation, 8 Vendémiaire an X (30 September 1801). ANOM CC9B 9. **58.** Toussaint proclamation, 16 Vendémiaire an X (8 October 1801). ANOM CC9B 9. **59.** Pluchon, *Toussaint Louverture*, p. 400. **60.** Toussaint proclamation, n.d. [early 1802]. ANOM CC9 B9. **61.** *Commerce de la colonie pendant l'An VIII*. ANOM CC9A 28. **62.** Report to Bonaparte, 1 Thermidor an IX (20 July 1801). AN AFIV 1213. **63.** Lundahl, 'Toussaint Louverture and the war economy of Saint-Domingue', p. 135. **64.** Claude Auguste and Marcel Auguste, *L'expédition Leclerc 1801–1803* (Port-au-Prince: Imprimerie H. Deschamps, 1985), p. 15. **65.** Vincent, 'Notice sur un grand nombre d'hommes civils et militaires'. **66.** After his expulsion to the United States, Roume noted in a letter to Pichon that Toussaint had been reading all his correspondence 'for the past eighteen months', New York, 1 Vendémiaire an X (23 September 1801). Archives Diplomatiques Paris-La Courneuve, 40CP/37. **67.** Letter to French Ministry of Navy, Cap, 6 Prairial an VIII (26 May 1800). AN AFIV 1212. **68.** Letter to Guiton de Maulévrier, Cap, 21 Frimaire an VIII (12 December 1799), cited in de Cauna (ed.), *Toussaint Louverture et l'indépendance d'Haïti*, p. 74. **69.** 'Quelques observations sur le parti à prendre, relativement à la colonie de Saint-Domingue', 27 Vendémiaire an IX (19 October 1800). ANOM CC9A 28. **70.** Malenfant, *Des colonies*, p. 78. **71.** Pierre-Jacques de la Ferronays letter,

April 1801, cited in Paul Cheney, *Cul de Sac: Patrimony, Capitalism, and Slavery in French Saint-Domingue* (Chicago: University of Chicago Press, 2017), p. 187. **72.** Duboys, *Précis historique*, vol. 2, p. 6. **73.** Guilhou letter, Port-Républicain, 10 Brumaire an IX (1 November 1800). ANOM CC9A 28. **74.** Guilhou to Toussaint, n.d. [late 1801]. ANOM CC9A 32. **75.** Letter from chief medical officer Decout, Les Cayes, 15 Brumaire an X (6 November 1801). ANOM CC9A 28. **76.** See Toussaint's letter to Deseulle, 23 Thermidor an V (10 August 1797), ANOM CC9A 15; see also Toussaint to Vincent, 30 Vendémiaire an VI (21 October 1797), AN AFIII 210. **77.** Toussaint to Roume, Port-de-Paix, 25 Thermidor an VII (12 August 1799). ANOM CC9A 25. **78.** Deseulle to Toussaint, Cap, 14 Fructidor an IX (1 September 1801). ANOM CC9B 2. **79.** Ibid. **80.** 'Mémoire sur la colonie de Saint-Domingue', 1801. AN AFIV 1212. **81.** 'Notice sur Toussaint Louverture, au général Bonaparte', 1801. AN AFIV 1212. **82.** 'Lettre d'un colon de Saint-Domingue au premier consul' (early 1802). AN AFIV 1213. **83.** 'Idées sur Saint-Domingue', 1801. AN AFIV 1212. **84.** Toussaint to Descourtilz, Cap, 14 Fructidor an IX (1 September 1801). Archives Départementales de la Gironde, Collection Marcel Chatillon, 61 J 18. **85.** Descourtilz, *Voyages d'un naturaliste*, vol. 3, pp. 245–6, 249 and 253. **86.** Jacques Périès, *La révolution de Saint-Domingue*. British Library MS 38074, f. 7. **87.** Ibid., ff. 18–19. **88.** Périès to Minister of Navy, 25 Brumaire an IX (16 November 1800). ANOM CC9B 18. **89.** See 'Demande de concession de la Compagnie Périès dans l'ancienne partie espagnole'. ANOM CC9A 23. **90.** Périès to Minister of Navy, 25 Germinal an IX (15 April 1801). ANOM CC9B 18. **91.** Périès letter, 15 Messidor an VIII (4 July 1800). ANOM CC9B 18. **92.** Périès letter, 25 Thermidor an VIII (13 August 1800). ANOM CC9B 18. **93.** Edward Corbet report to Balcarres, Port-Républicain, 31 March 1801. NAM, 6807/183/1, ff. 285–291. **94.** Périès letter, 25 Brumaire an IX (16 November 1800). ANOM CC9B 18. **95.** December 1802 letter, Port-au-Prince, quoted in Gabriel Debien, 'Réfugiés de Saint-Domingue aux Etats-Unis', *Revue de la Société d'histoire et de géographie d'Haïti* vol. 21, no. 79 (October 1950), pp. 20–21. **96.** Letter to French Minister of Navy, 1 Floréal an IX (21 April 1801). ANOM CC9A 24. **97.** Périès letter, 25 Germinal an IX (15 April 1801). ANOM CC9B 18. **98.** Périès letter, 30 Messidor an VIII (19 July 1800), ANOM CC9B 18. He repeated the point in his later memoir: 'whether free or enslaved', black people were 'criminal by their very nature' ('ne connaissent d'autre vertu que le crime'). Périès, *La révolution de Saint-Domingue*. British Library MS 38074, f. 38. **99.** Périès letter, 25 Thermidor an VIII (13 August 1800). ANOM CC9B 18. **100.** Périès letter, 27 Thermidor an IX (15 August 1801). ANOM CC9B 18. **101.** Letter, 8 Brumaire an X (30 October 1801). ANOM CC9B 18. **102.** Whitfield report to Nugent, Port-Républicain, 5 December 1801. National Archives, Kew, CO 137/106. **103.** Toussaint, *Récit des événements qui se sont passés dans la partie Nord de Saint-Domingue depuis le 29 Vendémiaire jusqu'au 13 Brumaire an X*, p. 11. ANOM CC9B 18. **104.** 'Coup d'oeil of the actual situation of the colony of Saint-Domingue', n.d. [1801]. National Archives, Kew, WO 1/72. **105.** This was notably the view of Périès; see *La révolution de Saint-Domingue*. British Library MS 38074, ff. 29–30. **106.** Roume to Minister of Navy, Philadelphia, 11 Frimaire an X (2 December 1801). ANOM CC9B 2. **107.** Ibid. **108.** Corbet report, 16 November 1801. National Archives, Kew, CO 137/106. **109.** Roume to Minister of Navy, New York, 3 Vendémiaire an X (25 November 1801). ANOM CC9B 2. **110.** Toussaint, *Récit des événements*, p. 3. **111.** See for example Moyse's letter to the municipal council of Montéchrist, 28 Ventôse an VIII (19 March 1800), in which he accused the authorities of complicity in human trafficking. ANOM CC9B 17. **112.** Cited in Delatte, 'Mémoire sur les évènements de Fort-Liberté', 16 Frimaire an VII (6 December 1798). ANOM CC9A 22. **113.** Claude B. Auguste, 'L'Affaire Moyse', *Revue de la Société haïtienne d'histoire et de géographie* nos 180–81 (July–October 1994), p. 9. **114.** Whitfield report to Nugent, Port-Républicain, 5 December 1801. National Archives, Kew, CO 137/106. **115.** Toussaint, *Récit des événements*, p. 11. **116.** Ibid. **117.** Pageot to Minister of Navy, Philadelphia, 10 Pluviôse an X (30 January 1802). ANOM CC9B 18. **118.** Madiou, *Histoire d'Haïti*, vol. 2, p. 123. **119.** Toussaint to British representative, 11 Germinal an IX (1 April 1801). NAM, 6807/183/1, ff. 302–320. **120.** See for example the letter vaunting Christophe's merits as a loyal French ally from Roume to the Minister of

Navy, New York, 3 Vendémiaire an X (25 September 1801). ANOM CC9 B2. **121.** Whitfield to Toussaint, 20 January 1801, National Archives, Kew, CO 245/1; Toussaint to Balcarres, Santo Domingo, 1 February 1801, CO 137/105. **122.** Whitfield report to John King, Whitehall, 17 June 1801. National Archives, Kew, CO 137/106. **123.** Corbet to Balcarres, 6 March 1801. National Archives, Kew, CO 245/1. **124.** Corbet reports to Balcarres, 31 March and 21 July 1801, and to Nugent, 9 September 1801. National Archives, Kew, CO 137/105 and CO 137/106. **125.** Balcarres to Vice-Admiral Hugh Seymour, 28 July 1801. National Archives, Kew, CO 137/105. **126.** See Corbet update to Nugent on the discussions, Kingston, 24 October 1801. National Archives, Kew, CO 137/106. **127.** Bunel-Corbet agreement, Kingston, Jamaica, 16 November 1801. NAM, 6807/183/1, ff. 131–142. **128.** Philip Wright (ed.), *Lady Nugent's Journal of her Residence in Jamaica from 1801 to 1805* (Kingston, Jamaica: University of West Indies Press, 2002), entry for 21 October 1801. **129.** 'Adresse des citoyens des États-Unis d'Amérique résidant au Cap Français', 21 Brumaire an X (12 November 1801). ANOM CC9B 18. **130.** Proclamation of Cap municipality, 19 Brumaire an X (10 November 1801). ANOM CC9B 18. **131.** Letter from Mr Law, Gonaïves, 26 October 1801. National Archives, Kew, CO 137/106. **132.** Toussaint decree, Cap, 19 Brumaire an X (10 November 1801). ANOM CC9B 18. **133.** Letter from Moyse to Toussaint, 15 Fructidor an VII (1 September 1799). ANOM CC9A 26. **134.** Moyse to Isaac and Placide Louverture, 12 Ventôse an IX (3 March 1801). Bibliothèque Municipale, Nantes. **135.** Toussaint decree, Cap, 4 Frimaire an X (25 November 1801). ANOM CC9B 9. **136.** Ibid. **137.** Decree of 10 January 1802, Santo Domingo, 'Diario de lo ocurrido en Santo Domingo'. **138.** Toussaint decree, Cap, 4 Frimaire an X (25 November 1801). ANOM CC9B 9. **139.** Ibid.

11: THE TREE OF BLACK LIBERTY

1. See for example the letter of Borgella to Toussaint, 30 January 1802, in which he mentions these rumours circulating in the colony 'for the past two months'. ANOM CC9B 19. **2.** Secret memorandum from Lord Hobart, Downing Street, London, 18 November 1801. National Archives, Kew, CO 137/106. **3.** Toussaint to Nugent, 8 December 1801, National Archives, Kew, CO 137/106; Nugent letter, Jamaica, 29 November 1801, NAM, 6807/183/1, ff. 439–40. **4.** Whitfield to Nugent, Port-Républicain, 9 December 1801. National Archives, Kew, CO 137/106. **5.** Whitfield to Corbet, Port-Républicain, 17 December 1801. National Archives, Kew, CO 137/107. **6.** After initially trying to get them back stealthily (see Chapter 8), he first formally asked for both of his children to be returned to him in February 1801. Toussaint to Minister of Navy, Santo Domingo, 23 Pluviôse an IX (12 February 1801). Archives Départementales de la Gironde, Collection Marcel Chatillon, 61 J 18. **7.** Toussaint proclamation, Port-Républicain, 19 Frimaire an X (20 December 1801). ANOM CC9 B9. **8.** Auguste Nemours, *Histoire de la guerre d'indépendance de Saint-Domingue* (Paris and Nancy: Berger-Levrault, 1925), vol. 1, p. 1. **9.** Nemours, *Histoire de la famille et de la descendance de Toussaint-Louverture*, p. 363. **10.** *Mémoires d'Isaac fils de Toussaint Louverture sur l'expédition des français sous le Consulat de Napoléon Bonaparte.* BNF NAF 12409. **11.** Rallier sent Bonaparte a copy of his *Observations sur la situation actuelle de la colonie de Saint-Domingue* (1800). AN AFIV 1212. **12.** The draft document, dated 17 Pluviôse an IX (6 February 1801), is still in Toussaint's personal folder in the Archives Nationales. AN EE 1991. **13.** Letter of Bonaparte, 13 Ventôse an IX (4 March 1801), cited in Sannon, *Histoire de Toussaint Louverture*, vol. 3, p. 36. **14.** Instructions to colonial prefect, cited in ibid., p. 37. **15.** Navy Minister to Toussaint, April 1801, ANOM CC9B 18; see also decree of consuls on Santo Domingo, 7 Brumaire an X. **16.** Instructions to Rear-Admiral Lacrosse, 4 January 1800. Napoleon Bonaparte, *Correspondance générale*, vol. 3, pp. 22–4. **17.** Gainot, 'Le général Laveaux, gouverneur de Saint-Domingue', p. 451. **18.** *Journal du Comte P.-L. Roederer, ministre et conseiller d'état* (Paris, 1909), quoted in Geggus (ed.), *The Haitian Revolution*, p. 171. **19.** Kerverseau report, 7 September 1801. ANOM CC9B 23. **20.** François Barbé de Marbois, *Réflexions sur la colonie de*

Saint-Domingue (Paris, 1796). **21.** Emmanuel de Las Cases, *Mémorial de Sainte-Hélène*, ed. M. Dunan (Paris: Flammarion, 1983), vol. 1, pp. 714–16. **22.** See notably Vincent's letter to the commander of the expedition, Paris, 27 Brumaire an X (18 November 1801). ANOM Collection Moreau de Saint-Méry F3 283. **23.** Charles Vincent, 'Réflexions sur l'état actuel de la colonie de Saint-Domingue et sur les moyens d'y rétablir l'autorité de la métropole', 21 Vendémiaire an X (13 October 1801). ANOM Collection Moreau de Saint-Méry F3 283. **24.** Vincent, *Notice sur Dominique Toussaint Louverture*. **25.** *Observations du général du génie Vincent*, p. 13. **26.** Quoted in Sannon, *Histoire de Toussaint Louverture*, vol. 3, p. 33; the decree banning black people and persons of colour was promulgated in July 1802. **27.** Quoted in Antoine-Clair Thibaudeau, *Mémoires sur le Consulat* (Paris, 1827), pp. 120–21. I am grateful to David Bell for bringing this passage to my attention. **28.** Quoted in Pamphile de Lacroix, *La Révolution de Haïti*, p. 283. **29.** Toussaint to Paul Louverture, 17 Pluviôse an X (6 February 1802). Boromé, 'A finding list'. **30.** See for example his agreement with the American merchant James Gillespie, 5 Vendémiaire an IX (27 September 1800), quoted in Nemours, *Relations internationales*, pp. 152–3. **31.** See the report by Whitfield to Corbet about the arrival in Cap of an American brig loaded with weapons, 19 May 1801. NAM, 6807/183/1, f. 341. See also report from French Agency official Liot to Pichon, Cap, 25 Thermidor an IX (13 August 1801) concerning an agreement for the sale of American weapons concluded between Toussaint and an American merchant named Holmes. Archives Diplomatiques Paris-La Courneuve, 40CP/37. **32.** Report from French commissioner, Philadelphia, 14 Prairial an IX (3 June 1801). ANOM CC9A 28. **33.** Military report to French minister of Navy, 2 Ventôse an XI (21 February 1803). ANOM CC9A 30. **34.** Toussaint note to Borgella, 12 December 1801; cited in Duboys, *Précis historique*, vol. 2, pp. 227–8. **35.** Pamphile de Lacroix, *La Révolution de Haïti*, p. 284. **36.** French military report, 20 February 1802. ANOM CC9B 23. See also Nemours, *Histoire militaire*, vol. 1, p. 114; a further 24,000 soldiers were sent during the course of the conflict. **37.** See for example the letter to Toussaint from Leandre, commander of La Saline, 4 Ventôse an X (23 February 1802); Archives départementales de la Gironde, 61 J 18. See also Nemours, *Histoire militaire*, vol. 1, p. 194. **38.** Toussaint wrote two letters from his Saint-Marc headquarters to his brother, one calling on him to continue to resist in Santo Domingo and the other (to be used only if the messenger was intercepted by the French) to co-operate with the French. Kerverseau's forces captured the messenger, and the French general then deceived Paul Louverture by sending him the second letter. Both texts, dated 20 Pluviôse an X (9 February 1802), are in Kerverseau's correspondence. Archives départementales de la Gironde, Collection Marcel Chatillon, 61 J 24. **39.** *Précis des services de Joseph Antoine Idlinger, commissaire ordonnateur à Saint-Domingue*. Archives de la Seine, Paris, DQ10-1418, dossier Joseph Idlinger. **40.** Toussaint to Leclerc, Gonaïves, 22 Pluviôse an X (11 February 1802). AN AB XIX 5002, Papiers Leclerc. **41.** Claude Auguste and Marcel Auguste, *L'expédition Leclerc 1801–1803*, p. 93. **42.** Maurepas report to Toussaint, 6 February 1802. Archives départementales de la Gironde, Collection Marcel Chatillon, 61 J 18. **43.** Maurepas reports to Toussaint, 11 and 14 February 1802. Archives départementales de la Gironde, Collection Marcel Chatillon, 61 J 18. **44.** Pluchon, *Toussaint Louverture*, p. 478. **45.** Girard, *The Slaves Who Defeated Napoleon*, pp. 90–91. **46.** Bonaparte proclamation, 17 Brumaire an X (8 November 1801). **47.** Bonaparte to Toussaint, 18 November 1801. **48.** Antoine Métral, *Histoire de l'expédition militaire des français à Saint-Domingue* (Paris, 1825), p. 59. Coisnon gave a more embellished account of the meeting in a letter to Leclerc. See Archives départementales de la Gironde, Collection Marcel Chatillon, 61 J 18. **49.** Bonaparte notes for instructions to Leclerc, 31 October 1801; Archives Nationales AFIV/863; also in Gustav Roloff, *Die Kolonialpolitik Napoleons I* (Munich, 1899), appendix. **50.** For a detailed study of the phenomenon, drawing on French archival sources, see Charles Bonaparte Auguste and Marcel Bonaparte Auguste, *Les déportés de Saint-Domingue* (Quebec: Éditions Naaman, 1979). **51.** Ibid. **52.** Leclerc to Minister of Navy, 17 Messidor (6 July 1802), *Lettres du général Leclerc* (Paris: Ernest Leroux, 1937), p. 182. **53.** Ibid., pp. 98–100. **54.** 'Notice sur un grand nombre d'hommes civils et militaires'. **55.** Girard, *The Slaves Who Defeated Napoleon*, pp. 121–2. **56.** Nemours, *Histoire militaire*, vol. 1,

p. 227; Auguste, *L'expédition Leclerc 1801–1803*, pp. 134–5. **57.** Madiou, *Histoire d'Haïti*, vol. 2, pp. 182–3. **58.** Toussaint speech, 19–20 Pluviôse an X (8–9 February 1802), quoted in Métral, *Histoire de l'expédition des français à Saint-Domingue*, pp. 67–8. **59.** Toussaint to Dommage, 9 February 1802, quoted in Sannon, *Histoire de Toussaint Louverture*, vol. 3, p. 59. **60.** Toussaint to Dessalines, 8 February 1802, quoted in ibid., p. 58. **61.** Admiral Villaret de Joyeuse to Leclerc, 3 Ventôse an X (22 February 1802). AN AB XIX 5002, Papiers Leclerc. **62.** Quoted in report by French officer Jean Figeac, 14 Vendémiaire an XI (6 October 1802). ANOM CC9A 32. **63.** Descourtilz, *Voyages d'un naturaliste*, vol. 3, pp. 304–6 and 359 n.1. **64.** A number of Vernet's letters to Toussaint from March and April 1802 are in the Rochambeau Papers; there is also a copy of Belair's letter to Toussaint, Habitation Mayance, 21 Germinal an X (11 April 1802). Rochambeau Papers, University of Florida. **65.** See for example the frustrated letter by General Desfourneaux to Leclerc, Plaisance, 15 Ventôse an X (16 March 1802). AN 135AP/6, Papiers Rochambeau. **66.** Letter of commander Dalton, 5 Germinal an X (26 March 1802), cited in Nemours, *Histoire militaire*, vol. 2, p. 410. **67.** Jacques de Norvins, *Souvenirs d'un historien de Napoléon*, vol. 2, p. 376. **68.** Pamphile de Lacroix, *La Révolution de Haïti*, p. 325. **69.** Leclerc to Decrès, 27 February 1802. ANOM CC9 B19. **70.** Leclerc to Bonaparte, 25 March 1802, in *Lettres du général Leclerc*, pp. 116–17. **71.** Leclerc to Minister of Navy, 21 April 1802, ibid., pp. 130–32. **72.** A few letters from Sans-Souci to Toussaint have survived; one is dated March 1802, written from his headquarters in Grande-Rivière, and is in the Kurt Fisher collection in the New York Public Library; another from April 1802 is cited in Auguste, *L'expédition Leclerc 1801–1803*, pp. 147–8; there are also two of his letters from early April 1802 in the Rochambeau Papers, University of Florida. **73.** Girard, *The Slaves Who Defeated Napoleon*, p. 121. **74.** Madiou, *Histoire d'Haïti*, vol. 2, p. 203. **75.** Dessalines letter 14 March 1802, in de Cauna (ed.), *Toussaint Louverture et l'indépendance d'Haïti*, p. 14; *Mémoires d'Isaac Louverture*, p. 261. **76.** Madiou, *Histoire d'Haïti*, vol. 2, p. 222; Saint-Rémy, *Vie de Toussaint*, p. 368. **77.** Nemours, *Histoire militaire*, vol. 1, p. 255. **78.** Métral, *Histoire de l'expédition des français à Saint-Domingue*, p. 69. **79.** Ibid., p. 87. **80.** Toussaint proclamation, 10 Ventôse an X (1 March 1802); quoted in Sannon, *Histoire de Toussaint Louverture*, vol. 3, pp. 75–81. **81.** Duboys, *Précis historique*, vol. 2, p. 259. **82.** Boudet to Toussaint, Port-Républicain, 11 Germinal an X (1 April 1802). AN AB XIX 5002, Papiers Leclerc. **83.** Toussaint to Boudet, Dondon headquarters, 21 Germinal an X (11 April 1802). AN AB XIX 5002, Papiers Leclerc. **84.** Ibid. **85.** Auguste, *L'expédition Leclerc 1801–1803*, p. 116. **86.** André Vernet to Toussaint, Saint-Michel, 10 Floréal an X (30 April 1802). Rochambeau Papers, University of Florida. **87.** Toussaint, *arrêté*, 9 Floréal an X (29 April 1802). ANOM CC9B 9. **88.** Toussaint to Christophe, 8 Floréal an X (28 April 1802). Archives Départementales de la Gironde, Collection Marcel Chatillon, 61 J 18; the envelope was marked 'service militaire très pressé'. On the second offensive see Nemours, *Histoire militaire*, vol. 1, pp. 266, 270–71. **89.** Norvins, *Souvenirs d'un historien de Napoléon*, vol. 2, pp. 308–9, 362–3. **90.** See his letter to Toussaint, 14 February 1802: 'even though this (French) army has come to deprive us of our liberty, I cannot help treat its captive soldiers with humanity. For it is not they we should direct our rage at, but their chiefs.' Archives Départementales de la Gironde, Collection Marcel Chatillon, 61 J 18. **91.** Toussaint to Leclerc, Verrettes, 25 Pluviôse an X (14 February 1802). AN AB XIX 5002, Papiers Leclerc. **92.** Pamphile de Lacroix, *La Révolution de Haïti*, p. 349. **93.** Norvins, *Souvenirs d'un historien*, vol. 2, pp. 395–6. **94.** *Mémoires d'Isaac Louverture*, p. 292. **95.** Leclerc to Toussaint, 17 Floréal an X (7 May 1802), and Toussaint reply 22 Floréal an X (12 May 1802); Toussaint in the end was allowed a guard of twelve soldiers. AN AB XIX 5002, Papiers Leclerc. **96.** Toussaint to Leclerc, 22 Floréal an X (12 May 1802). AN AB XIX 5002, Papiers Leclerc. **97.** *Mémoires d'Isaac Louverture*, pp. 295–6. **98.** Bonaparte to Leclerc, 16 March 1802, quoted in Sannon, *Histoire de Toussaint Louverture*, vol. 3, p. 102. **99.** Toussaint to Gonaïves commander, 25 Floréal (15 May 1802). AN 135AP/6, Papiers Rochambeau. **100.** Toussaint to Dugua, 25 May 1802. AN AB XIX 5002, Papiers Leclerc. **101.** In a letter to Leclerc dated 21 Prairial (22 May 1802), Dessalines complained that he had received emissaries from Toussaint from Plaisance seeking instructions about how to 'continue the rebellion'. AN 135AP/6, Papiers Rochambeau. On Sylla's resistance see Auguste, *L'expédition Leclerc 1801–1803*, pp. 163–7. **102.** Reported in Descourtilz, *Voyages d'un naturaliste*, vol. 3, p. 186. **103.** Toussaint to Brunet, 16 Prairial an X (5 June 1802). AN 135AP/6, Papiers Rochambeau. **104.** *Mémoires d'Isaac Louverture*, pp. 307–8. **105.** Leclerc proclamation, 22 Prairial an X (11 June 1802), *Gazette Officielle de Saint-Domingue*, 4 Messidor an X (23 June 1802). **106.** On the 'wonderful and superb' destiny of Gingembre, who ended up being deported to Corsica along with a number of Toussaint's most ardent supporters, see Nemours, *Histoire militaire*, vol. 2, pp. 300–43. **107.** Toussaint letter, 7 Prairial an X (27 May 1802), cited in Sannon, *Histoire de Toussaint Louverture*, vol. 3, p. 108, n.2. **108.** Toussaint to Leclerc, 22 Floréal an X (12 May 1802). AN AB XIX 5002, Papiers Leclerc. **109.** Report by Brigadier Pesquidon, 30 Floréal an X (20 May 1802). AN 135AP/6, Papiers Rochambeau. **110.** Brunet to Leclerc, Habitation Georges, 7 June 1802. AN 135AP/6, Papiers Rochambeau. **111.** Two 'emissaries' (spies) who were 'following the movements of Toussaint' were paid 1,200 francs. A separate entry of 4,000 francs for 'extraordinary expenses' also mentions 'presents to Dessalines and his wife, and funds paid to his officers'. Brunet to Leclerc, Habitation Georges, 19 June 1802. AN 135AP/6, Papiers Rochambeau. **112.** Toussaint to Bonaparte, Brest, 1 Thermidor an X (20 July 1802). AN AFIV 1213. **113.** Report of mayor of Bayonne, 14 Fructidor an X (1 September 1802). AN EE 1991. **114.** On this period see Nemours, *Histoire de la captivité et de la mort de Toussaint Louverture* (Paris and Nancy: Berger-Levrault, 1929). **115.** Leclerc to Minister of Navy, 17 Messidor an X (6 July 1802), in P. Roussier (ed.), *Lettres du général Leclerc*, p. 183. **116.** Nemours, *Histoire de la captivité*, pp. 51 and 57. **117.** The order came directly from Bonaparte, and was conveyed by his Minister of War, Berthier (letter of 13 Fructidor an X [31 August 1802] to Fouché). AN 135AP/6, Papiers Rochambeau. **118.** Baille to Minister of Navy, 10 Brumaire an XI (1 November 1802). ANOM CC9B 18. **119.** Testimony gathered by Dubois and relayed in his letter to Grégoire, Paris, 25 May 1823. BNF NAF 6864. **120.** Mars Plaisir to Isaac Louverture, Paris, 3 October 1815. BNF NAF 6864. **121.** See Whitfield report to Nugent, 5 December 1801. National Archives, Kew, CO 137/106. **122.** Pamphile de Lacroix, *La Révolution de Haïti*, p. 312; see also Périès, *La révolution de Saint-Domingue*, f. 35. **123.** Philippe Artières (ed.), *Journal du général Caffarelli* (Paris: Mercure de France, 2016), p. 126. **124.** Caffarelli report to Bonaparte, 2 Vendémiaire an XI (24 September 1802), AN EE 1991; see also Henry Gauthier-Villars, 'La captivité de Toussaint Louverture', *Revue Bleue*, 23 January 1892. **125.** Toussaint to Bonaparte, 30 Fructidor an X (17 September 1802). AN AFIV 1213. **126.** Jeannin to Isaac Louverture, Fort de Joux, 24 November 1810. BNF NAF 6864. **127.** Artières (ed.), Toussaint Louverture, *Mémoires*, p. 93. **128.** Ibid., pp. 99–100. **129.** Ibid., pp. 89–90. **130.** Ibid., p. 62. **131.** Ibid., p. 96. **132.** Ibid., p. 94. **133.** Ibid., p. 92. **134.** Ibid., p. 91. **135.** Ibid., p. 66. **136.** Ibid., p. 76. **137.** Duboys, *Précis historique*, vol. 2, p. 261. **138.** Letter of Follin, 22 March 1803, Cap, in Gabriel Debien, 'Vers la fin de l'expédition de Saint-Domingue', *Caribbean Studies* vol. 11, no. 2 (July 1971), p. 100. **139.** Toussaint to Bonaparte, 17 Vendémiaire an XI (8 October 1802). AN AFIV 1213. **140.** The fort's chapel was destroyed in 1879, and so Toussaint's remains have been for ever lost. **141.** Toussaint to Bonaparte, 17 Vendémiaire an XI (8 October 1802). AN AFIV 1213. **142.** See Julia Gaffield (ed.), *The Haitian Declaration of Independence* (Charlottesville and London: University of Virginia Press, 2016). **143.** Charles Tristan Montholon, *Récits de la captivité de l'empereur Napoléon à Sainte-Hélène* (Paris, 1847), vol. 2, p. 52. **144.** Letter of Minister of Navy Decrès to Leclerc, 25 Prairial an X (14 June 1802), in *Lettres du général Leclerc*, p. 285. **145.** Leclerc to Bonaparte, 15 Vendémiaire an XI (7 October 1802), ibid., p. 256. **146.** Métral, *Histoire de l'expédition des français à Saint-Domingue*, pp. 176–86. **147.** Toussaint to Simon Baptiste, 7 Pluviôse an X (27 January 1802), Santo Domingo; Boromé, 'A finding list'. **148.** Rochambeau to Bonaparte, Cap, 23 Germinal an XI (14 April 1803). AN AFIV 1213. **149.** Nemours, *Histoire militaire*, vol. 2, p. 173. **150.** General Hardÿ to Leclerc, 16 Ventôse an X (7 March 1802). AN AB XIX 5002, Papiers Leclerc. **151.** Quoted in Pamphile de Lacroix, *La Révolution de Haïti*, pp. 366–7. **152.** Quoted in Lélia Justin Lhérisson, *Les héros de l'indépendance dans l'histoire d'Haïti* (Port-au-Prince, 1954), p. 3.

12: A UNIVERSAL HERO

1. Letter of 15 April 1954, in Ann Bardach (ed.), *The Prison Letters of Fidel Castro* (New York: Nation Books, 2007). 2. On the 'cultural trauma' provoked by the Saint-Domingue revolution among white elites in the Atlantic region see Alejandro Gómez, *Le spectre de la révolution noire* (Rennes: Presses Universitaires de Rennes, 2013). 3. See David Geggus, 'Slave rebellion during the Age of Revolution', in Wim Klooster and Gert Oostindie (eds), *Curaçao in the Age of Revolutions* (Leiden: KITLV Press, 2011); Genovese, *From Rebellion to Revolution*, p. 3. 4. Examples cited in Geggus, *The Haitian Revolution*, p. 188; on Jamaica and the Haitian revolution see Michael Mullin, *African in America: Slave Acculturation and Resistance in the American South and the British Caribbean* (Chicago: University of Illinois Press, 1992), pp. 216–17. 5. Cited in Scott, *The Common Wind*, p. 180. 6. See Laurent Dubois, 'The promise of revolution: Saint-Domingue and the struggle for autonomy in Guadeloupe 1797–1802', in Geggus (ed.), *The Impact of the Haitian Revolution* pp. 113, 116 and 117. 7. Military report, quoted in Aline Helg, 'A fragmented majority: free "of all colours", Indians, and slaves in Caribbean Colombia during the Haitian Revolution', ibid., p. 159. 8. For further examples see Oruno D. Lara, 'L'influence de la Révolution haïtienne dans son environnement caraïbe', *Présence Africaine* 2004 (1), pp. 89–103. 9. Consuelo Naranjo Orovio, 'Le fantasme d'Haïti: l'élaboration intéressée d'une grande peur', in Yacou (ed.), *Saint-Domingue espagnol*, p. 639. 10. Quoted in James Sidbury, 'Saint-Domingue in Virginia: ideology, local meanings, and resistance to slavery 1790–1800', *Journal of Southern History* vol. 63, no. 3 (August 1997), p. 547. 11. Douglas Egerton, *Gabriel's Rebellion: The Virginia Slave Conspiracies of 1800 and 1802* (Chapel Hill: University of North Carolina Press, 1993), p. 48; see also Michael Nicholls, *Whispers of Rebellion: Narrating Gabriel's Conspiracy* (Charlottesville: University of Virginia Press, 2012). 12. June 1800 report, cited in Ada Ferrer, *Freedom's Mirror*, p. 152. 13. French consul report to Minister of Navy, Philadelphia, 30 September 1800. ANOM CC9B 2. 14. A list of *vodou* deities put together from nine sources in the Plaisance region in the mid twentieth century included one named 'Monsieur Toussaint'. George Eaton Simpson, 'The belief system of Haitian vodun', *American Anthropologist* vol. 47, no. 1 (January–March 1945), p. 45. 15. Odette Mennesson-Rigaud, 'Le rôle du vaudou dans l'indépendance d'Haïti', *Présence Africaine* 1958 (1), p. 64. 16. Quoted in Laurent Dubois, 'Thinking Haitian independence in Haitian vodou', in Gaffield (ed.), *The Haitian Declaration of Independence*, p. 209. 17. John Balfour to Henry Dundas, Tobago, 15 February 1794. Correspondence of Henry Dundas, Bodleian Library, Oxford, MSS W.Ind. S.8. 18. On the role of sailors see Chapter 2 in Scott, *The Common Wind*. 19. Matthias Assunçao, 'L'adhésion populaire aux projets révolutionnaires dans les sociétés esclavagistes', *Caravelle* no. 54 (1990), p. 295. 20. See Janet Polasky, *Revolutions Without Borders* (New Haven: Yale University Press, 2015). 21. Cited in Michael Craton, *Testing the Chains: Resistance to Slavery in the British West Indies* (Ithaca, NY and London: Cornell University Press, 1982), p. 236. 22. Kevin Whelan, 'The Green Atlantic: radical reciprocities between Ireland and America in the long eighteenth century', in Kathleen Wilson (ed.), *A New Imperial History* (Cambridge: Cambridge University Press, 2004), pp. 232 and 234. 23. On the political struggles of Cuban slaves during the first half of the nineteenth century see Alain Yacou, *La longue guerre des nègres marrons de Cuba (1796–1852)* (Paris: Karthala, 2009). 24. *Gaceta de Madrid*, 18 May 1804, quoted in Ada Ferrer, 'Speaking of Haiti', in Geggus (ed.), *The Impact of the Haitian Revolution*, p. 224. 25. Ibid., p. 235. 26. Ada Ferrer, 'La société esclavagiste cubaine et la révolution Haïtienne', *Annales. Histoire, sciences sociales* 2003–2, pp. 352–5. 27. Manuel Barcia, 'Revolts among enslaved Africans in nineteenth-century Cuba', *Journal of Caribbean History* 2005–2, pp. 178 and 179. 28. Matthew Childs, '"A French black general arrived to conquer the island": images of the Haitian revolution in Cuba's 1812 Aponte rebellion', in Geggus (ed.), *The Impact of the Haitian Revolution*, p. 148. 29. Ibid., pp. 136, 143–4. 30. Dessalines proclamation, Cap, 28 April 1804. ANOM CC9B 23. 31. Hérard Dumesle, *Voyage dans le nord d'Hayti* (Les Cayes, 1824), pp. 85–9. 32. Ibid.,

pp. 310–11. **33.** Ibid., pp. 159 and 176. **34.** For further discussion see Erin Zavitz, 'Revolutionary narrations: early nineteenth century Haitian historiography and the challenge of writing counter-history', *Atlantic Studies* vol. 14, no. 3 (2017). **35.** Thomas Madiou, *Histoire d'Haïti.* **36.** On the significant influences of Haïti on Bolívar's thinking see Sibylle Fischer, 'Bolívar in Haiti: republicanism in the revolutionary Atlantic', in Caria Calargé, Raphael Dalleo, Luis Duno-Gottberg and Clevis Headley (eds), *Haiti and the Americas* (Jackson: University Press of Mississipi, 2013). **37.** Sonthonax to Toussaint, Cap, 13 Prairial an V (1 June 1797). BNF NAF 8988, Papiers Sonthonax. **38.** Carlo Célius, 'Neoclassicism and the Haitian revolution', in Geggus (ed.), *The Impact of the Haitian Revolution*, p. 378. **39.** Approximately 21 billion dollars in twenty-first-century terms. **40.** For an excellent discussion of the international constraints on the early Haitian state, and their impact on domestic politics, see Robert Shilliam, 'What the Haitian Revolution might tell us about development, security, and the politics of race', *Comparative Studies in Society and History* vol. 50, no. 3 (July 2008), pp. 778–808. **41.** See Helen Weston, 'The many faces of Toussaint Louverture', in Agnes Lugo-Ortiz and Angela Rosenthal, *Slave Portraiture in the Atlantic World* (New York: Cambridge University Press, 2013), pp. 356–7. **42.** François Grenier, *Entrevue de Toussaint Louverture et du général Maitland* (1821). **43.** *Toussaint Louverture proclame la constitution de 1801*, undated, artist unknown (*c.*1822). **44.** *Entrevue de Toussaint Louverture et de ses enfants*, undated, artist unknown (*c.*1822). **45.** *Mort de Toussaint Louverture*, undated, artist unknown (*c.*1822). **46.** Célius, 'Neoclassicism and the Haitian revolution', p. 378. **47.** Jean Price-Mars, *Ainsi parla l'oncle* (New York: Parapsychology Foundation Inc., 1928), p. 28. **48.** 'O Muse, now to the new songs I tune to my lyre', excerpt from *The Haïtiade* (1827–8), in Doris Kadish and Deborah Jenson (eds), *Poetry of Haitian Independence* (New Haven and London: Yale University Press, 2015), p. 125; the authorship has not been conclusively established, but some literary critics believe the poem may have been written by Toussaint's son Isaac; ibid., pp. xxviii–xxix. **49.** *The Denison Review* (Denison, Iowa), 8 July 1903. Library of Congress, Historic American Newspapers. **50.** Alfred N. Hunt, *Haiti's Influence on Antebellum America* (Baton Rouge: Louisiana State University Press, 1988), p. 190. **51.** On the role of black seamen see more generally Gilroy, *Black Atlantic*, and Peter Linebaugh and Marcus Rediker, *The Many-Headed Hydra* (London: Verso, 2002). **52.** See Sara Fanning, *Caribbean Crossing: African Americans and the Haitian Emigration Movement* (New York: New York University Press, 2017); see also Matthew J. Smith, *Liberty, Fraternity, Exile: Haiti and Jamaica after Emancipation* (Durham, NC: University of North Carolina Press, 2014). **53.** David Walker, *Appeal to Coloured Citizens of the World*, ed. P. Hinks (University Park, PA: Pennsylvania State University Press, 2000), p. 23. **54.** *Anti-slavery Bugle*, 28 April 1855. Library of Congress, Historic American Newspapers. **55.** *Weekly Anglo-African*, 15 February 1862, quoted in Matthew Clavin, 'American Toussaints: symbol, subversion, and the Black Atlantic tradition in the American Civil War', in Maurice Jackson and Jacqueline Bacon (eds), *African Americans and the Haitian Revolution* (New York and London: Routledge, 2010), p. 115. **56.** Sara Fanning, 'The roots of early black nationalism: Northern African Americans' invocations of Haiti in the early nineteenth century', *Slavery and Abolition* vol. 28, no. 1 (April 2007), pp. 62–3. **57.** For further discussion of these two traditions see Michael O. West and William G. Martin, 'Haiti, I'm sorry: the Haitian revolution and the forging of the black international', in West, Martin and Wilkins (eds), *From Toussaint to Tupac*, pp. 91–7. **58.** For further analysis see Jacqueline Bacon, 'A revolution unexampled in the history of man: the Haitian revolution in *Freedom's Journal*, 1827–1829', in Jackson and Bacon (eds), *African Americans and the Haitian Revolution.* **59.** *Freedom's Journal*, Friday 4 May 1827. **60.** *Freedom's Journal*, Friday 11 May 1827. The main source here was Pamphile de Lacroix's work on the Haitian Revolution. **61.** *Freedom's Journal*, Friday 18 May 1827. **62.** *Freedom's Journal*, Friday 11 May 1827. **63.** Except from 'Theresa – a Haytien Tale', *Freedom's Journal*, January–February 1828, in Jackson and Bacon (eds), *African Americans and the Haitian Revolution*, pp. 174–5. **64.** *The Anti-Slavery Record*, vol.1, no. 4, April 1835. I am very grateful to Oliver Franklin for lending me his personal copy of this document. **65.** James McCune Smith, 'Lecture on the Haytien Revolutions', 26 February 1841, excerpts reproduced in Jackson and Bacon (eds), *African Americans and the Haitian Revolution*, pp. 177–83. **66.** Harriet Martineau, *The Hour and the Man* (London, 1841). **67.** John Relly Beard, *Toussaint L'Ouverture, a Biography and Autobiography* (Boston, 1863), p. 292; this version included a translation of Toussaint's memoir written in Fort de Joux. **68.** Brandon Byrd, 'Black republicans, black republic: African Americans, Haiti, and the promise of reconstruction', *Slavery and Abolition* vol. 36, no. 4 (2015), p. 550. **69.** James Theodore Holly, *A vindication of the capacity of the negro race for self-government, and civilised progress, as demonstrated by historical events of the Haytian revolution* (New Haven, 1857). **70.** Byrd, 'Black republicans, black republic', p. 551. **71.** Wendell Phillips, *One of the Greatest Men in History: Toussaint Louverture* (New York and Boston, 1861). **72.** Susan Belasco, 'Harriet Martineau's black hero and the American antislavery movement', *Nineteenth Century Literature* vol. 55, no. 2 (September 2000), p. 177. **73.** Schuyler Colfax, 'Recollections of Wendell Phillips' lecture in Washington in 1862', *The Indianapolis Journal*, 18 April 1884. **74.** See for example 'Wendell Phillips's oration on Toussaint Louverture', *New York Daily Tribune*, 13 March 1863. **75.** *Weekly Anglo-African*, 19 December 1863; and *New York Independent*, 4 February 1864, quoted in Clavin, 'American Toussaints', p. 110. **76.** Ibid., pp. 111–12 and 116. **77.** George Washington Williams, *A History of the Negro Troops in the War of the Rebellion* (New York, 1888), pp. 45–6. **78.** Robbie Shilliam, *The Black Pacific* (London: Bloomsbury, 2015), p. 147. **79.** See for example the articles on Maceo in the *Hawaiian Star*, 12 February 1897, and in *The Nashville Globe*, 22 January 1909. **80.** For further analysis see Robin Kelley, '"But a local phase of a world problem": black history's global vision 1883–1950', *Journal of American History* vol. 86, no. 3 (December 1999). **81.** Anténor Firmin, *De l'égalité des races humaines: anthropologie positive* (Paris, 1885), pp. 545–60. **82.** On the life of Douglass see David Blight's biography, *Frederick Douglass: Prophet of Freedom* (New York, 2018). **83.** Frederick Douglass, *Lecture on Haiti* (Chicago, 1893), pp. 209–10. **84.** Frederick Douglass, 'Toussaint Louverture', *The Colored American* July 1903, pp. 487, 489, 491 and 492; Frantz Fanon, *Black Skins, White Masks* (New York: Grove Press, 1967), p. 100. **85.** Ibid., pp. 490 and 491. **86.** Douglass, *Lecture on Haiti*, pp. 205, 208–9. **87.** Mitch Kachun, 'Antebellum African Americans, public commemoration, and the Haitian revolution', *Journal of the Early Republic* vol. 26, no. 2 (Summer 2006), p. 52. **88.** George Kilmer, 'A Black Spartacus', *The Roanoke Times* (Roanoke, VA), 3 October 1893. **89.** In its issue of 27 April 1906 the *Montana Plaindealer* offered this version: 'I may be sent to death, gentlemen, but Hayti will live free and independent, for I have planted the roots of liberty so deep in Haytien soil that France will never be able to tear them up.' Library of Congress, Historic American Newspapers. **90.** In April–May 1897, *The Broad Ax* (Salt Lake City) published a seven-part series on Toussaint. Library of Congress, Historic American Newspapers. **91.** Article in *The Kansas City Sun*, 17 April 1920. Library of Congress, Historic American Newspapers. **92.** Programme of Toussaint Louverture Literary Society for St Patrick's Day celebration, *St Paul Daily Globe* (Minn.), 15 March 1896. Library of Congress, Historic American Newspapers. **93.** *The Evening Star* (Washington), 21 February 1915. Library of Congress, Historic American Newspapers. **94.** Report in *Cayton's Weekly* (Seattle), 13 November 1920. Library of Congress, Historic American Newspapers. **95.** *The Detroit Tribune*, 13 July 1940. Library of Congress, Historic American Newspapers. **96.** On the American occupation see Dantès Bellegarde, *La résistance haïtienne* (Montreal: Éditions Beauchemin, 1937); see also his work *La nation haïtienne* (Paris: J. de Gigord, 1938). **97.** Quoted in Musab Younis, 'The Grand Machinery of the World: Race, Global Order, and the Black Atlantic', DPhil thesis, Oxford University, 2017, p. 276. **98.** On Haitian intellectual life during this period more generally see Magdaline Shannon, *Jean-Price Mars, the Haitian Elite, and the American Occupation 1915–1935* (London: Macmillan, 1996); on the formation of the *Société* see pp. 166–7. **99.** Quoted in Joseph Guerdy, 'Société Haïtienne d'Histoire, de géographie, et de géologie', *Le Nouvelliste*, 7 December 2012. **100.** Sannon, *Histoire de Toussaint Louverture*, vol. 3, p. 205. **101.** Garvey speech at UNIA meeting, New York, March 1920, in R. Hill (ed.), *The Marcus Garvey and Universal Negro Improvement Association Papers* (Berkeley: University of California Press,

1983), vol. 2, p. 255. **102.** Marcus Garvey, 'African Fundamentalism' (1925), in John Henrik Clarke and Amy Jacques Garvey (eds), *Marcus Garvey and the Vision of Africa* (New York: Vintage Books 1974), p. 156. **103.** Cited in Charles Forsdick and Christian Høgsbjerg, *Toussaint Louverture: A Black Jacobin*, p. 138. **104.** Quoted in Carolyn Williams, 'The Haitian Revolution and a North American Griot: the life of Toussaint L'Ouverture by Jacob Lawrence', in Martin Munroe and Elizabeth Walcott-Hackshaw (eds), *Echoes of the Haitian Revolution* (Kingston, Jamaica: University of the West Indies Press, 2009), p. 78. **105.** The accompanying texts for each of the images can be found in Patricia Hill, *Painting Harlem Modern: The Art of Jacob Lawrence* (Berkeley: University of California Press, 2009), pp. 62–8. **106.** C. L. R. James, 'Slavery to-day: a shocking exposure', *Tit-Bits*, 5 August 1933. **107.** Lindsey Swindall, *Paul Robeson: A Life of Activism and Art* (Lanham, MD: Rowman and Littlefield, 2013), p. 18. **108.** Christian Høgsbjerg (ed.), C. L. R. James, *Toussaint Louverture: The Story of the Only Successful Slave Revolt in History. A Play in Three Acts* (Durham, NC: Duke University Press, 2013), p. 127. **109.** Paul Robeson, 'Ho Chi Minh is the Toussaint L'Ouverture of Indo-China', *Freedom*, March 1954. **110.** Pablo Neruda, 'Toussaint Louverture', in *Canto General*, transl. Jack Schmitt (Berkeley: University of California Press, 2000), p. 117. **111.** 'Prière de paix', in *Hosties noires*; in Léopold Sédar Senghor, *Poèmes* (Paris, 1973), p. 90. **112.** René Depestre, 'Haiti as a myth and as a reality', *Tricontinental* 13 (July 1969), p. 7. I am grateful to Neha Shah for drawing my attention to this article. **113.** Édouard Glissant, Preface to *Monsieur Toussaint* (Paris: Gallimard, 1998 edn), p. 9. **114.** Bernard Dadié, *Îles de tempête* (Paris: Présence Africaine, 1973), p. 80. **115.** Aimé Césaire, *Cahier d'un retour au pays natal* (Paris: Présence Africaine, 1983 edn), p. 24. **116.** Ibid., pp. 25–6. **117.** Hurley, in Garraway (ed.), *Tree of Liberty*, p. 126. **118.** Aimé Césaire, *Toussaint Louverture. La Révolution française et le problème colonial* (Paris: Présence Africaine, 1981 edn), p. 24. **119.** Ibid., p. 185. **120.** Ibid., pp. 195–6. **121.** Ibid., p. 205. **122.** Ibid., p. 199. **123.** Ibid., p. 345. For a more general assessment of Césaire and Senghor's views on sovereignty see Gary Wilder, *Freedom Time: Negritude, Decolonisation, and the Future of the World* (Durham, NC: Duke University Press, 2015). **124.** Cora Kaplan, 'Black Heroes/White Writers: Toussaint L'Ouverture and the literary imagination', *History Workshop Journal* 46 (1998), p. 33. **125.** See Sudhir Hazareesingh, *The Legend of Napoleon* (London: Granta, 2004). **126.** Joseph Saint-Rémy, *Mémoires du général Toussaint Louverture, écrits par lui-même* (Paris, 1853). **127.** See Karma Nabulsi, *Traditions of War*. **128.** Ralph Ellison, 'Mister Toussan', in *Flying Home and Other Stories* (London: Random House, 1998), pp. 26, 27 and 30. **129.** See Tiffany Ruby Patterson and Robin Kelley, 'Unfinished migrations: reflections on the African diaspora and the making of the modern world', *African Studies Review* vol. 43, no. 1 (April 2000), pp. 30–32.

CONCLUSION: AN INSPIRATION FOR OUR TIMES

1. Ntozake Shange, *for colored girls who have considered suicide/when the rainbow is enuf* (London: Prentice Hall, 1997), pp. 26–9. **2.** Henry Blackwell, 'An interview with Ntozake Shange', *Black American Literature Forum* vol. 13, no. 4 (Winter 1979), pp. 135 and 137. **3.** See Karen McCarthy Brown, 'Art and resistance: Haiti's political murals, October 1994', *African Arts* vol. 29, no. 2 (October 1994). **4.** See notably the pamphlet *Toussaint Louverture, précurseur de l'indépendance d'Haïti* (Port-au-Prince, 2001). **5.** Pierre Lepidi, 'La route des esclaves', *Le Monde*, 22 January 2018. **6.** Stephen R. Davis, *The ANC's War Against Apartheid* (Bloomington: Indiana University Press, 2018). **7.** Shange, *for colored girls*. **8.** Jean Jonassaint, 'Towards new paradigms in Caribbean studies', in Garraway (ed.), *Cultural Legacies of the Haitian Revolution*, pp. 205–6. **9.** On the literary dimensions of the Toussaint myth see Philip Kaisary, *The Haitian Revolution in the Literary Imagination* (Charlottesville: University of Virginia Press, 2014); and Isabel Lamell, *Der Toussaint-Louverture-Mythos* (Bielefeld: De Gruyter, 2015). **10.** On nineteenth-century representations of Toussaint see Chapter 8 in Marlene Daut, *Tropics of Haiti: Race and the Literary History of the Haitian Revolution in the Atlantic World* (Liverpool: Liverpool

University Press, 2015). **11.** Alphonse de Lamartine, *Toussaint Louverture* (Paris, 1857 edn), p. 58. **12.** Alejo Carpentier, *The Kingdom of this World* (New York: Farrar, Straus and Giroux, 1989 edn), pp. 36, 108 and 109. **13.** Derek Walcott, 'The Haitian Earth', in *The Haitian Trilogy* (New York: Farrar, Straus and Giroux, 2002), p. 353. **14.** For further discussion of Walcott's writings on the Haitian Revolution see Edward Baugh, 'Of Men and Heroes: Walcott and the Haitian revolution', *Callaloo* vol. 28, no. 1 (Winter 2005), pp. 45–54. **15.** Maryse Condé, *In the Time of the Revolution*, pp. 466 and 488. **16.** Fabienne Pasquet, *La deuxième mort de Toussaint Louverture* (Arles: Actes Sud, 2001), p. 73. **17.** Jean-Claude Fignolé, *Moi Toussaint Louverture, avec la plume complice de l'auteur* (Mont-Royal, Quebec: Ville Mont-Royal Plume & Encre, 2004), pp. 23, 185, 205 and 277. **18.** Madison Smartt Bell, *All Souls' Rising* (New York: Pantheon, 1995), *Master of the Crossroads* (New York: Pantheon, 2000) and *The Stone that the Builder Refused* (New York: Pantheon, 2004). **19.** See Anthony Georges-Pierre, 'Toussaint Louverture face à l'histoire', *Le Nouvelliste*, 17 March 2014. **20.** Speech by Pierre Buteau at commemoration of the 214th anniversary of Toussaint's death, Université de la Fondation Aristide, Haïti. *Le Nouvelliste*, 6 April 2017. **21.** Jean Métellus, *Toussaint Louverture, le précurseur* (Paris: Le Temps des Cerises, 2014), p. 280. Métellus also wrote a play on Toussaint, published in 2003. **22.** For a more general discussion see Renaud Hourcade, 'L'esclavage dans la mémoire nationale française: cadres et enjeux d'une politique mémorielle en mutation', *Droit et Cultures* vol. 66 (2013), pp. 71–86. **23.** Lucie Poulvélarie, 'L'Isle-de-Noé: abolition de l'esclavage, un haut-lieu de mémoire', *La Dépêche*, 15 May 2013. **24.** François Bancel, Pascal Blanchard and Françoise Vergès, *La République coloniale, essai sur une utopie* (Paris: Albin Michel, 2003), p. 154. For further discussion see Christine Chivallon, 'L'émergence récente de la mémoire de l'esclavage dans l'espace public: enjeux et significations', *Revue d'Histoire Moderne et Contemporaine* no. 52 (2005-5), pp. 64–81; see also her more detailed study, *L'esclavage, du souvenir à la mémoire* (Paris: Karthala, 2012). **25.** On the cinematic representations of the revolution, and of slavery more generally, see Alyssa Goldstein Sepinwall, 'Slavery, memory, and the Haitian revolution in Chris Rock's *Top Five*', *Journal of American Culture* vol. 41, no. 1 (March 2018). **26.** *Toussaint Louverture*, directed by Philippe Niang, 180 mins, France-Télévisions, 2012. **27.** Julie Ménard, 'Pontoise: cette statue est scandaleuse, c'est un criminel de guerre', *Le Parisien*, 12 September 2017. See more generally Myriam Cottias, 'Faut-il déboulonner les statues des "héros' controversés"?', *La Croix*, 11 October 2017. **28.** See Amia Srinivasan, 'Under Rhodes', *London Review of Books* vol. 38, no. 7 (31 March 2016). **29.** 'Columbus statue should be replaced with Toussaint Louverture', *Chicago Defender*, 5 December 2017. **30.** See André Marie and Yinda Yinda, 'Mémoires indociles: de Louverture à Basquiat', *Tumultes* no. 27 (2006), pp. 69–88. **31.** John Agard, 'Toussaint L'Ouverture acknowledges Wordsworth's sonnet "To Toussaint L'Ouverture"', 2006. **32.** Lillian Thuram, *Mes étoiles noires* (Paris: Éditions des Noyelles, 2009). **33.** Fred Duval, Jean-Pierre Pécau and Dim. D, *Jour J: Les fantômes d'Hispaniola* (Paris: Delcourt, 2018). **34.** http://www.lycee-toussaint-louverture.com. **35.** Tony Crowley, 'Murals of Northern Ireland' http://ccdl.libraries.claremont.edu/cdm/singleitem/collection/mni/id/5993/rec/5. **36.** An article in the *Evening Journal* (Wilmington, Del.), 1 July 1893, mentioned this 'Toussaint Louverture club', noting that it was 'composed entirely of coloured men' and held its meetings at 109 West 34th Street. **37.** David Suisman, 'Co-workers in the kingdom of culture: Black Swan records and the political economy of African American music', *Journal of American History* vol. 90, no. 4 (March 2004), p. 1311. **38.** Maurice Jackson, '"Friends of the Negro! Fly with me, the Path is open to the sea": remembering the Haitian revolution in the history, music, and culture of the African American people', *Early American Studies* vol. 6, no. 1 (Spring 2008), pp. 98–9. **39.** See interview of David Blake with Gerald Larner in *The Musical Times* vol. 118, no. 1615 (September 1977), pp. 721–7. I am grateful to David Ekserdjian for drawing this opera to my attention. **40.** Jérôme Brie, *Les derniers jours de Toussaint Louverture* (Grinalbert Polymedia, 2012). **41.** Michael Gira, interview, *Stereogum*, 7 May 2014. **42.** Doug DeLoach, 'Chouk Bwa: deep roots, borderless energy', *Songlines*, 3 March 2018.

Index

Italic page numbers refer to illustrations.

A Note About the Author

Sudhir Hazareesingh was born in Mauritius. He is a Fellow of the British Academy and has been a fellow and tutor in politics at Balliol College, Oxford, since 1990. He has written extensively about French intellectual and cultural history, and among his books are *The Legend of Napoleon*, *In the Shadow of the General*, and *How the French Think*. He won the Prix du Mémorial d'Ajaccio and the Prix de la Fondation Napoléon for the first of these, a Prix d'Histoire du Sénat for the second, and the Grand Prix du Livre d'Idées for the third.